Copy editor: Kathleen Fraser.

drawnandquarterly.com | sarahglidden.com

First edition: October 2016. Printed in China. 10 9 8 7 6 5 4 3 2 1

Library and Archives Canada Cataloguing in Publication. Glidden, Sarah, author, illustrator. *Rolling Blackouts: Dispatches from Turkey, Syria, and Iraq*/Sarah Glidden.ISBN 978-1-77046-255-7 (hardback) 1. Glidden, Sarah—Travel—Middle East—Comic books, strips, etc. 2. Foreign news—Comic books, strips, etc. 3. Foreign news—United States—Comic books, strips, etc. 4. Journalism—Comic books, strips, etc. 5. Interviewing in journalism—Comic books, strips, etc. 6. Iraq War, 2003–2011—Influence—Comic books, strips, etc. 7. Turkey—Social conditions—21st century—Comic books, strips, etc. 8. Syria—Social conditions—21st century—Comic books, strips, etc. 9. Iraq—Social conditions—8. 21st century—Comic books, strips, etc. 10. Graphic novels. I. Title. PN4784.F6G554 2016 070.4'3320222 C2016-900987-4

Published in the USA by Drawn & Quarterly, a client publisher of Farrar, Straus and Giroux. Orders: 888.330.8477. Published in Canada by Drawn & Quarterly, a client publisher of Raincoast Books. Orders: 800.663.5714.

ROLLING BLACKOUTS

DISPATCHES FROM TURKEY, SYRIA, AND IRAQ

SARAH GLIDDEN

Drawn & Quarterly

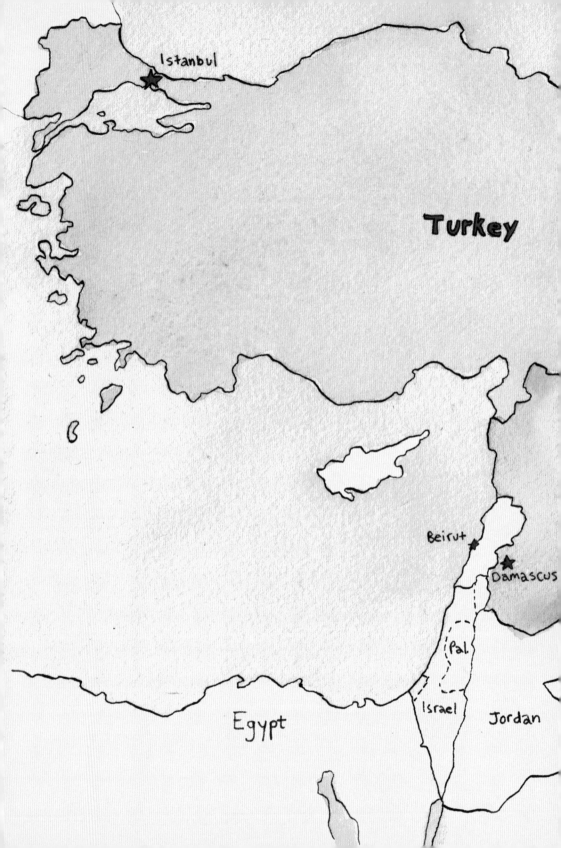

Istanbul

Turkey

Beirut

Damascus

Pal.

Egypt

Israel

Jordan

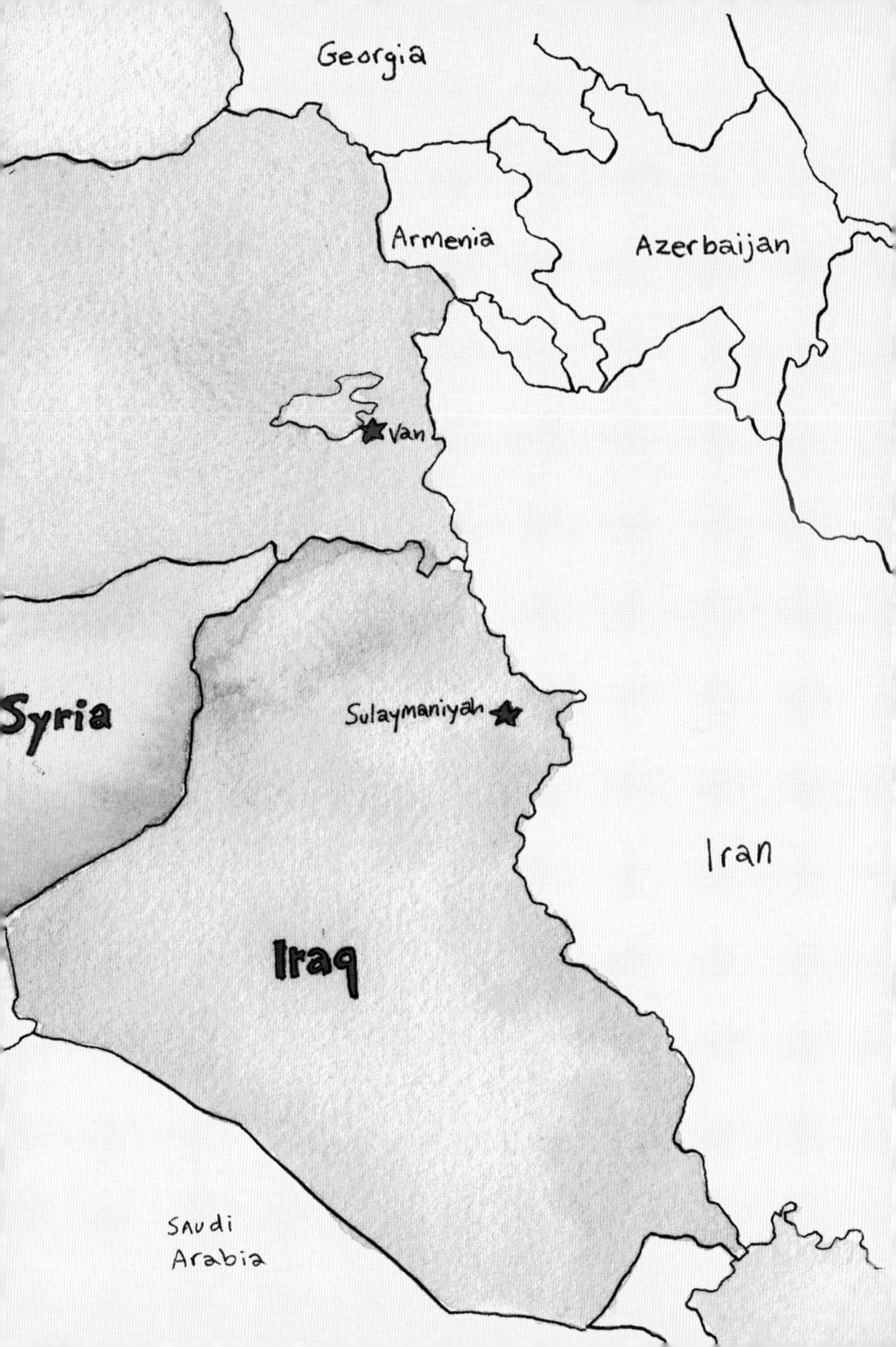
Georgia
Armenia
Azerbaijan
Van
Syria
Sulaymaniyah
Iran
Iraq
Saudi
Arabia

ABOUT THIS BOOK

This is a story based on true events and real dialogue.

I spent two months with the people portrayed in this book, observing and documenting them and capturing as much as I could with my little digital recorder. I recorded our conversations as we ate our meals, walked around cities, conducted interviews, and unwound at the end of the day with a beer or three. This means that when I returned home, I had hundreds of hours of recorded conversation to transcribe and sift through. It also means that almost all the dialogue in this book is taken directly from these recordings, with some minimal cleanup done for grammar or clarity. There are several instances where a recording was not possible; those have been noted at the back of the book.

I want to make clear, however, that these transcribed conversations have been edited and condensed in order to be transformed into a readable comic that isn't a thousand pages long. Like any journalist, I did my best to make sure that I never edited dialogue in a way that would alter the meaning or context of what was being said. Or at least, the meaning or context as I interpreted it.

These true events and real dialogue have been crafted into a story, but a person's life is not a story. We all create narratives of our own lives, highlighting some experiences, forgetting others. Our memories are stories that we rewrite and edit every time we recall them, not files stored away in a box somewhere, waiting to be taken out and looked at. When we tell our story to someone else, they pay attention to certain details and overlook others, and then this process is magnified again when they tell the story to someone new. For this reason, true objectivity is impossible in narrative journalism (and arguably in any kind of journalism). The idea that I was turning someone else's life into a story fit for consumption is not something I took lightly while I was working on this book, and it will probably always make me uncomfortable. But stories are how all of us try to make sense of a chaotic world, and I think it's worth it, discomfort and all.

A NOTE ON NAMES: Yes, there are two characters named Sarah in this book. One of them is Sarah Stuteville, a journalist from the *Seattle Globalist*, and one of them is me, Sarah Glidden. For a long time while working on the book, and with Sarah Stuteville's permission, I changed her character's name to Sal in order to avoid confusion. This never sat right with me, however, and in the end I had to go with my gut feeling that it wouldn't be right to change a person's name for the sake of clarity. Sarah and I have always had the same name, so there's really no reason for that to change now.

All other characters in this book are called by their actual names unless they have requested otherwise for reasons of safety concerns. Those changes have been noted in the back of the book.

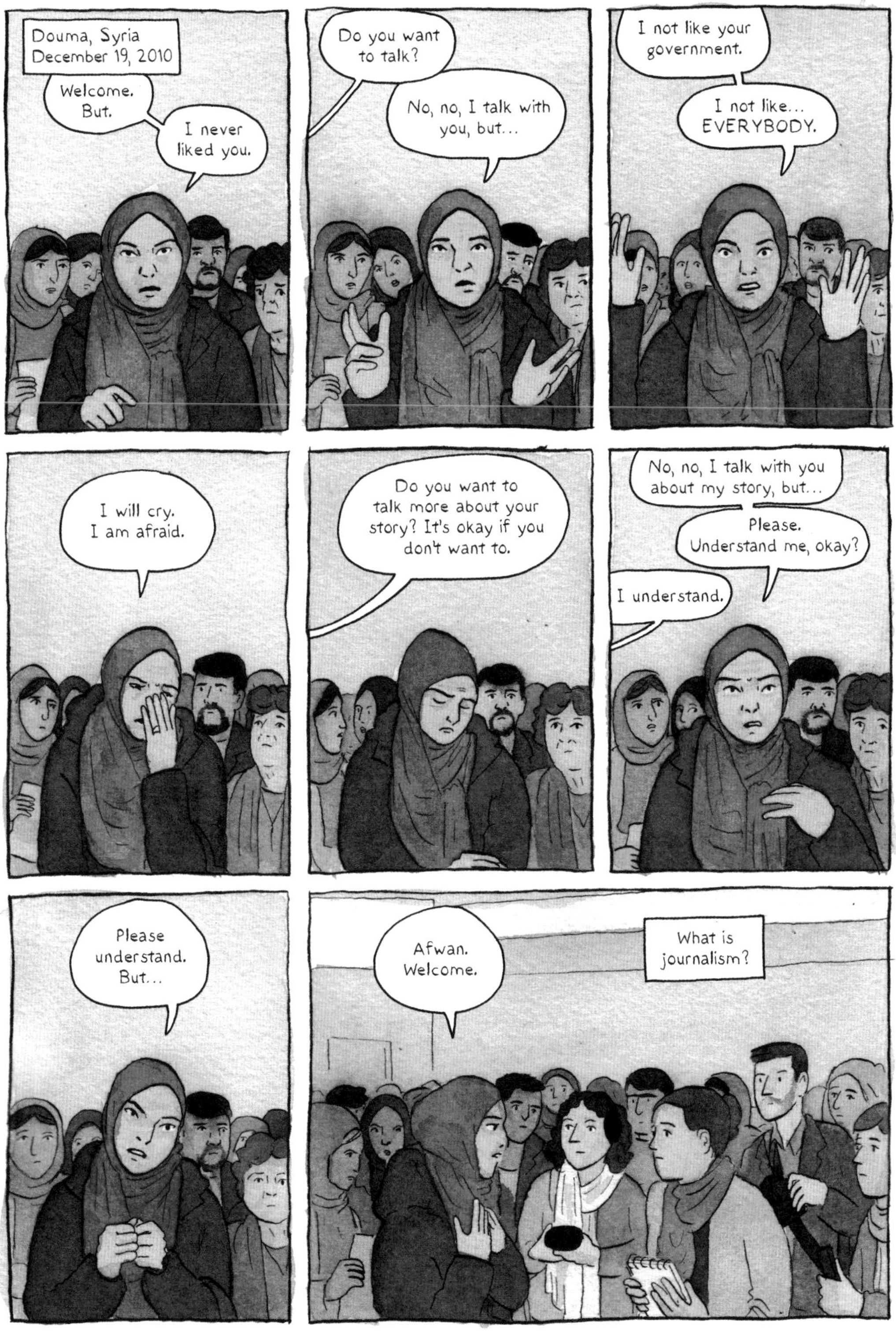

Douma, Syria December 19, 2010
Welcome. But.
I never liked you.
Do you want to talk?
No, no, I talk with you, but...
I not like your government.
I not like... EVERYBODY.
I will cry. I am afraid.
Do you want to talk more about your story? It's okay if you don't want to.
No, no, I talk with you about my story, but...
Please. Understand me, okay?
I understand.
Please understand. But...
Afwan. Welcome.
What is journalism?

STARTING OUT

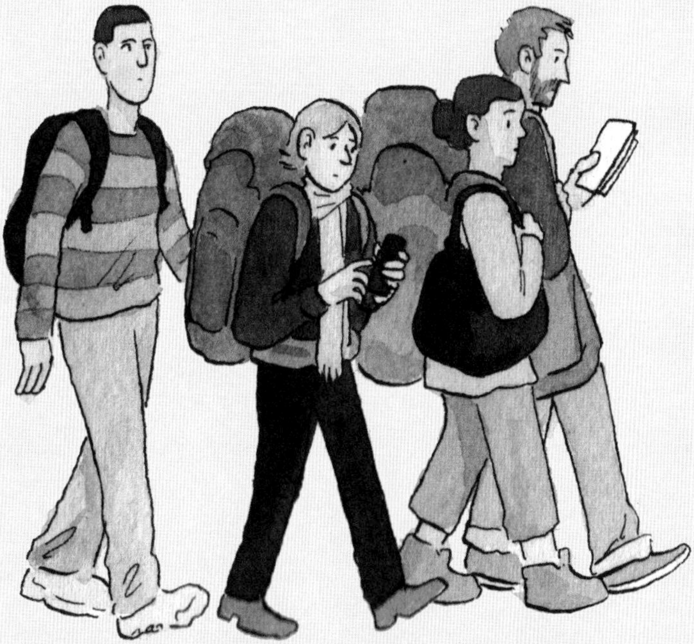

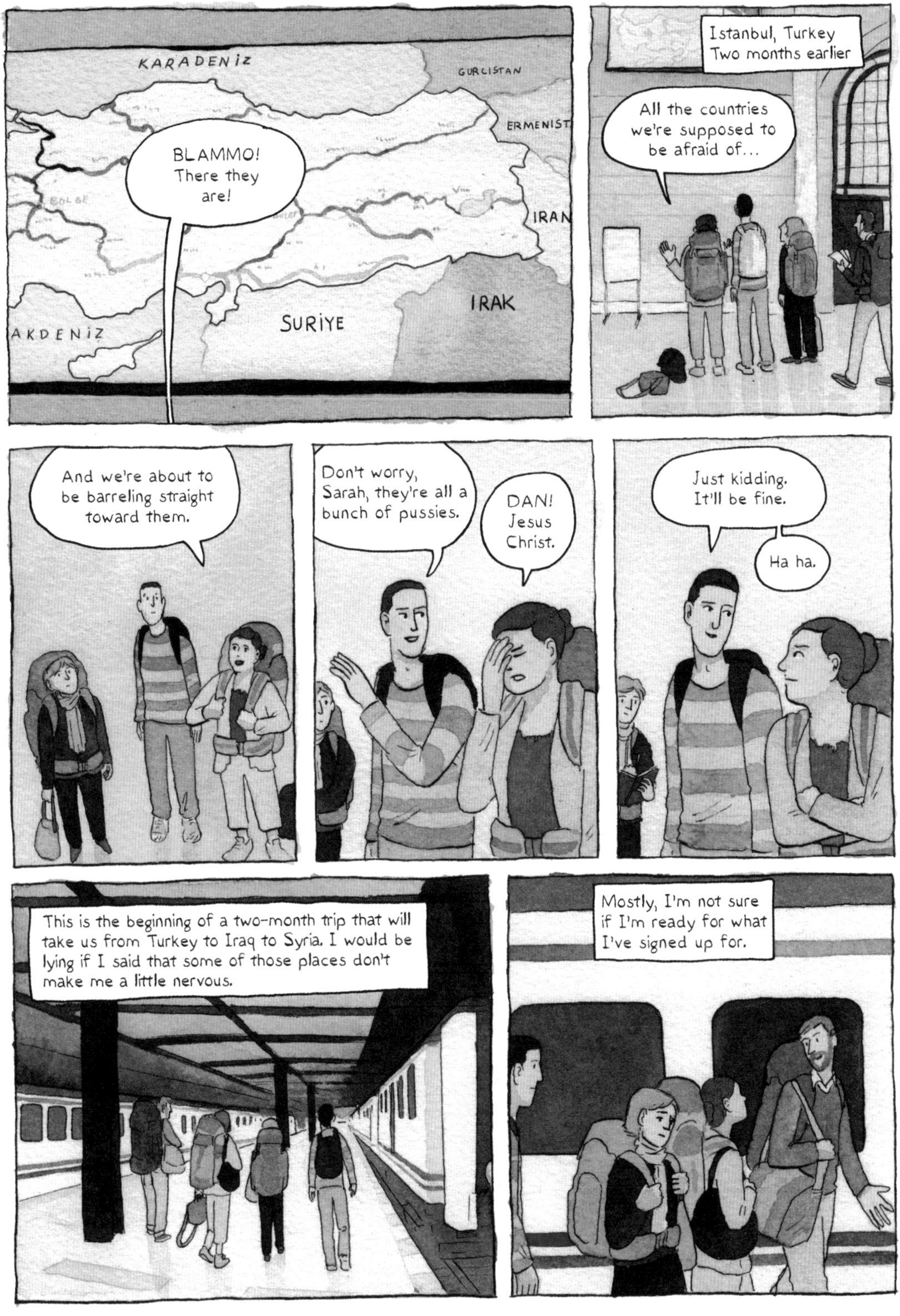
KARADENIZ
GURCISTAN
ERMENIST
IRAN
IRAK
SURIYE
AKDENIZ
BLAMMO! There they are!
Istanbul, Turkey Two months earlier
All the countries we're supposed to be afraid of...
And we're about to be barreling straight toward them.
Don't worry, Sarah, they're all a bunch of pussies.
DAN! Jesus Christ.
Just kidding. It'll be fine.
Ha ha.
This is the beginning of a two-month trip that will take us from Turkey to Iraq to Syria. I would be lying if I said that some of those places don't make me a little nervous.
Mostly, I'm not sure if I'm ready for what I've signed up for.

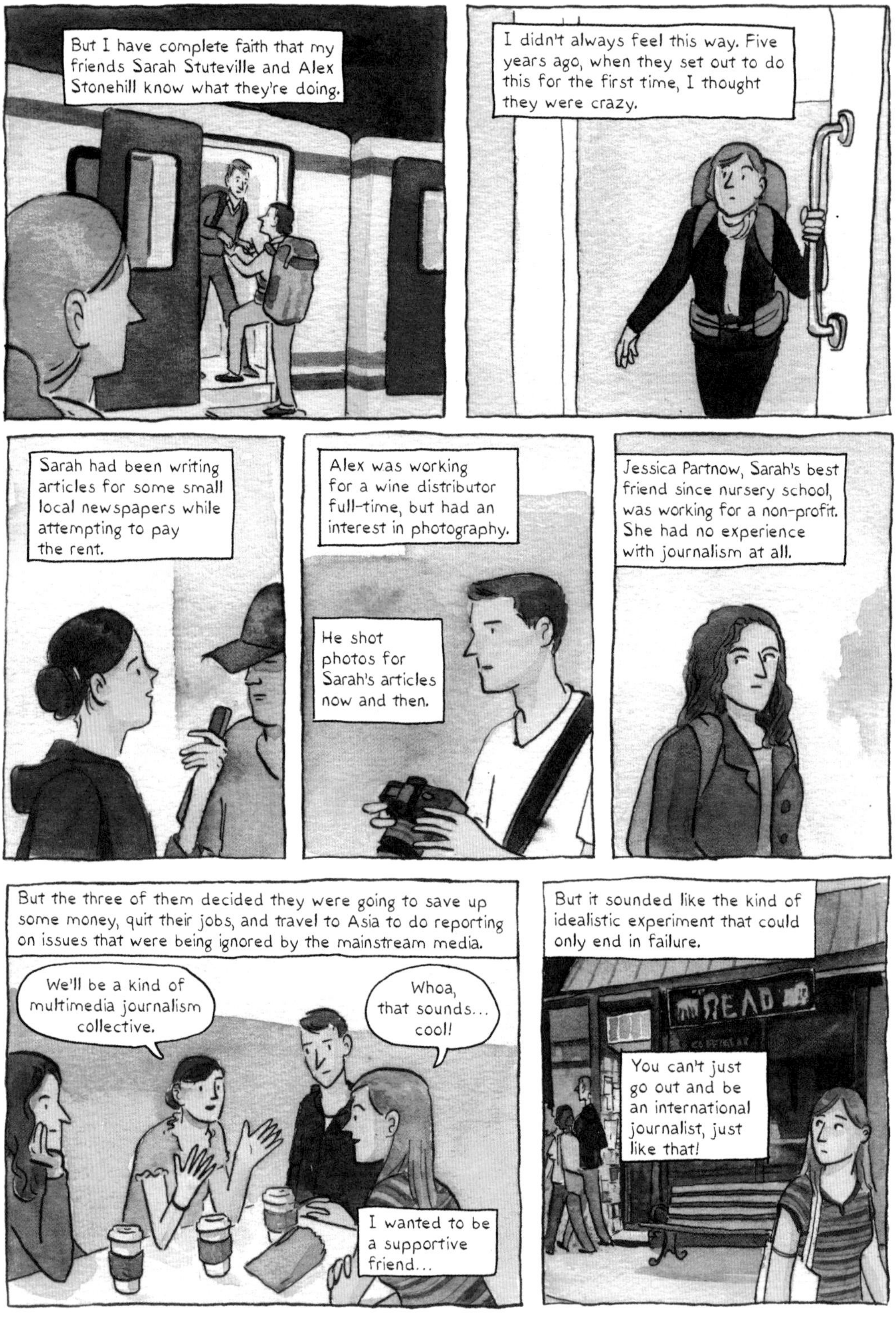
But I have complete faith that my friends Sarah Stuteville and Alex Stonehill know what they're doing.
I didn't always feel this way. Five years ago, when they set out to do this for the first time, I thought they were crazy.
Sarah had been writing articles for some small local newspapers while attempting to pay the rent.
Alex was working for a wine distributor full-time, but had an interest in photography.
He shot photos for Sarah's articles now and then.
Jessica Partnow, Sarah's best friend since nursery school, was working for a non-profit. She had no experience with journalism at all.
But the three of them decided they were going to save up some money, quit their jobs, and travel to Asia to do reporting on issues that were being ignored by the mainstream media.
We'll be a kind of multimedia journalism collective.
Whoa, that sounds... cool!
I wanted to be a supportive friend...
But it sounded like the kind of idealistic experiment that could only end in failure.
READ
You can't just go out and be an international journalist, just like that!

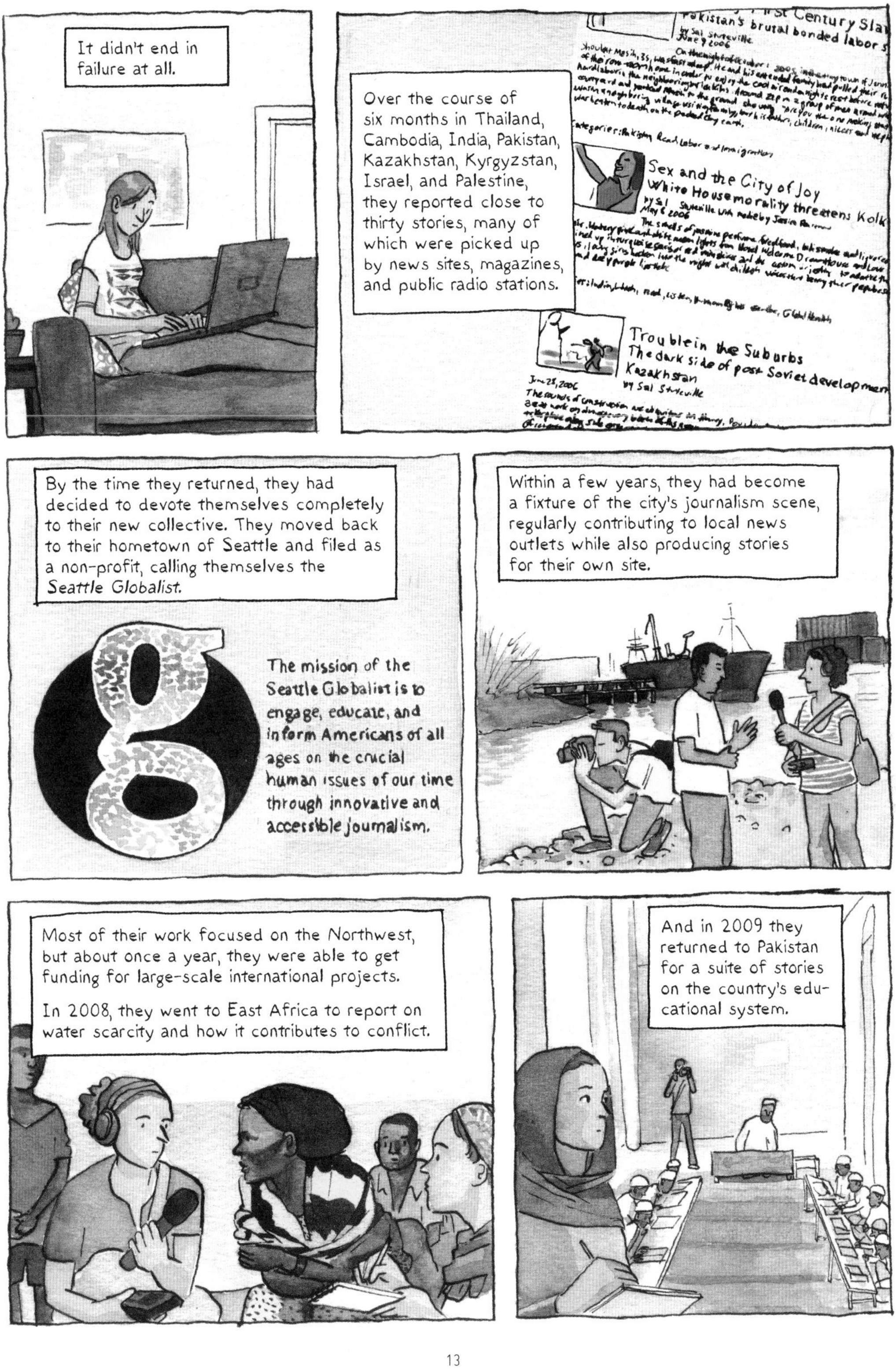
It didn't end in failure at all.
Over the course of six months in Thailand, Cambodia, India, Pakistan, Kazakhstan, Kyrgyzstan, Israel, and Palestine, they reported close to thirty stories, many of which were picked up by news sites, magazines, and public radio stations.
Pakistan's brutal bonded labor s
Sex and the City of Joy
White House morality threatens Kolk
Trouble in the Suburbs
The dark side of post Soviet developm
Kazakhstan
by Sal Stuteville
By the time they returned, they had decided to devote themselves completely to their new collective. They moved back to their hometown of Seattle and filed as a non-profit, calling themselves the *Seattle Globalist.*
The mission of the Seattle Globalist is to engage, educate, and inform Americans of all ages on the crucial human issues of our time through innovative and accessible journalism.
Within a few years, they had become a fixture of the city's journalism scene, regularly contributing to local news outlets while also producing stories for their own site.
Most of their work focused on the Northwest, but about once a year, they were able to get funding for large-scale international projects.
In 2008, they went to East Africa to report on water scarcity and how it contributes to conflict.
And in 2009 they returned to Pakistan for a suite of stories on the country's educational system.

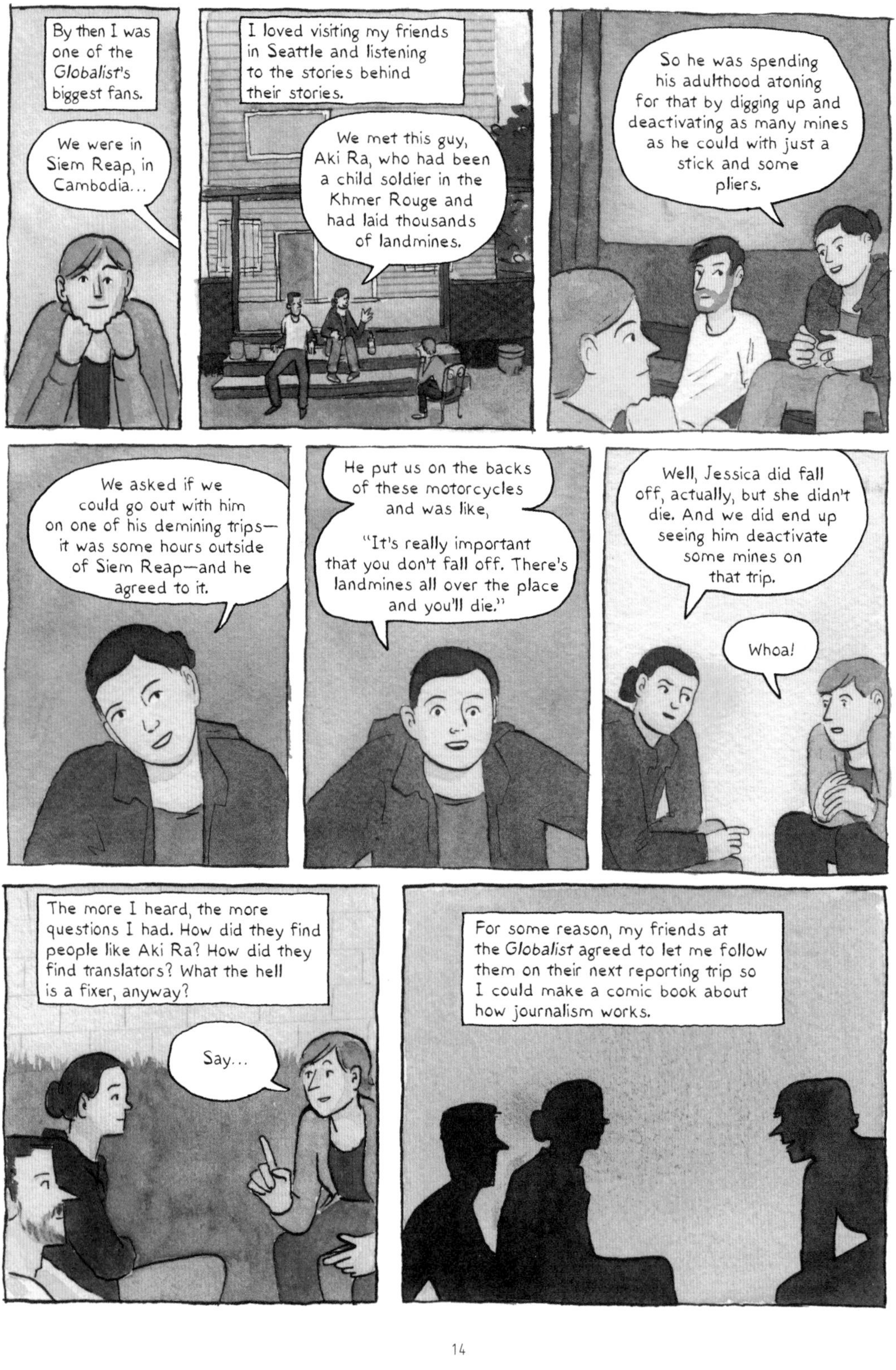
By then I was one of the *Globalist*'s biggest fans.
We were in Siem Reap, in Cambodia...
I loved visiting my friends in Seattle and listening to the stories behind their stories.
We met this guy, Aki Ra, who had been a child soldier in the Khmer Rouge and had laid thousands of landmines.
So he was spending his adulthood atoning for that by digging up and deactivating as many mines as he could with just a stick and some pliers.
We asked if we could go out with him on one of his demining trips—it was some hours outside of Siem Reap—and he agreed to it.
He put us on the backs of these motorcycles and was like, "It's really important that you don't fall off. There's landmines all over the place and you'll die."
Well, Jessica did fall off, actually, but she didn't die. And we did end up seeing him deactivate some mines on that trip.
Whoa!
The more I heard, the more questions I had. How did they find people like Aki Ra? How did they find translators? What the hell is a fixer, anyway?
Say...
For some reason, my friends at the *Globalist* agreed to let me follow them on their next reporting trip so I could make a comic book about how journalism works.

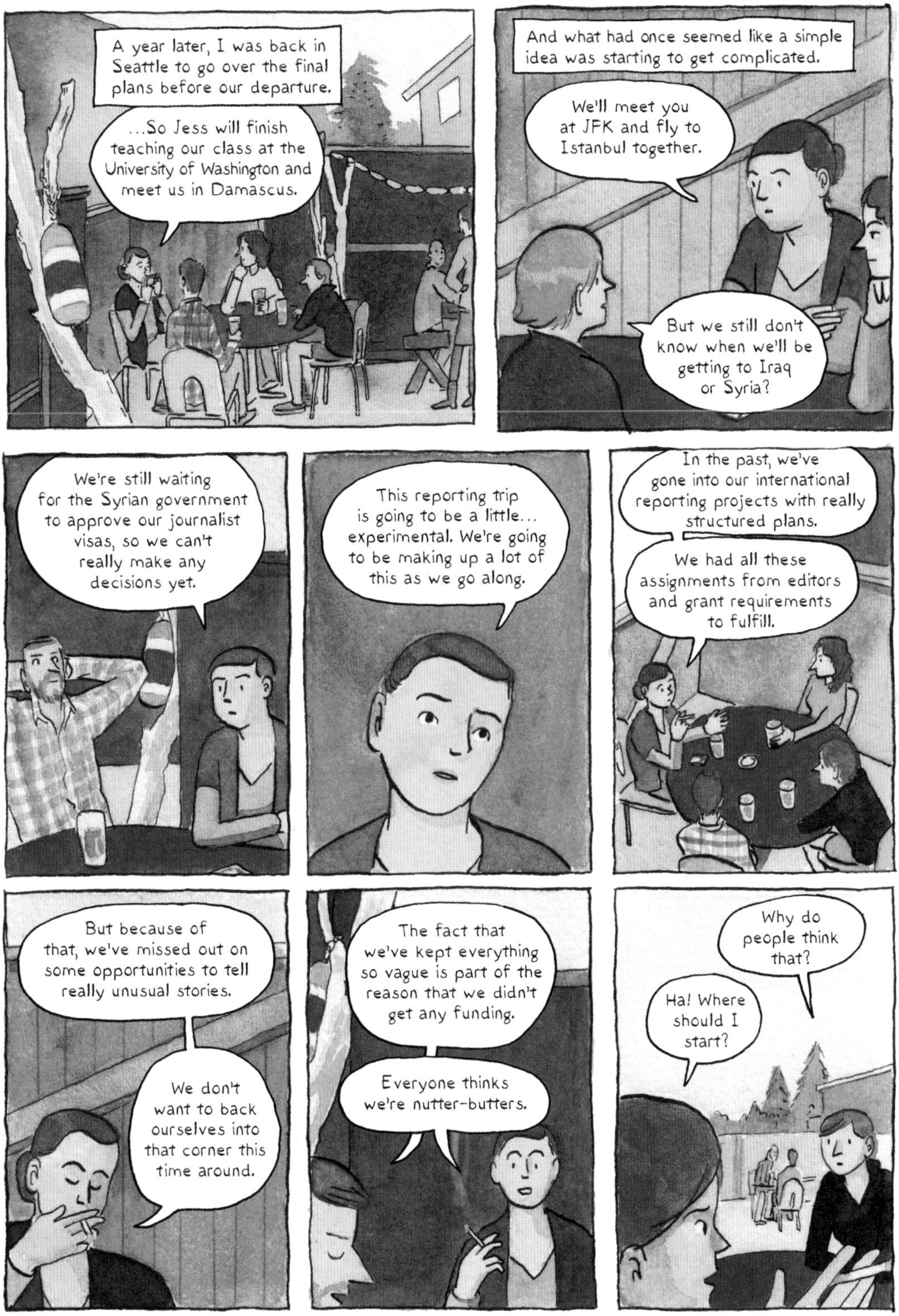
A year later, I was back in Seattle to go over the final plans before our departure.
...So Jess will finish teaching our class at the University of Washington and meet us in Damascus.
And what had once seemed like a simple idea was starting to get complicated.
We'll meet you at JFK and fly to Istanbul together.
But we still don't know when we'll be getting to Iraq or Syria?
We're still waiting for the Syrian government to approve our journalist visas, so we can't really make any decisions yet.
This reporting trip is going to be a little... experimental. We're going to be making up a lot of this as we go along.
In the past, we've gone into our international reporting projects with really structured plans.
We had all these assignments from editors and grant requirements to fulfill.
But because of that, we've missed out on some opportunities to tell really unusual stories.
We don't want to back ourselves into that corner this time around.
The fact that we've kept everything so vague is part of the reason that we didn't get any funding.
Everyone thinks we're nutter-butters.
Why do people think that?
Ha! Where should I start?

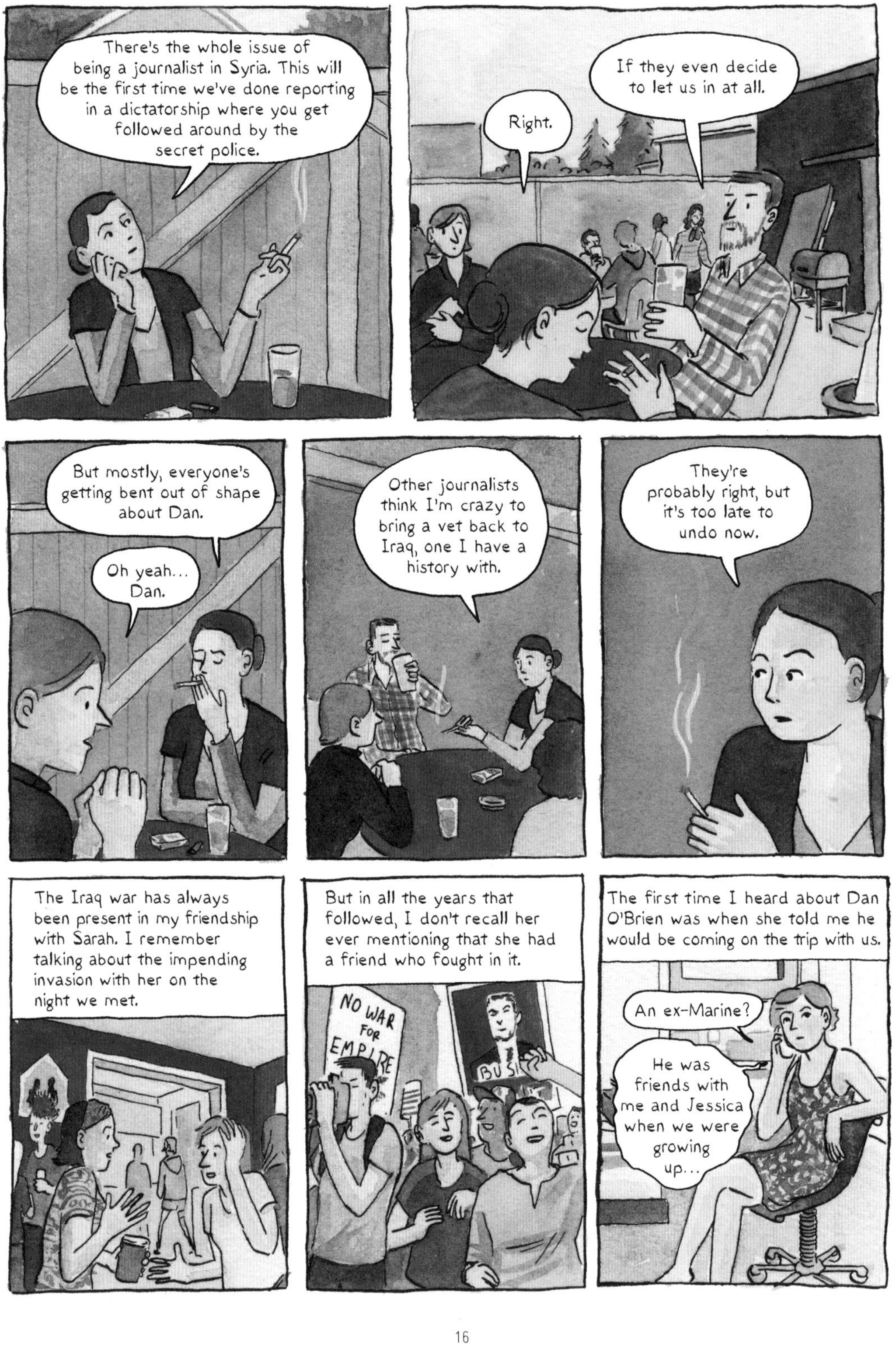
There's the whole issue of being a journalist in Syria. This will be the first time we've done reporting in a dictatorship where you get followed around by the secret police.
Right.
If they even decide to let us in at all.
But mostly, everyone's getting bent out of shape about Dan.
Oh yeah... Dan.
Other journalists think I'm crazy to bring a vet back to Iraq, one I have a history with.
They're probably right, but it's too late to undo now.
The Iraq war has always been present in my friendship with Sarah. I remember talking about the impending invasion with her on the night we met.
But in all the years that followed, I don't recall her ever mentioning that she had a friend who fought in it.
NO WAR FOR EMPIRE
BUSH
The first time I heard about Dan O'Brien was when she told me he would be coming on the trip with us.
An ex-Marine?
He was friends with me and Jessica when we were growing up...

There are certain stereo-types that civilians use to explain why people join the military.

There are the poverty draftees— people from poor families who can't afford college without the GI Bill and whose chances of finding a job are slim...

Or those who are following a family tradition of service...

But none of this was true for Sarah's childhood friend Dan. He certainly didn't come from a family who would have encouraged him to go to war.

Sarah describes his parents as "classic Seattle hippies."

Dan's mother even founded an organization with Jessica's mother called Families for Peace whose goal was to end the sale of violent toys.

G.I. Joe SAY NO

It was at these meetings that Sarah, Jessica, Dan, and his friend Nick became a close foursome whose friendship lasted into their teens.

No one was prepared for Dan's announcement at the age of twenty-five that he was joining the Marines. It seemed to come out of nowhere.

Gates 45-47

By the time Sarah, Jessica, and Alex were going out on their first reporting trip, Dan was nearing his first deployment.

Whose idea was it for him to come with us this time? Sarah says Dan asked her and Dan says she asked him.

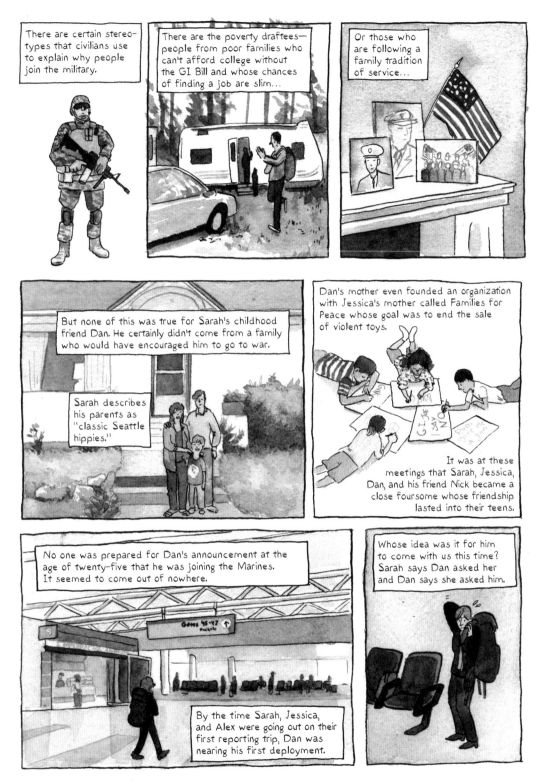

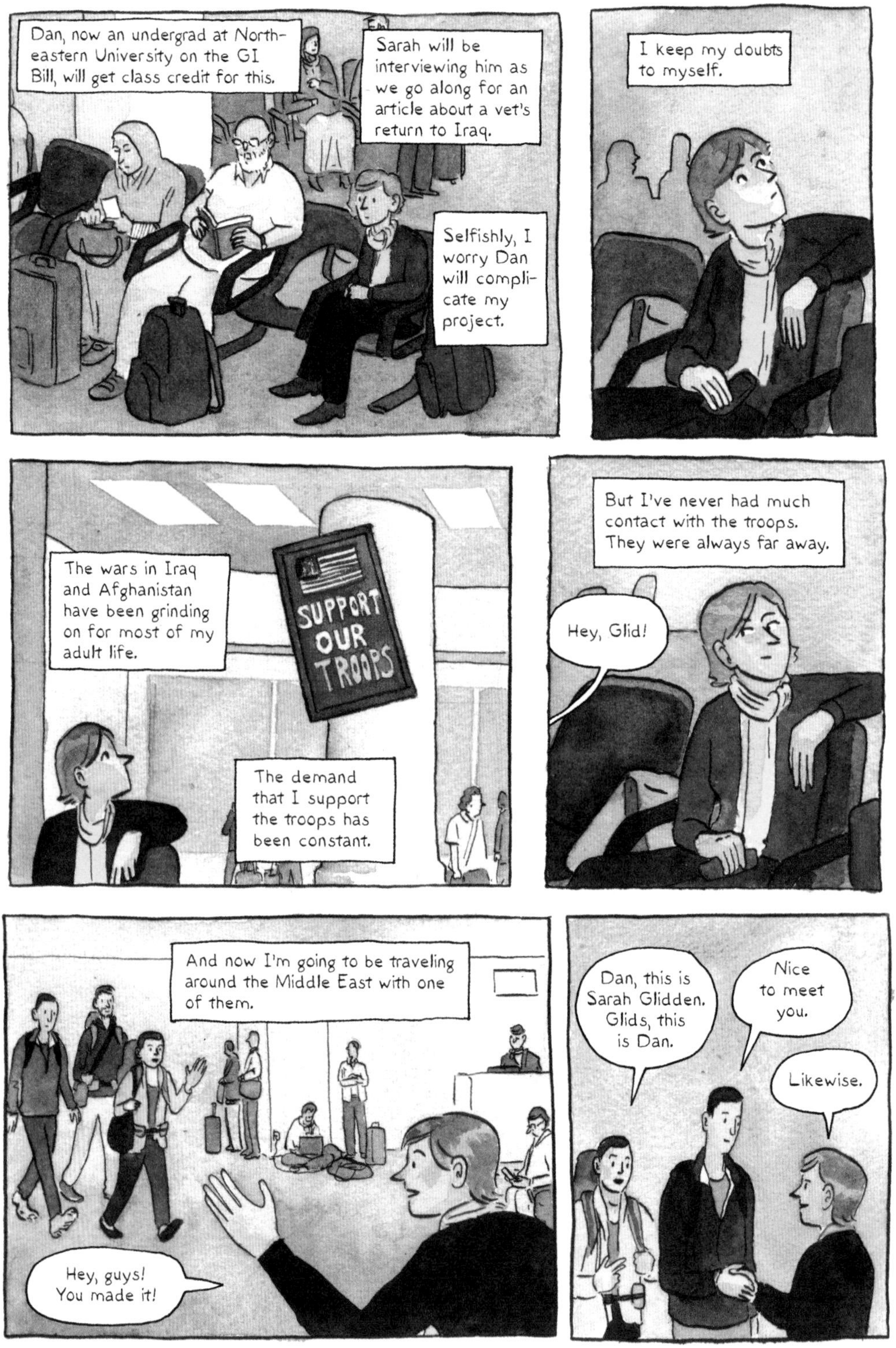
Dan, now an undergrad at Northeastern University on the GI Bill, will get class credit for this.
Sarah will be interviewing him as we go along for an article about a vet's return to Iraq.
Selfishly, I worry Dan will complicate my project.
I keep my doubts to myself.
The wars in Iraq and Afghanistan have been grinding on for most of my adult life.
SUPPORT OUR TROOPS
The demand that I support the troops has been constant.
But I've never had much contact with the troops. They were always far away.
Hey, Glid!
And now I'm going to be traveling around the Middle East with one of them.
Hey, guys! You made it!
Dan, this is Sarah Glidden. Glids, this is Dan.
Nice to meet you.
Likewise.

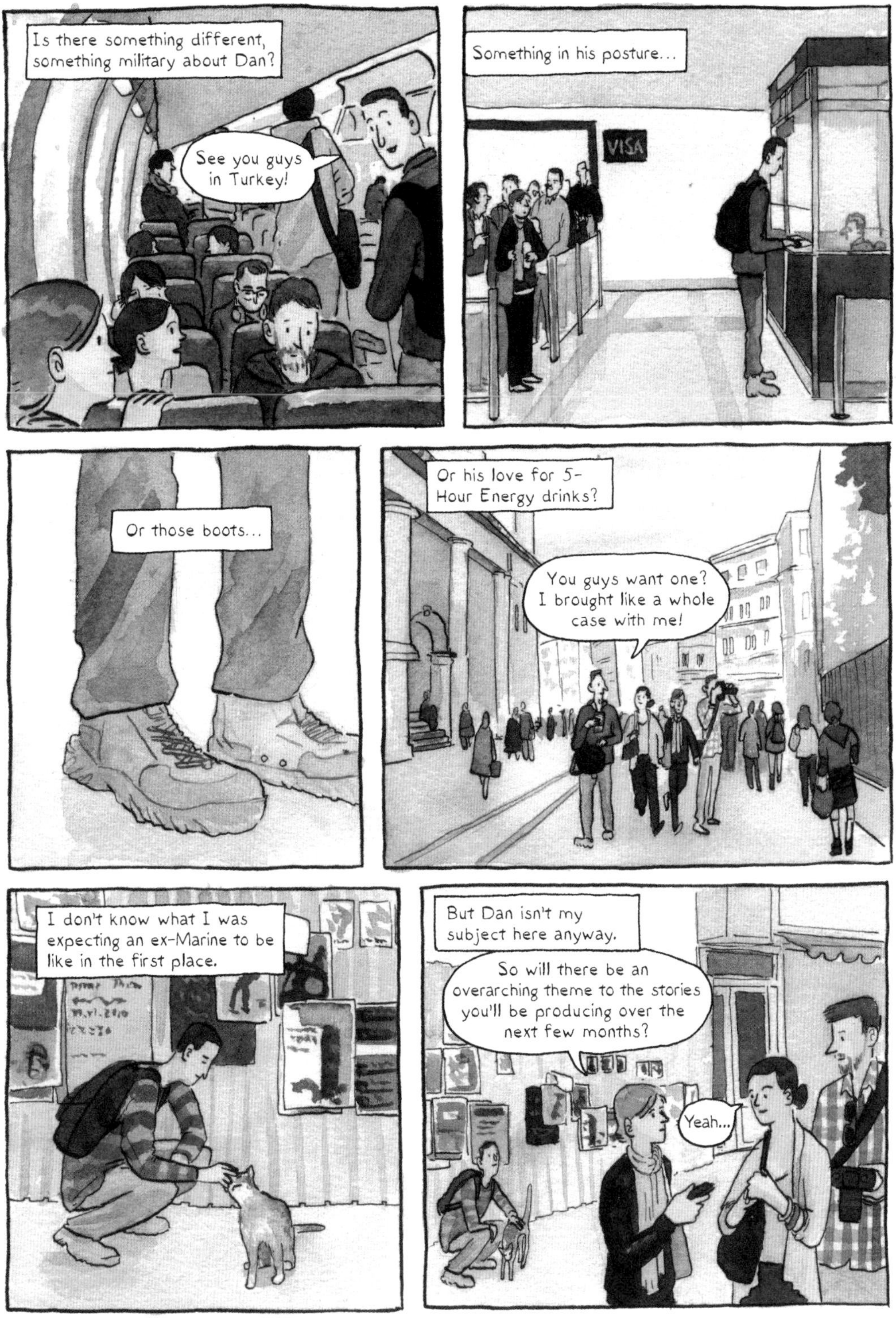
Is there something different, something military about Dan?
See you guys in Turkey!
Something in his posture...
VISA
Or those boots...
Or his love for 5-Hour Energy drinks?
You guys want one? I brought like a whole case with me!
I don't know what I was expecting an ex-Marine to be like in the first place.
But Dan isn't my subject here anyway.
So will there be an overarching theme to the stories you'll be producing over the next few months?
Yeah...

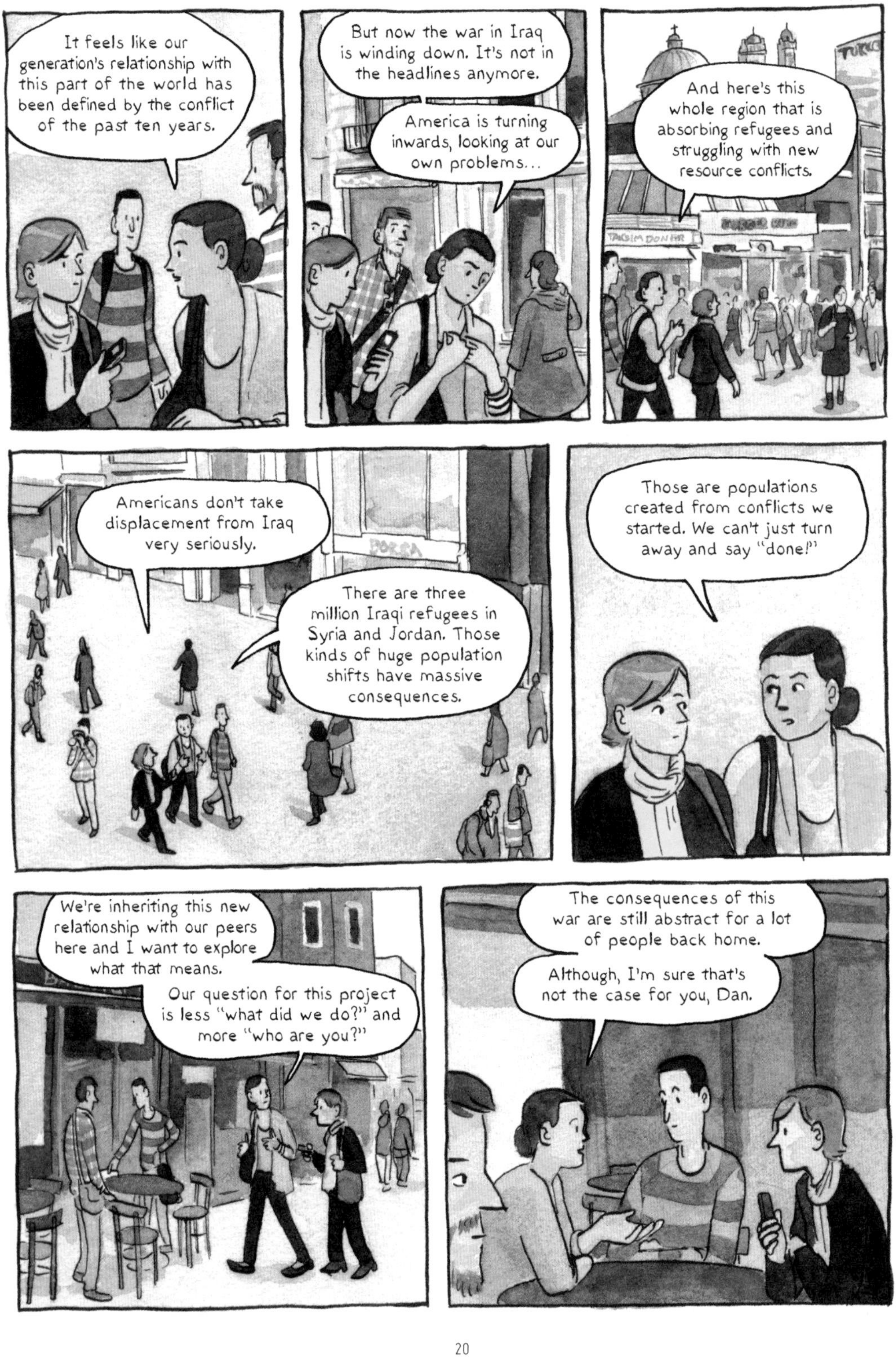
It feels like our generation's relationship with this part of the world has been defined by the conflict of the past ten years.
But now the war in Iraq is winding down. It's not in the headlines anymore.
America is turning inwards, looking at our own problems...
And here's this whole region that is absorbing refugees and struggling with new resource conflicts.
TAKSIM DONER
Americans don't take displacement from Iraq very seriously.
There are three million Iraqi refugees in Syria and Jordan. Those kinds of huge population shifts have massive consequences.
Those are populations created from conflicts we started. We can't just turn away and say "done!"
We're inheriting this new relationship with our peers here and I want to explore what that means.
Our question for this project is less "what did we do?" and more "who are you?"
The consequences of this war are still abstract for a lot of people back home.
Although, I'm sure that's not the case for you, Dan.

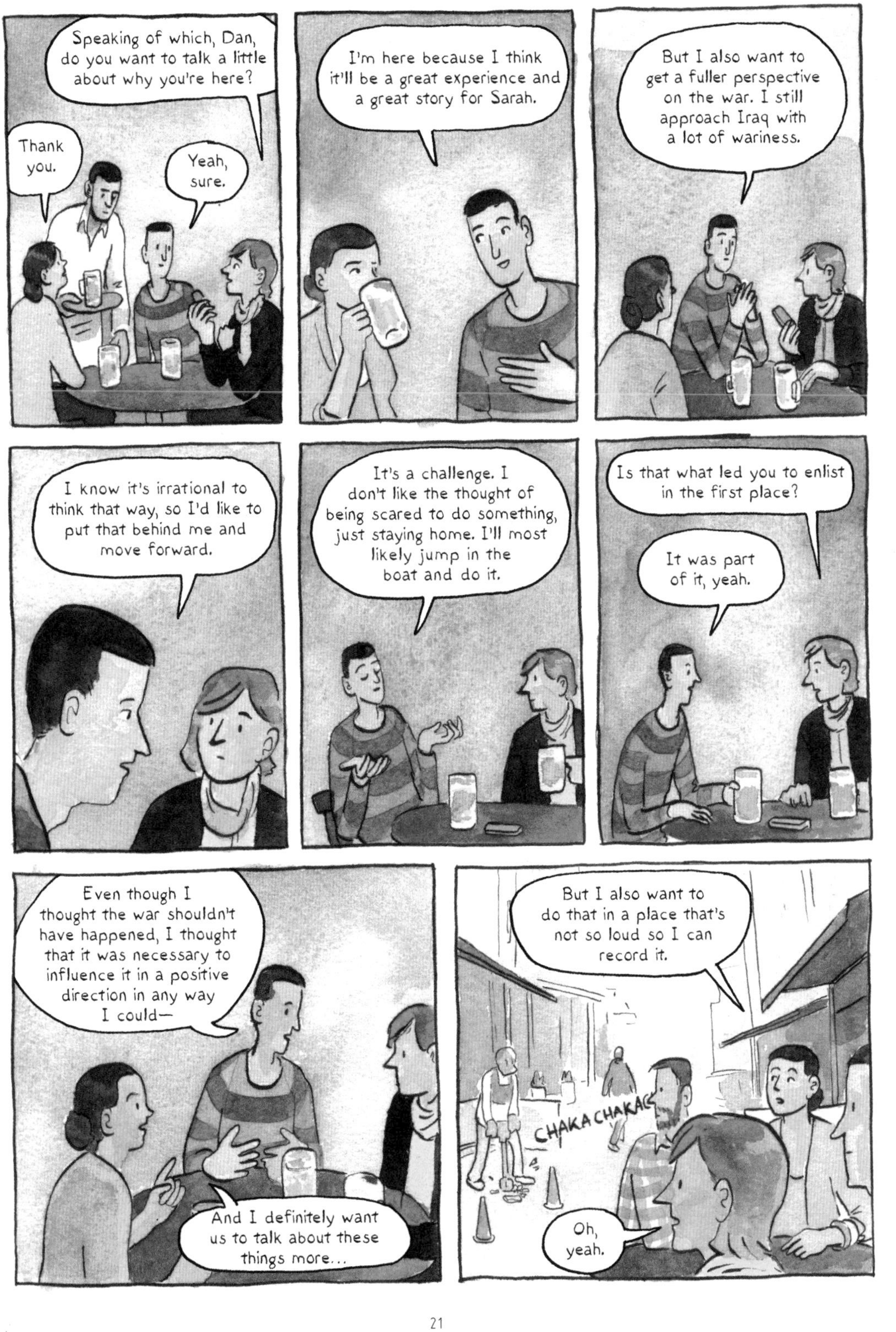
Speaking of which, Dan, do you want to talk a little about why you're here?
Thank you.
Yeah, sure.
I'm here because I think it'll be a great experience and a great story for Sarah.
But I also want to get a fuller perspective on the war. I still approach Iraq with a lot of wariness.
I know it's irrational to think that way, so I'd like to put that behind me and move forward.
It's a challenge. I don't like the thought of being scared to do something, just staying home. I'll most likely jump in the boat and do it.
Is that what led you to enlist in the first place?
It was part of it, yeah.
Even though I thought the war shouldn't have happened, I thought that it was necessary to influence it in a positive direction in any way I could—
And I definitely want us to talk about these things more...
But I also want to do that in a place that's not so loud so I can record it.
CHAKA CHAKAC
Oh, yeah.

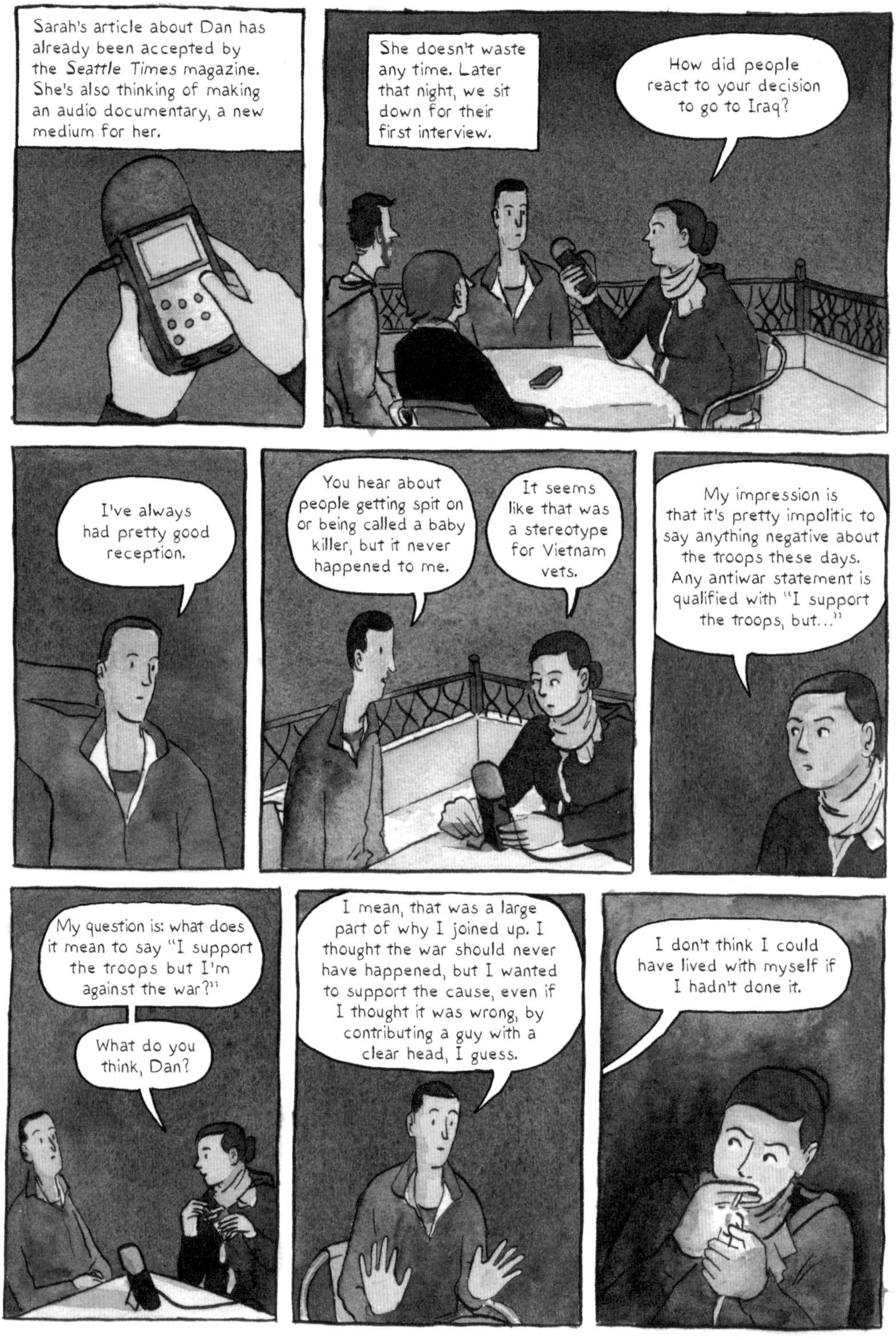
Sarah's article about Dan has already been accepted by the *Seattle Times* magazine. She's also thinking of making an audio documentary, a new medium for her.
She doesn't waste any time. Later that night, we sit down for their first interview.
How did people react to your decision to go to Iraq?
I've always had pretty good reception.
You hear about people getting spit on or being called a baby killer, but it never happened to me.
It seems like that was a stereotype for Vietnam vets.
My impression is that it's pretty impolitic to say anything negative about the troops these days. Any antiwar statement is qualified with "I support the troops, but..."
My question is: what does it mean to say "I support the troops but I'm against the war?"
What do you think, Dan?
I mean, that was a large part of why I joined up. I thought the war should never have happened, but I wanted to support the cause, even if I thought it was wrong, by contributing a guy with a clear head, I guess.
I don't think I could have lived with myself if I hadn't done it.

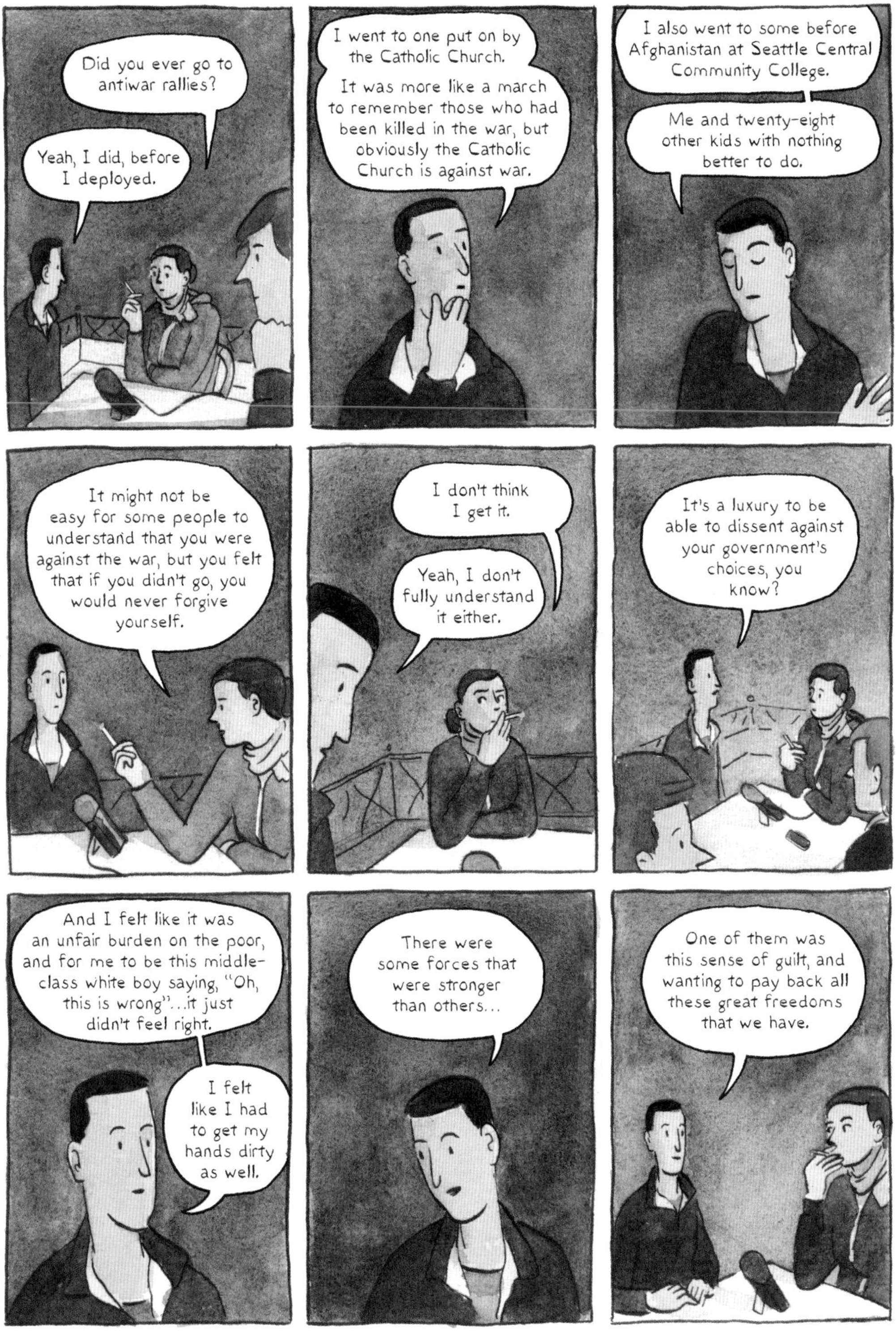
Did you ever go to antiwar rallies?
Yeah, I did, before I deployed.
I went to one put on by the Catholic Church.
It was more like a march to remember those who had been killed in the war, but obviously the Catholic Church is against war.
I also went to some before Afghanistan at Seattle Central Community College.
Me and twenty-eight other kids with nothing better to do.
It might not be easy for some people to understand that you were against the war, but you felt that if you didn't go, you would never forgive yourself.
I don't think I get it.
Yeah, I don't fully understand it either.
It's a luxury to be able to dissent against your government's choices, you know?
And I felt like it was an unfair burden on the poor, and for me to be this middle-class white boy saying, "Oh, this is wrong"...it just didn't feel right.
I felt like I had to get my hands dirty as well.
There were some forces that were stronger than others...
One of them was this sense of guilt, and wanting to pay back all these great freedoms that we have.

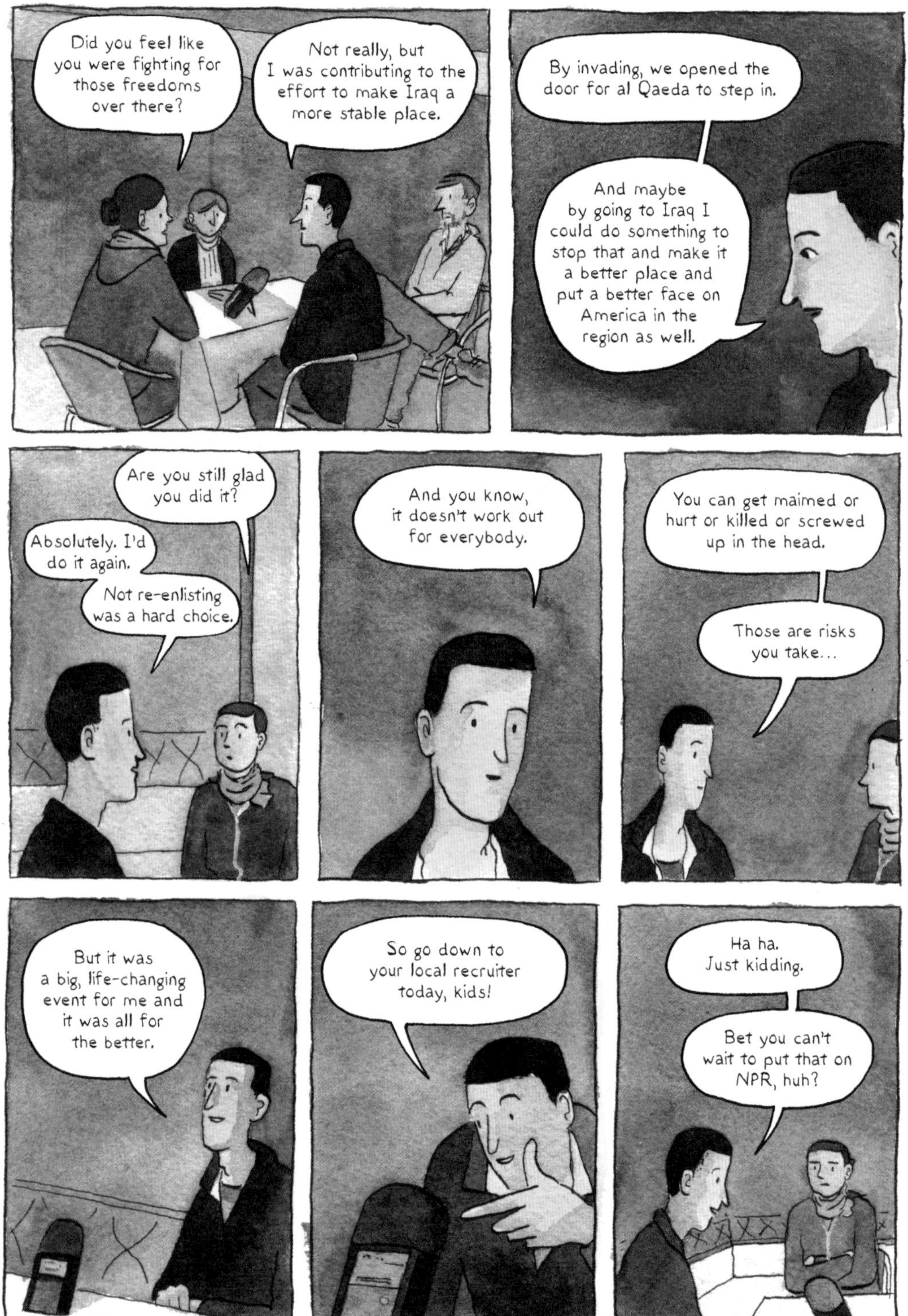
Did you feel like you were fighting for those freedoms over there?
Not really, but I was contributing to the effort to make Iraq a more stable place.
By invading, we opened the door for al Qaeda to step in.
And maybe by going to Iraq I could do something to stop that and make it a better place and put a better face on America in the region as well.
Are you still glad you did it?
Absolutely. I'd do it again.
Not re-enlisting was a hard choice.
And you know, it doesn't work out for everybody.
You can get maimed or hurt or killed or screwed up in the head.
Those are risks you take...
But it was a big, life-changing event for me and it was all for the better.
So go down to your local recruiter today, kids!
Ha ha. Just kidding.
Bet you can't wait to put that on NPR, huh?

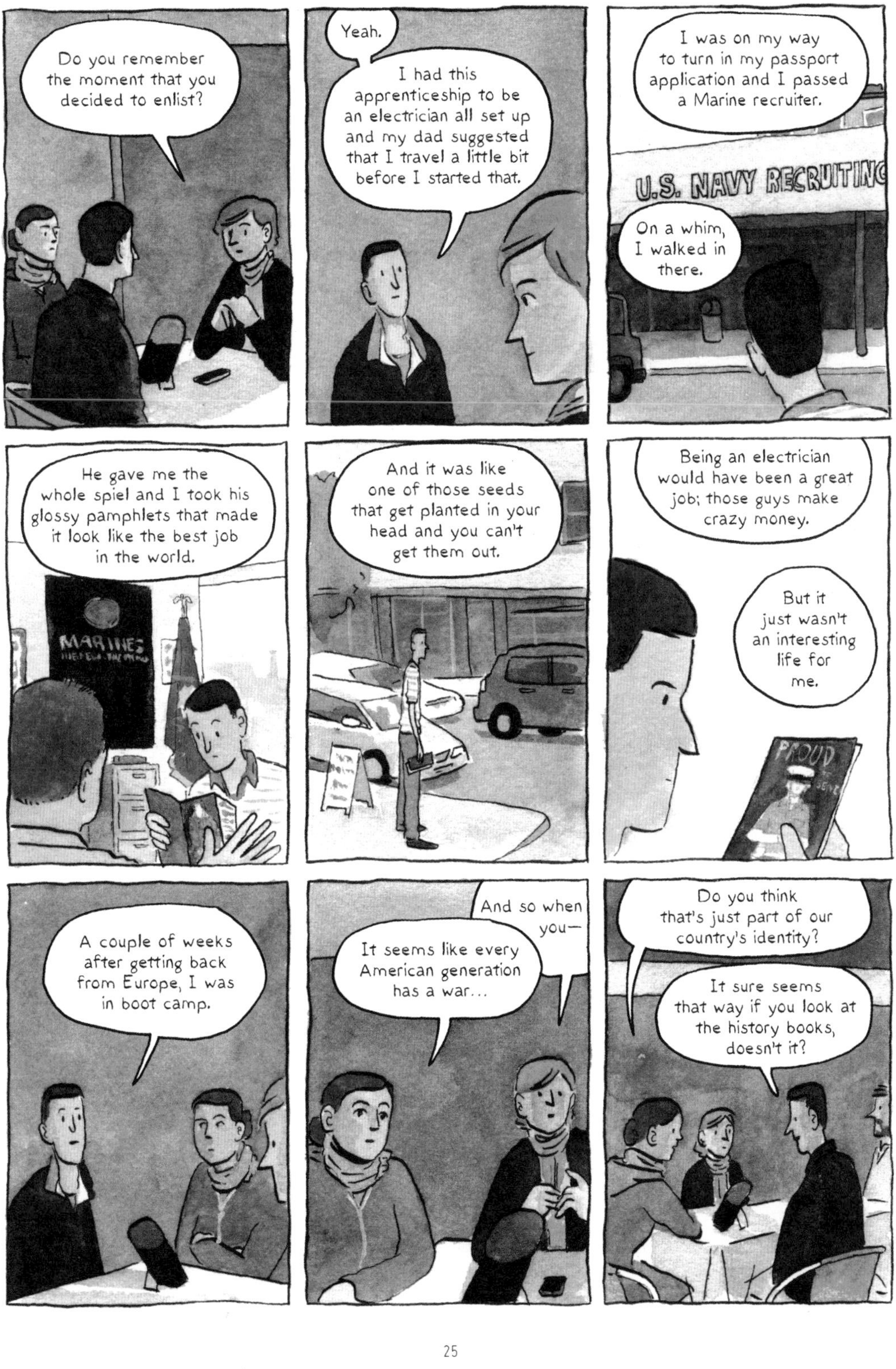
Do you remember the moment that you decided to enlist?
Yeah.
I had this apprenticeship to be an electrician all set up and my dad suggested that I travel a little bit before I started that.
I was on my way to turn in my passport application and I passed a Marine recruiter.
U.S. NAVY RECRUITIN
On a whim, I walked in there.
He gave me the whole spiel and I took his glossy pamphlets that made it look like the best job in the world.
MARINES
And it was like one of those seeds that get planted in your head and you can't get them out.
Being an electrician would have been a great job; those guys make crazy money.
But it just wasn't an interesting life for me.
PROUD
A couple of weeks after getting back from Europe, I was in boot camp.
And so when you—
It seems like every American generation has a war...
Do you think that's just part of our country's identity?
It sure seems that way if you look at the history books, doesn't it?

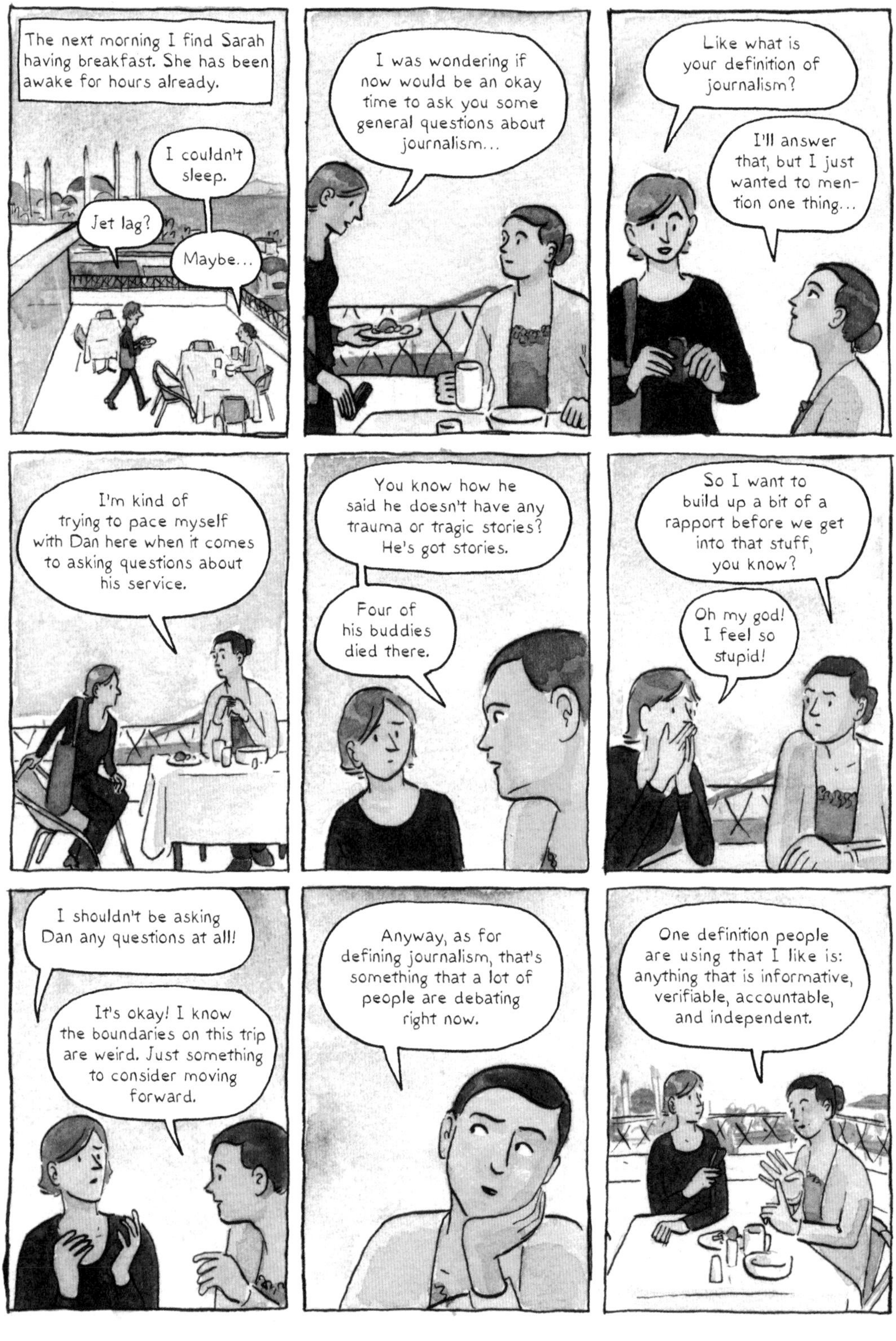
The next morning I find Sarah having breakfast. She has been awake for hours already.
I couldn't sleep.
Jet lag?
Maybe...
I was wondering if now would be an okay time to ask you some general questions about journalism...
Like what is your definition of journalism?
I'll answer that, but I just wanted to mention one thing...
I'm kind of trying to pace myself with Dan here when it comes to asking questions about his service.
You know how he said he doesn't have any trauma or tragic stories? He's got stories.
Four of his buddies died there.
So I want to build up a bit of a rapport before we get into that stuff, you know?
Oh my god! I feel so stupid!
I shouldn't be asking Dan any questions at all!
It's okay! I know the boundaries on this trip are weird. Just something to consider moving forward.
Anyway, as for defining journalism, that's something that a lot of people are debating right now.
One definition people are using that I like is: anything that is informative, verifiable, accountable, and independent.

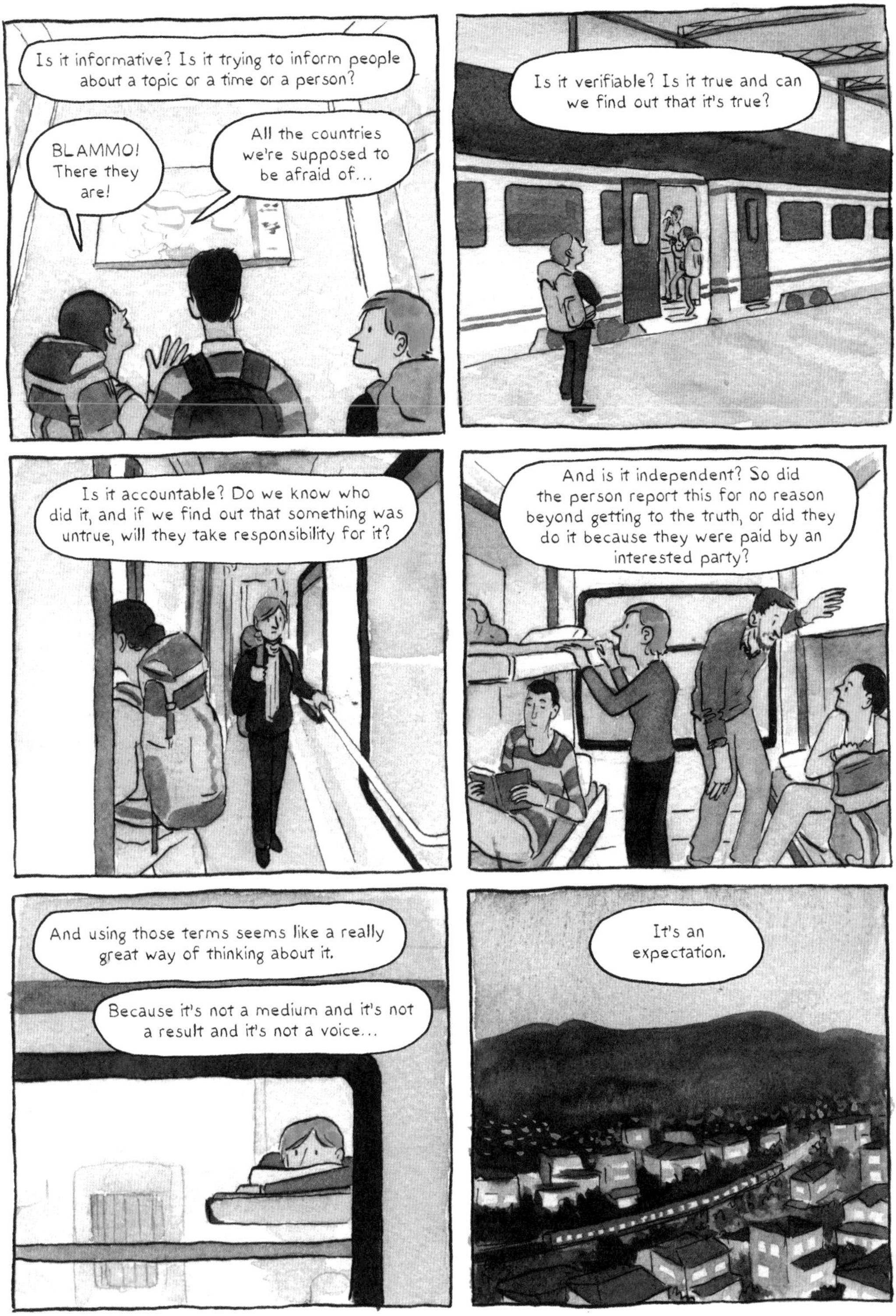
Is it informative? Is it trying to inform people about a topic or a time or a person?
BLAMMO! There they are!
All the countries we're supposed to be afraid of...
Is it verifiable? Is it true and can we find out that it's true?
Is it accountable? Do we know who did it, and if we find out that something was untrue, will they take responsibility for it?
And is it independent? So did the person report this for no reason beyond getting to the truth, or did they do it because they were paid by an interested party?
And using those terms seems like a really great way of thinking about it.
Because it's not a medium and it's not a result and it's not a voice...
It's an expectation.

THE TRANS-ASIA EXPRESS

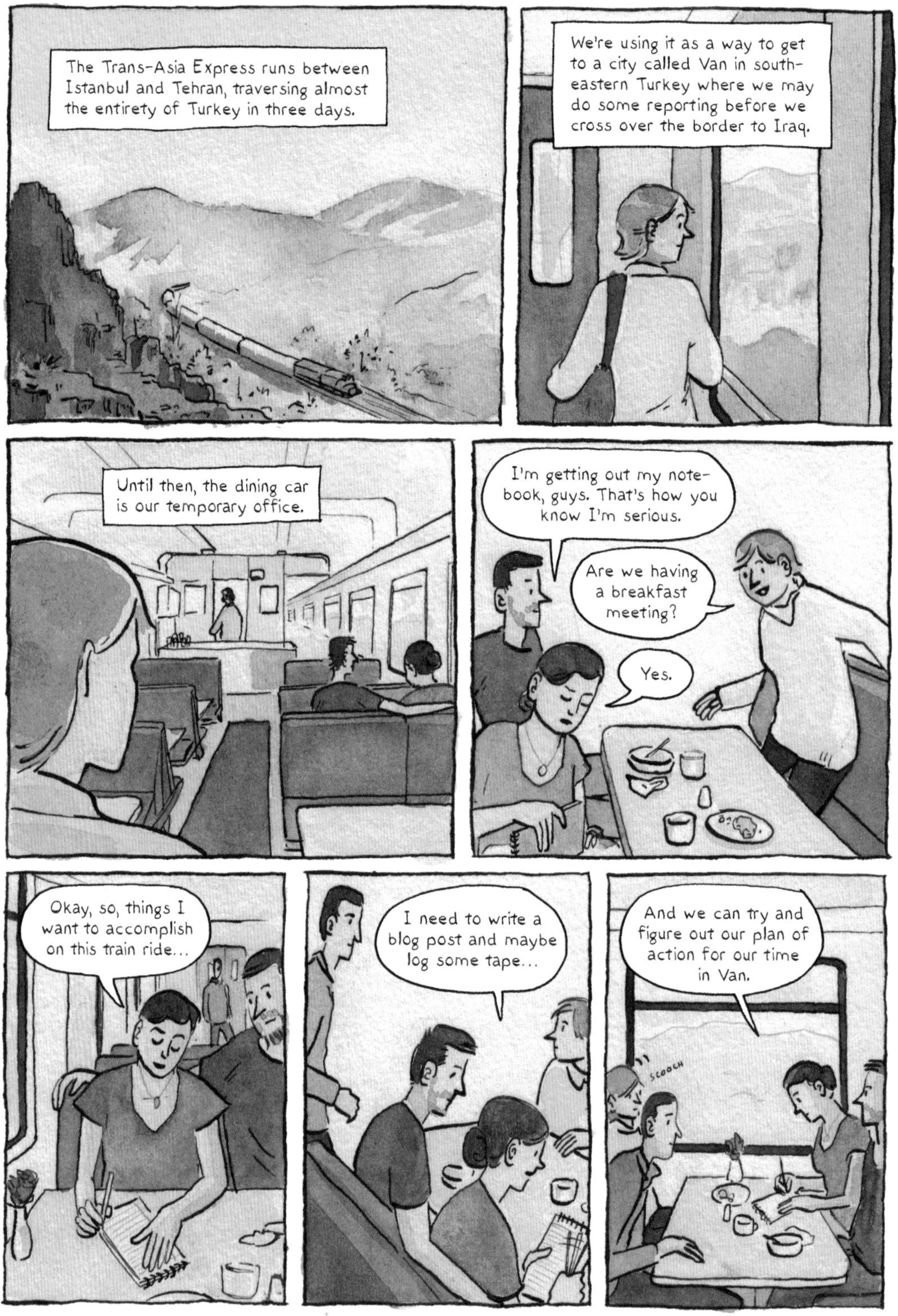
The Trans-Asia Express runs between Istanbul and Tehran, traversing almost the entirety of Turkey in three days.
We're using it as a way to get to a city called Van in south-eastern Turkey where we may do some reporting before we cross over the border to Iraq.
Until then, the dining car is our temporary office.
I'm getting out my note-book, guys. That's how you know I'm serious.
Are we having a breakfast meeting?
Yes.
Okay, so, things I want to accomplish on this train ride...
I need to write a blog post and maybe log some tape...
SCOOCH
And we can try and figure out our plan of action for our time in Van.

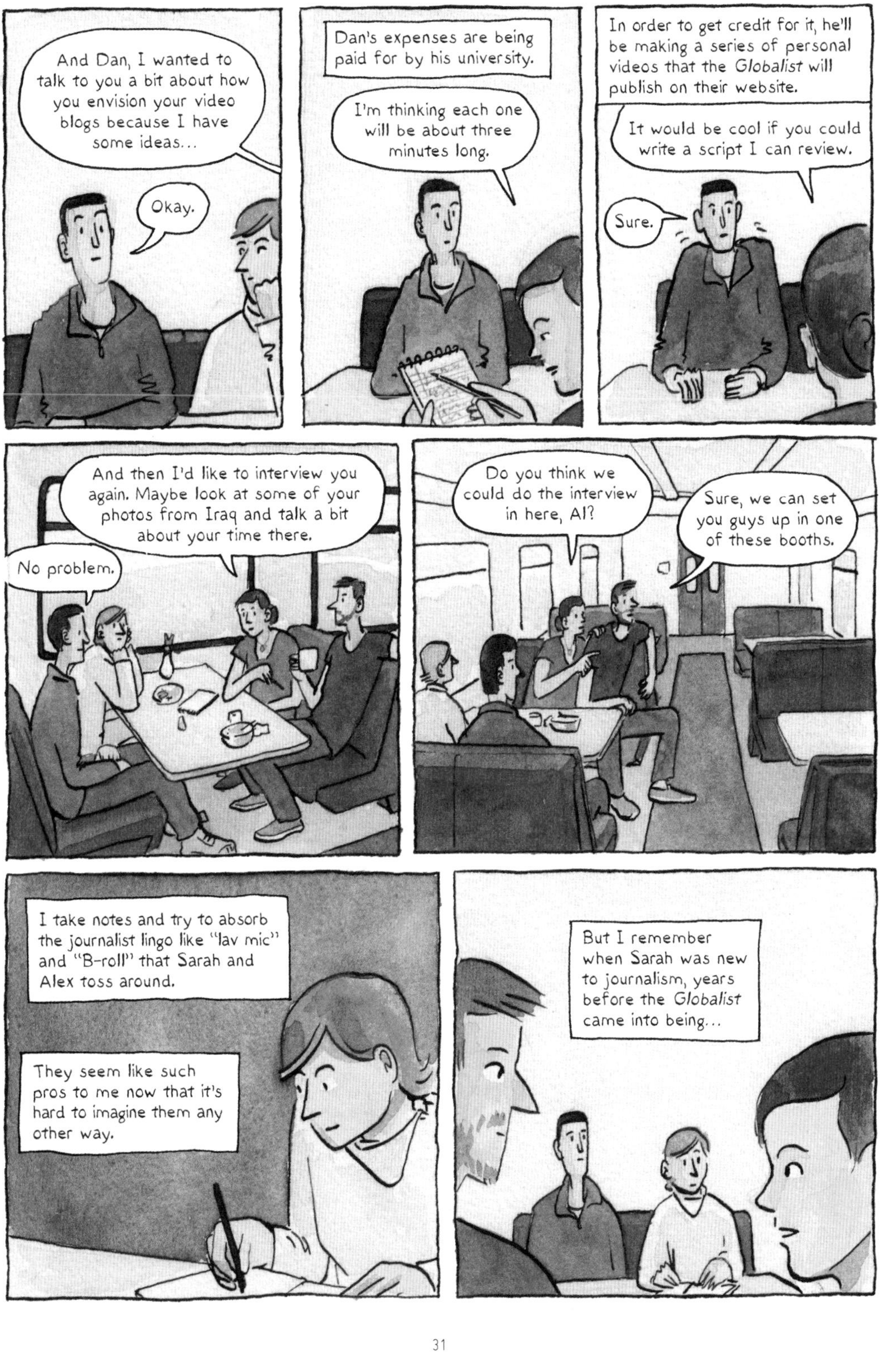
And Dan, I wanted to talk to you a bit about how you envision your video blogs because I have some ideas...
Okay.
Dan's expenses are being paid for by his university.
I'm thinking each one will be about three minutes long.
In order to get credit for it, he'll be making a series of personal videos that the *Globalist* will publish on their website.
It would be cool if you could write a script I can review.
Sure.
And then I'd like to interview you again. Maybe look at some of your photos from Iraq and talk a bit about your time there.
No problem.
Do you think we could do the interview in here, Al?
Sure, we can set you guys up in one of these booths.
I take notes and try to absorb the journalist lingo like "lav mic" and "B-roll" that Sarah and Alex toss around.
They seem like such pros to me now that it's hard to imagine them any other way.
But I remember when Sarah was new to journalism, years before the *Globalist* came into being...

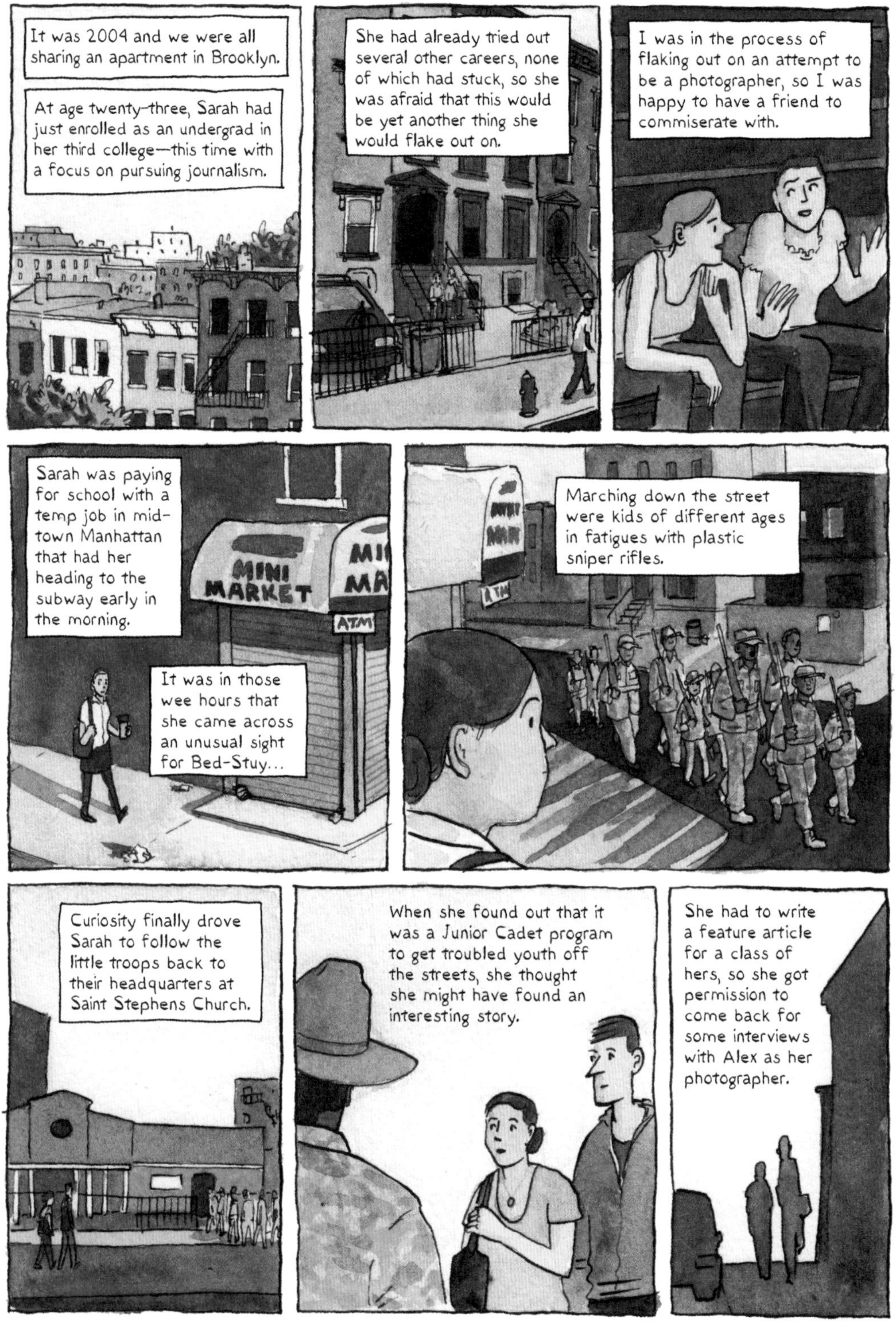
It was 2004 and we were all sharing an apartment in Brooklyn.
At age twenty-three, Sarah had just enrolled as an undergrad in her third college—this time with a focus on pursuing journalism.
She had already tried out several other careers, none of which had stuck, so she was afraid that this would be yet another thing she would flake out on.
I was in the process of flaking out on an attempt to be a photographer, so I was happy to have a friend to commiserate with.
Sarah was paying for school with a temp job in mid-town Manhattan that had her heading to the subway early in the morning.
MINI MARKET
ATM
It was in those wee hours that she came across an unusual sight for Bed-Stuy...
Marching down the street were kids of different ages in fatigues with plastic sniper rifles.
Curiosity finally drove Sarah to follow the little troops back to their headquarters at Saint Stephens Church.
When she found out that it was a Junior Cadet program to get troubled youth off the streets, she thought she might have found an interesting story.
She had to write a feature article for a class of hers, so she got permission to come back for some interviews with Alex as her photographer.

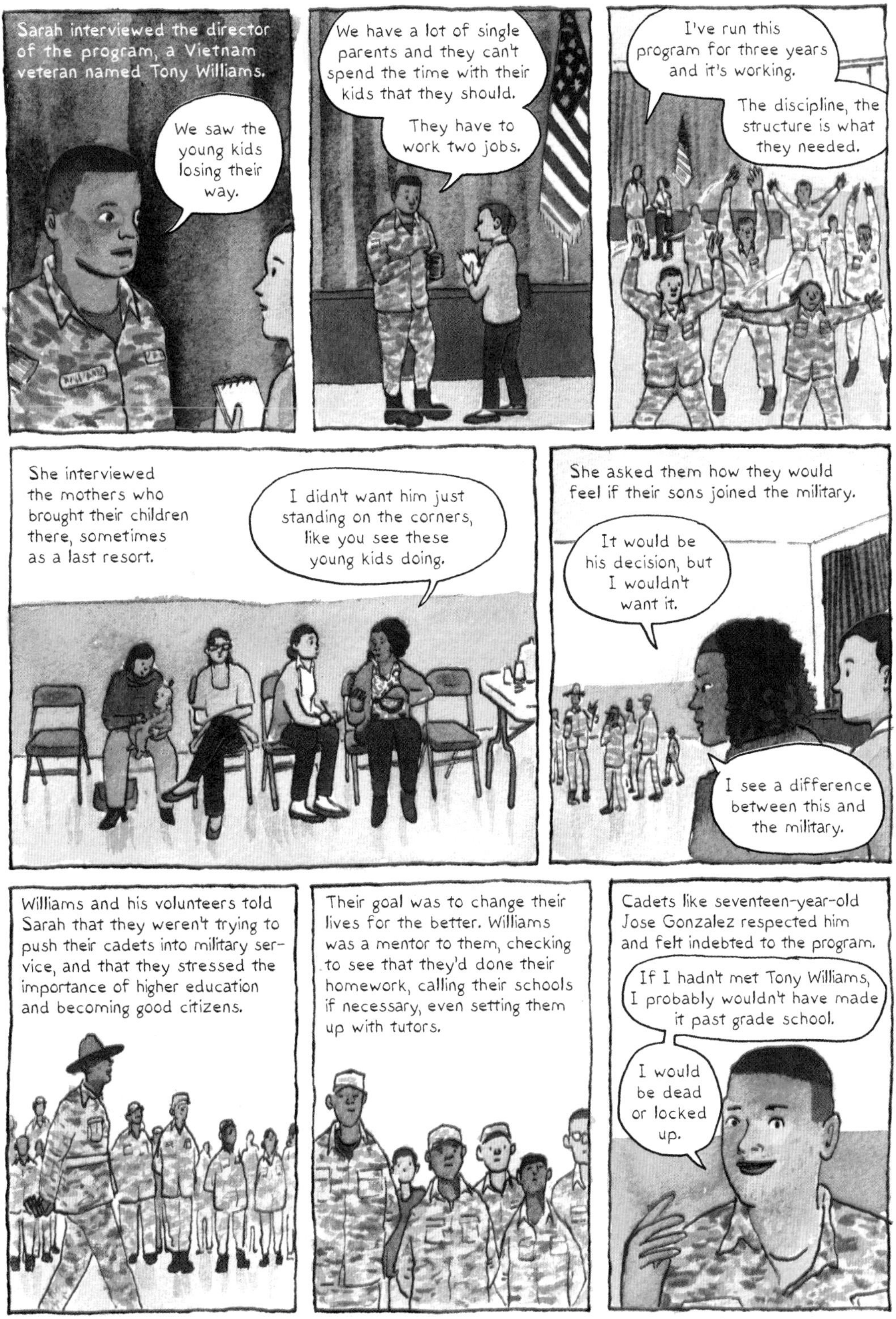
Sarah interviewed the director of the program, a Vietnam veteran named Tony Williams.
We saw the young kids losing their way.
We have a lot of single parents and they can't spend the time with their kids that they should.
They have to work two jobs.
I've run this program for three years and it's working.
The discipline, the structure is what they needed.
She interviewed the mothers who brought their children there, sometimes as a last resort.
I didn't want him just standing on the corners, like you see these young kids doing.
She asked them how they would feel if their sons joined the military.
It would be his decision, but I wouldn't want it.
I see a difference between this and the military.
Williams and his volunteers told Sarah that they weren't trying to push their cadets into military service, and that they stressed the importance of higher education and becoming good citizens.
Their goal was to change their lives for the better. Williams was a mentor to them, checking to see that they'd done their homework, calling their schools if necessary, even setting them up with tutors.
Cadets like seventeen-year-old Jose Gonzalez respected him and felt indebted to the program.
If I hadn't met Tony Williams, I probably wouldn't have made it past grade school.
I would be dead or locked up.

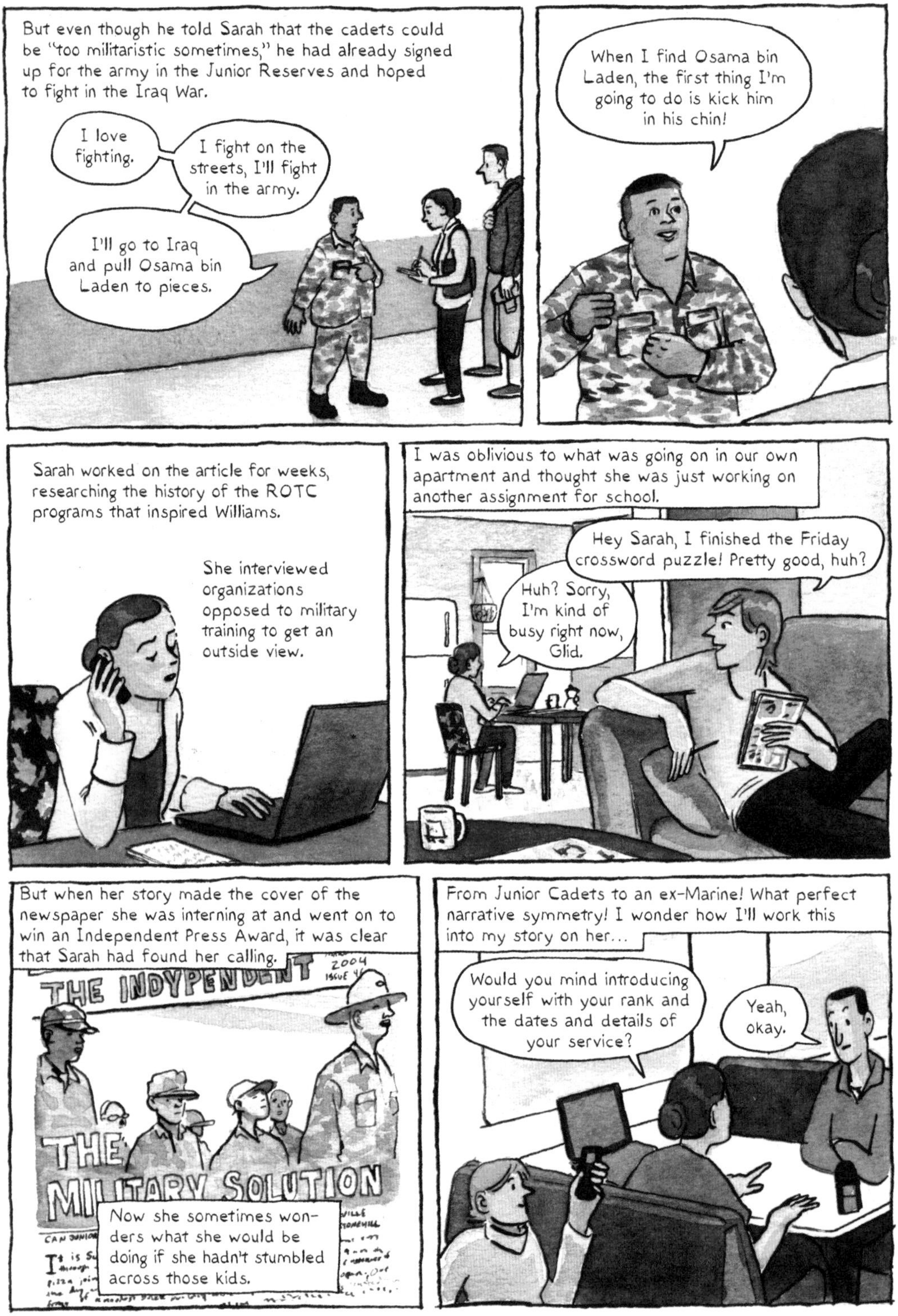
But even though he told Sarah that the cadets could be "too militaristic sometimes," he had already signed up for the army in the Junior Reserves and hoped to fight in the Iraq War.
I love fighting.
I fight on the streets, I'll fight in the army.
I'll go to Iraq and pull Osama bin Laden to pieces.
When I find Osama bin Laden, the first thing I'm going to do is kick him in his chin!
Sarah worked on the article for weeks, researching the history of the ROTC programs that inspired Williams.
She interviewed organizations opposed to military training to get an outside view.
I was oblivious to what was going on in our own apartment and thought she was just working on another assignment for school.
Hey Sarah, I finished the Friday crossword puzzle! Pretty good, huh?
Huh? Sorry, I'm kind of busy right now, Glid.
But when her story made the cover of the newspaper she was interning at and went on to win an Independent Press Award, it was clear that Sarah had found her calling.
THE INDYPENDENT
2004
THE MILITARY SOLUTION
Now she sometimes wonders what she would be doing if she hadn't stumbled across those kids.
From Junior Cadets to an ex-Marine! What perfect narrative symmetry! I wonder how I'll work this into my story on her...
Would you mind introducing yourself with your rank and the dates and details of your service?
Yeah, okay.

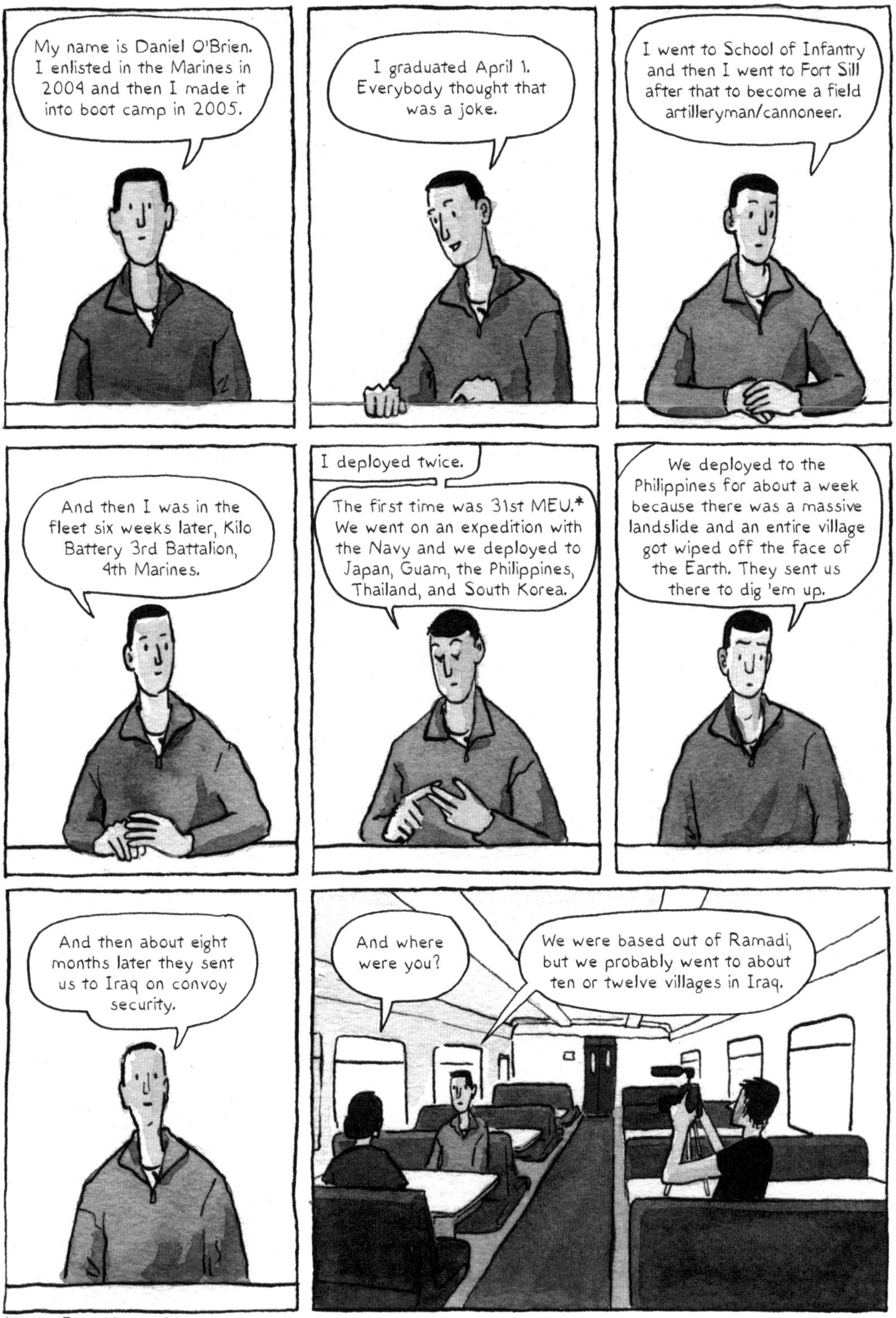
My name is Daniel O'Brien. I enlisted in the Marines in 2004 and then I made it into boot camp in 2005.
I graduated April 1. Everybody thought that was a joke.
I went to School of Infantry and then I went to Fort Sill after that to become a field artilleryman/cannoneer.
And then I was in the fleet six weeks later, Kilo Battery 3rd Battalion, 4th Marines.
I deployed twice.
The first time was 31st MEU.* We went on an expedition with the Navy and we deployed to Japan, Guam, the Philippines, Thailand, and South Korea.
We deployed to the Philippines for about a week because there was a massive landslide and an entire village got wiped off the face of the Earth. They sent us there to dig 'em up.
And then about eight months later they sent us to Iraq on convoy security.
And where were you?
We were based out of Ramadi, but we probably went to about ten or twelve villages in Iraq.

*Marine Expeditionary Unit

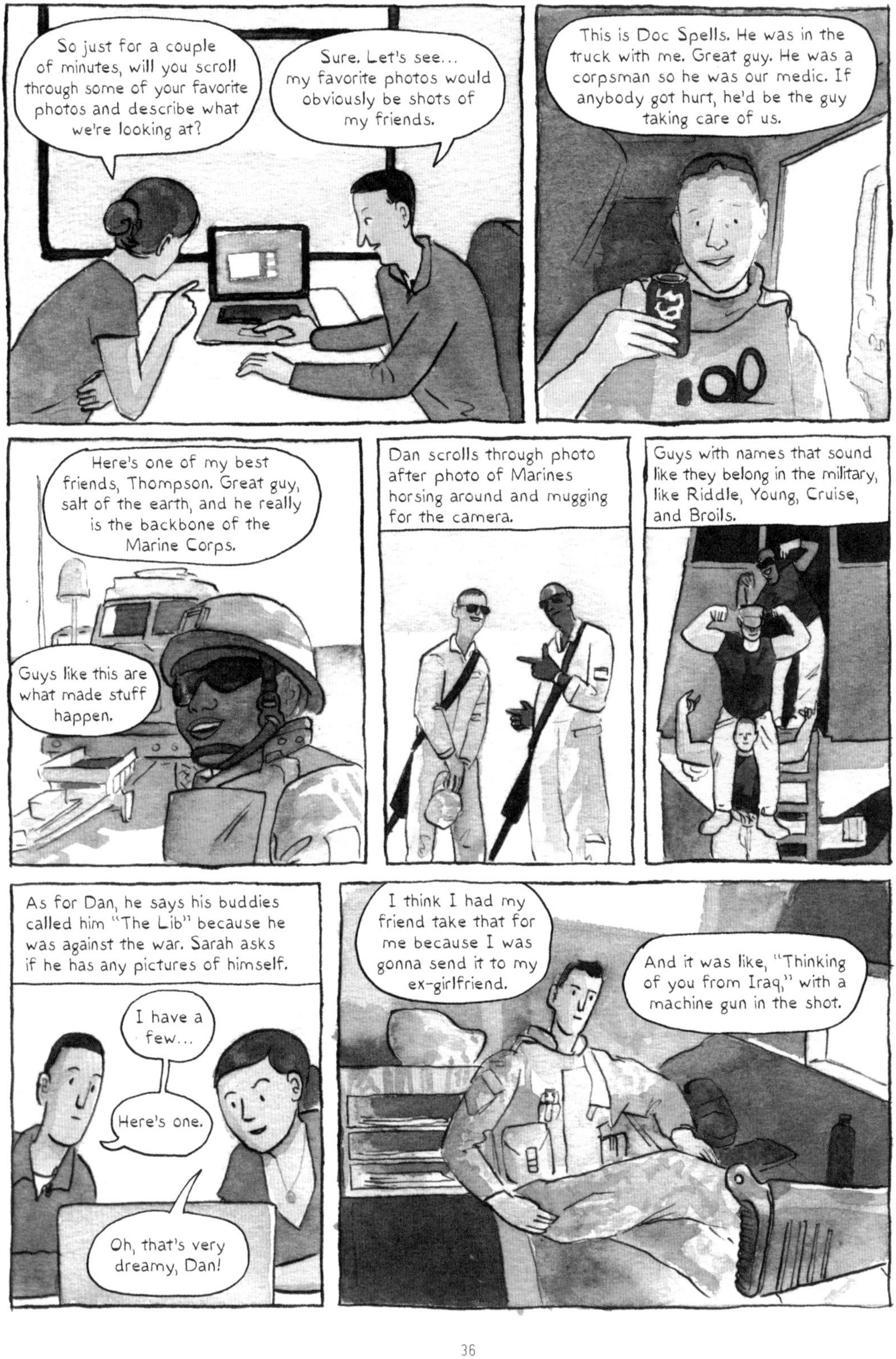
So just for a couple of minutes, will you scroll through some of your favorite photos and describe what we're looking at?
Sure. Let's see... my favorite photos would obviously be shots of my friends.
This is Doc Spells. He was in the truck with me. Great guy. He was a corpsman so he was our medic. If anybody got hurt, he'd be the guy taking care of us.
Here's one of my best friends, Thompson. Great guy, salt of the earth, and he really is the backbone of the Marine Corps.
Guys like this are what made stuff happen.
Dan scrolls through photo after photo of Marines horsing around and mugging for the camera.
Guys with names that sound like they belong in the military, like Riddle, Young, Cruise, and Broils.
As for Dan, he says his buddies called him "The Lib" because he was against the war. Sarah asks if he has any pictures of himself.
I have a few...
Here's one.
Oh, that's very dreamy, Dan!
I think I had my friend take that for me because I was gonna send it to my ex-girlfriend.
And it was like, "Thinking of you from Iraq," with a machine gun in the shot.

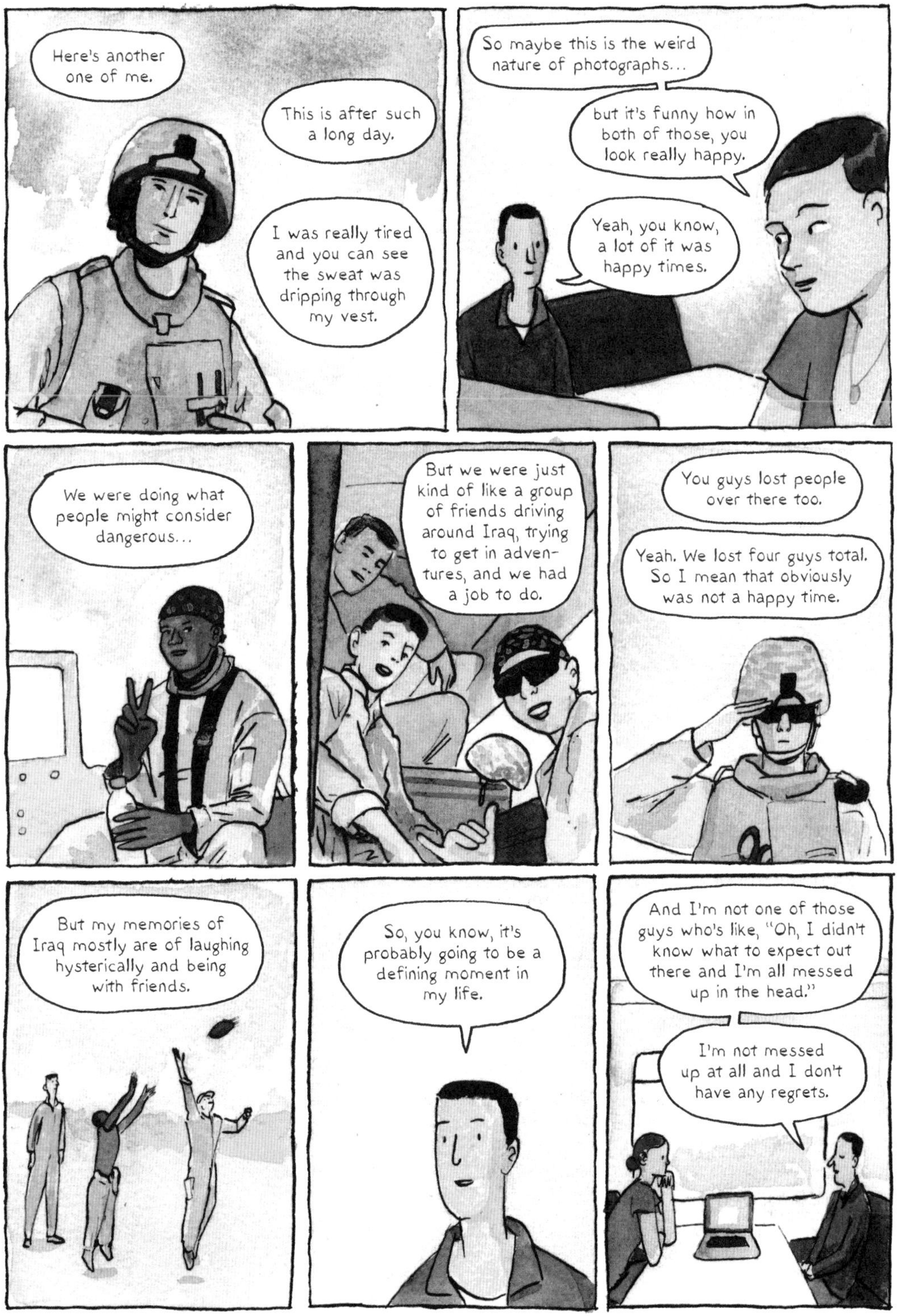
Here's another one of me.
This is after such a long day.
I was really tired and you can see the sweat was dripping through my vest.
So maybe this is the weird nature of photographs...
but it's funny how in both of those, you look really happy.
Yeah, you know, a lot of it was happy times.
We were doing what people might consider dangerous...
But we were just kind of like a group of friends driving around Iraq, trying to get in adventures, and we had a job to do.
You guys lost people over there too.
Yeah. We lost four guys total. So I mean that obviously was not a happy time.
But my memories of Iraq mostly are of laughing hysterically and being with friends.
So, you know, it's probably going to be a defining moment in my life.
And I'm not one of those guys who's like, "Oh, I didn't know what to expect out there and I'm all messed up in the head."
I'm not messed up at all and I don't have any regrets.

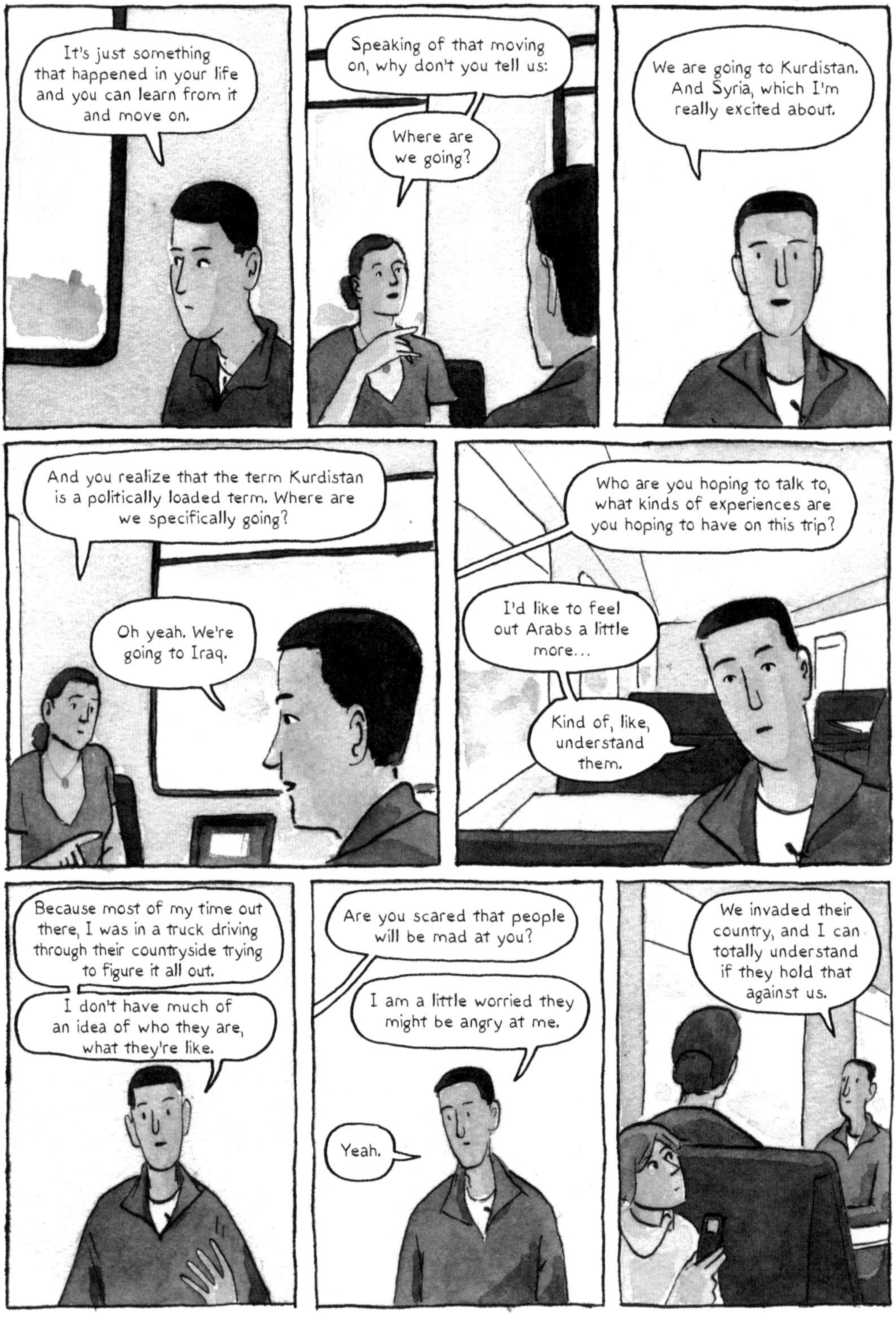
It's just something that happened in your life and you can learn from it and move on.
Speaking of that moving on, why don't you tell us:
Where are we going?
We are going to Kurdistan. And Syria, which I'm really excited about.
And you realize that the term Kurdistan is a politically loaded term. Where are we specifically going?
Oh yeah. We're going to Iraq.
Who are you hoping to talk to, what kinds of experiences are you hoping to have on this trip?
I'd like to feel out Arabs a little more...
Kind of, like, understand them.
Because most of my time out there, I was in a truck driving through their countryside trying to figure it all out.
I don't have much of an idea of who they are, what they're like.
Are you scared that people will be mad at you?
I am a little worried they might be angry at me.
Yeah.
We invaded their country, and I can totally understand if they hold that against us.

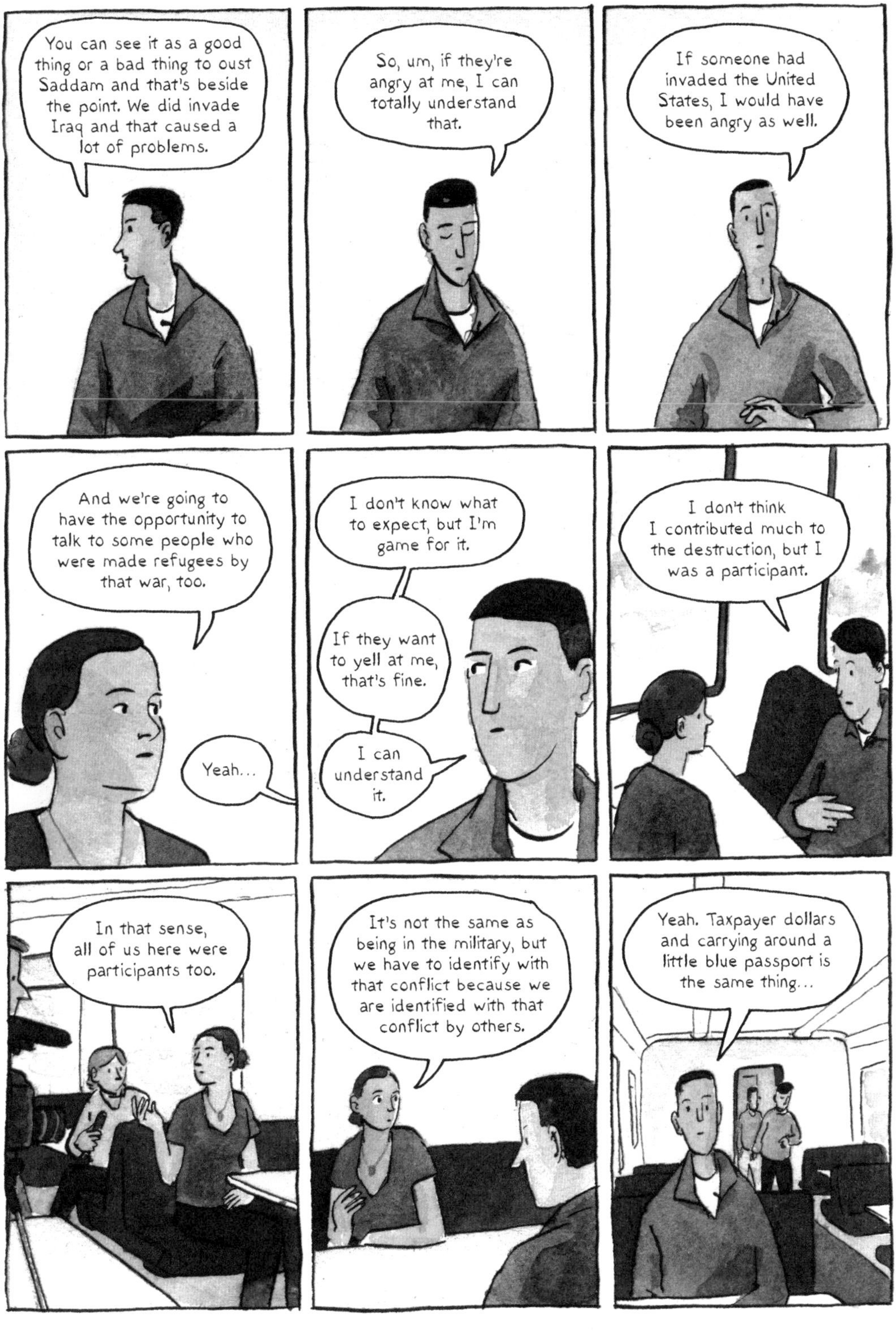
You can see it as a good thing or a bad thing to oust Saddam and that's beside the point. We did invade Iraq and that caused a lot of problems.
So, um, if they're angry at me, I can totally understand that.
If someone had invaded the United States, I would have been angry as well.
And we're going to have the opportunity to talk to some people who were made refugees by that war, too.
Yeah...
I don't know what to expect, but I'm game for it.
If they want to yell at me, that's fine.
I can understand it.
I don't think I contributed much to the destruction, but I was a participant.
In that sense, all of us here were participants too.
It's not the same as being in the military, but we have to identify with that conflict because we are identified with that conflict by others.
Yeah. Taxpayer dollars and carrying around a little blue passport is the same thing...

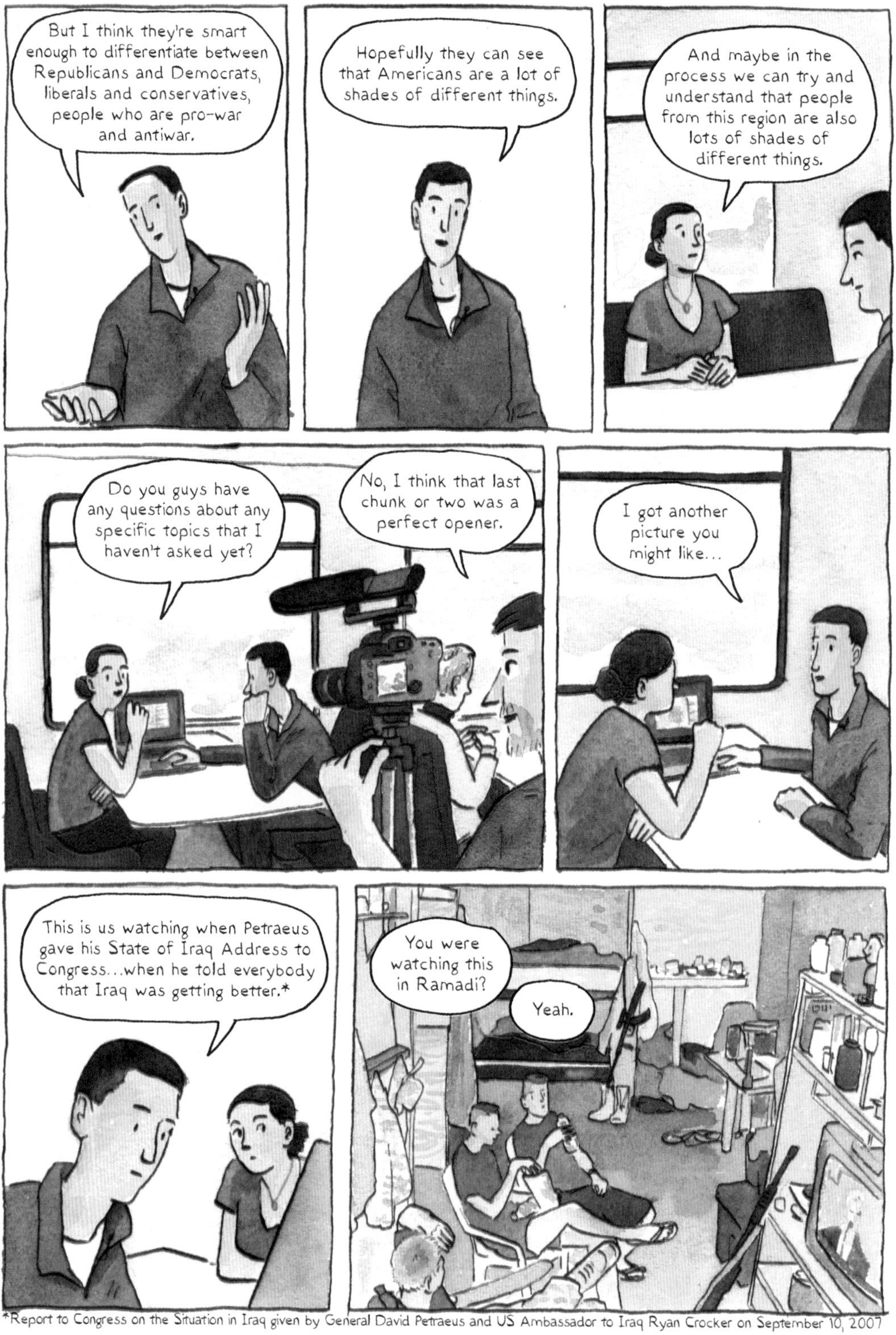
But I think they're smart enough to differentiate between Republicans and Democrats, liberals and conservatives, people who are pro-war and antiwar.
Hopefully they can see that Americans are a lot of shades of different things.
And maybe in the process we can try and understand that people from this region are also lots of shades of different things.
Do you guys have any questions about any specific topics that I haven't asked yet?
No, I think that last chunk or two was a perfect opener.
I got another picture you might like...
This is us watching when Petraeus gave his State of Iraq Address to Congress...when he told everybody that Iraq was getting better.*
You were watching this in Ramadi?
Yeah.

*Report to Congress on the Situation in Iraq given by General David Petraeus and US Ambassador to Iraq Ryan Crocker on September 10, 2007

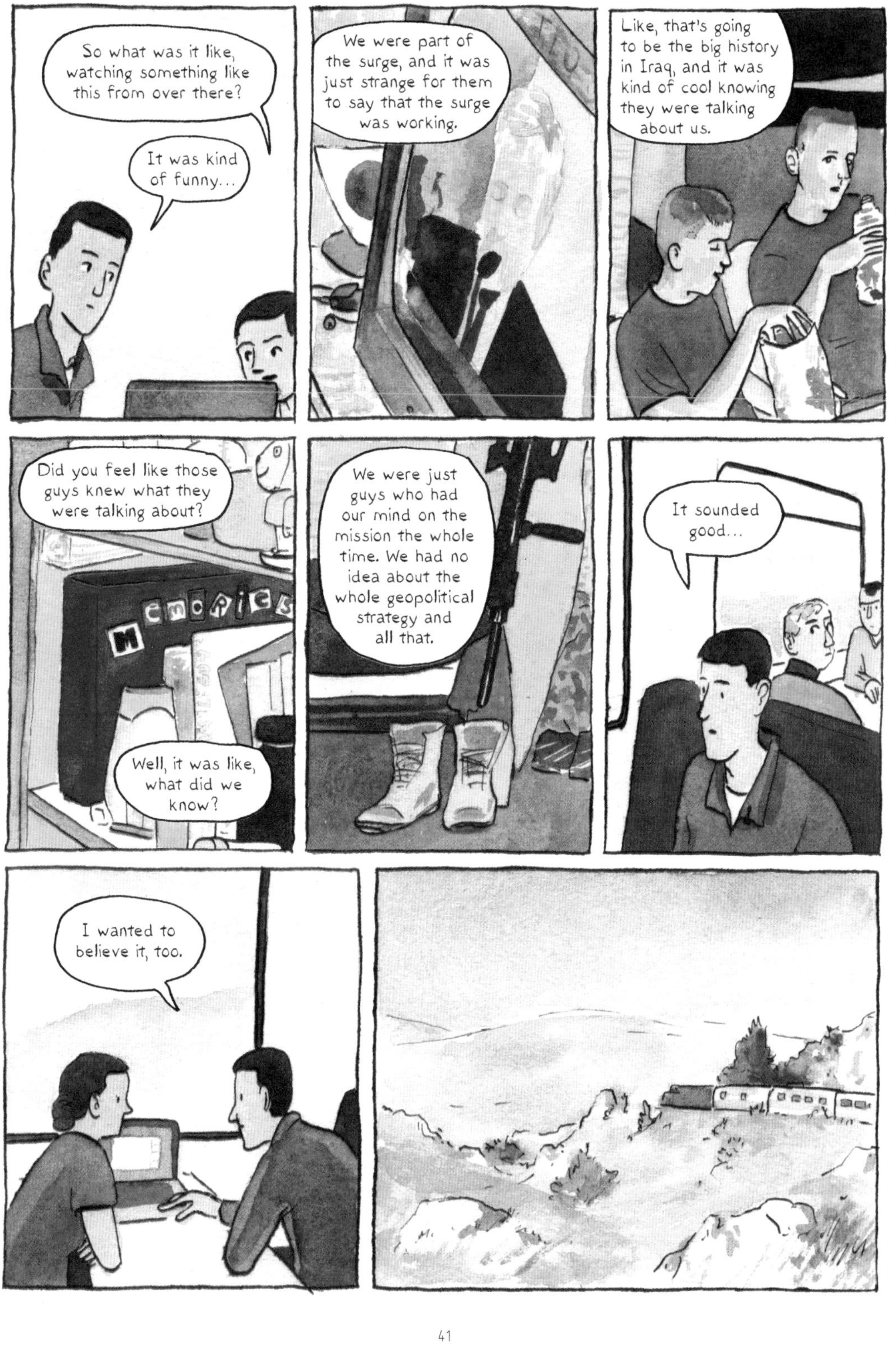

So what was it like, watching something like this from over there?
It was kind of funny...
We were part of the surge, and it was just strange for them to say that the surge was working.
Like, that's going to be the big history in Iraq, and it was kind of cool knowing they were talking about us.
Did you feel like those guys knew what they were talking about?
Memories
Well, it was like, what did we know?
We were just guys who had our mind on the mission the whole time. We had no idea about the whole geopolitical strategy and all that.
It sounded good...
I wanted to believe it, too.

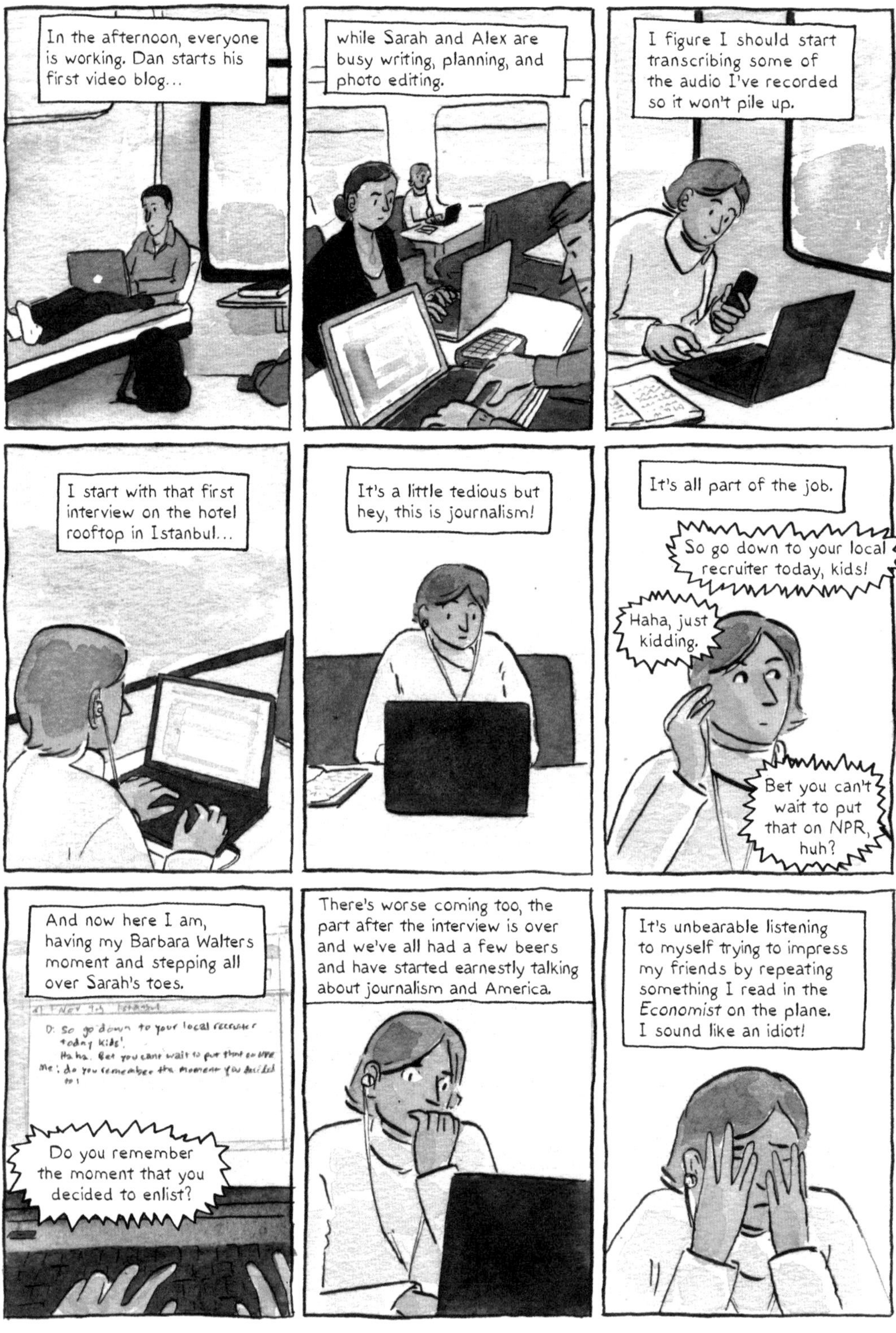
In the afternoon, everyone is working. Dan starts his first video blog...
while Sarah and Alex are busy writing, planning, and photo editing.
I figure I should start transcribing some of the audio I've recorded so it won't pile up.
I start with that first interview on the hotel rooftop in Istanbul...
It's a little tedious but hey, this is journalism!
It's all part of the job.
So go down to your local recruiter today, kids!
Haha, just kidding.
Bet you can't wait to put that on NPR, huh?
And now here I am, having my Barbara Walters moment and stepping all over Sarah's toes.
Do you remember the moment that you decided to enlist?
There's worse coming too, the part after the interview is over and we've all had a few beers and have started earnestly talking about journalism and America.
It's unbearable listening to myself trying to impress my friends by repeating something I read in the *Economist* on the plane. I sound like an idiot!

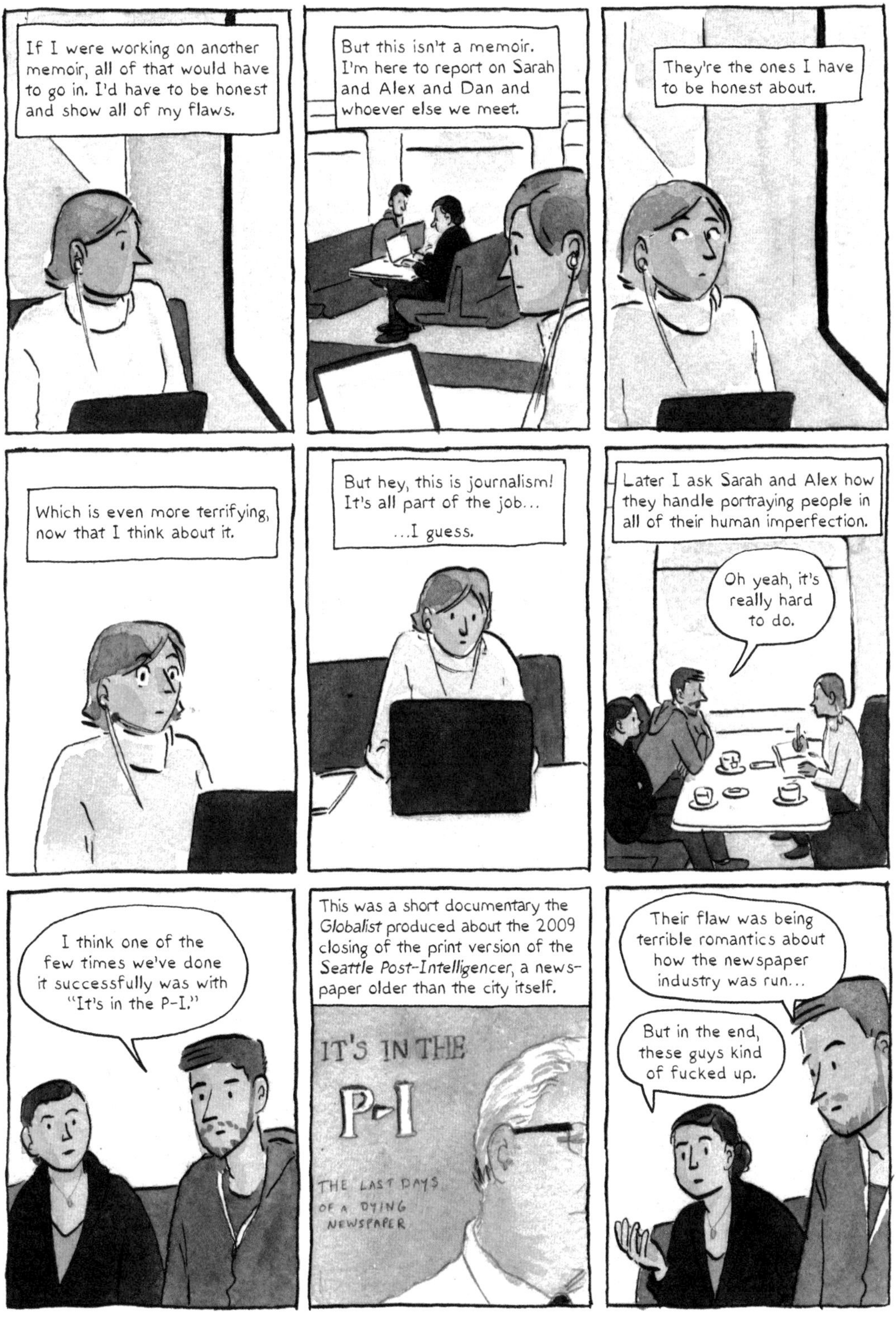
If I were working on another memoir, all of that would have to go in. I'd have to be honest and show all of my flaws.
But this isn't a memoir. I'm here to report on Sarah and Alex and Dan and whoever else we meet.
They're the ones I have to be honest about.
Which is even more terrifying, now that I think about it.
But hey, this is journalism! It's all part of the job... ...I guess.
Later I ask Sarah and Alex how they handle portraying people in all of their human imperfection.
Oh yeah, it's really hard to do.
I think one of the few times we've done it successfully was with "It's in the P-I."
This was a short documentary the *Globalist* produced about the 2009 closing of the print version of the *Seattle Post-Intelligencer*, a newspaper older than the city itself.
IT'S IN THE P-I
THE LAST DAYS OF A DYING NEWSPAPER
Their flaw was being terrible romantics about how the newspaper industry was run...
But in the end, these guys kind of fucked up.

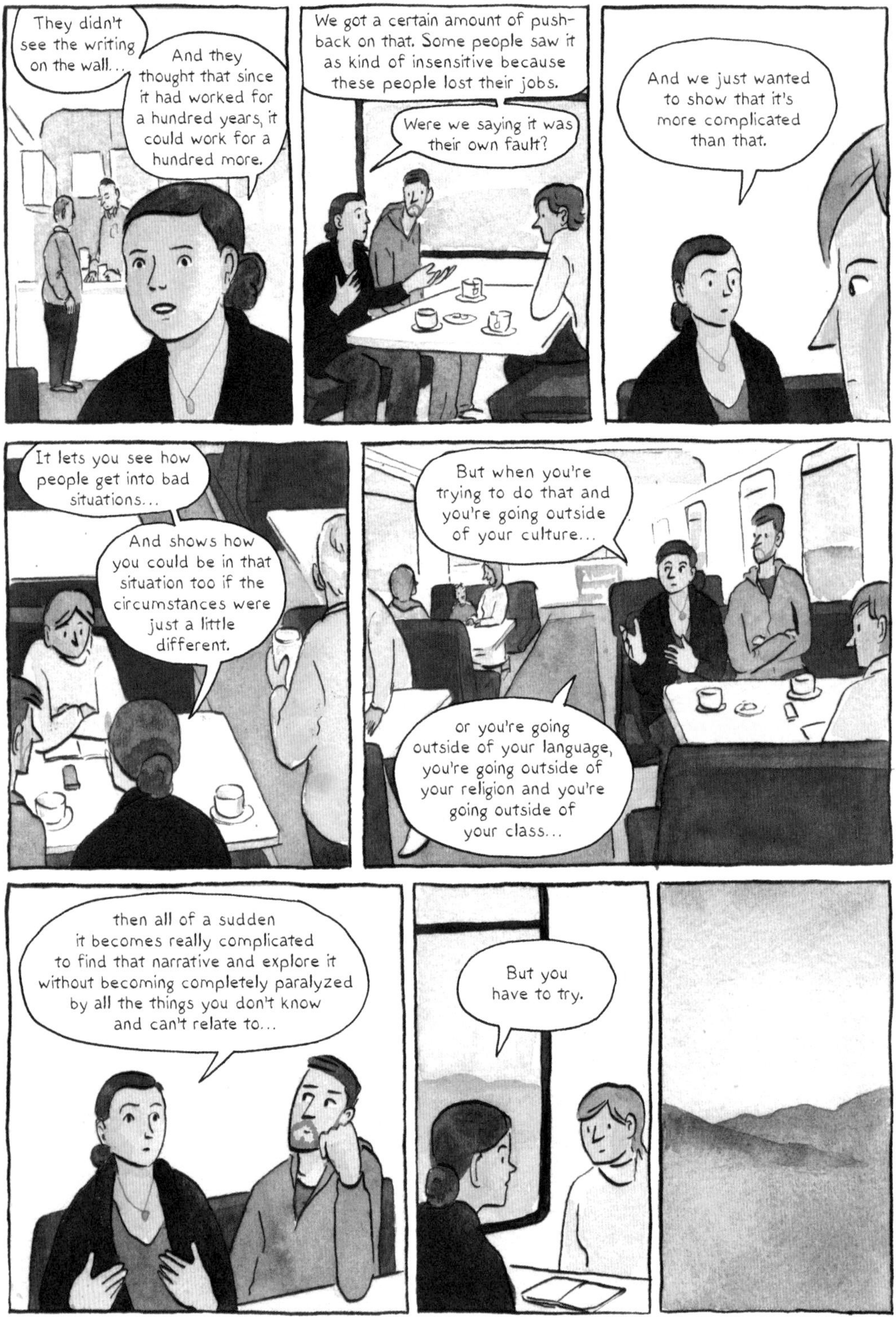
They didn't see the writing on the wall...
And they thought that since it had worked for a hundred years, it could work for a hundred more.
We got a certain amount of push-back on that. Some people saw it as kind of insensitive because these people lost their jobs.
Were we saying it was their own fault?
And we just wanted to show that it's more complicated than that.
It lets you see how people get into bad situations...
And shows how you could be in that situation too if the circumstances were just a little different.
But when you're trying to do that and you're going outside of your culture...
or you're going outside of your language, you're going outside of your religion and you're going outside of your class...
then all of a sudden it becomes really complicated to find that narrative and explore it without becoming completely paralyzed by all the things you don't know and can't relate to...
But you have to try.

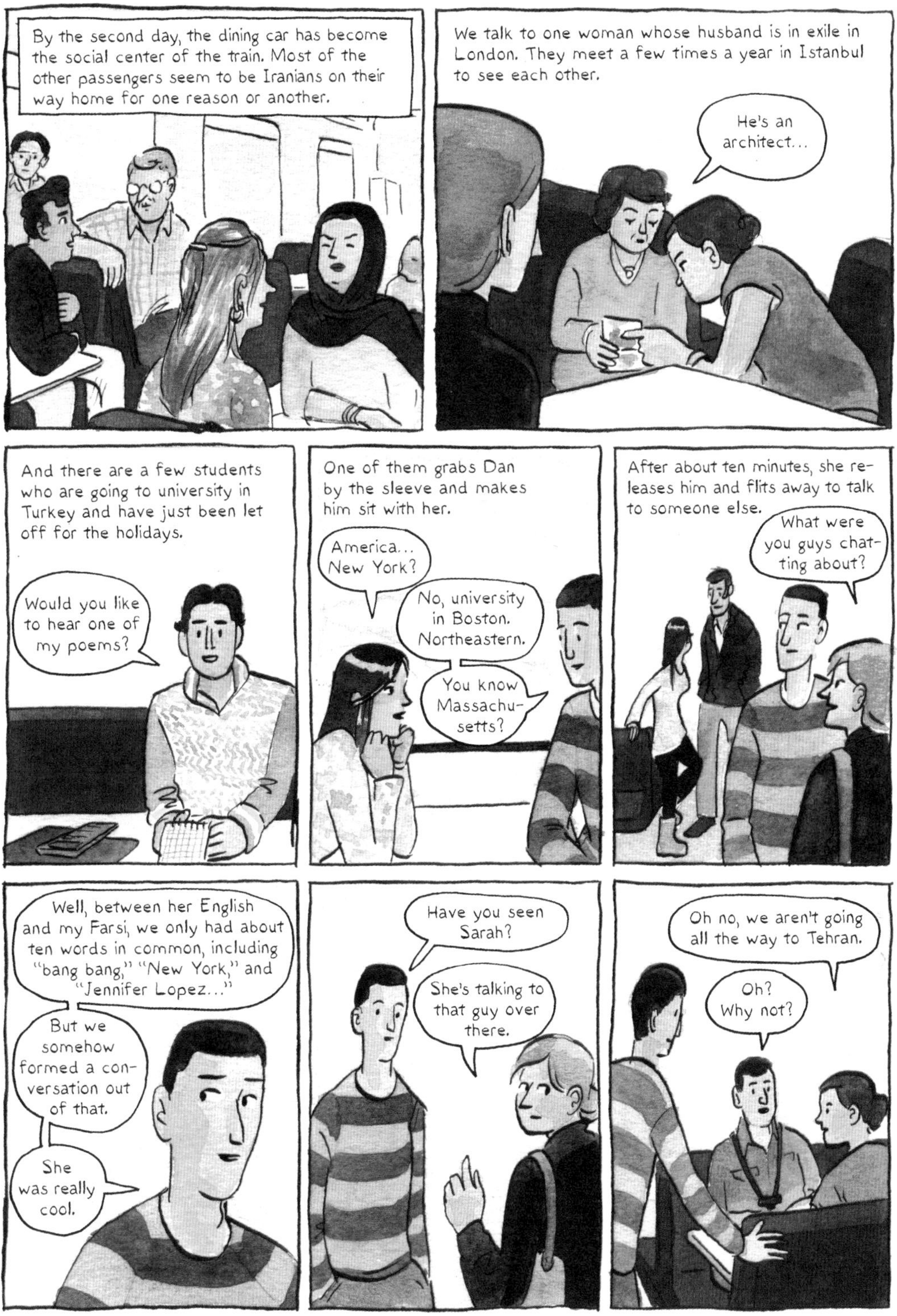
By the second day, the dining car has become the social center of the train. Most of the other passengers seem to be Iranians on their way home for one reason or another.
We talk to one woman whose husband is in exile in London. They meet a few times a year in Istanbul to see each other.
He's an architect...
And there are a few students who are going to university in Turkey and have just been let off for the holidays.
Would you like to hear one of my poems?
One of them grabs Dan by the sleeve and makes him sit with her.
America... New York?
No, university in Boston. Northeastern.
You know Massachusetts?
After about ten minutes, she releases him and flits away to talk to someone else.
What were you guys chatting about?
Well, between her English and my Farsi, we only had about ten words in common, including "bang bang," "New York," and "Jennifer Lopez..."
But we somehow formed a conversation out of that.
She was really cool.
Have you seen Sarah?
She's talking to that guy over there.
Oh no, we aren't going all the way to Tehran.
Oh? Why not?

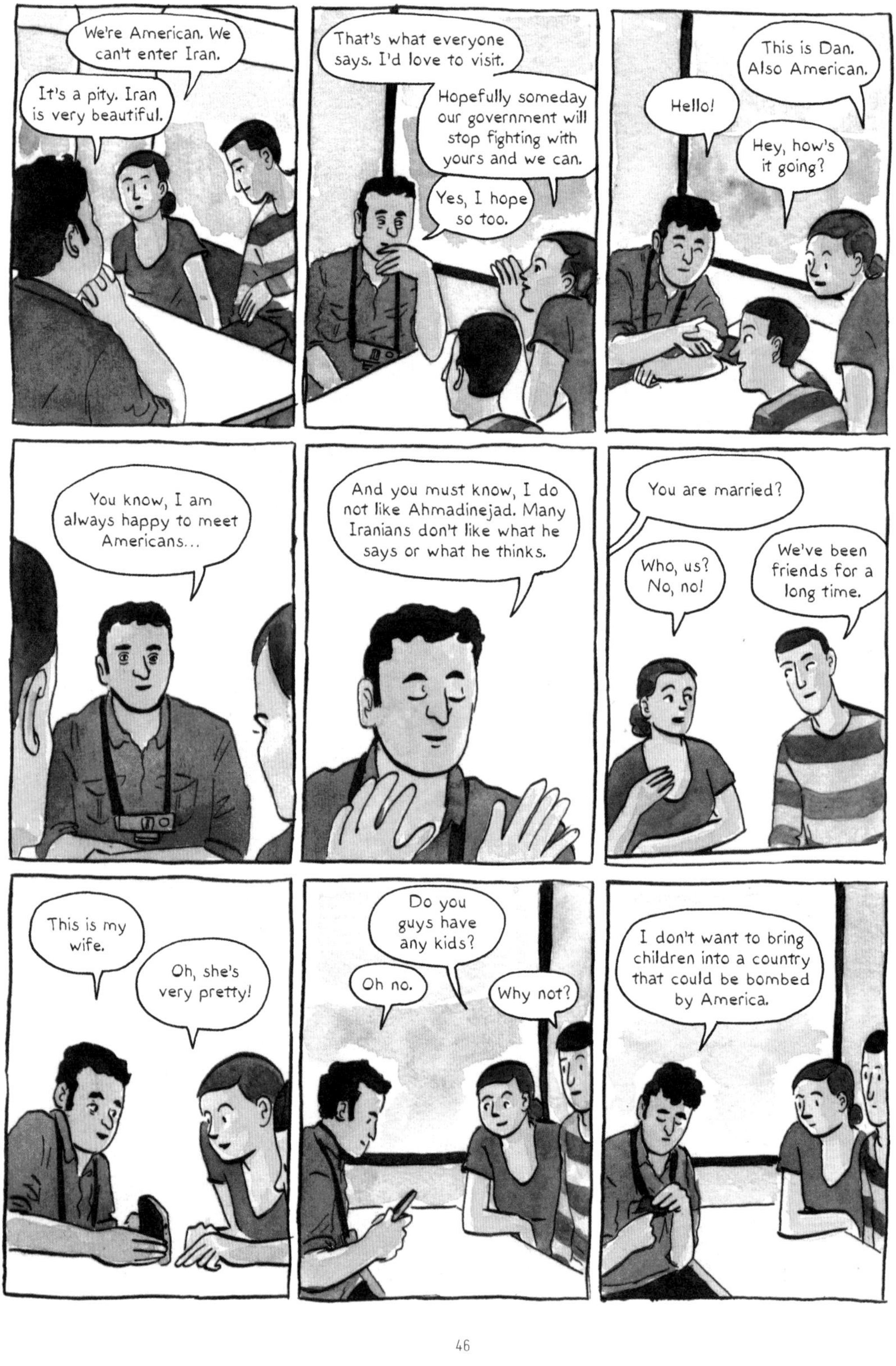
We're American. We can't enter Iran.
It's a pity. Iran is very beautiful.
That's what everyone says. I'd love to visit.
Hopefully someday our government will stop fighting with yours and we can.
Yes, I hope so too.
This is Dan. Also American.
Hello!
Hey, how's it going?
You know, I am always happy to meet Americans...
And you must know, I do not like Ahmadinejad. Many Iranians don't like what he says or what he thinks.
You are married?
Who, us? No, no!
We've been friends for a long time.
This is my wife.
Oh, she's very pretty!
Do you guys have any kids?
Oh no.
Why not?
I don't want to bring children into a country that could be bombed by America.

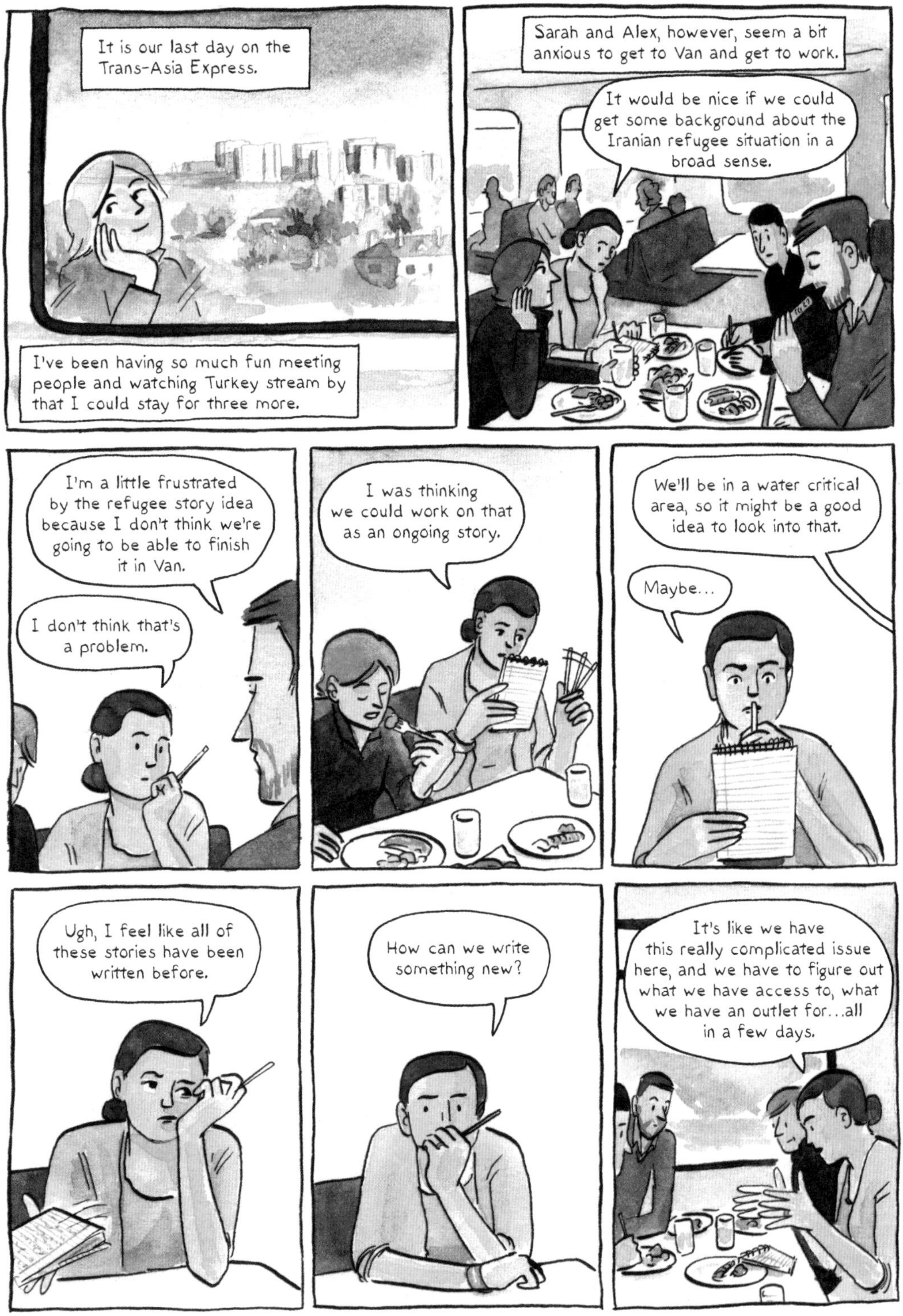

It is our last day on the Trans-Asia Express.
I've been having so much fun meeting people and watching Turkey stream by that I could stay for three more.
Sarah and Alex, however, seem a bit anxious to get to Van and get to work.
It would be nice if we could get some background about the Iranian refugee situation in a broad sense.
I'm a little frustrated by the refugee story idea because I don't think we're going to be able to finish it in Van.
I don't think that's a problem.
I was thinking we could work on that as an ongoing story.
We'll be in a water critical area, so it might be a good idea to look into that.
Maybe...
Ugh, I feel like all of these stories have been written before.
How can we write something new?
It's like we have this really complicated issue here, and we have to figure out what we have access to, what we have an outlet for...all in a few days.

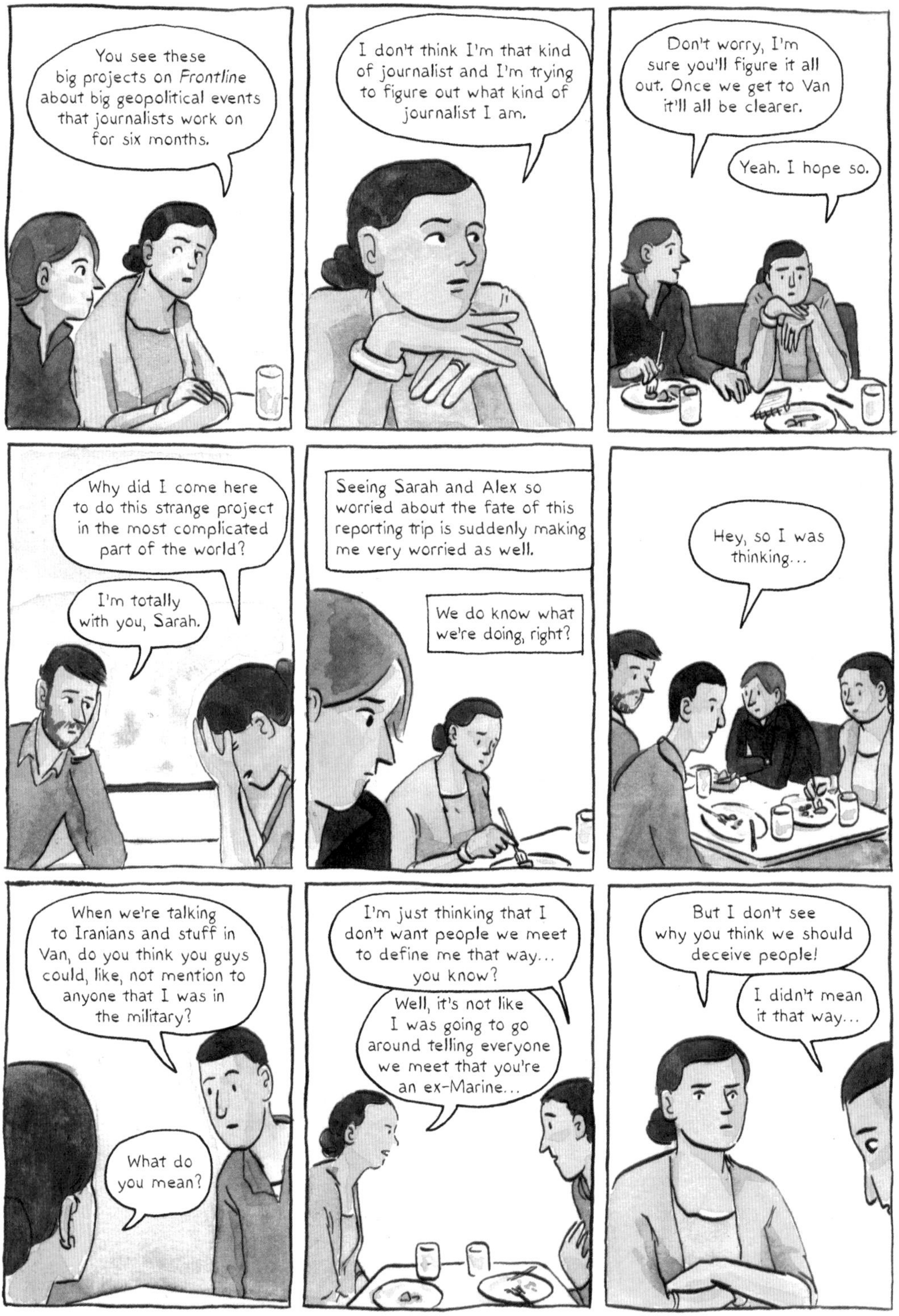
You see these big projects on *Frontline* about big geopolitical events that journalists work on for six months.
I don't think I'm that kind of journalist and I'm trying to figure out what kind of journalist I am.
Don't worry, I'm sure you'll figure it all out. Once we get to Van it'll all be clearer.
Yeah. I hope so.
Why did I come here to do this strange project in the most complicated part of the world?
I'm totally with you, Sarah.
Seeing Sarah and Alex so worried about the fate of this reporting trip is suddenly making me very worried as well.
We do know what we're doing, right?
Hey, so I was thinking...
When we're talking to Iranians and stuff in Van, do you think you guys could, like, not mention to anyone that I was in the military?
What do you mean?
I'm just thinking that I don't want people we meet to define me that way... you know?
Well, it's not like I was going to go around telling everyone we meet that you're an ex-Marine...
But I don't see why you think we should deceive people!
I didn't mean it that way...

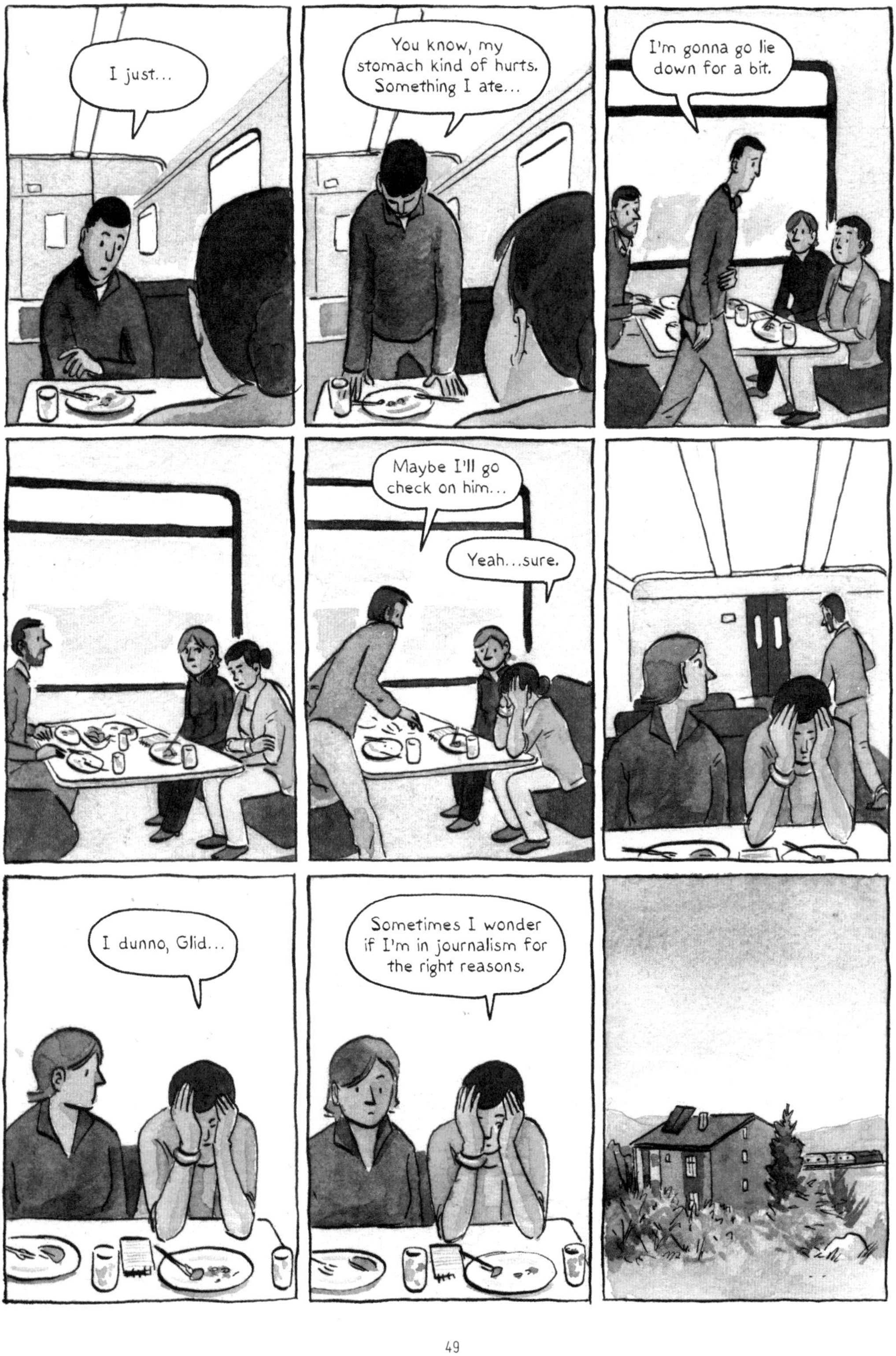
I just...
You know, my stomach kind of hurts. Something I ate...
I'm gonna go lie down for a bit.
Maybe I'll go check on him...
Yeah...sure.
I dunno, Glid...
Sometimes I wonder if I'm in journalism for the right reasons.

VAN, TURKEY

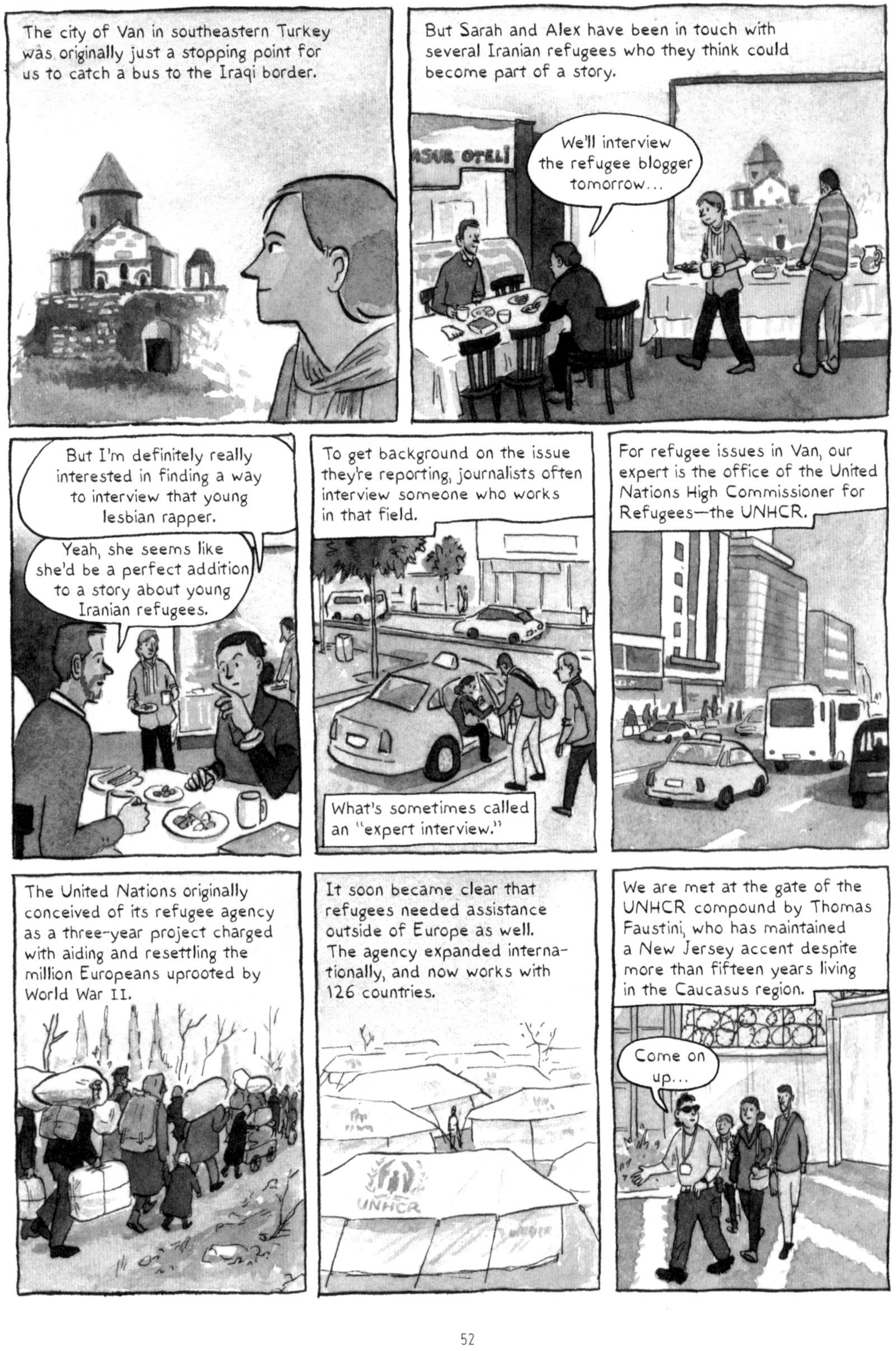

The city of Van in southeastern Turkey was originally just a stopping point for us to catch a bus to the Iraqi border.
But Sarah and Alex have been in touch with several Iranian refugees who they think could become part of a story.
We'll interview the refugee blogger tomorrow...
But I'm definitely really interested in finding a way to interview that young lesbian rapper.
Yeah, she seems like she'd be a perfect addition to a story about young Iranian refugees.
To get background on the issue they're reporting, journalists often interview someone who works in that field.
What's sometimes called an "expert interview."
For refugee issues in Van, our expert is the office of the United Nations High Commissioner for Refugees—the UNHCR.
The United Nations originally conceived of its refugee agency as a three-year project charged with aiding and resettling the million Europeans uprooted by World War II.
It soon became clear that refugees needed assistance outside of Europe as well. The agency expanded internationally, and now works with 126 countries.
UNHCR
We are met at the gate of the UNHCR compound by Thomas Faustini, who has maintained a New Jersey accent despite more than fifteen years living in the Caucasus region.
Come on up...

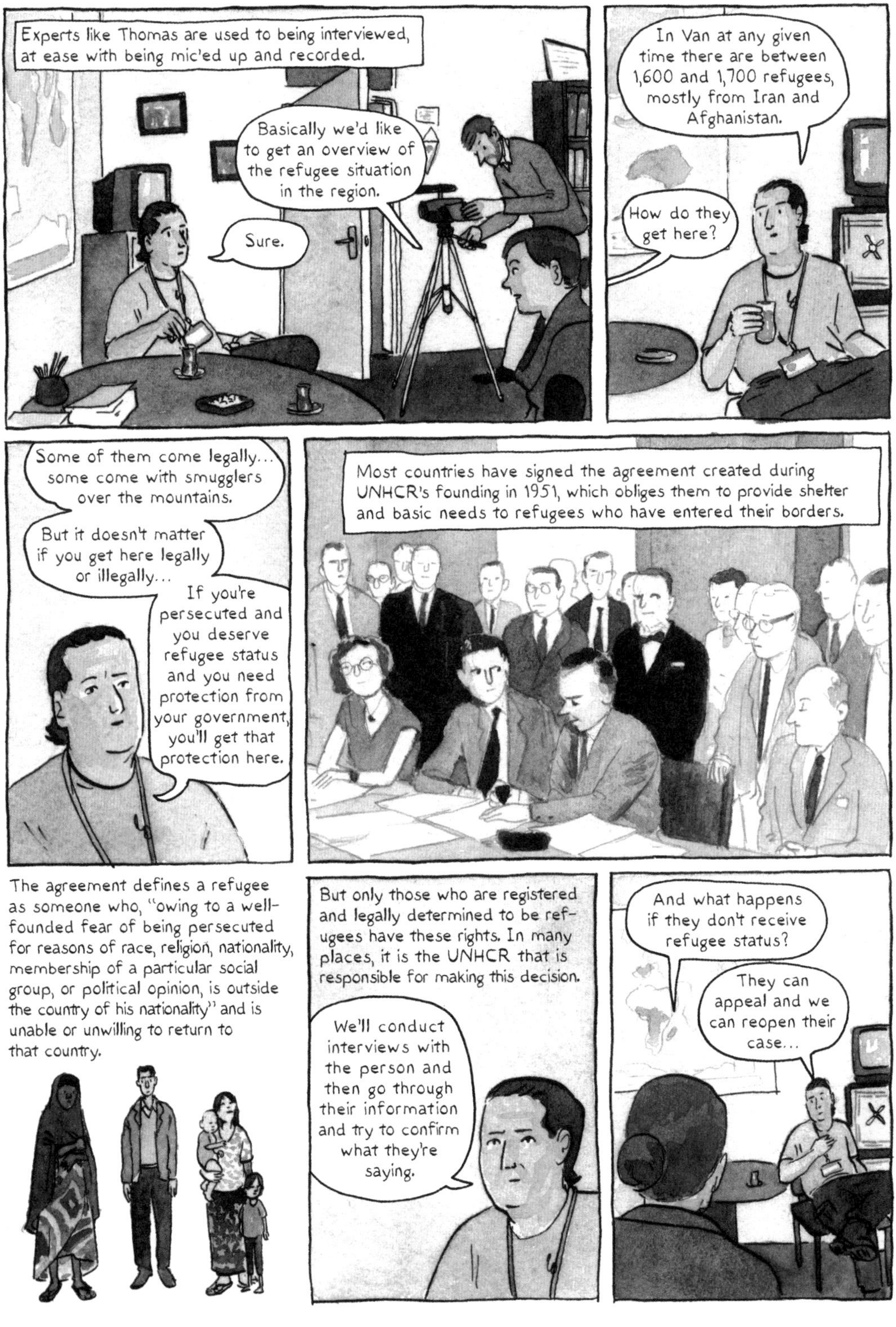
Experts like Thomas are used to being interviewed, at ease with being mic'ed up and recorded.
Basically we'd like to get an overview of the refugee situation in the region.
Sure.
In Van at any given time there are between 1,600 and 1,700 refugees, mostly from Iran and Afghanistan.
How do they get here?
Some of them come legally... some come with smugglers over the mountains.
But it doesn't matter if you get here legally or illegally...
If you're persecuted and you deserve refugee status and you need protection from your government, you'll get that protection here.
Most countries have signed the agreement created during UNHCR's founding in 1951, which obliges them to provide shelter and basic needs to refugees who have entered their borders.
The agreement defines a refugee as someone who, "owing to a well-founded fear of being persecuted for reasons of race, religion, nationality, membership of a particular social group, or political opinion, is outside the country of his nationality" and is unable or unwilling to return to that country.
But only those who are registered and legally determined to be refugees have these rights. In many places, it is the UNHCR that is responsible for making this decision.
We'll conduct interviews with the person and then go through their information and try to confirm what they're saying.
And what happens if they don't receive refugee status?
They can appeal and we can reopen their case...

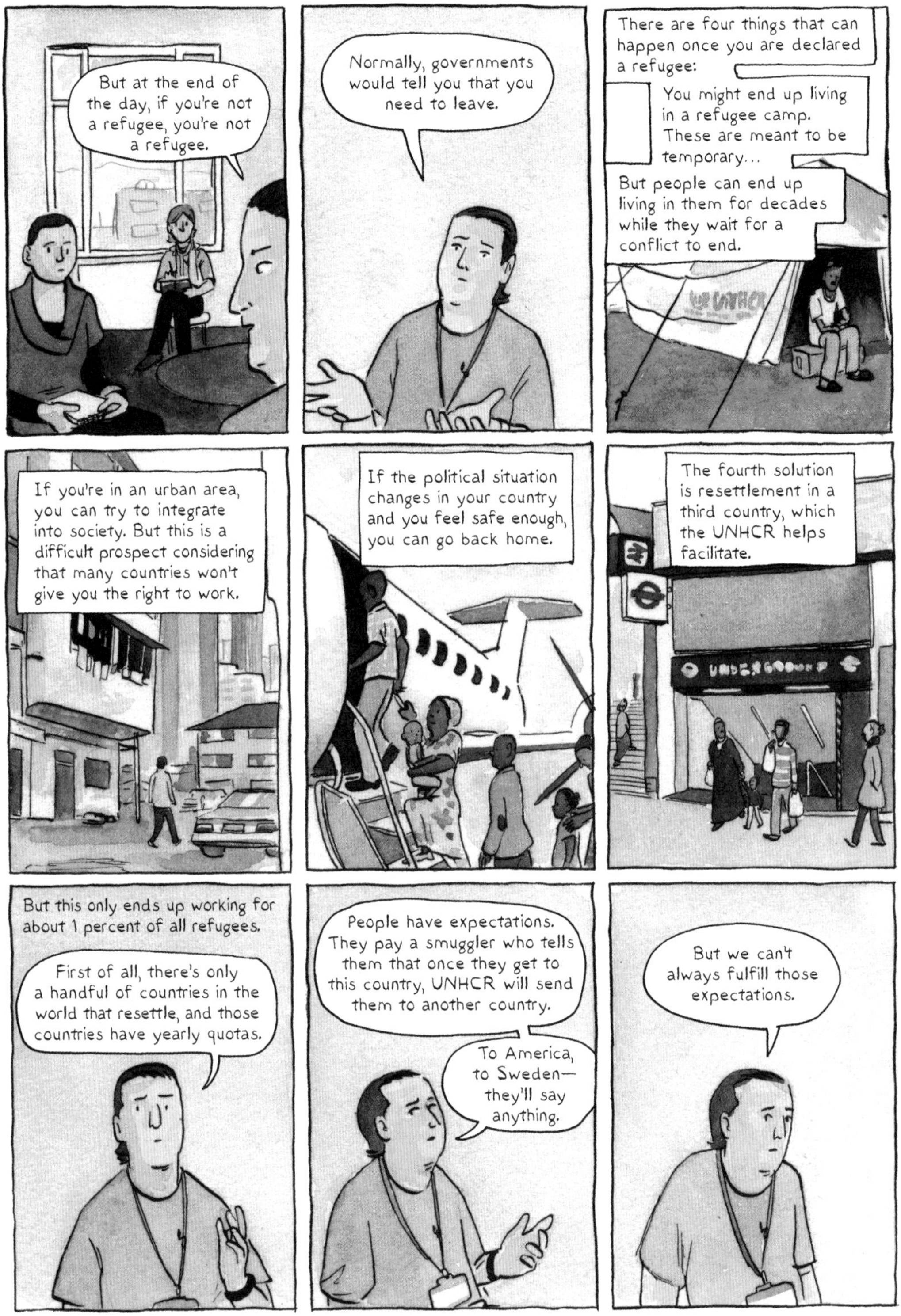
But at the end of the day, if you're not a refugee, you're not a refugee.
Normally, governments would tell you that you need to leave.
There are four things that can happen once you are declared a refugee:
You might end up living in a refugee camp. These are meant to be temporary...
But people can end up living in them for decades while they wait for a conflict to end.
UNHCR
If you're in an urban area, you can try to integrate into society. But this is a difficult prospect considering that many countries won't give you the right to work.
If the political situation changes in your country and you feel safe enough, you can go back home.
The fourth solution is resettlement in a third country, which the UNHCR helps facilitate.
UNDERGROUND
But this only ends up working for about 1 percent of all refugees.
First of all, there's only a handful of countries in the world that resettle, and those countries have yearly quotas.
People have expectations. They pay a smuggler who tells them that once they get to this country, UNHCR will send them to another country.
To America, to Sweden— they'll say anything.
But we can't always fulfill those expectations.

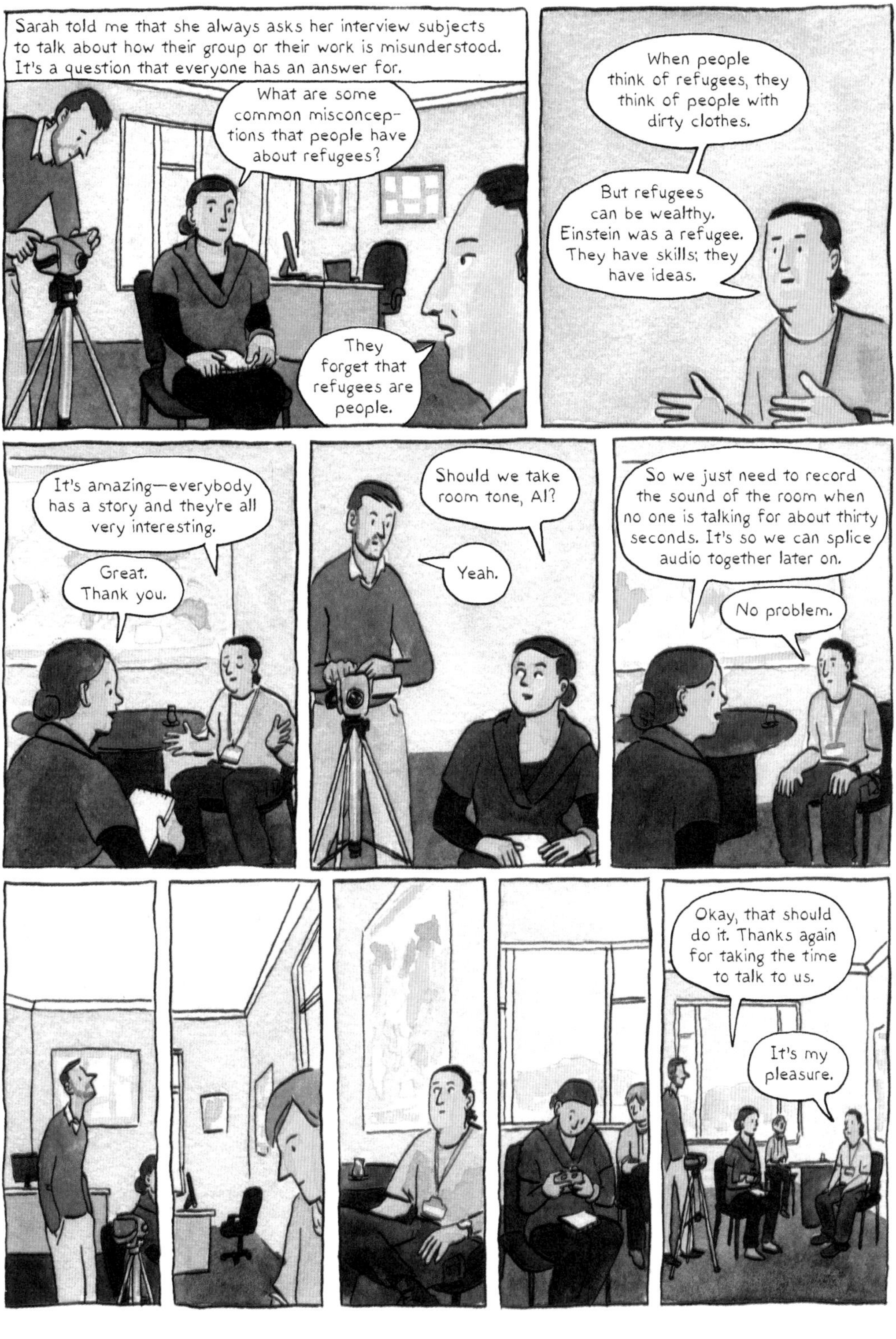
Sarah told me that she always asks her interview subjects to talk about how their group or their work is misunderstood. It's a question that everyone has an answer for.
What are some common misconceptions that people have about refugees?
They forget that refugees are people.
When people think of refugees, they think of people with dirty clothes.
But refugees can be wealthy. Einstein was a refugee. They have skills; they have ideas.
It's amazing—everybody has a story and they're all very interesting.
Great. Thank you.
Should we take room tone, Al?
Yeah.
So we just need to record the sound of the room when no one is talking for about thirty seconds. It's so we can splice audio together later on.
No problem.
Okay, that should do it. Thanks again for taking the time to talk to us.
It's my pleasure.

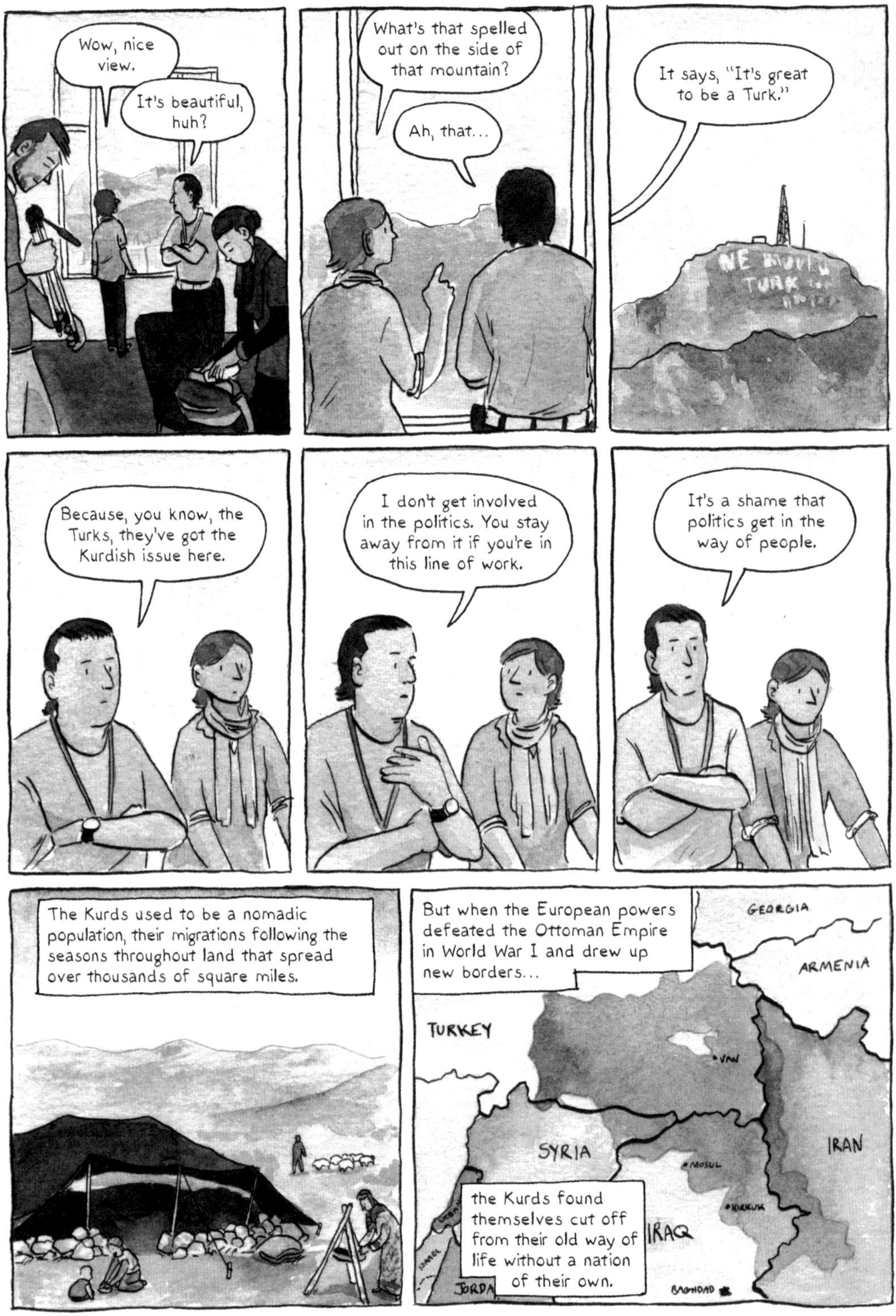

Wow, nice view.
It's beautiful, huh?
What's that spelled out on the side of that mountain?
Ah, that...
It says, "It's great to be a Turk."
Because, you know, the Turks, they've got the Kurdish issue here.
I don't get involved in the politics. You stay away from it if you're in this line of work.
It's a shame that politics get in the way of people.
The Kurds used to be a nomadic population, their migrations following the seasons throughout land that spread over thousands of square miles.
But when the European powers defeated the Ottoman Empire in World War I and drew up new borders...
GEORGIA
ARMENIA
TURKEY
VAN
SYRIA
MOSUL
IRAN
KIRKUK
IRAQ
BAGHDAD
the Kurds found themselves cut off from their old way of life without a nation of their own.

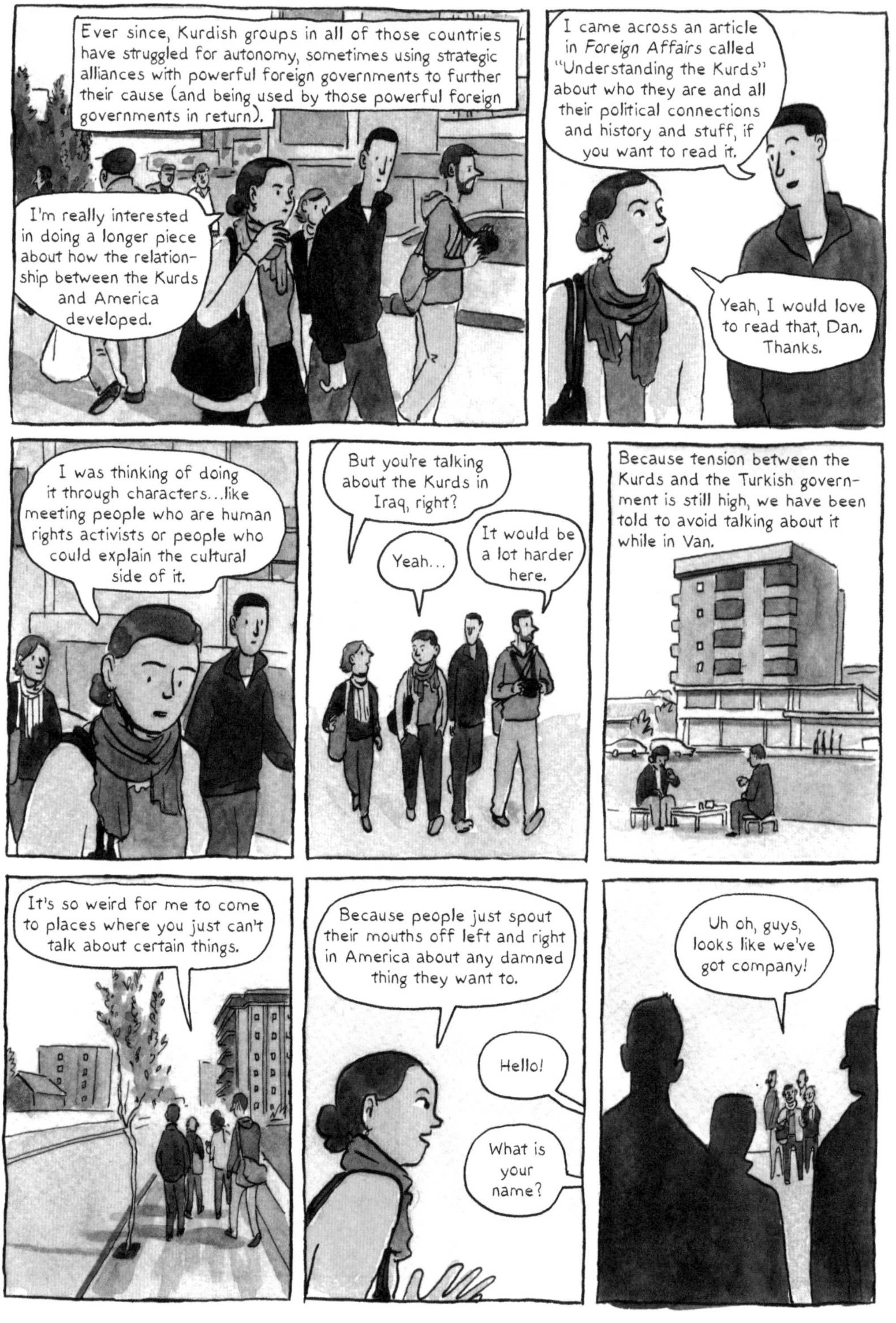
Ever since, Kurdish groups in all of those countries have struggled for autonomy, sometimes using strategic alliances with powerful foreign governments to further their cause (and being used by those powerful foreign governments in return).
I'm really interested in doing a longer piece about how the relationship between the Kurds and America developed.
I came across an article in *Foreign Affairs* called "Understanding the Kurds" about who they are and all their political connections and history and stuff, if you want to read it.
Yeah, I would love to read that, Dan. Thanks.
I was thinking of doing it through characters...like meeting people who are human rights activists or people who could explain the cultural side of it.
But you're talking about the Kurds in Iraq, right?
Yeah...
It would be a lot harder here.
Because tension between the Kurds and the Turkish government is still high, we have been told to avoid talking about it while in Van.
It's so weird for me to come to places where you just can't talk about certain things.
Because people just spout their mouths off left and right in America about any damned thing they want to.
Hello!
What is your name?
Uh oh, guys, looks like we've got company!

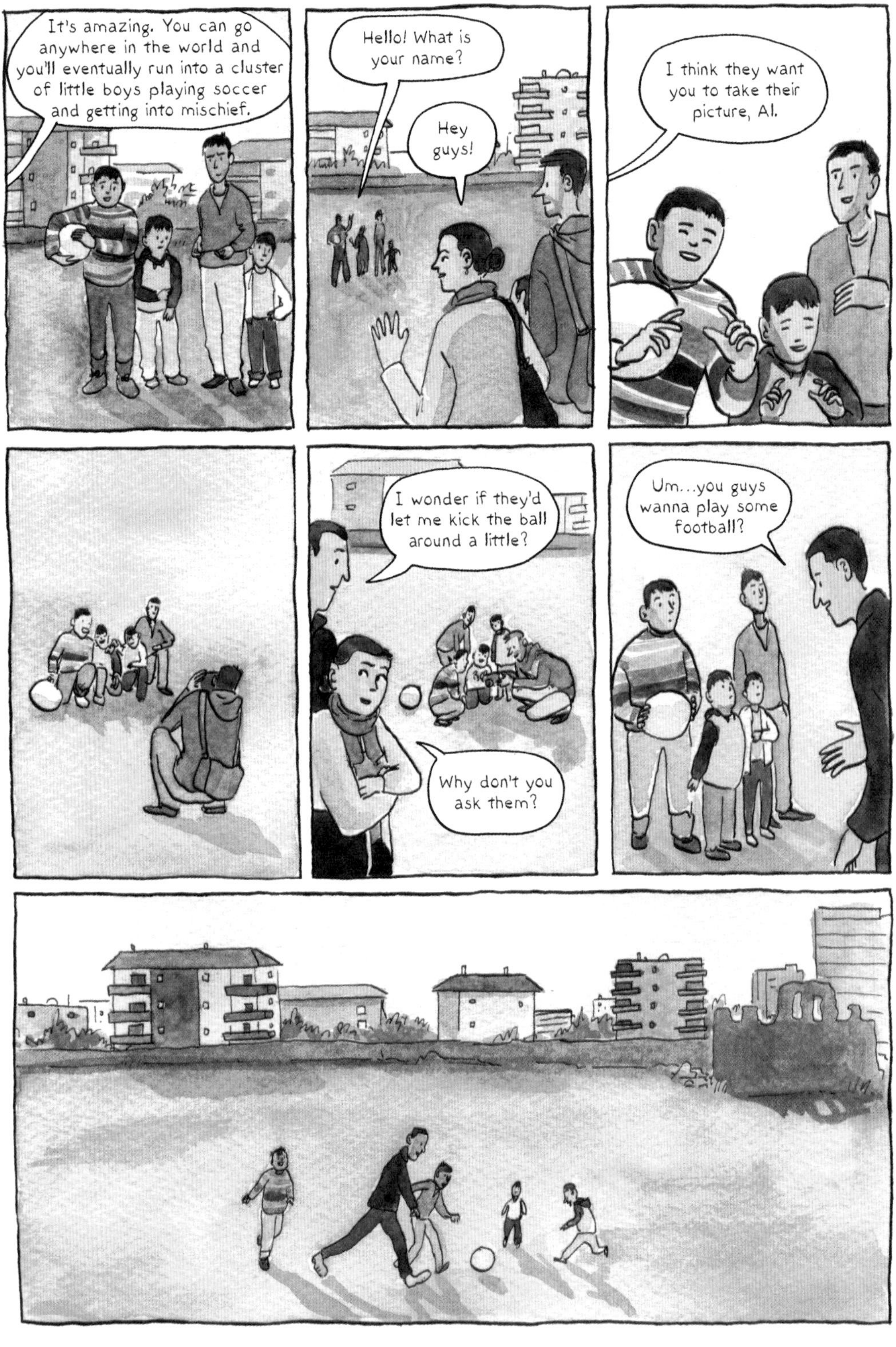
It's amazing. You can go anywhere in the world and you'll eventually run into a cluster of little boys playing soccer and getting into mischief.
Hello! What is your name?
Hey guys!
I think they want you to take their picture, Al.
I wonder if they'd let me kick the ball around a little?
Why don't you ask them?
Um...you guys wanna play some football?

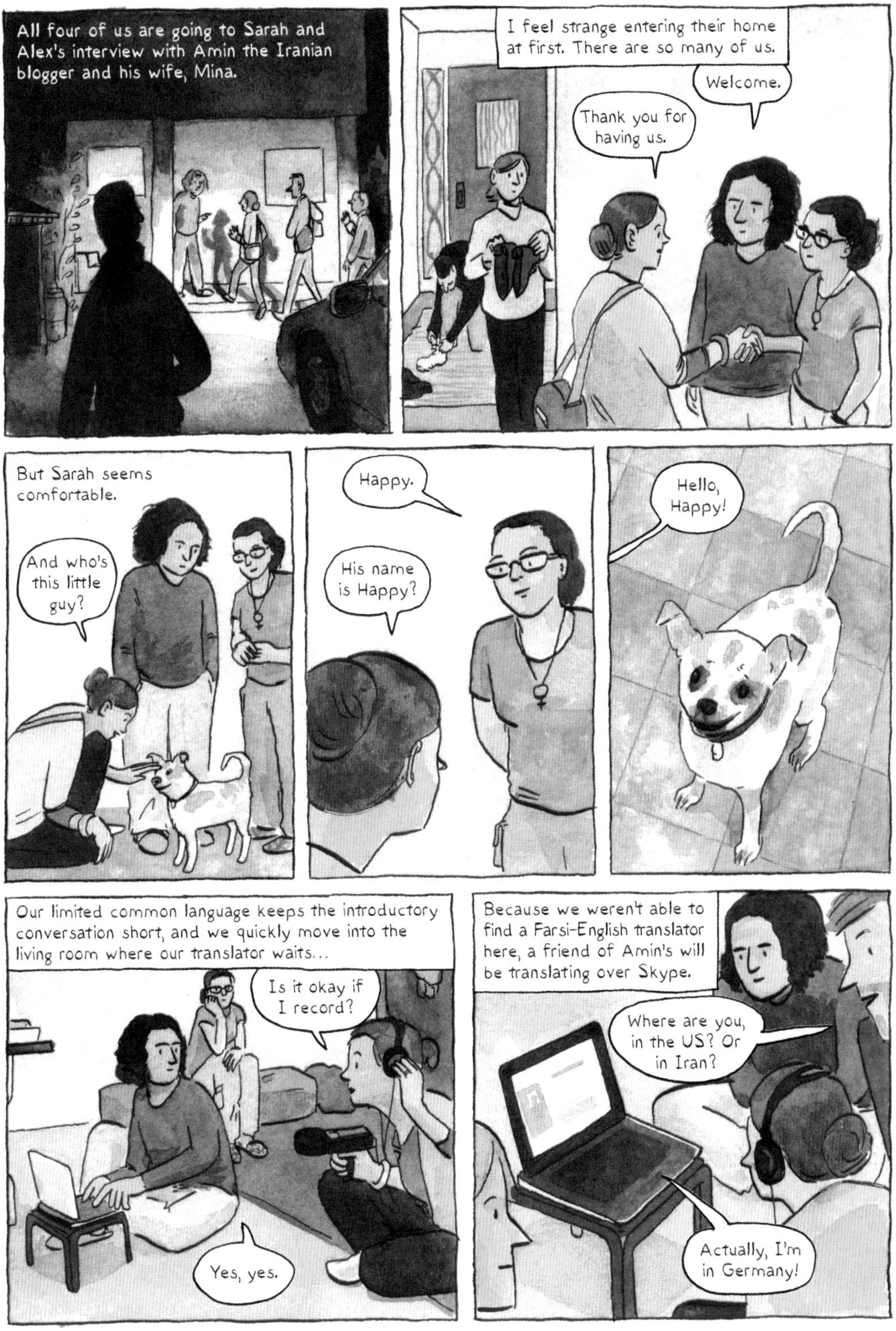
All four of us are going to Sarah and Alex's interview with Amin the Iranian blogger and his wife, Mina.
I feel strange entering their home at first. There are so many of us.
Thank you for having us.
Welcome.
But Sarah seems comfortable.
And who's this little guy?
Happy.
His name is Happy?
Hello, Happy!
Our limited common language keeps the introductory conversation short, and we quickly move into the living room where our translator waits...
Is it okay if I record?
Yes, yes.
Because we weren't able to find a Farsi-English translator here, a friend of Amin's will be translating over Skype.
Where are you, in the US? Or in Iran?
Actually, I'm in Germany!

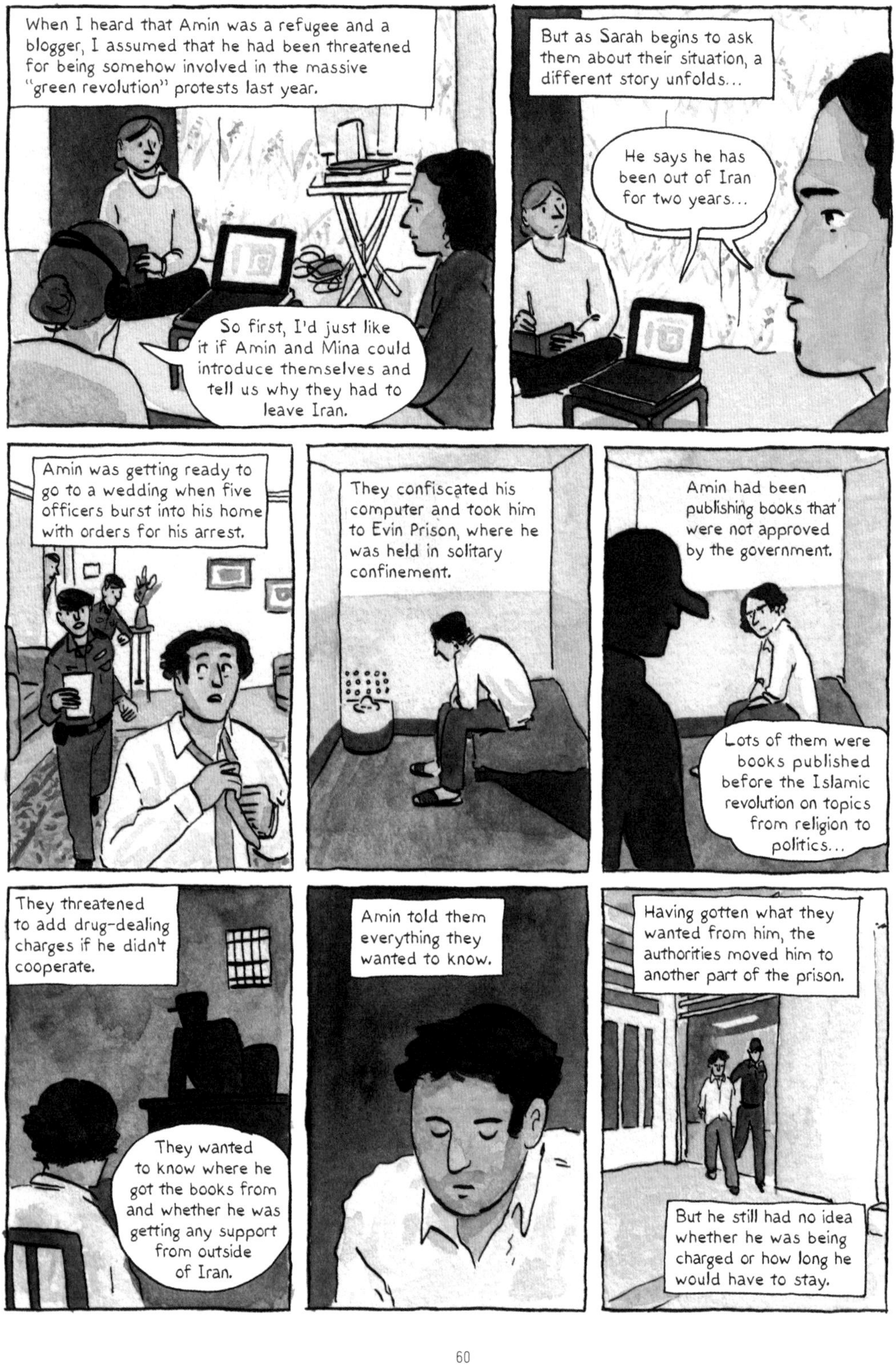
When I heard that Amin was a refugee and a blogger, I assumed that he had been threatened for being somehow involved in the massive "green revolution" protests last year.
So first, I'd just like it if Amin and Mina could introduce themselves and tell us why they had to leave Iran.
But as Sarah begins to ask them about their situation, a different story unfolds...
He says he has been out of Iran for two years...
Amin was getting ready to go to a wedding when five officers burst into his home with orders for his arrest.
They confiscated his computer and took him to Evin Prison, where he was held in solitary confinement.
Amin had been publishing books that were not approved by the government.
Lots of them were books published before the Islamic revolution on topics from religion to politics...
They threatened to add drug-dealing charges if he didn't cooperate.
They wanted to know where he got the books from and whether he was getting any support from outside of Iran.
Amin told them everything they wanted to know.
Having gotten what they wanted from him, the authorities moved him to another part of the prison.
But he still had no idea whether he was being charged or how long he would have to stay.

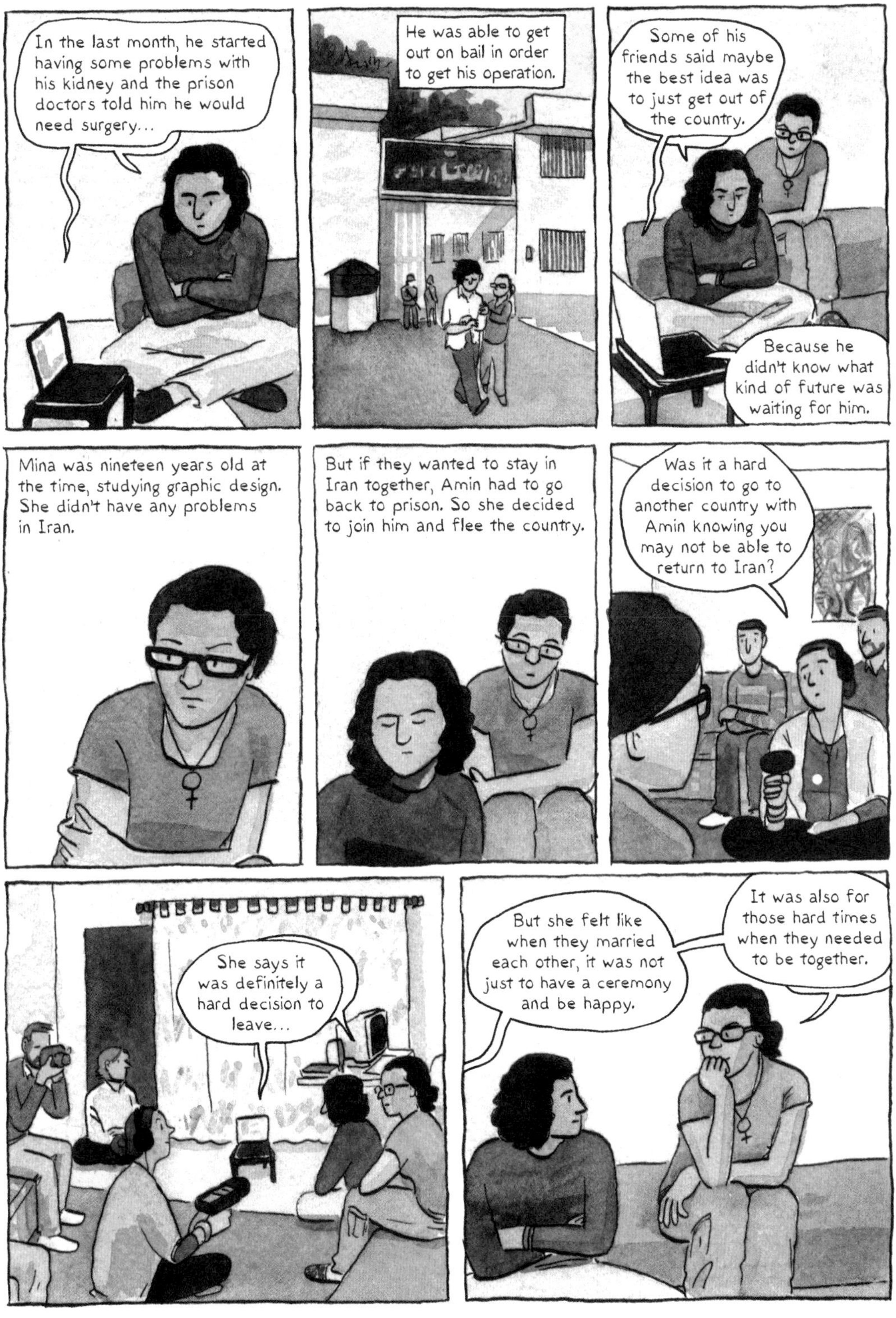
In the last month, he started having some problems with his kidney and the prison doctors told him he would need surgery...
He was able to get out on bail in order to get his operation.
Some of his friends said maybe the best idea was to just get out of the country.
Because he didn't know what kind of future was waiting for him.
Mina was nineteen years old at the time, studying graphic design. She didn't have any problems in Iran.
But if they wanted to stay in Iran together, Amin had to go back to prison. So she decided to join him and flee the country.
Was it a hard decision to go to another country with Amin knowing you may not be able to return to Iran?
She says it was definitely a hard decision to leave...
But she felt like when they married each other, it was not just to have a ceremony and be happy.
It was also for those hard times when they needed to be together.

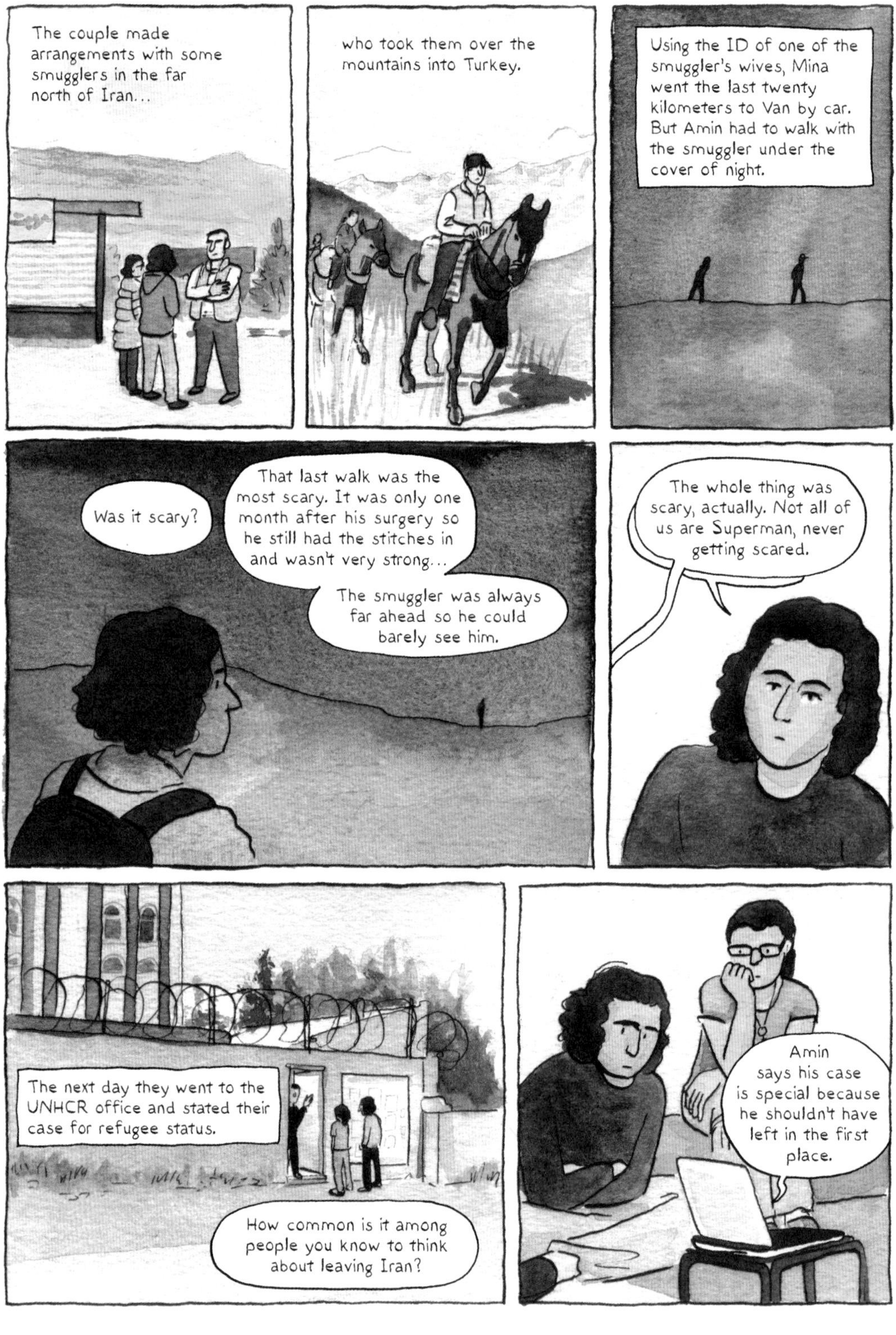

The couple made arrangements with some smugglers in the far north of Iran...
who took them over the mountains into Turkey.
Using the ID of one of the smuggler's wives, Mina went the last twenty kilometers to Van by car. But Amin had to walk with the smuggler under the cover of night.
Was it scary?
That last walk was the most scary. It was only one month after his surgery so he still had the stitches in and wasn't very strong...
The smuggler was always far ahead so he could barely see him.
The whole thing was scary, actually. Not all of us are Superman, never getting scared.
The next day they went to the UNHCR office and stated their case for refugee status.
How common is it among people you know to think about leaving Iran?
Amin says his case is special because he shouldn't have left in the first place.

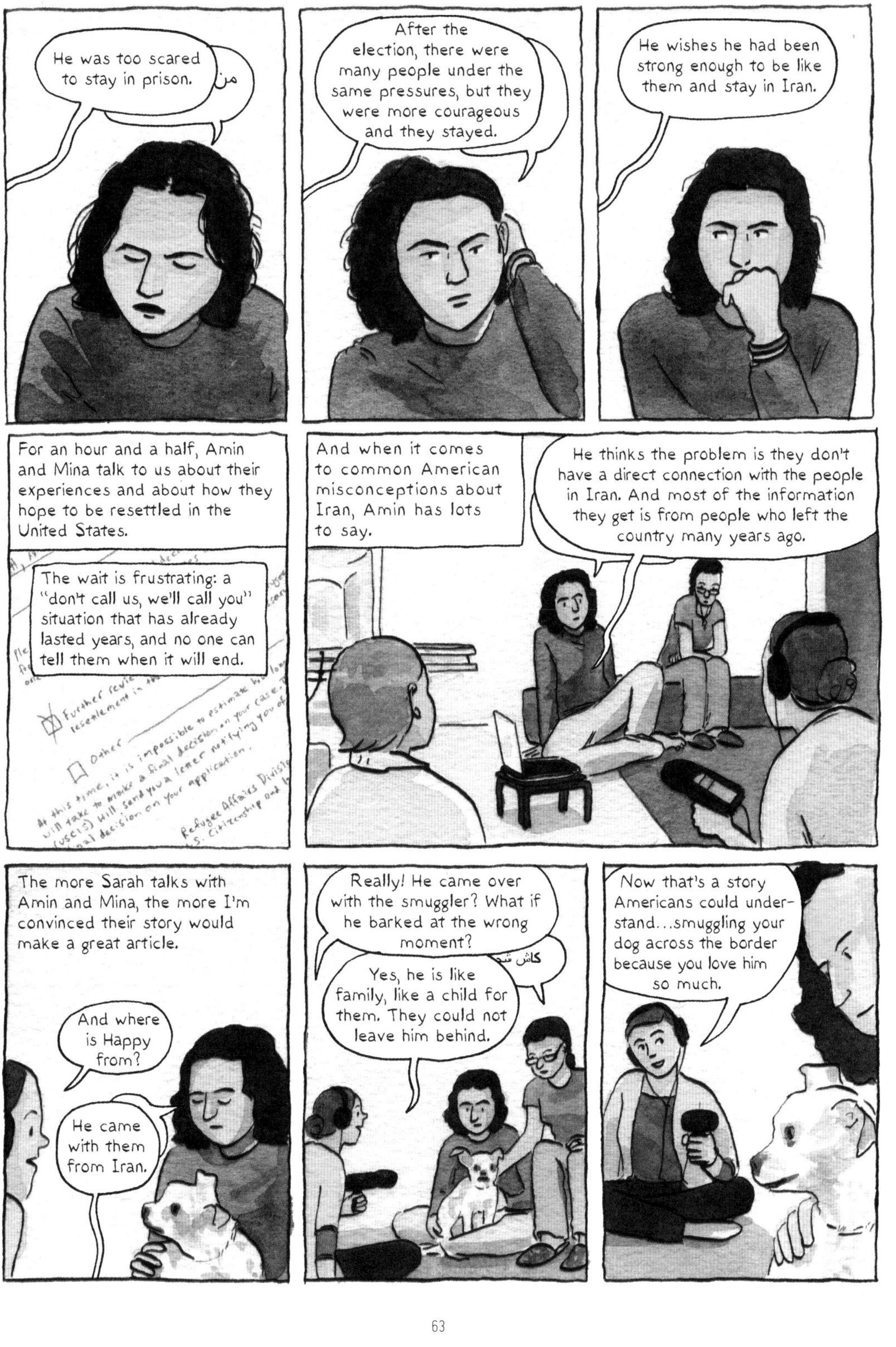
He was too scared to stay in prison.
من
After the election, there were many people under the same pressures, but they were more courageous and they stayed.
He wishes he had been strong enough to be like them and stay in Iran.
For an hour and a half, Amin and Mina talk to us about their experiences and about how they hope to be resettled in the United States.
The wait is frustrating: a "don't call us, we'll call you" situation that has already lasted years, and no one can tell them when it will end.
And when it comes to common American misconceptions about Iran, Amin has lots to say.
He thinks the problem is they don't have a direct connection with the people in Iran. And most of the information they get is from people who left the country many years ago.
The more Sarah talks with Amin and Mina, the more I'm convinced their story would make a great article.
And where is Happy from?
He came with them from Iran.
Really! He came over with the smuggler? What if he barked at the wrong moment?
Yes, he is like family, like a child for them. They could not leave him behind.
Now that's a story Americans could understand...smuggling your dog across the border because you love him so much.

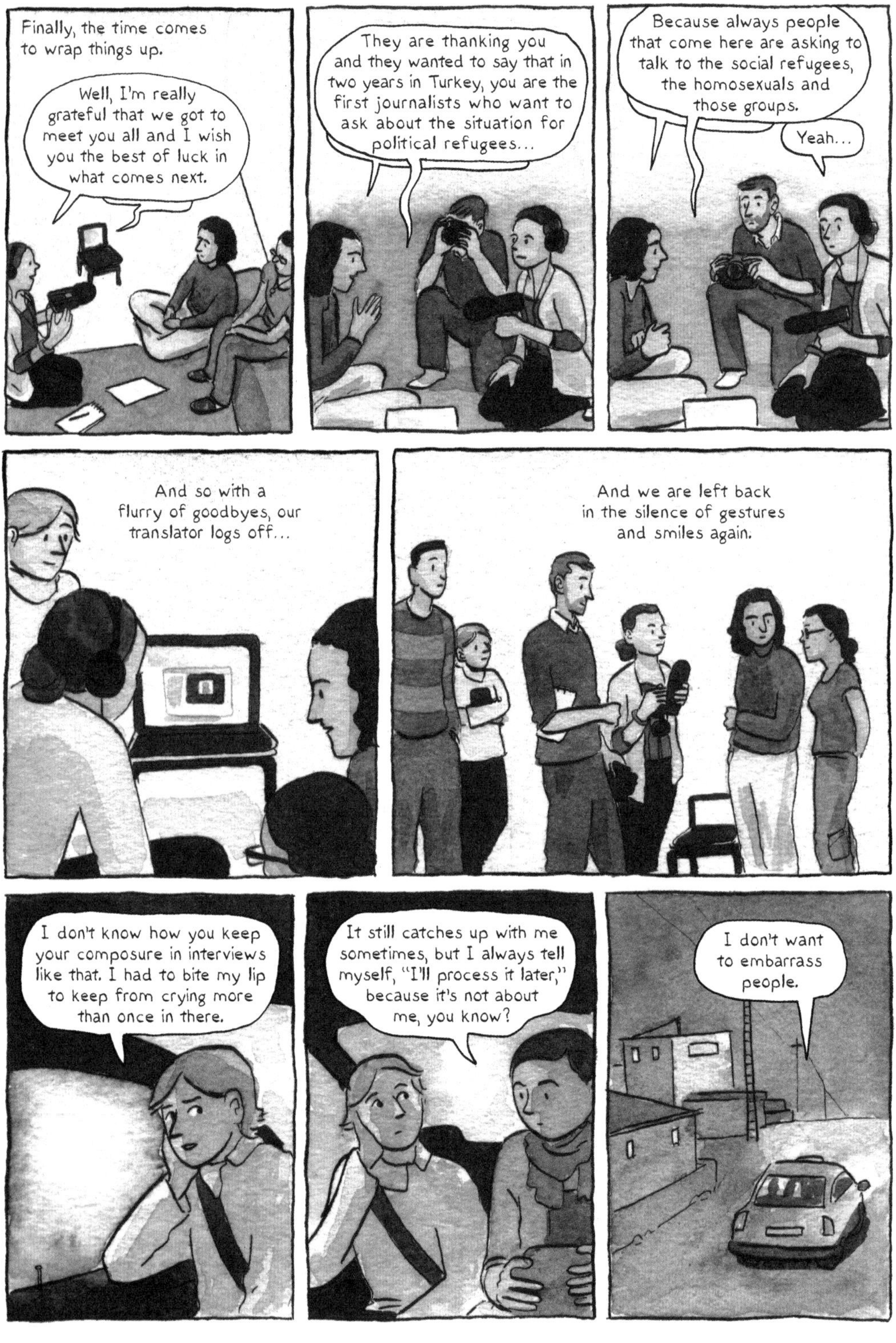

Finally, the time comes to wrap things up.
Well, I'm really grateful that we got to meet you all and I wish you the best of luck in what comes next.
They are thanking you and they wanted to say that in two years in Turkey, you are the first journalists who want to ask about the situation for political refugees...
Because always people that come here are asking to talk to the social refugees, the homosexuals and those groups.
Yeah...
And so with a flurry of goodbyes, our translator logs off...
And we are left back in the silence of gestures and smiles again.
I don't know how you keep your composure in interviews like that. I had to bite my lip to keep from crying more than once in there.
It still catches up with me sometimes, but I always tell myself, "I'll process it later," because it's not about me, you know?
I don't want to embarrass people.

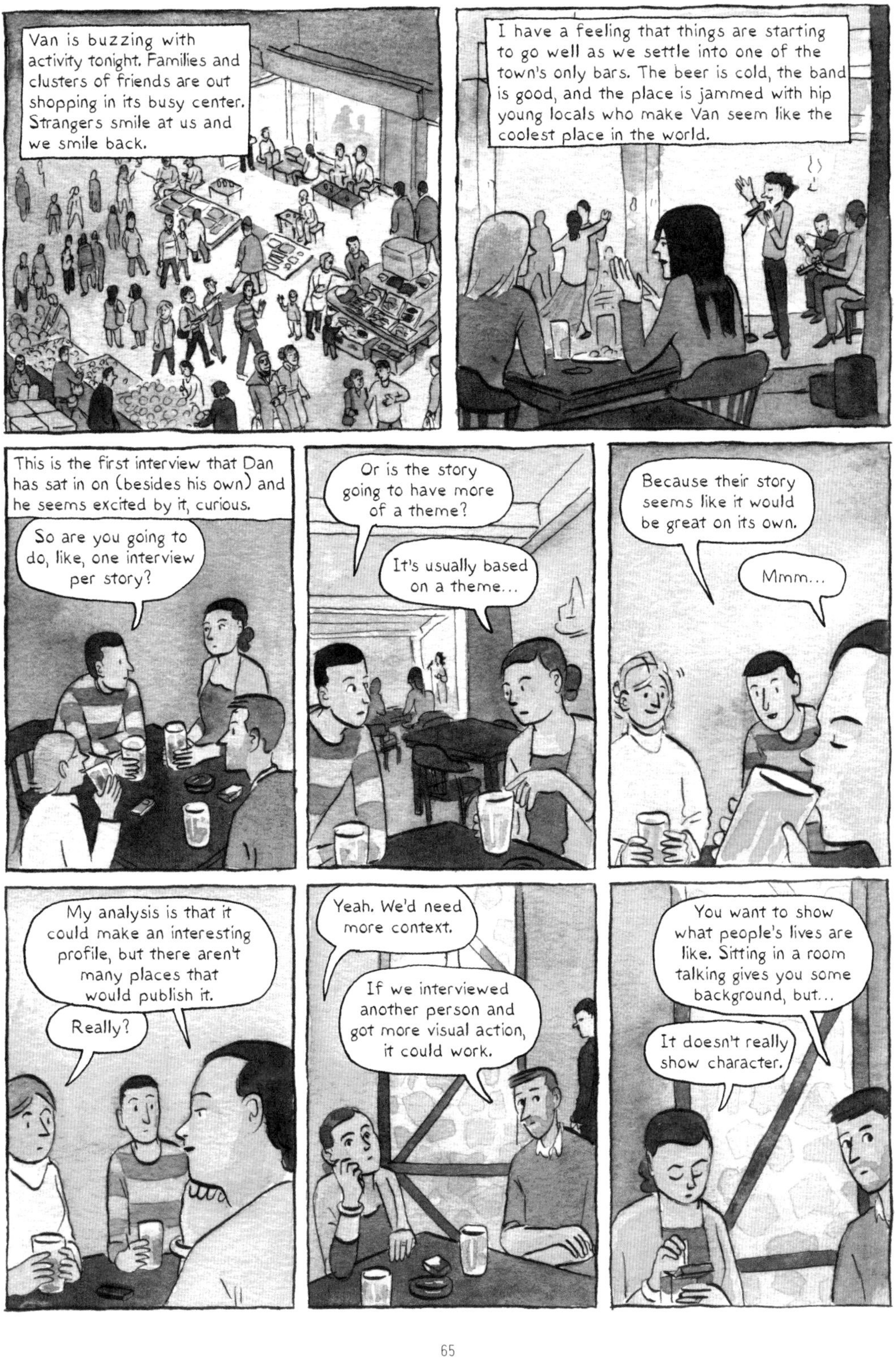
Van is buzzing with activity tonight. Families and clusters of friends are out shopping in its busy center. Strangers smile at us and we smile back.
I have a feeling that things are starting to go well as we settle into one of the town's only bars. The beer is cold, the band is good, and the place is jammed with hip young locals who make Van seem like the coolest place in the world.
This is the first interview that Dan has sat in on (besides his own) and he seems excited by it, curious.
So are you going to do, like, one interview per story?
Or is the story going to have more of a theme?
It's usually based on a theme...
Because their story seems like it would be great on its own.
Mmm...
My analysis is that it could make an interesting profile, but there aren't many places that would publish it.
Really?
Yeah. We'd need more context.
If we interviewed another person and got more visual action, it could work.
You want to show what people's lives are like. Sitting in a room talking gives you some background, but...
It doesn't really show character.

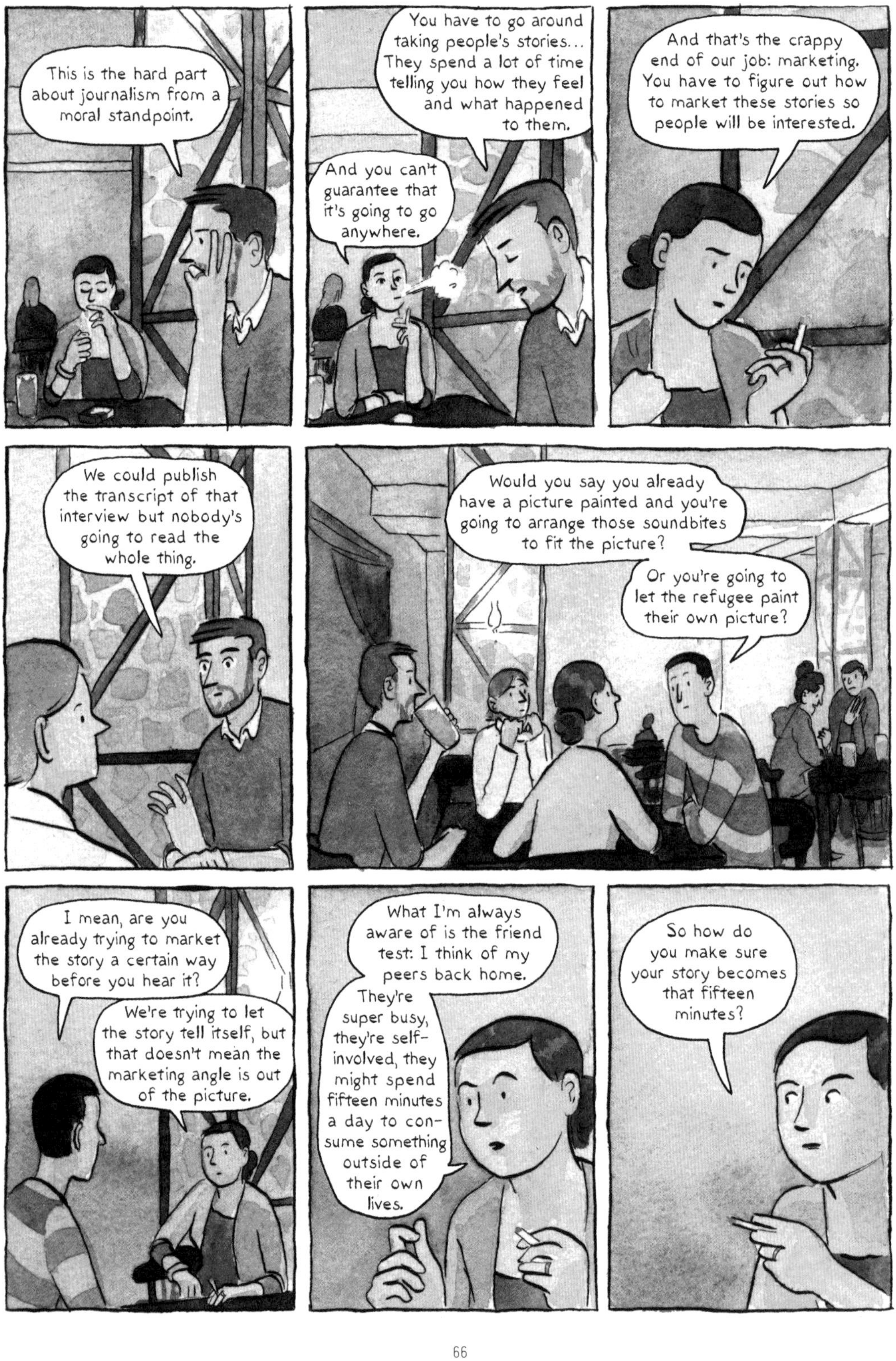
This is the hard part about journalism from a moral standpoint.
You have to go around taking people's stories... They spend a lot of time telling you how they feel and what happened to them.
And you can't guarantee that it's going to go anywhere.
And that's the crappy end of our job: marketing. You have to figure out how to market these stories so people will be interested.
We could publish the transcript of that interview but nobody's going to read the whole thing.
Would you say you already have a picture painted and you're going to arrange those soundbites to fit the picture?
Or you're going to let the refugee paint their own picture?
I mean, are you already trying to market the story a certain way before you hear it?
We're trying to let the story tell itself, but that doesn't mean the marketing angle is out of the picture.
What I'm always aware of is the friend test: I think of my peers back home.
They're super busy, they're self-involved, they might spend fifteen minutes a day to consume something outside of their own lives.
So how do you make sure your story becomes that fifteen minutes?

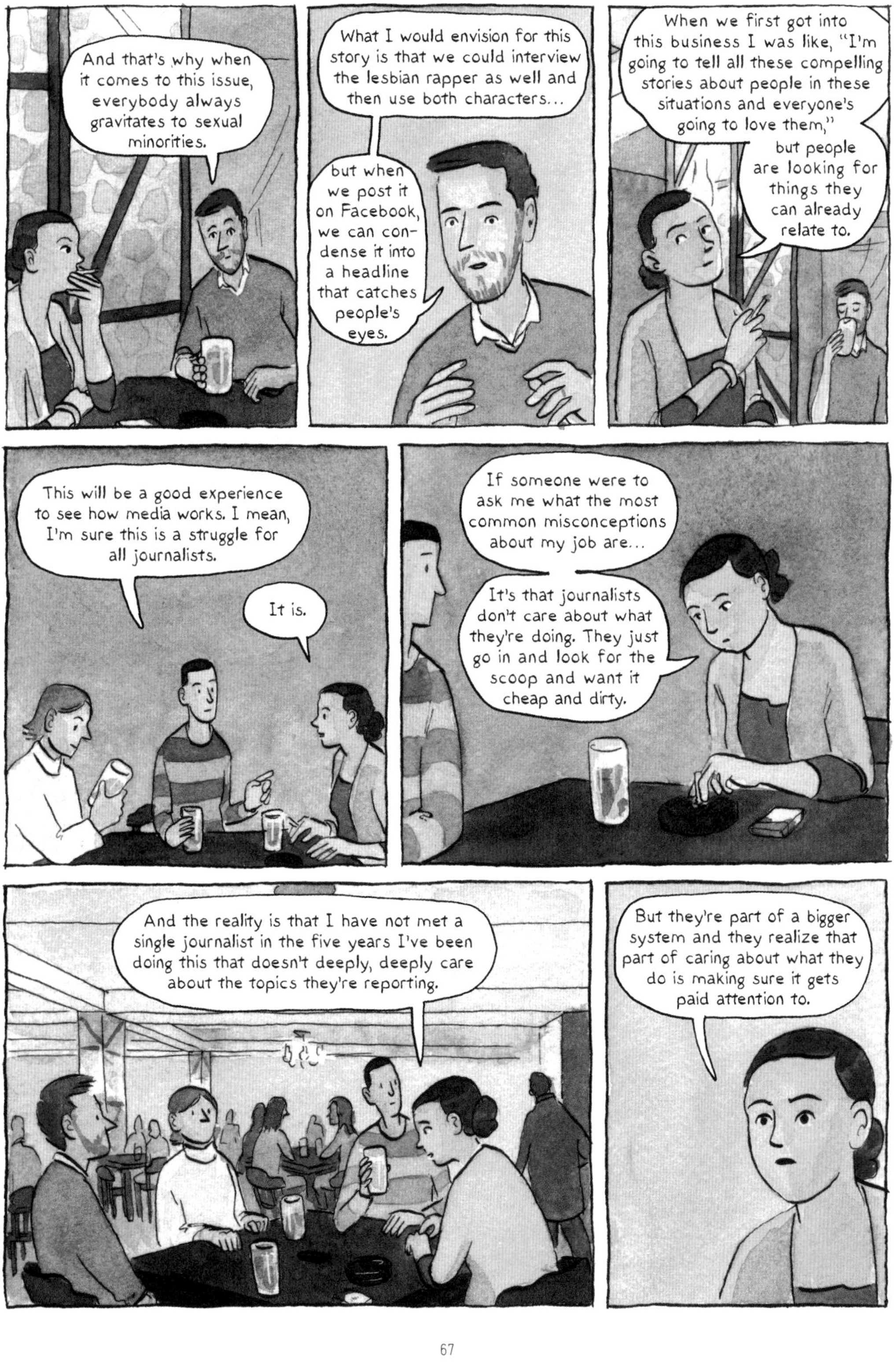
And that's why when it comes to this issue, everybody always gravitates to sexual minorities.
What I would envision for this story is that we could interview the lesbian rapper as well and then use both characters...
but when we post it on Facebook, we can condense it into a headline that catches people's eyes.
When we first got into this business I was like, "I'm going to tell all these compelling stories about people in these situations and everyone's going to love them,"
but people are looking for things they can already relate to.
This will be a good experience to see how media works. I mean, I'm sure this is a struggle for all journalists.
It is.
If someone were to ask me what the most common misconceptions about my job are...
It's that journalists don't care about what they're doing. They just go in and look for the scoop and want it cheap and dirty.
And the reality is that I have not met a single journalist in the five years I've been doing this that doesn't deeply, deeply care about the topics they're reporting.
But they're part of a bigger system and they realize that part of caring about what they do is making sure it gets paid attention to.

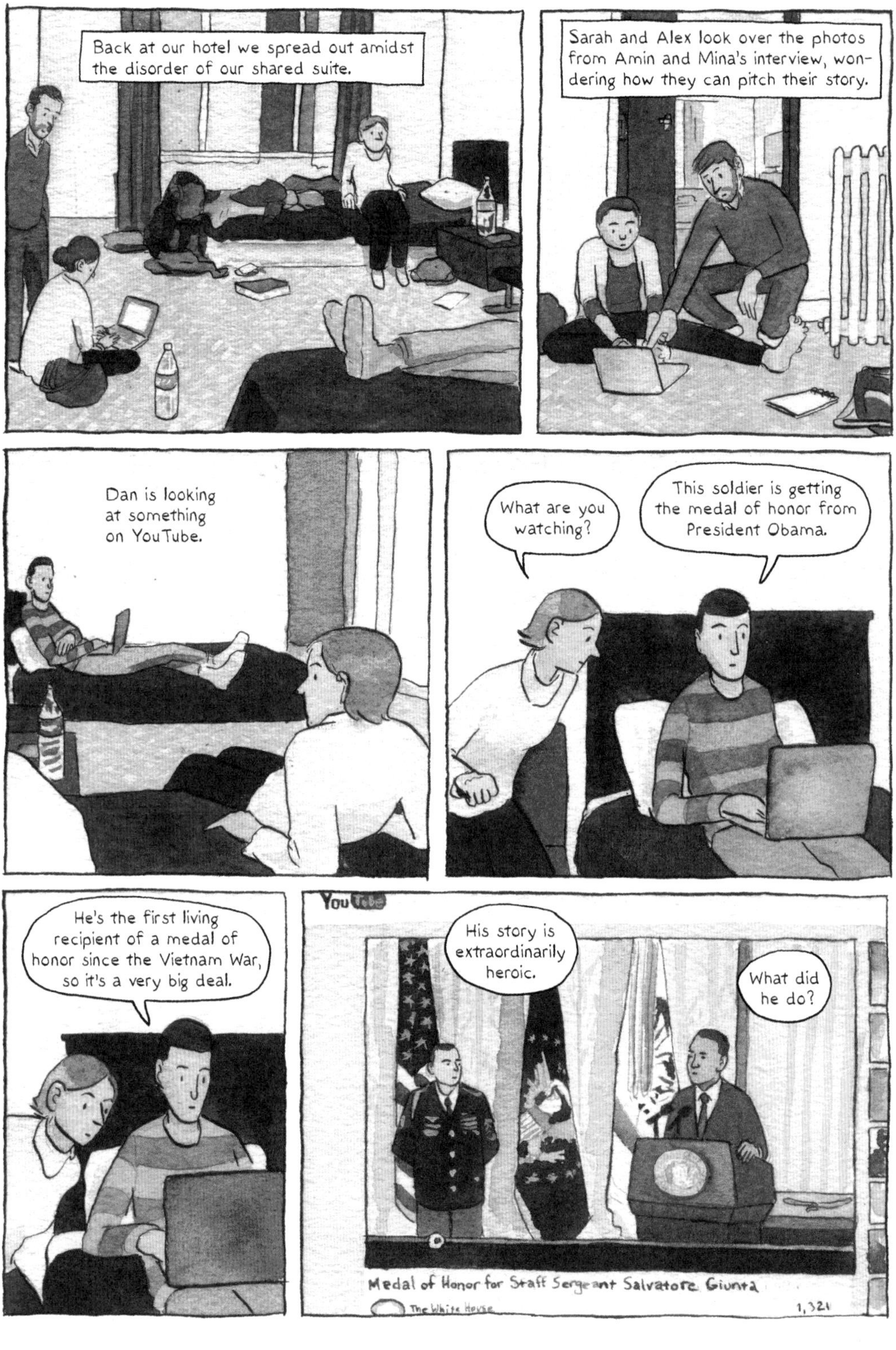
Back at our hotel we spread out amidst the disorder of our shared suite.
Sarah and Alex look over the photos from Amin and Mina's interview, wondering how they can pitch their story.
Dan is looking at something on YouTube.
What are you watching?
This soldier is getting the medal of honor from President Obama.
He's the first living recipient of a medal of honor since the Vietnam War, so it's a very big deal.
YouTube
His story is extraordinarily heroic.
What did he do?
Medal of Honor for Staff Sergeant Salvatore Giunta
The White House
1,321

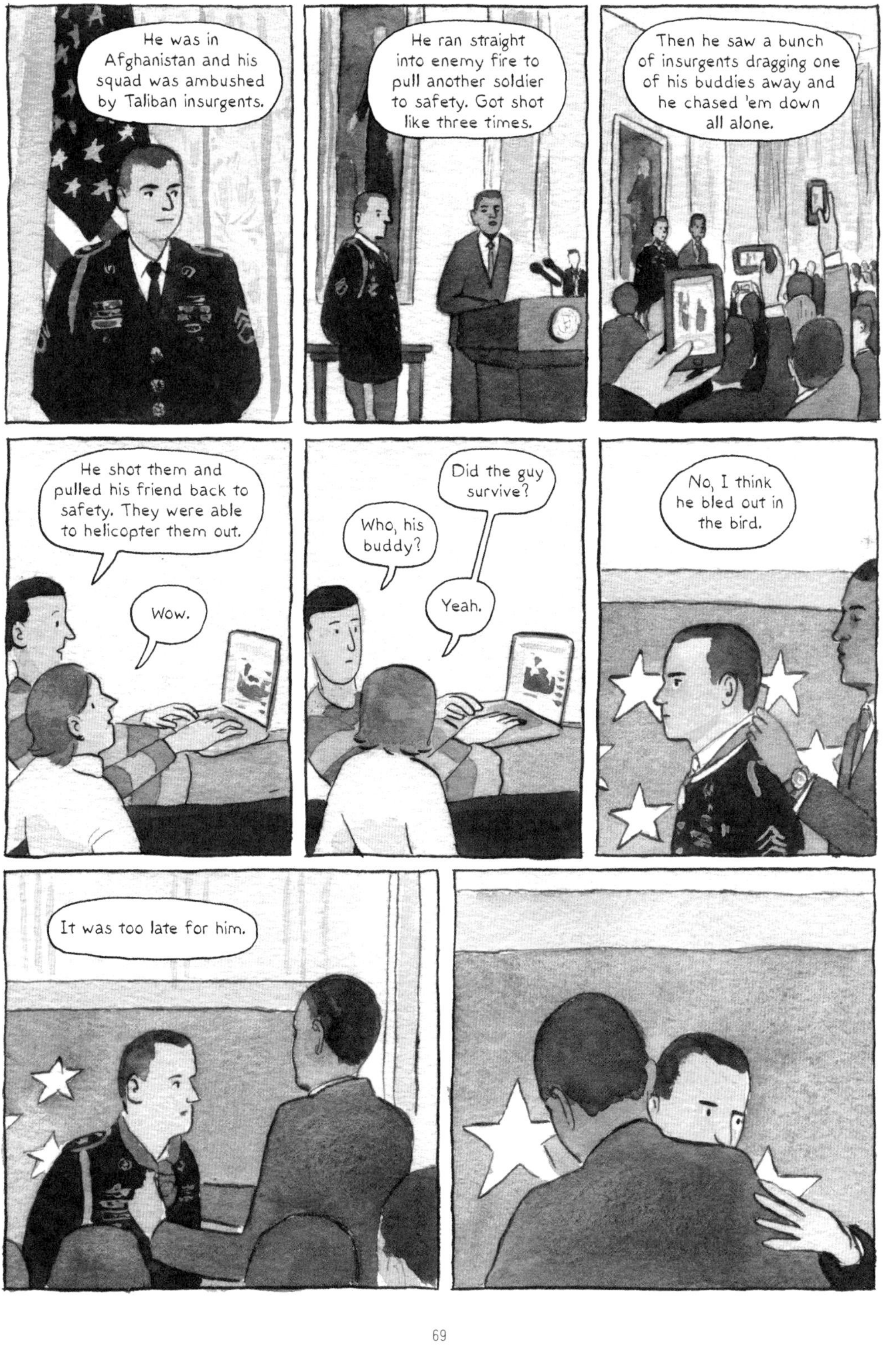
He was in Afghanistan and his squad was ambushed by Taliban insurgents.
He ran straight into enemy fire to pull another soldier to safety. Got shot like three times.
Then he saw a bunch of insurgents dragging one of his buddies away and he chased 'em down all alone.
He shot them and pulled his friend back to safety. They were able to helicopter them out.
Wow.
Did the guy survive?
Who, his buddy?
Yeah.
No, I think he bled out in the bird.
It was too late for him.

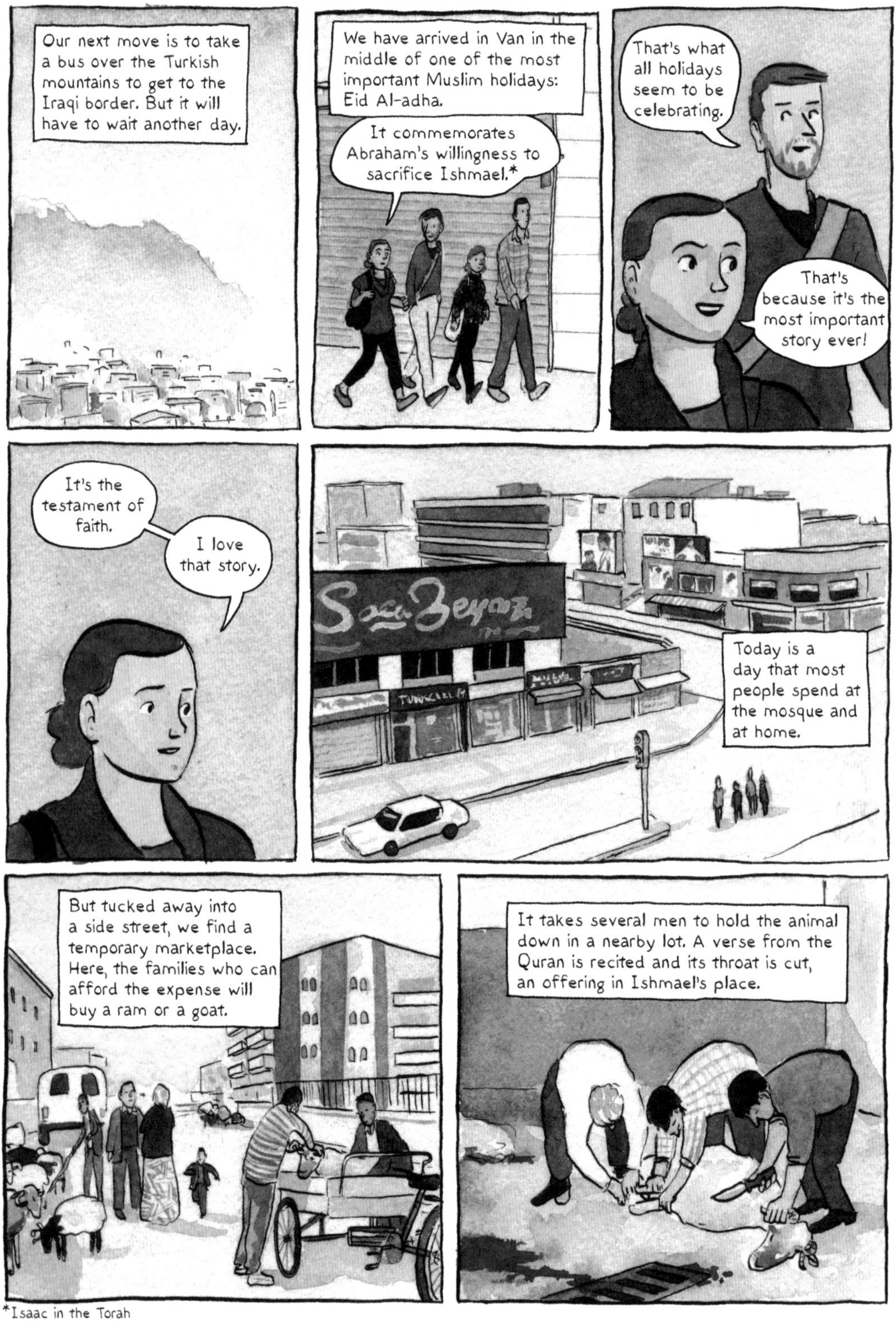

Our next move is to take a bus over the Turkish mountains to get to the Iraqi border. But it will have to wait another day.
We have arrived in Van in the middle of one of the most important Muslim holidays: Eid Al-adha.
It commemorates Abraham's willingness to sacrifice Ishmael.*
That's what all holidays seem to be celebrating.
That's because it's the most important story ever!
It's the testament of faith.
I love that story.
Today is a day that most people spend at the mosque and at home.
But tucked away into a side street, we find a temporary marketplace. Here, the families who can afford the expense will buy a ram or a goat.
It takes several men to hold the animal down in a nearby lot. A verse from the Quran is recited and its throat is cut, an offering in Ishmael's place.

*Isaac in the Torah

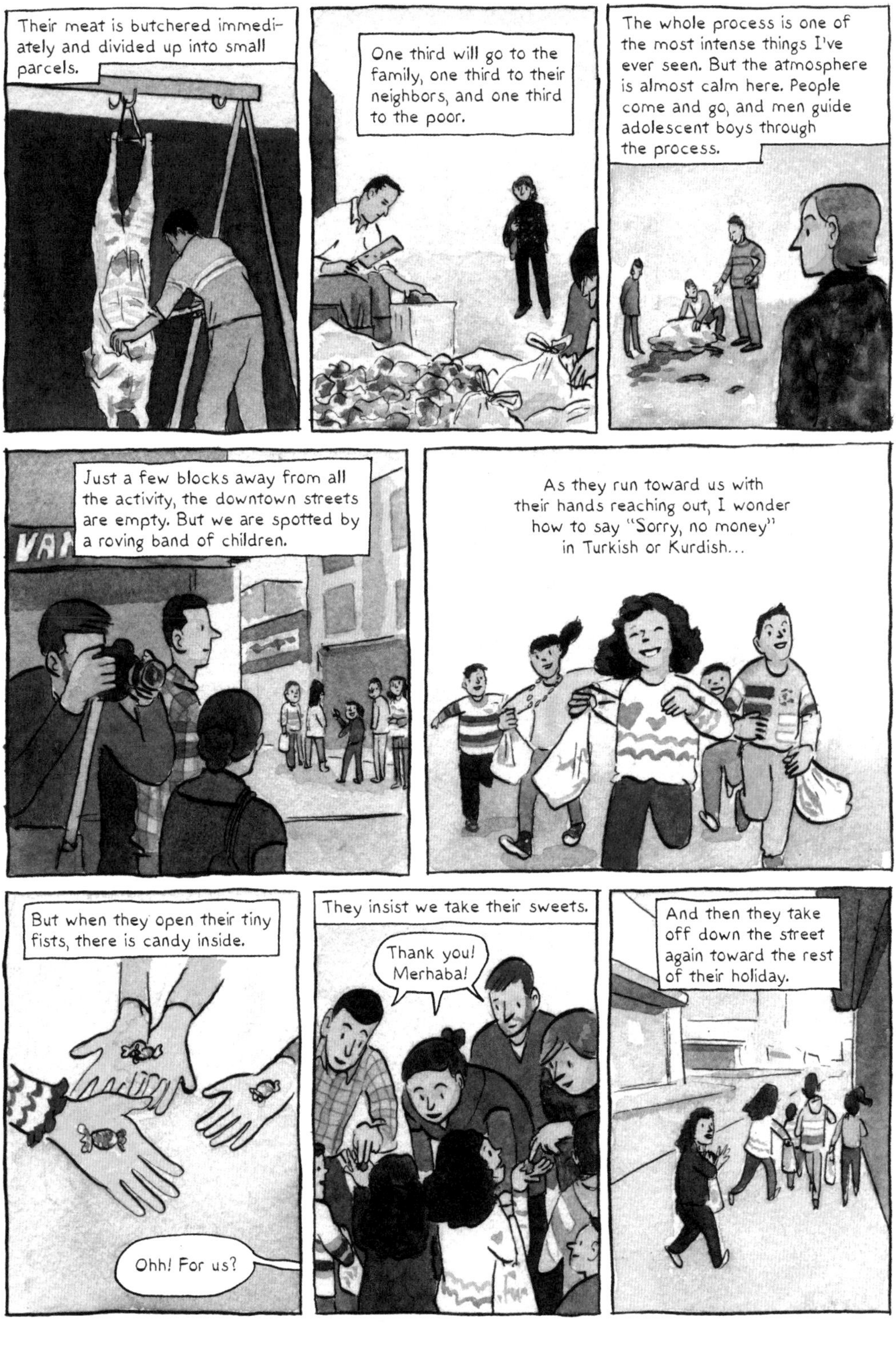
Their meat is butchered immediately and divided up into small parcels.
One third will go to the family, one third to their neighbors, and one third to the poor.
The whole process is one of the most intense things I've ever seen. But the atmosphere is almost calm here. People come and go, and men guide adolescent boys through the process.
Just a few blocks away from all the activity, the downtown streets are empty. But we are spotted by a roving band of children.
VAN
As they run toward us with their hands reaching out, I wonder how to say "Sorry, no money" in Turkish or Kurdish...
But when they open their tiny fists, there is candy inside.
Ohh! For us?
They insist we take their sweets.
Thank you! Merhaba!
And then they take off down the street again toward the rest of their holiday.

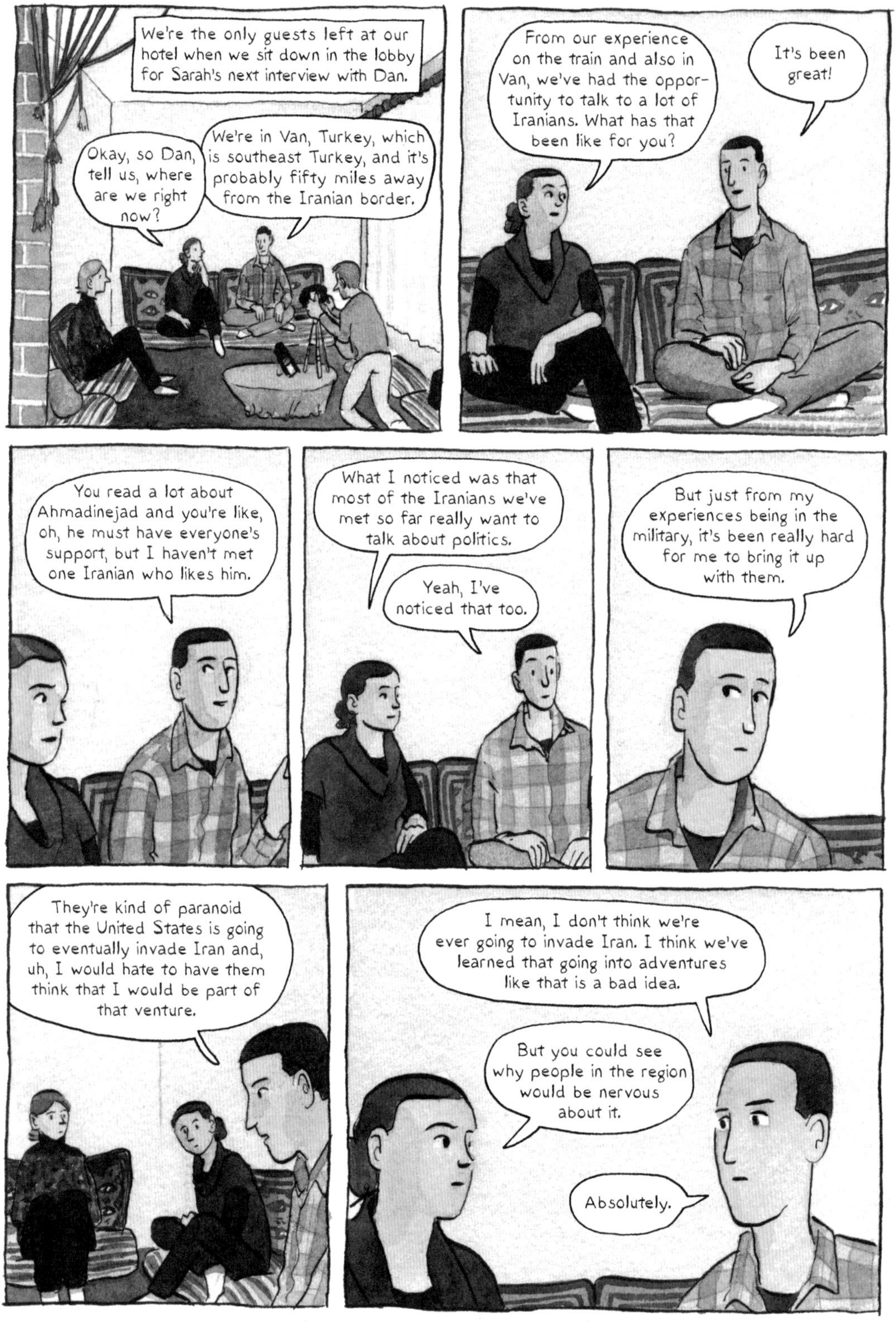

We're the only guests left at our hotel when we sit down in the lobby for Sarah's next interview with Dan.
Okay, so Dan, tell us, where are we right now?
We're in Van, Turkey, which is southeast Turkey, and it's probably fifty miles away from the Iranian border.
From our experience on the train and also in Van, we've had the opportunity to talk to a lot of Iranians. What has that been like for you?
It's been great!
You read a lot about Ahmadinejad and you're like, oh, he must have everyone's support, but I haven't met one Iranian who likes him.
What I noticed was that most of the Iranians we've met so far really want to talk about politics.
Yeah, I've noticed that too.
But just from my experiences being in the military, it's been really hard for me to bring it up with them.
They're kind of paranoid that the United States is going to eventually invade Iran and, uh, I would hate to have them think that I would be part of that venture.
I mean, I don't think we're ever going to invade Iran. I think we've learned that going into adventures like that is a bad idea.
But you could see why people in the region would be nervous about it.
Absolutely.

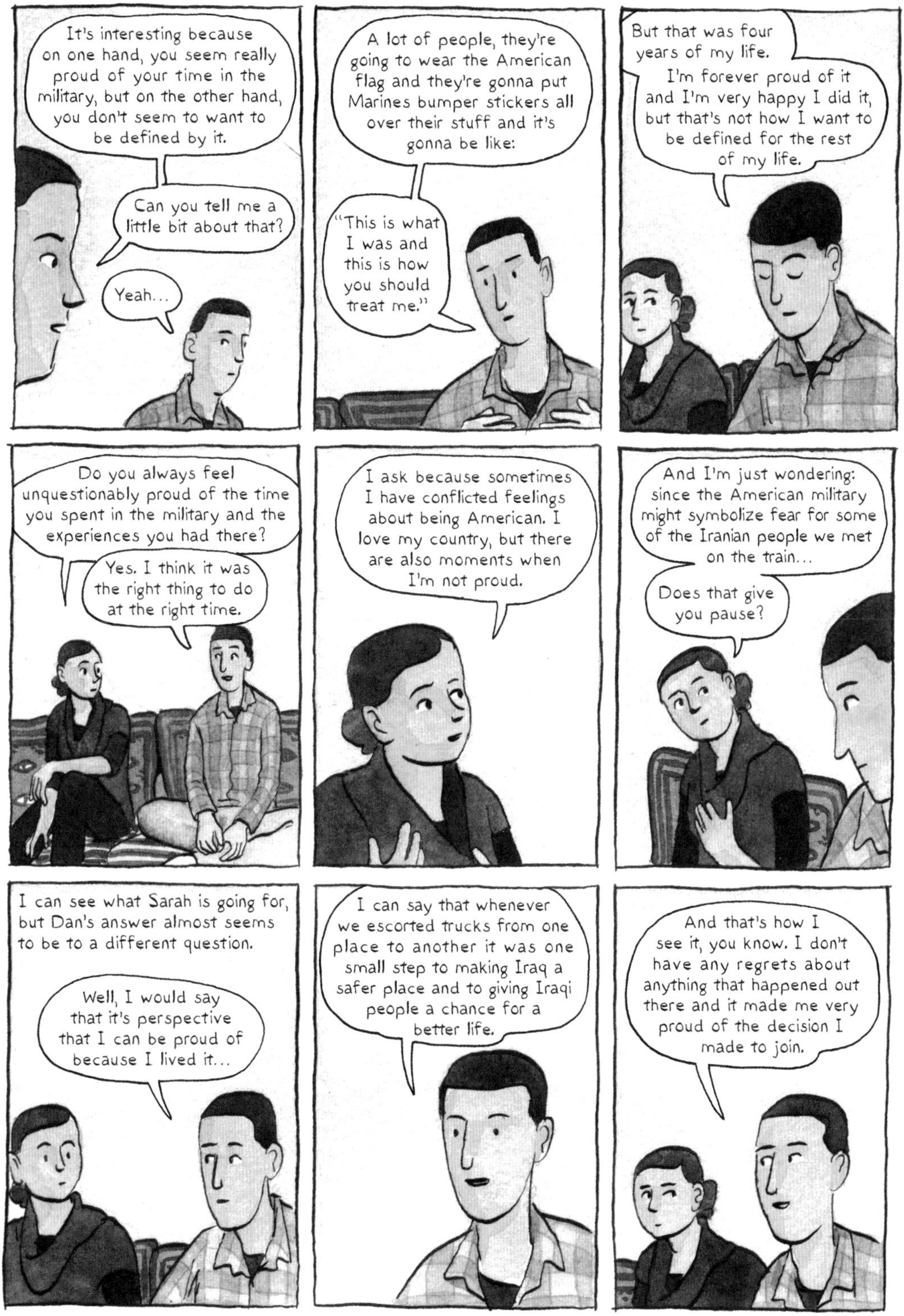

It's interesting because on one hand, you seem really proud of your time in the military, but on the other hand, you don't seem to want to be defined by it.
Can you tell me a little bit about that?
Yeah...
A lot of people, they're going to wear the American flag and they're gonna put Marines bumper stickers all over their stuff and it's gonna be like:
"This is what I was and this is how you should treat me."
But that was four years of my life.
I'm forever proud of it and I'm very happy I did it, but that's not how I want to be defined for the rest of my life.
Do you always feel unquestionably proud of the time you spent in the military and the experiences you had there?
Yes. I think it was the right thing to do at the right time.
I ask because sometimes I have conflicted feelings about being American. I love my country, but there are also moments when I'm not proud.
And I'm just wondering: since the American military might symbolize fear for some of the Iranian people we met on the train...
Does that give you pause?
I can see what Sarah is going for, but Dan's answer almost seems to be to a different question.
Well, I would say that it's perspective that I can be proud of because I lived it...
I can say that whenever we escorted trucks from one place to another it was one small step to making Iraq a safer place and to giving Iraqi people a chance for a better life.
And that's how I see it, you know. I don't have any regrets about anything that happened out there and it made me very proud of the decision I made to join.

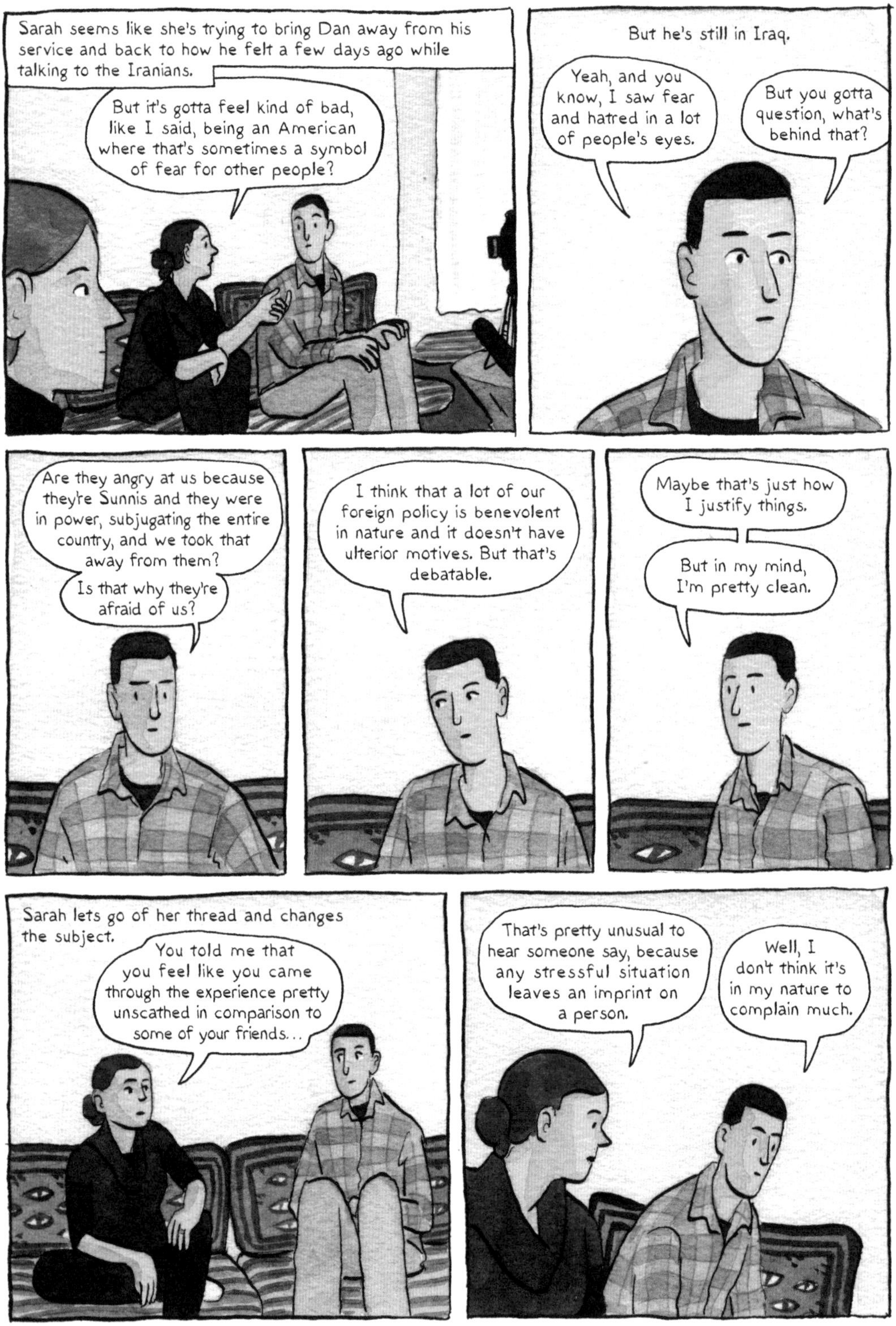
Sarah seems like she's trying to bring Dan away from his service and back to how he felt a few days ago while talking to the Iranians.
But it's gotta feel kind of bad, like I said, being an American where that's sometimes a symbol of fear for other people?
But he's still in Iraq.
Yeah, and you know, I saw fear and hatred in a lot of people's eyes.
But you gotta question, what's behind that?
Are they angry at us because they're Sunnis and they were in power, subjugating the entire country, and we took that away from them?
Is that why they're afraid of us?
I think that a lot of our foreign policy is benevolent in nature and it doesn't have ulterior motives. But that's debatable.
Maybe that's just how I justify things.
But in my mind, I'm pretty clean.
Sarah lets go of her thread and changes the subject.
You told me that you feel like you came through the experience pretty unscathed in comparison to some of your friends...
That's pretty unusual to hear someone say, because any stressful situation leaves an imprint on a person.
Well, I don't think it's in my nature to complain much.

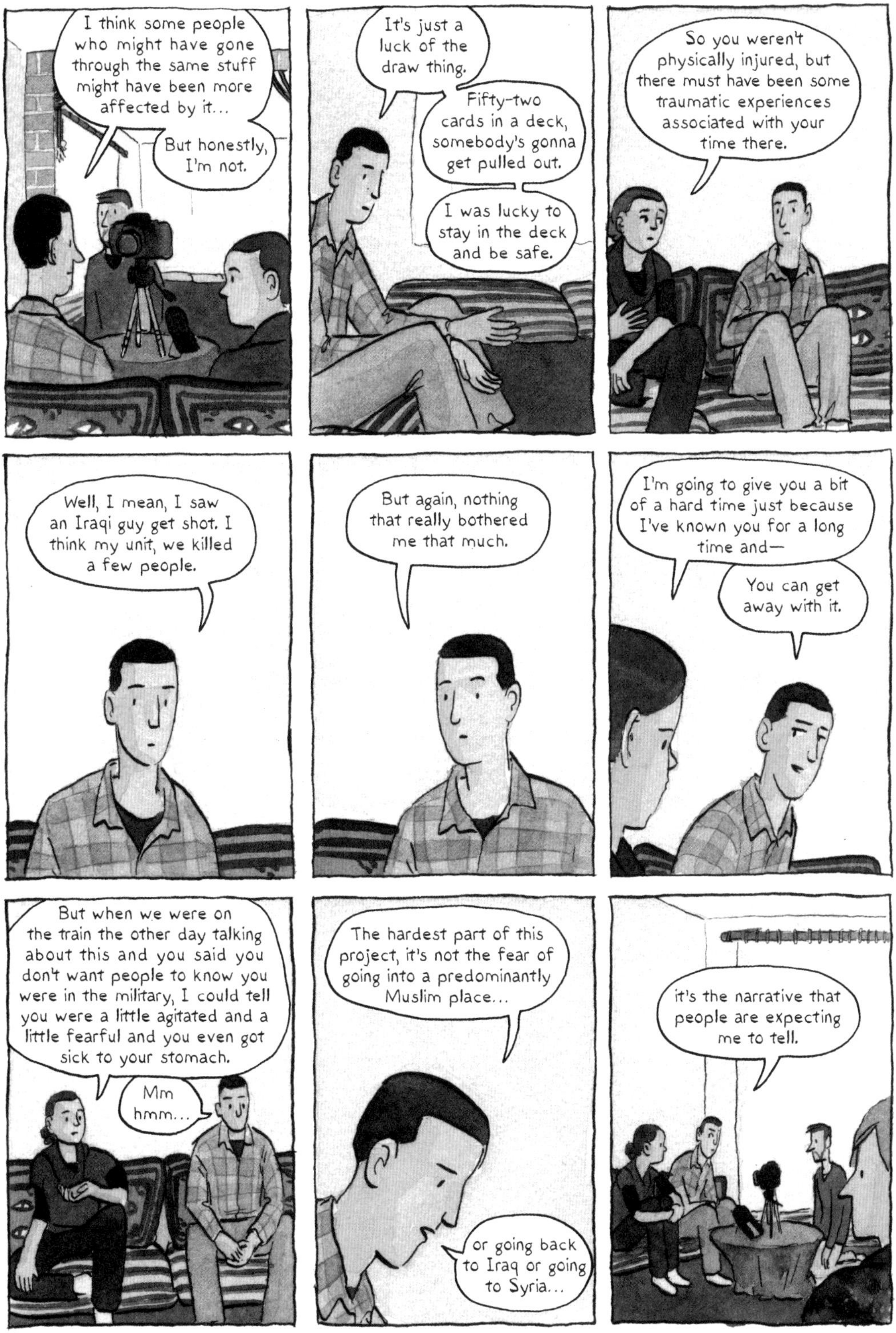
I think some people who might have gone through the same stuff might have been more affected by it...
But honestly, I'm not.
It's just a luck of the draw thing.
Fifty-two cards in a deck, somebody's gonna get pulled out.
I was lucky to stay in the deck and be safe.
So you weren't physically injured, but there must have been some traumatic experiences associated with your time there.
Well, I mean, I saw an Iraqi guy get shot. I think my unit, we killed a few people.
But again, nothing that really bothered me that much.
I'm going to give you a bit of a hard time just because I've known you for a long time and—
You can get away with it.
But when we were on the train the other day talking about this and you said you don't want people to know you were in the military, I could tell you were a little agitated and a little fearful and you even got sick to your stomach.
Mm hmm...
The hardest part of this project, it's not the fear of going into a predominantly Muslim place...
or going back to Iraq or going to Syria...
it's the narrative that people are expecting me to tell.

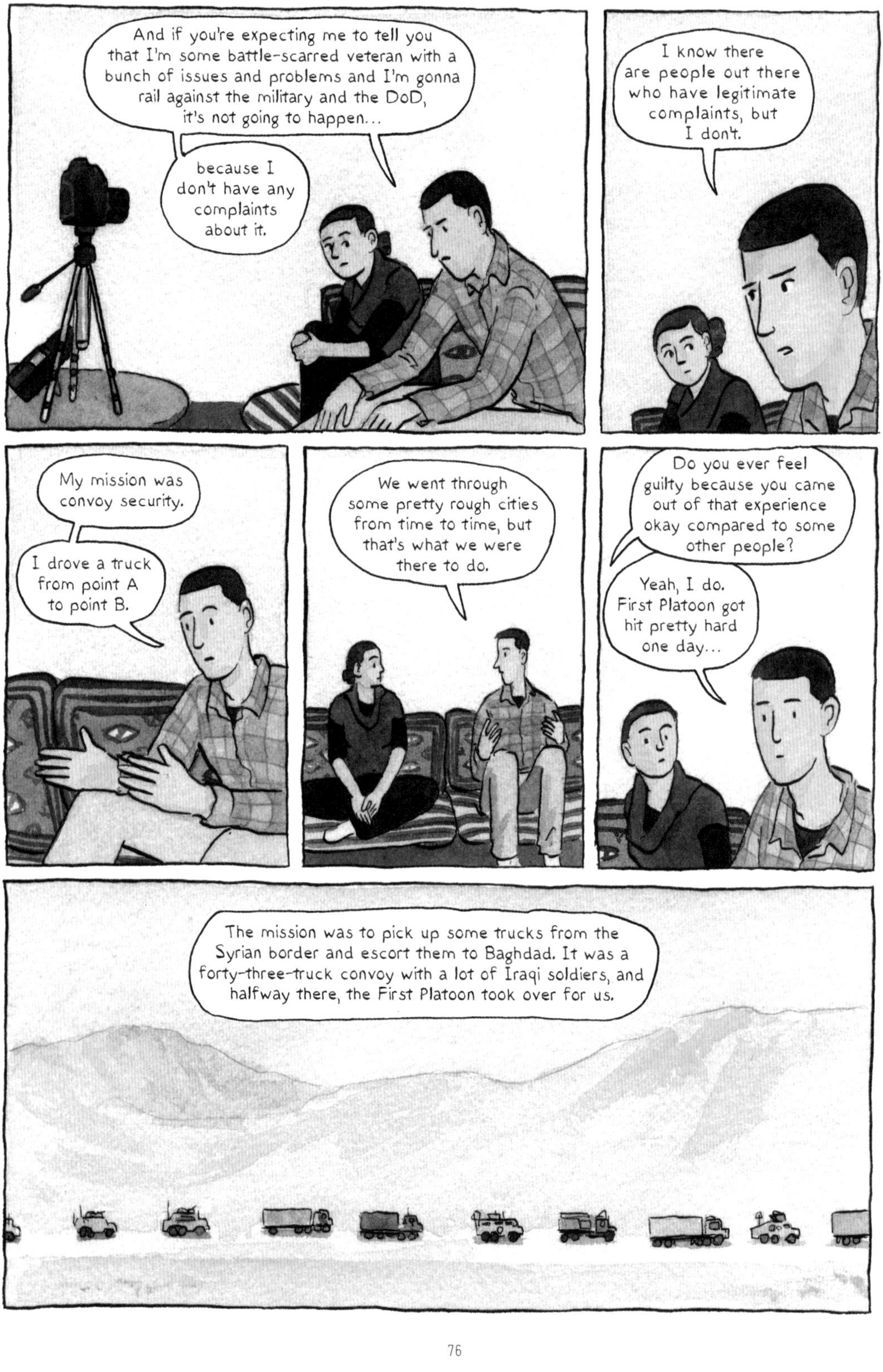
And if you're expecting me to tell you that I'm some battle-scarred veteran with a bunch of issues and problems and I'm gonna rail against the military and the DoD, it's not going to happen...
because I don't have any complaints about it.
I know there are people out there who have legitimate complaints, but I don't.
My mission was convoy security.
I drove a truck from point A to point B.
We went through some pretty rough cities from time to time, but that's what we were there to do.
Do you ever feel guilty because you came out of that experience okay compared to some other people?
Yeah, I do. First Platoon got hit pretty hard one day...
The mission was to pick up some trucks from the Syrian border and escort them to Baghdad. It was a forty-three-truck convoy with a lot of Iraqi soldiers, and halfway there, the First Platoon took over for us.

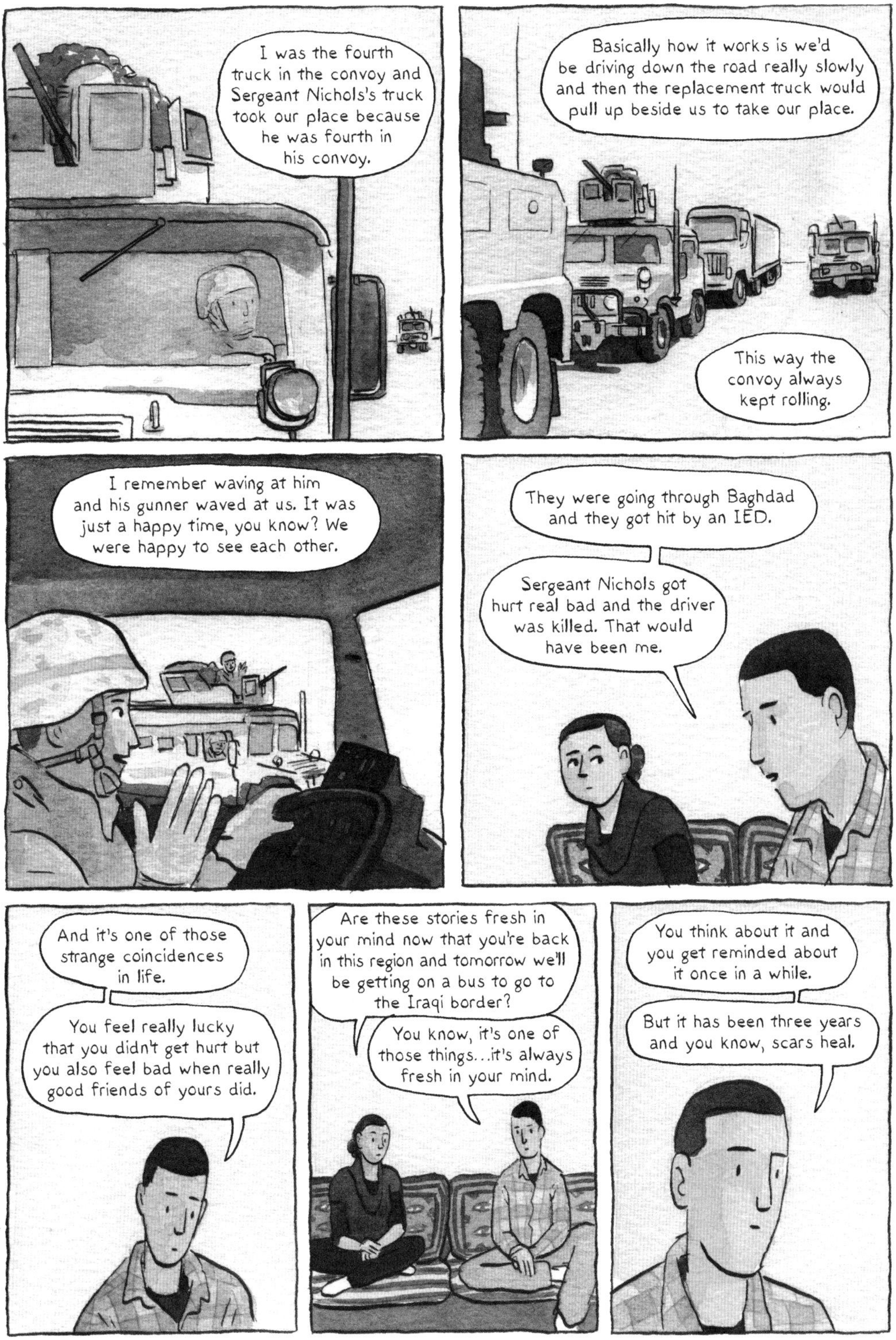
I was the fourth truck in the convoy and Sergeant Nichols's truck took our place because he was fourth in his convoy.
Basically how it works is we'd be driving down the road really slowly and then the replacement truck would pull up beside us to take our place.
This way the convoy always kept rolling.
I remember waving at him and his gunner waved at us. It was just a happy time, you know? We were happy to see each other.
They were going through Baghdad and they got hit by an IED.
Sergeant Nichols got hurt real bad and the driver was killed. That would have been me.
And it's one of those strange coincidences in life.
You feel really lucky that you didn't get hurt but you also feel bad when really good friends of yours did.
Are these stories fresh in your mind now that you're back in this region and tomorrow we'll be getting on a bus to go to the Iraqi border?
You know, it's one of those things...it's always fresh in your mind.
You think about it and you get reminded about it once in a while.
But it has been three years and you know, scars heal.

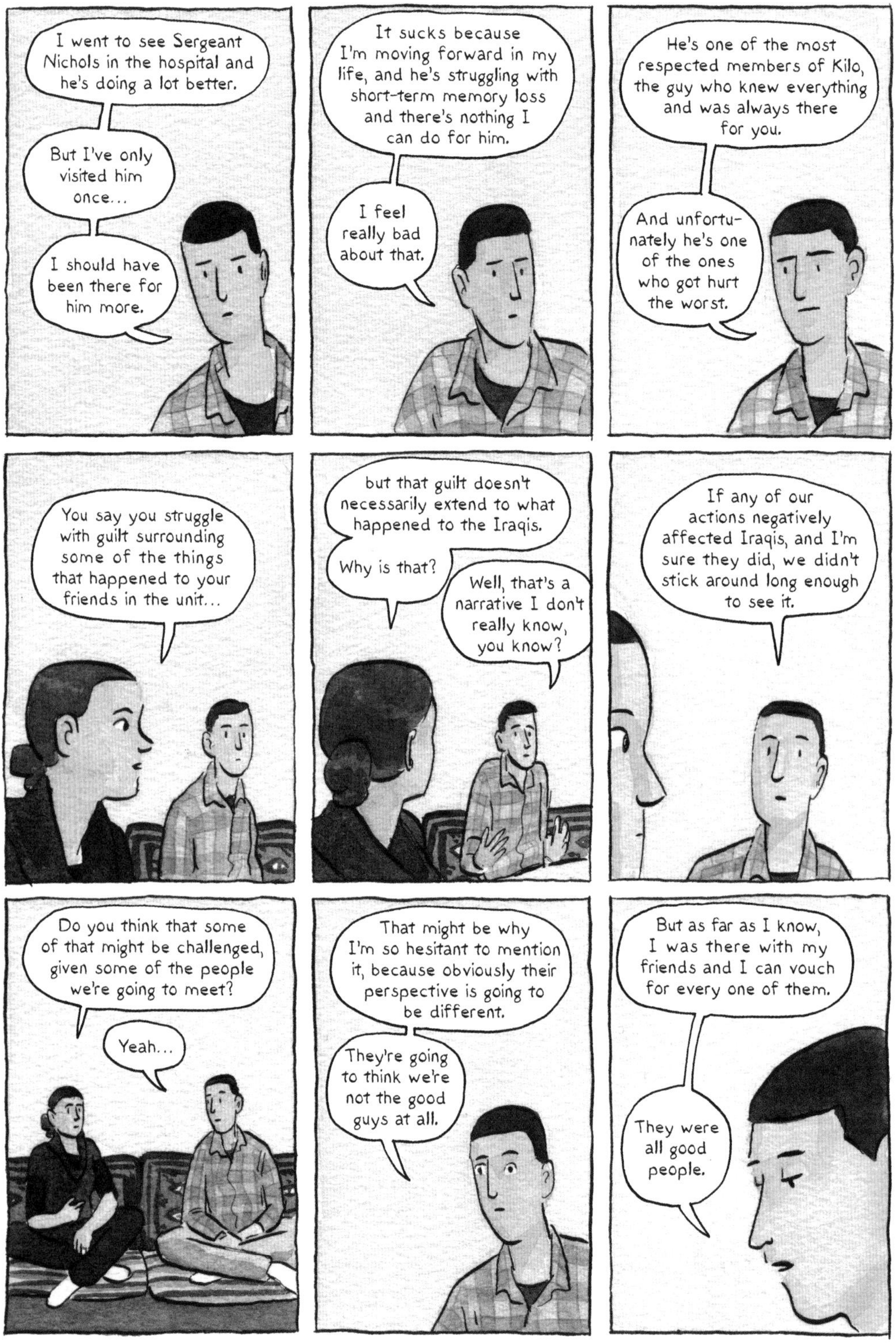
I went to see Sergeant Nichols in the hospital and he's doing a lot better.
But I've only visited him once...
I should have been there for him more.
It sucks because I'm moving forward in my life, and he's struggling with short-term memory loss and there's nothing I can do for him.
I feel really bad about that.
He's one of the most respected members of Kilo, the guy who knew everything and was always there for you.
And unfortunately he's one of the ones who got hurt the worst.
You say you struggle with guilt surrounding some of the things that happened to your friends in the unit...
but that guilt doesn't necessarily extend to what happened to the Iraqis.
Why is that?
Well, that's a narrative I don't really know, you know?
If any of our actions negatively affected Iraqis, and I'm sure they did, we didn't stick around long enough to see it.
Do you think that some of that might be challenged, given some of the people we're going to meet?
Yeah...
That might be why I'm so hesitant to mention it, because obviously their perspective is going to be different.
They're going to think we're not the good guys at all.
But as far as I know, I was there with my friends and I can vouch for every one of them.
They were all good people.

TRAVERSING THE KRG

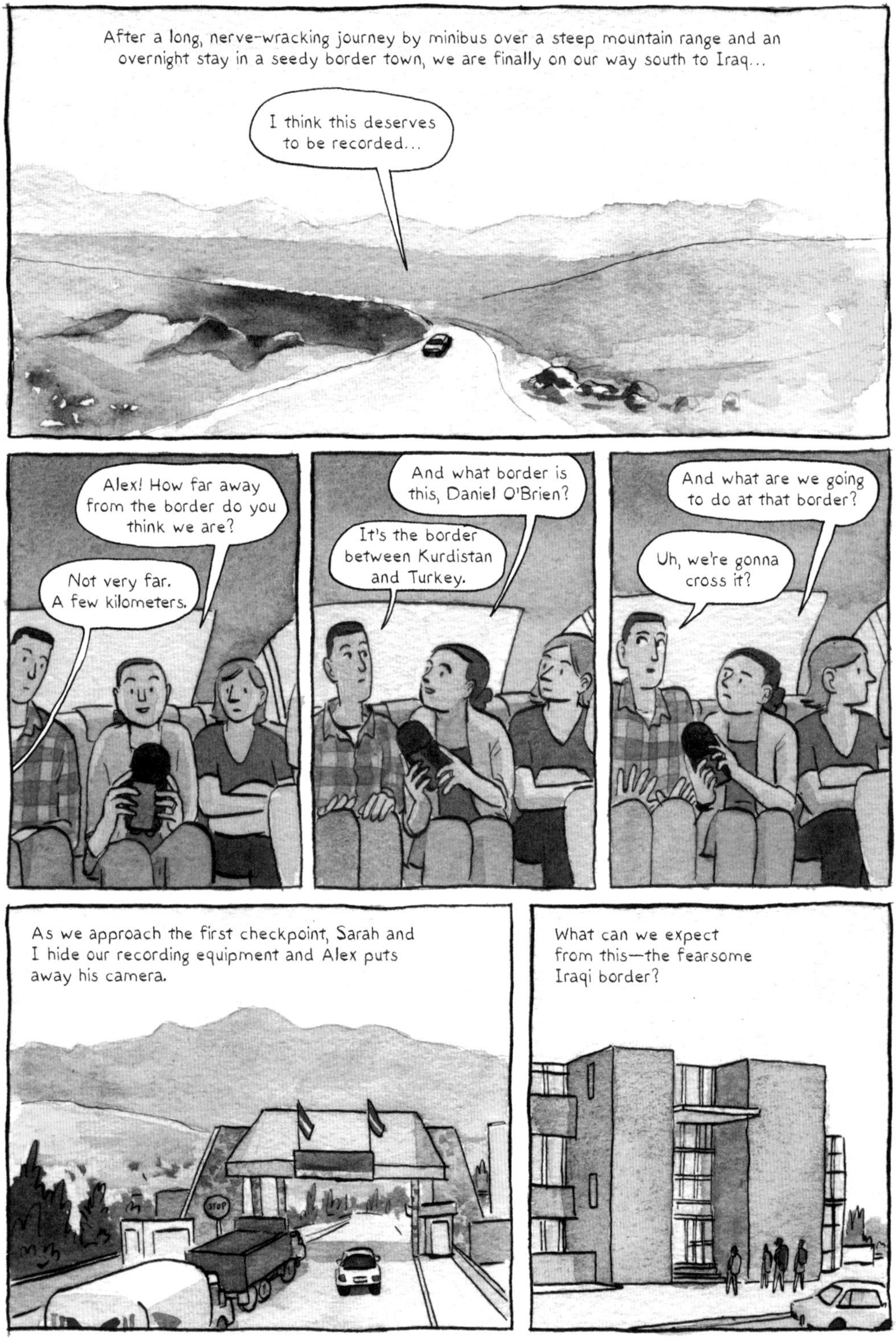
After a long, nerve-wracking journey by minibus over a steep mountain range and an overnight stay in a seedy border town, we are finally on our way south to Iraq...
I think this deserves to be recorded...
Alex! How far away from the border do you think we are?
Not very far. A few kilometers.
And what border is this, Daniel O'Brien?
It's the border between Kurdistan and Turkey.
And what are we going to do at that border?
Uh, we're gonna cross it?
As we approach the first checkpoint, Sarah and I hide our recording equipment and Alex puts away his camera.
STOP
What can we expect from this—the fearsome Iraqi border?

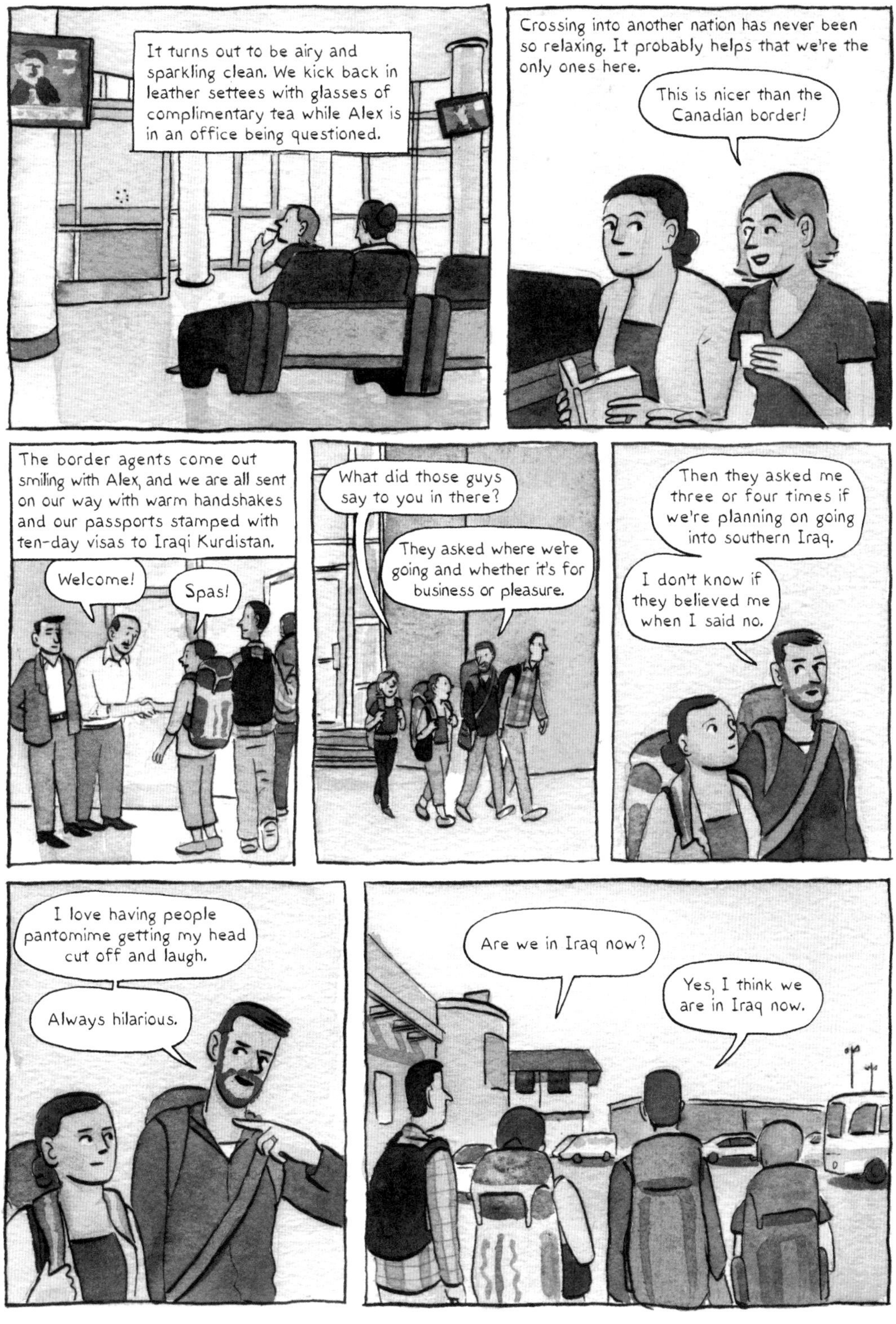
It turns out to be airy and sparkling clean. We kick back in leather settees with glasses of complimentary tea while Alex is in an office being questioned.
Crossing into another nation has never been so relaxing. It probably helps that we're the only ones here.
This is nicer than the Canadian border!
The border agents come out smiling with Alex, and we are all sent on our way with warm handshakes and our passports stamped with ten-day visas to Iraqi Kurdistan.
Welcome!
Spas!
What did those guys say to you in there?
They asked where we're going and whether it's for business or pleasure.
Then they asked me three or four times if we're planning on going into southern Iraq.
I don't know if they believed me when I said no.
I love having people pantomime getting my head cut off and laugh.
Always hilarious.
Are we in Iraq now?
Yes, I think we are in Iraq now.

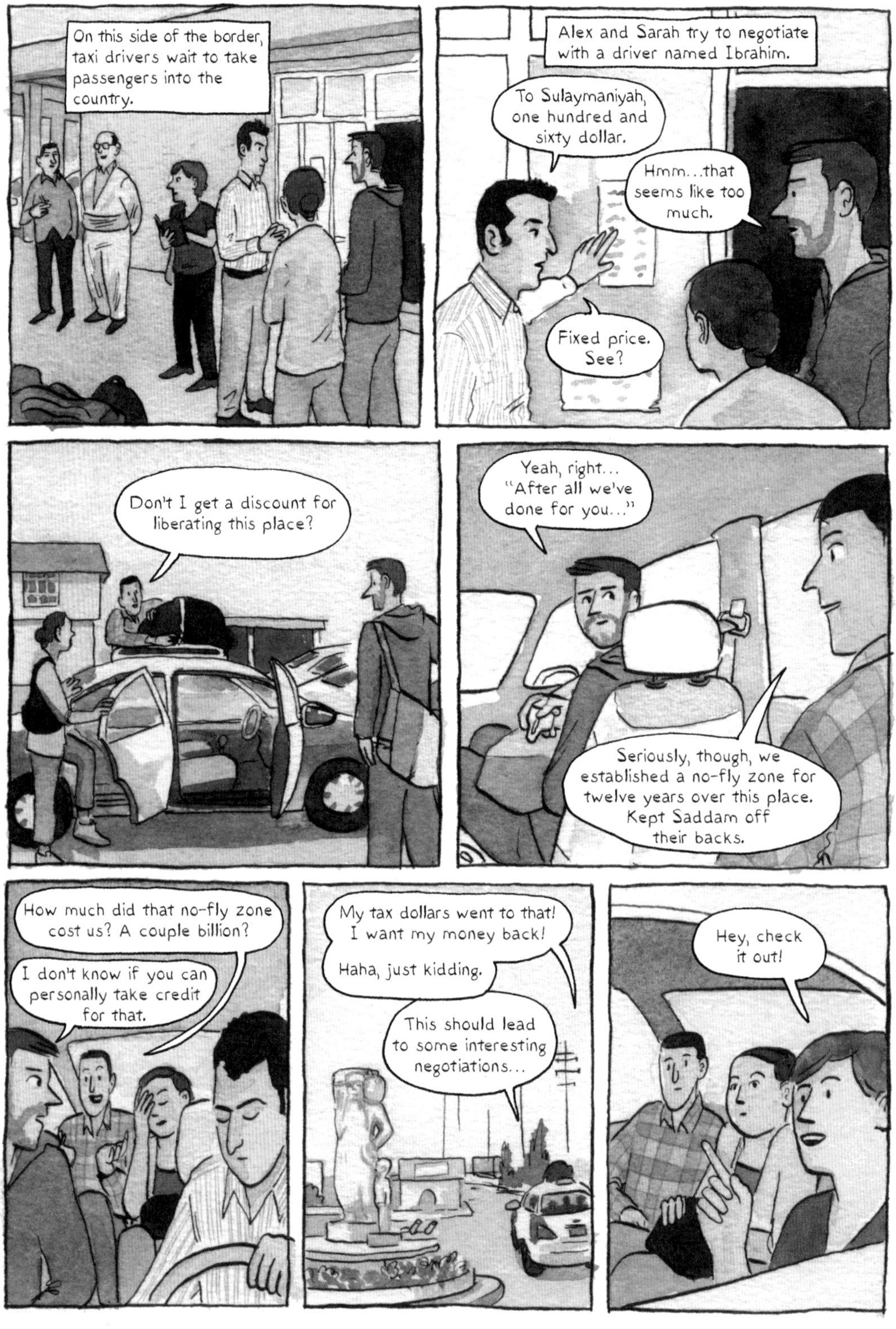

On this side of the border, taxi drivers wait to take passengers into the country.
Alex and Sarah try to negotiate with a driver named Ibrahim.
To Sulaymaniyah, one hundred and sixty dollar.
Hmm...that seems like too much.
Fixed price. See?
Don't I get a discount for liberating this place?
Yeah, right... "After all we've done for you..."
Seriously, though, we established a no-fly zone for twelve years over this place. Kept Saddam off their backs.
How much did that no-fly zone cost us? A couple billion?
I don't know if you can personally take credit for that.
My tax dollars went to that! I want my money back!
Haha, just kidding.
This should lead to some interesting negotiations...
Hey, check it out!

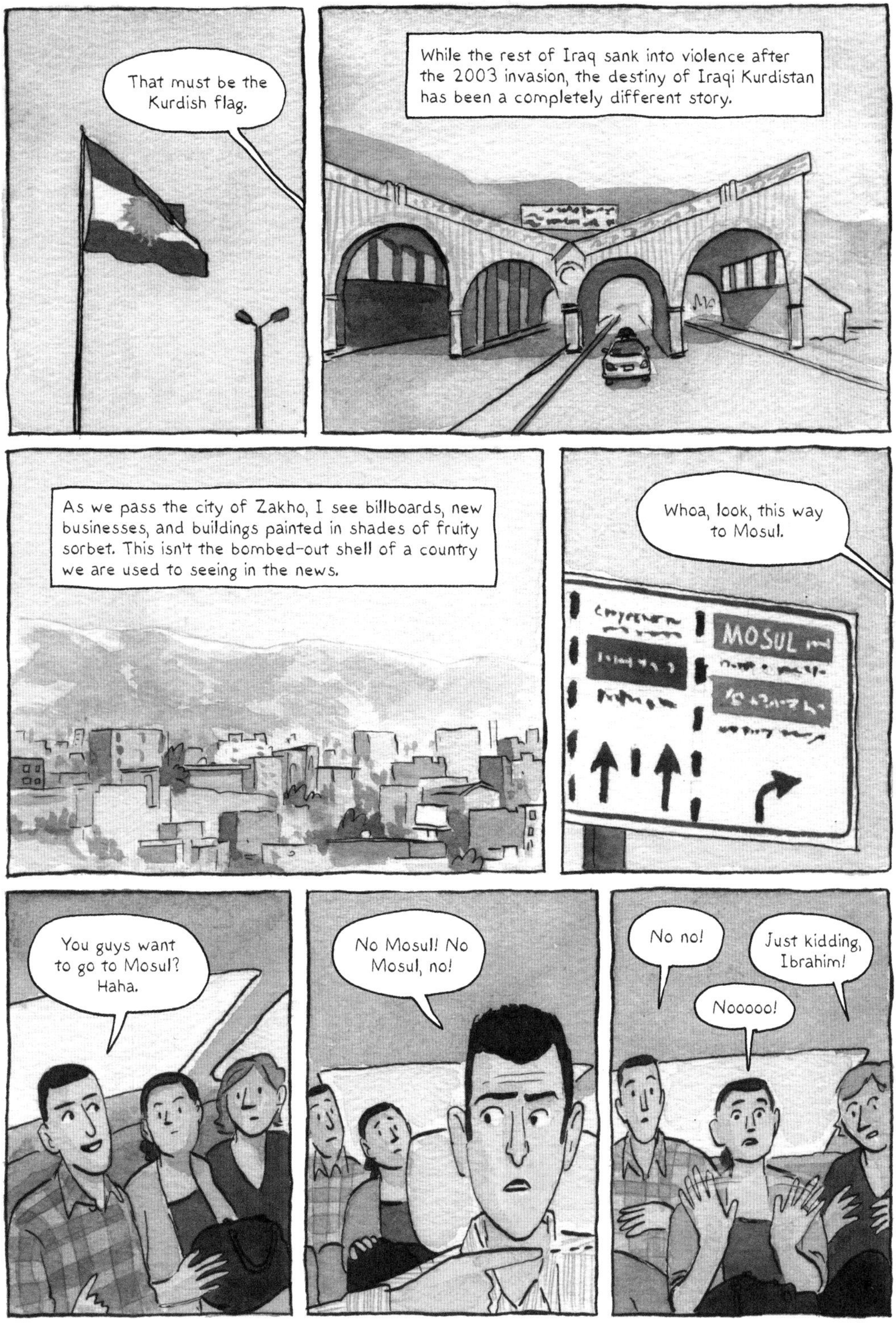
That must be the Kurdish flag.
While the rest of Iraq sank into violence after the 2003 invasion, the destiny of Iraqi Kurdistan has been a completely different story.
As we pass the city of Zakho, I see billboards, new businesses, and buildings painted in shades of fruity sorbet. This isn't the bombed-out shell of a country we are used to seeing in the news.
Whoa, look, this way to Mosul.
MOSUL
You guys want to go to Mosul? Haha.
No Mosul! No Mosul, no!
No no!
Just kidding, Ibrahim!
Nooooo!

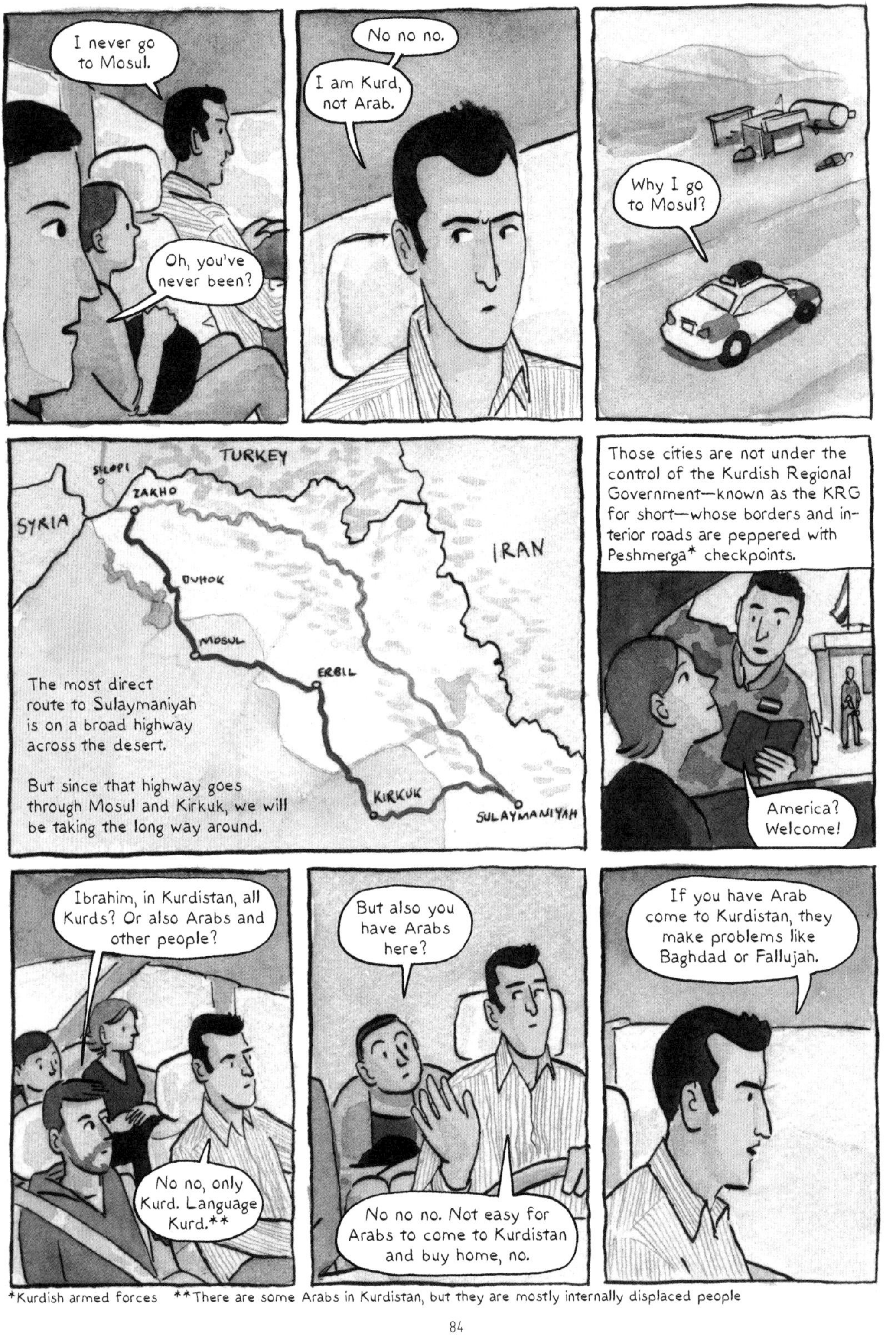
I never go to Mosul.
Oh, you've never been?
No no no.
I am Kurd, not Arab.
Why I go to Mosul?
TURKEY
SILOPI
ZAKHO
SYRIA
IRAN
DUHOK
MOSUL
ERBIL
KIRKUK
SULAYMANIYAH
The most direct route to Sulaymaniyah is on a broad highway across the desert.
But since that highway goes through Mosul and Kirkuk, we will be taking the long way around.
Those cities are not under the control of the Kurdish Regional Government—known as the KRG for short—whose borders and interior roads are peppered with Peshmerga* checkpoints.
America? Welcome!
Ibrahim, in Kurdistan, all Kurds? Or also Arabs and other people?
No no, only Kurd. Language Kurd.**
But also you have Arabs here?
No no no. Not easy for Arabs to come to Kurdistan and buy home, no.
If you have Arab come to Kurdistan, they make problems like Baghdad or Fallujah.

*Kurdish armed forces **There are some Arabs in Kurdistan, but they are mostly internally displaced people

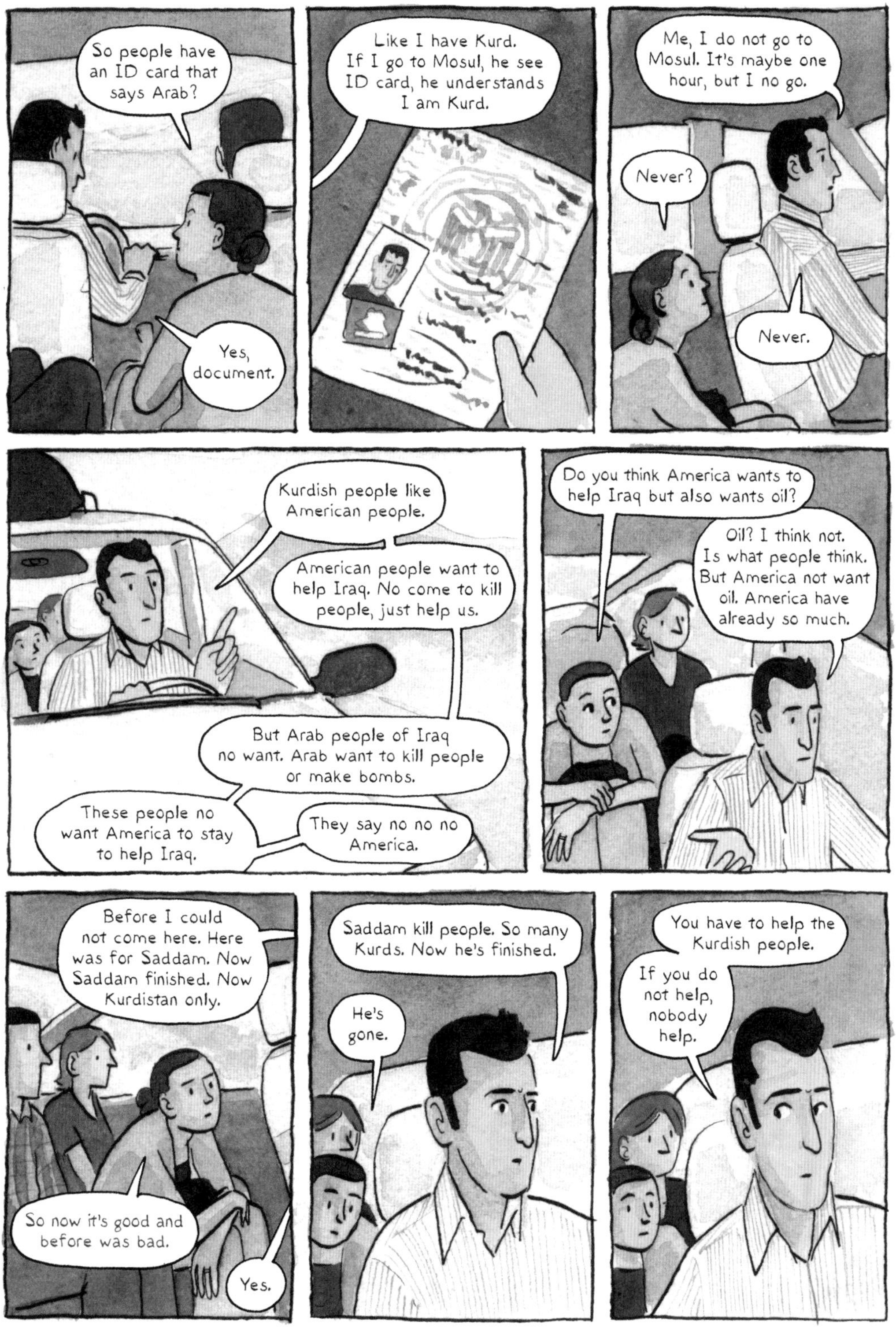
So people have an ID card that says Arab?
Yes, document.
Like I have Kurd. If I go to Mosul, he see ID card, he understands I am Kurd.
Me, I do not go to Mosul. It's maybe one hour, but I no go.
Never?
Never.
Kurdish people like American people.
American people want to help Iraq. No come to kill people, just help us.
But Arab people of Iraq no want. Arab want to kill people or make bombs.
These people no want America to stay to help Iraq.
They say no no no America.
Do you think America wants to help Iraq but also wants oil?
Oil? I think not. Is what people think. But America not want oil. America have already so much.
Before I could not come here. Here was for Saddam. Now Saddam finished. Now Kurdistan only.
So now it's good and before was bad.
Yes.
Saddam kill people. So many Kurds. Now he's finished.
He's gone.
You have to help the Kurdish people.
If you do not help, nobody help.

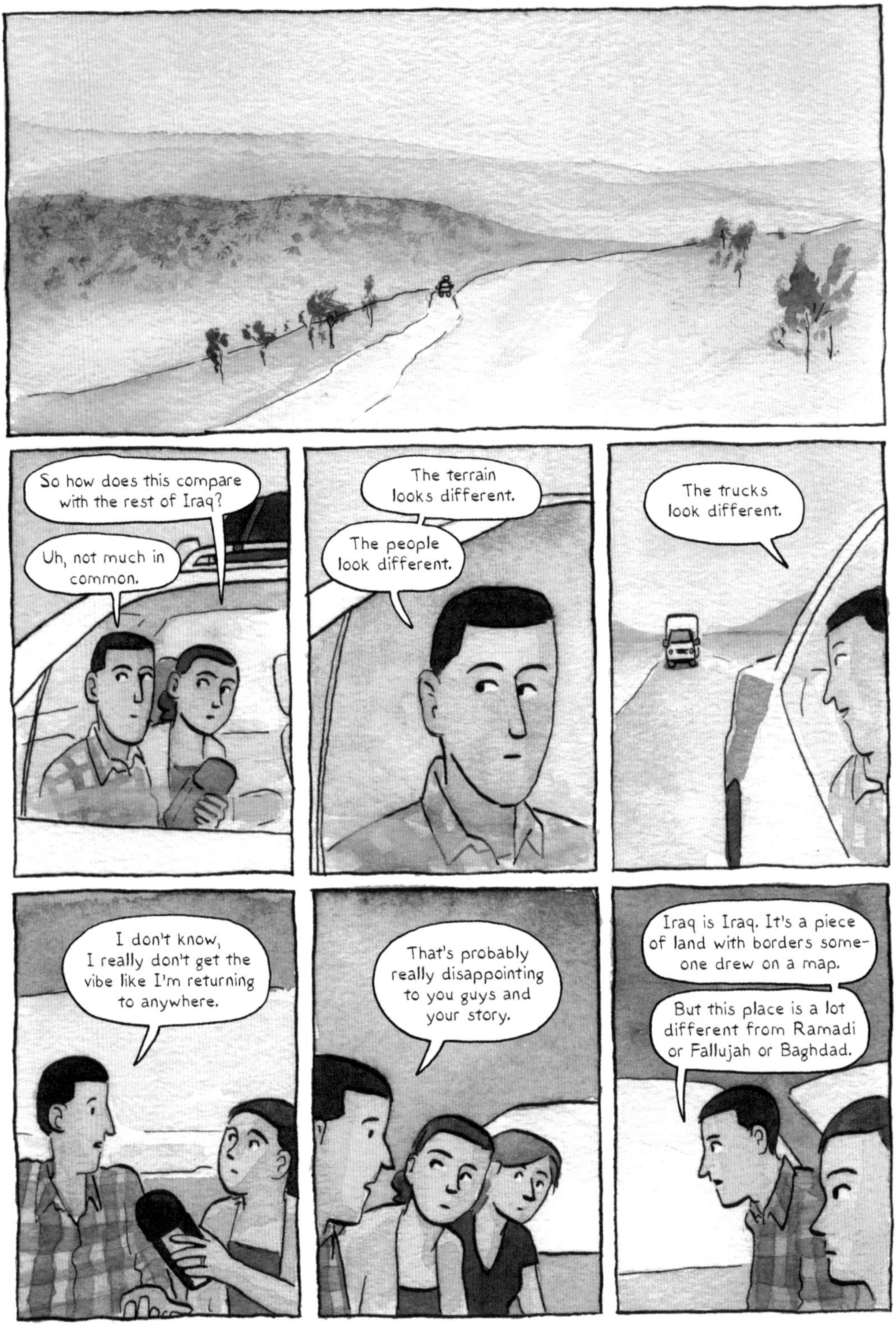
So how does this compare with the rest of Iraq?
Uh, not much in common.
The terrain looks different.
The people look different.
The trucks look different.
I don't know, I really don't get the vibe like I'm returning to anywhere.
That's probably really disappointing to you guys and your story.
Iraq is Iraq. It's a piece of land with borders some-one drew on a map.
But this place is a lot different from Ramadi or Fallujah or Baghdad.

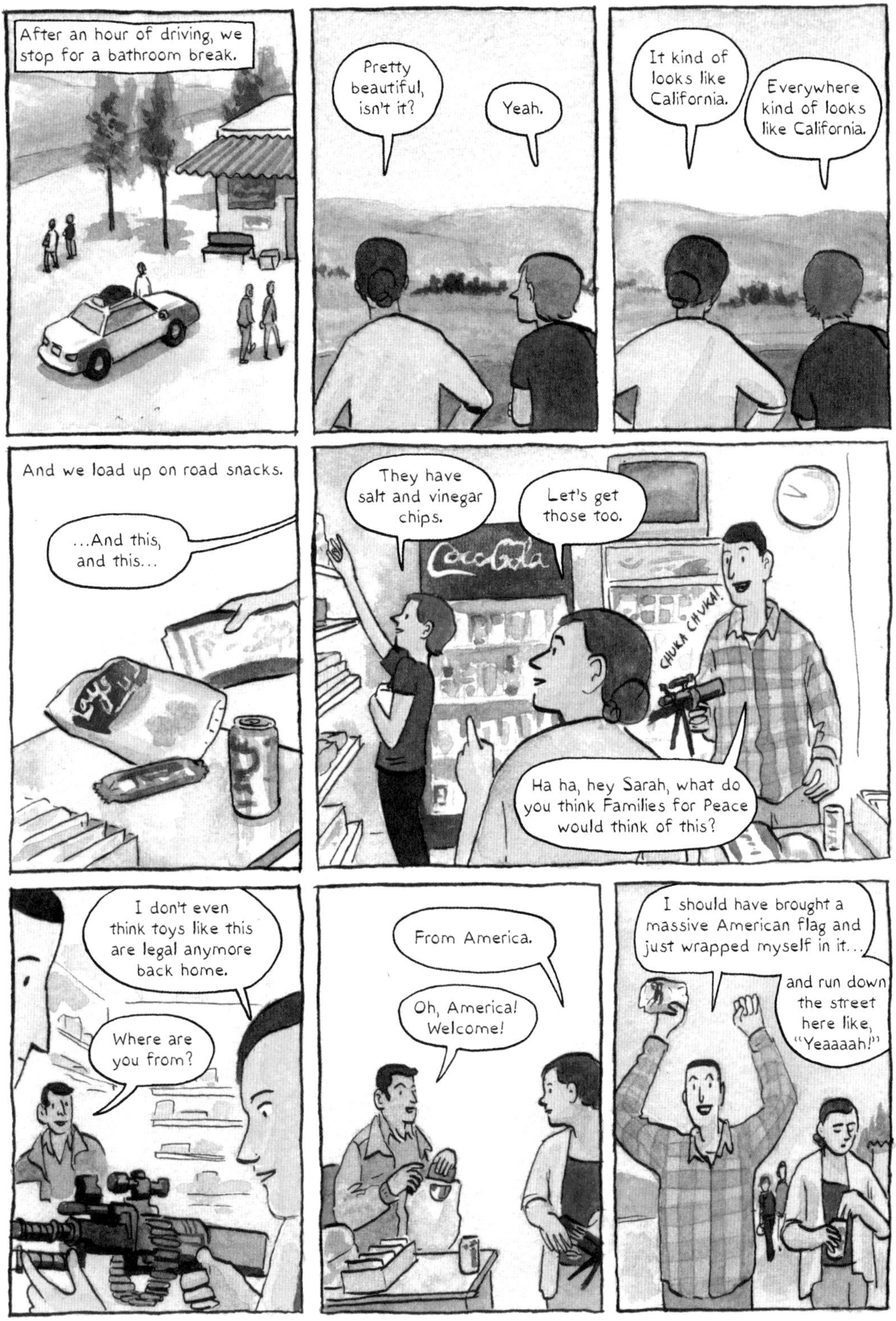
After an hour of driving, we stop for a bathroom break.
Pretty beautiful, isn't it?
Yeah.
It kind of looks like California.
Everywhere kind of looks like California.
And we load up on road snacks.
...And this, and this...
They have salt and vinegar chips.
Let's get those too.
Coca-Cola
CHUKA CHUKA!
Ha ha, hey Sarah, what do you think Families for Peace would think of this?
I don't even think toys like this are legal anymore back home.
Where are you from?
From America.
Oh, America! Welcome!
I should have brought a massive American flag and just wrapped myself in it...
and run down the street here like, "Yeaaaah!"

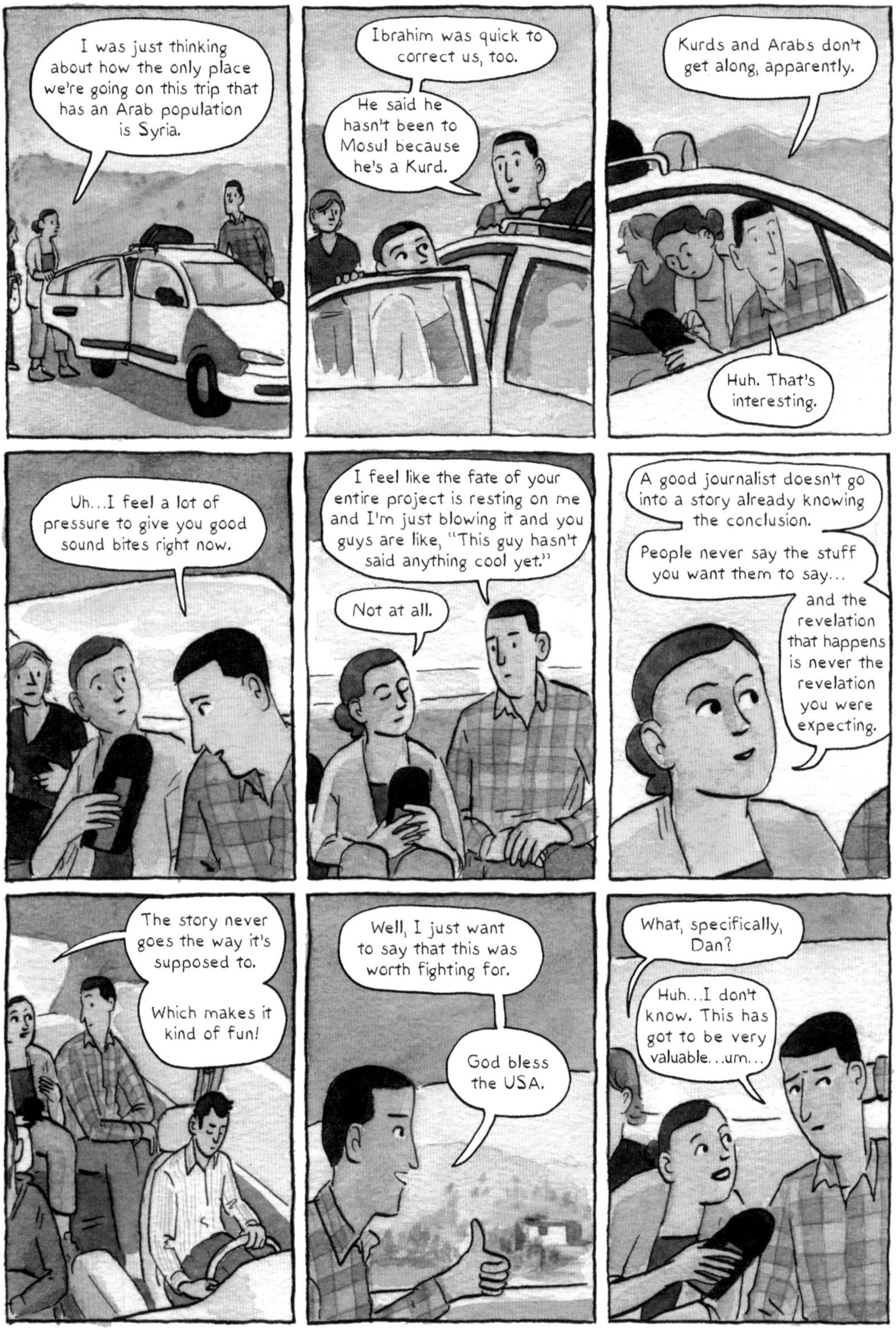
I was just thinking about how the only place we're going on this trip that has an Arab population is Syria.
Ibrahim was quick to correct us, too.
He said he hasn't been to Mosul because he's a Kurd.
Kurds and Arabs don't get along, apparently.
Huh. That's interesting.
Uh...I feel a lot of pressure to give you good sound bites right now.
I feel like the fate of your entire project is resting on me and I'm just blowing it and you guys are like, "This guy hasn't said anything cool yet."
Not at all.
A good journalist doesn't go into a story already knowing the conclusion.
People never say the stuff you want them to say...
and the revelation that happens is never the revelation you were expecting.
The story never goes the way it's supposed to.
Which makes it kind of fun!
Well, I just want to say that this was worth fighting for.
God bless the USA.
What, specifically, Dan?
Huh...I don't know. This has got to be very valuable...um...

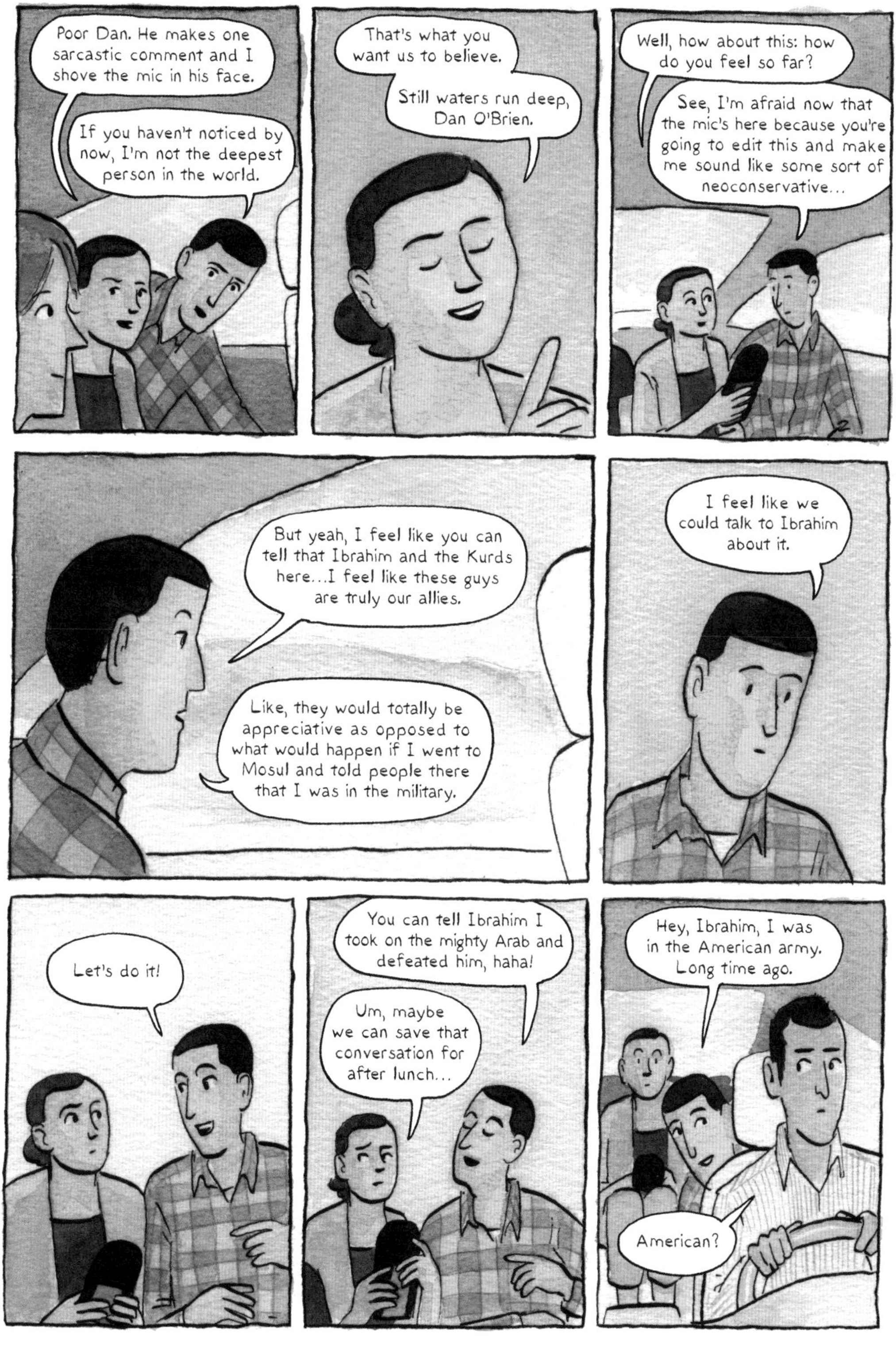

Poor Dan. He makes one sarcastic comment and I shove the mic in his face.
If you haven't noticed by now, I'm not the deepest person in the world.
That's what you want us to believe.
Still waters run deep, Dan O'Brien.
Well, how about this: how do you feel so far?
See, I'm afraid now that the mic's here because you're going to edit this and make me sound like some sort of neoconservative...
But yeah, I feel like you can tell that Ibrahim and the Kurds here...I feel like these guys are truly our allies.
Like, they would totally be appreciative as opposed to what would happen if I went to Mosul and told people there that I was in the military.
I feel like we could talk to Ibrahim about it.
Let's do it!
You can tell Ibrahim I took on the mighty Arab and defeated him, haha!
Um, maybe we can save that conversation for after lunch...
Hey, Ibrahim, I was in the American army. Long time ago.
American?

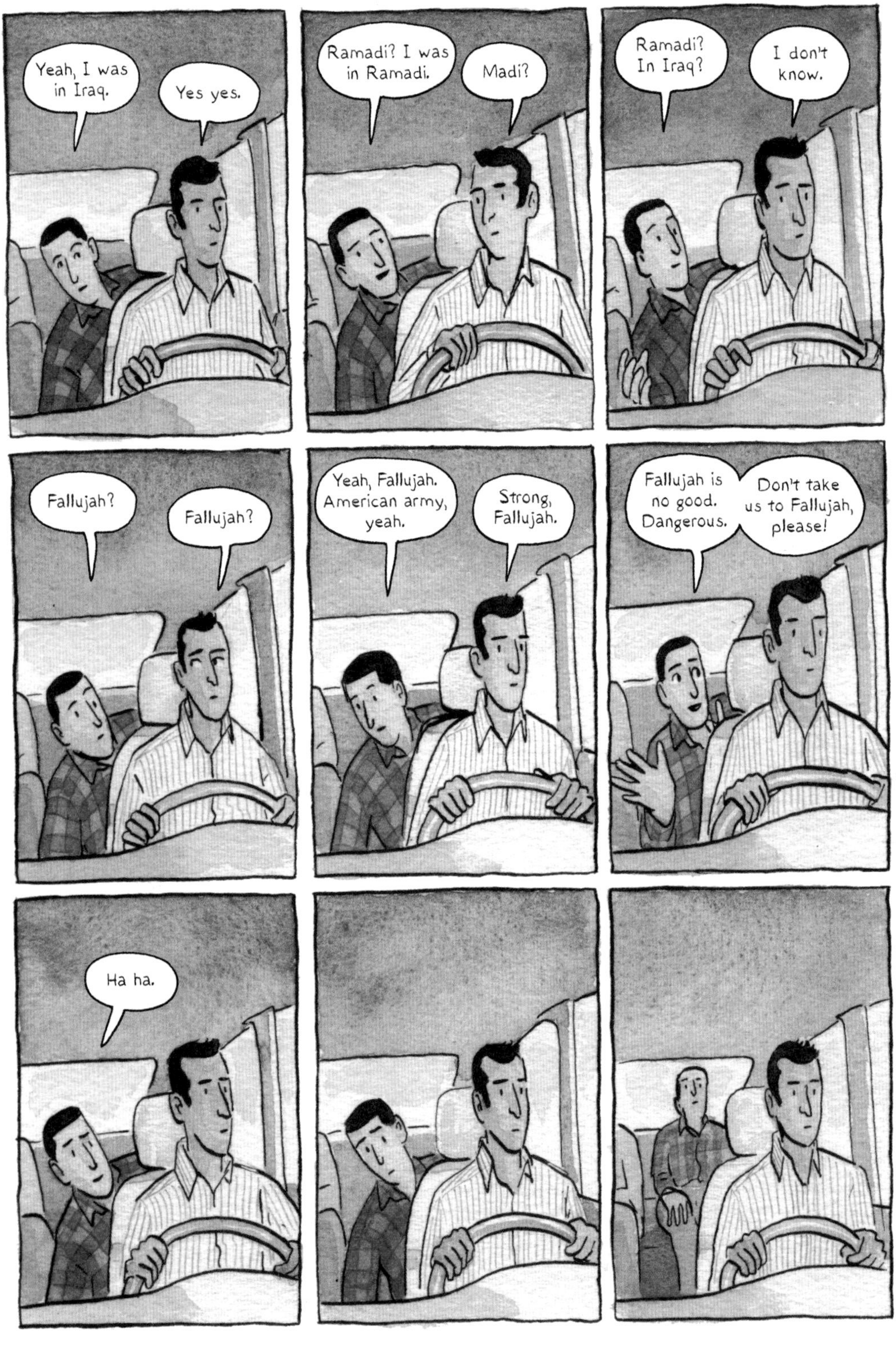
Yeah, I was in Iraq.
Yes yes.
Ramadi? I was in Ramadi.
Madi?
Ramadi? In Iraq?
I don't know.
Fallujah?
Fallujah?
Yeah, Fallujah. American army, yeah.
Strong, Fallujah.
Fallujah is no good. Dangerous.
Don't take us to Fallujah, please!
Ha ha.

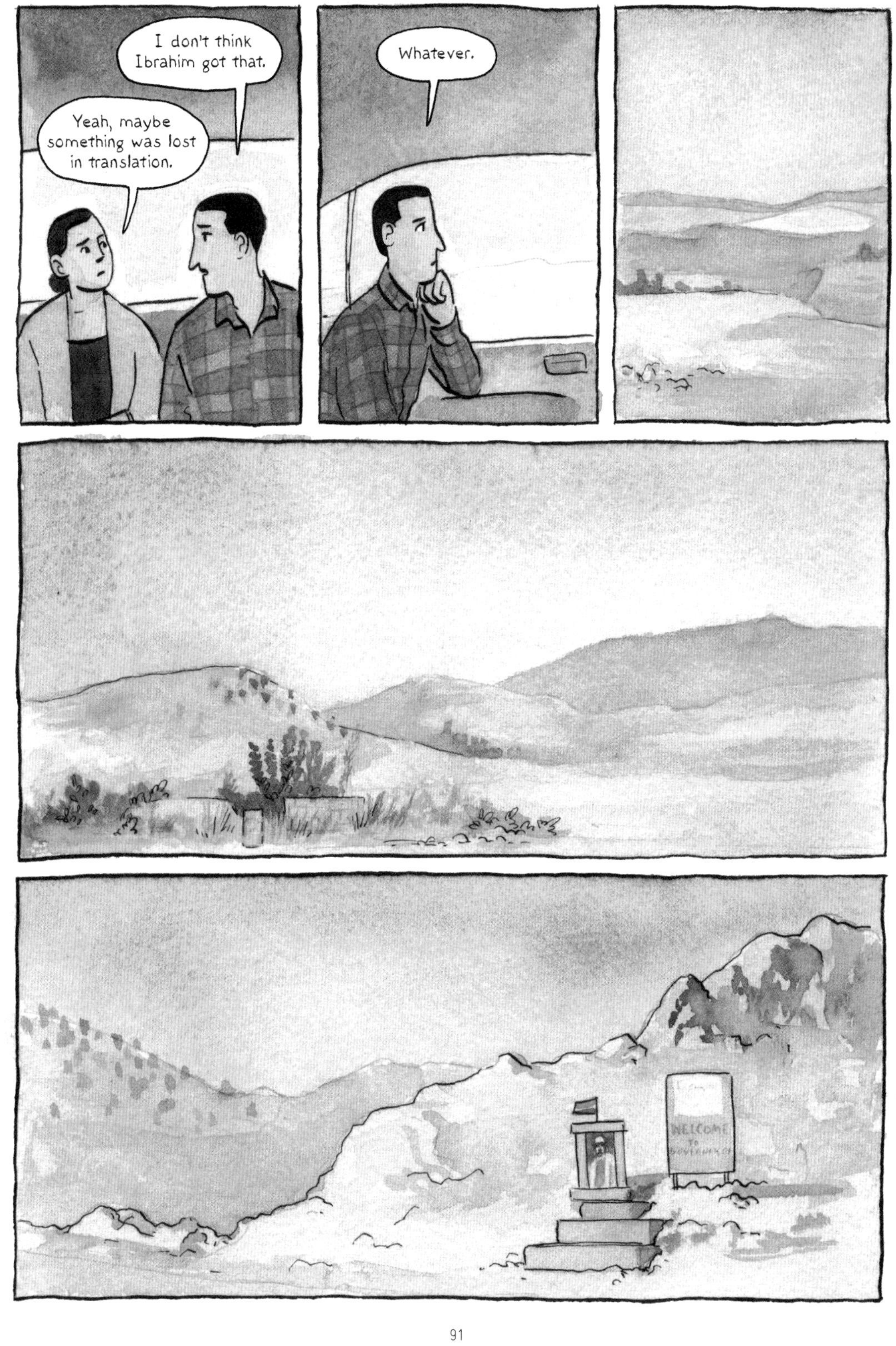
I don't think Ibrahim got that.
Yeah, maybe something was lost in translation.
Whatever.
WELCOME
TO

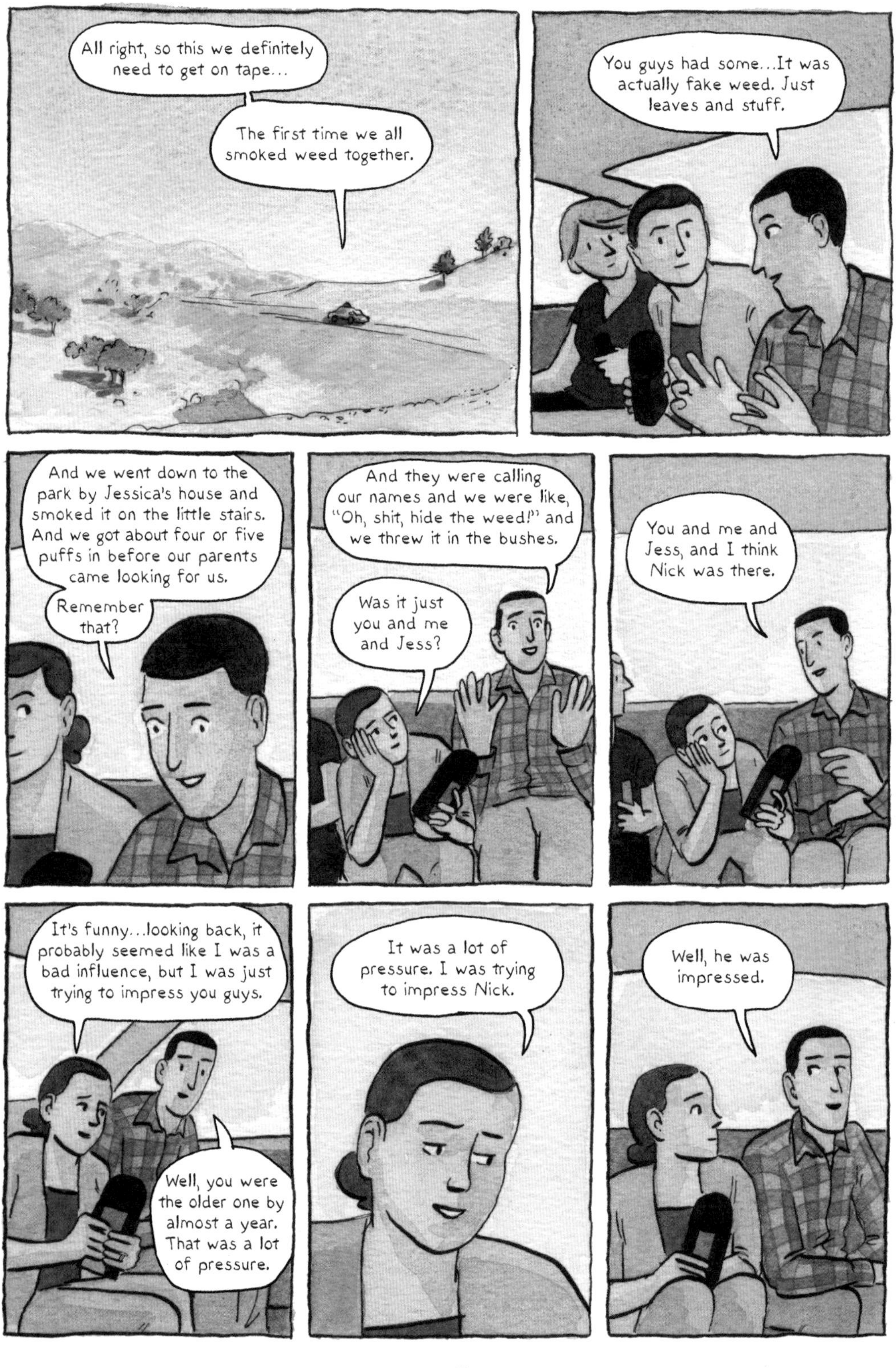
All right, so this we definitely need to get on tape...
The first time we all smoked weed together.
You guys had some...It was actually fake weed. Just leaves and stuff.
And we went down to the park by Jessica's house and smoked it on the little stairs. And we got about four or five puffs in before our parents came looking for us.
Remember that?
And they were calling our names and we were like, "Oh, shit, hide the weed!" and we threw it in the bushes.
Was it just you and me and Jess?
You and me and Jess, and I think Nick was there.
It's funny...looking back, it probably seemed like I was a bad influence, but I was just trying to impress you guys.
Well, you were the older one by almost a year. That was a lot of pressure.
It was a lot of pressure. I was trying to impress Nick.
Well, he was impressed.

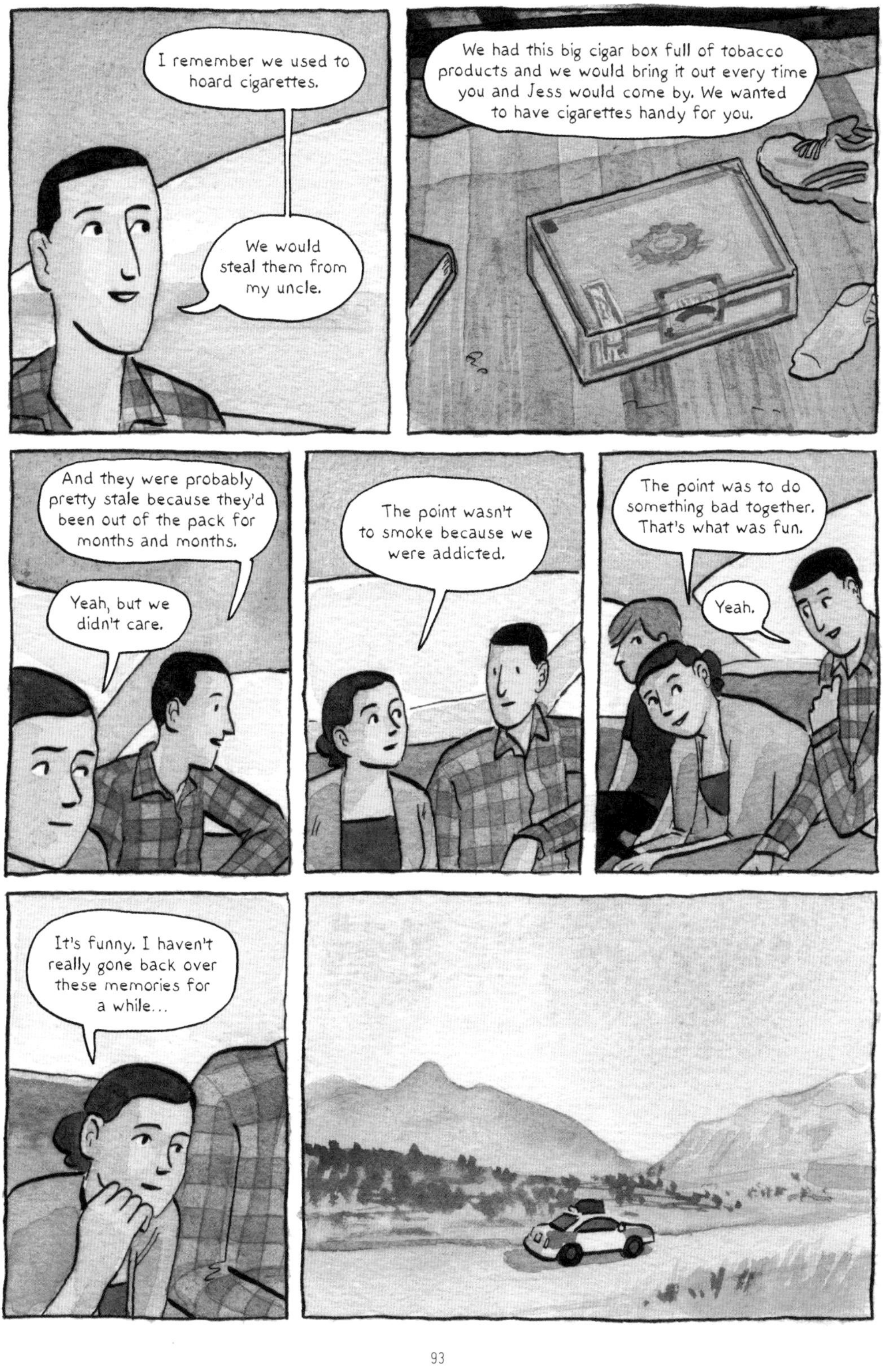
I remember we used to hoard cigarettes.
We would steal them from my uncle.
We had this big cigar box full of tobacco products and we would bring it out every time you and Jess would come by. We wanted to have cigarettes handy for you.
And they were probably pretty stale because they'd been out of the pack for months and months.
Yeah, but we didn't care.
The point wasn't to smoke because we were addicted.
The point was to do something bad together. That's what was fun.
Yeah.
It's funny. I haven't really gone back over these memories for a while...

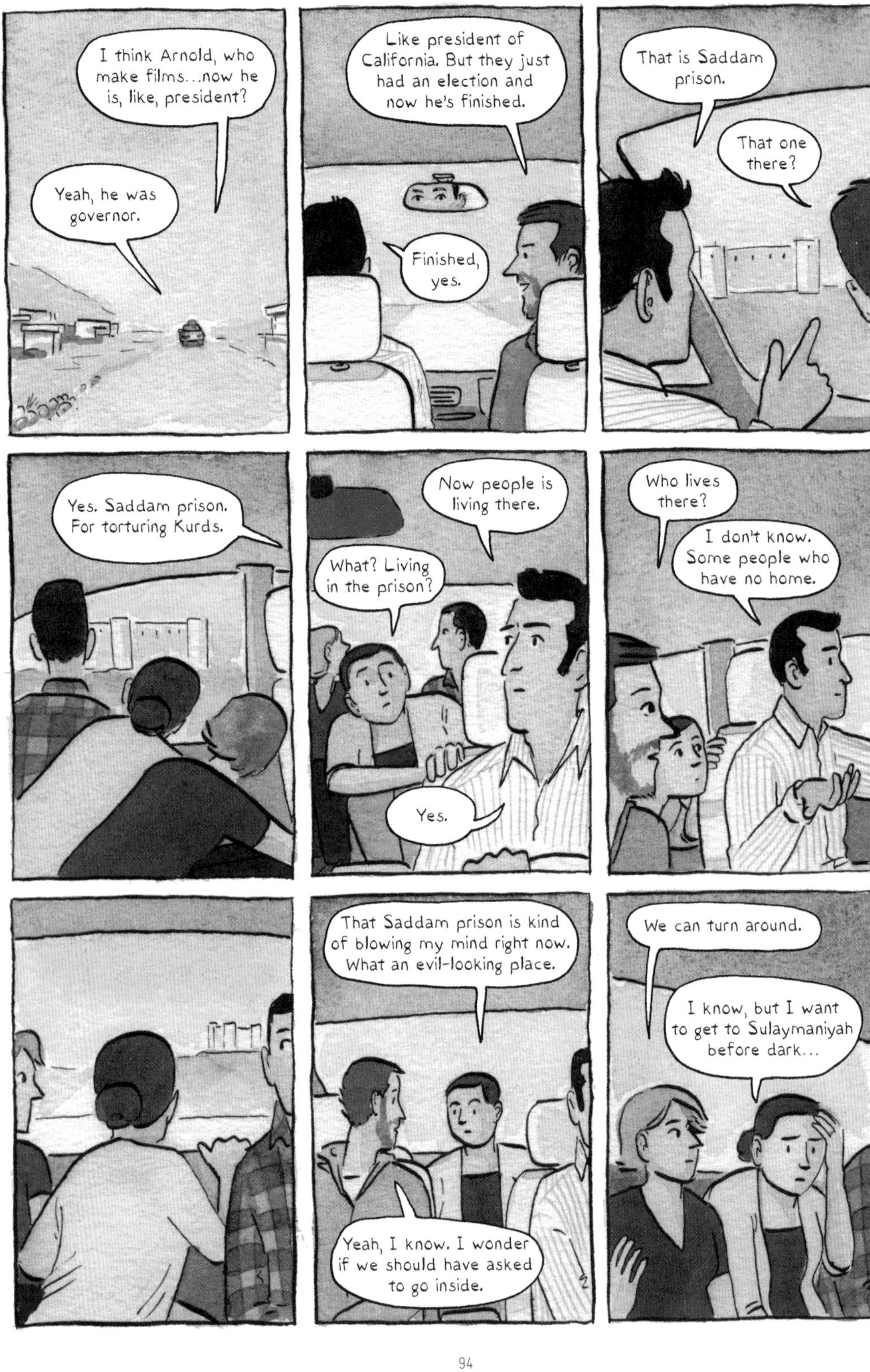
I think Arnold, who make films...now he is, like, president?
Yeah, he was governor.
Like president of California. But they just had an election and now he's finished.
Finished, yes.
That is Saddam prison.
That one there?
Yes. Saddam prison. For torturing Kurds.
Now people is living there.
What? Living in the prison?
Yes.
Who lives there?
I don't know. Some people who have no home.
That Saddam prison is kind of blowing my mind right now. What an evil-looking place.
Yeah, I know. I wonder if we should have asked to go inside.
We can turn around.
I know, but I want to get to Sulaymaniyah before dark...

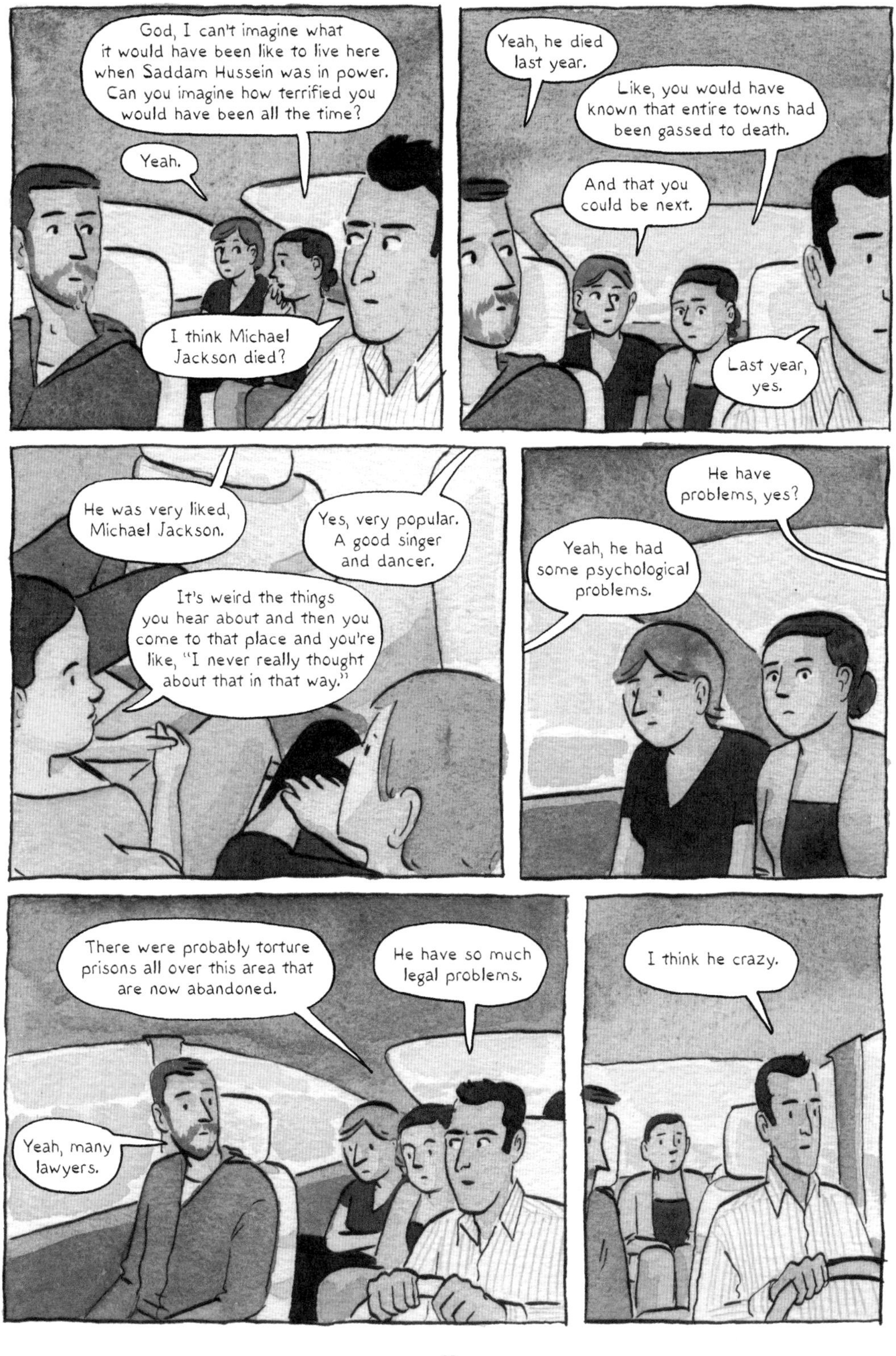
God, I can't imagine what it would have been like to live here when Saddam Hussein was in power. Can you imagine how terrified you would have been all the time?
Yeah.
I think Michael Jackson died?
Yeah, he died last year.
Like, you would have known that entire towns had been gassed to death.
And that you could be next.
Last year, yes.
He was very liked, Michael Jackson.
Yes, very popular. A good singer and dancer.
It's weird the things you hear about and then you come to that place and you're like, "I never really thought about that in that way."
He have problems, yes?
Yeah, he had some psychological problems.
There were probably torture prisons all over this area that are now abandoned.
He have so much legal problems.
Yeah, many lawyers.
I think he crazy.

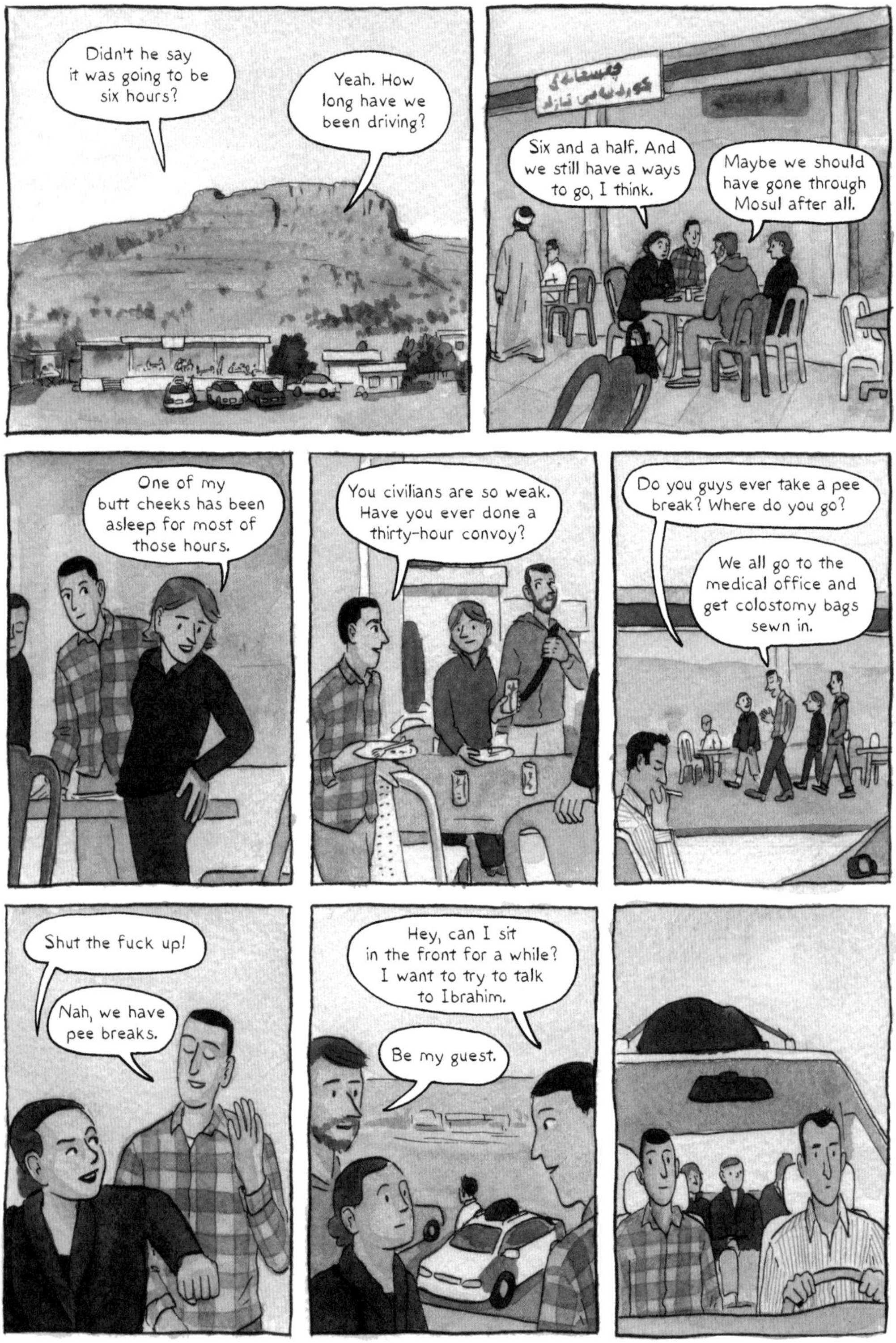
Didn't he say it was going to be six hours?
Yeah. How long have we been driving?
Six and a half. And we still have a ways to go, I think.
Maybe we should have gone through Mosul after all.
One of my butt cheeks has been asleep for most of those hours.
You civilians are so weak. Have you ever done a thirty-hour convoy?
Do you guys ever take a pee break? Where do you go?
We all go to the medical office and get colostomy bags sewn in.
Shut the fuck up!
Nah, we have pee breaks.
Hey, can I sit in the front for a while? I want to try to talk to Ibrahim.
Be my guest.

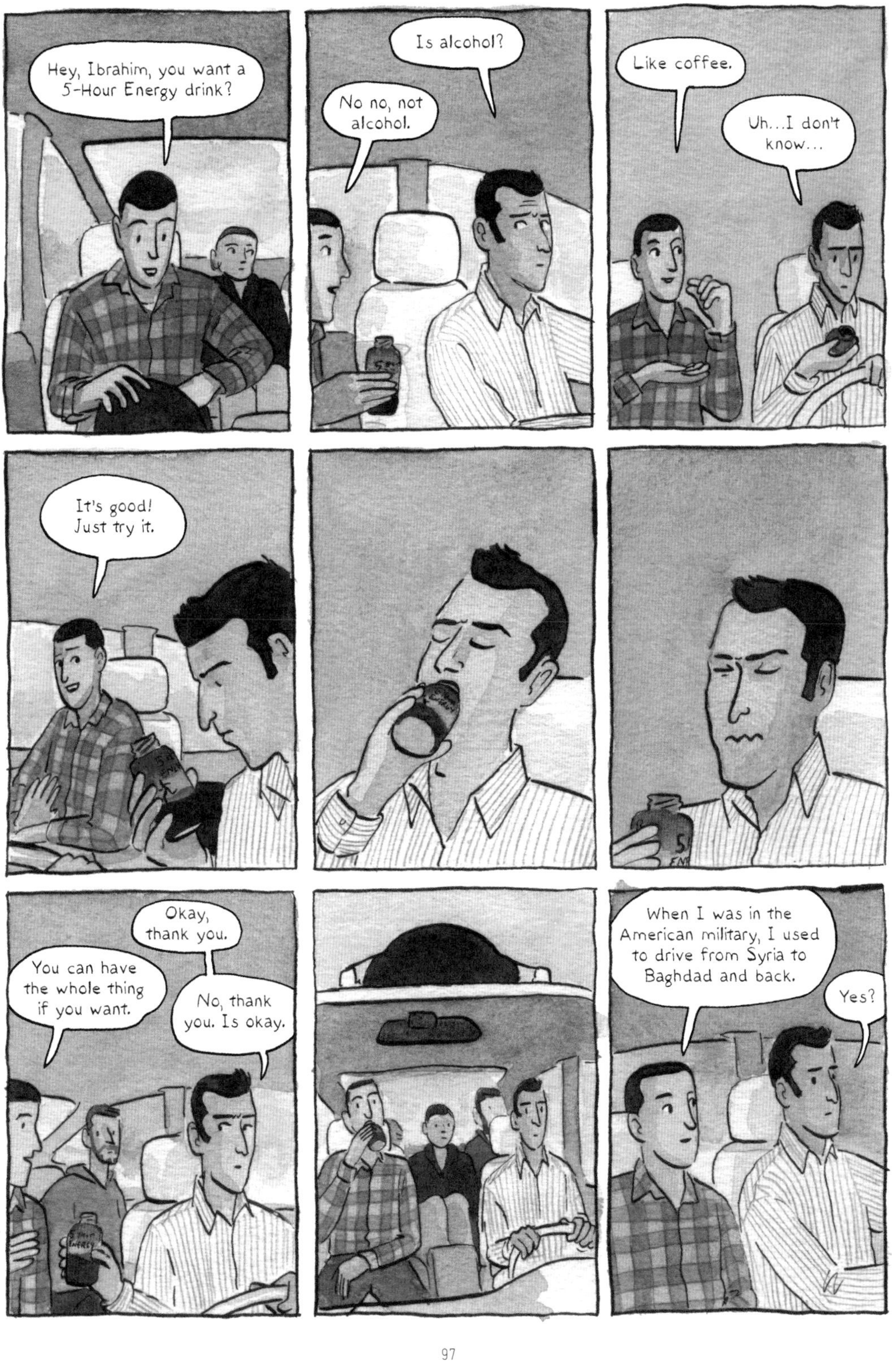
Hey, Ibrahim, you want a 5-Hour Energy drink?
Is alcohol?
No no, not alcohol.
Like coffee.
Uh...I don't know...
It's good! Just try it.
Okay, thank you.
You can have the whole thing if you want.
No, thank you. Is okay.
When I was in the American military, I used to drive from Syria to Baghdad and back.
Yes?

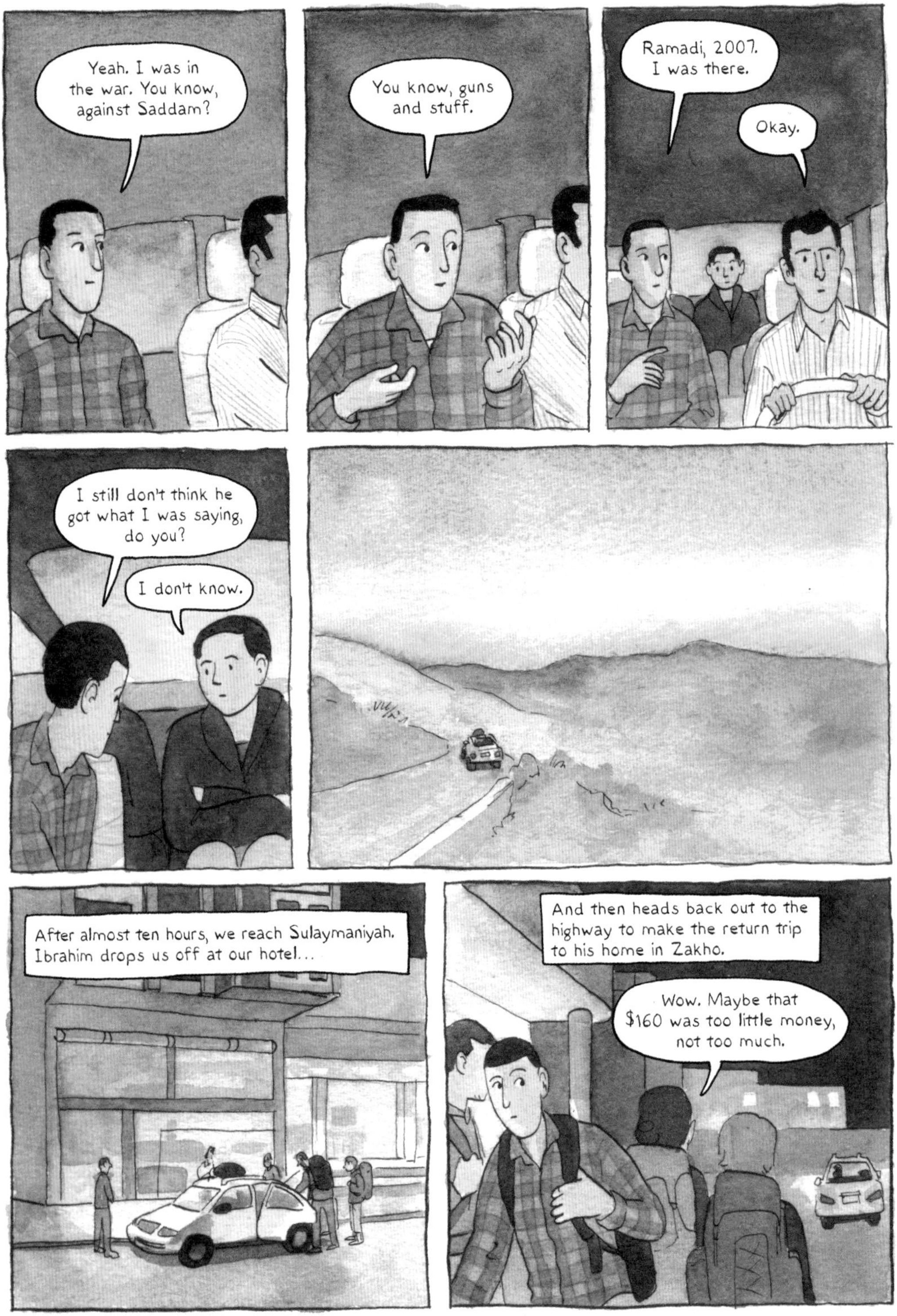
Yeah. I was in the war. You know, against Saddam?
You know, guns and stuff.
Ramadi, 2007. I was there.
Okay.
I still don't think he got what I was saying, do you?
I don't know.
After almost ten hours, we reach Sulaymaniyah. Ibrahim drops us off at our hotel...
And then heads back out to the highway to make the return trip to his home in Zakho.
Wow. Maybe that $160 was too little money, not too much.

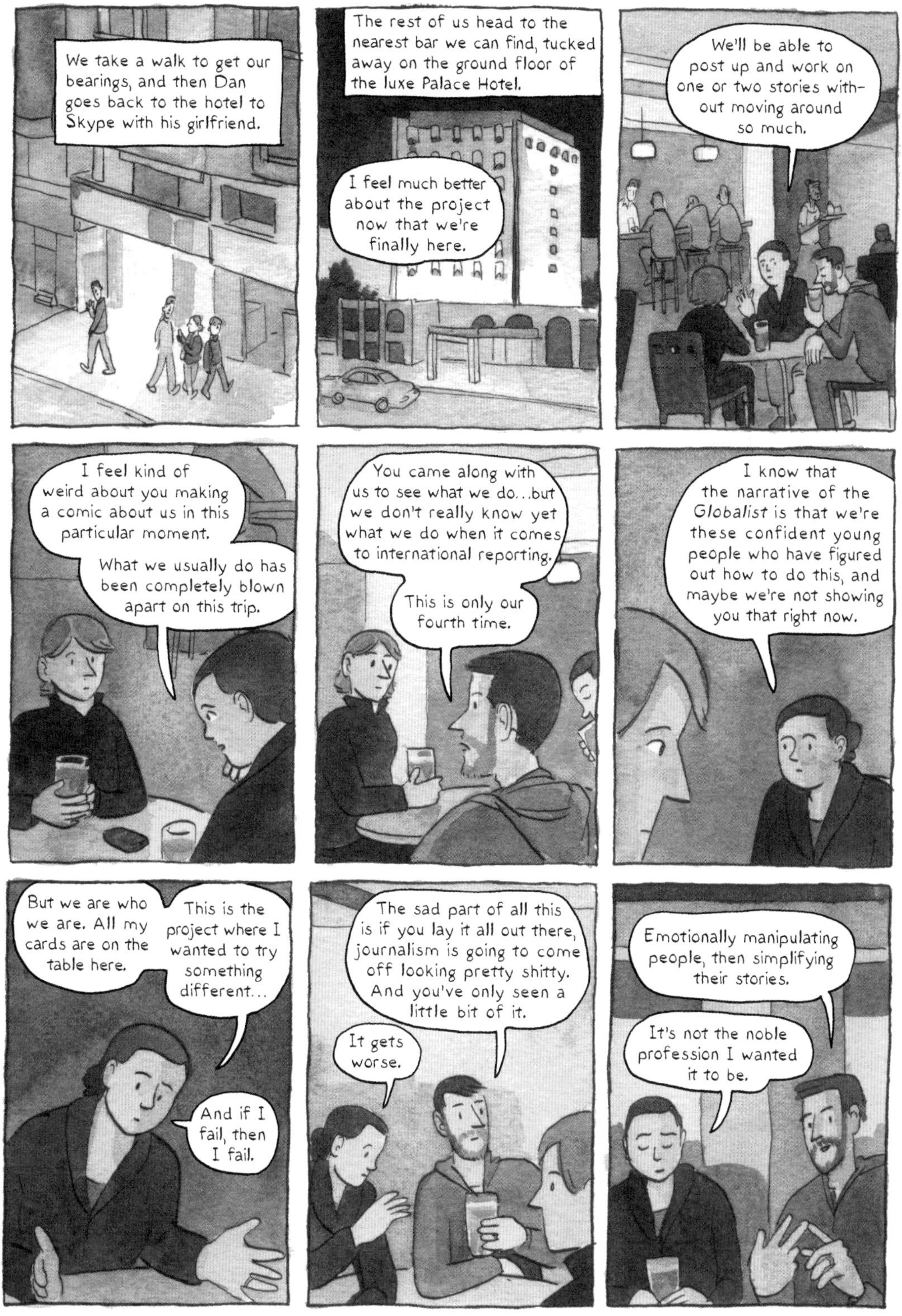
We take a walk to get our bearings, and then Dan goes back to the hotel to Skype with his girlfriend.
The rest of us head to the nearest bar we can find, tucked away on the ground floor of the luxe Palace Hotel.
I feel much better about the project now that we're finally here.
We'll be able to post up and work on one or two stories without moving around so much.
I feel kind of weird about you making a comic about us in this particular moment.
What we usually do has been completely blown apart on this trip.
You came along with us to see what we do...but we don't really know yet what we do when it comes to international reporting.
This is only our fourth time.
I know that the narrative of the *Globalist* is that we're these confident young people who have figured out how to do this, and maybe we're not showing you that right now.
But we are who we are. All my cards are on the table here.
This is the project where I wanted to try something different...
And if I fail, then I fail.
The sad part of all this is if you lay it all out there, journalism is going to come off looking pretty shitty. And you've only seen a little bit of it.
It gets worse.
Emotionally manipulating people, then simplifying their stories.
It's not the noble profession I wanted it to be.

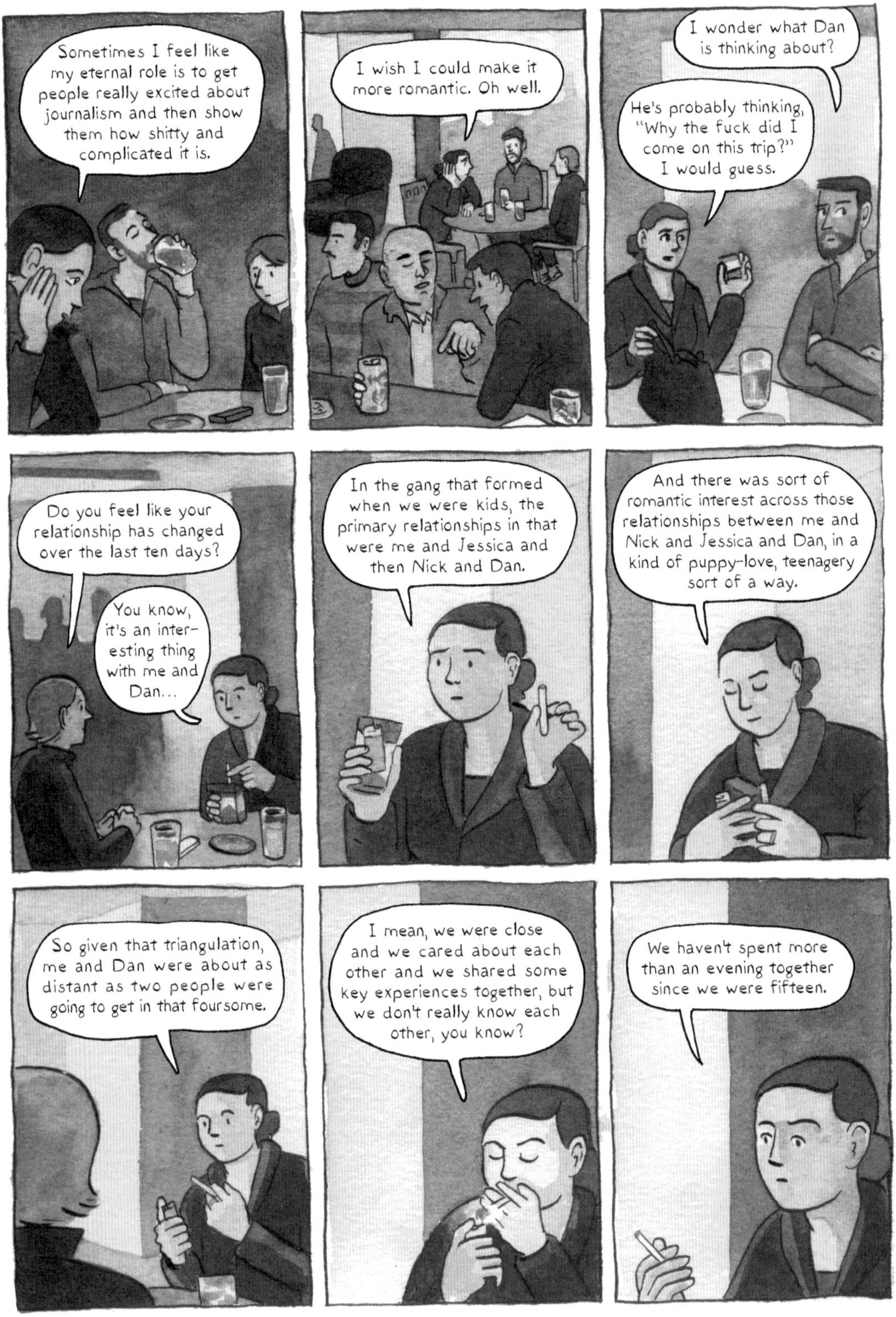

Sometimes I feel like my eternal role is to get people really excited about journalism and then show them how shitty and complicated it is.
I wish I could make it more romantic. Oh well.
I wonder what Dan is thinking about?
He's probably thinking, "Why the fuck did I come on this trip?" I would guess.
Do you feel like your relationship has changed over the last ten days?
You know, it's an interesting thing with me and Dan...
In the gang that formed when we were kids, the primary relationships in that were me and Jessica and then Nick and Dan.
And there was sort of romantic interest across those relationships between me and Nick and Jessica and Dan, in a kind of puppy-love, teenagery sort of a way.
So given that triangulation, me and Dan were about as distant as two people were going to get in that foursome.
I mean, we were close and we cared about each other and we shared some key experiences together, but we don't really know each other, you know?
We haven't spent more than an evening together since we were fifteen.

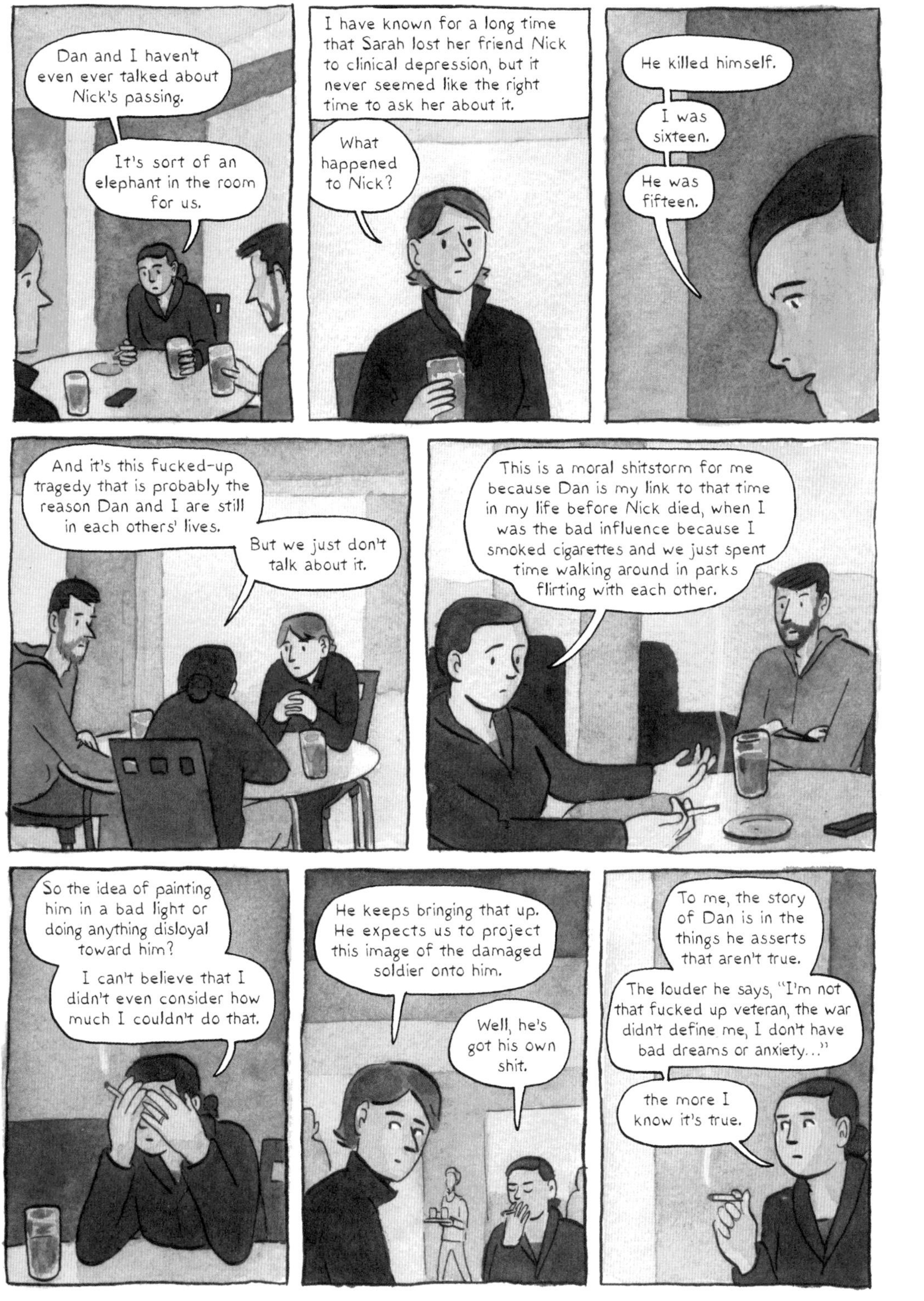
Dan and I haven't even ever talked about Nick's passing.
It's sort of an elephant in the room for us.
I have known for a long time that Sarah lost her friend Nick to clinical depression, but it never seemed like the right time to ask her about it.
What happened to Nick?
He killed himself.
I was sixteen.
He was fifteen.
And it's this fucked-up tragedy that is probably the reason Dan and I are still in each others' lives.
But we just don't talk about it.
This is a moral shitstorm for me because Dan is my link to that time in my life before Nick died, when I was the bad influence because I smoked cigarettes and we just spent time walking around in parks flirting with each other.
So the idea of painting him in a bad light or doing anything disloyal toward him?
I can't believe that I didn't even consider how much I couldn't do that.
He keeps bringing that up. He expects us to project this image of the damaged soldier onto him.
Well, he's got his own shit.
To me, the story of Dan is in the things he asserts that aren't true.
The louder he says, "I'm not that fucked up veteran, the war didn't define me, I don't have bad dreams or anxiety..."
the more I know it's true.

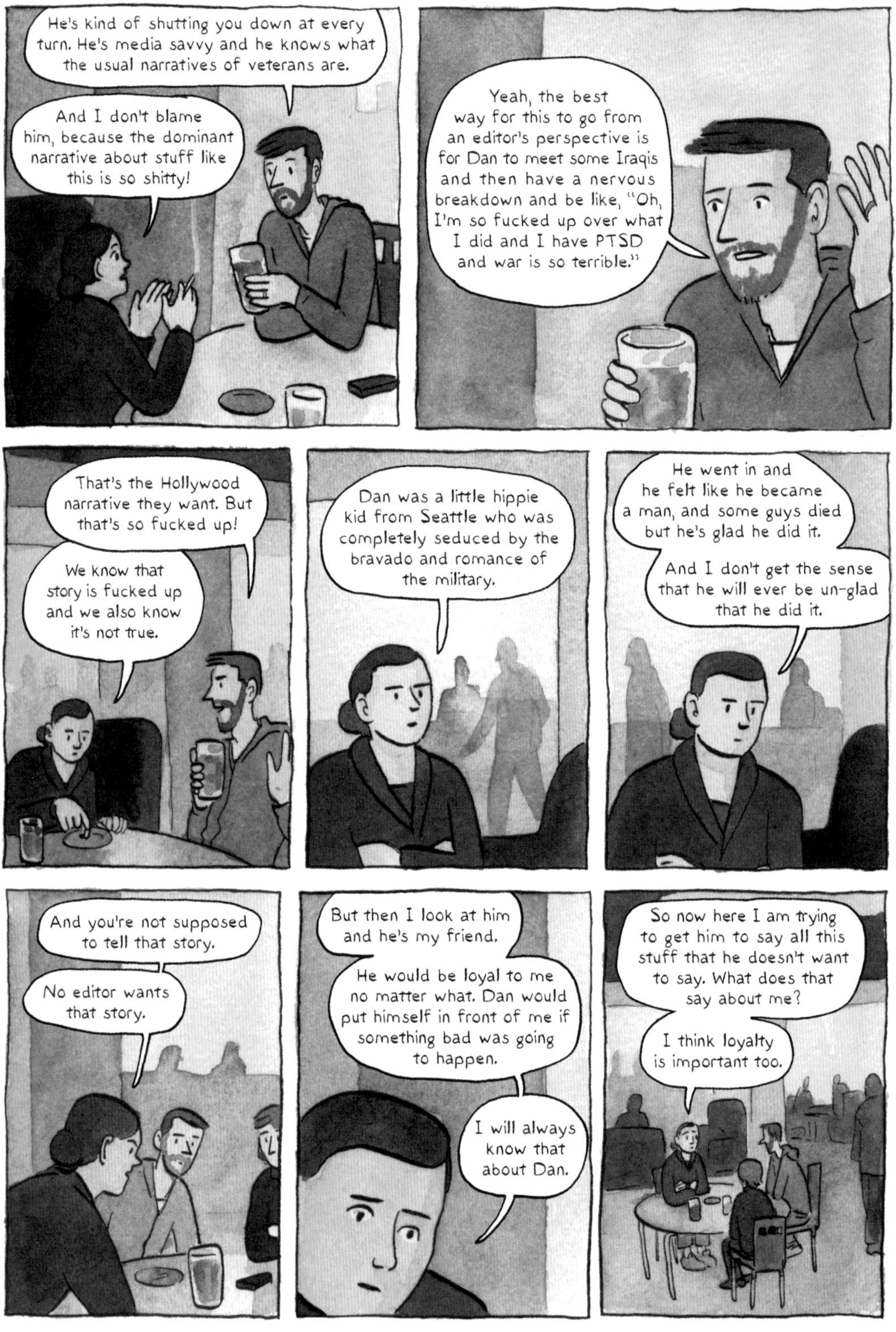
He's kind of shutting you down at every turn. He's media savvy and he knows what the usual narratives of veterans are.
And I don't blame him, because the dominant narrative about stuff like this is so shitty!
Yeah, the best way for this to go from an editor's perspective is for Dan to meet some Iraqis and then have a nervous breakdown and be like, "Oh, I'm so fucked up over what I did and I have PTSD and war is so terrible."
That's the Hollywood narrative they want. But that's so fucked up!
We know that story is fucked up and we also know it's not true.
Dan was a little hippie kid from Seattle who was completely seduced by the bravado and romance of the military.
He went in and he felt like he became a man, and some guys died but he's glad he did it.
And I don't get the sense that he will ever be un-glad that he did it.
And you're not supposed to tell that story.
No editor wants that story.
But then I look at him and he's my friend.
He would be loyal to me no matter what. Dan would put himself in front of me if something bad was going to happen.
I will always know that about Dan.
So now here I am trying to get him to say all this stuff that he doesn't want to say. What does that say about me?
I think loyalty is important too.

SULAYMANIYAH, IRAQ

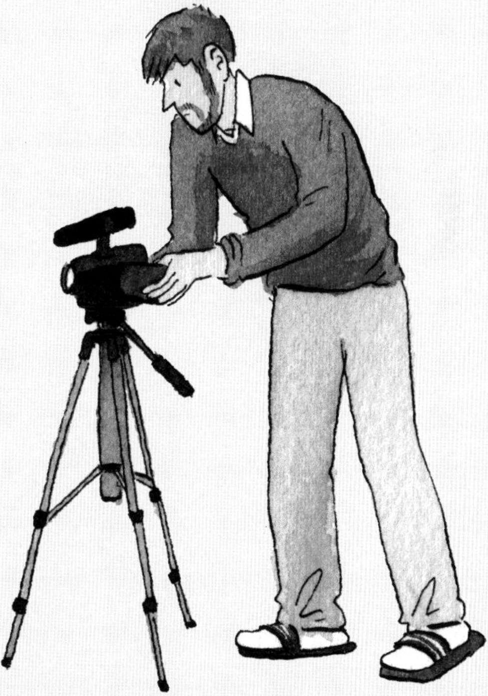

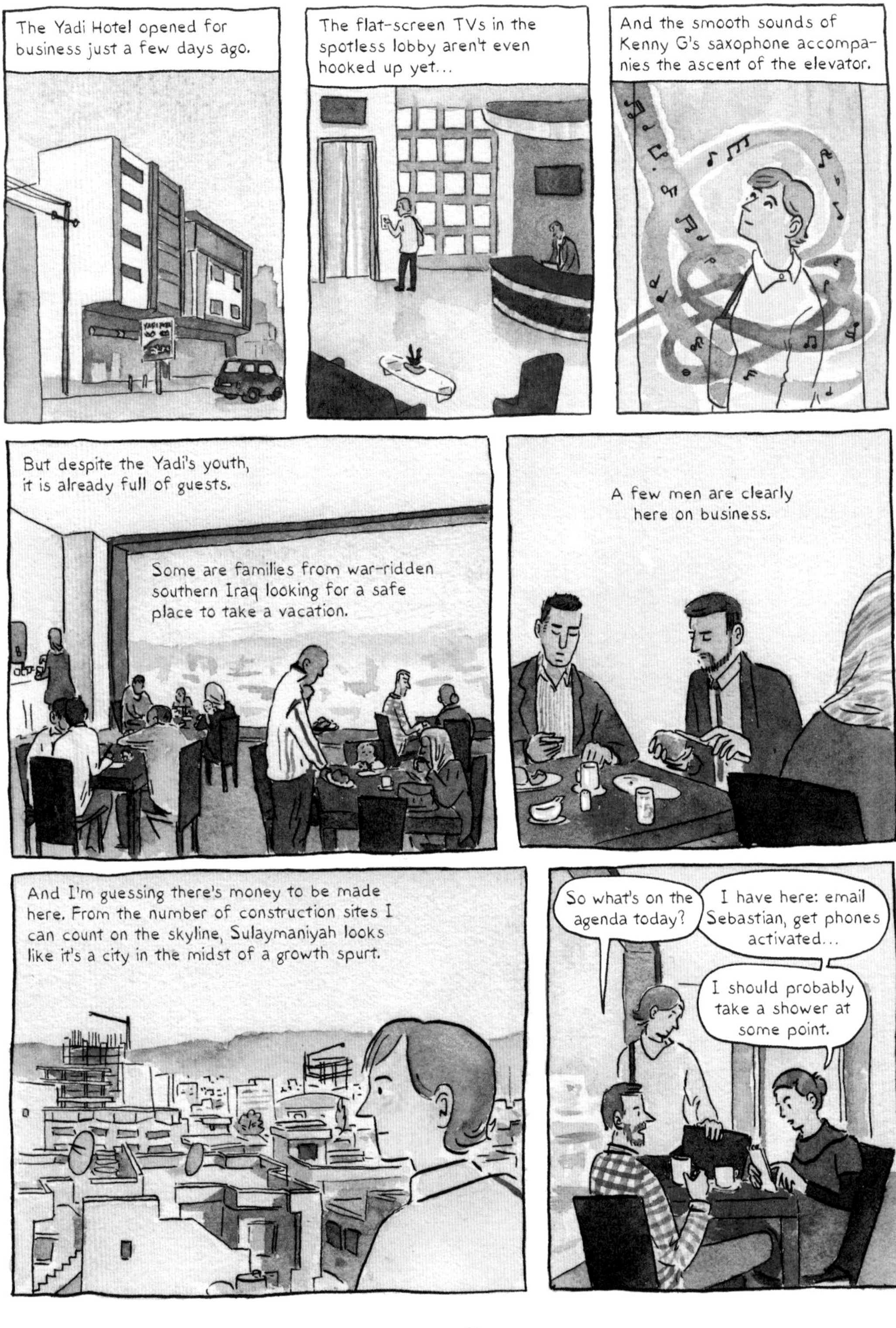

The Yadi Hotel opened for business just a few days ago.
The flat-screen TVs in the spotless lobby aren't even hooked up yet...
And the smooth sounds of Kenny G's saxophone accompanies the ascent of the elevator.
But despite the Yadi's youth, it is already full of guests.
Some are families from war-ridden southern Iraq looking for a safe place to take a vacation.
A few men are clearly here on business.
And I'm guessing there's money to be made here. From the number of construction sites I can count on the skyline, Sulaymaniyah looks like it's a city in the midst of a growth spurt.
So what's on the agenda today?
I have here: email Sebastian, get phones activated...
I should probably take a shower at some point.

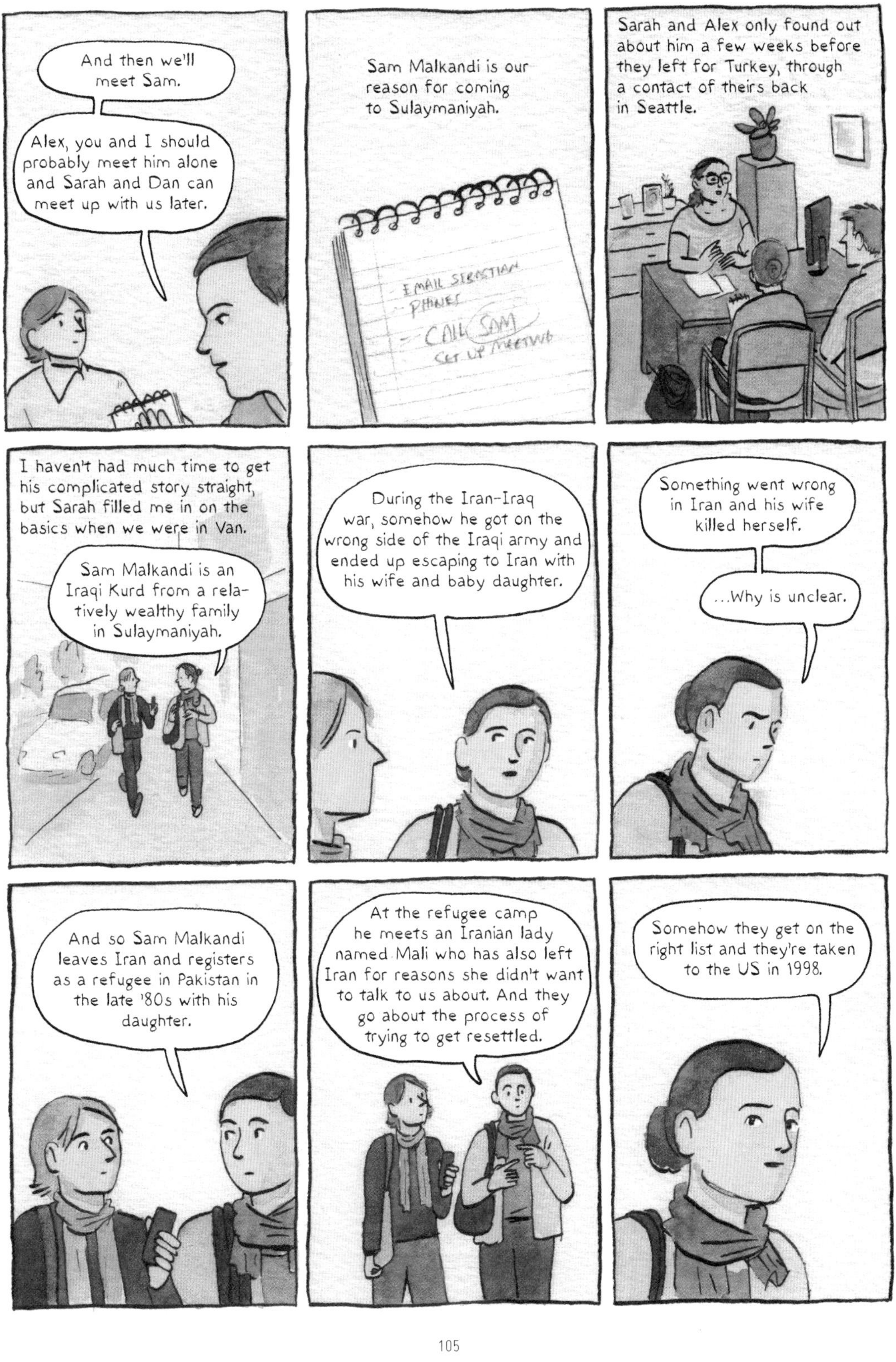
And then we'll meet Sam.
Alex, you and I should probably meet him alone and Sarah and Dan can meet up with us later.
Sam Malkandi is our reason for coming to Sulaymaniyah.
EMAIL SEBASTIAN
PHONES
CALL SAM
SET UP MEETING
Sarah and Alex only found out about him a few weeks before they left for Turkey, through a contact of theirs back in Seattle.
I haven't had much time to get his complicated story straight, but Sarah filled me in on the basics when we were in Van.
Sam Malkandi is an Iraqi Kurd from a relatively wealthy family in Sulaymaniyah.
During the Iran-Iraq war, somehow he got on the wrong side of the Iraqi army and ended up escaping to Iran with his wife and baby daughter.
Something went wrong in Iran and his wife killed herself.
...Why is unclear.
And so Sam Malkandi leaves Iran and registers as a refugee in Pakistan in the late '80s with his daughter.
At the refugee camp he meets an Iranian lady named Mali who has also left Iran for reasons she didn't want to talk to us about. And they go about the process of trying to get resettled.
Somehow they get on the right list and they're taken to the US in 1998.

Sam's story up until this point is the refugee American dream we love to hear about...

So they get to Texas and they don't really like Texas that much, but they have a friend in Seattle so they go up there.

Here's someone who went from exile in Iran to suffering a tragic loss to a decade living in refugee camps in Pakistan. Despite hardship, he was able to rebuild a family and, once in the US, a new life.

Sam worked in a restaurant. His wife, Mali, became a dental hygienist. The kids were in school...

They're super into America and when Baghdad falls in 2003, Sam is celebrating with American flags and stuff.

But something else was happening in 2003.

Thousands of miles away in Pakistan, a one-legged al Qaeda operative with the nom-de-guerre Khallad was captured and taken to an American black site prison.

Khallad had been up there on America's Most Wanted list as the alleged mastermind of the USS *Cole* bombing as well as the US embassy bombings in Kenya and Tanzania.

Originally, he had been hand-picked by Osama bin Laden to be one of the hijackers in the 9/11 attacks.

Walid bin-Attash (Khallad)

Khalid al-Mihdhar

Abu Bara al-Taizi

Nawaf al-Hazmi

The only reason he didn't end up on one of those planes was because his application for a US visa was denied.

Under a fake name, Salah Mohammed, he had made up a story for his application about coming to be fitted for a new prosthesis at a clinic in Bothell, Washington, where a contact had already made an appointment for him.

PLEASE TYPE OR PRINT YOUR ANSWER
SURNAME OR FAMILY NAME (exactly as

BIN YOUSAF

FIRST NAME AND MIDDLE NAME (exactly

SALAH SAEED MOHAN

OTHER NAMES (Maiden, Religious, P

OF BIRTH (D

His interrogators wanted to know who had helped him. He told them that it was a man whose name sounded like:

Barzan.

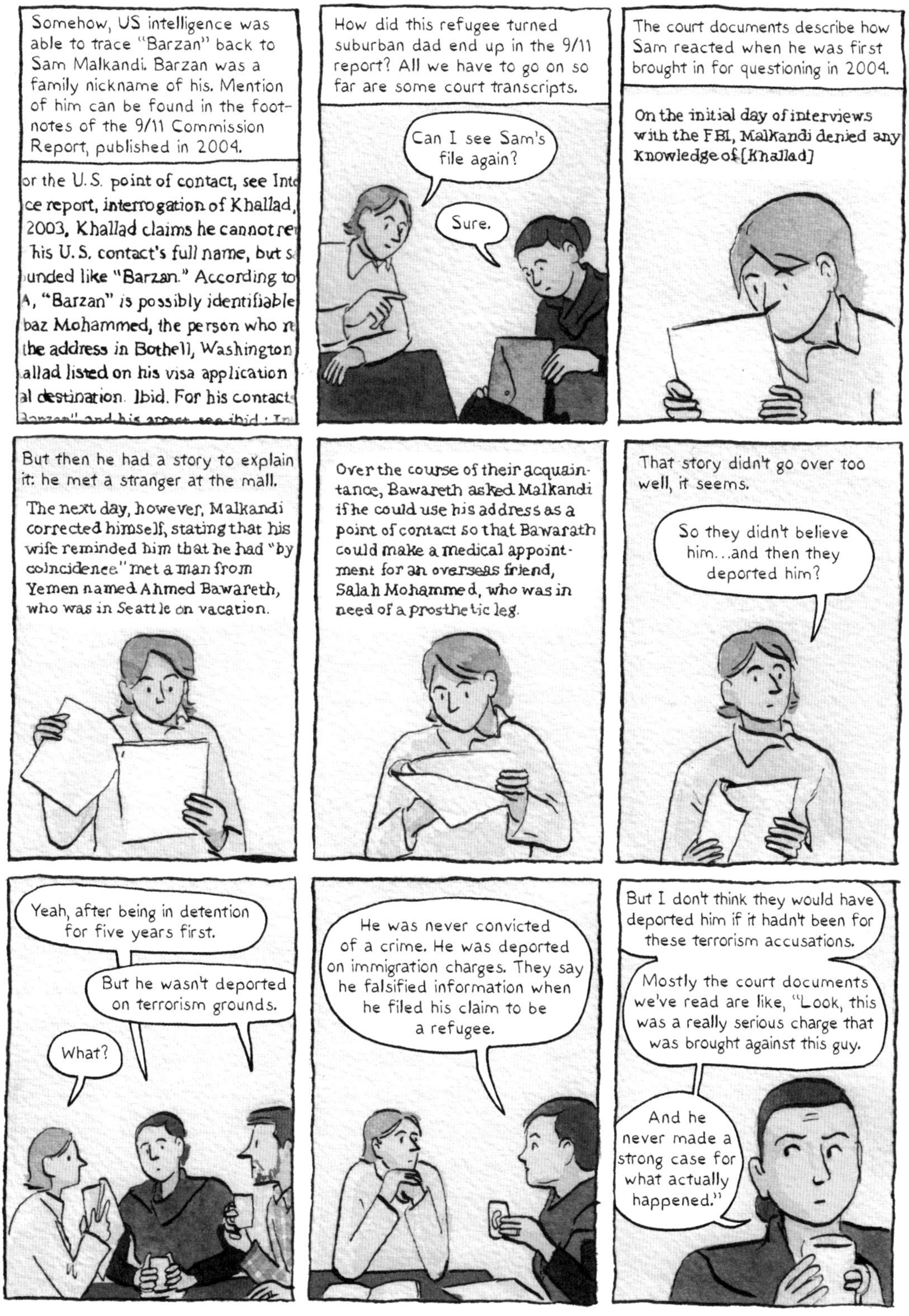

Somehow, US intelligence was able to trace "Barzan" back to Sam Malkandi. Barzan was a family nickname of his. Mention of him can be found in the footnotes of the 9/11 Commission Report, published in 2004.
or the U.S. point of contact, see Int
ce report, interrogation of Khallad,
2003. Khallad claims he cannot re
his U.S. contact's full name, but s
unded like "Barzan." According to
A, "Barzan" is possibly identifiable
baz Mohammed, the person who r
the address in Bothell, Washington
allad listed on his visa application
al destination. Ibid. For his contact
How did this refugee turned suburban dad end up in the 9/11 report? All we have to go on so far are some court transcripts.
Can I see Sam's file again?
Sure.
The court documents describe how Sam reacted when he was first brought in for questioning in 2004.
On the initial day of interviews with the FBI, Malkandi denied any knowledge of [Khallad]
But then he had a story to explain it: he met a stranger at the mall.
The next day, however, Malkandi corrected himself, stating that his wife reminded him that he had "by coincidence" met a man from Yemen named Ahmed Bawareth, who was in Seattle on vacation.
Over the course of their acquaintance, Bawareth asked Malkandi if he could use his address as a point of contact so that Bawarath could make a medical appointment for an overseas friend, Salah Mohammed, who was in need of a prosthetic leg.
That story didn't go over too well, it seems.
So they didn't believe him...and then they deported him?
Yeah, after being in detention for five years first.
But he wasn't deported on terrorism grounds.
What?
He was never convicted of a crime. He was deported on immigration charges. They say he falsified information when he filed his claim to be a refugee.
But I don't think they would have deported him if it hadn't been for these terrorism accusations.
Mostly the court documents we've read are like, "Look, this was a really serious charge that was brought against this guy.
And he never made a strong case for what actually happened."

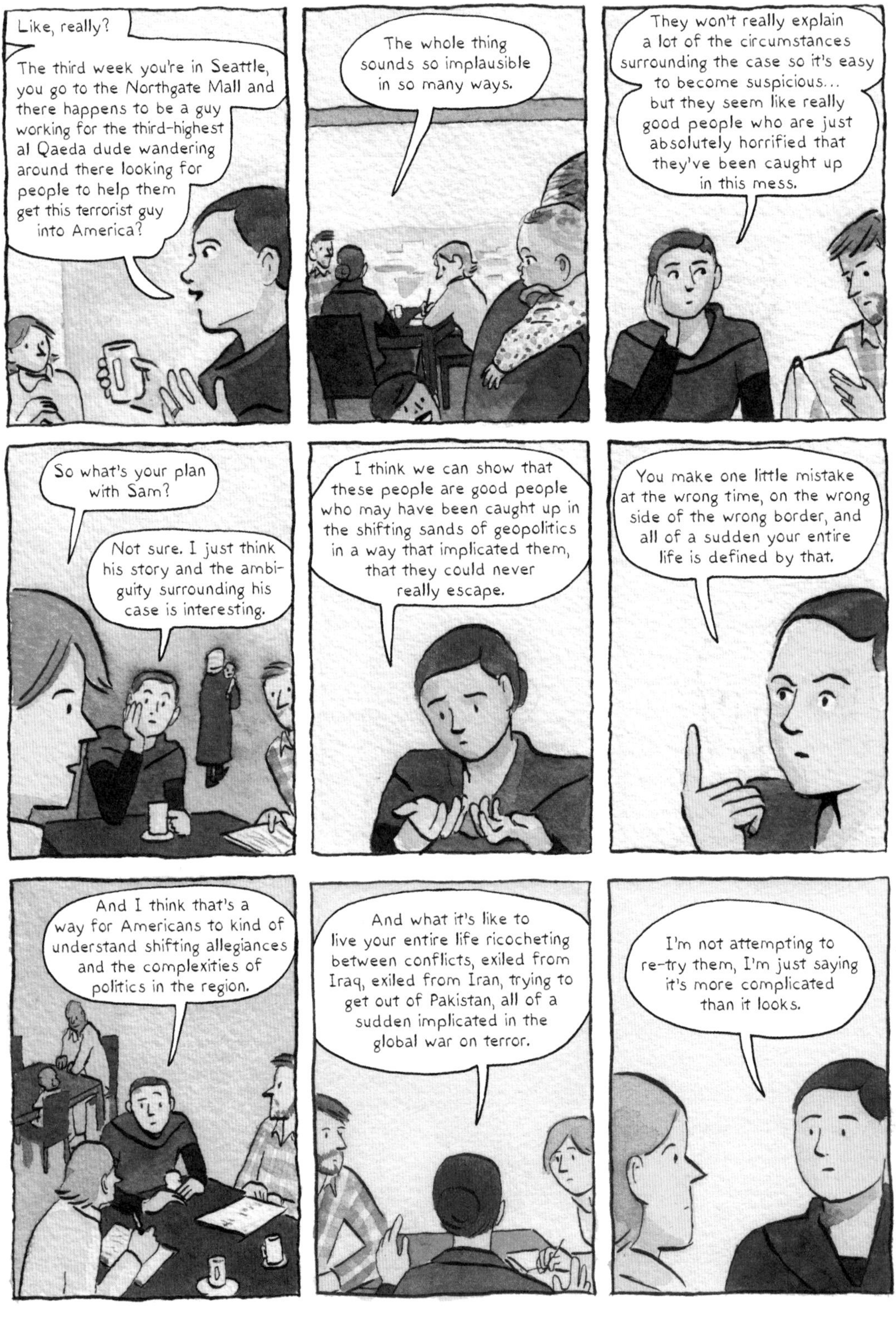
Like, really?
The third week you're in Seattle, you go to the Northgate Mall and there happens to be a guy working for the third-highest al Qaeda dude wandering around there looking for people to help them get this terrorist guy into America?
The whole thing sounds so implausible in so many ways.
They won't really explain a lot of the circumstances surrounding the case so it's easy to become suspicious... but they seem like really good people who are just absolutely horrified that they've been caught up in this mess.
So what's your plan with Sam?
Not sure. I just think his story and the ambiguity surrounding his case is interesting.
I think we can show that these people are good people who may have been caught up in the shifting sands of geopolitics in a way that implicated them, that they could never really escape.
You make one little mistake at the wrong time, on the wrong side of the wrong border, and all of a sudden your entire life is defined by that.
And I think that's a way for Americans to kind of understand shifting allegiances and the complexities of politics in the region.
And what it's like to live your entire life ricocheting between conflicts, exiled from Iraq, exiled from Iran, trying to get out of Pakistan, all of a sudden implicated in the global war on terror.
I'm not attempting to re-try them, I'm just saying it's more complicated than it looks.

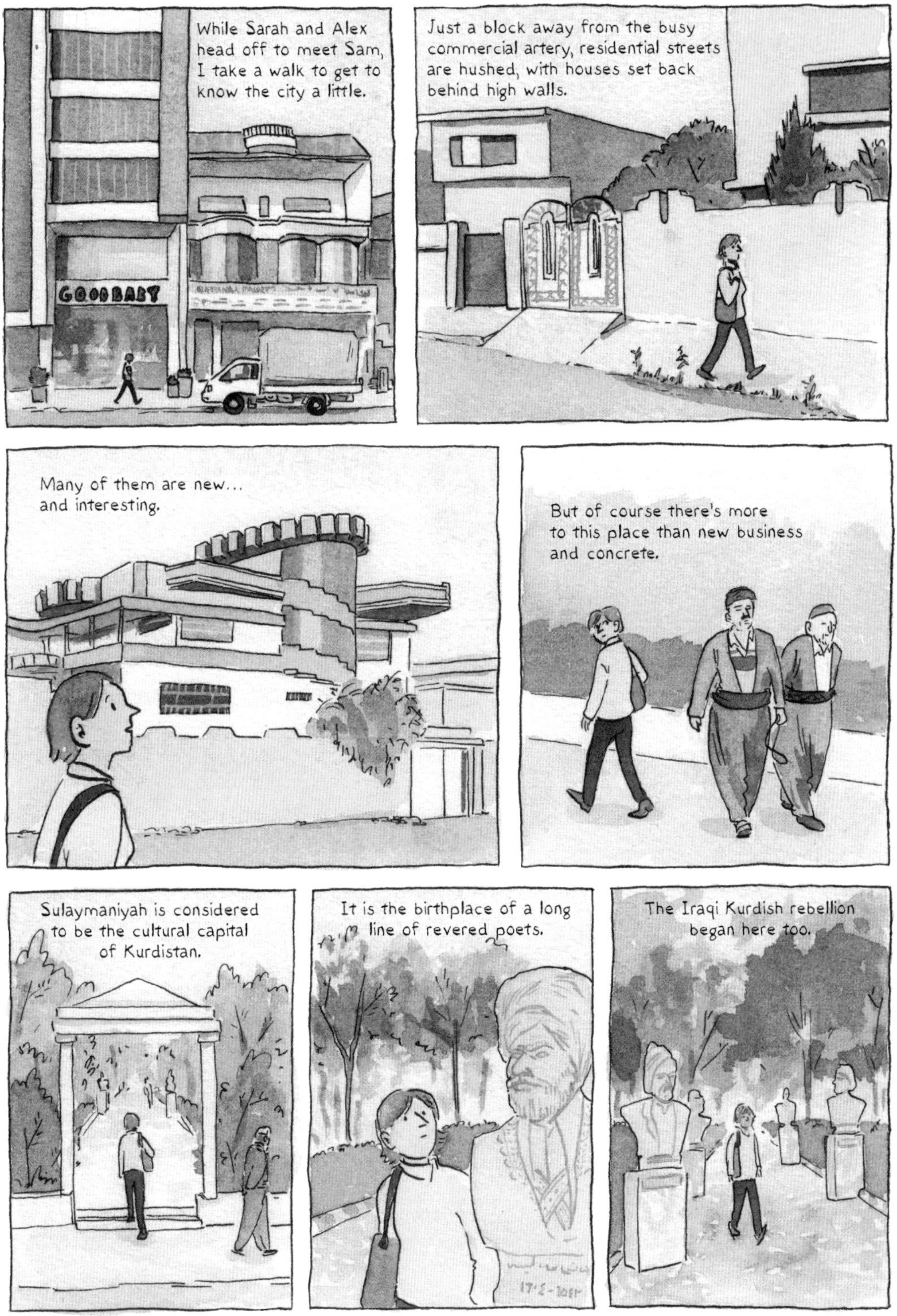
While Sarah and Alex head off to meet Sam, I take a walk to get to know the city a little.
GOODBABY
Just a block away from the busy commercial artery, residential streets are hushed, with houses set back behind high walls.
Many of them are new... and interesting.
But of course there's more to this place than new business and concrete.
Sulaymaniyah is considered to be the cultural capital of Kurdistan.
It is the birthplace of a long line of revered poets.
The Iraqi Kurdish rebellion began here too.

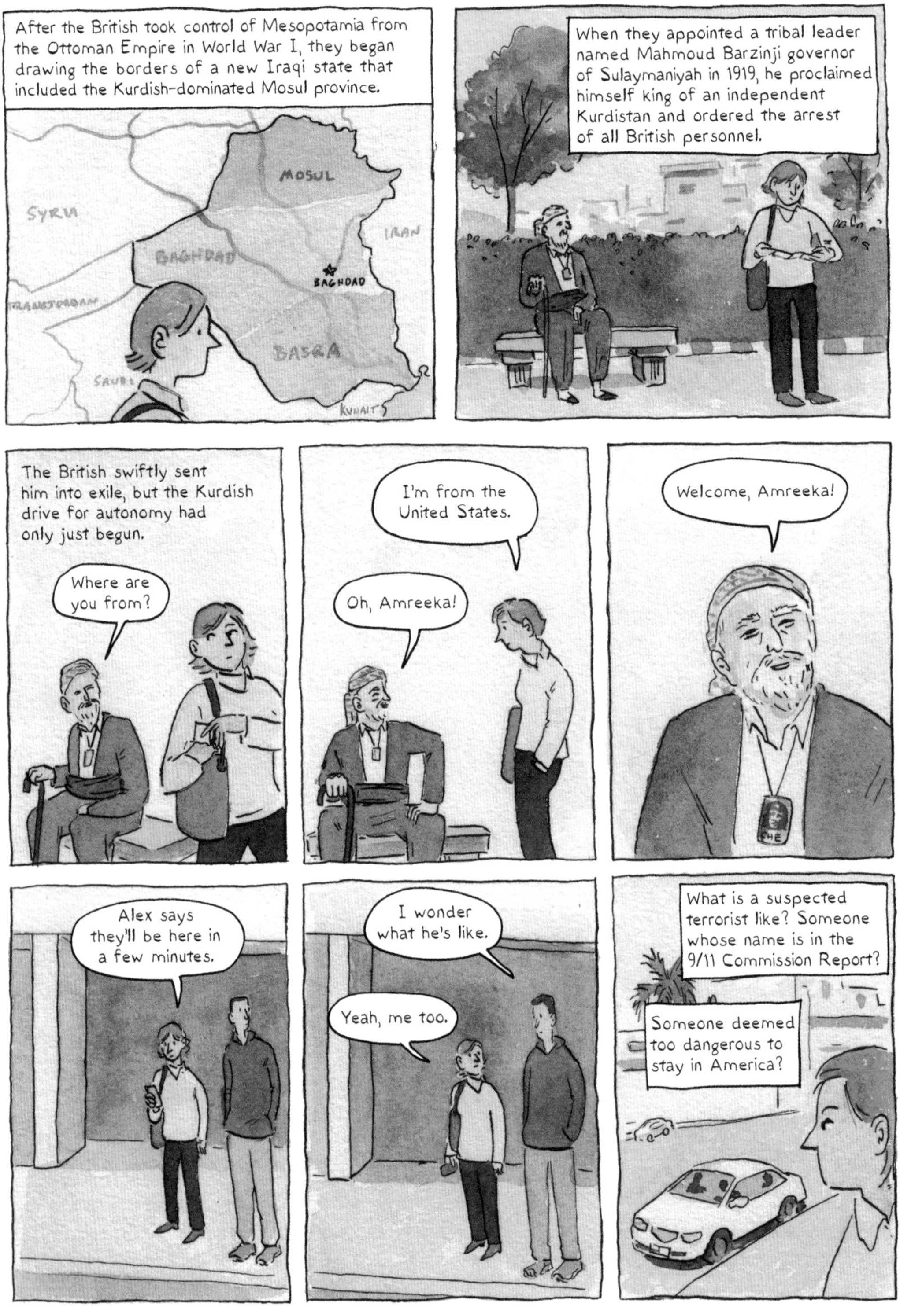

After the British took control of Mesopotamia from the Ottoman Empire in World War I, they began drawing the borders of a new Iraqi state that included the Kurdish-dominated Mosul province.
MOSUL
SYRIA
IRAN
BAGHDAD
BAGHDAD
TRANSJORDAN
BASRA
SAUDI
KUWAIT
When they appointed a tribal leader named Mahmoud Barzinji governor of Sulaymaniyah in 1919, he proclaimed himself king of an independent Kurdistan and ordered the arrest of all British personnel.
The British swiftly sent him into exile, but the Kurdish drive for autonomy had only just begun.
Where are you from?
I'm from the United States.
Oh, Amreeka!
Welcome, Amreeka!
CHE
Alex says they'll be here in a few minutes.
I wonder what he's like.
Yeah, me too.
What is a suspected terrorist like? Someone whose name is in the 9/11 Commission Report?
Someone deemed too dangerous to stay in America?

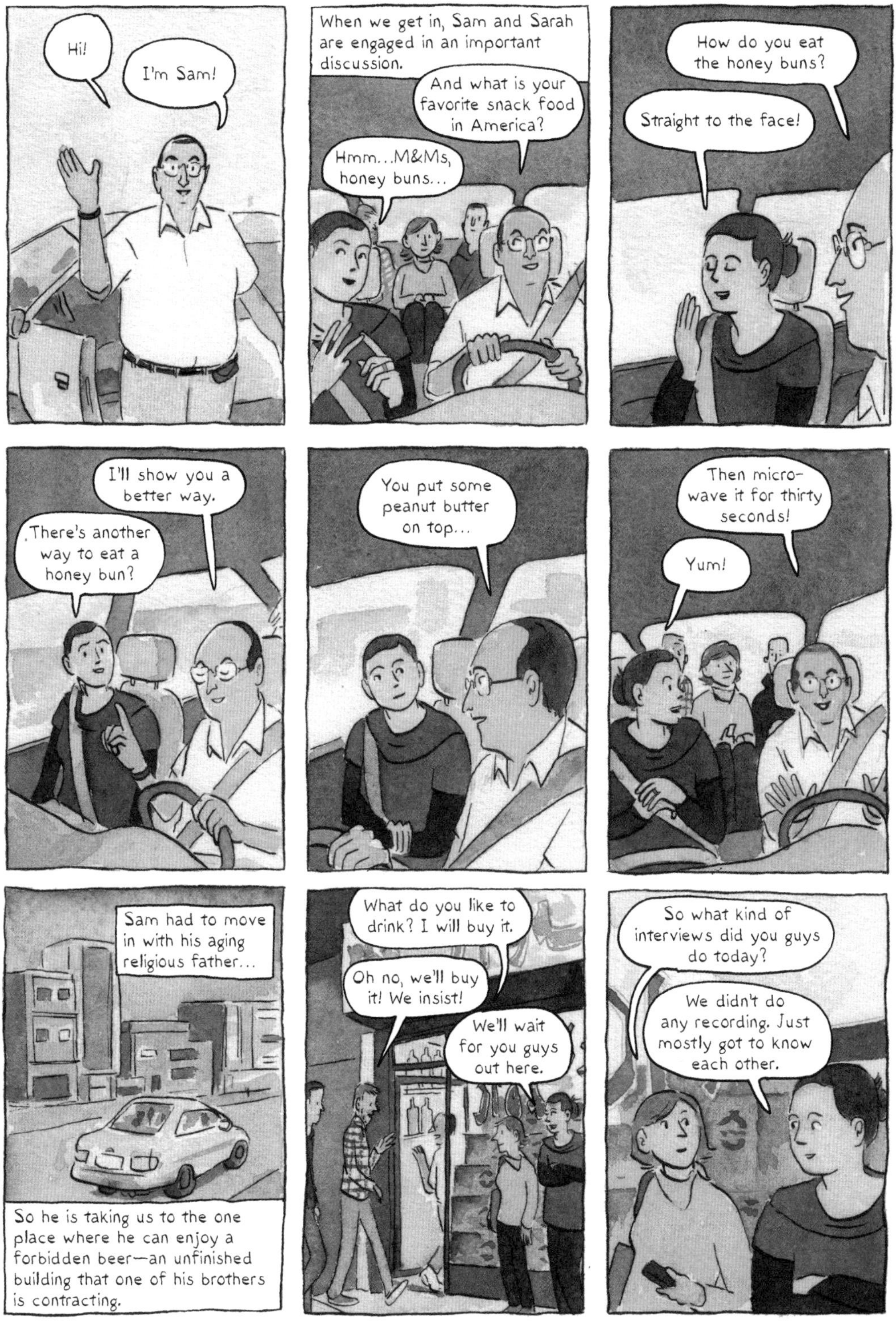
Hi!
I'm Sam!
When we get in, Sam and Sarah are engaged in an important discussion.
And what is your favorite snack food in America?
Hmm...M&Ms, honey buns...
How do you eat the honey buns?
Straight to the face!
I'll show you a better way.
There's another way to eat a honey bun?
You put some peanut butter on top...
Then microwave it for thirty seconds!
Yum!
Sam had to move in with his aging religious father...
So he is taking us to the one place where he can enjoy a forbidden beer—an unfinished building that one of his brothers is contracting.
What do you like to drink? I will buy it.
Oh no, we'll buy it! We insist!
We'll wait for you guys out here.
So what kind of interviews did you guys do today?
We didn't do any recording. Just mostly got to know each other.

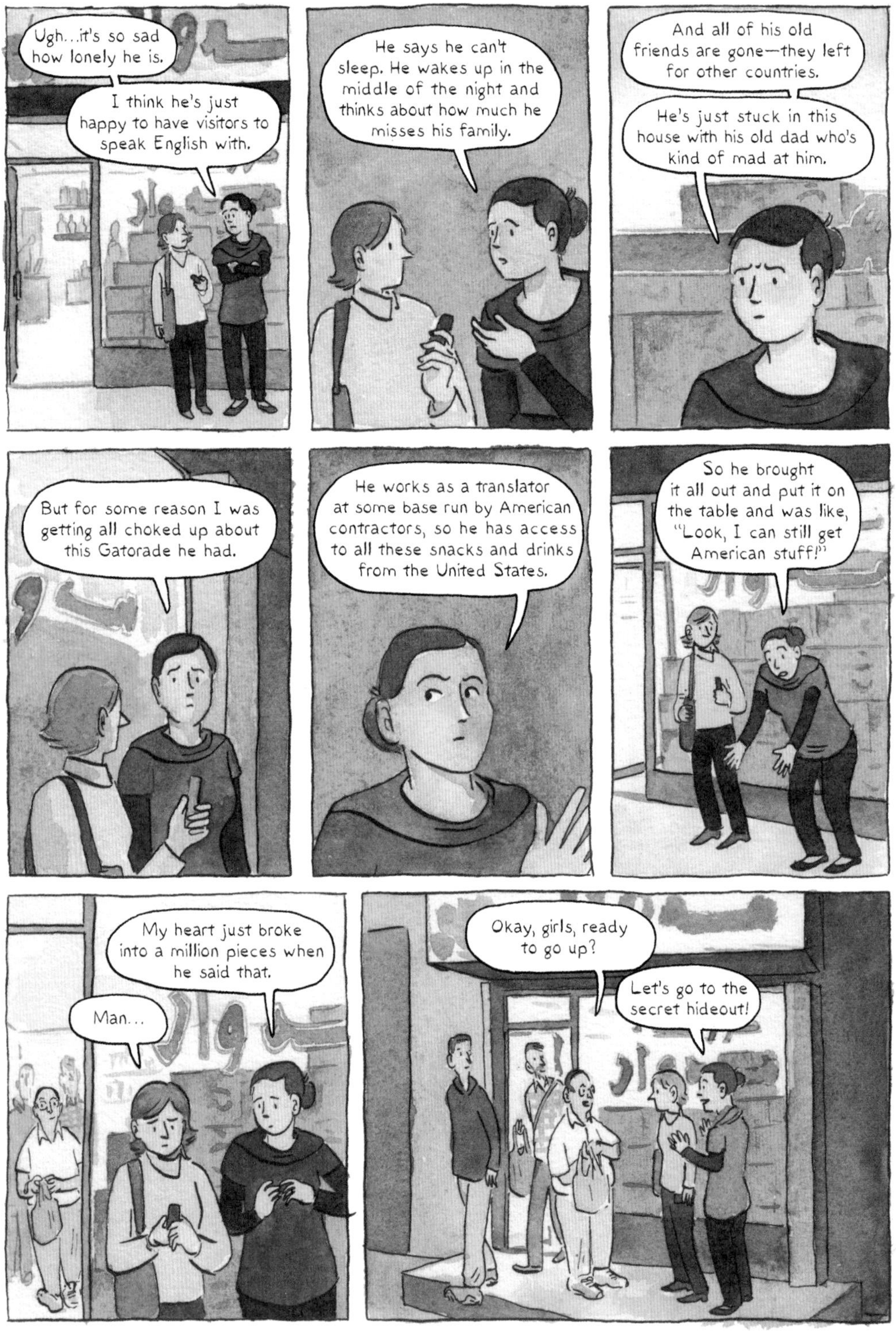
Ugh...it's so sad how lonely he is.
I think he's just happy to have visitors to speak English with.
He says he can't sleep. He wakes up in the middle of the night and thinks about how much he misses his family.
And all of his old friends are gone—they left for other countries.
He's just stuck in this house with his old dad who's kind of mad at him.
But for some reason I was getting all choked up about this Gatorade he had.
He works as a translator at some base run by American contractors, so he has access to all these snacks and drinks from the United States.
So he brought it all out and put it on the table and was like, "Look, I can still get American stuff!"
My heart just broke into a million pieces when he said that.
Man...
Okay, girls, ready to go up?
Let's go to the secret hideout!

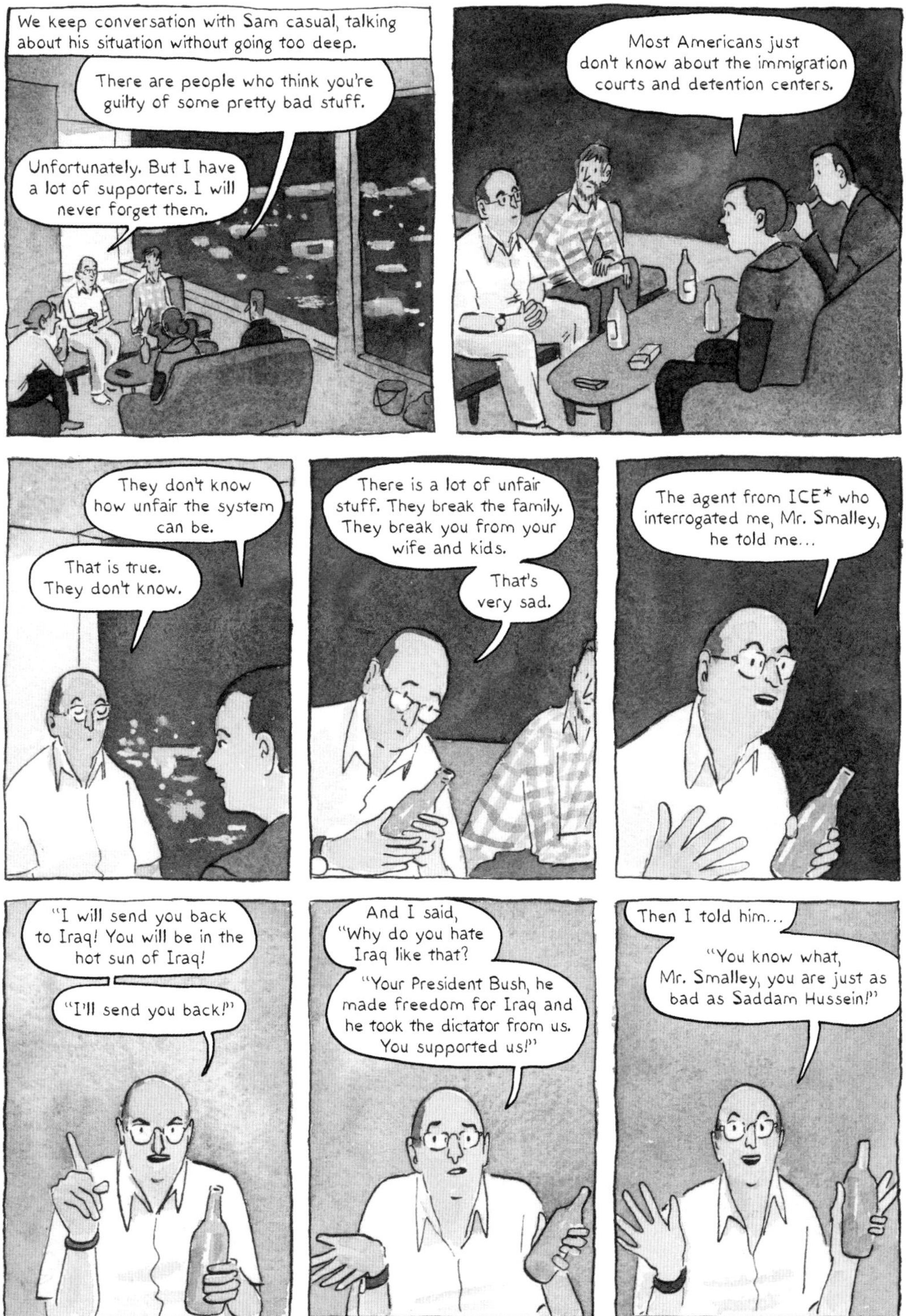
We keep conversation with Sam casual, talking about his situation without going too deep.
There are people who think you're guilty of some pretty bad stuff.
Unfortunately. But I have a lot of supporters. I will never forget them.
Most Americans just don't know about the immigration courts and detention centers.
They don't know how unfair the system can be.
That is true. They don't know.
There is a lot of unfair stuff. They break the family. They break you from your wife and kids.
That's very sad.
The agent from ICE* who interrogated me, Mr. Smalley, he told me...
"I will send you back to Iraq! You will be in the hot sun of Iraq!
"I'll send you back!"
And I said, "Why do you hate Iraq like that?
"Your President Bush, he made freedom for Iraq and he took the dictator from us. You supported us!"
Then I told him...
"You know what, Mr. Smalley, you are just as bad as Saddam Hussein!"

*Immigration and Customs Enforcement

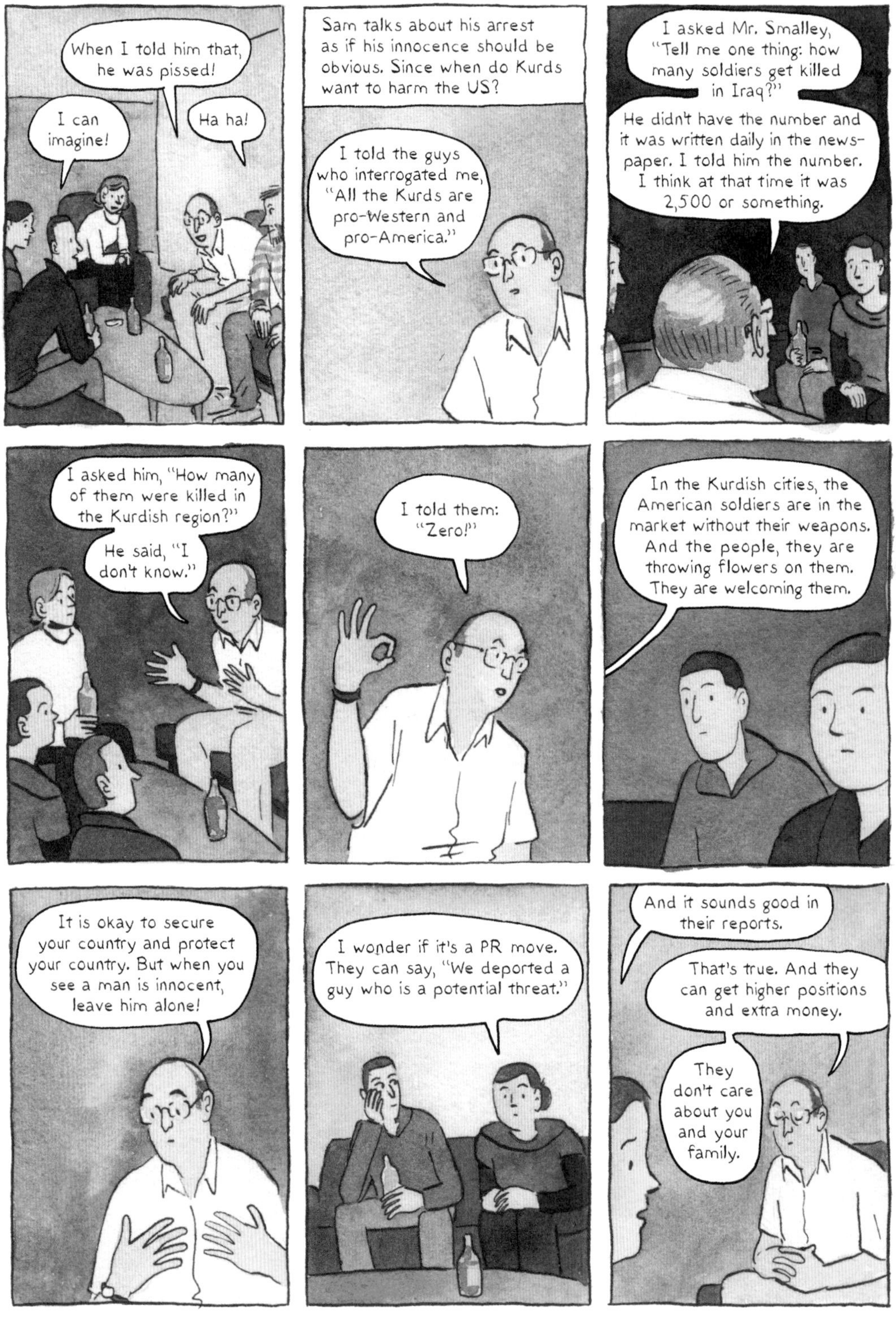
When I told him that, he was pissed!
I can imagine!
Ha ha!
Sam talks about his arrest as if his innocence should be obvious. Since when do Kurds want to harm the US?
I told the guys who interrogated me, "All the Kurds are pro-Western and pro-America."
I asked Mr. Smalley, "Tell me one thing: how many soldiers get killed in Iraq?"
He didn't have the number and it was written daily in the newspaper. I told him the number. I think at that time it was 2,500 or something.
I asked him, "How many of them were killed in the Kurdish region?"
He said, "I don't know."
I told them: "Zero!"
In the Kurdish cities, the American soldiers are in the market without their weapons. And the people, they are throwing flowers on them. They are welcoming them.
It is okay to secure your country and protect your country. But when you see a man is innocent, leave him alone!
I wonder if it's a PR move. They can say, "We deported a guy who is a potential threat."
And it sounds good in their reports.
That's true. And they can get higher positions and extra money.
They don't care about you and your family.

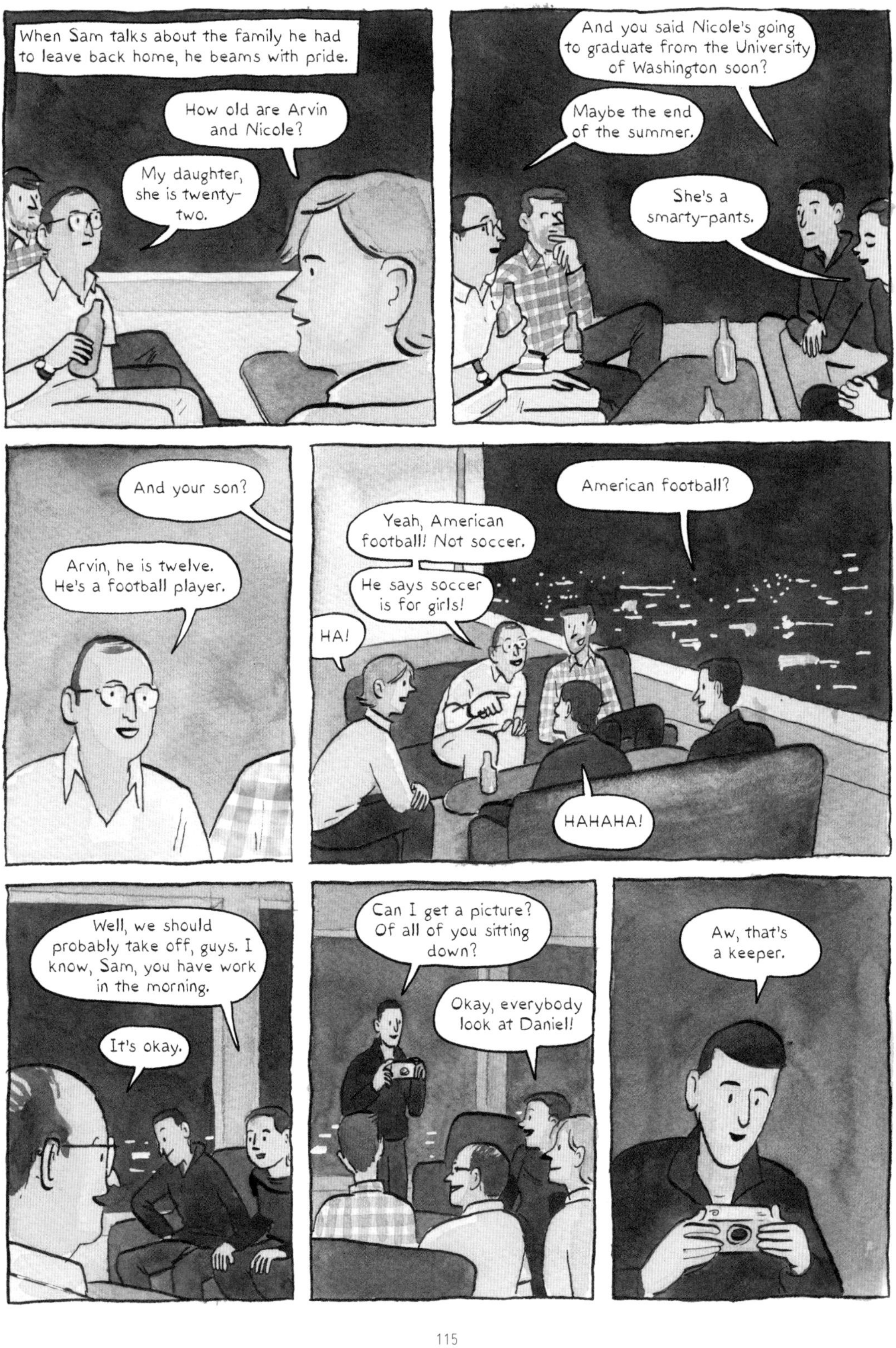
When Sam talks about the family he had to leave back home, he beams with pride.
How old are Arvin and Nicole?
My daughter, she is twenty-two.
And you said Nicole's going to graduate from the University of Washington soon?
Maybe the end of the summer.
She's a smarty-pants.
And your son?
Arvin, he is twelve. He's a football player.
American football?
Yeah, American football! Not soccer.
He says soccer is for girls!
HA!
HAHAHA!
Well, we should probably take off, guys. I know, Sam, you have work in the morning.
It's okay.
Can I get a picture? Of all of you sitting down?
Okay, everybody look at Daniel!
Aw, that's a keeper.

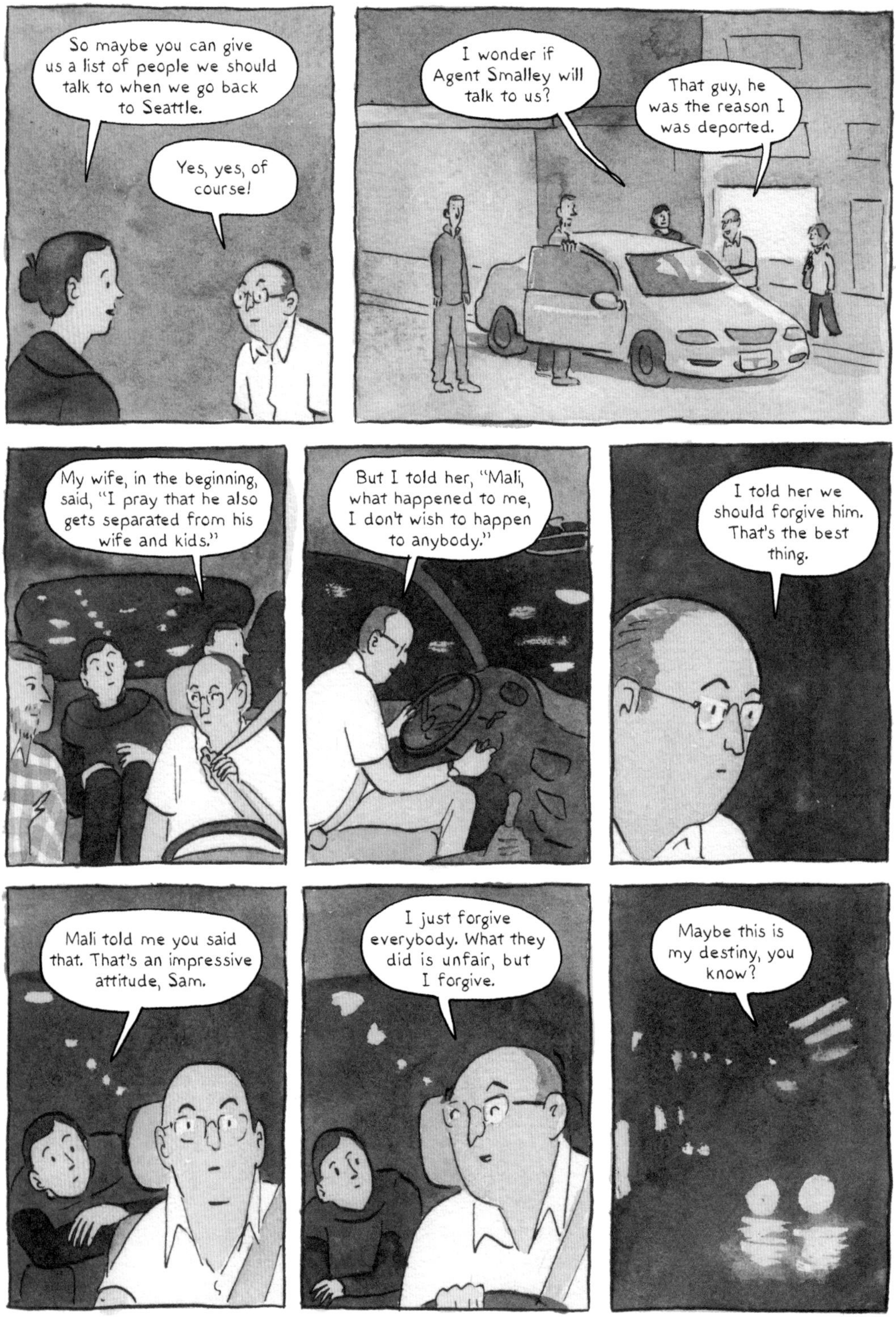
So maybe you can give us a list of people we should talk to when we go back to Seattle.
Yes, yes, of course!
I wonder if Agent Smalley will talk to us?
That guy, he was the reason I was deported.
My wife, in the beginning, said, "I pray that he also gets separated from his wife and kids."
But I told her, "Mali, what happened to me, I don't wish to happen to anybody."
I told her we should forgive him. That's the best thing.
Mali told me you said that. That's an impressive attitude, Sam.
I just forgive everybody. What they did is unfair, but I forgive.
Maybe this is my destiny, you know?

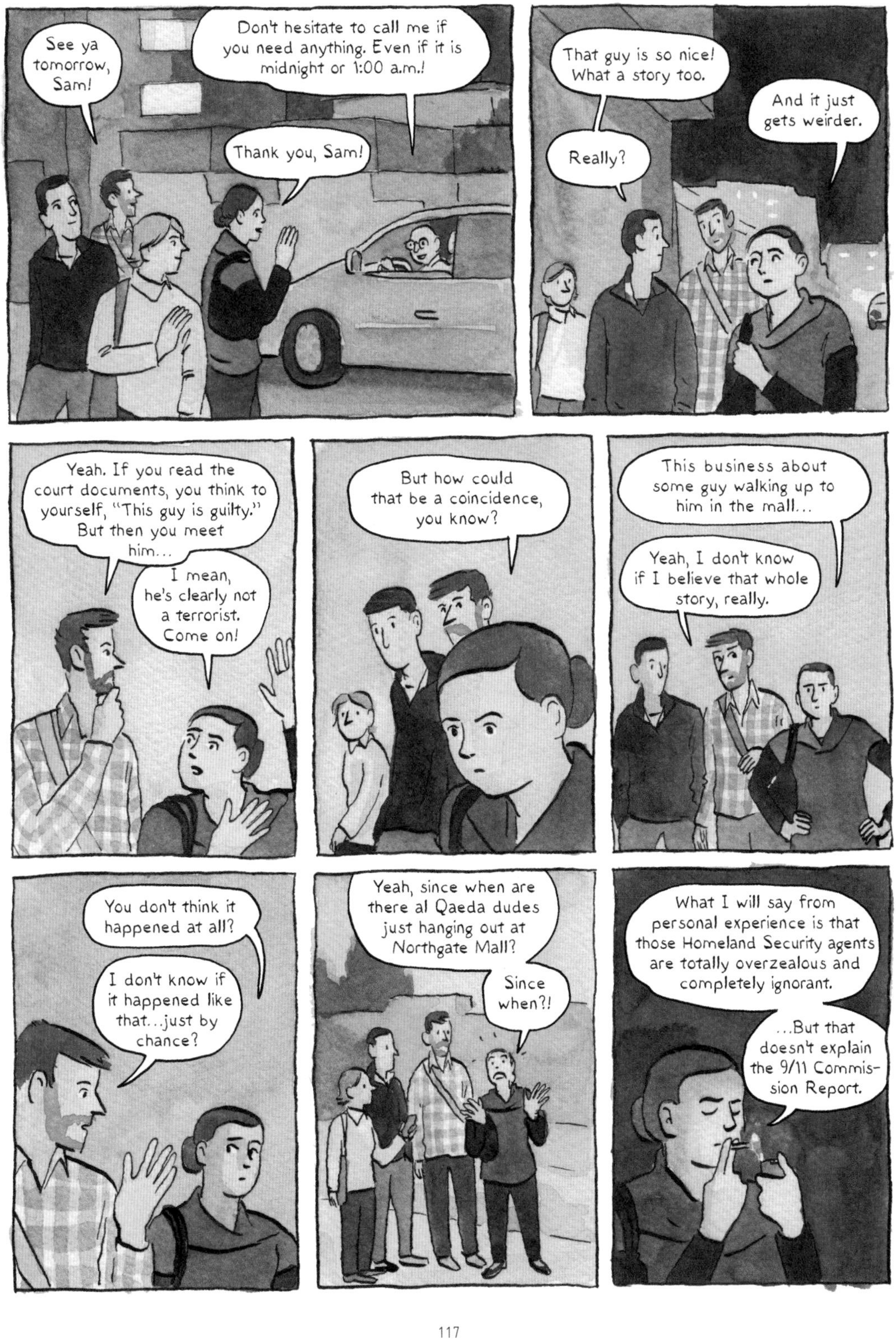

See ya tomorrow, Sam!
Don't hesitate to call me if you need anything. Even if it is midnight or 1:00 a.m.!
Thank you, Sam!
That guy is so nice! What a story too.
Really?
And it just gets weirder.
Yeah. If you read the court documents, you think to yourself, "This guy is guilty." But then you meet him...
I mean, he's clearly not a terrorist. Come on!
But how could that be a coincidence, you know?
This business about some guy walking up to him in the mall...
Yeah, I don't know if I believe that whole story, really.
You don't think it happened at all?
I don't know if it happened like that...just by chance?
Yeah, since when are there al Qaeda dudes just hanging out at Northgate Mall?
Since when?!
What I will say from personal experience is that those Homeland Security agents are totally overzealous and completely ignorant.
...But that doesn't explain the 9/11 Commission Report.

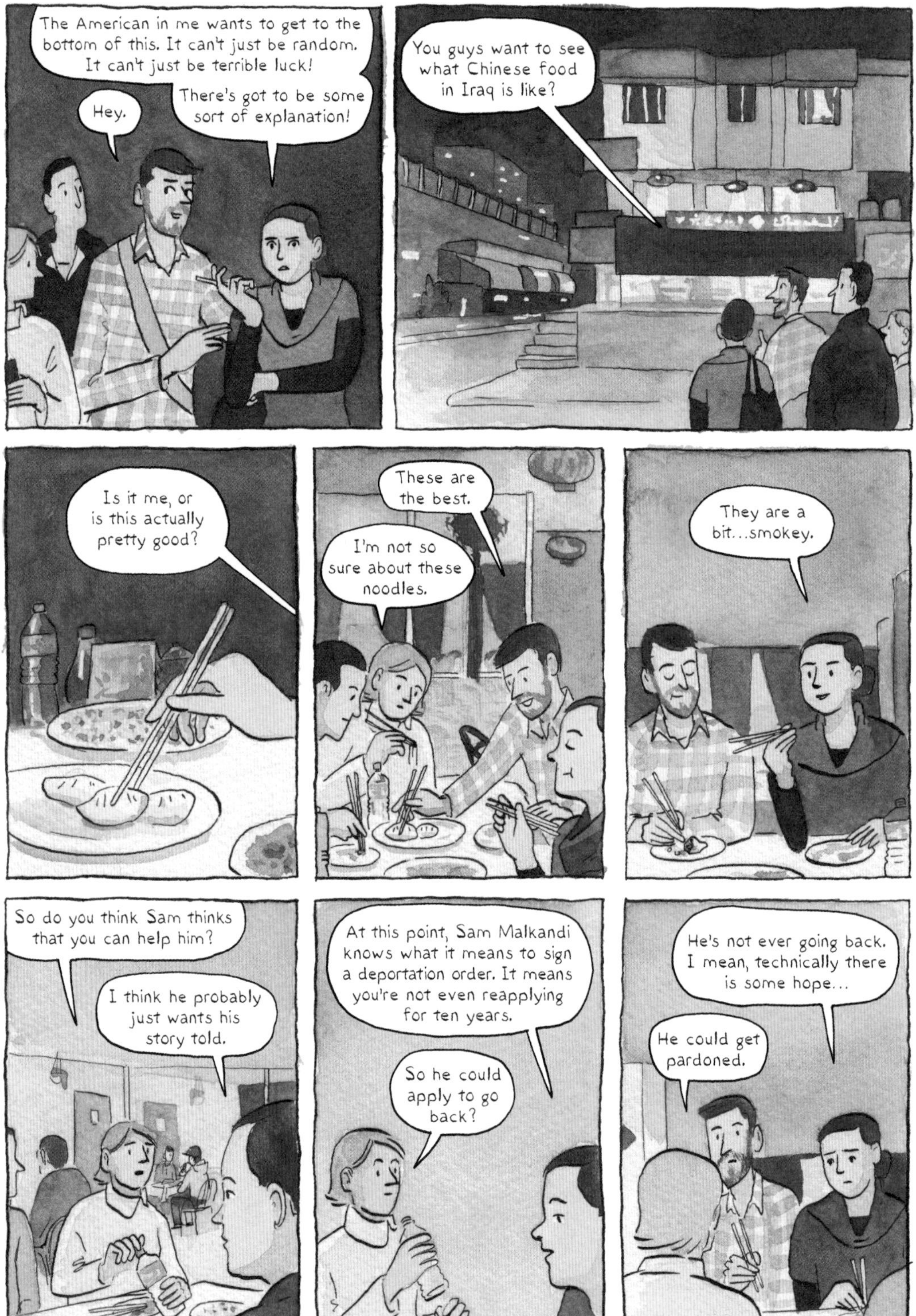
The American in me wants to get to the bottom of this. It can't just be random. It can't just be terrible luck!
Hey.
There's got to be some sort of explanation!
You guys want to see what Chinese food in Iraq is like?
Is it me, or is this actually pretty good?
These are the best.
I'm not so sure about these noodles.
They are a bit...smokey.
So do you think Sam thinks that you can help him?
I think he probably just wants his story told.
At this point, Sam Malkandi knows what it means to sign a deportation order. It means you're not even reapplying for ten years.
So he could apply to go back?
He's not ever going back. I mean, technically there is some hope...
He could get pardoned.

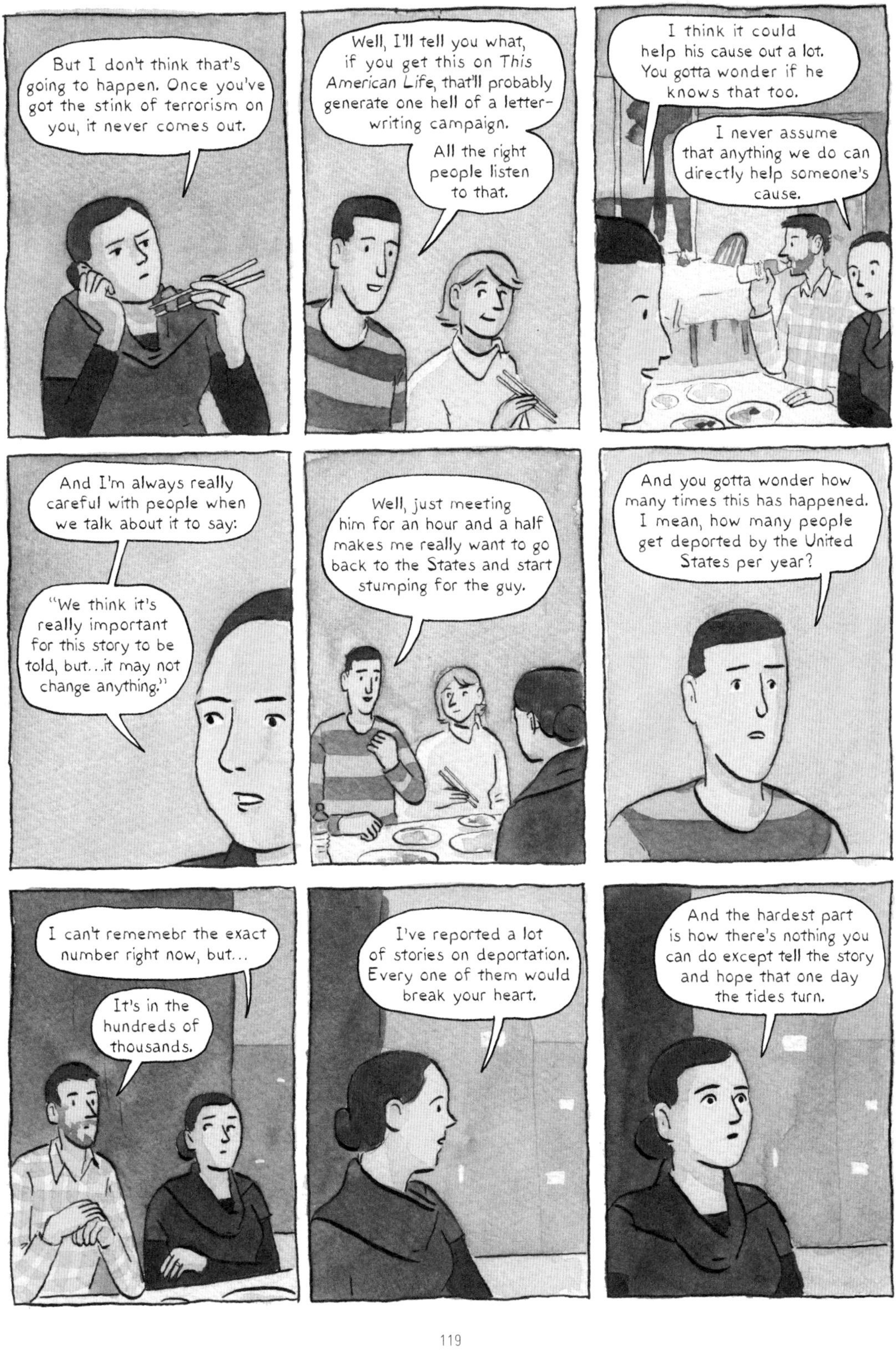
But I don't think that's going to happen. Once you've got the stink of terrorism on you, it never comes out.
Well, I'll tell you what, if you get this on *This American Life*, that'll probably generate one hell of a letter-writing campaign.
All the right people listen to that.
I think it could help his cause out a lot. You gotta wonder if he knows that too.
I never assume that anything we do can directly help someone's cause.
And I'm always really careful with people when we talk about it to say:
"We think it's really important for this story to be told, but...it may not change anything."
Well, just meeting him for an hour and a half makes me really want to go back to the States and start stumping for the guy.
And you gotta wonder how many times this has happened. I mean, how many people get deported by the United States per year?
I can't rememebr the exact number right now, but...
It's in the hundreds of thousands.
I've reported a lot of stories on deportation. Every one of them would break your heart.
And the hardest part is how there's nothing you can do except tell the story and hope that one day the tides turn.

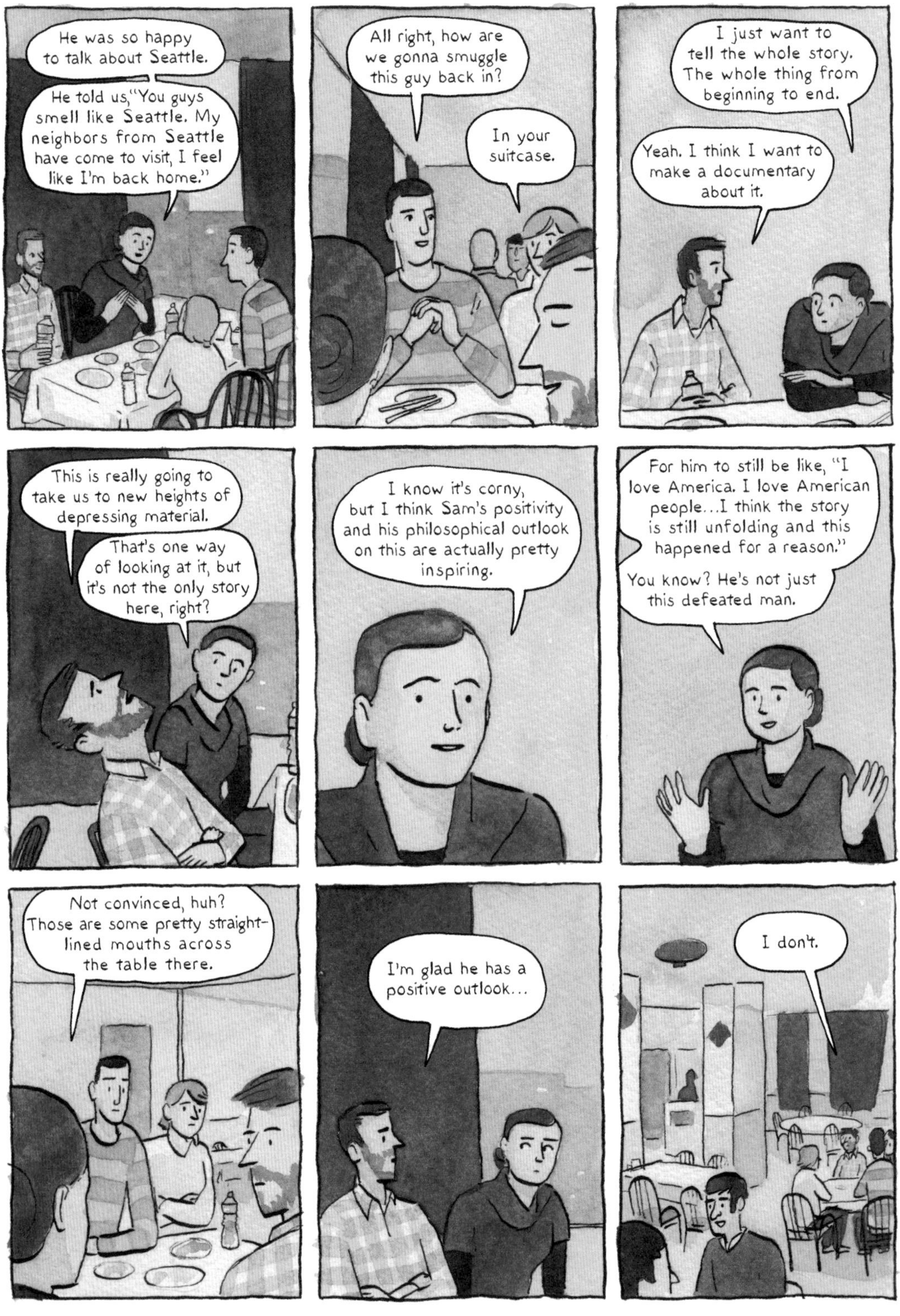
He was so happy to talk about Seattle.
He told us, "You guys smell like Seattle. My neighbors from Seattle have come to visit, I feel like I'm back home."
All right, how are we gonna smuggle this guy back in?
In your suitcase.
I just want to tell the whole story. The whole thing from beginning to end.
Yeah. I think I want to make a documentary about it.
This is really going to take us to new heights of depressing material.
That's one way of looking at it, but it's not the only story here, right?
I know it's corny, but I think Sam's positivity and his philosophical outlook on this are actually pretty inspiring.
For him to still be like, "I love America. I love American people...I think the story is still unfolding and this happened for a reason."
You know? He's not just this defeated man.
Not convinced, huh? Those are some pretty straight-lined mouths across the table there.
I'm glad he has a positive outlook...
I don't.

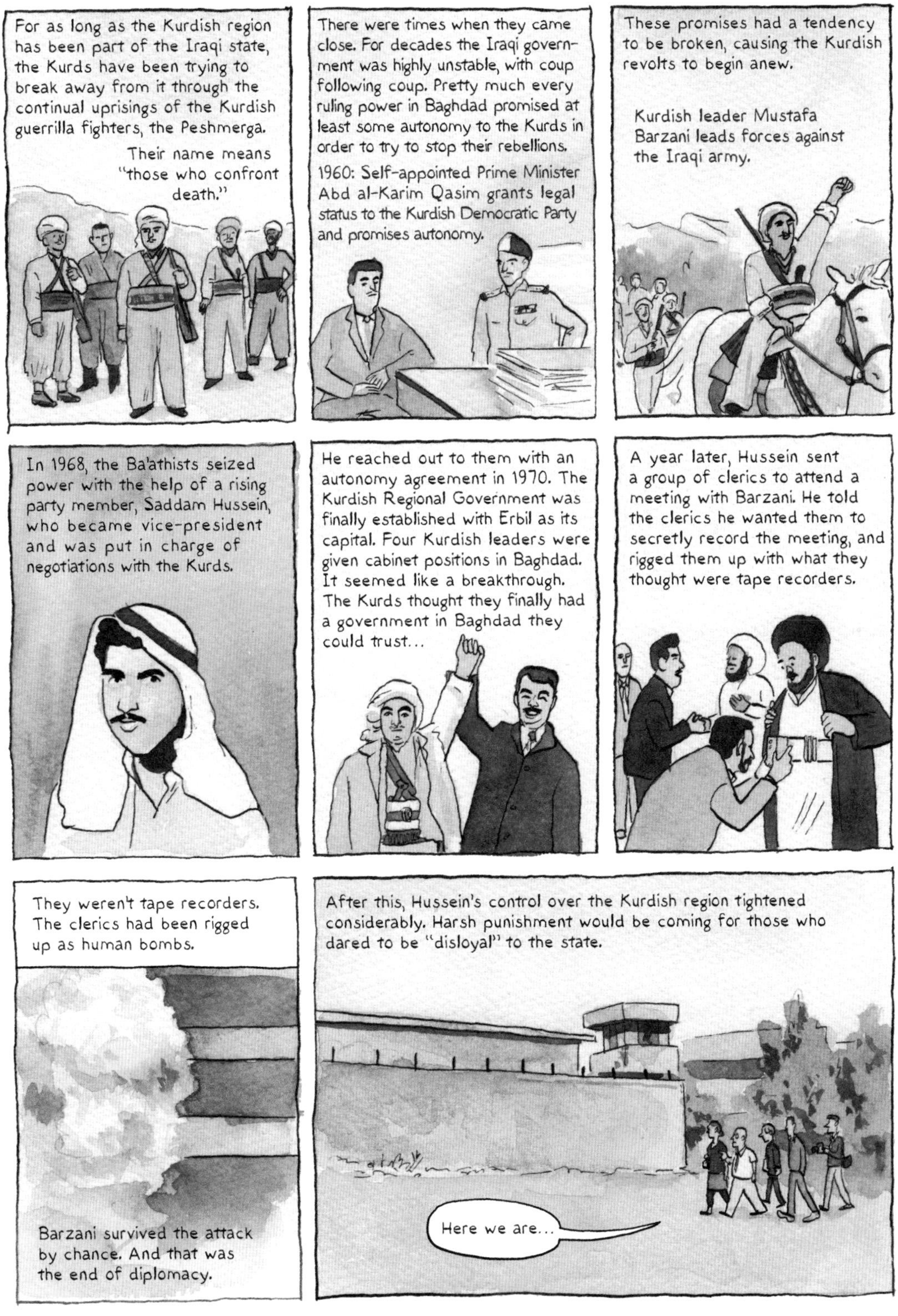
For as long as the Kurdish region has been part of the Iraqi state, the Kurds have been trying to break away from it through the continual uprisings of the Kurdish guerrilla fighters, the Peshmerga.
Their name means "those who confront death."
There were times when they came close. For decades the Iraqi government was highly unstable, with coup following coup. Pretty much every ruling power in Baghdad promised at least some autonomy to the Kurds in order to try to stop their rebellions.
1960: Self-appointed Prime Minister Abd al-Karim Qasim grants legal status to the Kurdish Democratic Party and promises autonomy.
These promises had a tendency to be broken, causing the Kurdish revolts to begin anew.
Kurdish leader Mustafa Barzani leads forces against the Iraqi army.
In 1968, the Ba'athists seized power with the help of a rising party member, Saddam Hussein, who became vice-president and was put in charge of negotiations with the Kurds.
He reached out to them with an autonomy agreement in 1970. The Kurdish Regional Government was finally established with Erbil as its capital. Four Kurdish leaders were given cabinet positions in Baghdad. It seemed like a breakthrough. The Kurds thought they finally had a government in Baghdad they could trust...
A year later, Hussein sent a group of clerics to attend a meeting with Barzani. He told the clerics he wanted them to secretly record the meeting, and rigged them up with what they thought were tape recorders.
They weren't tape recorders. The clerics had been rigged up as human bombs.
Barzani survived the attack by chance. And that was the end of diplomacy.
After this, Hussein's control over the Kurdish region tightened considerably. Harsh punishment would be coming for those who dared to be "disloyal" to the state.
Here we are...

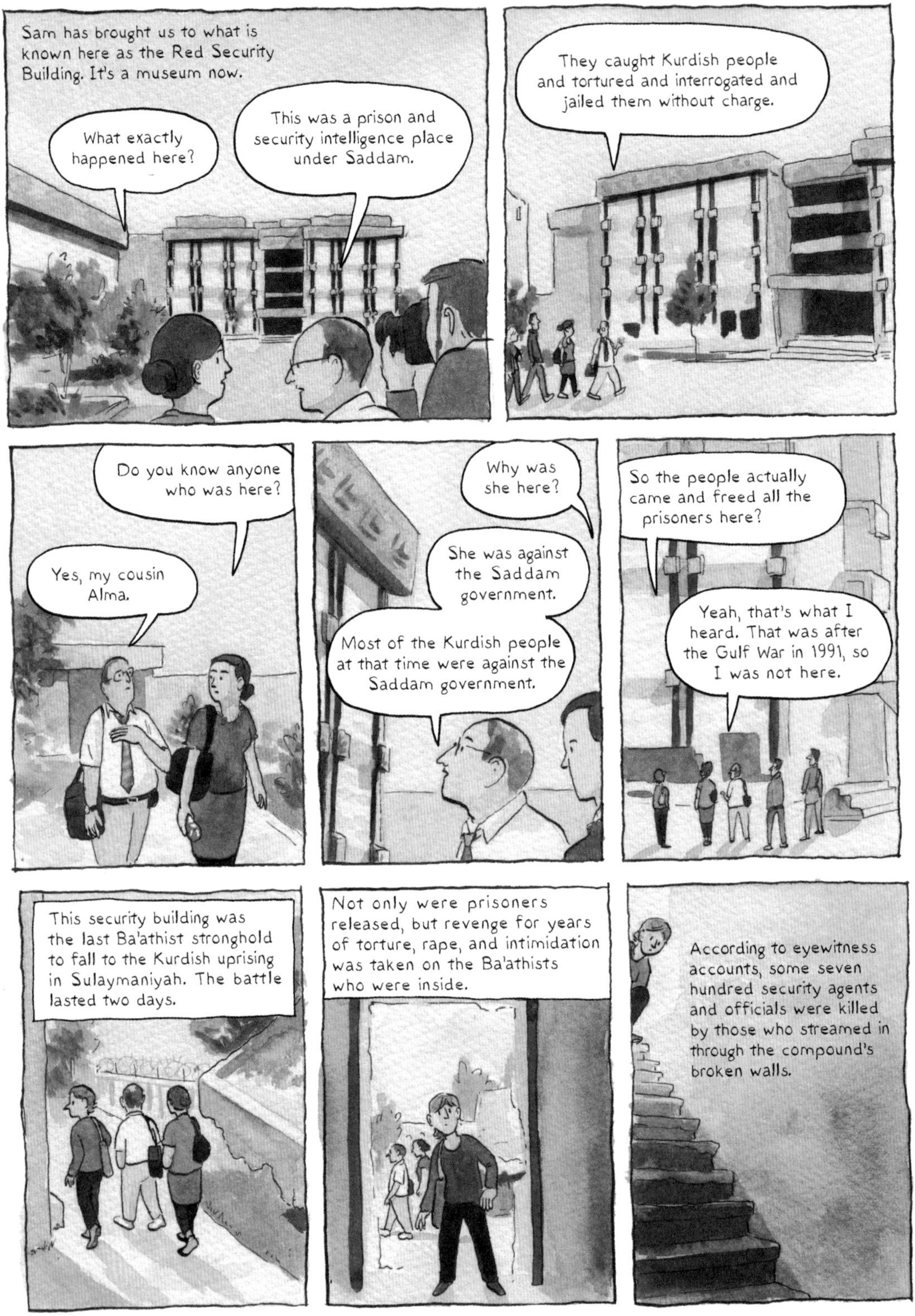
Sam has brought us to what is known here as the Red Security Building. It's a museum now.
What exactly happened here?
This was a prison and security intelligence place under Saddam.
They caught Kurdish people and tortured and interrogated and jailed them without charge.
Do you know anyone who was here?
Yes, my cousin Alma.
Why was she here?
She was against the Saddam government.
Most of the Kurdish people at that time were against the Saddam government.
So the people actually came and freed all the prisoners here?
Yeah, that's what I heard. That was after the Gulf War in 1991, so I was not here.
This security building was the last Ba'athist stronghold to fall to the Kurdish uprising in Sulaymaniyah. The battle lasted two days.
Not only were prisoners released, but revenge for years of torture, rape, and intimidation was taken on the Ba'athists who were inside.
According to eyewitness accounts, some seven hundred security agents and officials were killed by those who streamed in through the compound's broken walls.

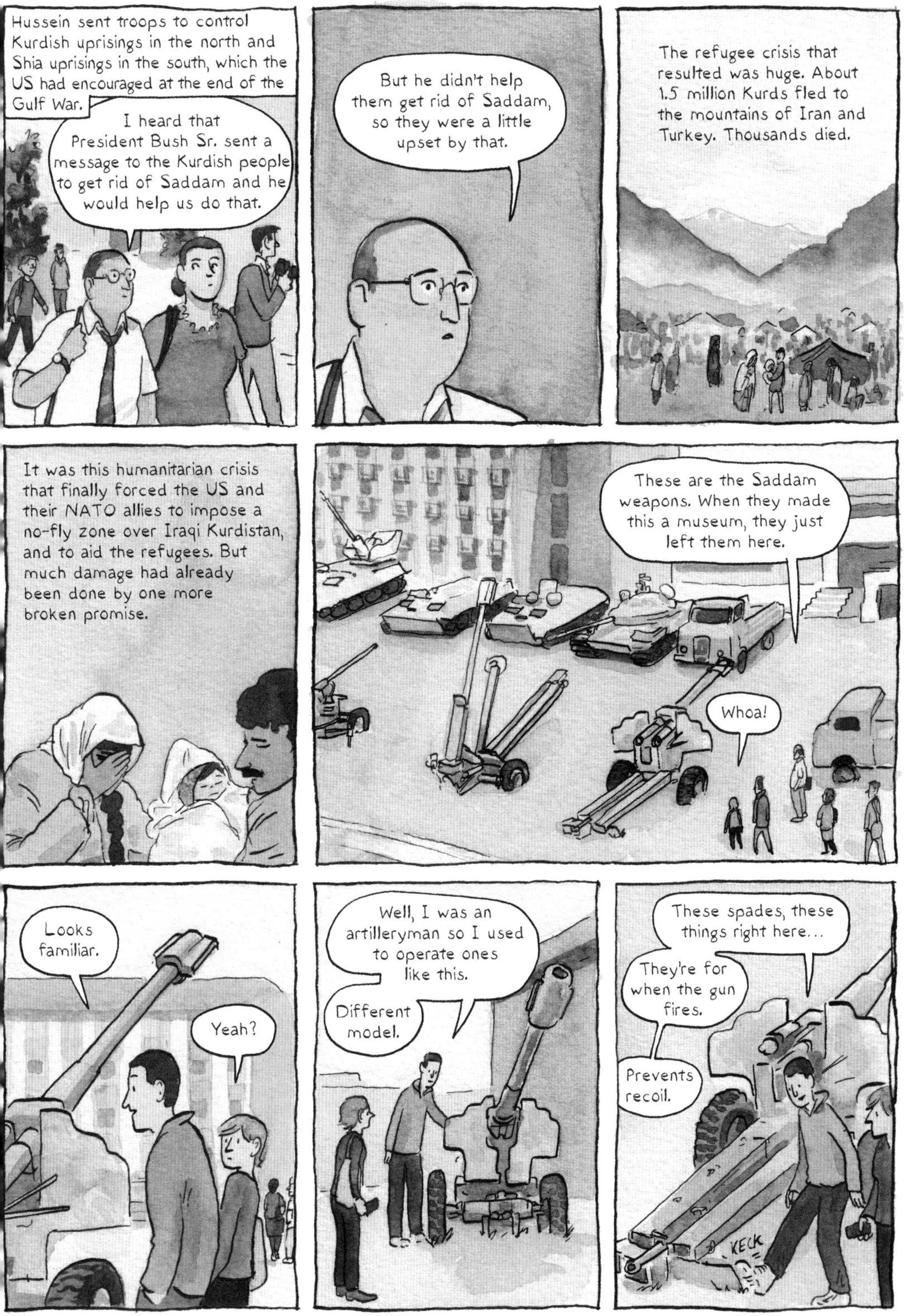
Hussein sent troops to control Kurdish uprisings in the north and Shia uprisings in the south, which the US had encouraged at the end of the Gulf War.
I heard that President Bush Sr. sent a message to the Kurdish people to get rid of Saddam and he would help us do that.
But he didn't help them get rid of Saddam, so they were a little upset by that.
The refugee crisis that resulted was huge. About 1.5 million Kurds fled to the mountains of Iran and Turkey. Thousands died.
It was this humanitarian crisis that finally forced the US and their NATO allies to impose a no-fly zone over Iraqi Kurdistan, and to aid the refugees. But much damage had already been done by one more broken promise.
These are the Saddam weapons. When they made this a museum, they just left them here.
Whoa!
Looks familiar.
Yeah?
Well, I was an artilleryman so I used to operate ones like this.
Different model.
These spades, these things right here...
They're for when the gun fires.
Prevents recoil.
KECK

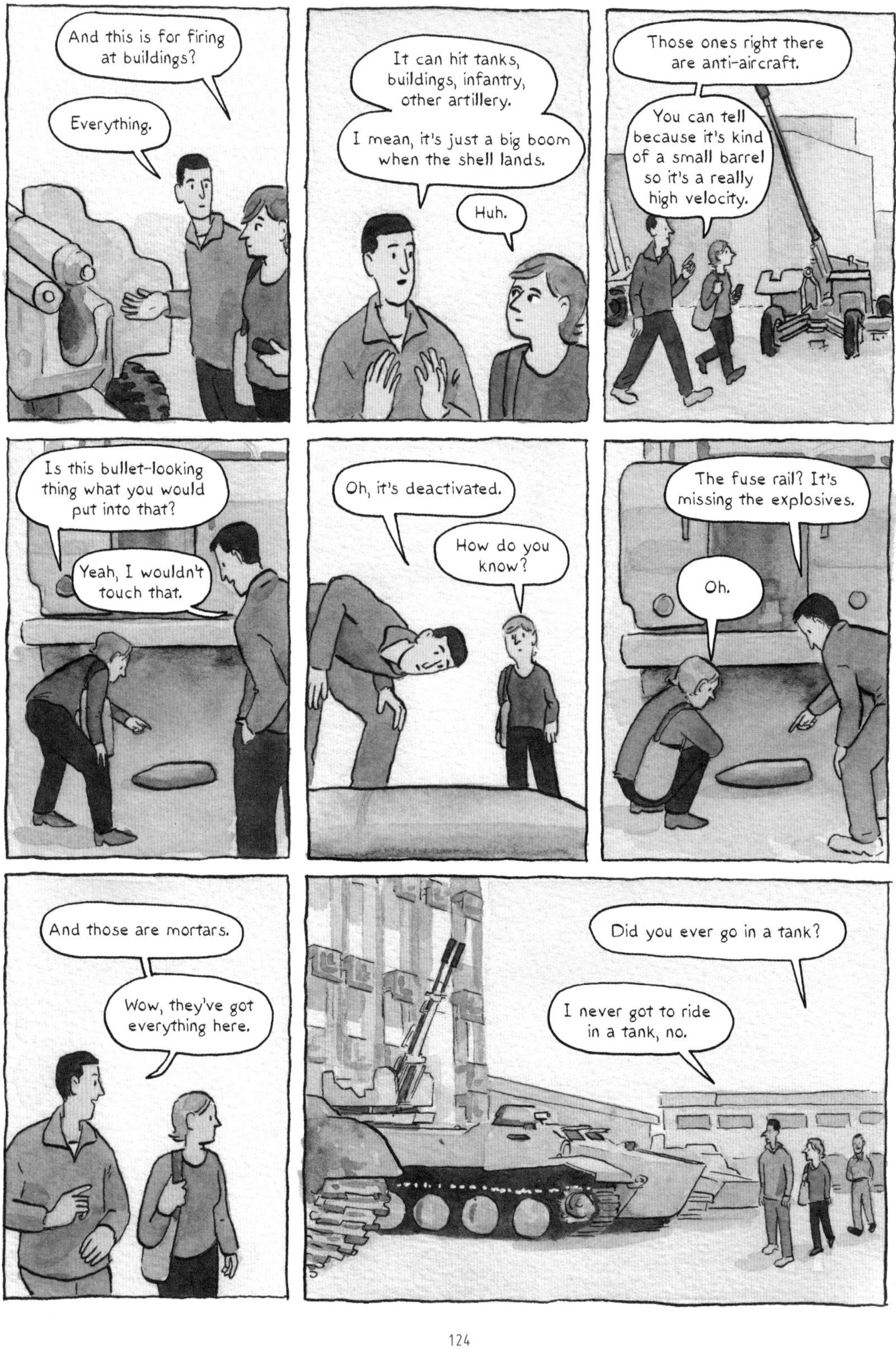
And this is for firing at buildings?
Everything.
It can hit tanks, buildings, infantry, other artillery.
I mean, it's just a big boom when the shell lands.
Huh.
Those ones right there are anti-aircraft.
You can tell because it's kind of a small barrel so it's a really high velocity.
Is this bullet-looking thing what you would put into that?
Yeah, I wouldn't touch that.
Oh, it's deactivated.
How do you know?
The fuse rail? It's missing the explosives.
Oh.
And those are mortars.
Wow, they've got everything here.
Did you ever go in a tank?
I never got to ride in a tank, no.

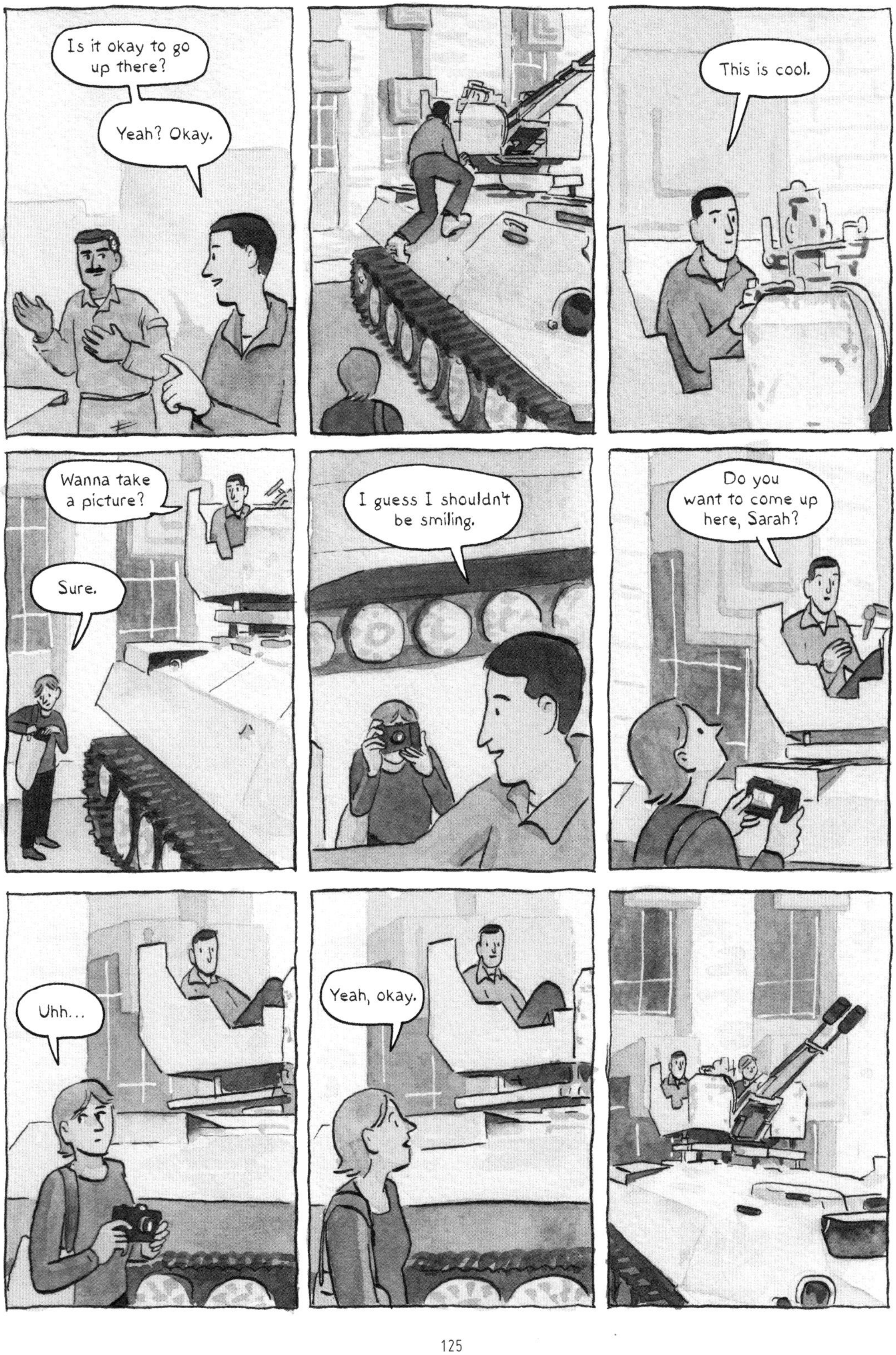
Is it okay to go up there?
Yeah? Okay.
This is cool.
Wanna take a picture?
Sure.
I guess I shouldn't be smiling.
Do you want to come up here, Sarah?
Uhh...
Yeah, okay.

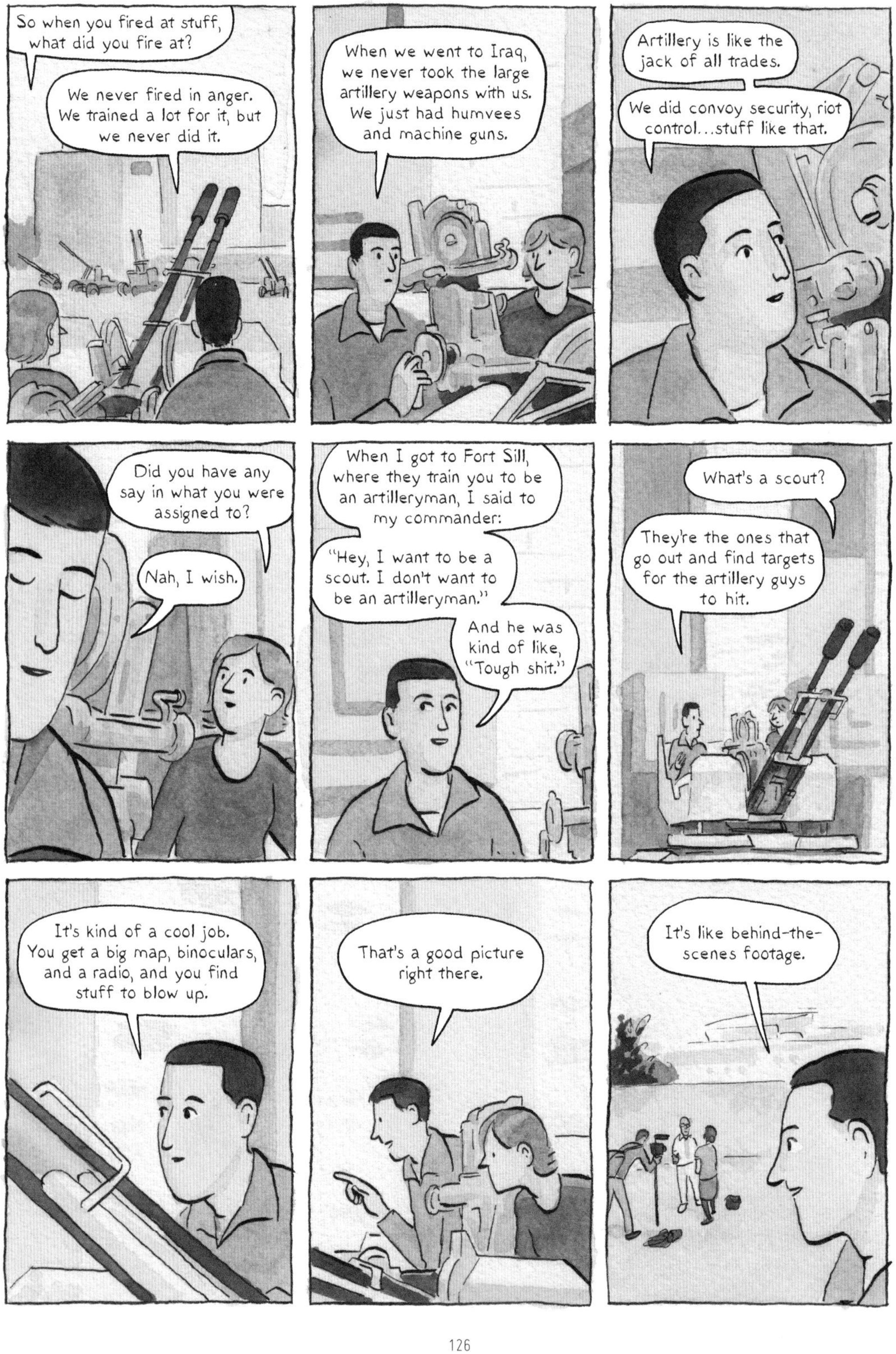
So when you fired at stuff, what did you fire at?
We never fired in anger. We trained a lot for it, but we never did it.
When we went to Iraq, we never took the large artillery weapons with us. We just had humvees and machine guns.
Artillery is like the jack of all trades.
We did convoy security, riot control...stuff like that.
Did you have any say in what you were assigned to?
Nah, I wish.
When I got to Fort Sill, where they train you to be an artilleryman, I said to my commander:
"Hey, I want to be a scout. I don't want to be an artilleryman."
And he was kind of like, "Tough shit."
What's a scout?
They're the ones that go out and find targets for the artillery guys to hit.
It's kind of a cool job. You get a big map, binoculars, and a radio, and you find stuff to blow up.
That's a good picture right there.
It's like behind-the-scenes footage.

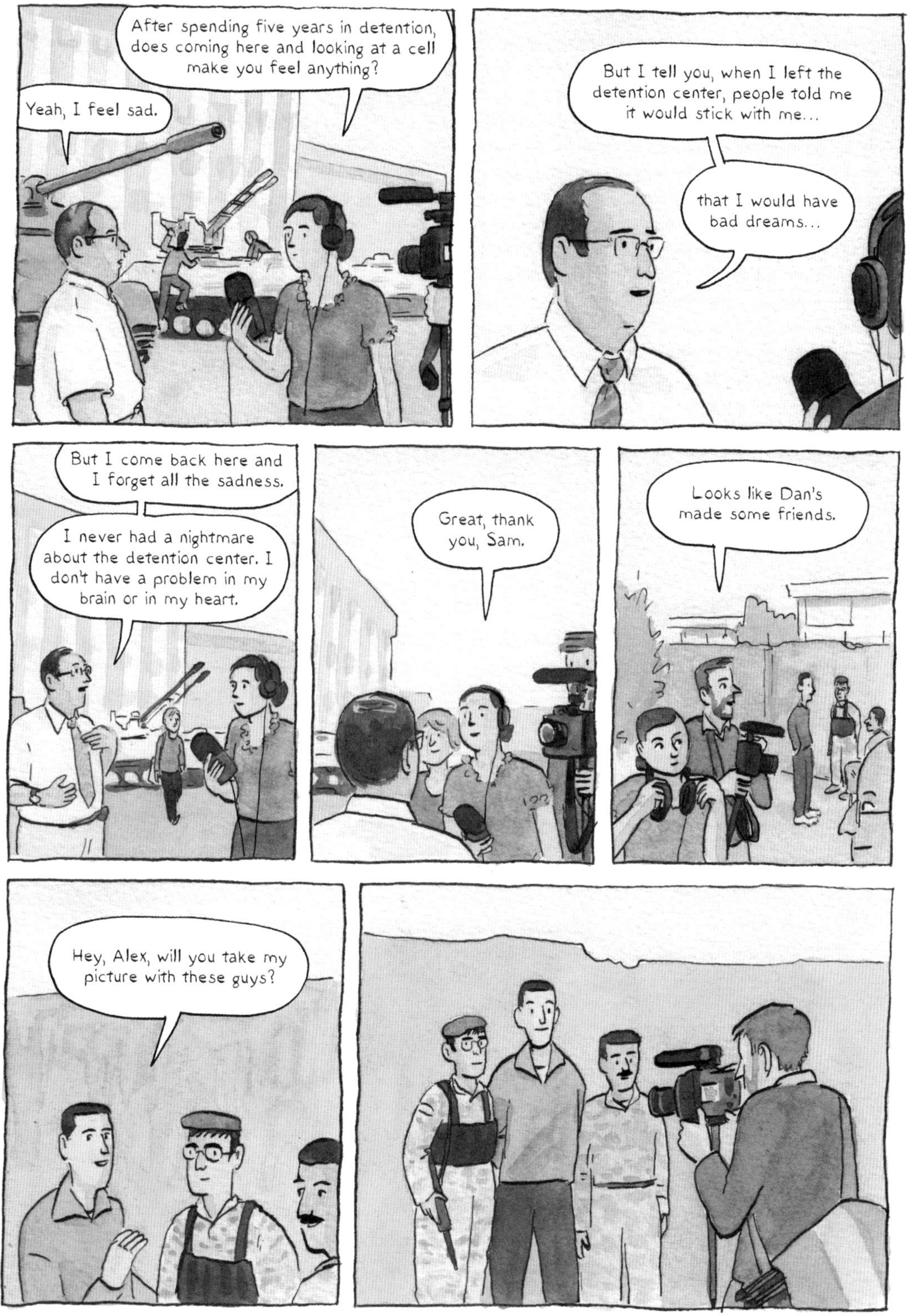

After spending five years in detention, does coming here and looking at a cell make you feel anything?
Yeah, I feel sad.
But I tell you, when I left the detention center, people told me it would stick with me...
that I would have bad dreams...
But I come back here and I forget all the sadness.
I never had a nightmare about the detention center. I don't have a problem in my brain or in my heart.
Great, thank you, Sam.
Looks like Dan's made some friends.
Hey, Alex, will you take my picture with these guys?

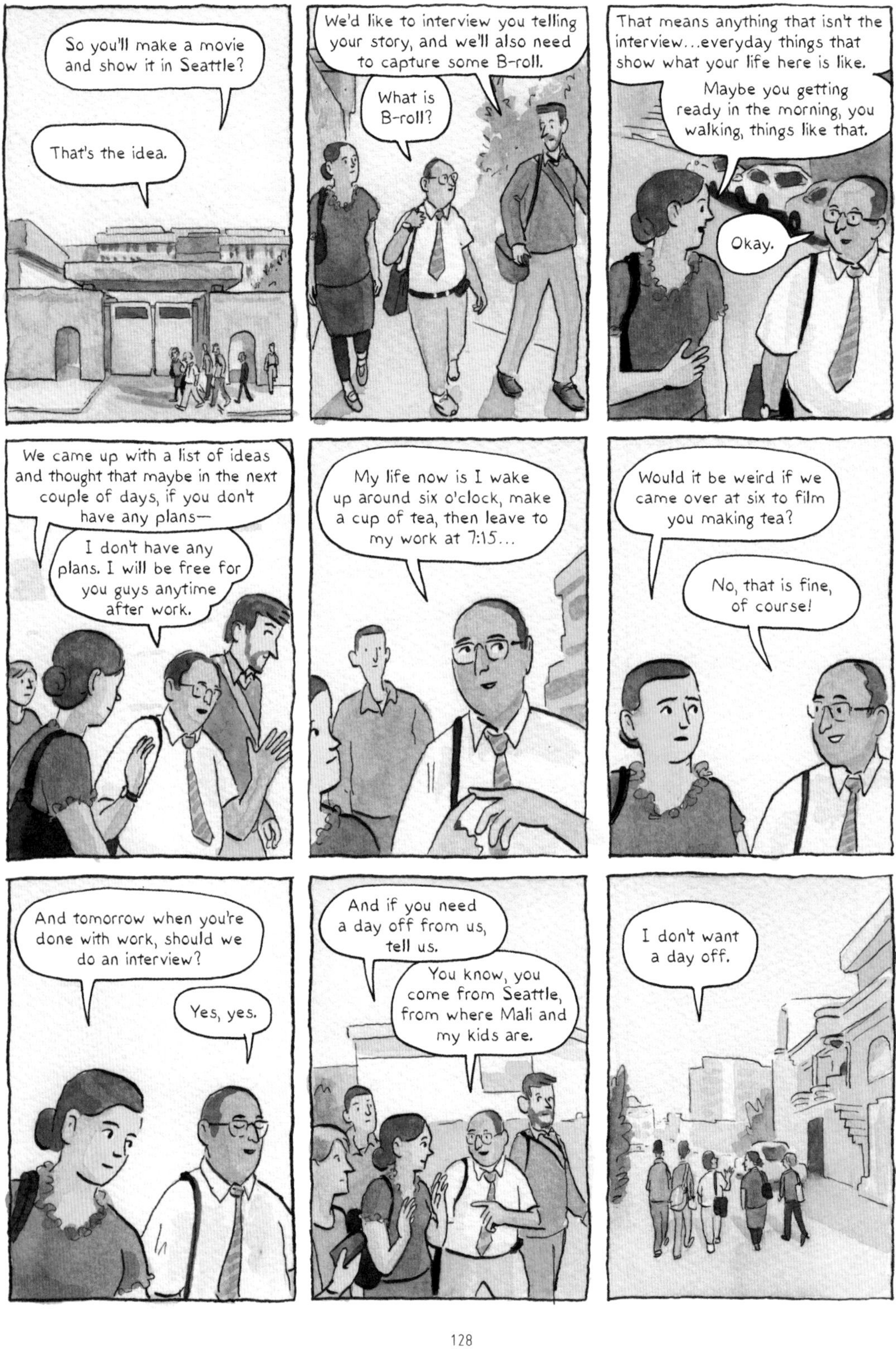

So you'll make a movie and show it in Seattle?
That's the idea.
We'd like to interview you telling your story, and we'll also need to capture some B-roll.
What is B-roll?
That means anything that isn't the interview...everyday things that show what your life here is like.
Maybe you getting ready in the morning, you walking, things like that.
Okay.
We came up with a list of ideas and thought that maybe in the next couple of days, if you don't have any plans—
I don't have any plans. I will be free for you guys anytime after work.
My life now is I wake up around six o'clock, make a cup of tea, then leave to my work at 7:15...
Would it be weird if we came over at six to film you making tea?
No, that is fine, of course!
And tomorrow when you're done with work, should we do an interview?
Yes, yes.
And if you need a day off from us, tell us.
You know, you come from Seattle, from where Mali and my kids are.
I don't want a day off.

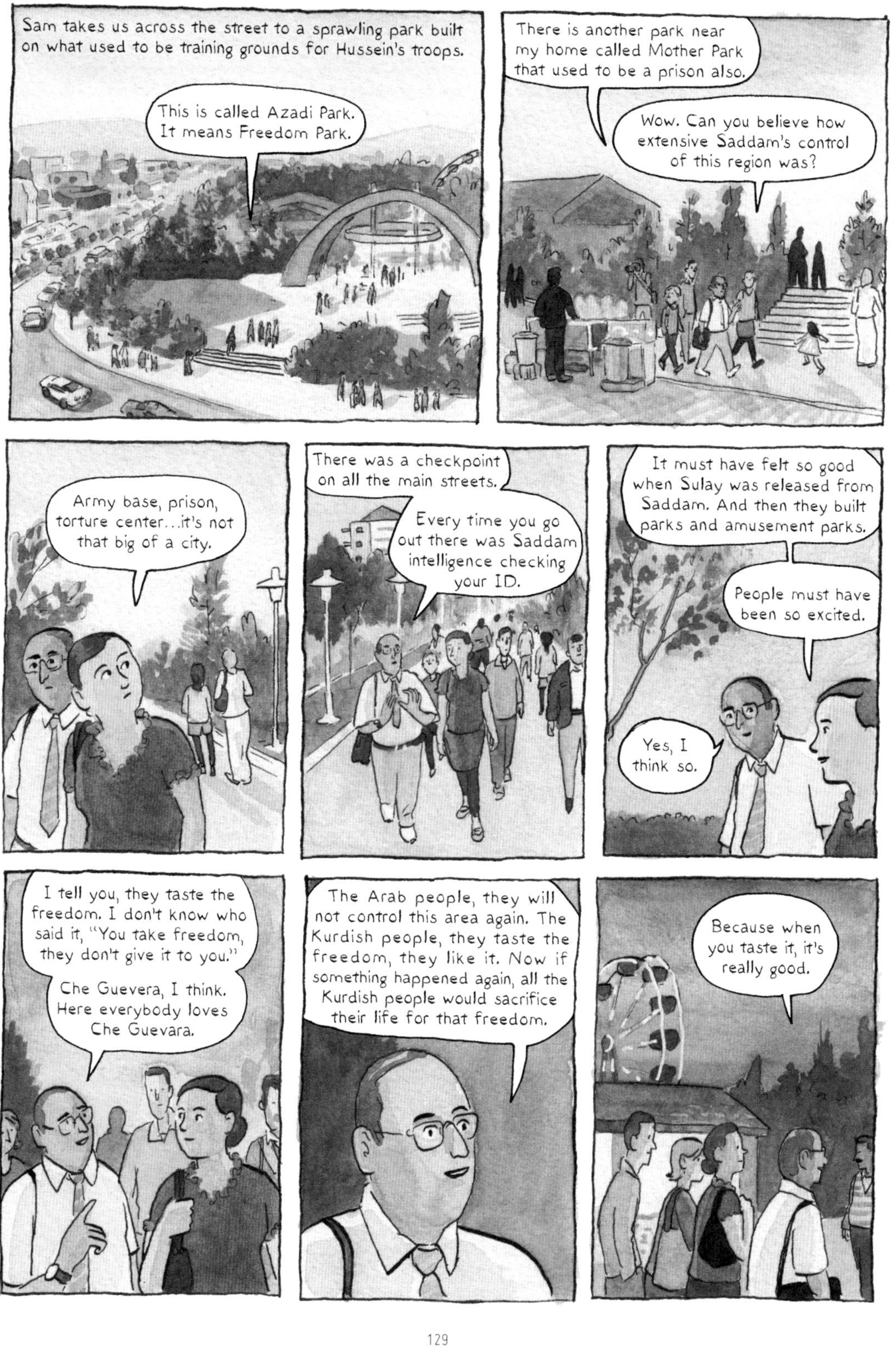
Sam takes us across the street to a sprawling park built on what used to be training grounds for Hussein's troops.
This is called Azadi Park. It means Freedom Park.
There is another park near my home called Mother Park that used to be a prison also.
Wow. Can you believe how extensive Saddam's control of this region was?
Army base, prison, torture center...it's not that big of a city.
There was a checkpoint on all the main streets.
Every time you go out there was Saddam intelligence checking your ID.
It must have felt so good when Sulay was released from Saddam. And then they built parks and amusement parks.
People must have been so excited.
Yes, I think so.
I tell you, they taste the freedom. I don't know who said it, "You take freedom, they don't give it to you."
Che Guevera, I think. Here everybody loves Che Guevara.
The Arab people, they will not control this area again. The Kurdish people, they taste the freedom, they like it. Now if something happened again, all the Kurdish people would sacrifice their life for that freedom.
Because when you taste it, it's really good.

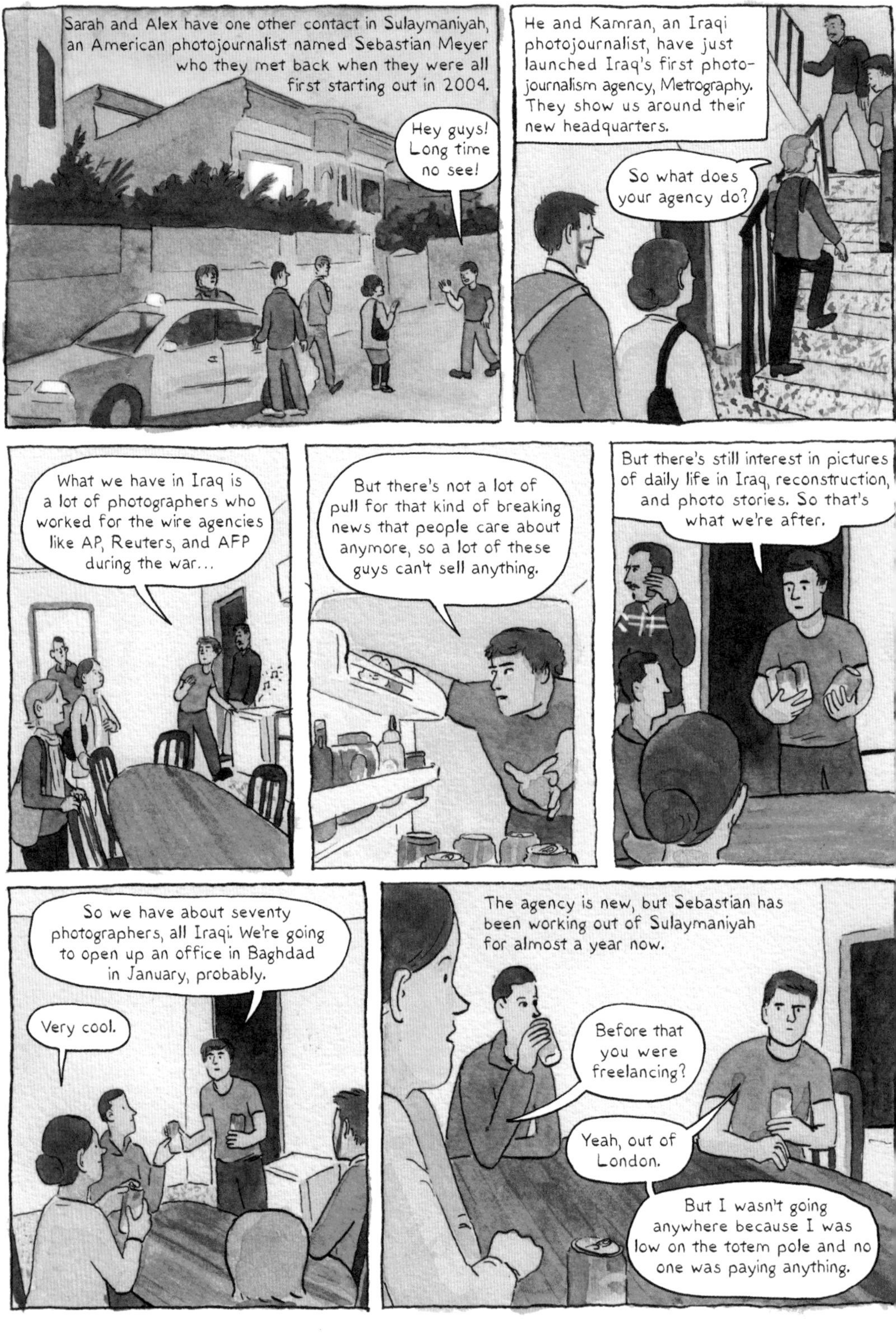

Sarah and Alex have one other contact in Sulaymaniyah, an American photojournalist named Sebastian Meyer who they met back when they were all first starting out in 2004.
Hey guys! Long time no see!
He and Kamran, an Iraqi photojournalist, have just launched Iraq's first photojournalism agency, Metrography. They show us around their new headquarters.
So what does your agency do?
What we have in Iraq is a lot of photographers who worked for the wire agencies like AP, Reuters, and AFP during the war...
But there's not a lot of pull for that kind of breaking news that people care about anymore, so a lot of these guys can't sell anything.
But there's still interest in pictures of daily life in Iraq, reconstruction, and photo stories. So that's what we're after.
So we have about seventy photographers, all Iraqi. We're going to open up an office in Baghdad in January, probably.
Very cool.
The agency is new, but Sebastian has been working out of Sulaymaniyah for almost a year now.
Before that you were freelancing?
Yeah, out of London.
But I wasn't going anywhere because I was low on the totem pole and no one was paying anything.

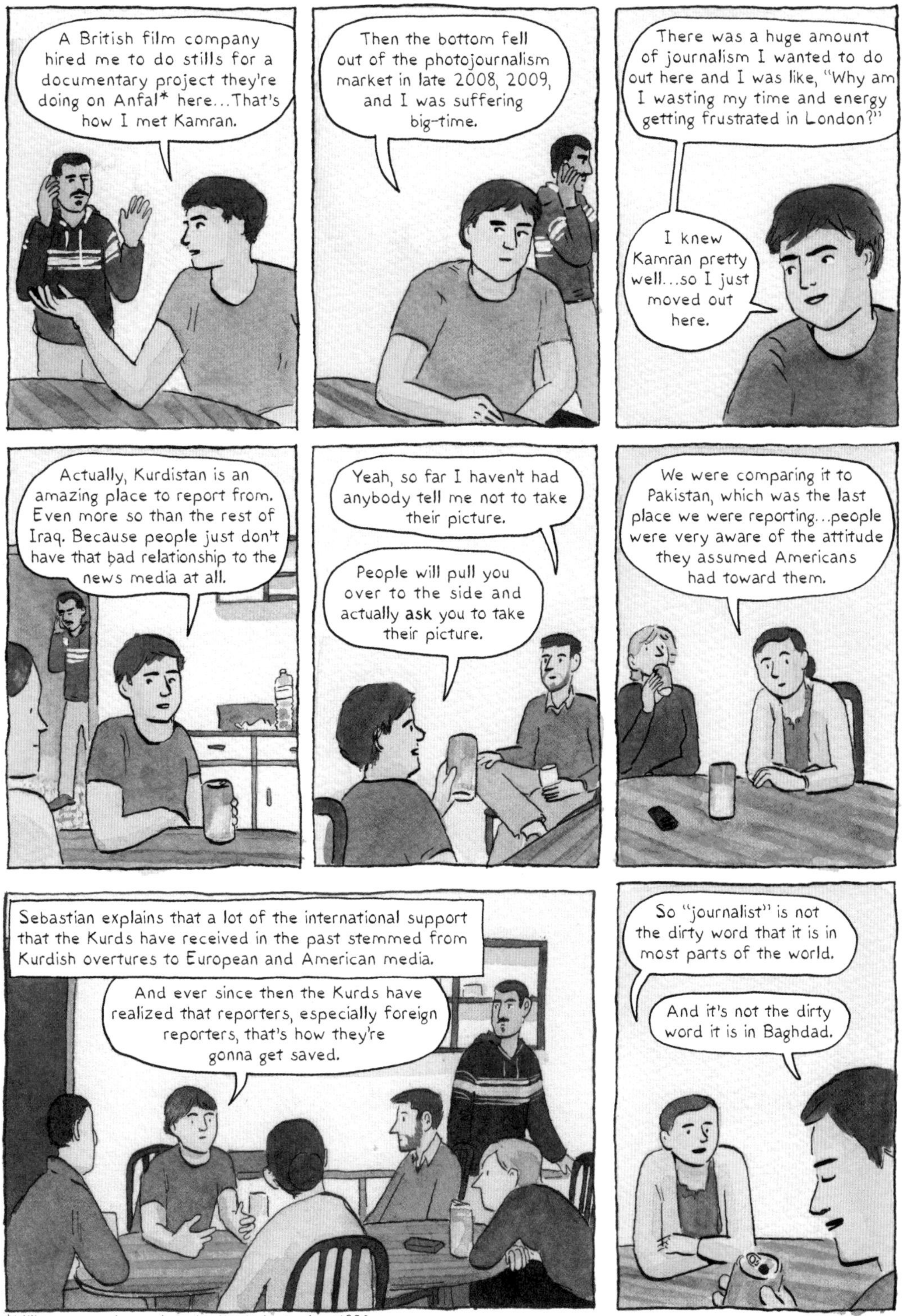
A British film company hired me to do stills for a documentary project they're doing on Anfal* here...That's how I met Kamran.
Then the bottom fell out of the photojournalism market in late 2008, 2009, and I was suffering big-time.
There was a huge amount of journalism I wanted to do out here and I was like, "Why am I wasting my time and energy getting frustrated in London?"
I knew Kamran pretty well...so I just moved out here.
Actually, Kurdistan is an amazing place to report from. Even more so than the rest of Iraq. Because people just don't have that bad relationship to the news media at all.
Yeah, so far I haven't had anybody tell me not to take their picture.
People will pull you over to the side and actually **ask** you to take their picture.
We were comparing it to Pakistan, which was the last place we were reporting...people were very aware of the attitude they assumed Americans had toward them.
Sebastian explains that a lot of the international support that the Kurds have received in the past stemmed from Kurdish overtures to European and American media.
And ever since then the Kurds have realized that reporters, especially foreign reporters, that's how they're gonna get saved.
So "journalist" is not the dirty word that it is in most parts of the world.
And it's not the dirty word it is in Baghdad.

*Military campaign against the Kurds in the late 1980s

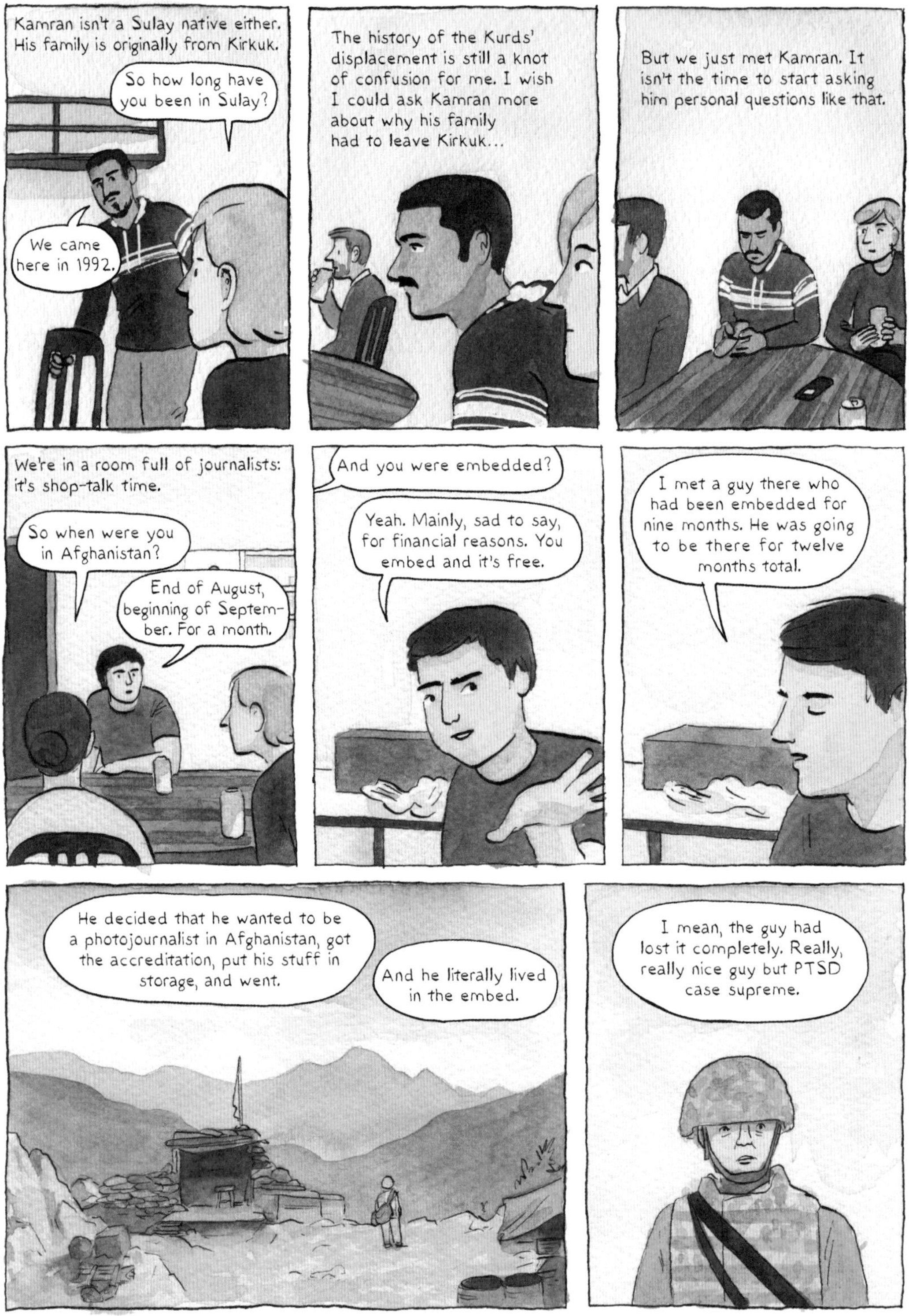
Kamran isn't a Sulay native either. His family is originally from Kirkuk.
So how long have you been in Sulay?
We came here in 1992.
The history of the Kurds' displacement is still a knot of confusion for me. I wish I could ask Kamran more about why his family had to leave Kirkuk...
But we just met Kamran. It isn't the time to start asking him personal questions like that.
We're in a room full of journalists: it's shop-talk time.
So when were you in Afghanistan?
End of August, beginning of September. For a month.
And you were embedded?
Yeah. Mainly, sad to say, for financial reasons. You embed and it's free.
I met a guy there who had been embedded for nine months. He was going to be there for twelve months total.
He decided that he wanted to be a photojournalist in Afghanistan, got the accreditation, put his stuff in storage, and went.
And he literally lived in the embed.
I mean, the guy had lost it completely. Really, really nice guy but PTSD case supreme.

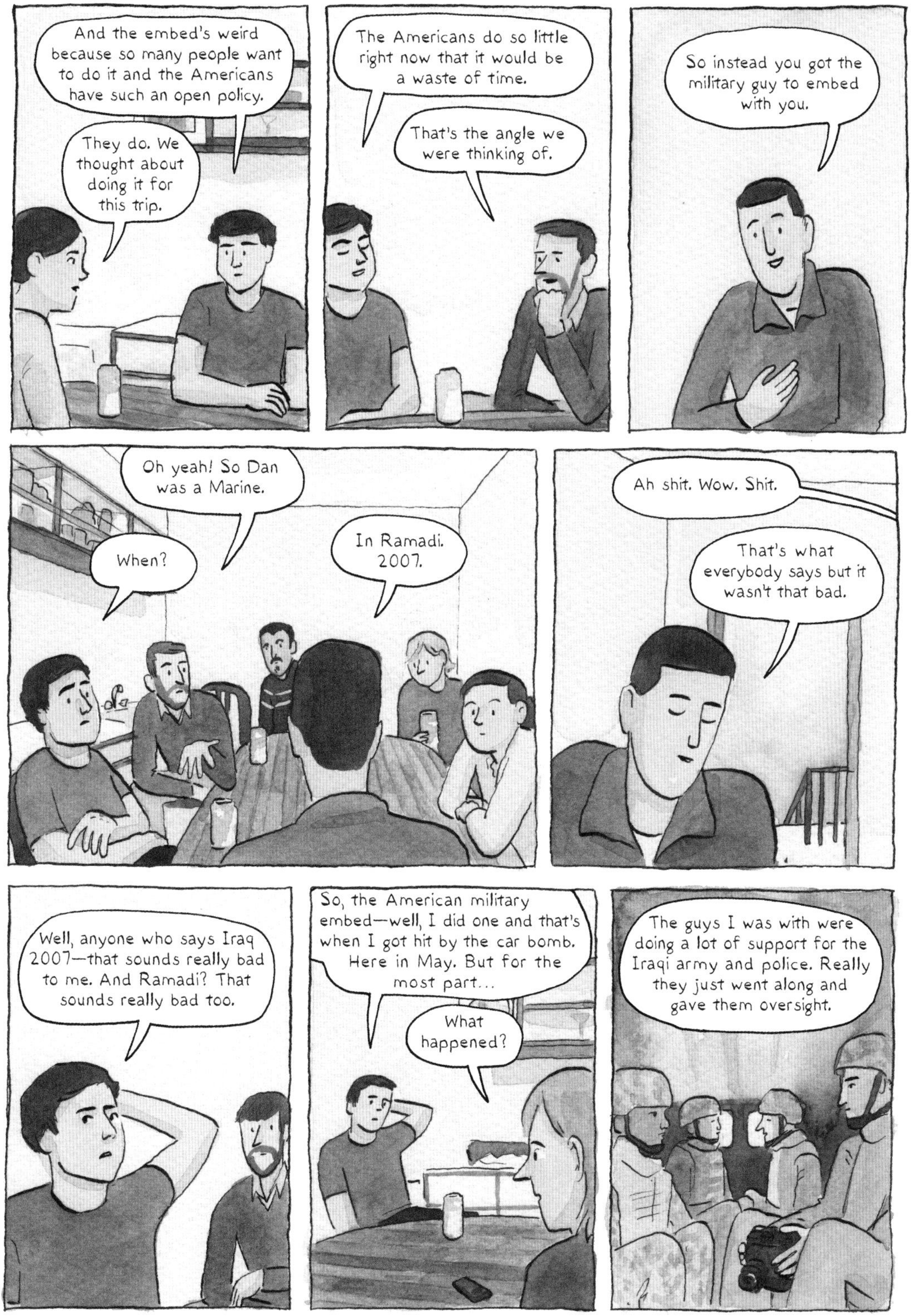
And the embed's weird because so many people want to do it and the Americans have such an open policy.
They do. We thought about doing it for this trip.
The Americans do so little right now that it would be a waste of time.
That's the angle we were thinking of.
So instead you got the military guy to embed with you.
Oh yeah! So Dan was a Marine.
When?
In Ramadi. 2007.
Ah shit. Wow. Shit.
That's what everybody says but it wasn't that bad.
Well, anyone who says Iraq 2007—that sounds really bad to me. And Ramadi? That sounds really bad too.
So, the American military embed—well, I did one and that's when I got hit by the car bomb. Here in May. But for the most part...
What happened?
The guys I was with were doing a lot of support for the Iraqi army and police. Really they just went along and gave them oversight.

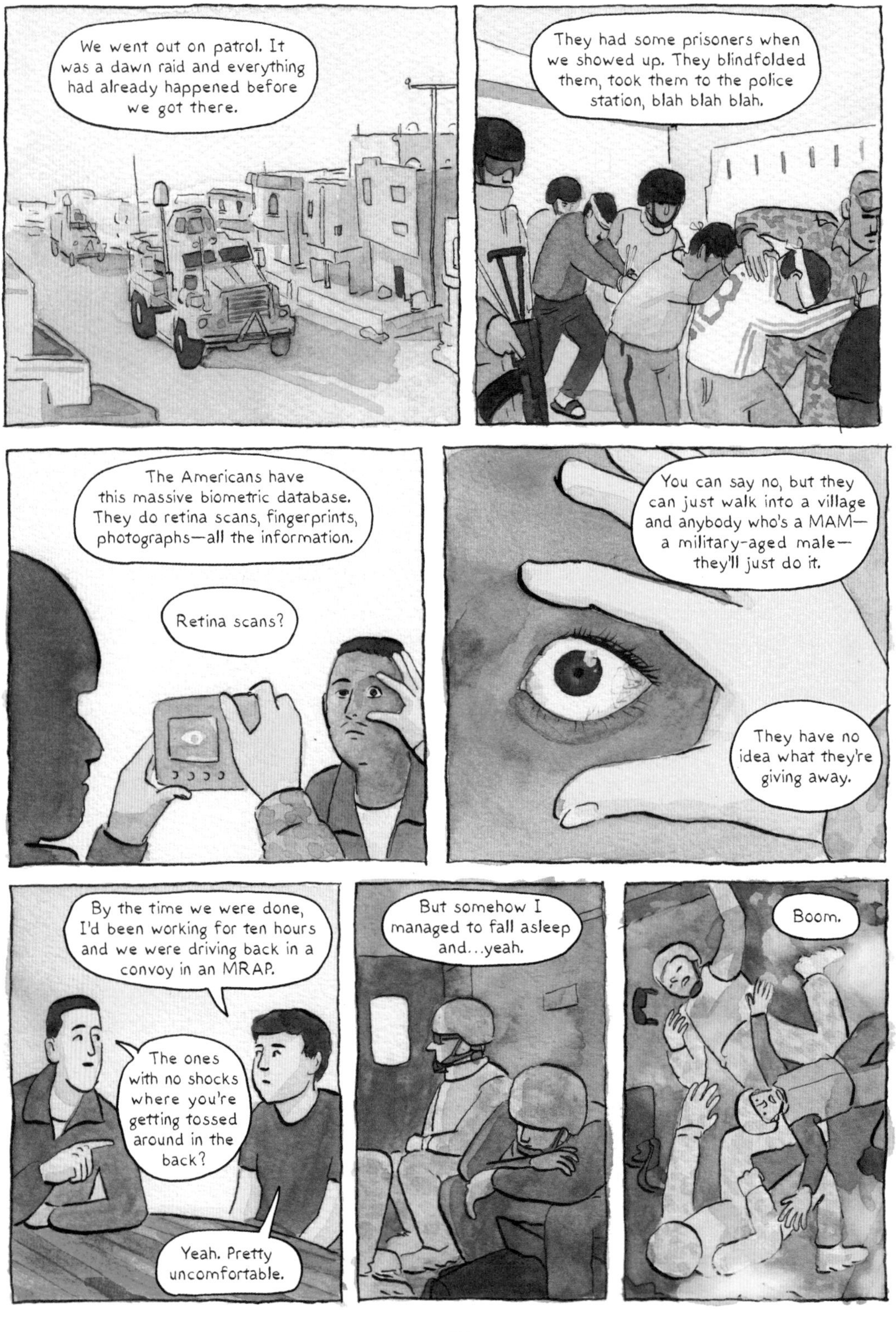
We went out on patrol. It was a dawn raid and everything had already happened before we got there.
They had some prisoners when we showed up. They blindfolded them, took them to the police station, blah blah blah.
The Americans have this massive biometric database. They do retina scans, fingerprints, photographs—all the information.
Retina scans?
You can say no, but they can just walk into a village and anybody who's a MAM—a military-aged male—they'll just do it.
They have no idea what they're giving away.
By the time we were done, I'd been working for ten hours and we were driving back in a convoy in an MRAP.
The ones with no shocks where you're getting tossed around in the back?
Yeah. Pretty uncomfortable.
But somehow I managed to fall asleep and...yeah.
Boom.

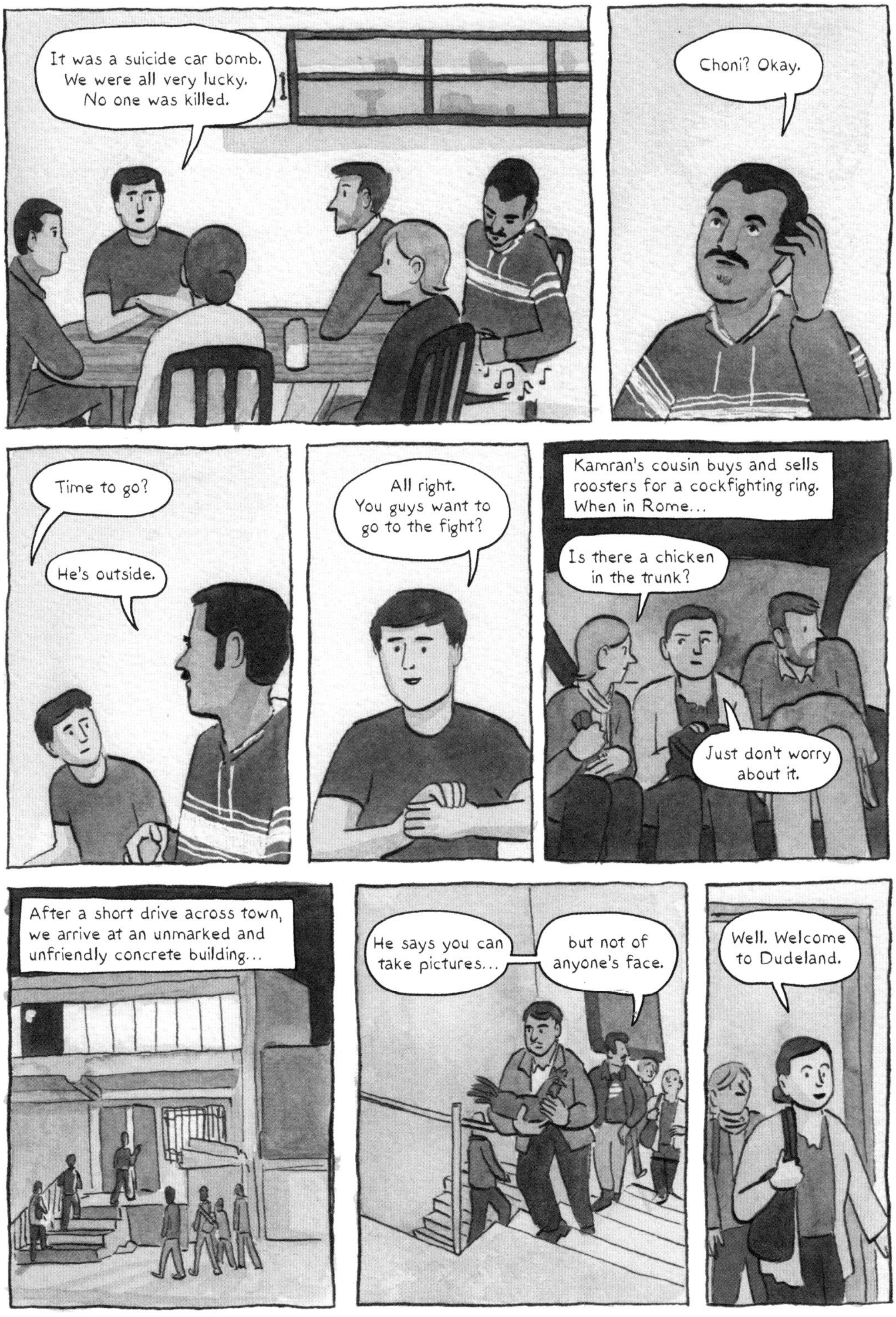

It was a suicide car bomb. We were all very lucky. No one was killed.
Choni? Okay.
Time to go?
He's outside.
All right. You guys want to go to the fight?
Kamran's cousin buys and sells roosters for a cockfighting ring. When in Rome...
Is there a chicken in the trunk?
Just don't worry about it.
After a short drive across town, we arrive at an unmarked and unfriendly concrete building...
He says you can take pictures...
but not of anyone's face.
Well. Welcome to Dudeland.

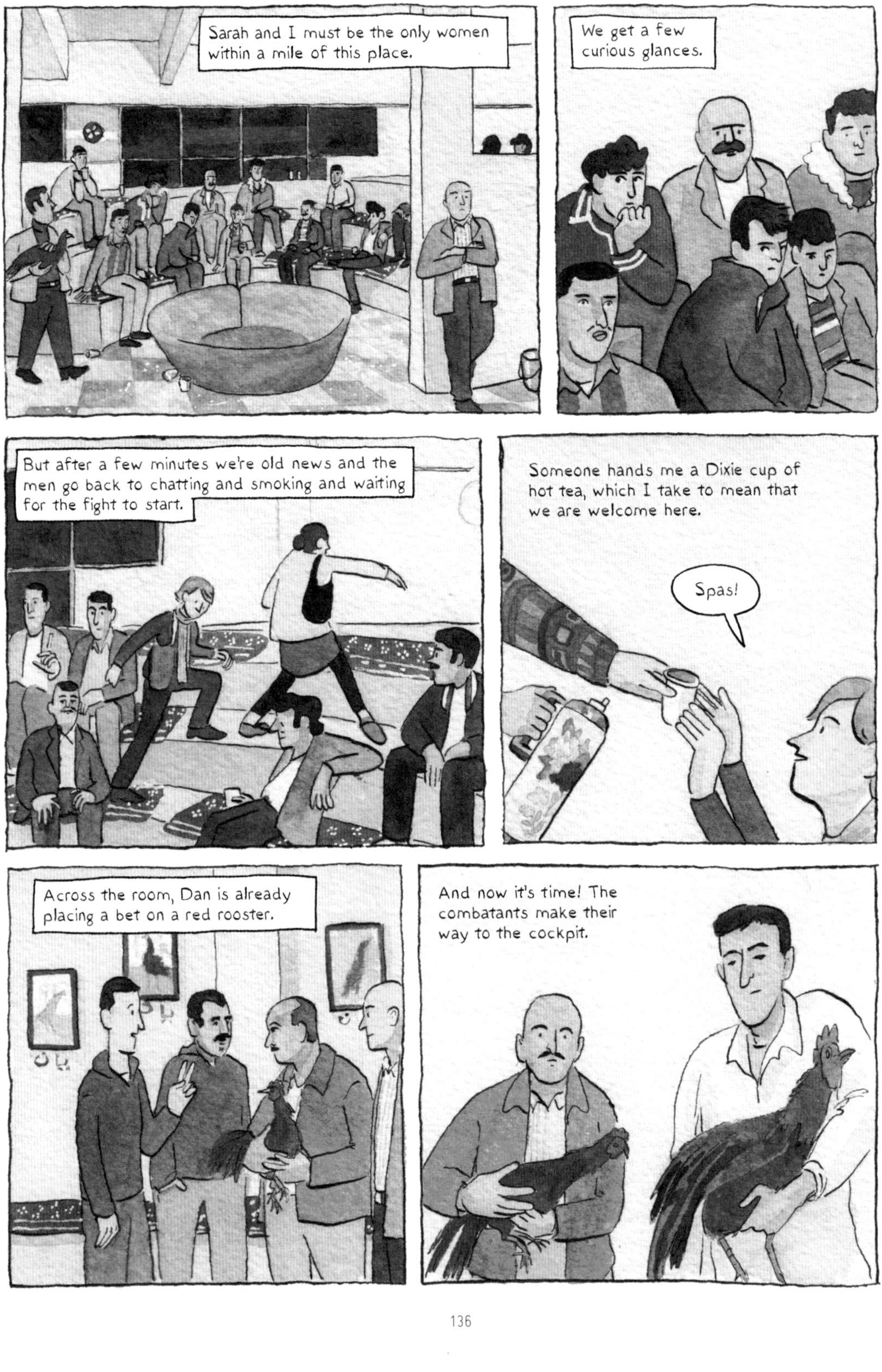

Sarah and I must be the only women within a mile of this place.
We get a few curious glances.
But after a few minutes we're old news and the men go back to chatting and smoking and waiting for the fight to start.
Someone hands me a Dixie cup of hot tea, which I take to mean that we are welcome here.
Spas!
Across the room, Dan is already placing a bet on a red rooster.
And now it's time! The combatants make their way to the cockpit.

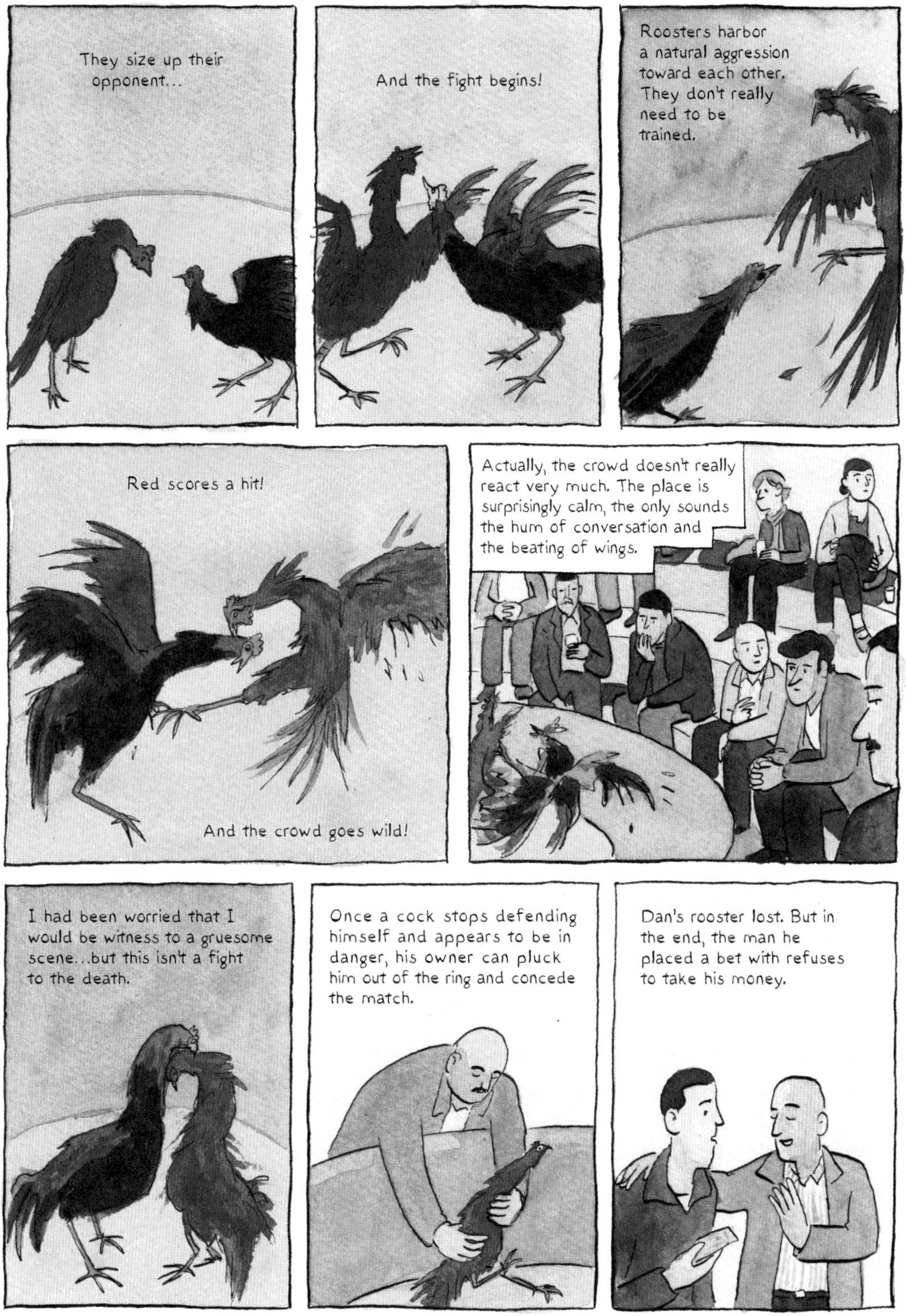
They size up their opponent...
And the fight begins!
Roosters harbor a natural aggression toward each other. They don't really need to be trained.
Red scores a hit!
And the crowd goes wild!
Actually, the crowd doesn't really react very much. The place is surprisingly calm, the only sounds the hum of conversation and the beating of wings.
I had been worried that I would be witness to a gruesome scene...but this isn't a fight to the death.
Once a cock stops defending himself and appears to be in danger, his owner can pluck him out of the ring and concede the match.
Dan's rooster lost. But in the end, the man he placed a bet with refuses to take his money.

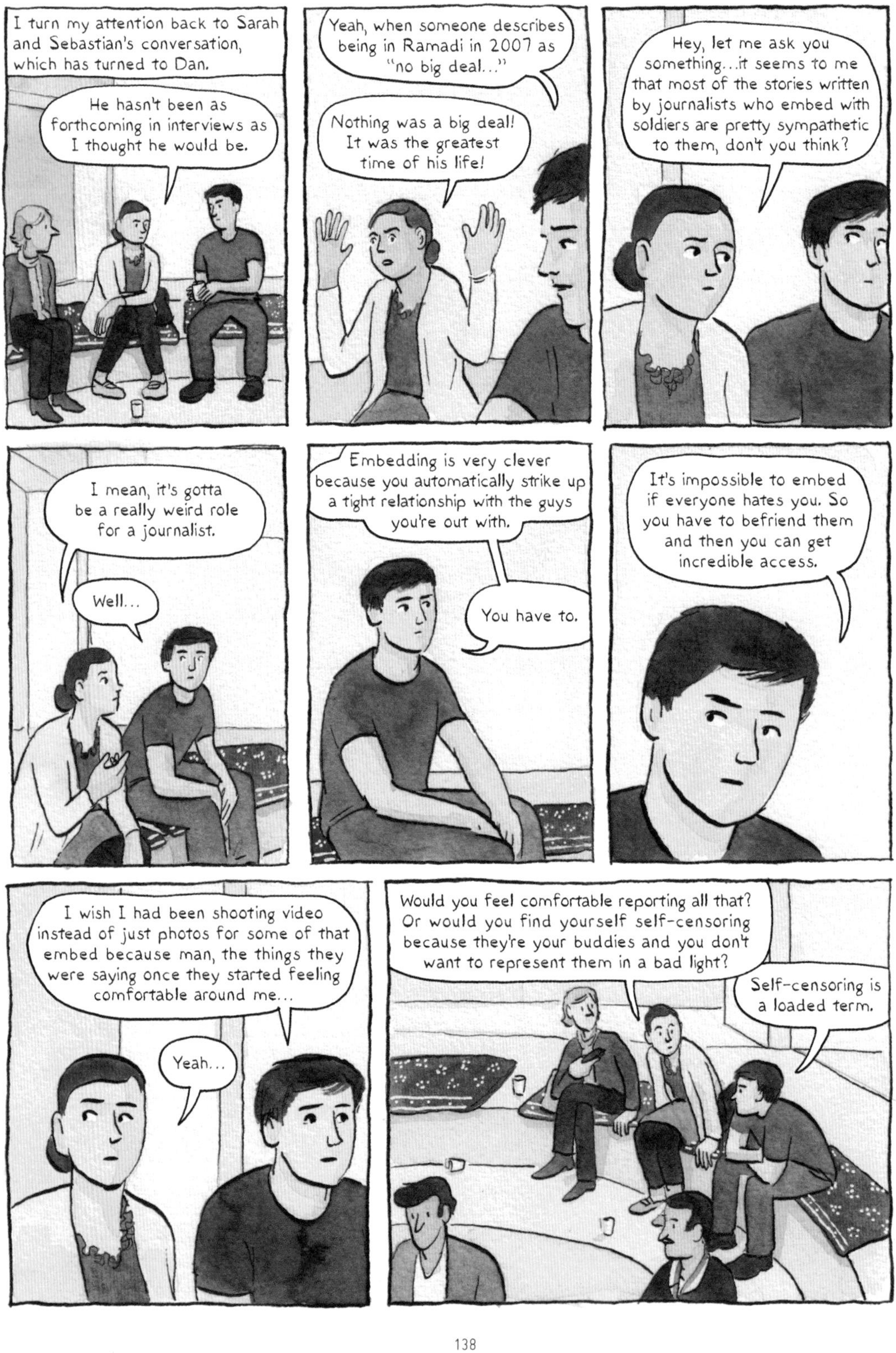

I turn my attention back to Sarah and Sebastian's conversation, which has turned to Dan.
He hasn't been as forthcoming in interviews as I thought he would be.
Yeah, when someone describes being in Ramadi in 2007 as "no big deal..."
Nothing was a big deal! It was the greatest time of his life!
Hey, let me ask you something...it seems to me that most of the stories written by journalists who embed with soldiers are pretty sympathetic to them, don't you think?
I mean, it's gotta be a really weird role for a journalist.
Well...
Embedding is very clever because you automatically strike up a tight relationship with the guys you're out with.
You have to.
It's impossible to embed if everyone hates you. So you have to befriend them and then you can get incredible access.
I wish I had been shooting video instead of just photos for some of that embed because man, the things they were saying once they started feeling comfortable around me...
Yeah...
Would you feel comfortable reporting all that? Or would you find yourself self-censoring because they're your buddies and you don't want to represent them in a bad light?
Self-censoring is a loaded term.

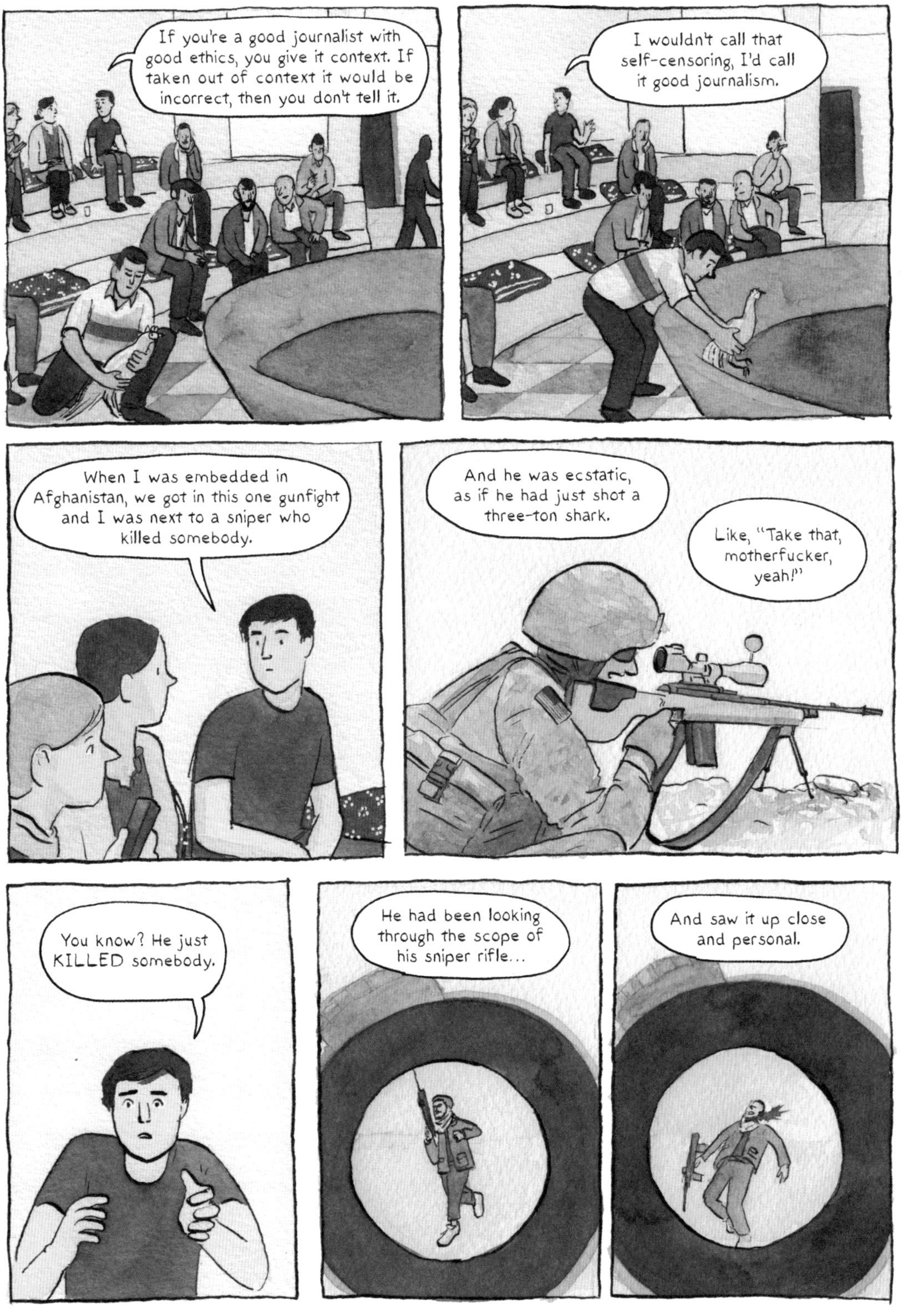
If you're a good journalist with good ethics, you give it context. If taken out of context it would be incorrect, then you don't tell it.
I wouldn't call that self-censoring, I'd call it good journalism.
When I was embedded in Afghanistan, we got in this one gunfight and I was next to a sniper who killed somebody.
And he was ecstatic, as if he had just shot a three-ton shark.
Like, "Take that, motherfucker, yeah!"
You know? He just KILLED somebody.
He had been looking through the scope of his sniper rifle...
And saw it up close and personal.

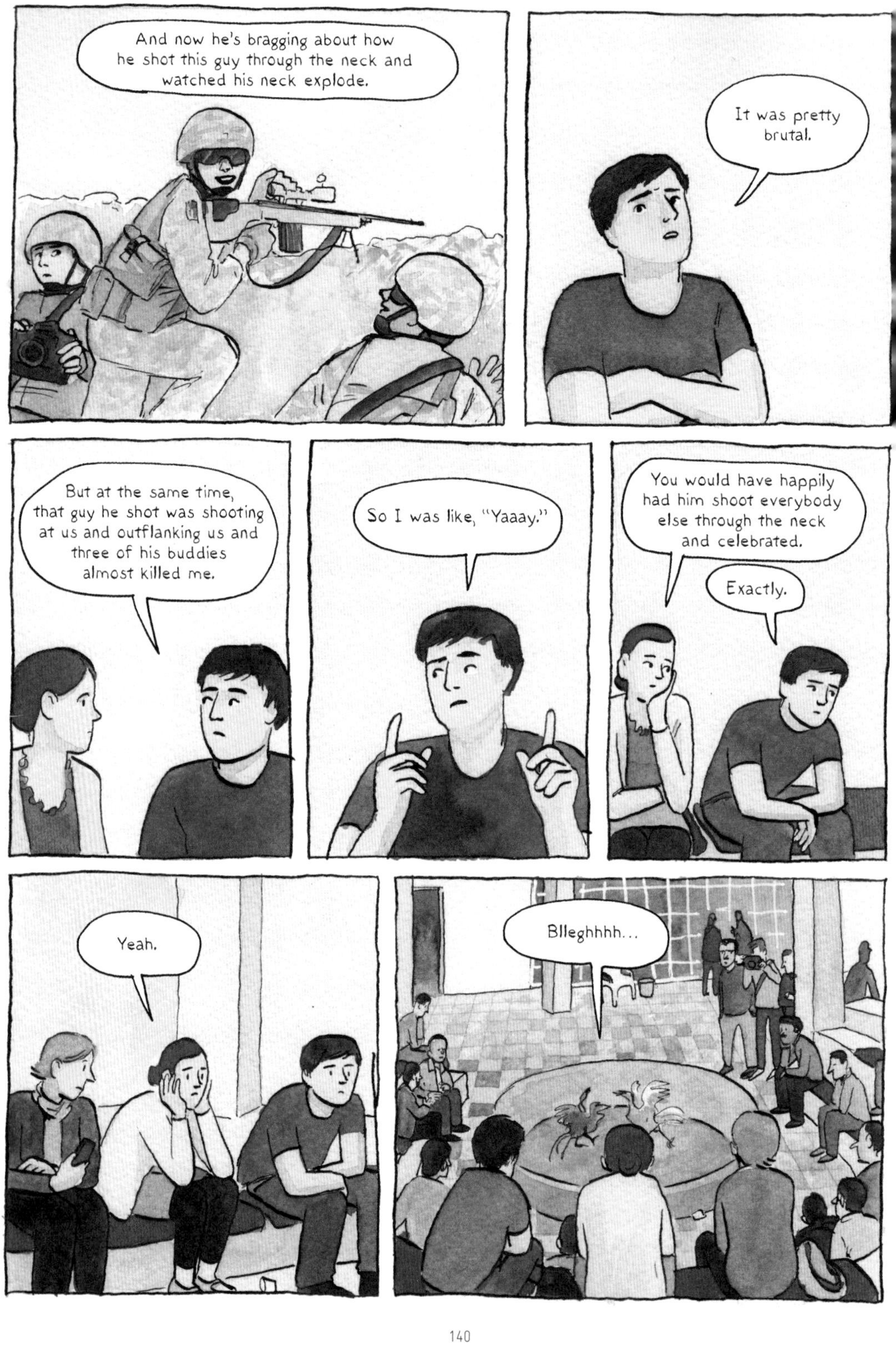
And now he's bragging about how he shot this guy through the neck and watched his neck explode.
It was pretty brutal.
But at the same time, that guy he shot was shooting at us and outflanking us and three of his buddies almost killed me.
So I was like, "Yaaay."
You would have happily had him shoot everybody else through the neck and celebrated.
Exactly.
Yeah.
Blleghhhh...

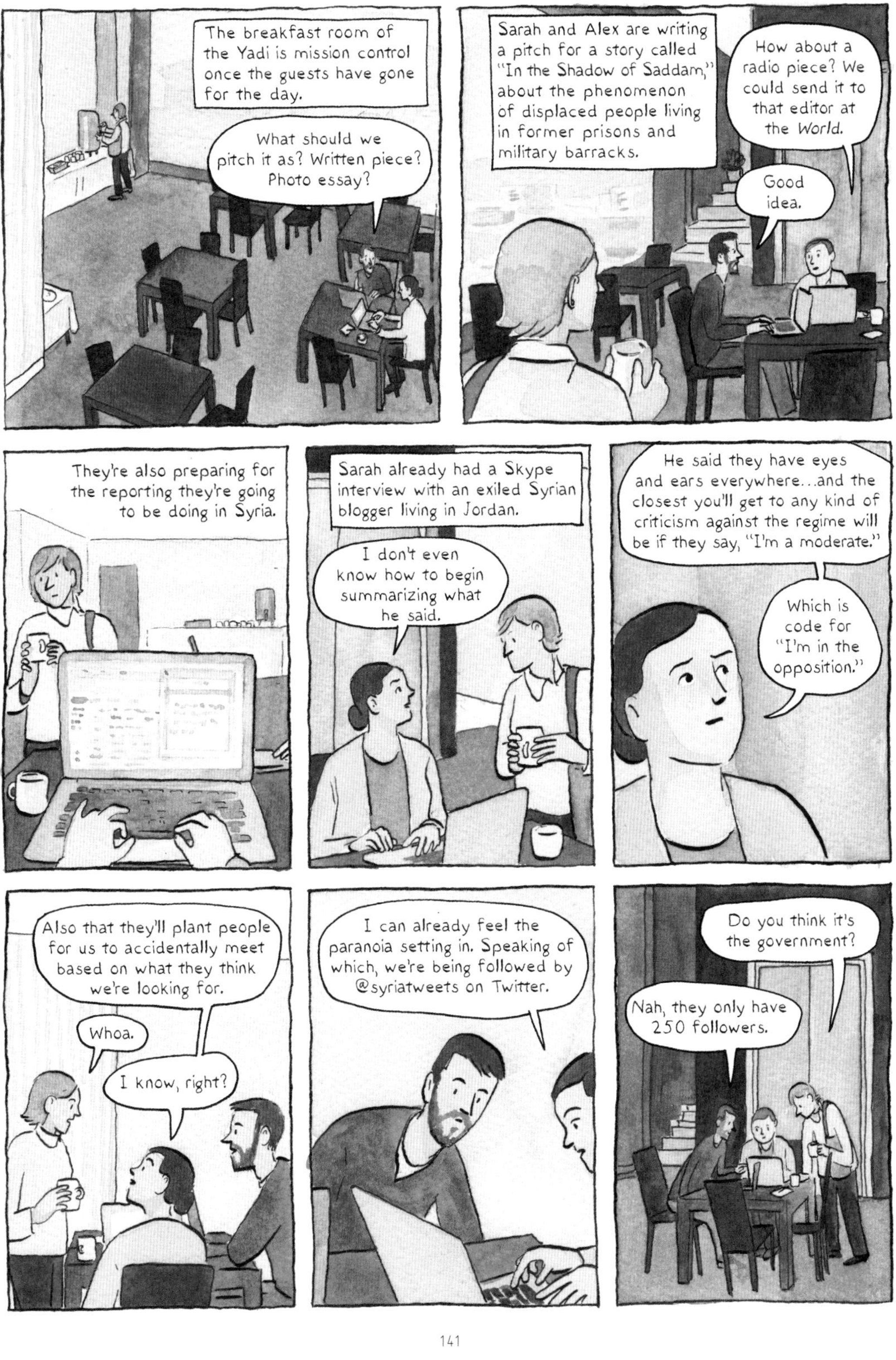
The breakfast room of the Yadi is mission control once the guests have gone for the day.
What should we pitch it as? Written piece? Photo essay?
Sarah and Alex are writing a pitch for a story called "In the Shadow of Saddam," about the phenomenon of displaced people living in former prisons and military barracks.
How about a radio piece? We could send it to that editor at the *World*.
Good idea.
They're also preparing for the reporting they're going to be doing in Syria.
Sarah already had a Skype interview with an exiled Syrian blogger living in Jordan.
I don't even know how to begin summarizing what he said.
He said they have eyes and ears everywhere...and the closest you'll get to any kind of criticism against the regime will be if they say, "I'm a moderate."
Which is code for "I'm in the opposition."
Also that they'll plant people for us to accidentally meet based on what they think we're looking for.
Whoa.
I know, right?
I can already feel the paranoia setting in. Speaking of which, we're being followed by @syriatweets on Twitter.
Do you think it's the government?
Nah, they only have 250 followers.

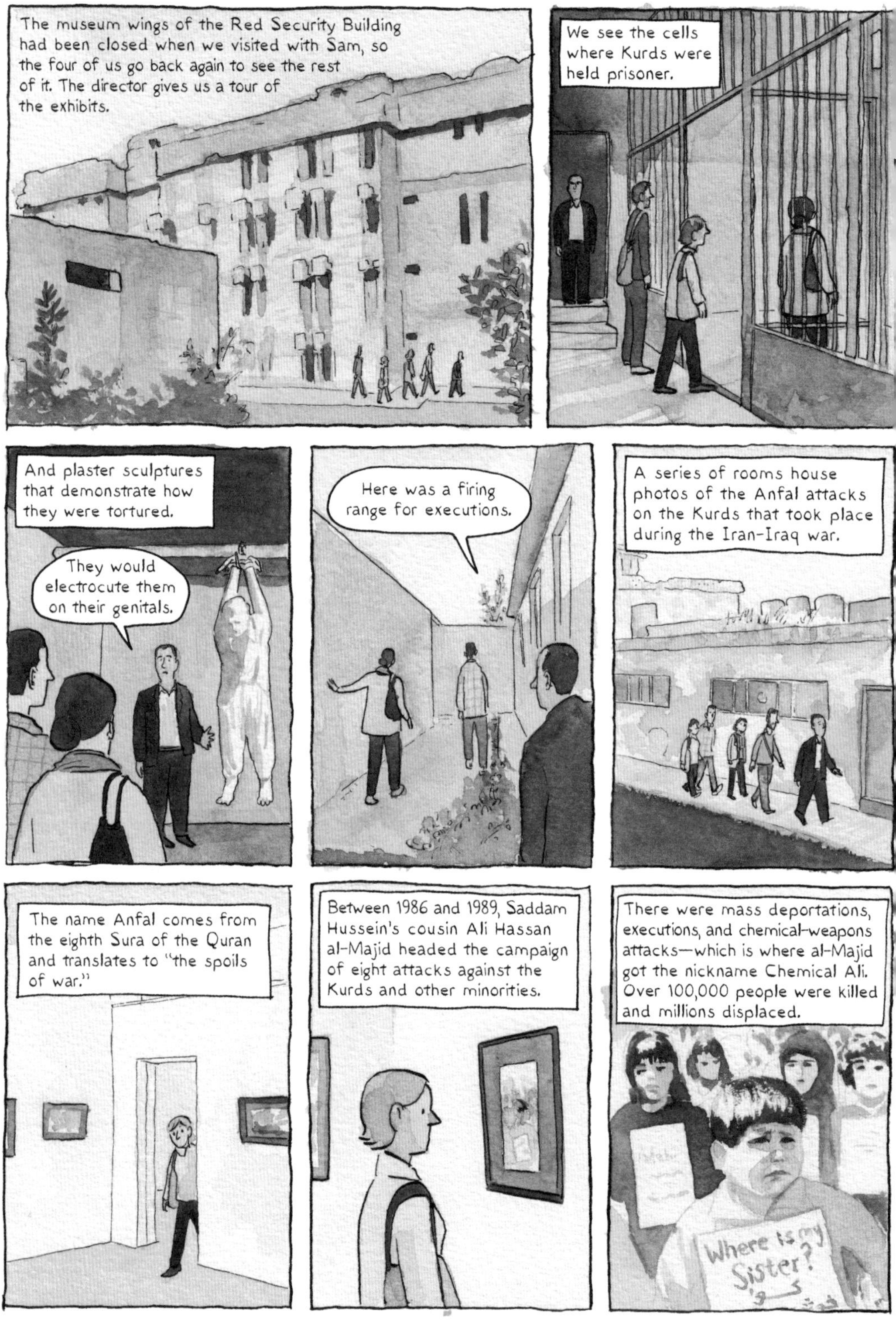

The museum wings of the Red Security Building had been closed when we visited with Sam, so the four of us go back again to see the rest of it. The director gives us a tour of the exhibits.
We see the cells where Kurds were held prisoner.
And plaster sculptures that demonstrate how they were tortured.
They would electrocute them on their genitals.
Here was a firing range for executions.
A series of rooms house photos of the Anfal attacks on the Kurds that took place during the Iran-Iraq war.
The name Anfal comes from the eighth Sura of the Quran and translates to "the spoils of war."
Between 1986 and 1989, Saddam Hussein's cousin Ali Hassan al-Majid headed the campaign of eight attacks against the Kurds and other minorities.
There were mass deportations, executions, and chemical-weapons attacks—which is where al-Majid got the nickname Chemical Ali. Over 100,000 people were killed and millions displaced.
Where is my Sister?

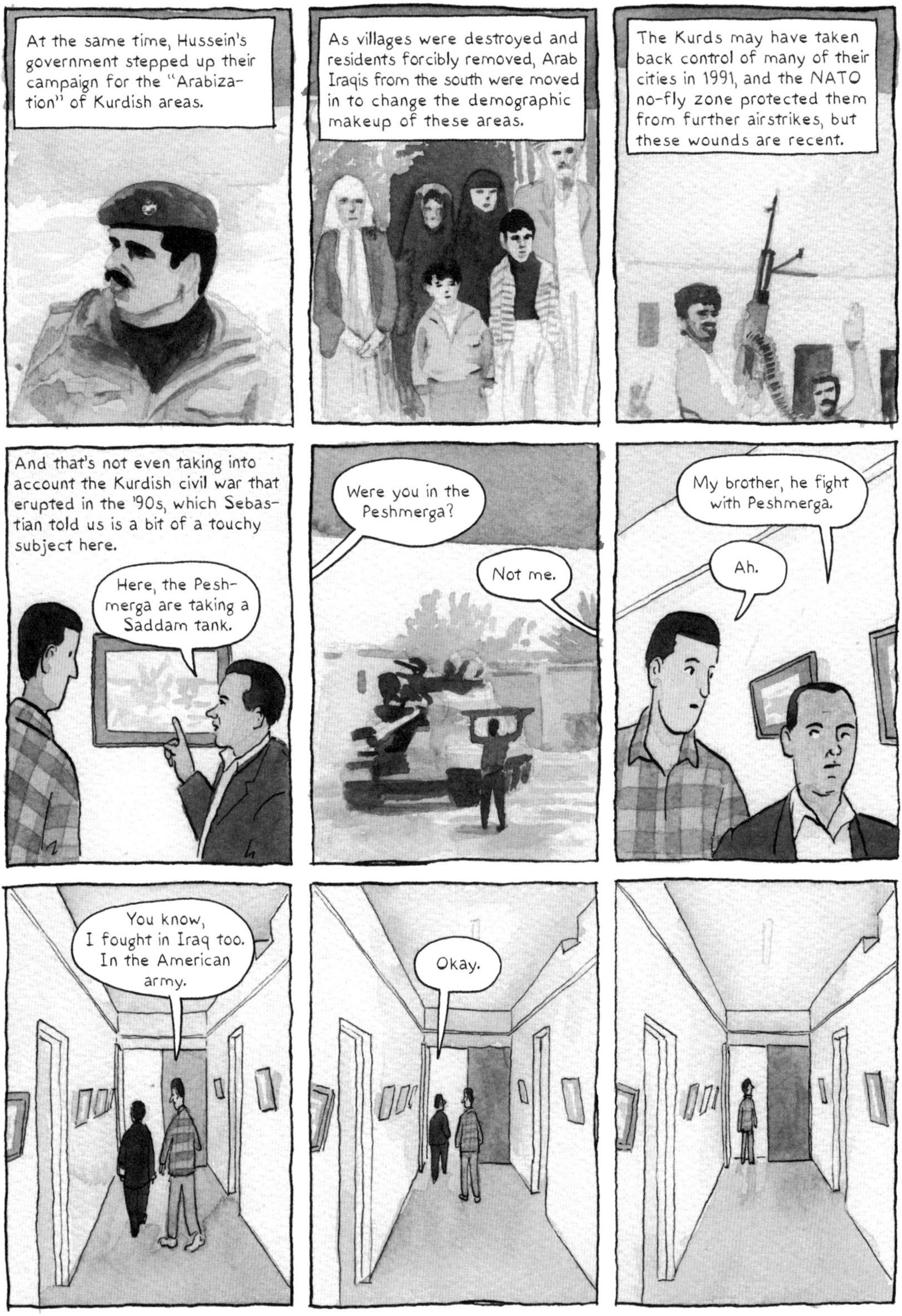
At the same time, Hussein's government stepped up their campaign for the "Arabization" of Kurdish areas.
As villages were destroyed and residents forcibly removed, Arab Iraqis from the south were moved in to change the demographic makeup of these areas.
The Kurds may have taken back control of many of their cities in 1991, and the NATO no-fly zone protected them from further airstrikes, but these wounds are recent.
And that's not even taking into account the Kurdish civil war that erupted in the '90s, which Sebastian told us is a bit of a touchy subject here.
Here, the Peshmerga are taking a Saddam tank.
Were you in the Peshmerga?
Not me.
My brother, he fight with Peshmerga.
Ah.
You know, I fought in Iraq too. In the American army.
Okay.

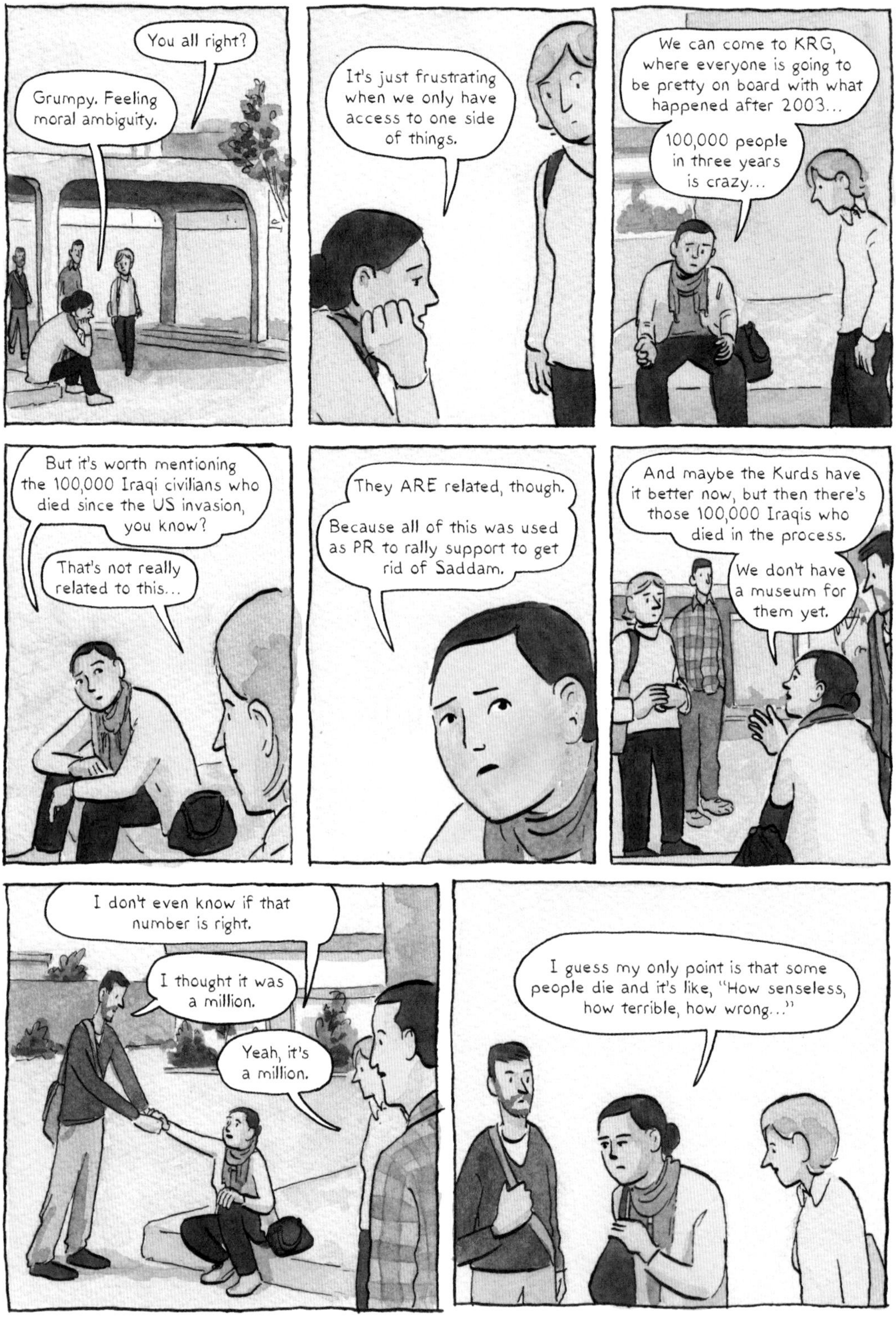
You all right?
Grumpy. Feeling moral ambiguity.
It's just frustrating when we only have access to one side of things.
We can come to KRG, where everyone is going to be pretty on board with what happened after 2003...
100,000 people in three years is crazy...
But it's worth mentioning the 100,000 Iraqi civilians who died since the US invasion, you know?
That's not really related to this...
They ARE related, though.
Because all of this was used as PR to rally support to get rid of Saddam.
And maybe the Kurds have it better now, but then there's those 100,000 Iraqis who died in the process.
We don't have a museum for them yet.
I don't even know if that number is right.
I thought it was a million.
Yeah, it's a million.
I guess my only point is that some people die and it's like, "How senseless, how terrible, how wrong..."

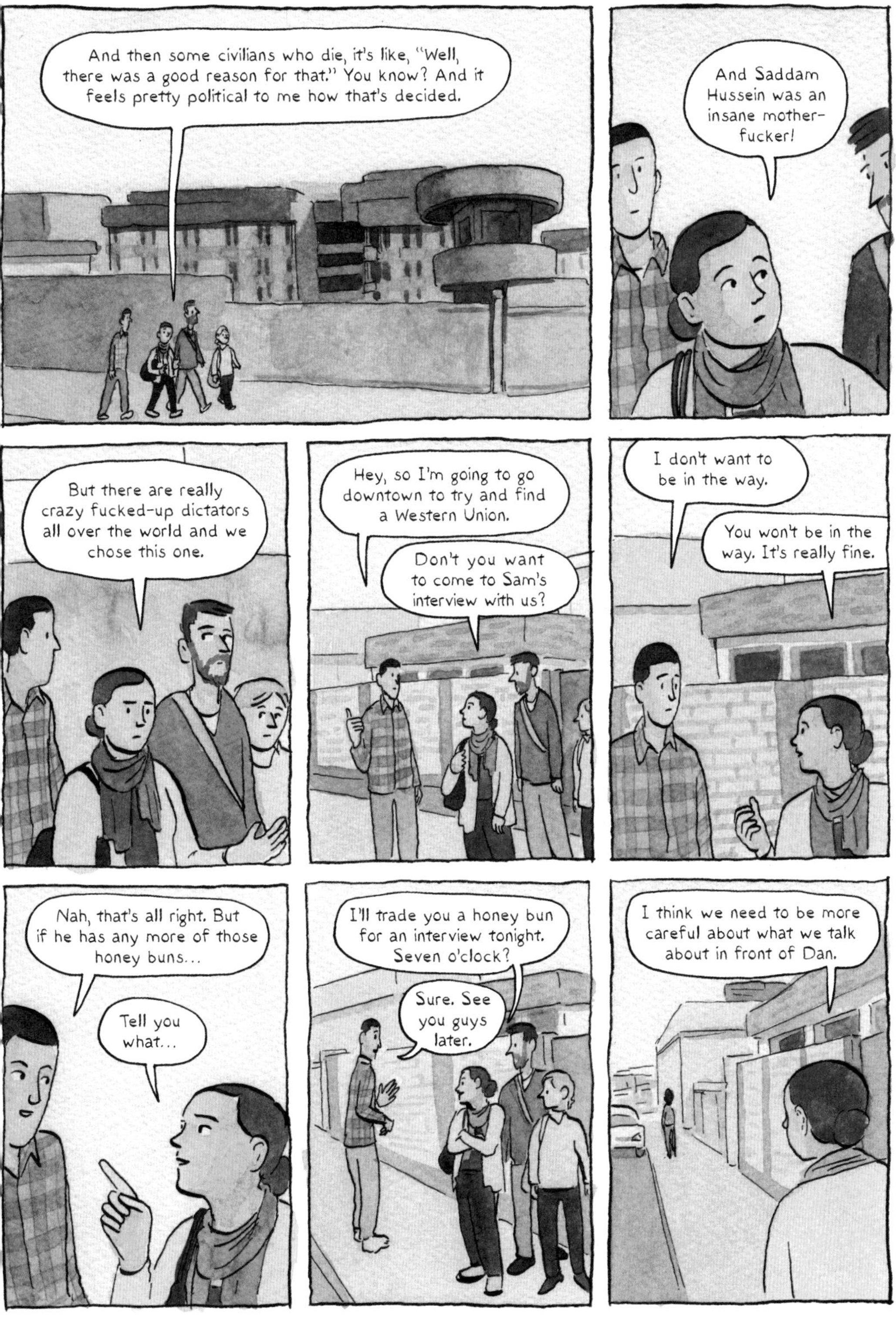
And then some civilians who die, it's like, "Well, there was a good reason for that." You know? And it feels pretty political to me how that's decided.
And Saddam Hussein was an insane mother-fucker!
But there are really crazy fucked-up dictators all over the world and we chose this one.
Hey, so I'm going to go downtown to try and find a Western Union.
Don't you want to come to Sam's interview with us?
I don't want to be in the way.
You won't be in the way. It's really fine.
Nah, that's all right. But if he has any more of those honey buns...
Tell you what...
I'll trade you a honey bun for an interview tonight. Seven o'clock?
Sure. See you guys later.
I think we need to be more careful about what we talk about in front of Dan.

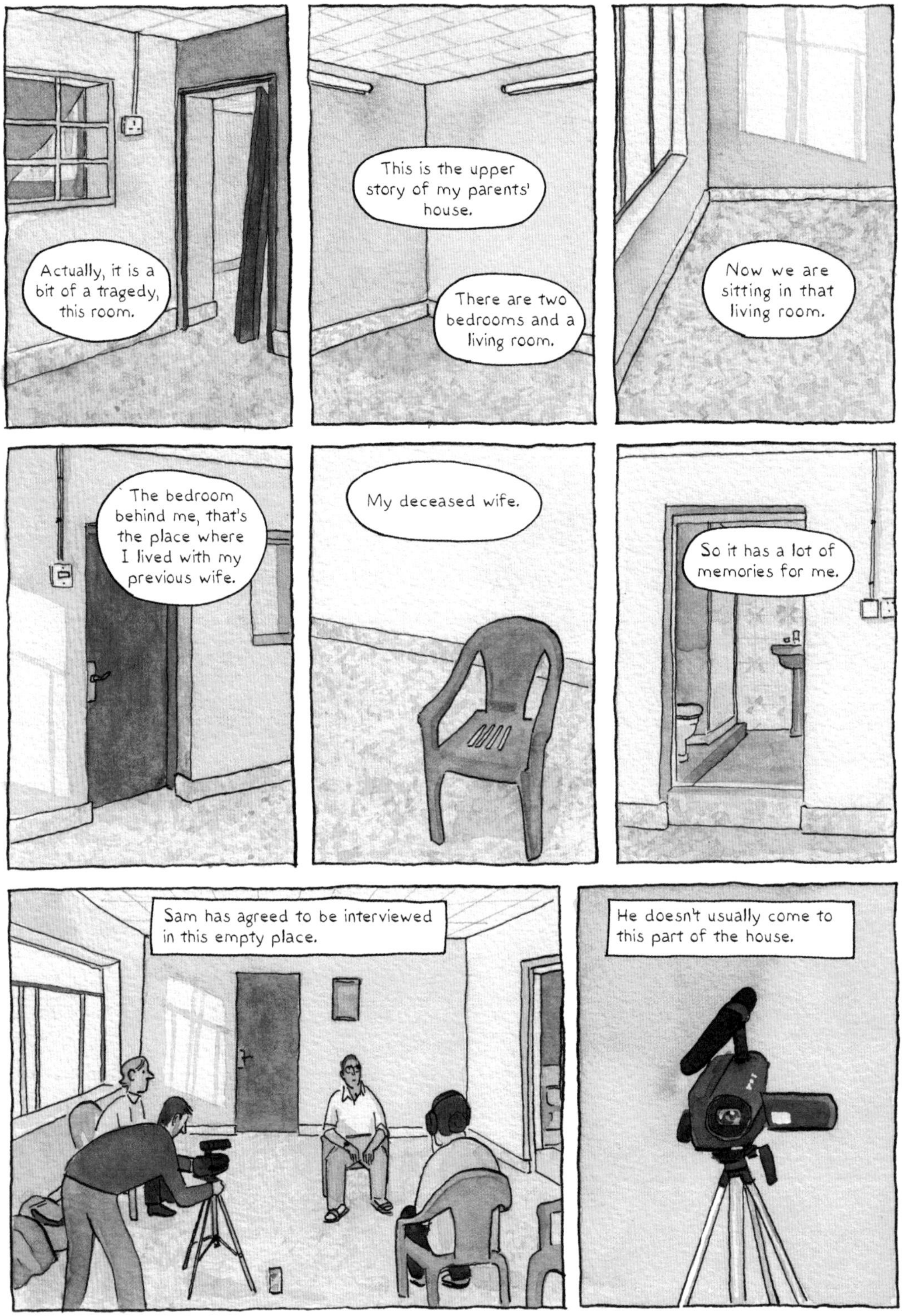
Actually, it is a bit of a tragedy, this room.
This is the upper story of my parents' house.
There are two bedrooms and a living room.
Now we are sitting in that living room.
The bedroom behind me, that's the place where I lived with my previous wife.
My deceased wife.
So it has a lot of memories for me.
Sam has agreed to be interviewed in this empty place.
He doesn't usually come to this part of the house.

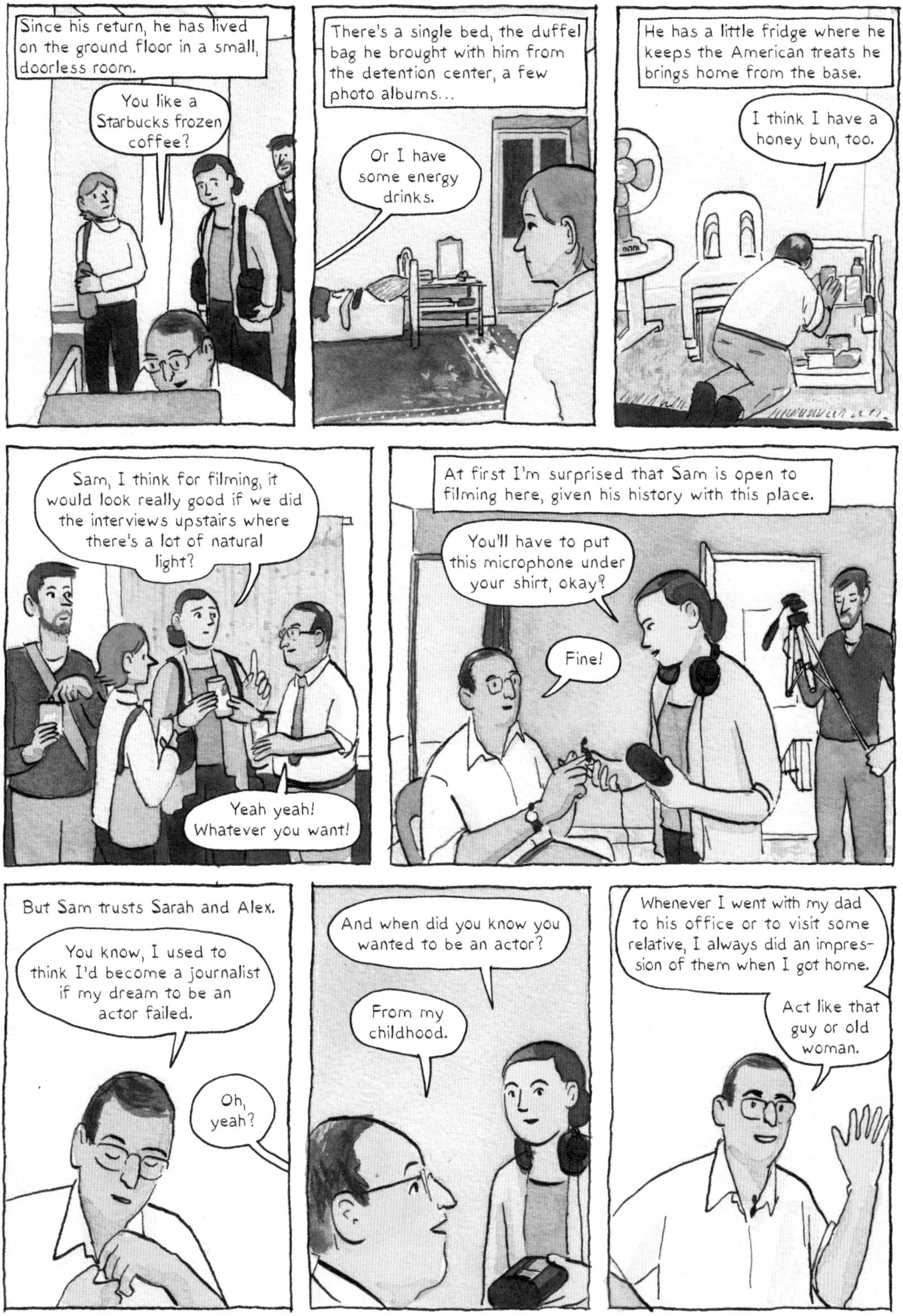
Since his return, he has lived on the ground floor in a small, doorless room.
You like a Starbucks frozen coffee?
There's a single bed, the duffel bag he brought with him from the detention center, a few photo albums...
Or I have some energy drinks.
He has a little fridge where he keeps the American treats he brings home from the base.
I think I have a honey bun, too.
Sam, I think for filming, it would look really good if we did the interviews upstairs where there's a lot of natural light?
Yeah yeah! Whatever you want!
At first I'm surprised that Sam is open to filming here, given his history with this place.
You'll have to put this microphone under your shirt, okay?
Fine!
But Sam trusts Sarah and Alex.
You know, I used to think I'd become a journalist if my dream to be an actor failed.
Oh, yeah?
And when did you know you wanted to be an actor?
From my childhood.
Whenever I went with my dad to his office or to visit some relative, I always did an impression of them when I got home.
Act like that guy or old woman.

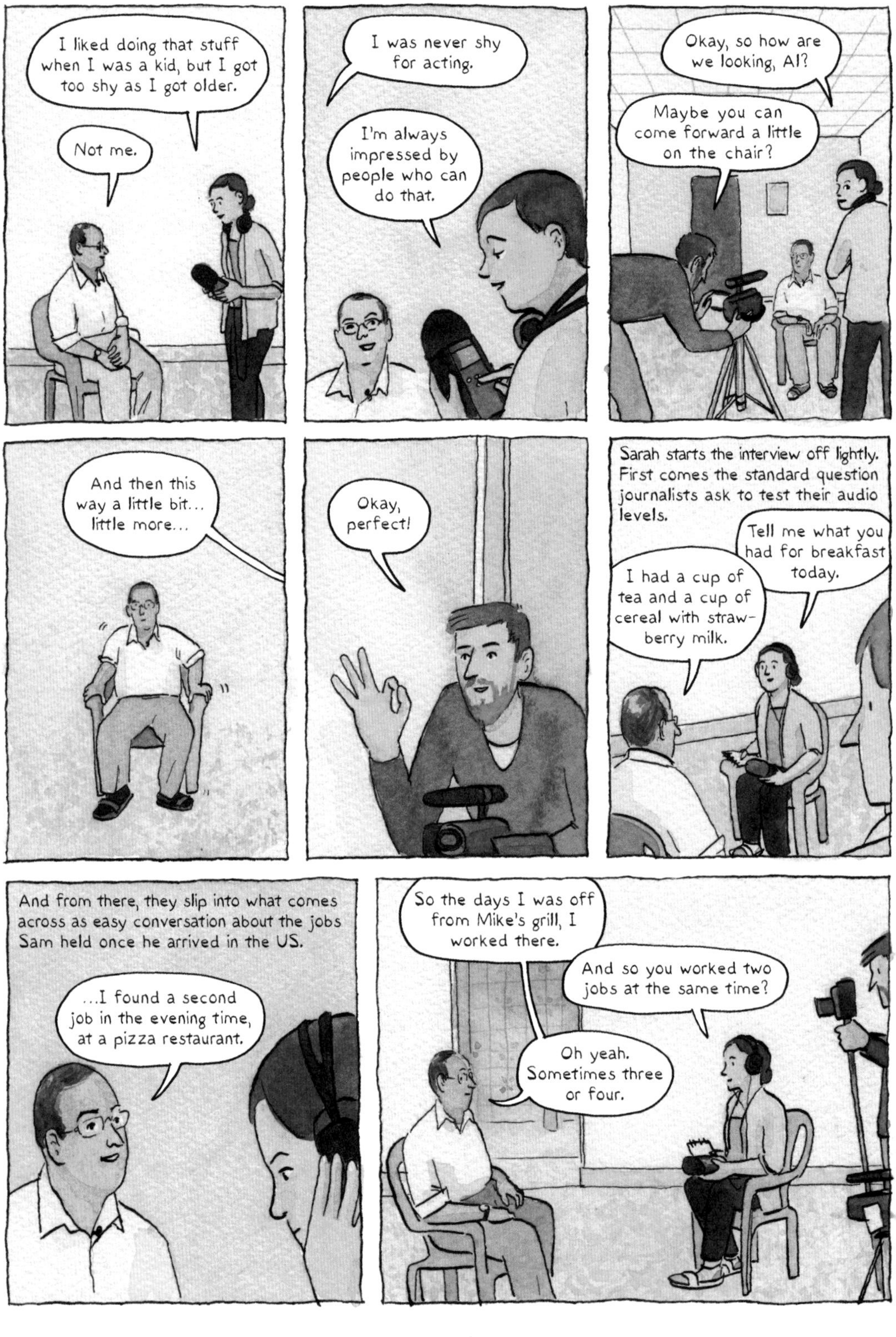
I liked doing that stuff when I was a kid, but I got too shy as I got older.
Not me.
I was never shy for acting.
I'm always impressed by people who can do that.
Okay, so how are we looking, Al?
Maybe you can come forward a little on the chair?
And then this way a little bit... little more...
Okay, perfect!
Sarah starts the interview off lightly. First comes the standard question journalists ask to test their audio levels.
Tell me what you had for breakfast today.
I had a cup of tea and a cup of cereal with straw-berry milk.
And from there, they slip into what comes across as easy conversation about the jobs Sam held once he arrived in the US.
...I found a second job in the evening time, at a pizza restaurant.
So the days I was off from Mike's grill, I worked there.
And so you worked two jobs at the same time?
Oh yeah. Sometimes three or four.

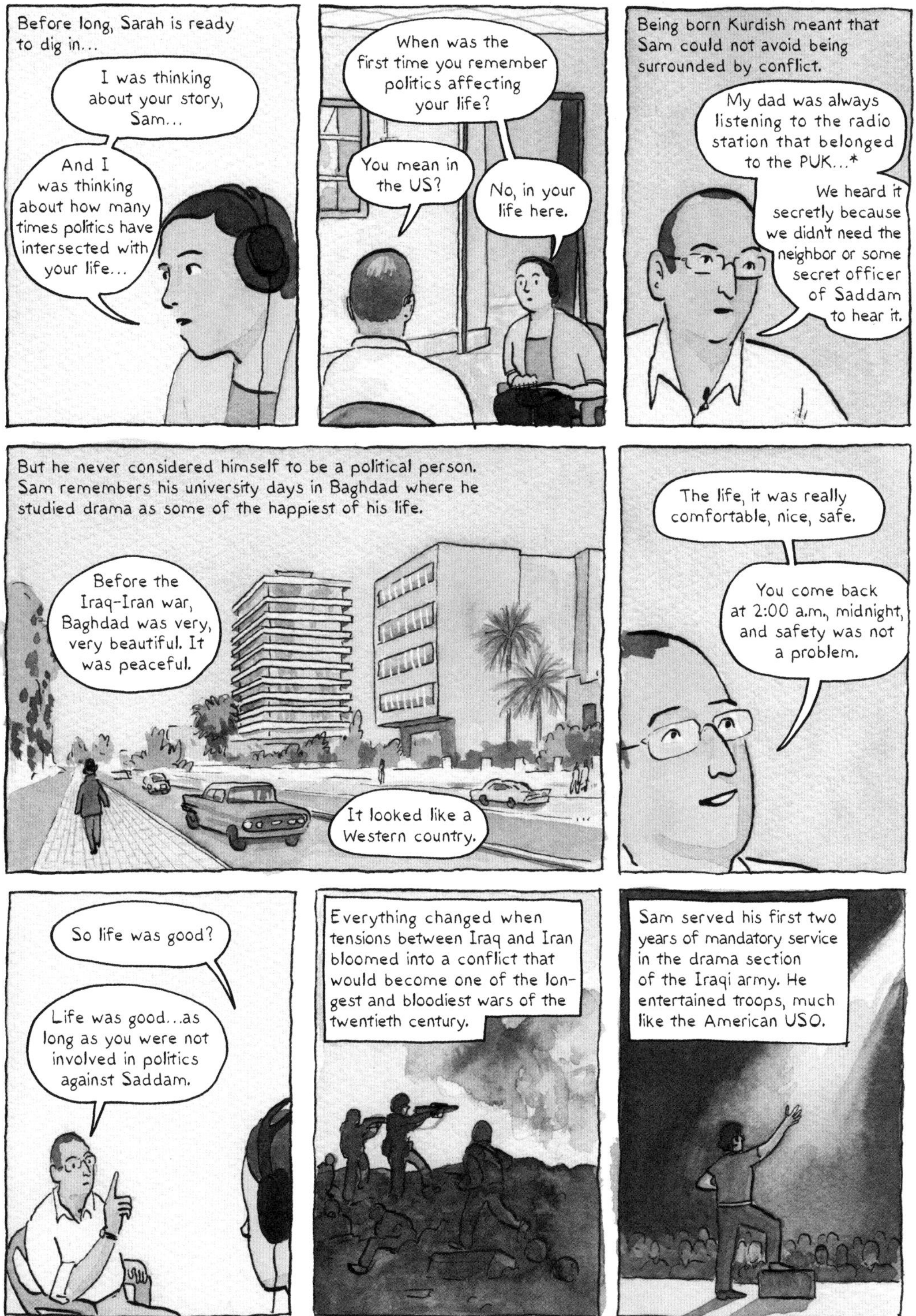
Before long, Sarah is ready to dig in...
I was thinking about your story, Sam...
And I was thinking about how many times politics have intersected with your life...
When was the first time you remember politics affecting your life?
You mean in the US?
No, in your life here.
Being born Kurdish meant that Sam could not avoid being surrounded by conflict.
My dad was always listening to the radio station that belonged to the PUK...*
We heard it secretly because we didn't need the neighbor or some secret officer of Saddam to hear it.
But he never considered himself to be a political person. Sam remembers his university days in Baghdad where he studied drama as some of the happiest of his life.
Before the Iraq-Iran war, Baghdad was very, very beautiful. It was peaceful.
It looked like a Western country.
The life, it was really comfortable, nice, safe.
You come back at 2:00 a.m., midnight, and safety was not a problem.
So life was good?
Life was good...as long as you were not involved in politics against Saddam.
Everything changed when tensions between Iraq and Iran bloomed into a conflict that would become one of the longest and bloodiest wars of the twentieth century.
Sam served his first two years of mandatory service in the drama section of the Iraqi army. He entertained troops, much like the American USO.

*One of two Kurdish politial parties

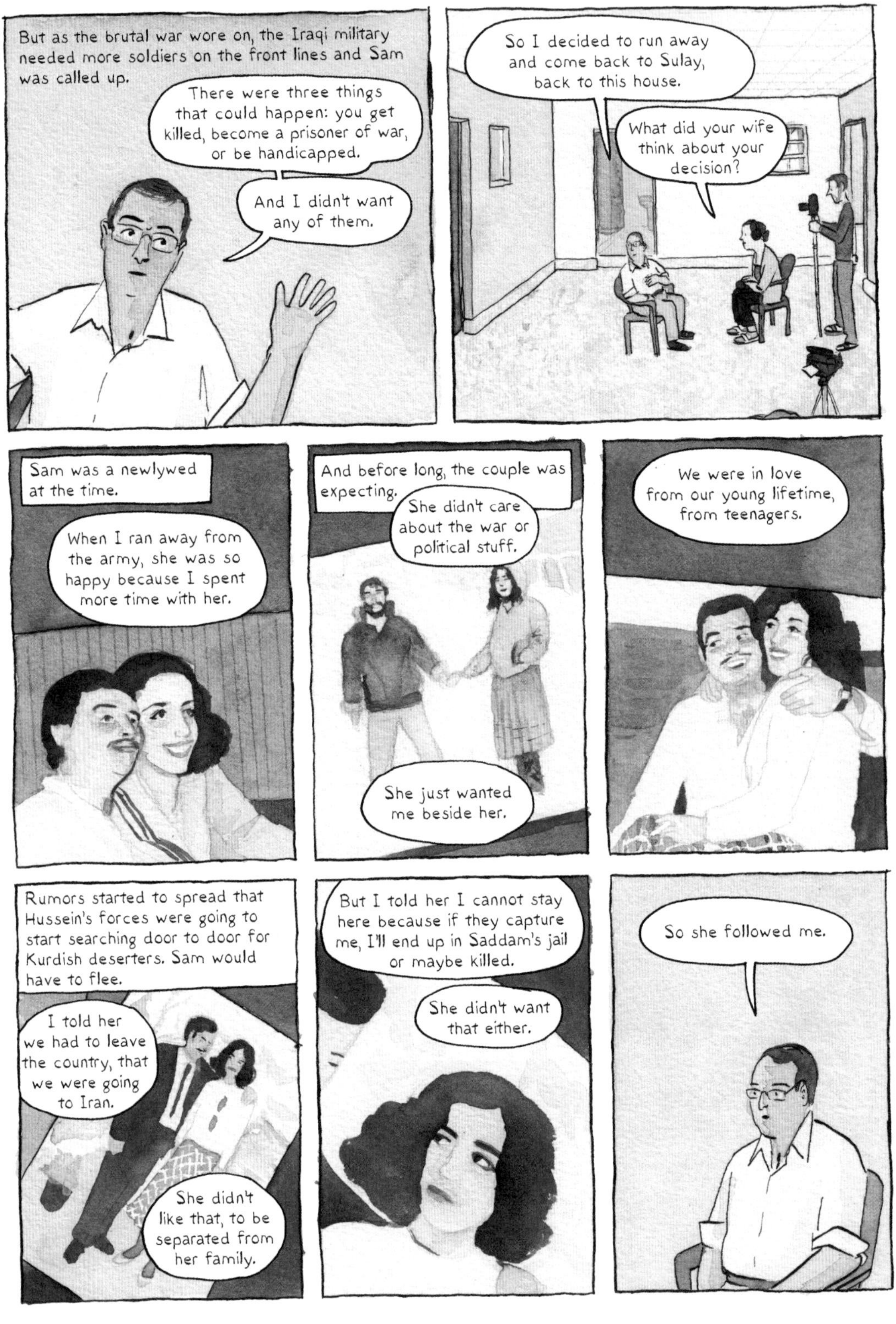
But as the brutal war wore on, the Iraqi military needed more soldiers on the front lines and Sam was called up.
There were three things that could happen: you get killed, become a prisoner of war, or be handicapped.
And I didn't want any of them.
So I decided to run away and come back to Sulay, back to this house.
What did your wife think about your decision?
Sam was a newlywed at the time.
When I ran away from the army, she was so happy because I spent more time with her.
And before long, the couple was expecting.
She didn't care about the war or political stuff.
She just wanted me beside her.
We were in love from our young lifetime, from teenagers.
Rumors started to spread that Hussein's forces were going to start searching door to door for Kurdish deserters. Sam would have to flee.
I told her we had to leave the country, that we were going to Iran.
She didn't like that, to be separated from her family.
But I told her I cannot stay here because if they capture me, I'll end up in Saddam's jail or maybe killed.
She didn't want that either.
So she followed me.

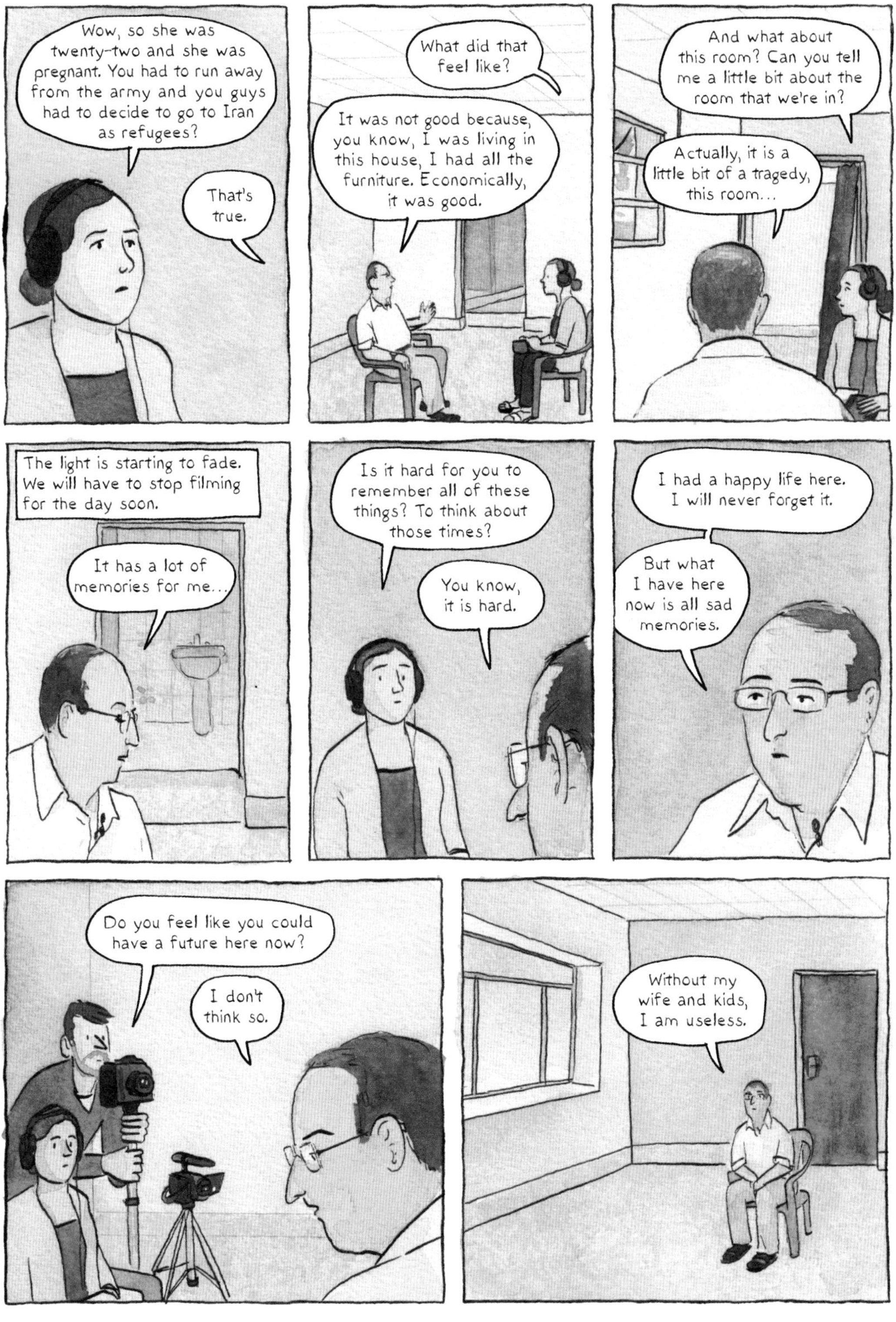
Wow, so she was twenty-two and she was pregnant. You had to run away from the army and you guys had to decide to go to Iran as refugees?
That's true.
What did that feel like?
It was not good because, you know, I was living in this house, I had all the furniture. Economically, it was good.
And what about this room? Can you tell me a little bit about the room that we're in?
Actually, it is a little bit of a tragedy, this room...
The light is starting to fade. We will have to stop filming for the day soon.
It has a lot of memories for me...
Is it hard for you to remember all of these things? To think about those times?
You know, it is hard.
I had a happy life here. I will never forget it.
But what I have here now is all sad memories.
Do you feel like you could have a future here now?
I don't think so.
Without my wife and kids, I am useless.

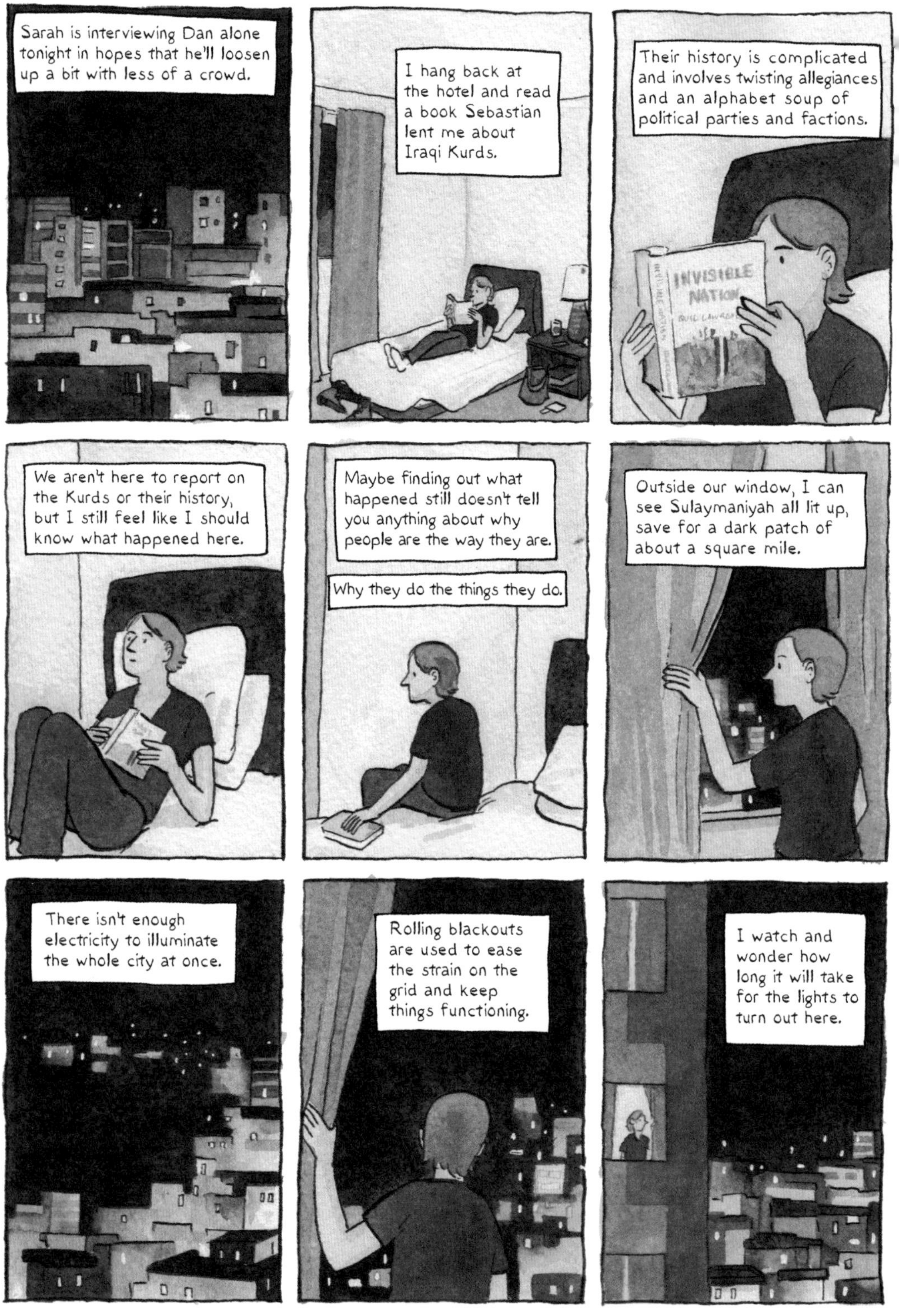
Sarah is interviewing Dan alone tonight in hopes that he'll loosen up a bit with less of a crowd.
I hang back at the hotel and read a book Sebastian lent me about Iraqi Kurds.
Their history is complicated and involves twisting allegiances and an alphabet soup of political parties and factions.
INVISIBLE NATION
We aren't here to report on the Kurds or their history, but I still feel like I should know what happened here.
Maybe finding out what happened still doesn't tell you anything about why people are the way they are.
Why they do the things they do.
Outside our window, I can see Sulaymaniyah all lit up, save for a dark patch of about a square mile.
There isn't enough electricity to illuminate the whole city at once.
Rolling blackouts are used to ease the strain on the grid and keep things functioning.
I watch and wonder how long it will take for the lights to turn out here.

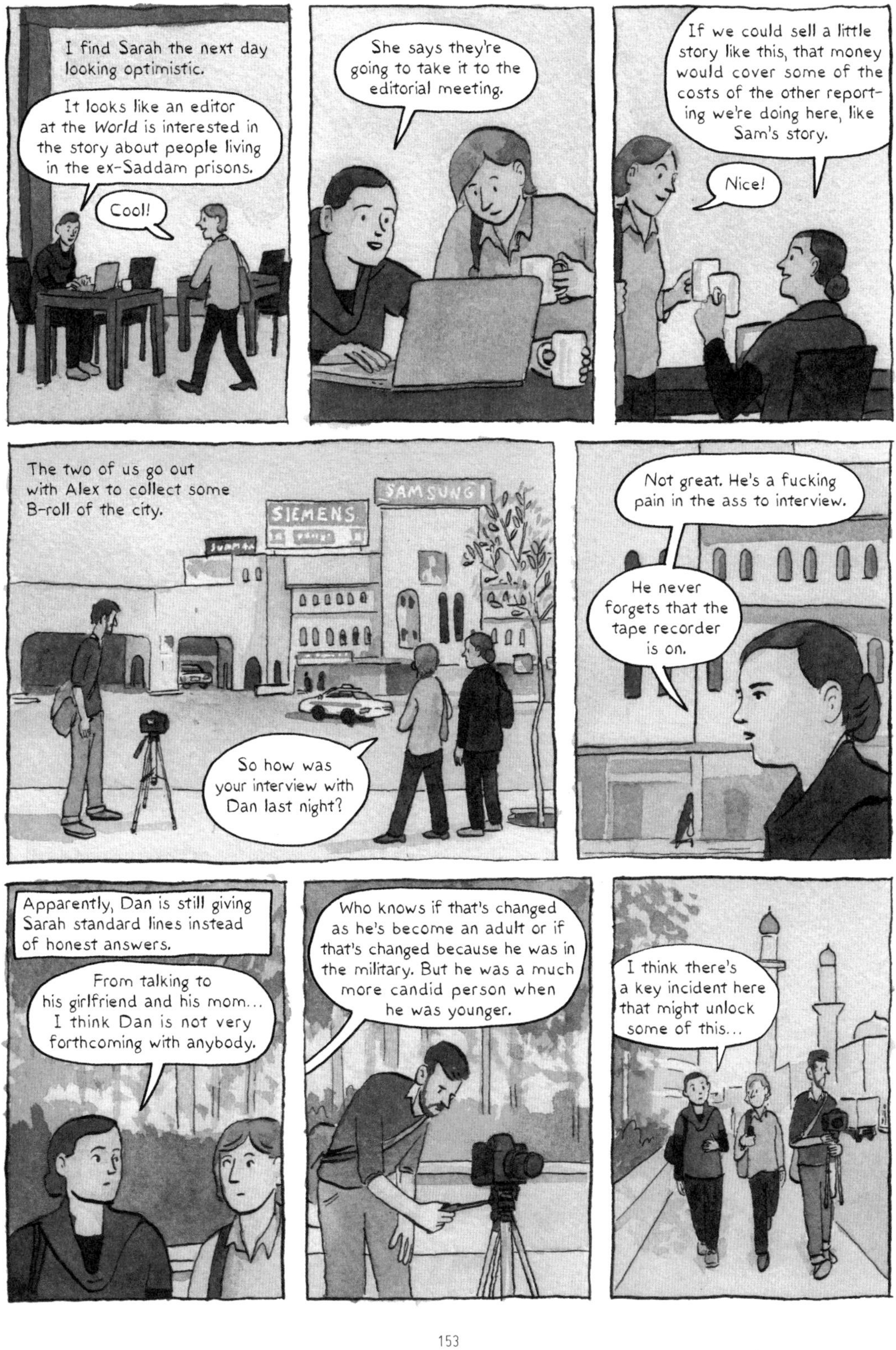
I find Sarah the next day looking optimistic.
It looks like an editor at the *World* is interested in the story about people living in the ex-Saddam prisons.
Cool!
She says they're going to take it to the editorial meeting.
If we could sell a little story like this, that money would cover some of the costs of the other reporting we're doing here, like Sam's story.
Nice!
The two of us go out with Alex to collect some B-roll of the city.
SIEMENS
SAMSUNG
So how was your interview with Dan last night?
Not great. He's a fucking pain in the ass to interview.
He never forgets that the tape recorder is on.
Apparently, Dan is still giving Sarah standard lines instead of honest answers.
From talking to his girlfriend and his mom... I think Dan is not very forthcoming with anybody.
Who knows if that's changed as he's become an adult or if that's changed because he was in the military. But he was a much more candid person when he was younger.
I think there's a key incident here that might unlock some of this...

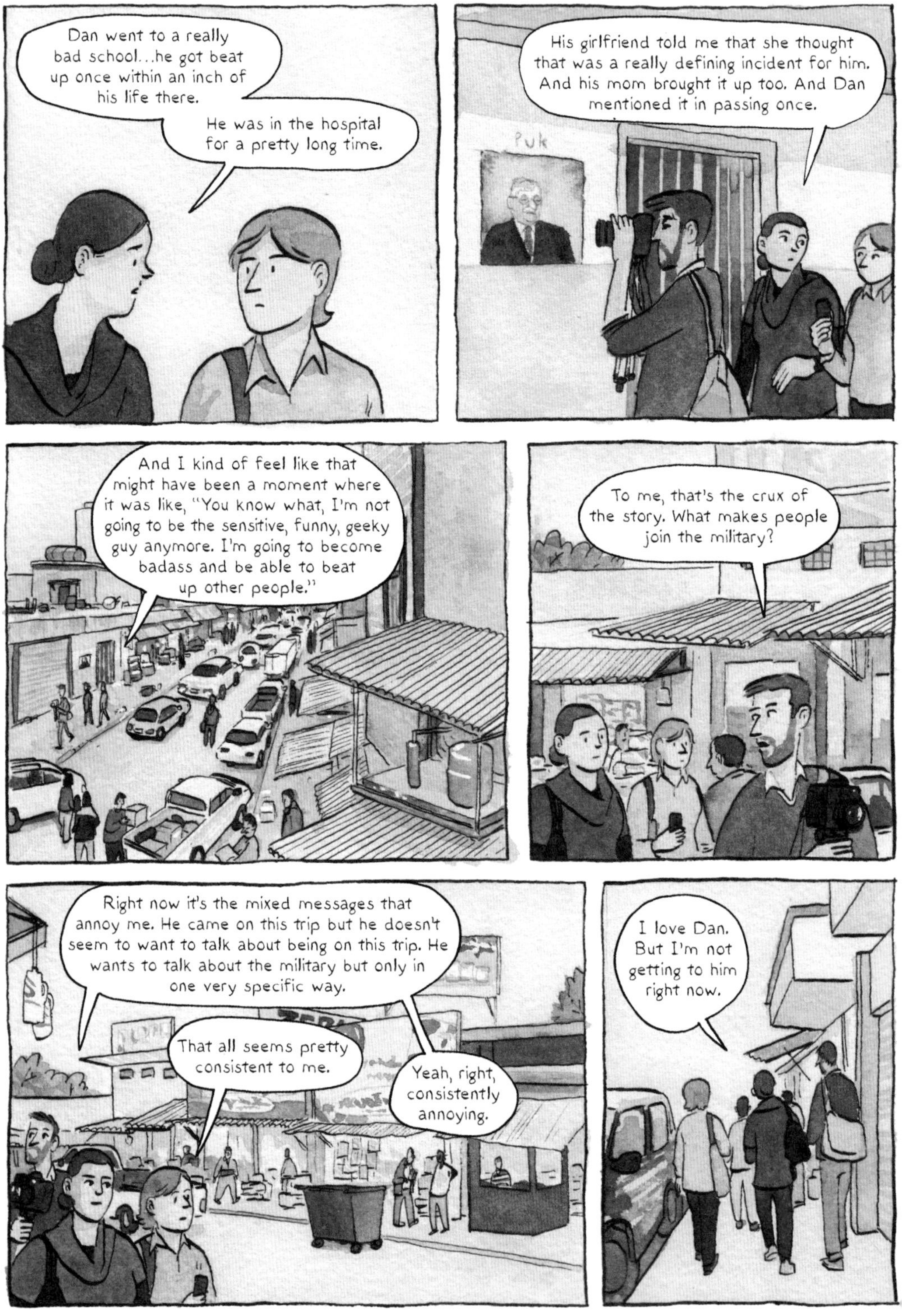
Dan went to a really bad school...he got beat up once within an inch of his life there.
He was in the hospital for a pretty long time.
Puk
His girlfriend told me that she thought that was a really defining incident for him. And his mom brought it up too. And Dan mentioned it in passing once.
And I kind of feel like that might have been a moment where it was like, "You know what, I'm not going to be the sensitive, funny, geeky guy anymore. I'm going to become badass and be able to beat up other people."
To me, that's the crux of the story. What makes people join the military?
Right now it's the mixed messages that annoy me. He came on this trip but he doesn't seem to want to talk about being on this trip. He wants to talk about the military but only in one very specific way.
That all seems pretty consistent to me.
Yeah, right, consistently annoying.
I love Dan. But I'm not getting to him right now.

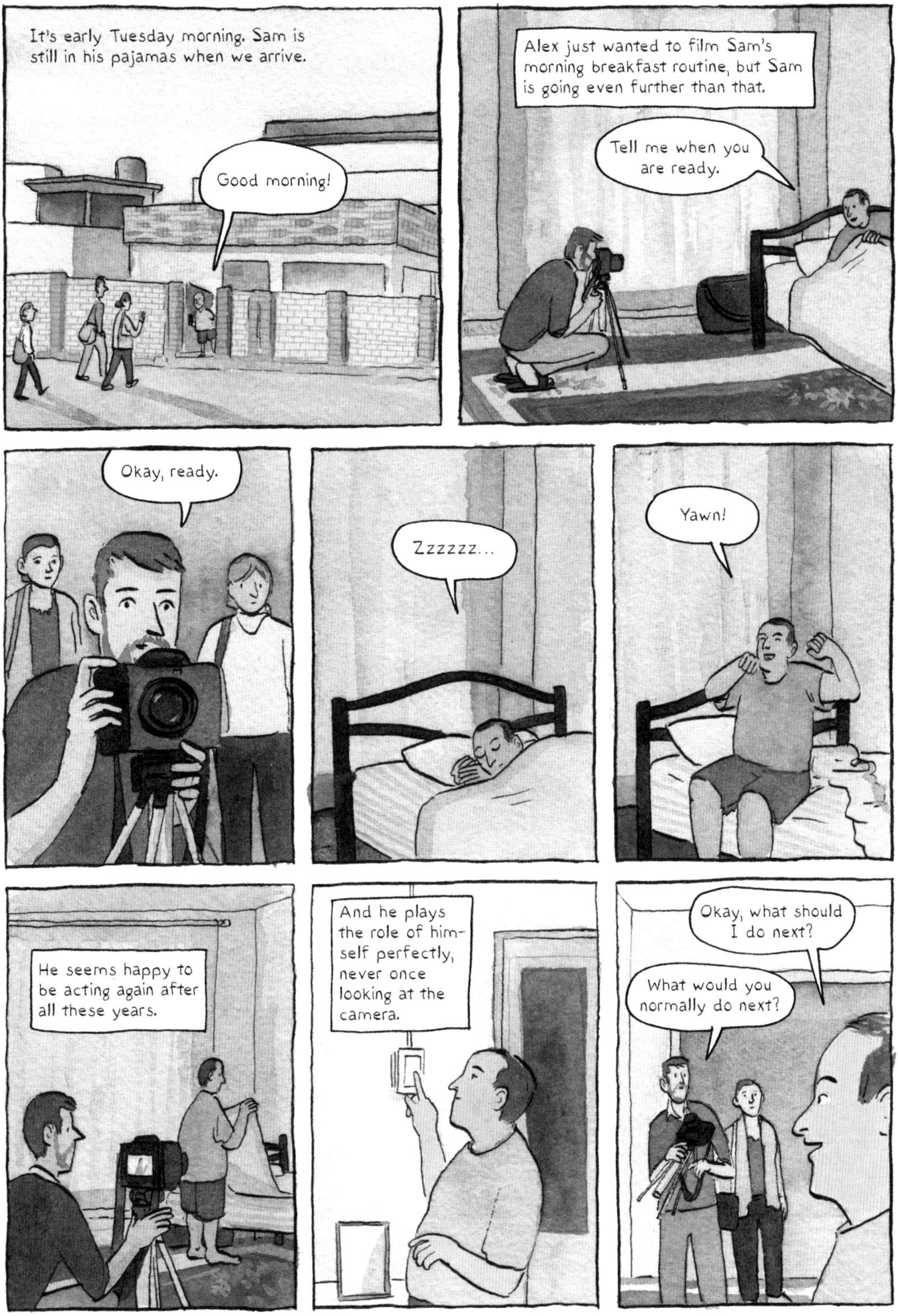
It's early Tuesday morning. Sam is still in his pajamas when we arrive.
Good morning!
Alex just wanted to film Sam's morning breakfast routine, but Sam is going even further than that.
Tell me when you are ready.
Okay, ready.
Zzzzzz...
Yawn!
He seems happy to be acting again after all these years.
And he plays the role of himself perfectly, never once looking at the camera.
Okay, what should I do next?
What would you normally do next?

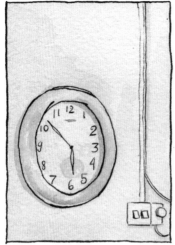

Do you guys usually do this?

We've done stuff like this before.

It gives people a sense of what someone's life is like.

And morning is when people seem to be the most themselves, in a way.

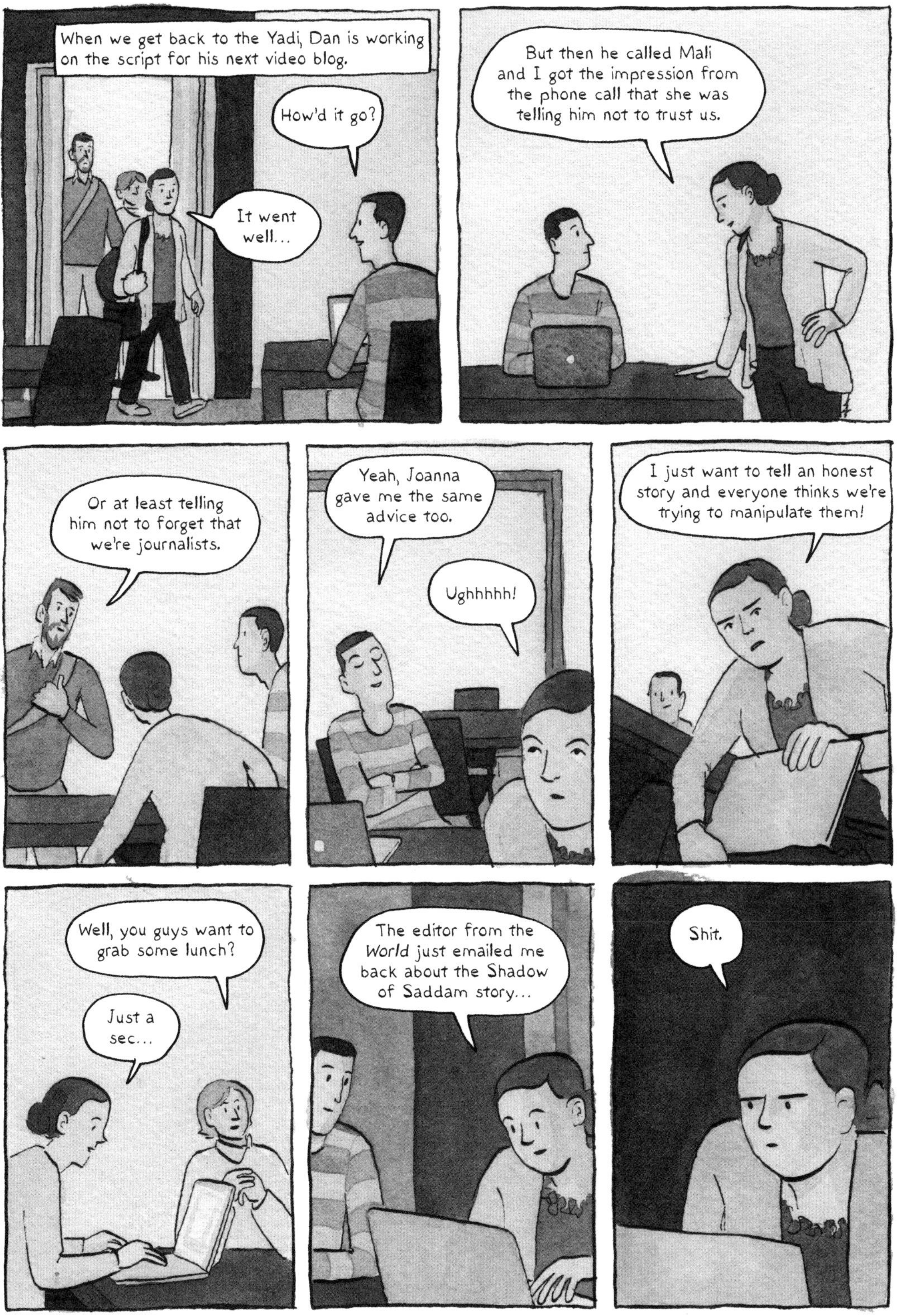
When we get back to the Yadi, Dan is working on the script for his next video blog.
How'd it go?
It went well...
But then he called Mali and I got the impression from the phone call that she was telling him not to trust us.
Or at least telling him not to forget that we're journalists.
Yeah, Joanna gave me the same advice too.
Ughhhhh!
I just want to tell an honest story and everyone thinks we're trying to manipulate them!
Well, you guys want to grab some lunch?
Just a sec...
The editor from the *World* just emailed me back about the Shadow of Saddam story...
Shit.

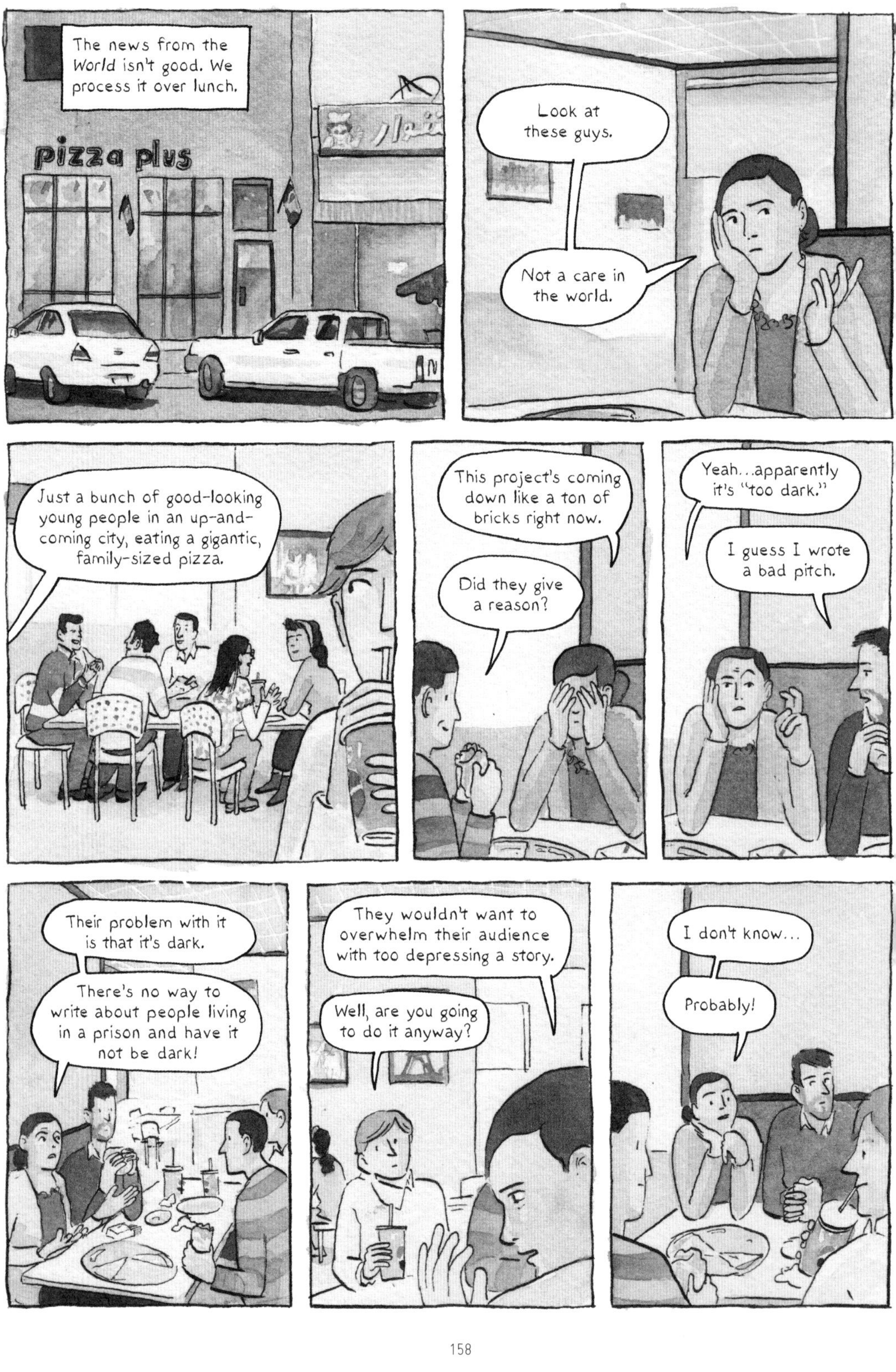
The news from the *World* isn't good. We process it over lunch.
pizza plus
Look at these guys.
Not a care in the world.
Just a bunch of good-looking young people in an up-and-coming city, eating a gigantic, family-sized pizza.
This project's coming down like a ton of bricks right now.
Did they give a reason?
Yeah...apparently it's "too dark."
I guess I wrote a bad pitch.
Their problem with it is that it's dark.
There's no way to write about people living in a prison and have it not be dark!
They wouldn't want to overwhelm their audience with too depressing a story.
Well, are you going to do it anyway?
I don't know...
Probably!

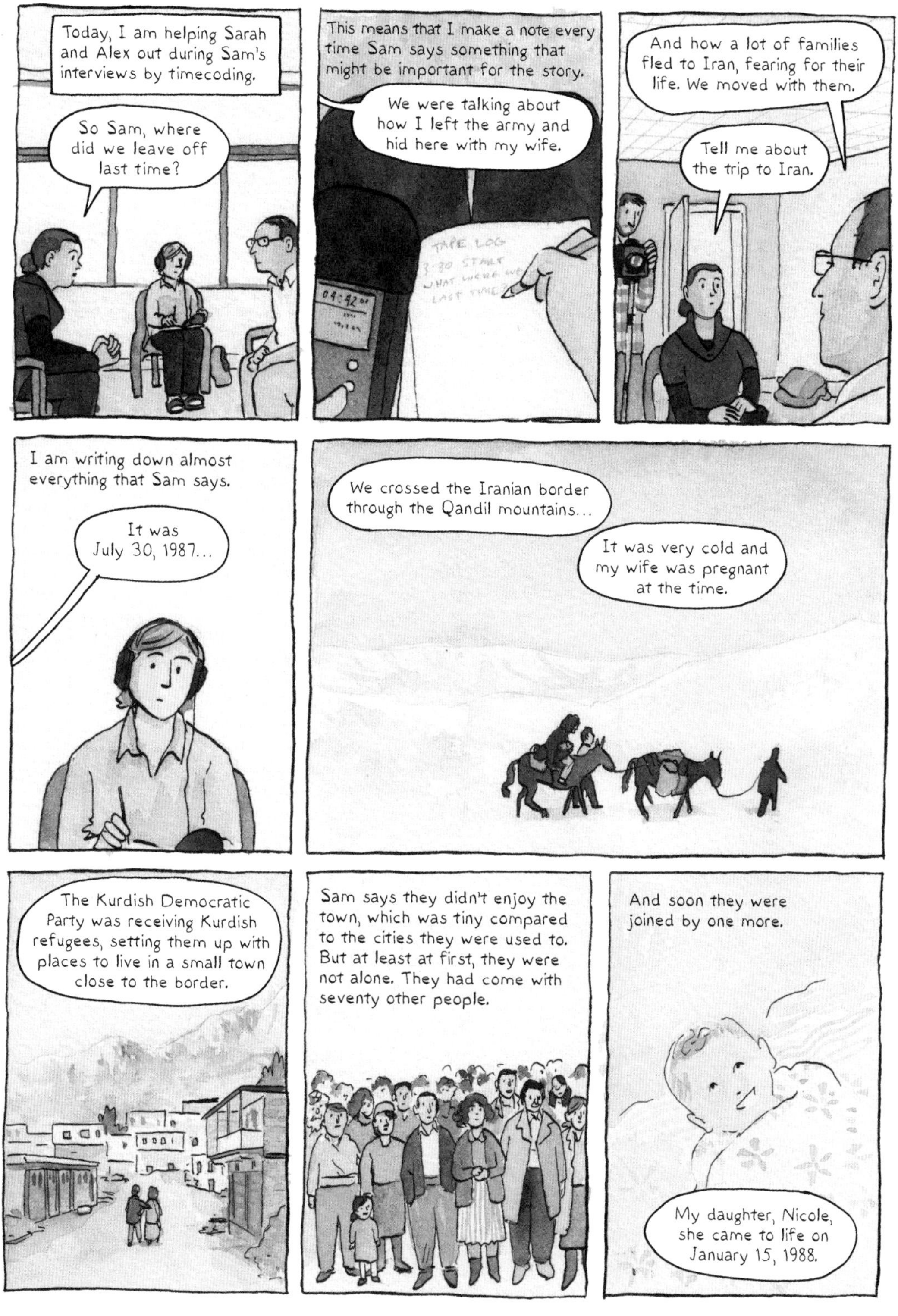

Today, I am helping Sarah and Alex out during Sam's interviews by timecoding.
So Sam, where did we leave off last time?
This means that I make a note every time Sam says something that might be important for the story.
We were talking about how I left the army and hid here with my wife.
And how a lot of families fled to Iran, fearing for their life. We moved with them.
Tell me about the trip to Iran.
I am writing down almost everything that Sam says.
It was July 30, 1987...
We crossed the Iranian border through the Qandil mountains...
It was very cold and my wife was pregnant at the time.
The Kurdish Democratic Party was receiving Kurdish refugees, setting them up with places to live in a small town close to the border.
Sam says they didn't enjoy the town, which was tiny compared to the cities they were used to. But at least at first, they were not alone. They had come with seventy other people.
And soon they were joined by one more.
My daughter, Nicole, she came to life on January 15, 1988.

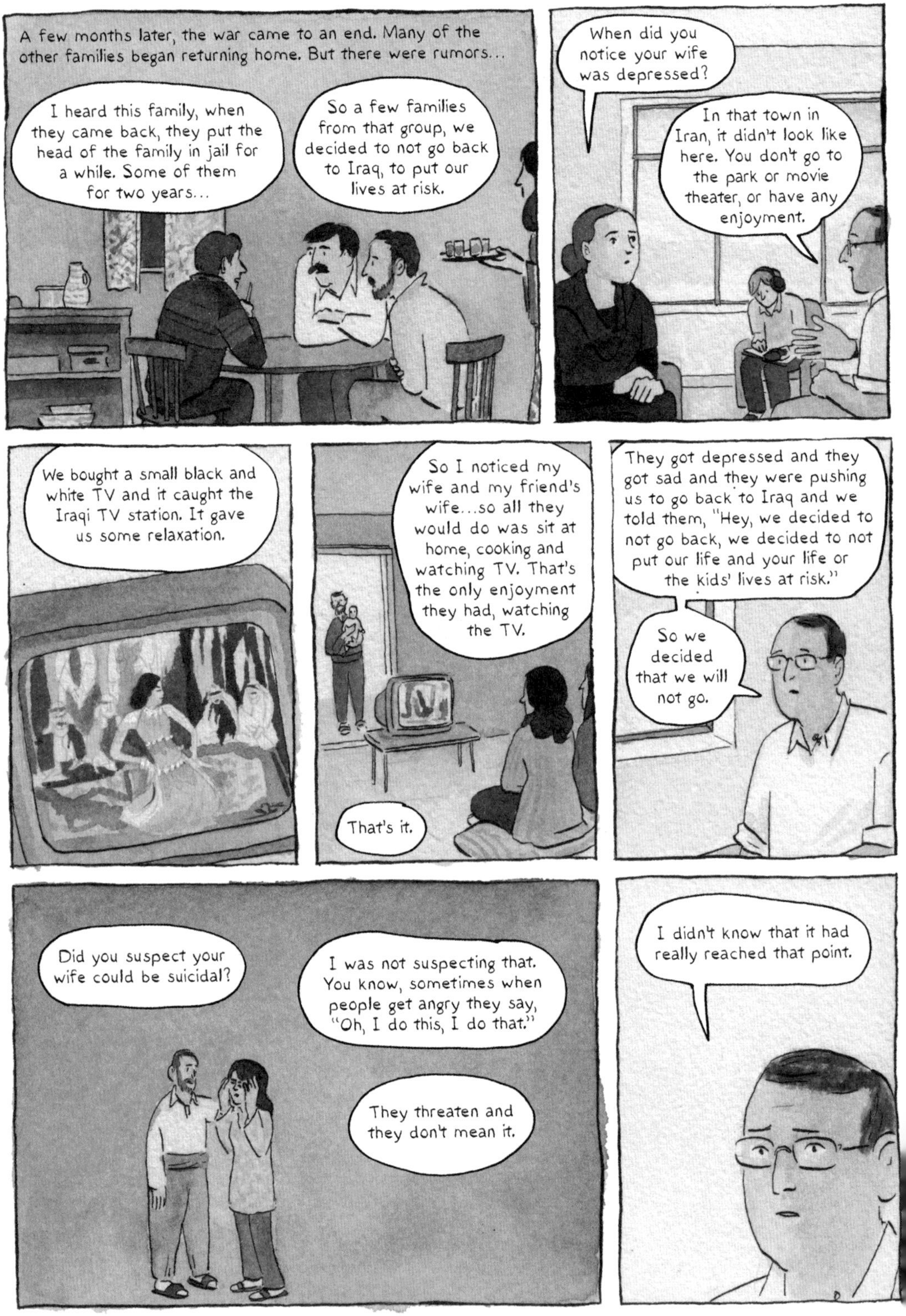

A few months later, the war came to an end. Many of the other families began returning home. But there were rumors...
I heard this family, when they came back, they put the head of the family in jail for a while. Some of them for two years...
So a few families from that group, we decided to not go back to Iraq, to put our lives at risk.
When did you notice your wife was depressed?
In that town in Iran, it didn't look like here. You don't go to the park or movie theater, or have any enjoyment.
We bought a small black and white TV and it caught the Iraqi TV station. It gave us some relaxation.
So I noticed my wife and my friend's wife...so all they would do was sit at home, cooking and watching TV. That's the only enjoyment they had, watching the TV.
That's it.
They got depressed and they got sad and they were pushing us to go back to Iraq and we told them, "Hey, we decided to not go back, we decided to not put our life and your life or the kids' lives at risk."
So we decided that we will not go.
Did you suspect your wife could be suicidal?
I was not suspecting that. You know, sometimes when people get angry they say, "Oh, I do this, I do that."
They threaten and they don't mean it.
I didn't know that it had really reached that point.

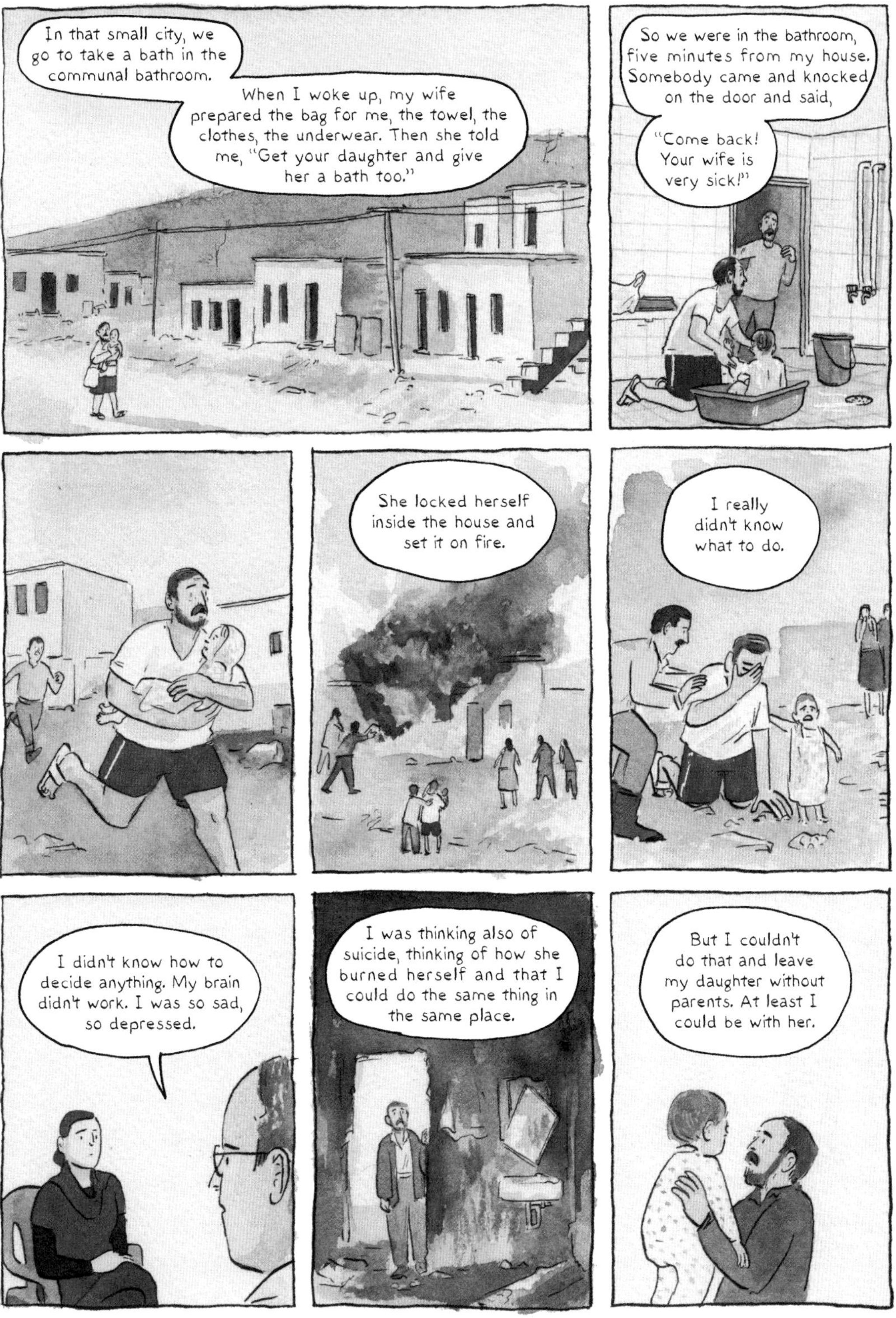
In that small city, we go to take a bath in the communal bathroom.
When I woke up, my wife prepared the bag for me, the towel, the clothes, the underwear. Then she told me, "Get your daughter and give her a bath too."
So we were in the bathroom, five minutes from my house. Somebody came and knocked on the door and said,
"Come back! Your wife is very sick!"
She locked herself inside the house and set it on fire.
I really didn't know what to do.
I didn't know how to decide anything. My brain didn't work. I was so sad, so depressed.
I was thinking also of suicide, thinking of how she burned herself and that I could do the same thing in the same place.
But I couldn't do that and leave my daughter without parents. At least I could be with her.

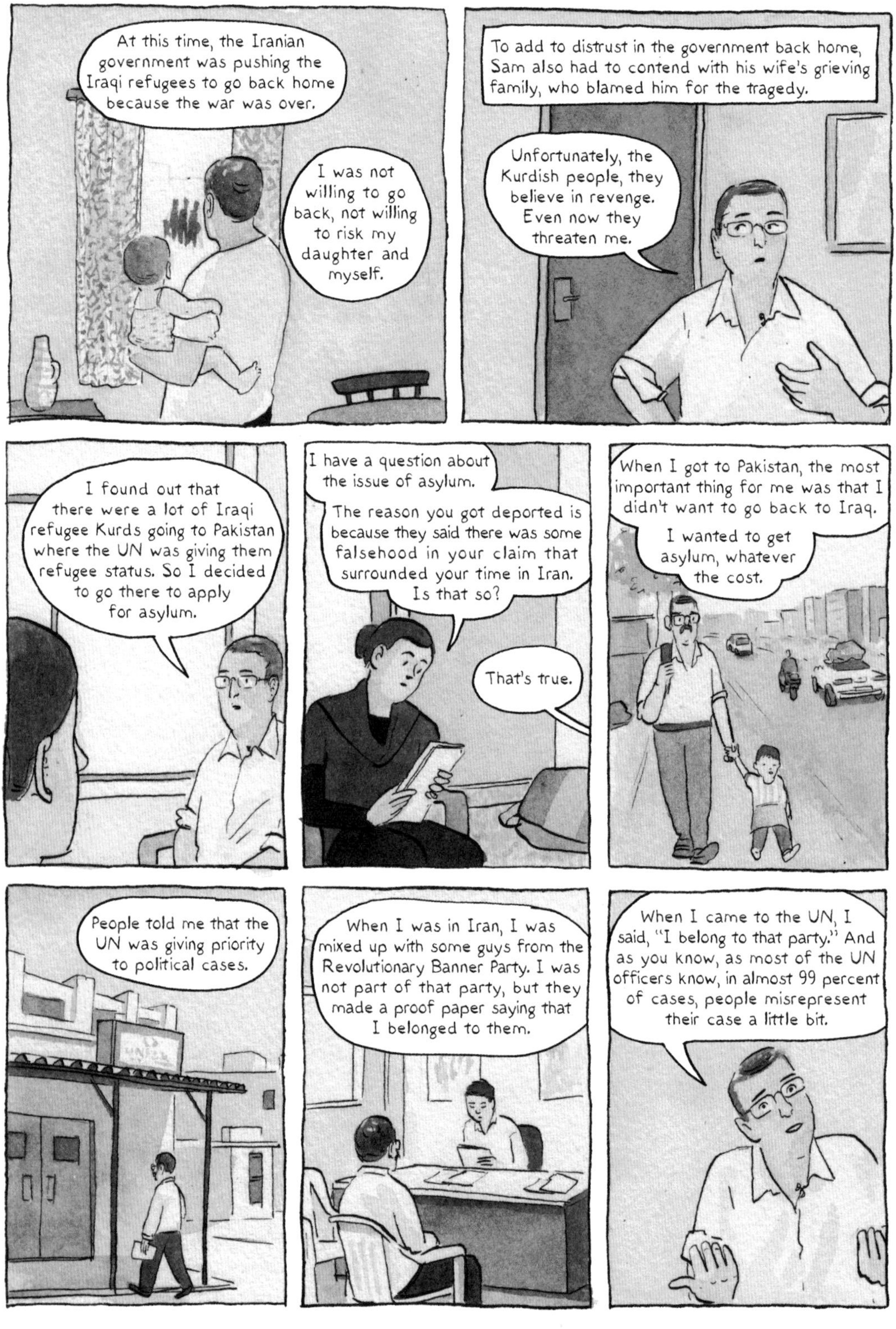
At this time, the Iranian government was pushing the Iraqi refugees to go back home because the war was over.
I was not willing to go back, not willing to risk my daughter and myself.
To add to distrust in the government back home, Sam also had to contend with his wife's grieving family, who blamed him for the tragedy.
Unfortunately, the Kurdish people, they believe in revenge. Even now they threaten me.
I found out that there were a lot of Iraqi refugee Kurds going to Pakistan where the UN was giving them refugee status. So I decided to go there to apply for asylum.
I have a question about the issue of asylum.
The reason you got deported is because they said there was some falsehood in your claim that surrounded your time in Iran. Is that so?
That's true.
When I got to Pakistan, the most important thing for me was that I didn't want to go back to Iraq.
I wanted to get asylum, whatever the cost.
People told me that the UN was giving priority to political cases.
When I was in Iran, I was mixed up with some guys from the Revolutionary Banner Party. I was not part of that party, but they made a proof paper saying that I belonged to them.
When I came to the UN, I said, "I belong to that party." And as you know, as most of the UN officers know, in almost 99 percent of cases, people misrepresent their case a little bit.

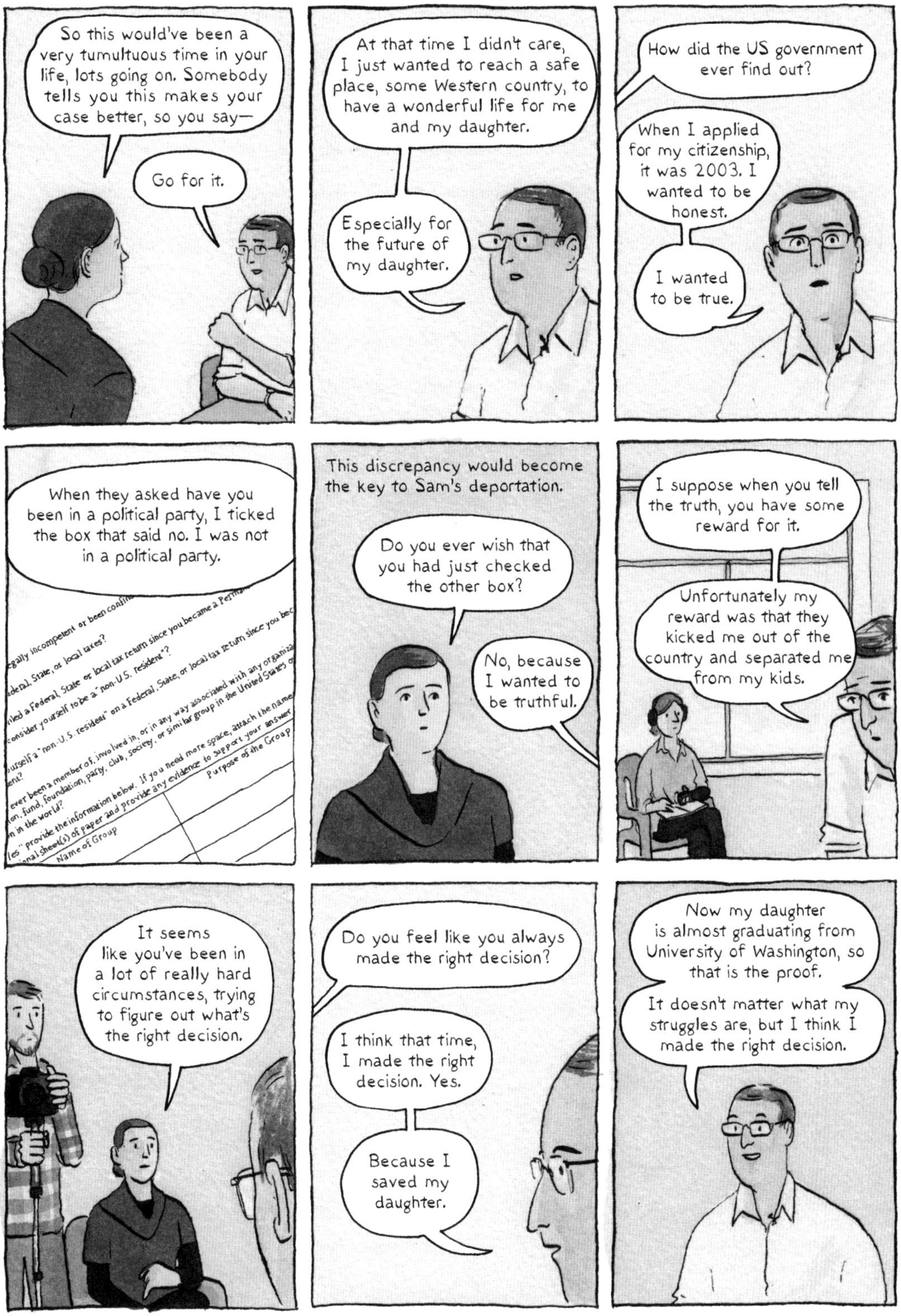
So this would've been a very tumultuous time in your life, lots going on. Somebody tells you this makes your case better, so you say—
Go for it.
At that time I didn't care, I just wanted to reach a safe place, some Western country, to have a wonderful life for me and my daughter.
Especially for the future of my daughter.
How did the US government ever find out?
When I applied for my citizenship, it was 2003. I wanted to be honest.
I wanted to be true.
When they asked have you been in a political party, I ticked the box that said no. I was not in a political party.
Name of Group
Purpose of the Group
This discrepancy would become the key to Sam's deportation.
Do you ever wish that you had just checked the other box?
No, because I wanted to be truthful.
I suppose when you tell the truth, you have some reward for it.
Unfortunately my reward was that they kicked me out of the country and separated me from my kids.
It seems like you've been in a lot of really hard circumstances, trying to figure out what's the right decision.
Do you feel like you always made the right decision?
I think that time, I made the right decision. Yes.
Because I saved my daughter.
Now my daughter is almost graduating from University of Washington, so that is the proof.
It doesn't matter what my struggles are, but I think I made the right decision.

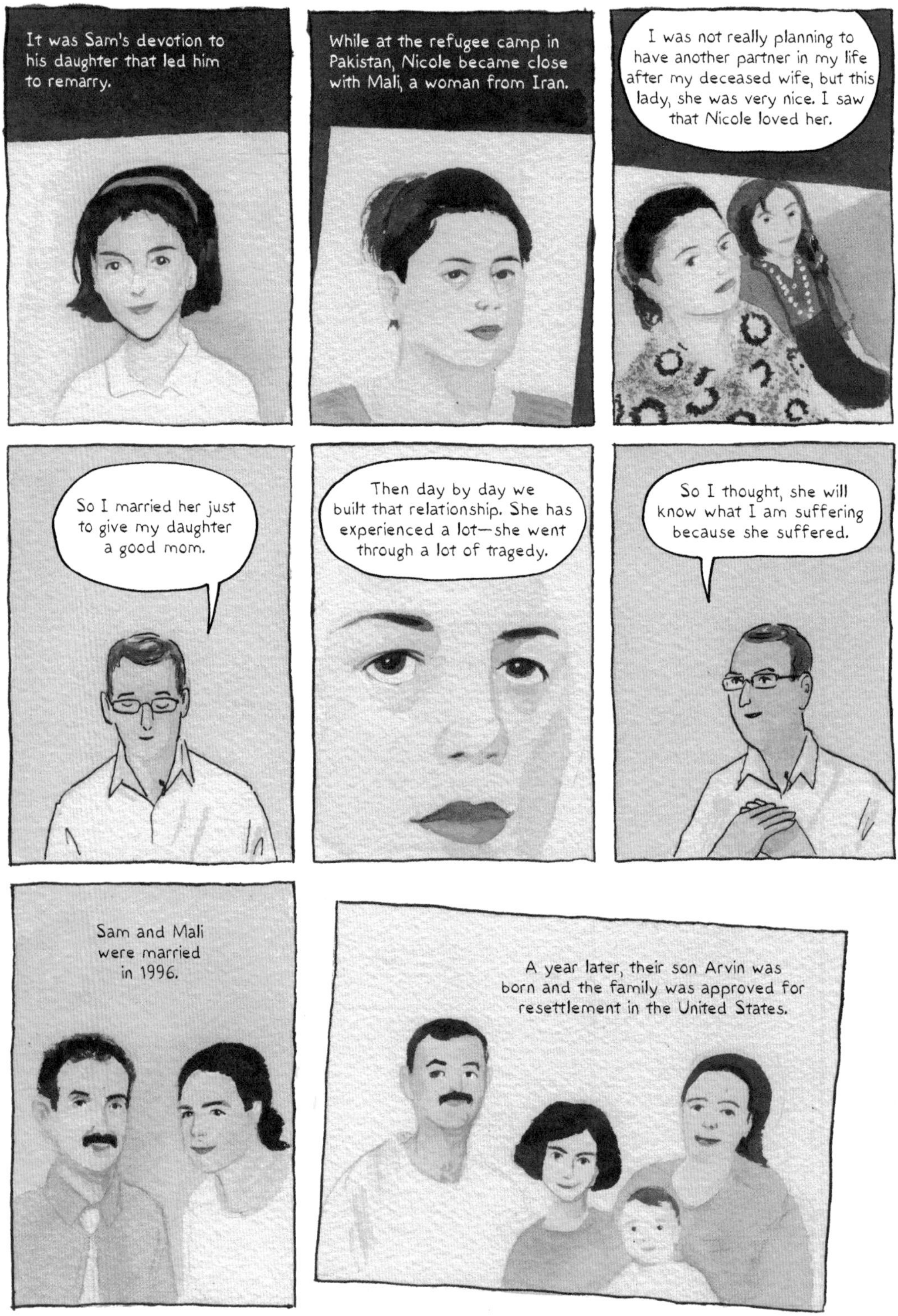
It was Sam's devotion to his daughter that led him to remarry.
While at the refugee camp in Pakistan, Nicole became close with Mali, a woman from Iran.
I was not really planning to have another partner in my life after my deceased wife, but this lady, she was very nice. I saw that Nicole loved her.
So I married her just to give my daughter a good mom.
Then day by day we built that relationship. She has experienced a lot—she went through a lot of tragedy.
So I thought, she will know what I am suffering because she suffered.
Sam and Mali were married in 1996.
A year later, their son Arvin was born and the family was approved for resettlement in the United States.

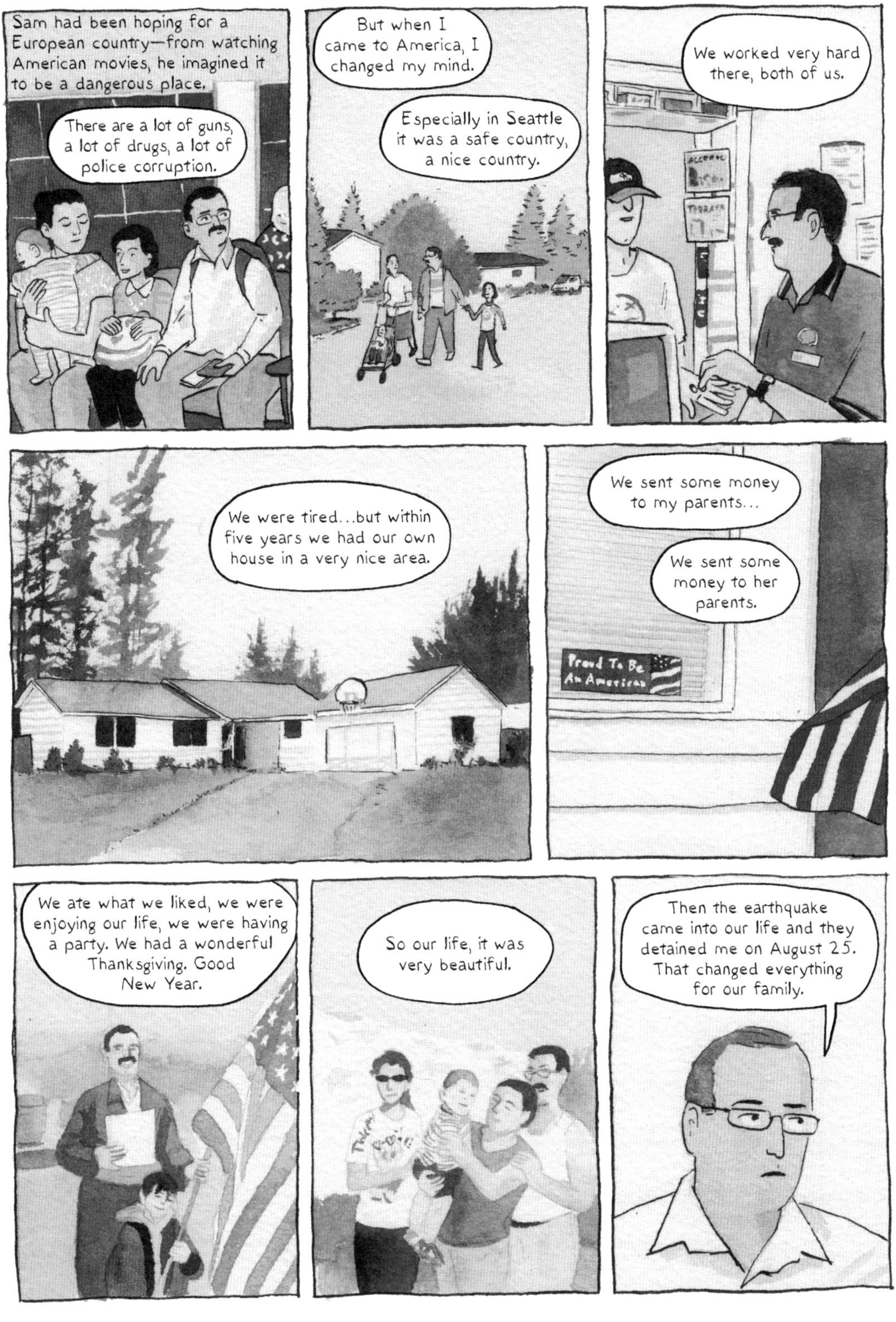
Sam had been hoping for a European country—from watching American movies, he imagined it to be a dangerous place.
There are a lot of guns, a lot of drugs, a lot of police corruption.
But when I came to America, I changed my mind.
Especially in Seattle it was a safe country, a nice country.
We worked very hard there, both of us.
We were tired...but within five years we had our own house in a very nice area.
We sent some money to my parents...
We sent some money to her parents.
Proud To Be An American
We ate what we liked, we were enjoying our life, we were having a party. We had a wonderful Thanksgiving. Good New Year.
So our life, it was very beautiful.
Then the earthquake came into our life and they detained me on August 25. That changed everything for our family.

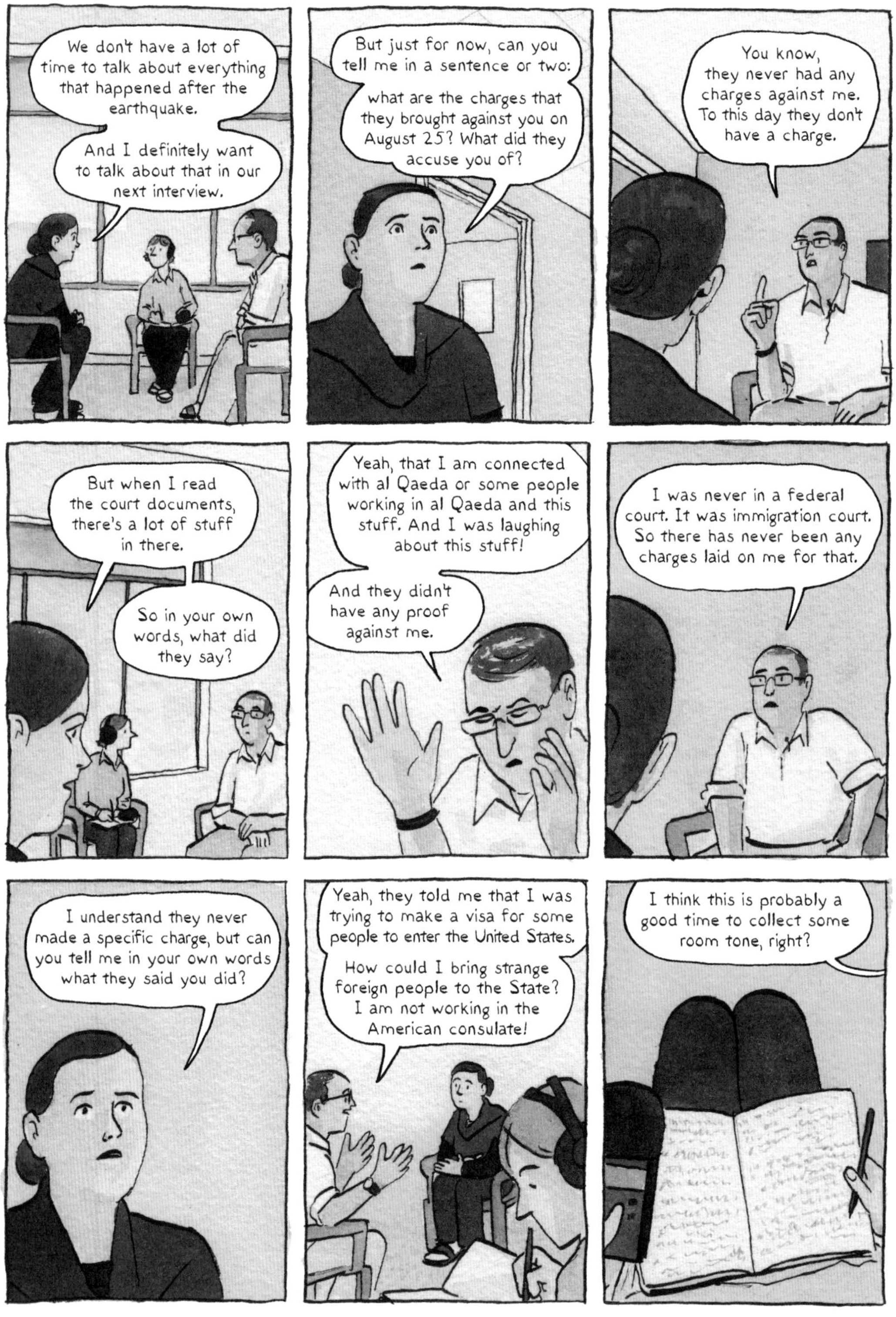
We don't have a lot of time to talk about everything that happened after the earthquake.
And I definitely want to talk about that in our next interview.
But just for now, can you tell me in a sentence or two:
what are the charges that they brought against you on August 25? What did they accuse you of?
You know, they never had any charges against me. To this day they don't have a charge.
But when I read the court documents, there's a lot of stuff in there.
So in your own words, what did they say?
Yeah, that I am connected with al Qaeda or some people working in al Qaeda and this stuff. And I was laughing about this stuff!
And they didn't have any proof against me.
I was never in a federal court. It was immigration court. So there has never been any charges laid on me for that.
I understand they never made a specific charge, but can you tell me in your own words what they said you did?
Yeah, they told me that I was trying to make a visa for some people to enter the United States.
How could I bring strange foreign people to the State? I am not working in the American consulate!
I think this is probably a good time to collect some room tone, right?

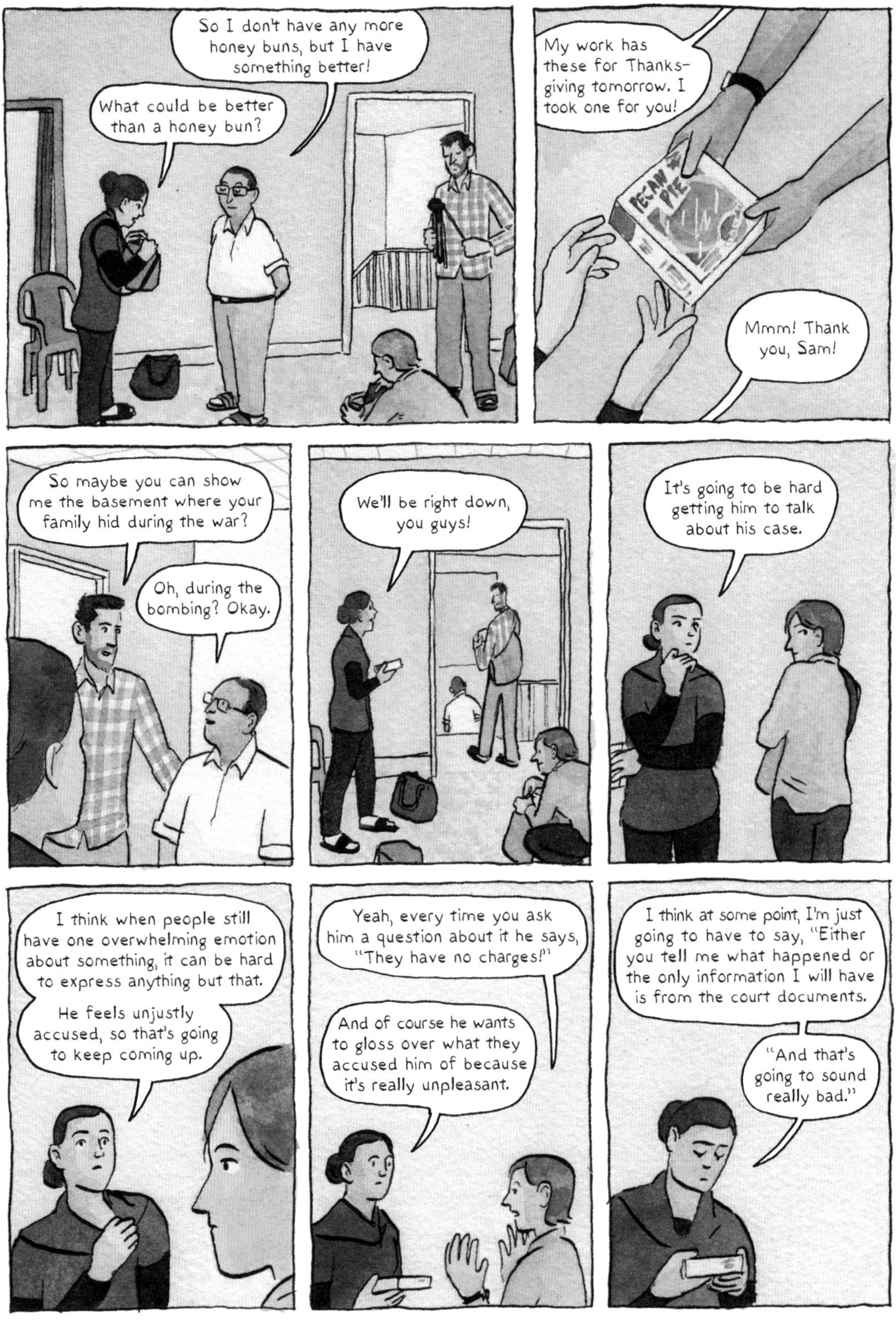

So I don't have any more honey buns, but I have something better!
What could be better than a honey bun?
My work has these for Thanksgiving tomorrow. I took one for you!
PECAN PIE
Mmm! Thank you, Sam!
So maybe you can show me the basement where your family hid during the war?
Oh, during the bombing? Okay.
We'll be right down, you guys!
It's going to be hard getting him to talk about his case.
I think when people still have one overwhelming emotion about something, it can be hard to express anything but that.
He feels unjustly accused, so that's going to keep coming up.
Yeah, every time you ask him a question about it he says, "They have no charges!"
And of course he wants to gloss over what they accused him of because it's really unpleasant.
I think at some point, I'm just going to have to say, "Either you tell me what happened or the only information I will have is from the court documents.
"And that's going to sound really bad."

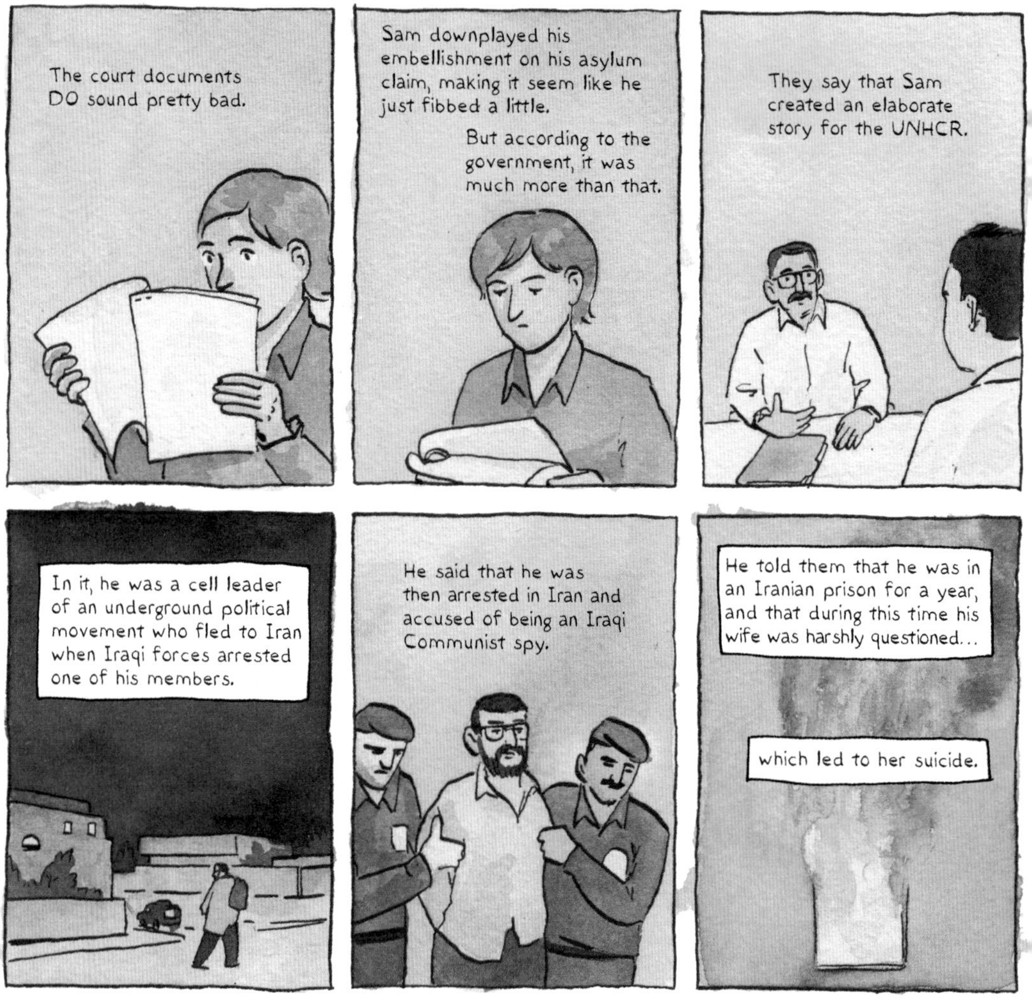

The court documents DO sound pretty bad.
Sam downplayed his embellishment on his asylum claim, making it seem like he just fibbed a little.
But according to the government, it was much more than that.
They say that Sam created an elaborate story for the UNHCR.
In it, he was a cell leader of an underground political movement who fled to Iran when Iraqi forces arrested one of his members.
He said that he was then arrested in Iran and accused of being an Iraqi Communist spy.
He told them that he was in an Iranian prison for a year, and that during this time his wife was harshly questioned...
which led to her suicide.

This is why, in the Ninth Circuit Court of Appeals ruling, the judge writes:

Malkandi's history of misrepresentations about his past and continued evasion of the truth casts a shadow over his present story. Though it cannot be overlooked that these statements were made initially in furtherance of his refugee status, he nonetheless spun quite a tale and continued to do so for a long time.

No wonder the "mall story" was suspicious after that.

Given his history, it is no surprise that the Board of Immigration Appeals discounted his improbable story of a chance meeting and a willingness to follow-up with a medical appointment for a perfect stranger. A pattern of misrepresentation has developed that cannot be ignored.

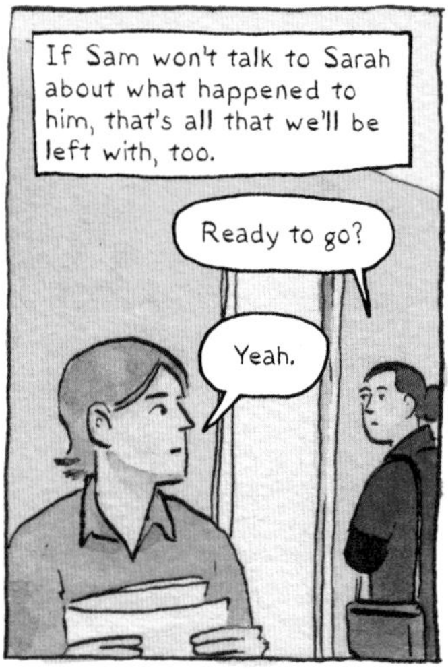

If Sam won't talk to Sarah about what happened to him, that's all that we'll be left with, too.
Ready to go?
Yeah.

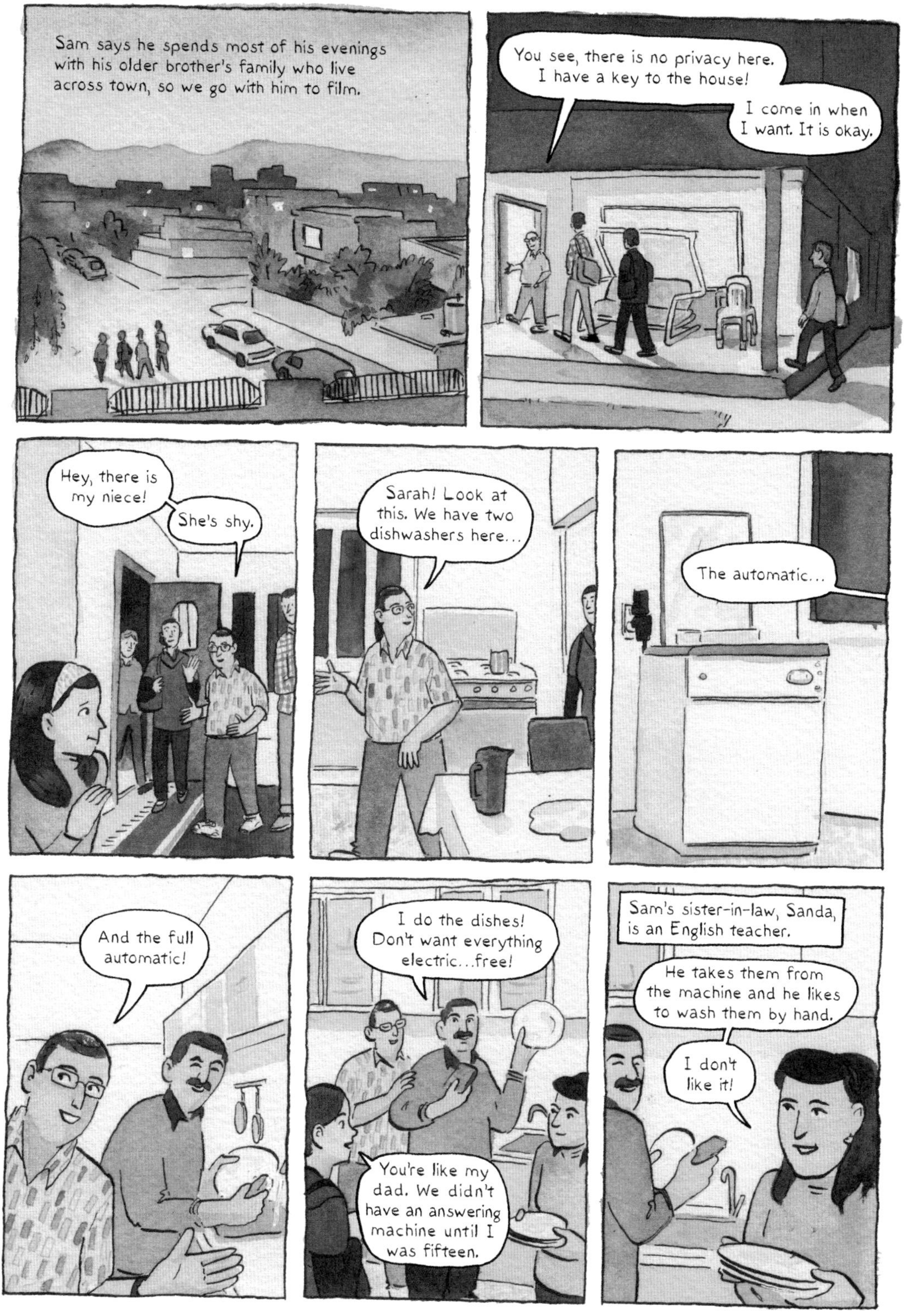
Sam says he spends most of his evenings with his older brother's family who live across town, so we go with him to film.
You see, there is no privacy here. I have a key to the house!
I come in when I want. It is okay.
Hey, there is my niece!
She's shy.
Sarah! Look at this. We have two dishwashers here...
The automatic...
And the full automatic!
I do the dishes! Don't want everything electric...free!
You're like my dad. We didn't have an answering machine until I was fifteen.
Sam's sister-in-law, Sanda, is an English teacher.
He takes them from the machine and he likes to wash them by hand.
I don't like it!

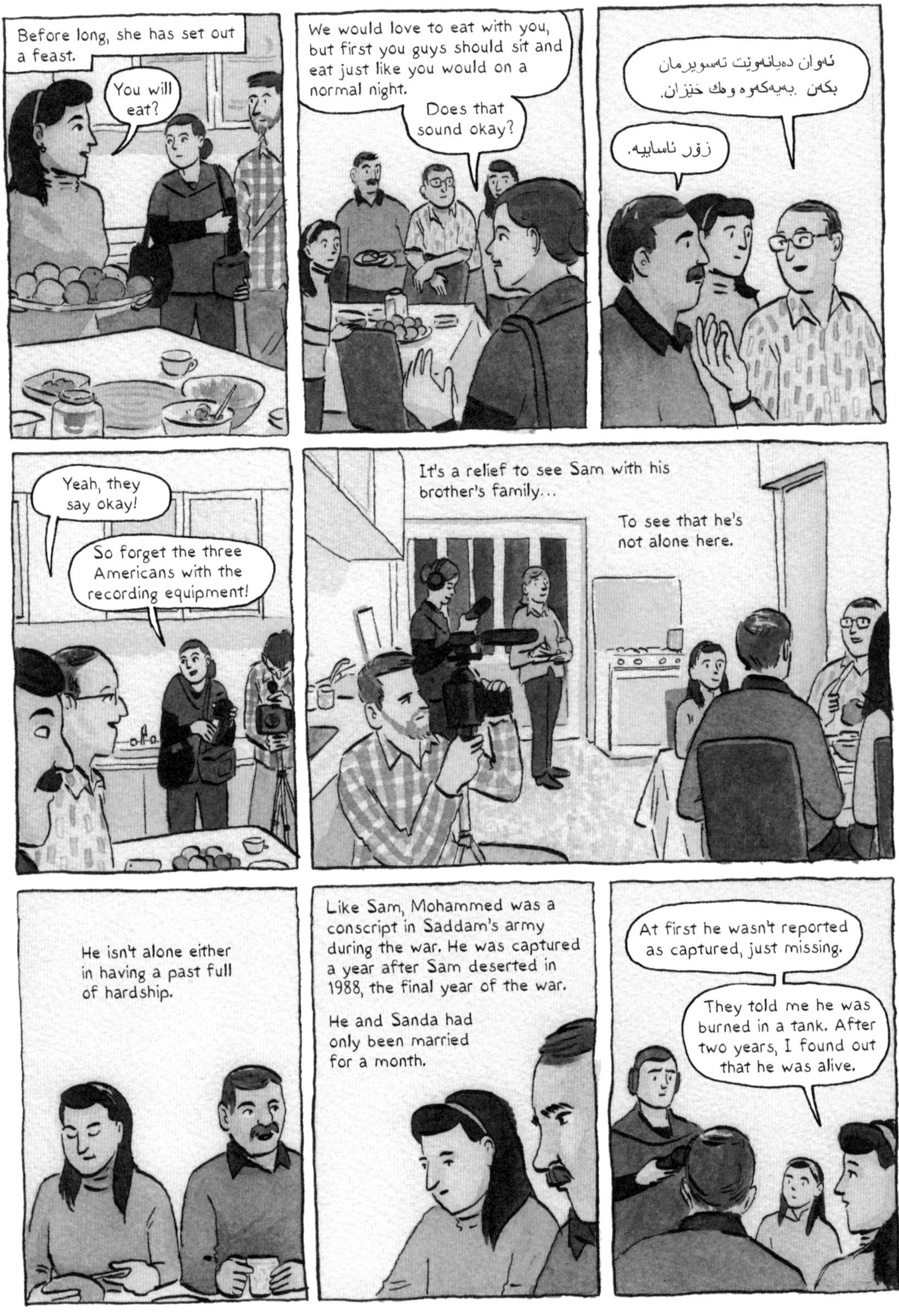
Before long, she has set out a feast.
You will eat?
We would love to eat with you, but first you guys should sit and eat just like you would on a normal night.
Does that sound okay?
ئەوان دەیانەوێت تەسویرمان بکەن .بەیەکەوە وەك خێزان.
زۆر ئاساییە.
Yeah, they say okay!
So forget the three Americans with the recording equipment!
It's a relief to see Sam with his brother's family...
To see that he's not alone here.
He isn't alone either in having a past full of hardship.
Like Sam, Mohammed was a conscript in Saddam's army during the war. He was captured a year after Sam deserted in 1988, the final year of the war.
He and Sanda had only been married for a month.
At first he wasn't reported as captured, just missing.
They told me he was burned in a tank. After two years, I found out that he was alive.

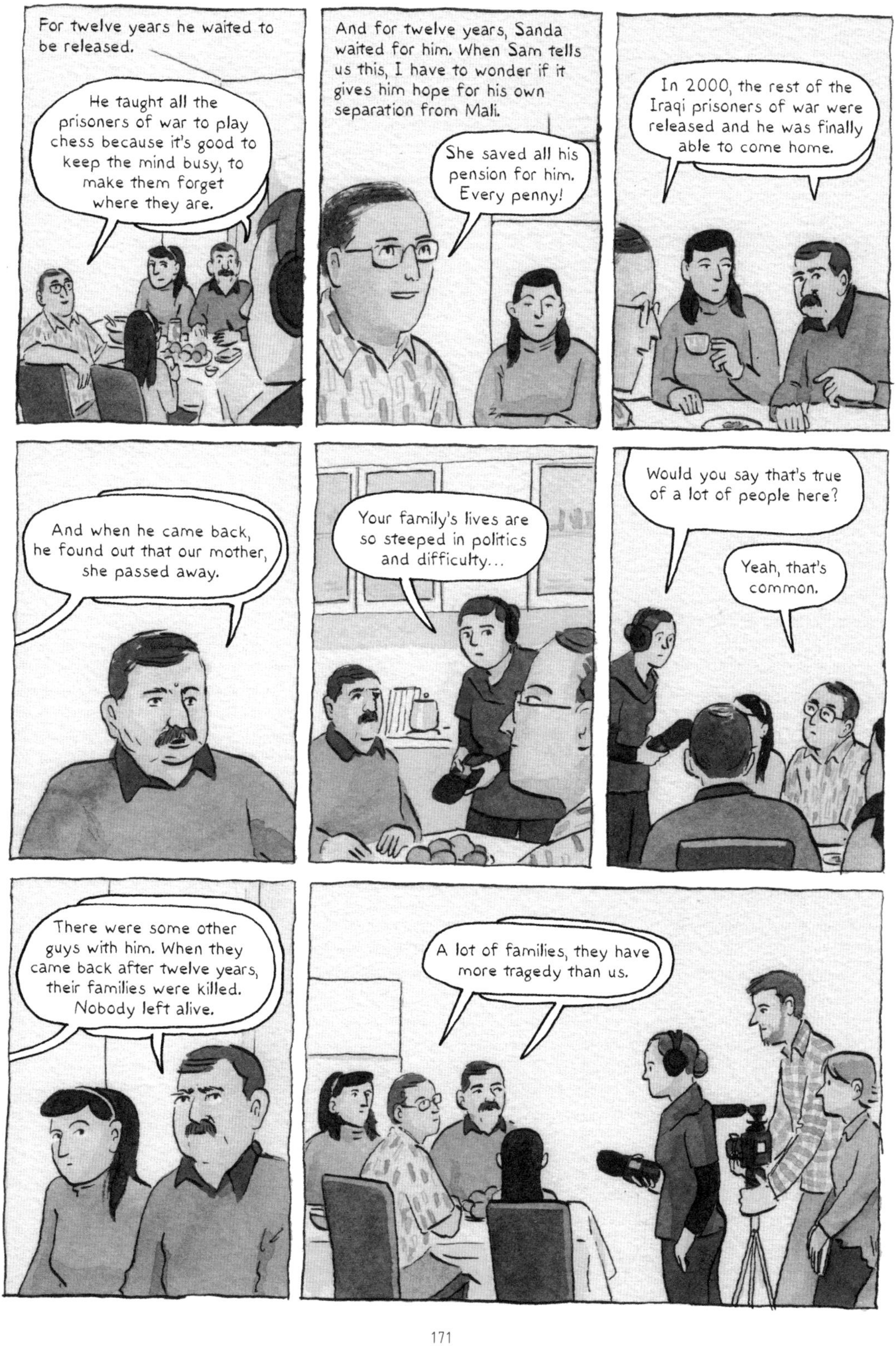
For twelve years he waited to be released.
He taught all the prisoners of war to play chess because it's good to keep the mind busy, to make them forget where they are.
And for twelve years, Sanda waited for him. When Sam tells us this, I have to wonder if it gives him hope for his own separation from Mali.
She saved all his pension for him. Every penny!
In 2000, the rest of the Iraqi prisoners of war were released and he was finally able to come home.
And when he came back, he found out that our mother, she passed away.
Your family's lives are so steeped in politics and difficulty...
Would you say that's true of a lot of people here?
Yeah, that's common.
There were some other guys with him. When they came back after twelve years, their families were killed. Nobody left alive.
A lot of families, they have more tragedy than us.

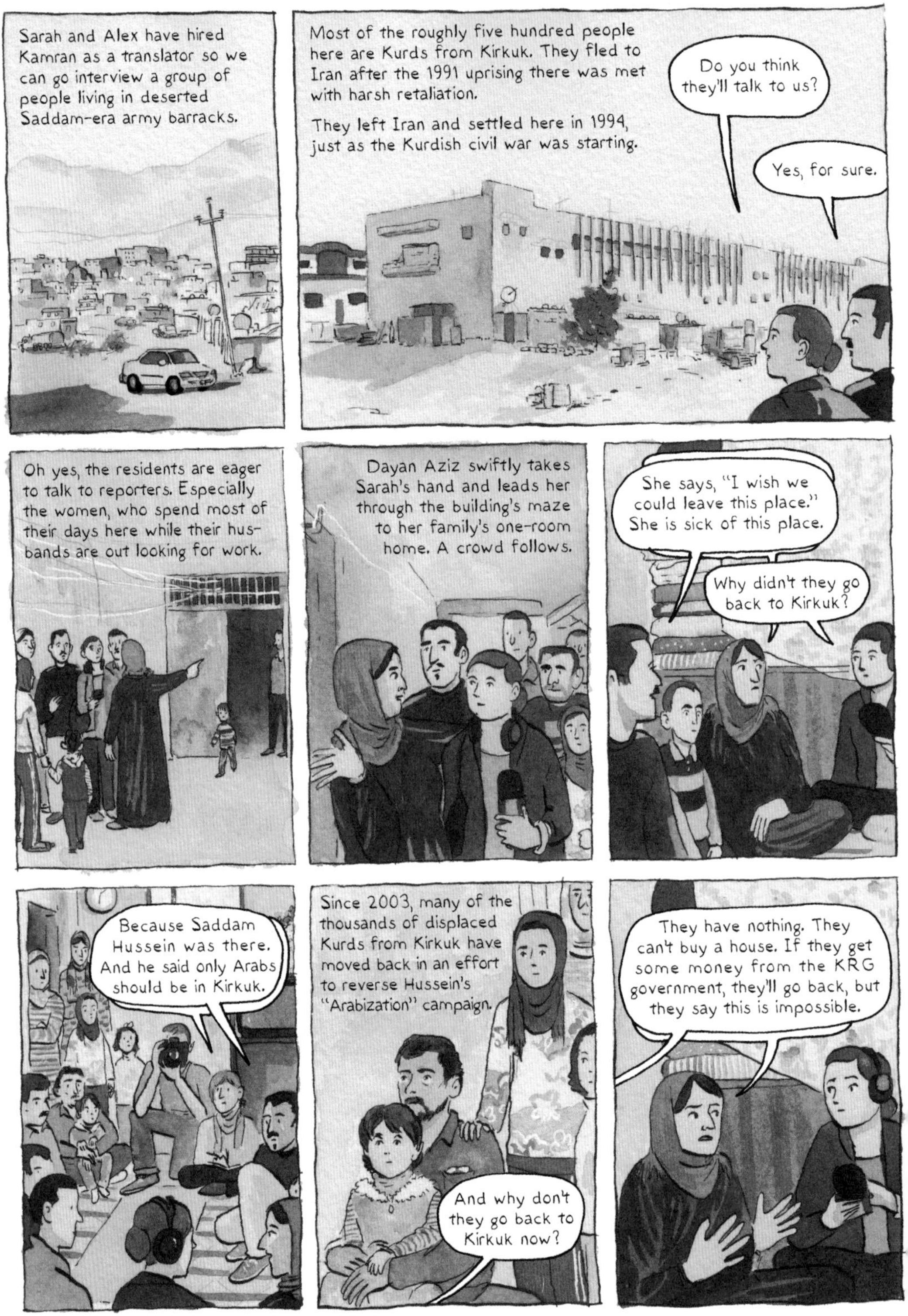
Sarah and Alex have hired Kamran as a translator so we can go interview a group of people living in deserted Saddam-era army barracks.
Most of the roughly five hundred people here are Kurds from Kirkuk. They fled to Iran after the 1991 uprising there was met with harsh retaliation.
They left Iran and settled here in 1994, just as the Kurdish civil war was starting.
Do you think they'll talk to us?
Yes, for sure.
Oh yes, the residents are eager to talk to reporters. Especially the women, who spend most of their days here while their husbands are out looking for work.
Dayan Aziz swiftly takes Sarah's hand and leads her through the building's maze to her family's one-room home. A crowd follows.
She says, "I wish we could leave this place." She is sick of this place.
Why didn't they go back to Kirkuk?
Because Saddam Hussein was there. And he said only Arabs should be in Kirkuk.
Since 2003, many of the thousands of displaced Kurds from Kirkuk have moved back in an effort to reverse Hussein's "Arabization" campaign.
And why don't they go back to Kirkuk now?
They have nothing. They can't buy a house. If they get some money from the KRG government, they'll go back, but they say this is impossible.

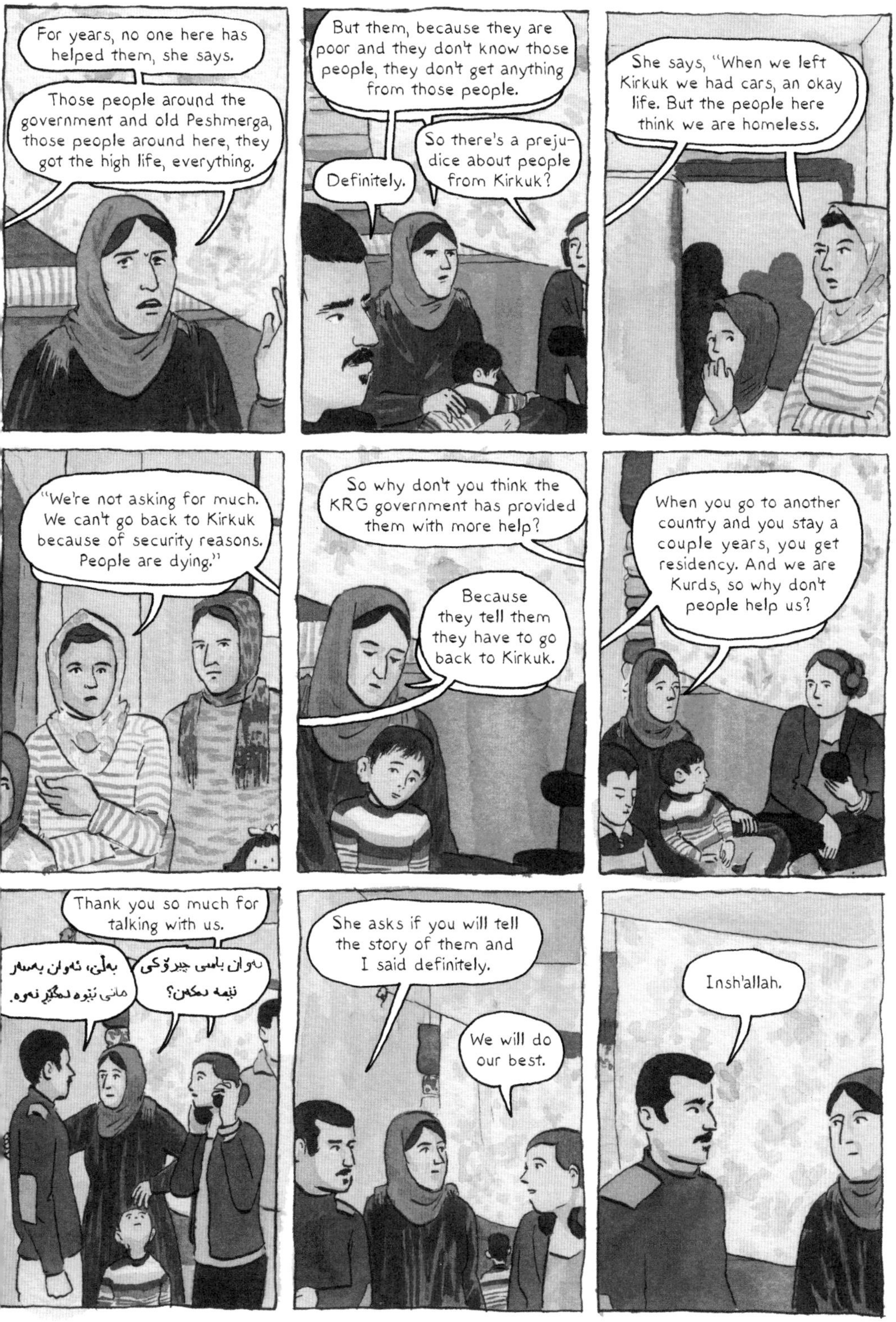
For years, no one here has helped them, she says.
Those people around the government and old Peshmerga, those people around here, they got the high life, everything.
But them, because they are poor and they don't know those people, they don't get anything from those people.
Definitely.
So there's a prejudice about people from Kirkuk?
She says, "When we left Kirkuk we had cars, an okay life. But the people here think we are homeless.
"We're not asking for much. We can't go back to Kirkuk because of security reasons. People are dying."
So why don't you think the KRG government has provided them with more help?
Because they tell them they have to go back to Kirkuk.
When you go to another country and you stay a couple years, you get residency. And we are Kurds, so why don't people help us?
Thank you so much for talking with us.
ئەوان باسی چیرۆکی ئێمە دەکەن؟
بەڵێ، ئەوان بەسەرهاتی ئێوە دەگێڕنەوە.
She asks if you will tell the story of them and I said definitely.
We will do our best.
Insh'allah.

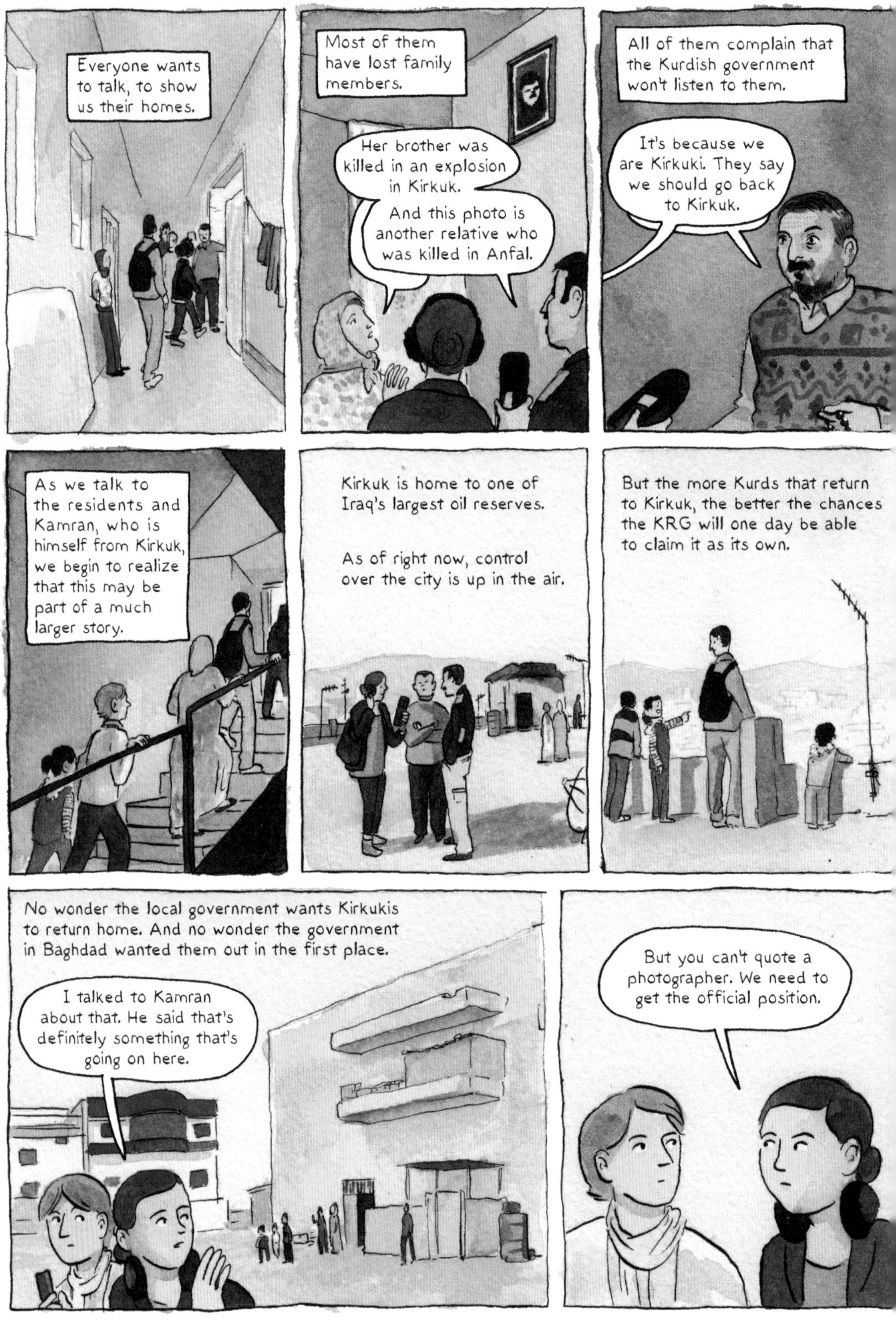
Everyone wants to talk, to show us their homes.
Most of them have lost family members.
Her brother was killed in an explosion in Kirkuk.
And this photo is another relative who was killed in Anfal.
All of them complain that the Kurdish government won't listen to them.
It's because we are Kirkuki. They say we should go back to Kirkuk.
As we talk to the residents and Kamran, who is himself from Kirkuk, we begin to realize that this may be part of a much larger story.
Kirkuk is home to one of Iraq's largest oil reserves.
As of right now, control over the city is up in the air.
But the more Kurds that return to Kirkuk, the better the chances the KRG will one day be able to claim it as its own.
No wonder the local government wants Kirkukis to return home. And no wonder the government in Baghdad wanted them out in the first place.
I talked to Kamran about that. He said that's definitely something that's going on here.
But you can't quote a photographer. We need to get the official position.

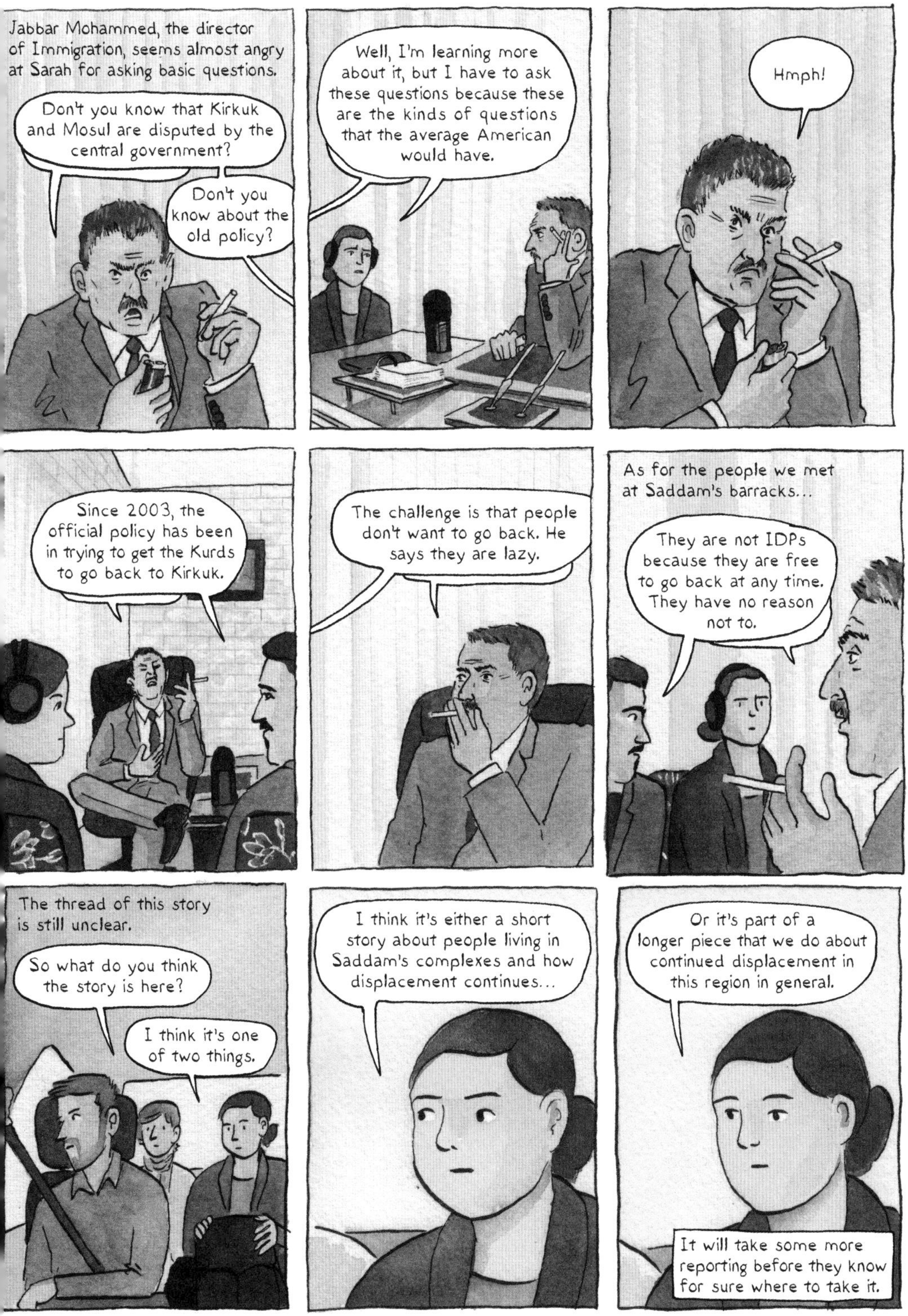

Jabbar Mohammed, the director of Immigration, seems almost angry at Sarah for asking basic questions.
Don't you know that Kirkuk and Mosul are disputed by the central government?
Don't you know about the old policy?
Well, I'm learning more about it, but I have to ask these questions because these are the kinds of questions that the average American would have.
Hmph!
Since 2003, the official policy has been in trying to get the Kurds to go back to Kirkuk.
The challenge is that people don't want to go back. He says they are lazy.
As for the people we met at Saddam's barracks...
They are not IDPs because they are free to go back at any time. They have no reason not to.
The thread of this story is still unclear.
So what do you think the story is here?
I think it's one of two things.
I think it's either a short story about people living in Saddam's complexes and how displacement continues...
Or it's part of a longer piece that we do about continued displacement in this region in general.
It will take some more reporting before they know for sure where to take it.

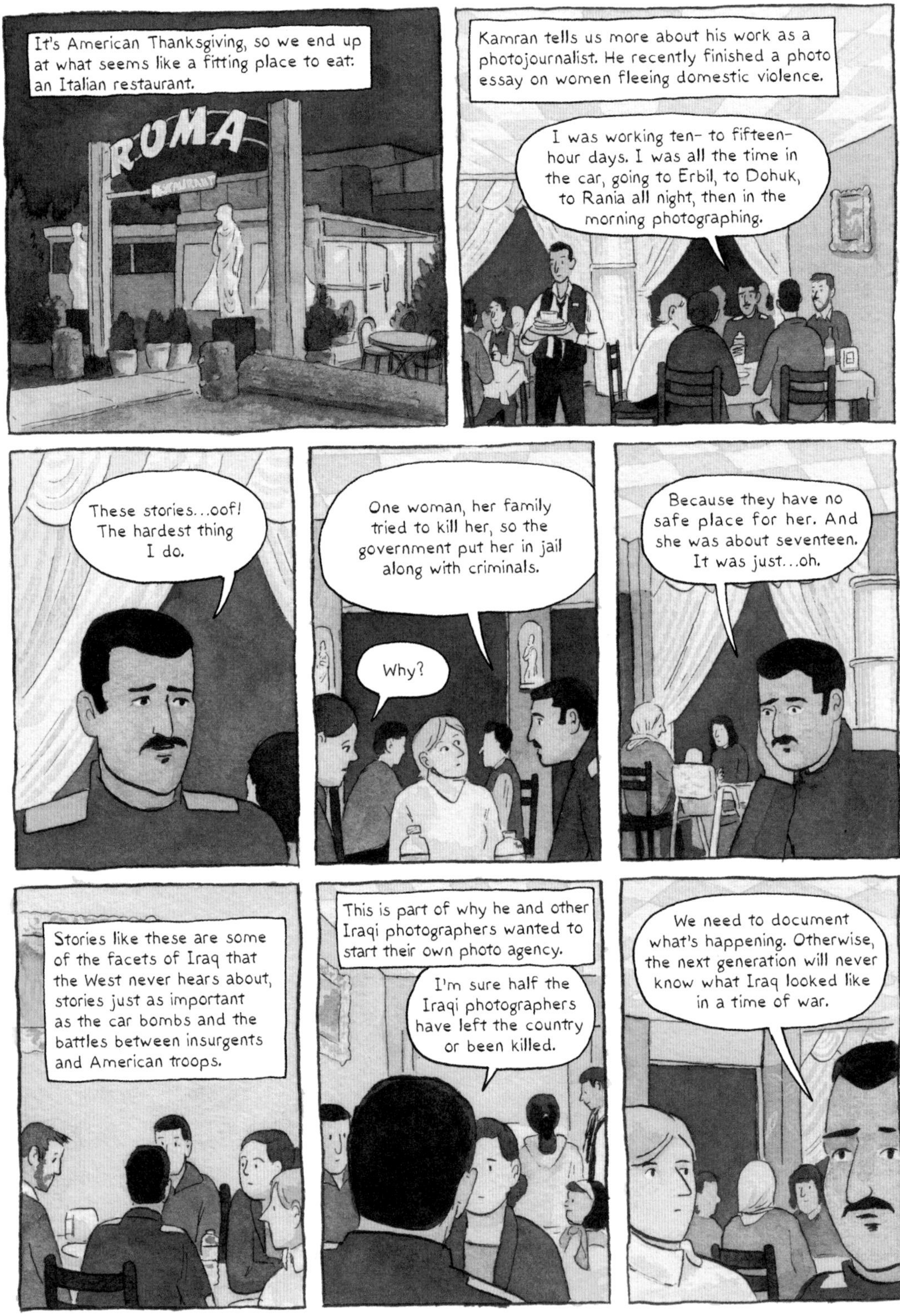
It's American Thanksgiving, so we end up at what seems like a fitting place to eat: an Italian restaurant.
ROMA
RESTAURANT
Kamran tells us more about his work as a photojournalist. He recently finished a photo essay on women fleeing domestic violence.
I was working ten- to fifteen-hour days. I was all the time in the car, going to Erbil, to Dohuk, to Rania all night, then in the morning photographing.
These stories...oof! The hardest thing I do.
One woman, her family tried to kill her, so the government put her in jail along with criminals.
Why?
Because they have no safe place for her. And she was about seventeen. It was just...oh.
Stories like these are some of the facets of Iraq that the West never hears about, stories just as important as the car bombs and the battles between insurgents and American troops.
This is part of why he and other Iraqi photographers wanted to start their own photo agency.
I'm sure half the Iraqi photographers have left the country or been killed.
We need to document what's happening. Otherwise, the next generation will never know what Iraq looked like in a time of war.

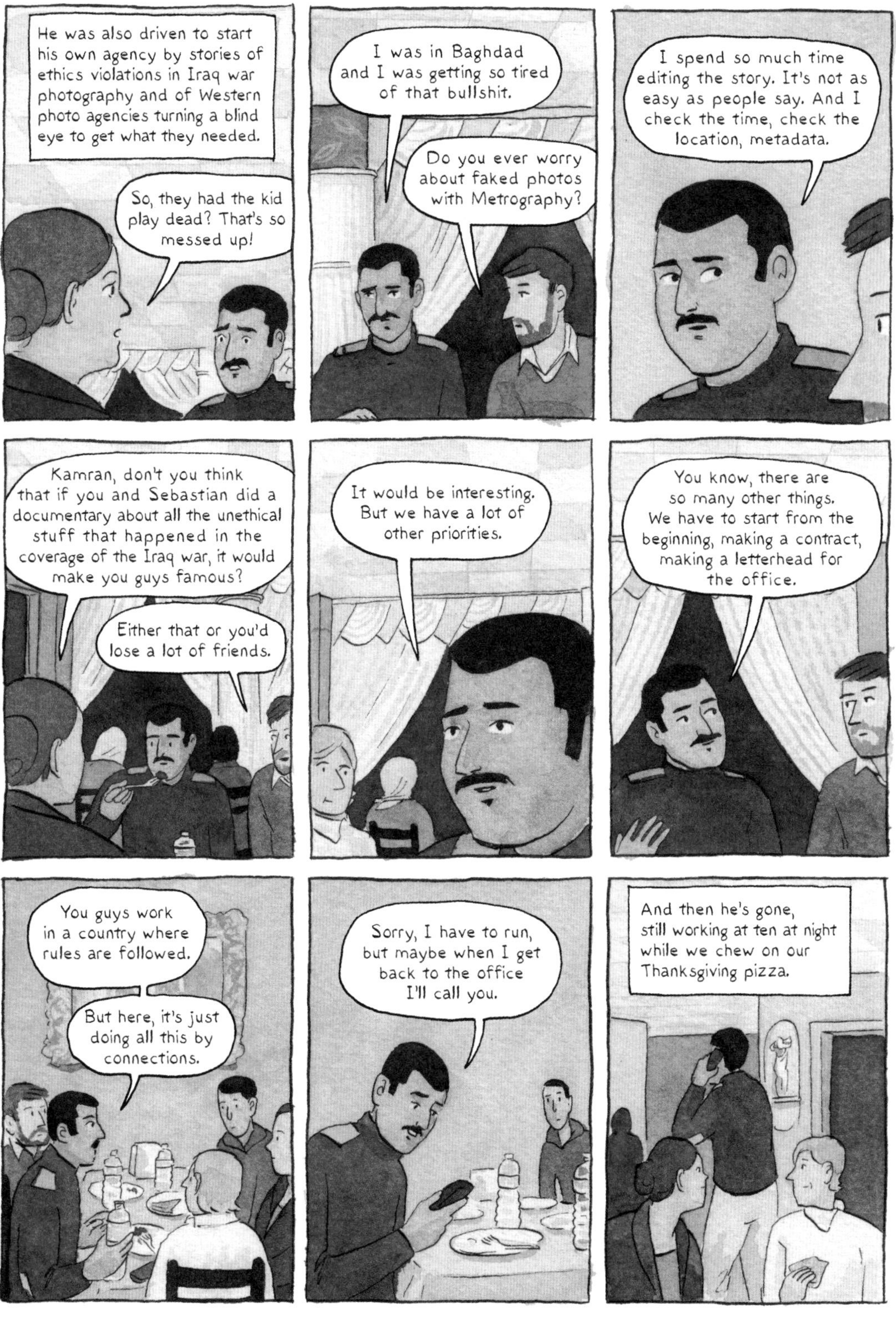
He was also driven to start his own agency by stories of ethics violations in Iraq war photography and of Western photo agencies turning a blind eye to get what they needed.
So, they had the kid play dead? That's so messed up!
I was in Baghdad and I was getting so tired of that bullshit.
Do you ever worry about faked photos with Metrography?
I spend so much time editing the story. It's not as easy as people say. And I check the time, check the location, metadata.
Kamran, don't you think that if you and Sebastian did a documentary about all the unethical stuff that happened in the coverage of the Iraq war, it would make you guys famous?
Either that or you'd lose a lot of friends.
It would be interesting. But we have a lot of other priorities.
You know, there are so many other things. We have to start from the beginning, making a contract, making a letterhead for the office.
You guys work in a country where rules are followed.
But here, it's just doing all this by connections.
Sorry, I have to run, but maybe when I get back to the office I'll call you.
And then he's gone, still working at ten at night while we chew on our Thanksgiving pizza.

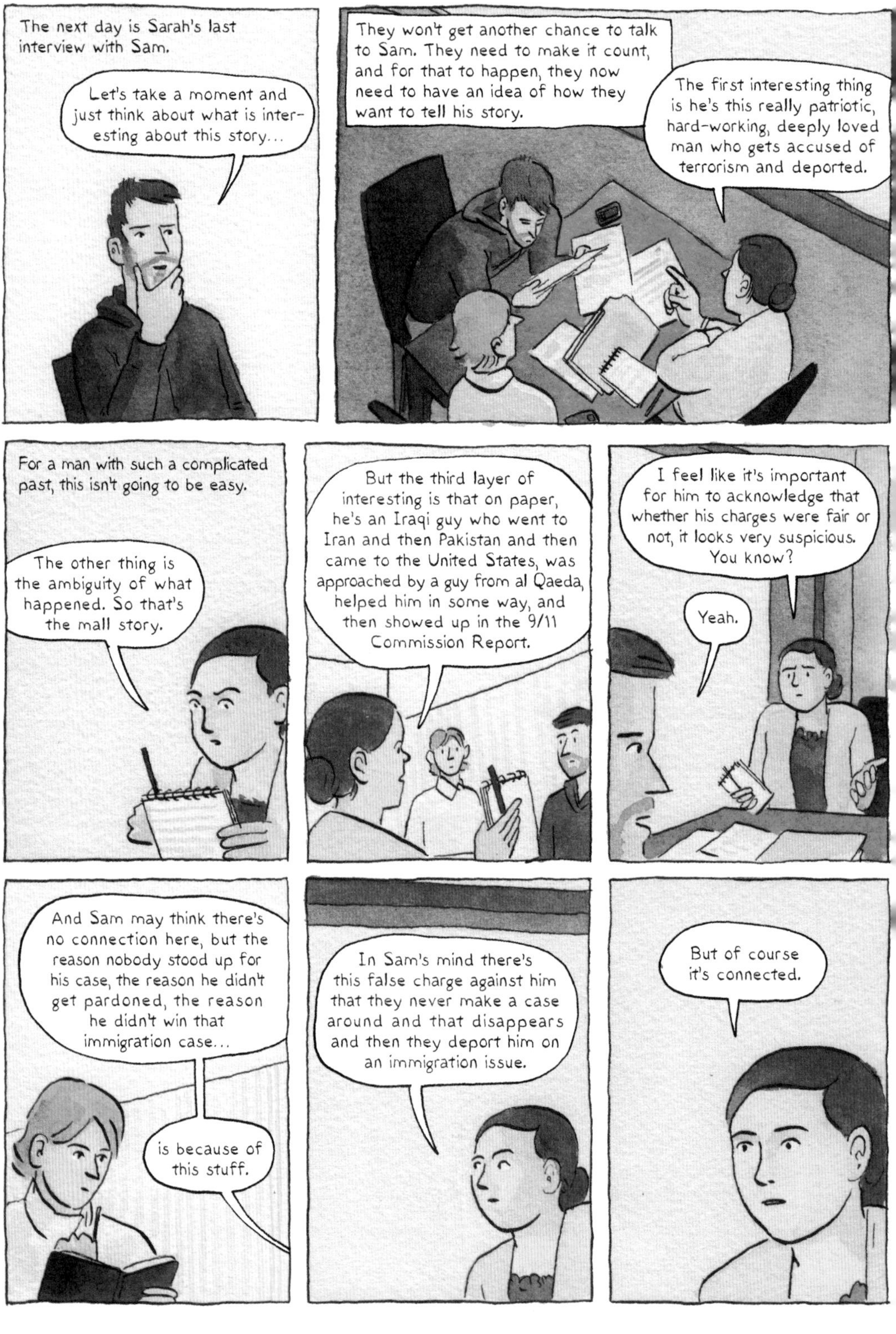
The next day is Sarah's last interview with Sam.
Let's take a moment and just think about what is interesting about this story...
They won't get another chance to talk to Sam. They need to make it count, and for that to happen, they now need to have an idea of how they want to tell his story.
The first interesting thing is he's this really patriotic, hard-working, deeply loved man who gets accused of terrorism and deported.
For a man with such a complicated past, this isn't going to be easy.
The other thing is the ambiguity of what happened. So that's the mall story.
But the third layer of interesting is that on paper, he's an Iraqi guy who went to Iran and then Pakistan and then came to the United States, was approached by a guy from al Qaeda, helped him in some way, and then showed up in the 9/11 Commission Report.
I feel like it's important for him to acknowledge that whether his charges were fair or not, it looks very suspicious. You know?
Yeah.
And Sam may think there's no connection here, but the reason nobody stood up for his case, the reason he didn't get pardoned, the reason he didn't win that immigration case...
is because of this stuff.
In Sam's mind there's this false charge against him that they never make a case around and that disappears and then they deport him on an immigration issue.
But of course it's connected.

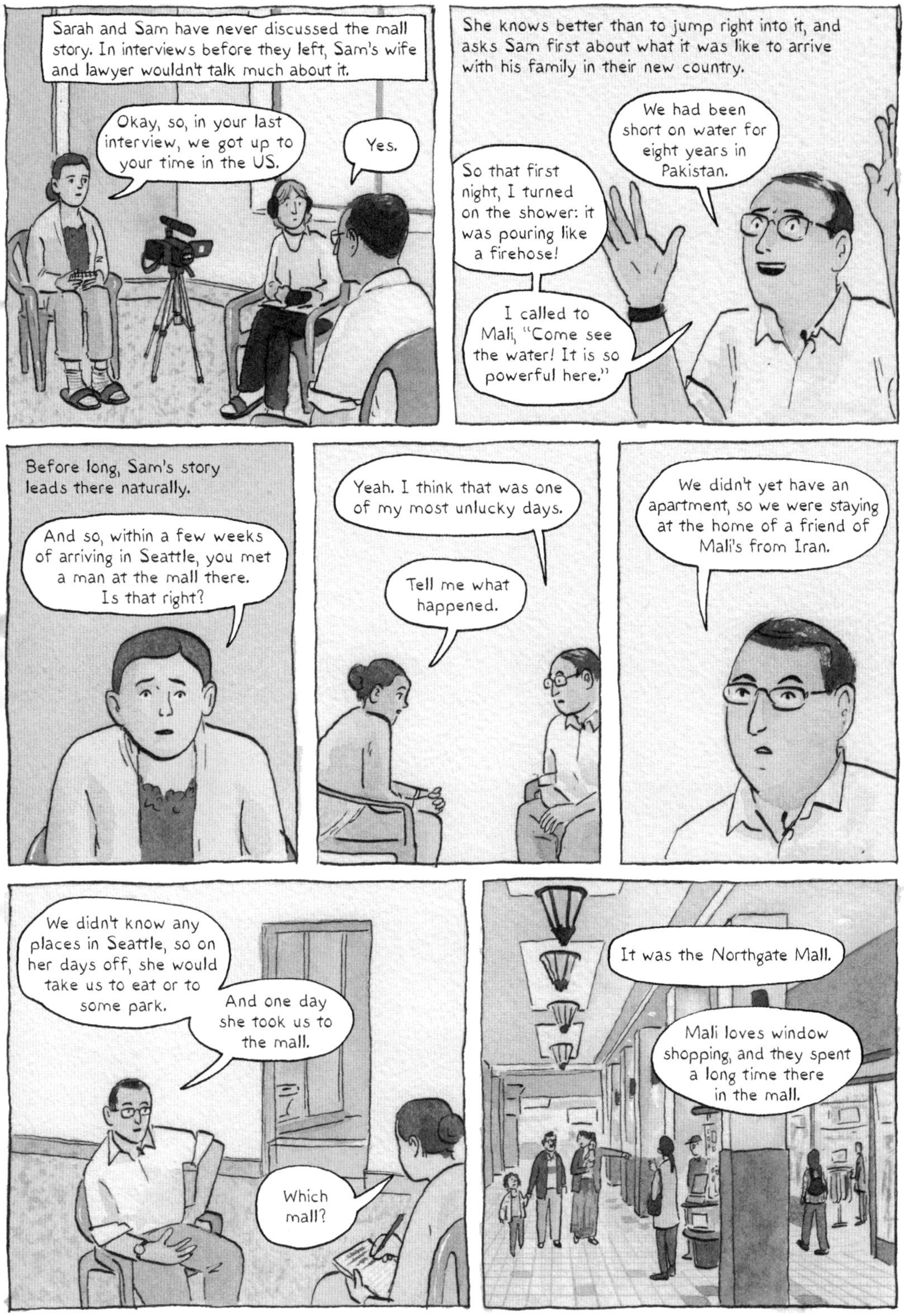
Sarah and Sam have never discussed the mall story. In interviews before they left, Sam's wife and lawyer wouldn't talk much about it.
Okay, so, in your last interview, we got up to your time in the US.
Yes.
She knows better than to jump right into it, and asks Sam first about what it was like to arrive with his family in their new country.
We had been short on water for eight years in Pakistan.
So that first night, I turned on the shower: it was pouring like a firehose!
I called to Mali, "Come see the water! It is so powerful here."
Before long, Sam's story leads there naturally.
And so, within a few weeks of arriving in Seattle, you met a man at the mall there. Is that right?
Yeah. I think that was one of my most unlucky days.
Tell me what happened.
We didn't yet have an apartment, so we were staying at the home of a friend of Mali's from Iran.
We didn't know any places in Seattle, so on her days off, she would take us to eat or to some park.
And one day she took us to the mall.
Which mall?
It was the Northgate Mall.
Mali loves window shopping, and they spent a long time there in the mall.

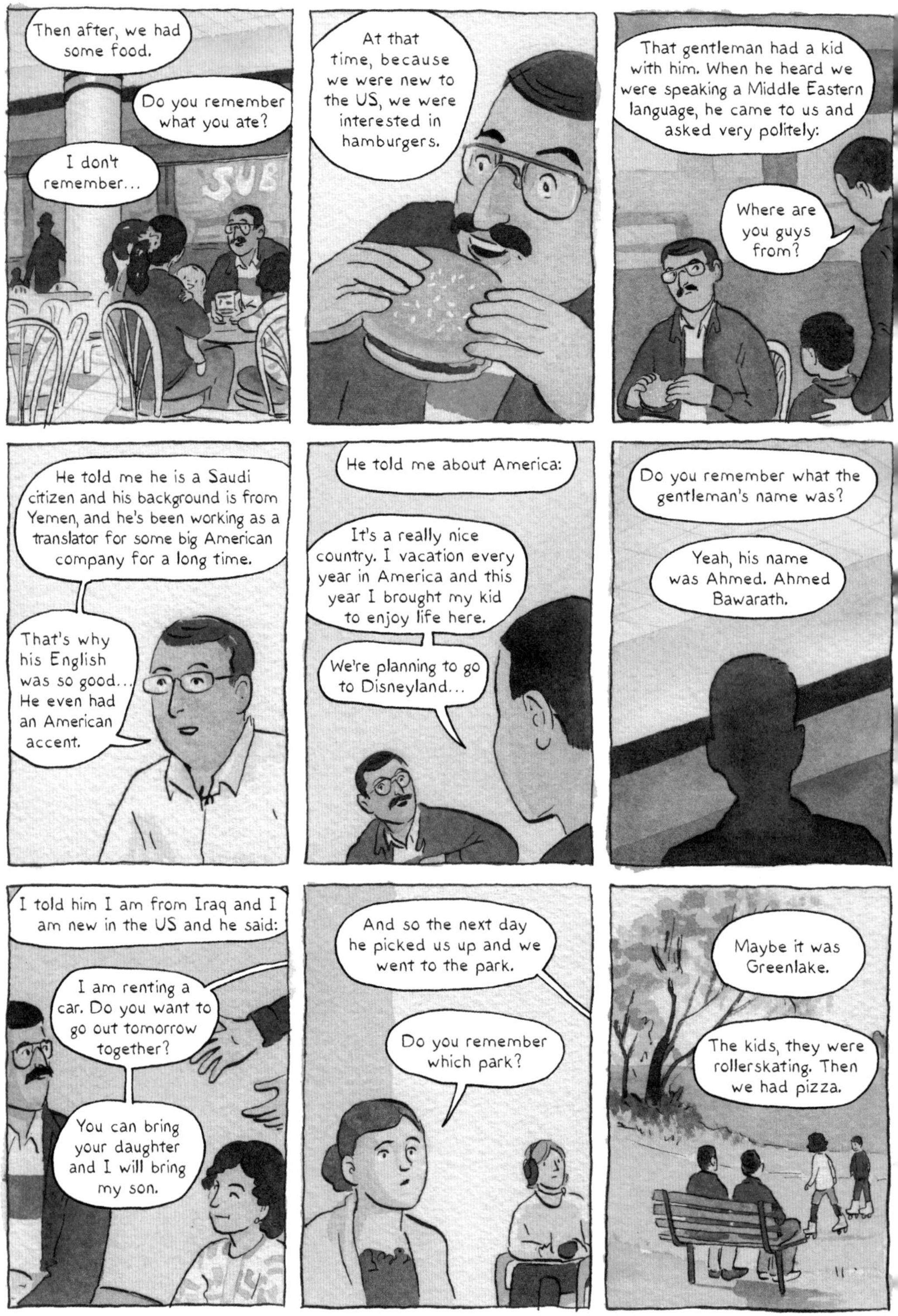
Then after, we had some food.
Do you remember what you ate?
I don't remember...
At that time, because we were new to the US, we were interested in hamburgers.
That gentleman had a kid with him. When he heard we were speaking a Middle Eastern language, he came to us and asked very politely:
Where are you guys from?
He told me he is a Saudi citizen and his background is from Yemen, and he's been working as a translator for some big American company for a long time.
That's why his English was so good... He even had an American accent.
He told me about America:
It's a really nice country. I vacation every year in America and this year I brought my kid to enjoy life here.
We're planning to go to Disneyland...
Do you remember what the gentleman's name was?
Yeah, his name was Ahmed. Ahmed Bawarath.
I told him I am from Iraq and I am new in the US and he said:
I am renting a car. Do you want to go out tomorrow together?
You can bring your daughter and I will bring my son.
And so the next day he picked us up and we went to the park.
Do you remember which park?
Maybe it was Greenlake.
The kids, they were rollerskating. Then we had pizza.

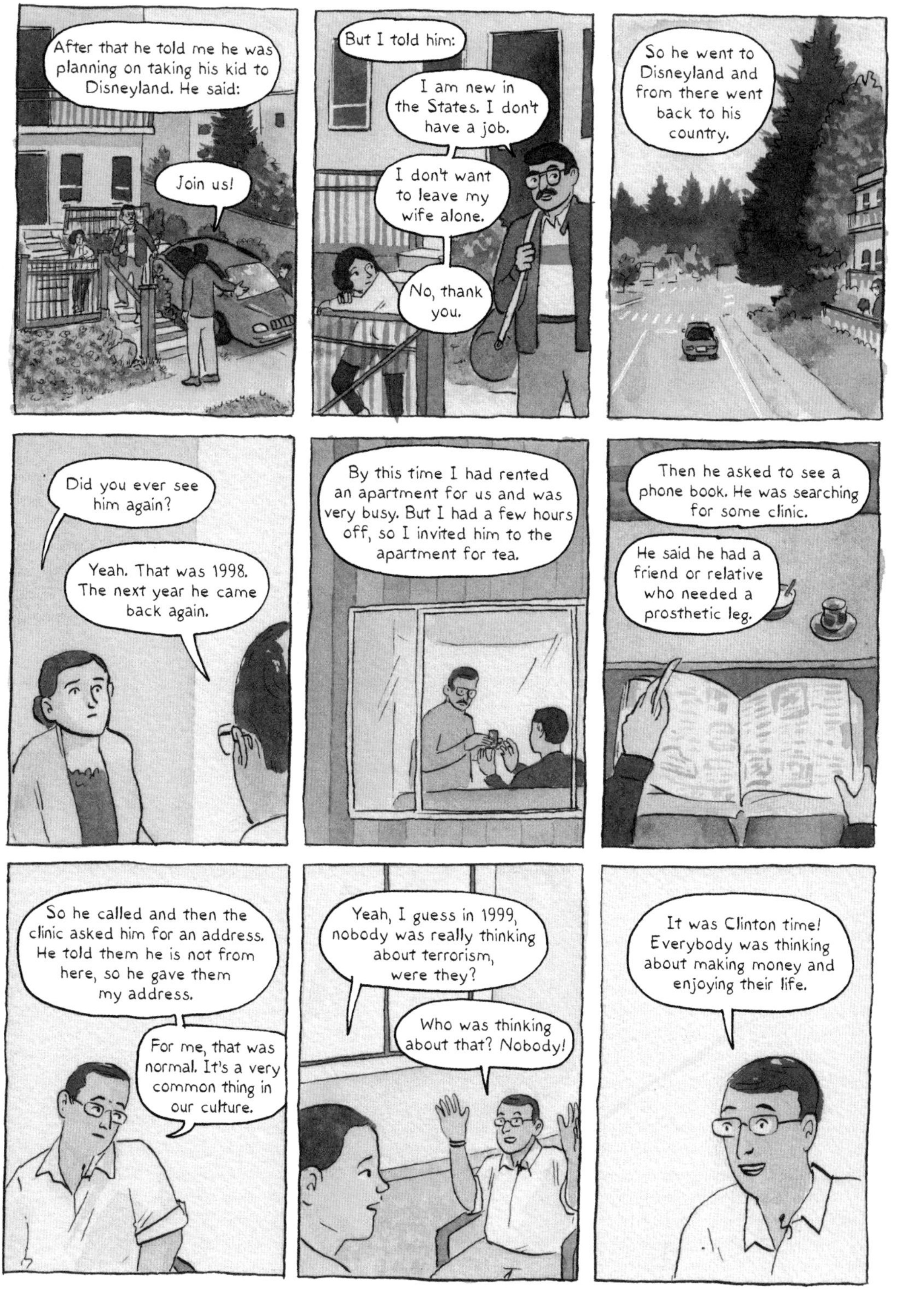
After that he told me he was planning on taking his kid to Disneyland. He said:
Join us!
But I told him:
I am new in the States. I don't have a job.
I don't want to leave my wife alone.
No, thank you.
So he went to Disneyland and from there went back to his country.
Did you ever see him again?
Yeah. That was 1998. The next year he came back again.
By this time I had rented an apartment for us and was very busy. But I had a few hours off, so I invited him to the apartment for tea.
Then he asked to see a phone book. He was searching for some clinic.
He said he had a friend or relative who needed a prosthetic leg.
So he called and then the clinic asked him for an address. He told them he is not from here, so he gave them my address.
For me, that was normal. It's a very common thing in our culture.
Yeah, I guess in 1999, nobody was really thinking about terrorism, were they?
Who was thinking about that? Nobody!
It was Clinton time! Everybody was thinking about making money and enjoying their life.

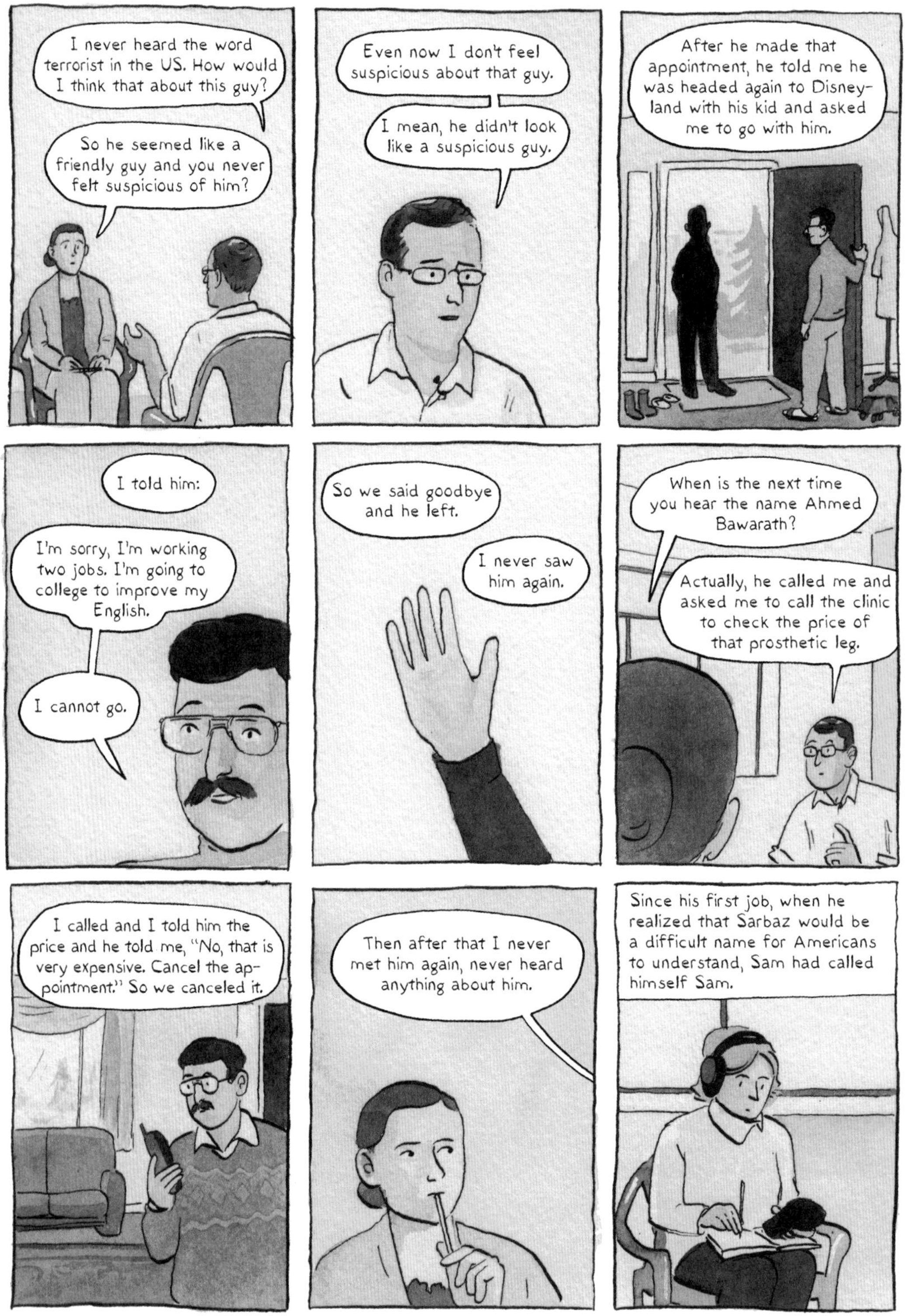
I never heard the word terrorist in the US. How would I think that about this guy?
So he seemed like a friendly guy and you never felt suspicious of him?
Even now I don't feel suspicious about that guy.
I mean, he didn't look like a suspicious guy.
After he made that appointment, he told me he was headed again to Disneyland with his kid and asked me to go with him.
I told him:
I'm sorry, I'm working two jobs. I'm going to college to improve my English.
I cannot go.
So we said goodbye and he left.
I never saw him again.
When is the next time you hear the name Ahmed Bawarath?
Actually, he called me and asked me to call the clinic to check the price of that prosthetic leg.
I called and I told him the price and he told me, "No, that is very expensive. Cancel the appointment." So we canceled it.
Then after that I never met him again, never heard anything about him.
Since his first job, when he realized that Sarbaz would be a difficult name for Americans to understand, Sam had called himself Sam.

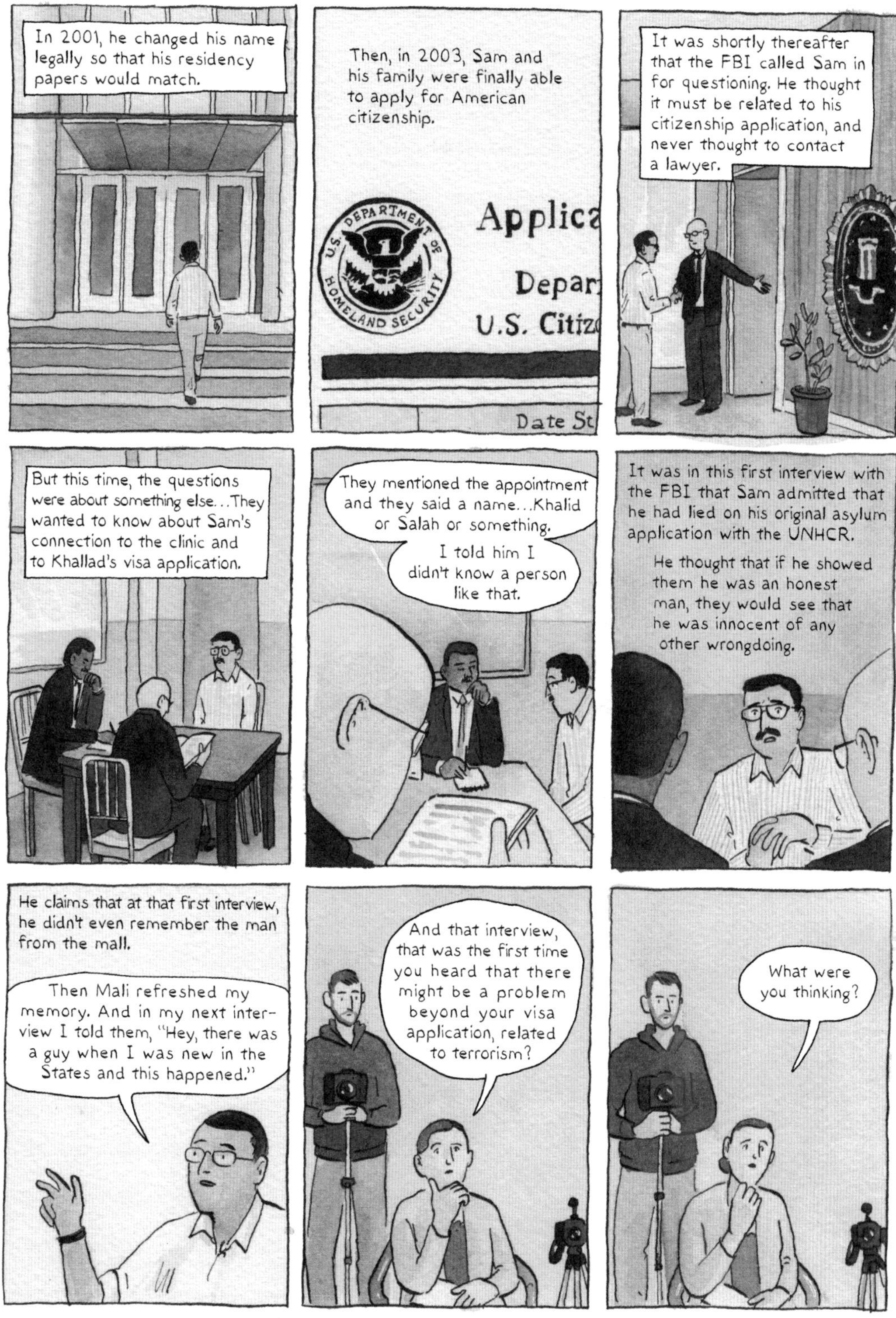
In 2001, he changed his name legally so that his residency papers would match.
Then, in 2003, Sam and his family were finally able to apply for American citizenship.
Applica
Depar
U.S. Citiz
Date St
It was shortly thereafter that the FBI called Sam in for questioning. He thought it must be related to his citizenship application, and never thought to contact a lawyer.
But this time, the questions were about something else... They wanted to know about Sam's connection to the clinic and to Khallad's visa application.
They mentioned the appointment and they said a name... Khalid or Salah or something.
I told him I didn't know a person like that.
It was in this first interview with the FBI that Sam admitted that he had lied on his original asylum application with the UNHCR.
He thought that if he showed them he was an honest man, they would see that he was innocent of any other wrongdoing.
He claims that at that first interview, he didn't even remember the man from the mall.
Then Mali refreshed my memory. And in my next interview I told them, "Hey, there was a guy when I was new in the States and this happened."
And that interview, that was the first time you heard that there might be a problem beyond your visa application, related to terrorism?
What were you thinking?

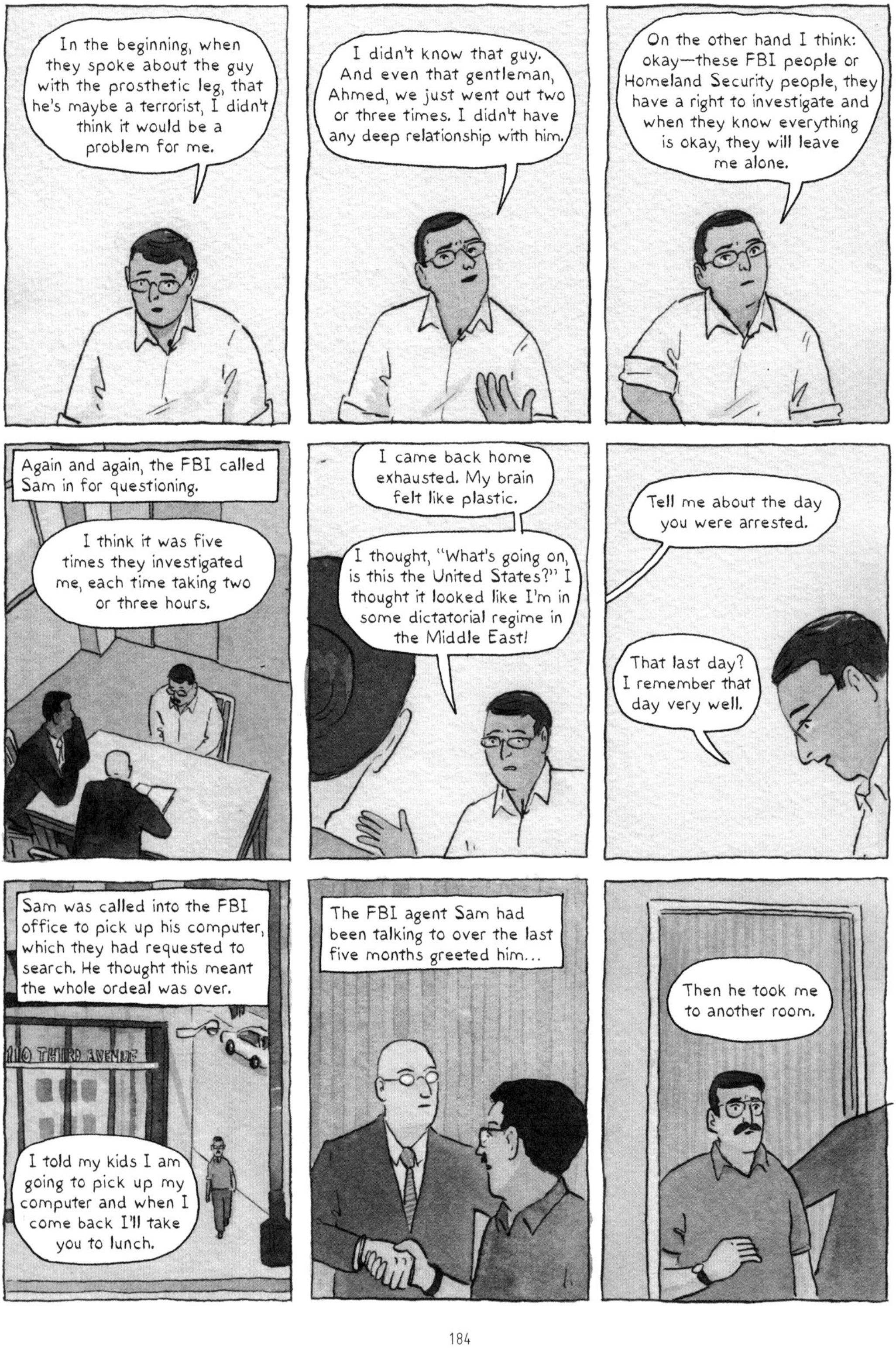
In the beginning, when they spoke about the guy with the prosthetic leg, that he's maybe a terrorist, I didn't think it would be a problem for me.
I didn't know that guy. And even that gentleman, Ahmed, we just went out two or three times. I didn't have any deep relationship with him.
On the other hand I think: okay—these FBI people or Homeland Security people, they have a right to investigate and when they know everything is okay, they will leave me alone.
Again and again, the FBI called Sam in for questioning.
I think it was five times they investigated me, each time taking two or three hours.
I came back home exhausted. My brain felt like plastic.
I thought, "What's going on, is this the United States?" I thought it looked like I'm in some dictatorial regime in the Middle East!
Tell me about the day you were arrested.
That last day? I remember that day very well.
Sam was called into the FBI office to pick up his computer, which they had requested to search. He thought this meant the whole ordeal was over.
110 THIRD AVENUE
I told my kids I am going to pick up my computer and when I come back I'll take you to lunch.
The FBI agent Sam had been talking to over the last five months greeted him...
Then he took me to another room.

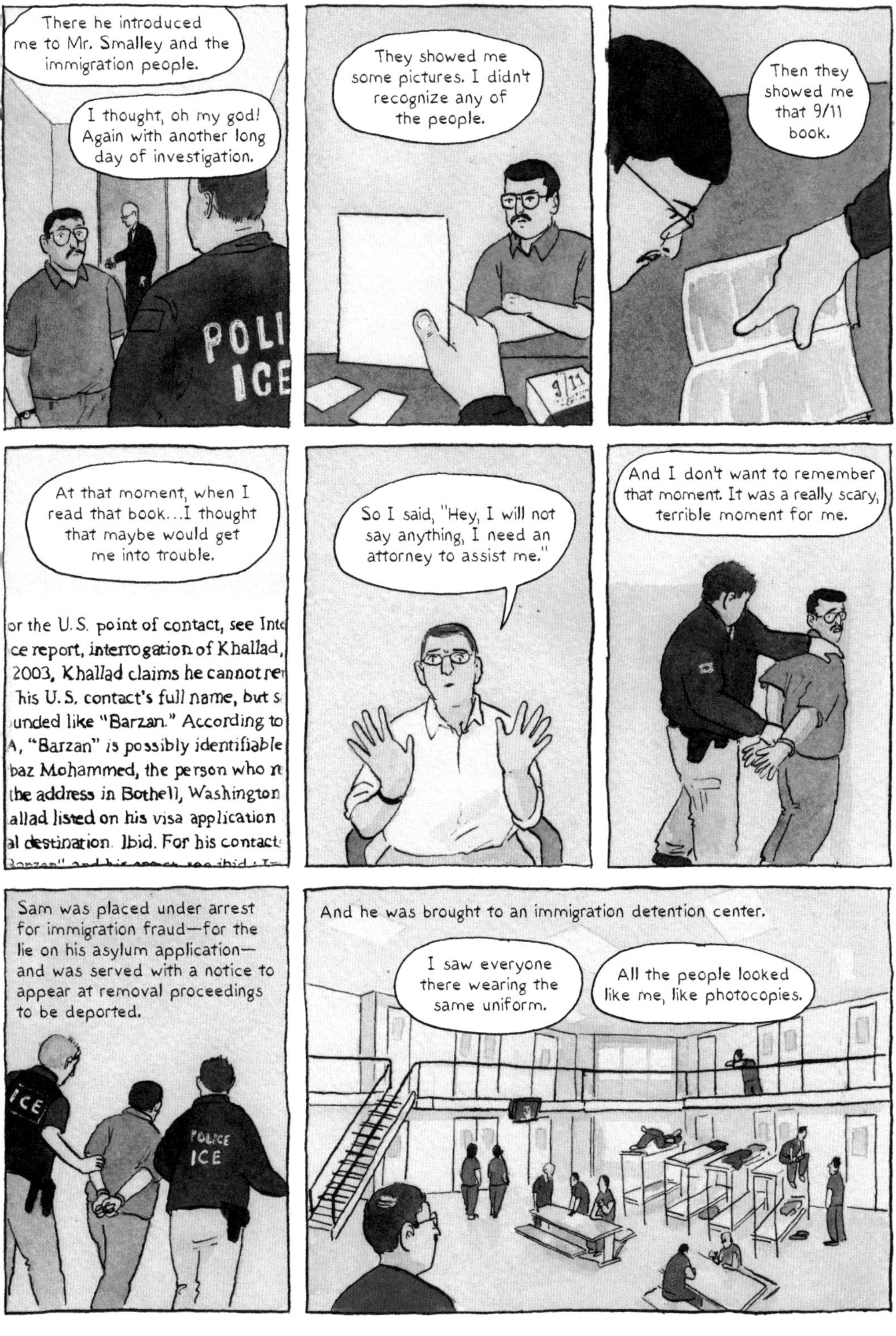

There he introduced me to Mr. Smalley and the immigration people.
I thought, oh my god! Again with another long day of investigation.
POLI ICE
They showed me some pictures. I didn't recognize any of the people.
9/11
Then they showed me that 9/11 book.
At that moment, when I read that book...I thought that maybe would get me into trouble.
or the U.S. point of contact, see Inte
ce report, interrogation of Khallad,
2003, Khallad claims he cannot re
his U.S. contact's full name, but s
unded like "Barzan." According to
A, "Barzan" is possibly identifiable
baz Mohammed, the person who r
the address in Bothell, Washington
allad listed on his visa application
al destination. Ibid. For his contact
So I said, "Hey, I will not say anything, I need an attorney to assist me."
And I don't want to remember that moment. It was a really scary, terrible moment for me.
Sam was placed under arrest for immigration fraud—for the lie on his asylum application—and was served with a notice to appear at removal proceedings to be deported.
ICE
POLICE ICE
And he was brought to an immigration detention center.
I saw everyone there wearing the same uniform.
All the people looked like me, like photocopies.

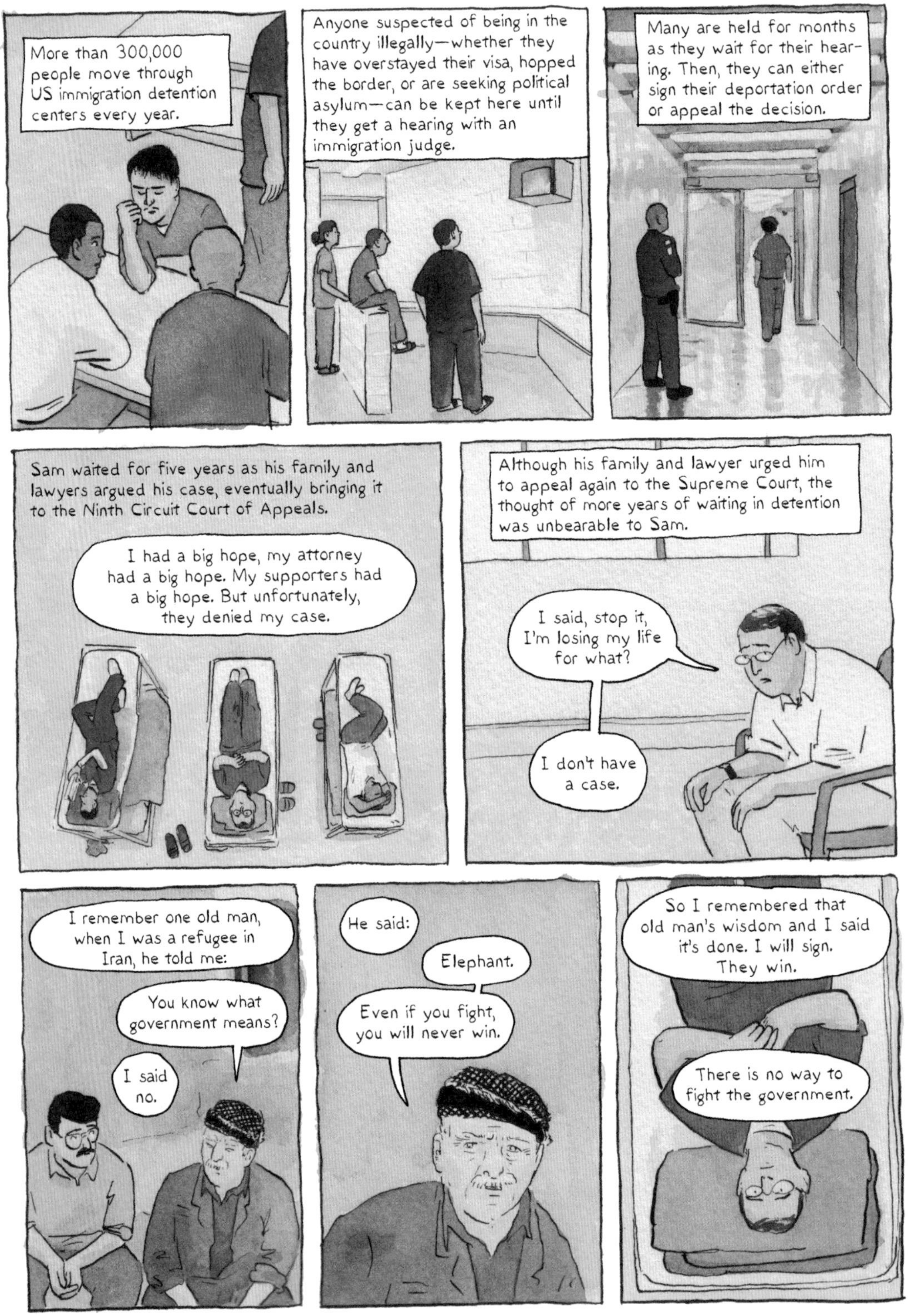
More than 300,000 people move through US immigration detention centers every year.
Anyone suspected of being in the country illegally—whether they have overstayed their visa, hopped the border, or are seeking political asylum—can be kept here until they get a hearing with an immigration judge.
Many are held for months as they wait for their hearing. Then, they can either sign their deportation order or appeal the decision.
Sam waited for five years as his family and lawyers argued his case, eventually bringing it to the Ninth Circuit Court of Appeals.
I had a big hope, my attorney had a big hope. My supporters had a big hope. But unfortunately, they denied my case.
Although his family and lawyer urged him to appeal again to the Supreme Court, the thought of more years of waiting in detention was unbearable to Sam.
I said, stop it, I'm losing my life for what?
I don't have a case.
I remember one old man, when I was a refugee in Iran, he told me:
You know what government means?
I said no.
He said:
Elephant.
Even if you fight, you will never win.
So I remembered that old man's wisdom and I said it's done. I will sign. They win.
There is no way to fight the government.

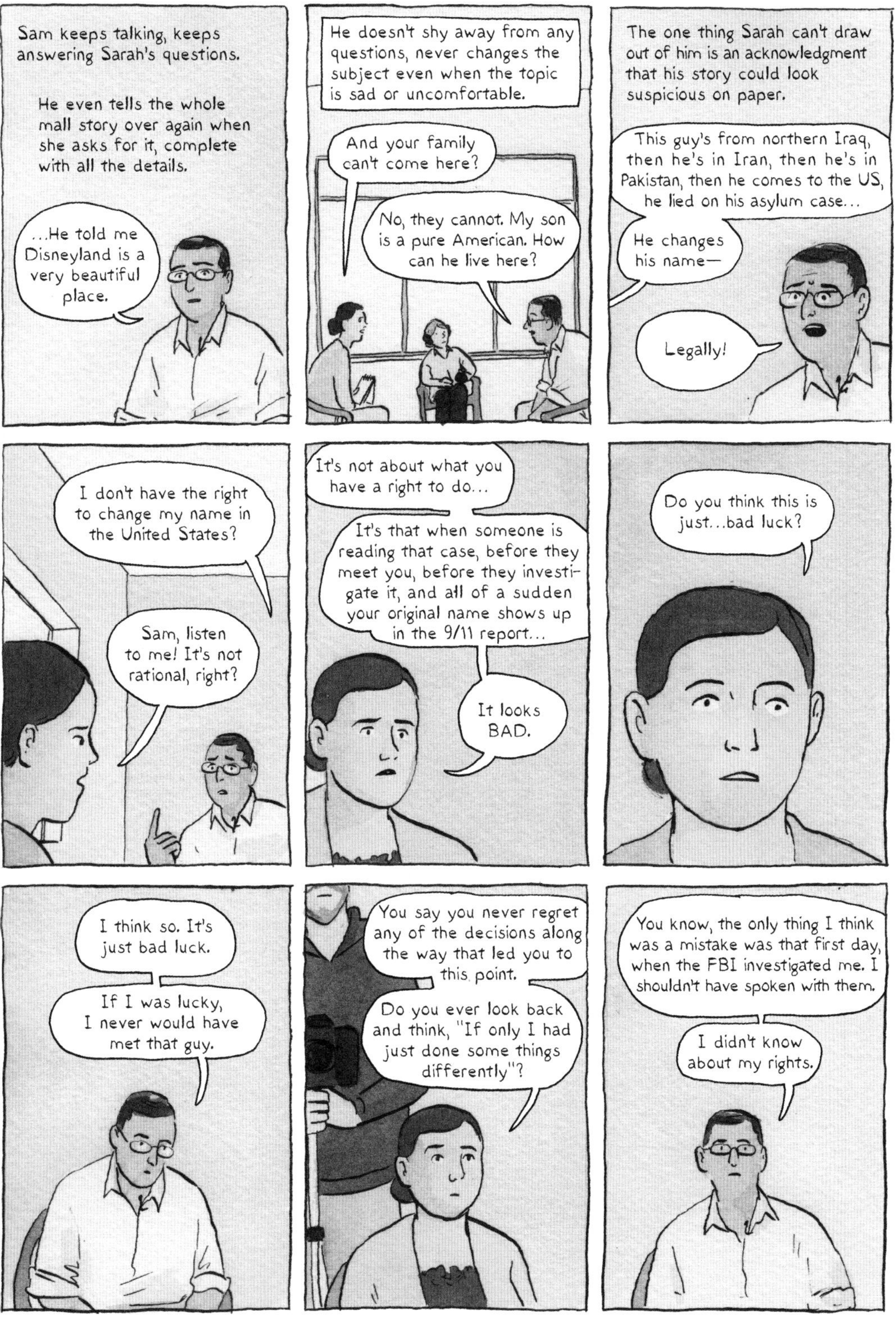

Sam keeps talking, keeps answering Sarah's questions.
He even tells the whole mall story over again when she asks for it, complete with all the details.
...He told me Disneyland is a very beautiful place.
He doesn't shy away from any questions, never changes the subject even when the topic is sad or uncomfortable.
And your family can't come here?
No, they cannot. My son is a pure American. How can he live here?
The one thing Sarah can't draw out of him is an acknowledgment that his story could look suspicious on paper.
This guy's from northern Iraq, then he's in Iran, then he's in Pakistan, then he comes to the US, he lied on his asylum case...
He changes his name—
Legally!
I don't have the right to change my name in the United States?
Sam, listen to me! It's not rational, right?
It's not about what you have a right to do...
It's that when someone is reading that case, before they meet you, before they investigate it, and all of a sudden your original name shows up in the 9/11 report...
It looks BAD.
Do you think this is just...bad luck?
I think so. It's just bad luck.
If I was lucky, I never would have met that guy.
You say you never regret any of the decisions along the way that led you to this point.
Do you ever look back and think, "If only I had just done some things differently"?
You know, the only thing I think was a mistake was that first day, when the FBI investigated me. I shouldn't have spoken with them.
I didn't know about my rights.

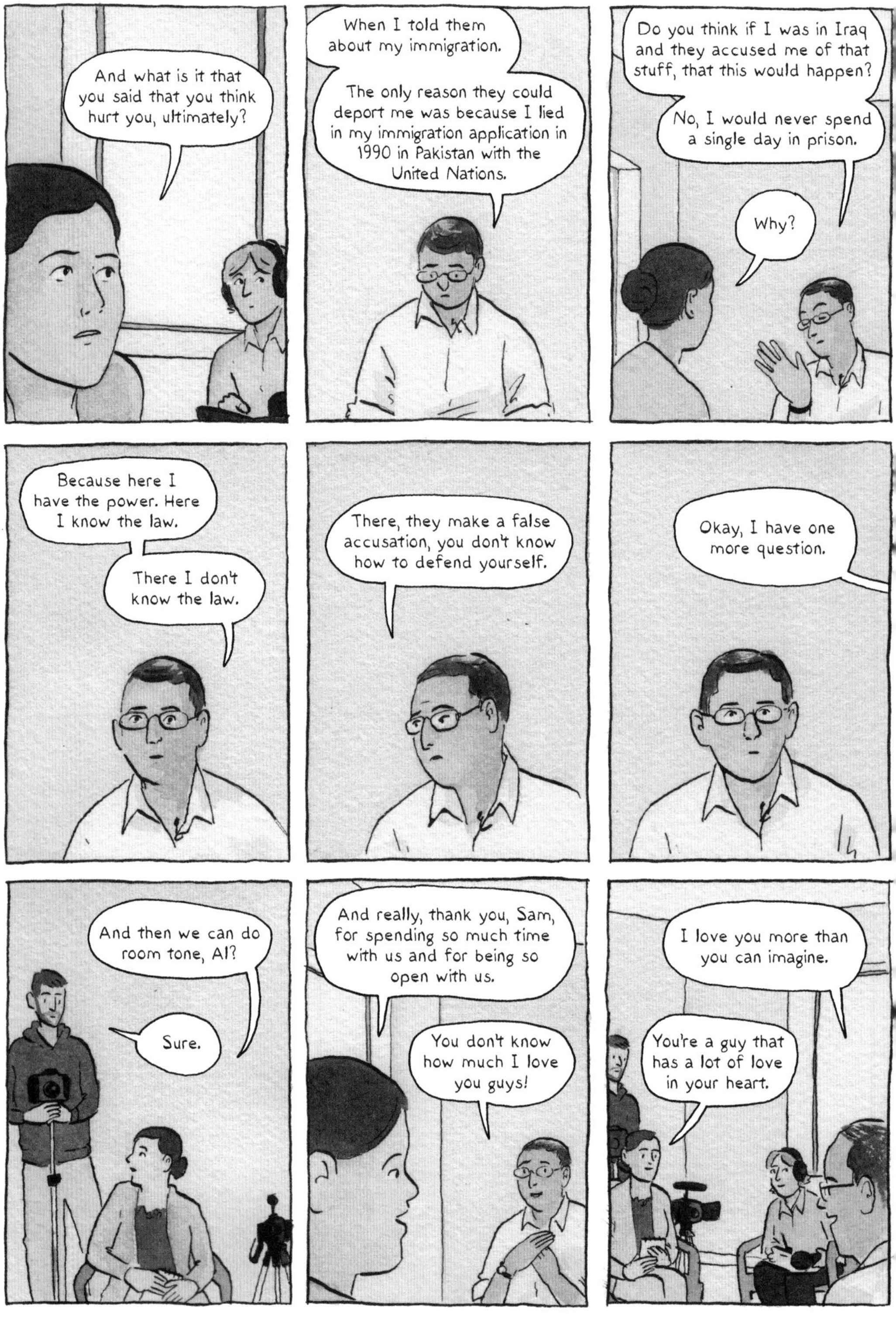
And what is it that you said that you think hurt you, ultimately?
When I told them about my immigration.
The only reason they could deport me was because I lied in my immigration application in 1990 in Pakistan with the United Nations.
Do you think if I was in Iraq and they accused me of that stuff, that this would happen?
No, I would never spend a single day in prison.
Why?
Because here I have the power. Here I know the law.
There I don't know the law.
There, they make a false accusation, you don't know how to defend yourself.
Okay, I have one more question.
And then we can do room tone, Al?
Sure.
And really, thank you, Sam, for spending so much time with us and for being so open with us.
You don't know how much I love you guys!
I love you more than you can imagine.
You're a guy that has a lot of love in your heart.

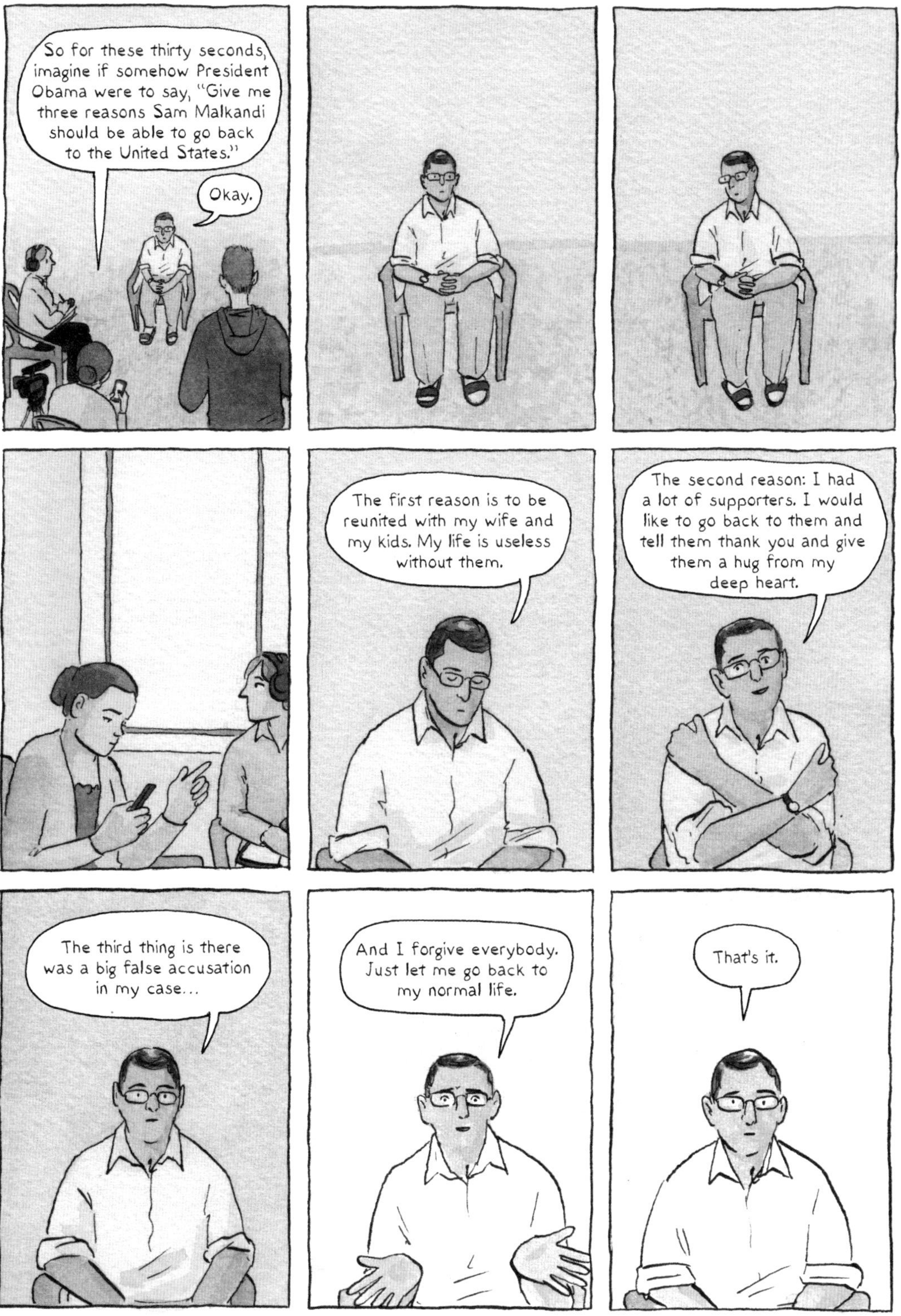
So for these thirty seconds, imagine if somehow President Obama were to say, "Give me three reasons Sam Malkandi should be able to go back to the United States."
Okay.
The first reason is to be reunited with my wife and my kids. My life is useless without them.
The second reason: I had a lot of supporters. I would like to go back to them and tell them thank you and give them a hug from my deep heart.
The third thing is there was a big false accusation in my case...
And I forgive everybody. Just let me go back to my normal life.
That's it.

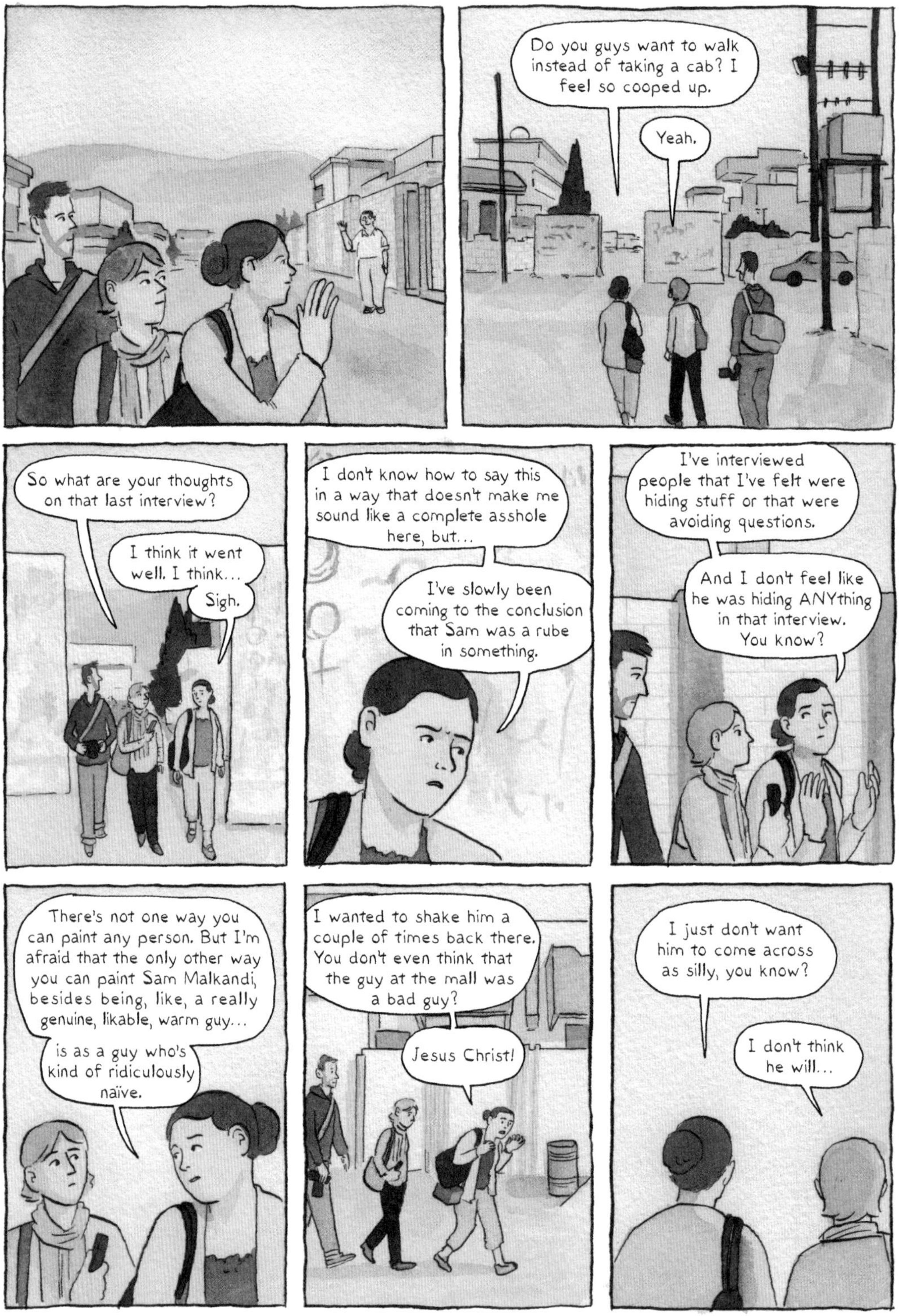
Do you guys want to walk instead of taking a cab? I feel so cooped up.
Yeah.
So what are your thoughts on that last interview?
I think it went well. I think...
Sigh.
I don't know how to say this in a way that doesn't make me sound like a complete asshole here, but...
I've slowly been coming to the conclusion that Sam was a rube in something.
I've interviewed people that I've felt were hiding stuff or that were avoiding questions.
And I don't feel like he was hiding ANYthing in that interview. You know?
There's not one way you can paint any person. But I'm afraid that the only other way you can paint Sam Malkandi, besides being, like, a really genuine, likable, warm guy...
is as a guy who's kind of ridiculously naïve.
I wanted to shake him a couple of times back there. You don't even think that the guy at the mall was a bad guy?
Jesus Christ!
I just don't want him to come across as silly, you know?
I don't think he will...

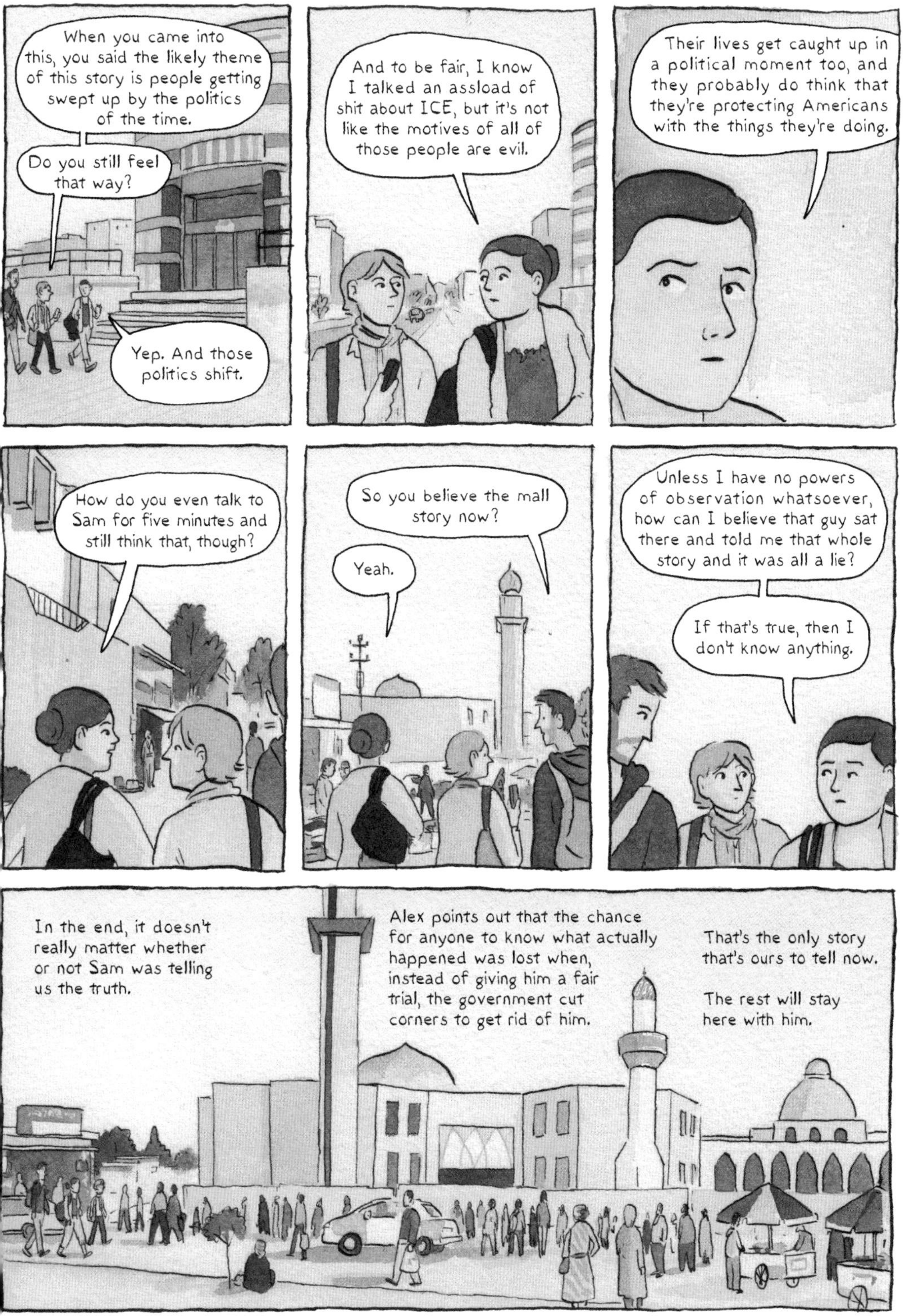
When you came into this, you said the likely theme of this story is people getting swept up by the politics of the time.
Do you still feel that way?
Yep. And those politics shift.
And to be fair, I know I talked an assload of shit about ICE, but it's not like the motives of all of those people are evil.
Their lives get caught up in a political moment too, and they probably do think that they're protecting Americans with the things they're doing.
How do you even talk to Sam for five minutes and still think that, though?
So you believe the mall story now?
Yeah.
Unless I have no powers of observation whatsoever, how can I believe that guy sat there and told me that whole story and it was all a lie?
If that's true, then I don't know anything.
In the end, it doesn't really matter whether or not Sam was telling us the truth.
Alex points out that the chance for anyone to know what actually happened was lost when, instead of giving him a fair trial, the government cut corners to get rid of him.
That's the only story that's ours to tell now.
The rest will stay here with him.

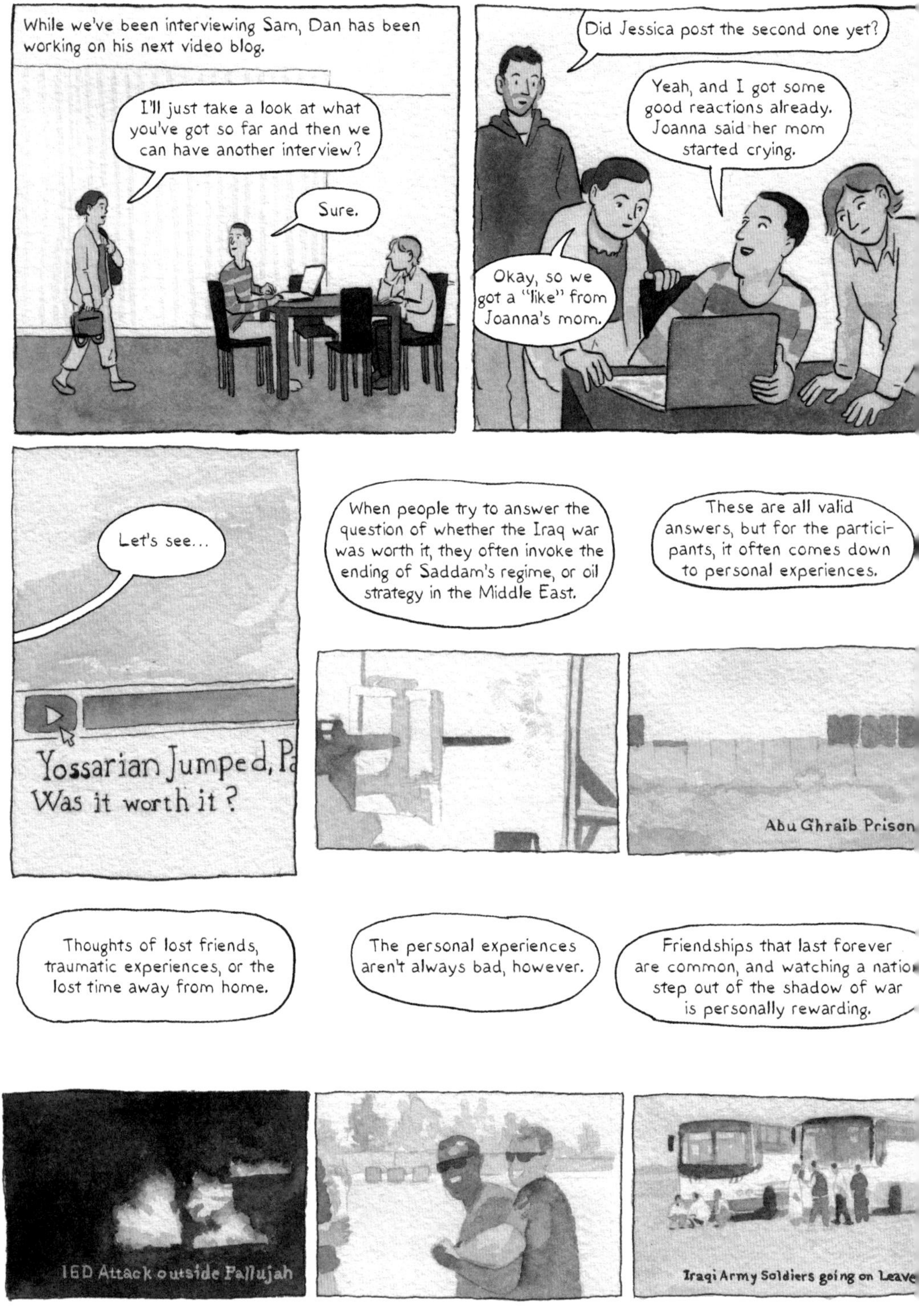
While we've been interviewing Sam, Dan has been working on his next video blog.
I'll just take a look at what you've got so far and then we can have another interview?
Sure.
Did Jessica post the second one yet?
Yeah, and I got some good reactions already. Joanna said her mom started crying.
Okay, so we got a "like" from Joanna's mom.
Let's see...
Yossarian Jumped, Pa
Was it worth it?
When people try to answer the question of whether the Iraq war was worth it, they often invoke the ending of Saddam's regime, or oil strategy in the Middle East.
These are all valid answers, but for the participants, it often comes down to personal experiences.
Abu Ghraib Prison
Thoughts of lost friends, traumatic experiences, or the lost time away from home.
The personal experiences aren't always bad, however.
Friendships that last forever are common, and watching a natio step out of the shadow of war is personally rewarding.
IED Attack outside Fallujah
Iraqi Army Soldiers going on Leave

For me, Iraq was the climax of an otherwise monotonous military career. It was a chance to apply years of tedious training.

By the time I arrived, I had largely forgotten all the grandiose reasons for joining up in the first place.

Gone were the notions of keeping the world safe from al Qaeda. And by 2007, avenging 9/11 in Iraq seemed like a joke.

No. I was there for my friends. I was there because we were part of a unit. We were there for each other.

Having had four years to reflect on the question, I still struggle to come up with an answer that doesn't seem selfish.

I have been personally rewarded with scholarships, healthcare coverage, and respect that I don't feel worthy of. It seems like I have been given so much while I gave so little.

Four members of my unit are dead and buried. And if you asked their families if the war in Iraq was worth it, what would their answer be?

I couldn't even begin to try and answer for them.

Then I think of the Kurds...

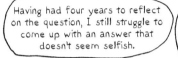
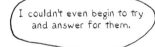

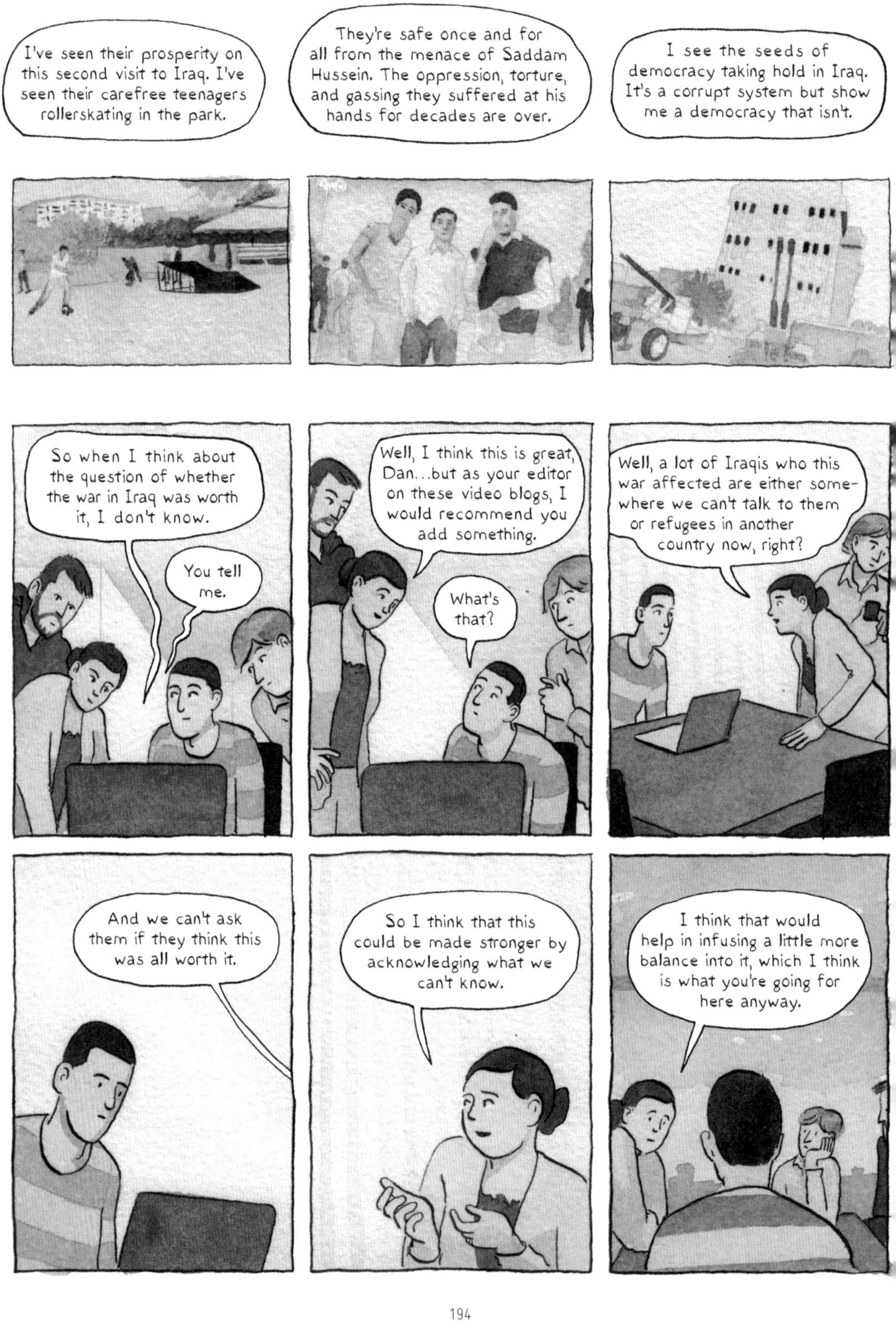
I've seen their prosperity on this second visit to Iraq. I've seen their carefree teenagers rollerskating in the park.
They're safe once and for all from the menace of Saddam Hussein. The oppression, torture, and gassing they suffered at his hands for decades are over.
I see the seeds of democracy taking hold in Iraq. It's a corrupt system but show me a democracy that isn't.
So when I think about the question of whether the war in Iraq was worth it, I don't know.
You tell me.
Well, I think this is great, Dan...but as your editor on these video blogs, I would recommend you add something.
What's that?
Well, a lot of Iraqis who this war affected are either somewhere we can't talk to them or refugees in another country now, right?
And we can't ask them if they think this was all worth it.
So I think that this could be made stronger by acknowledging what we can't know.
I think that would help in infusing a little more balance into it, which I think is what you're going for here anyway.

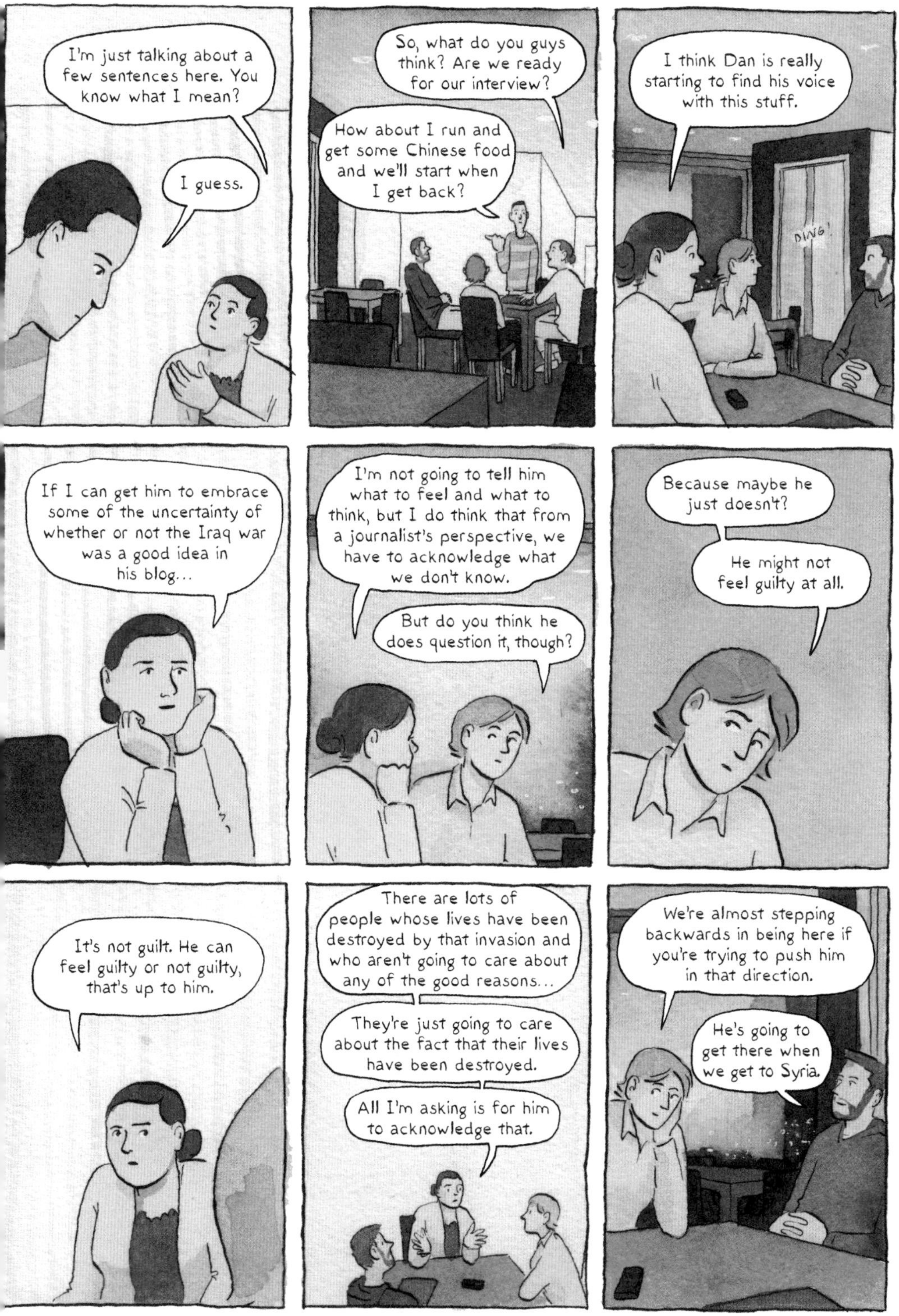
I'm just talking about a few sentences here. You know what I mean?
I guess.
So, what do you guys think? Are we ready for our interview?
How about I run and get some Chinese food and we'll start when I get back?
I think Dan is really starting to find his voice with this stuff.
DING!
If I can get him to embrace some of the uncertainty of whether or not the Iraq war was a good idea in his blog...
I'm not going to tell him what to feel and what to think, but I do think that from a journalist's perspective, we have to acknowledge what we don't know.
But do you think he does question it, though?
Because maybe he just doesn't?
He might not feel guilty at all.
It's not guilt. He can feel guilty or not guilty, that's up to him.
There are lots of people whose lives have been destroyed by that invasion and who aren't going to care about any of the good reasons...
They're just going to care about the fact that their lives have been destroyed.
All I'm asking is for him to acknowledge that.
We're almost stepping backwards in being here if you're trying to push him in that direction.
He's going to get there when we get to Syria.

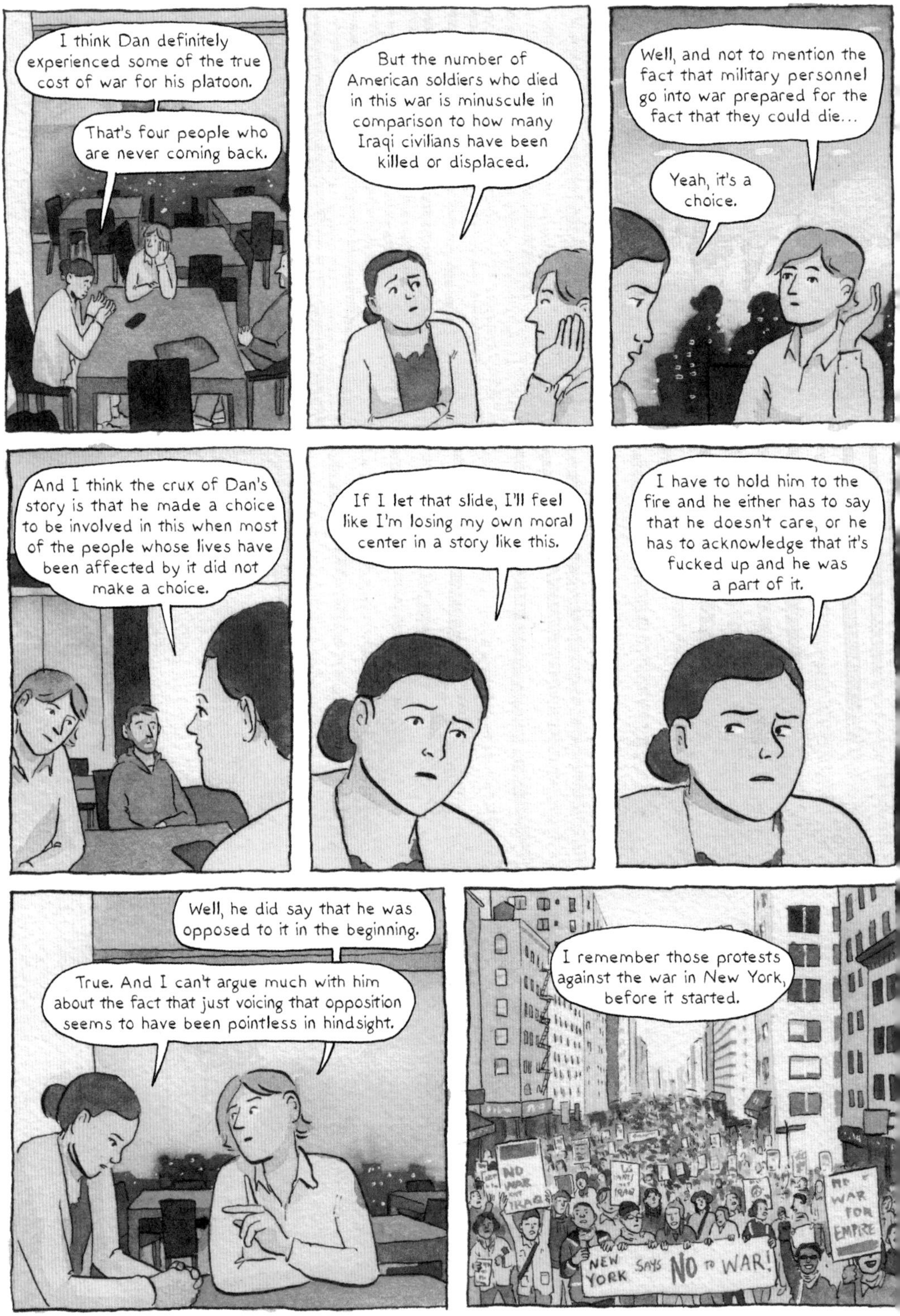
I think Dan definitely experienced some of the true cost of war for his platoon.
That's four people who are never coming back.
But the number of American soldiers who died in this war is minuscule in comparison to how many Iraqi civilians have been killed or displaced.
Well, and not to mention the fact that military personnel go into war prepared for the fact that they could die...
Yeah, it's a choice.
And I think the crux of Dan's story is that he made a choice to be involved in this when most of the people whose lives have been affected by it did not make a choice.
If I let that slide, I'll feel like I'm losing my own moral center in a story like this.
I have to hold him to the fire and he either has to say that he doesn't care, or he has to acknowledge that it's fucked up and he was a part of it.
Well, he did say that he was opposed to it in the beginning.
True. And I can't argue much with him about the fact that just voicing that opposition seems to have been pointless in hindsight.
I remember those protests against the war in New York, before it started.
NO WAR ON IRAQ
NO WAR FOR EMPIRE
NEW YORK SAYS NO TO WAR!

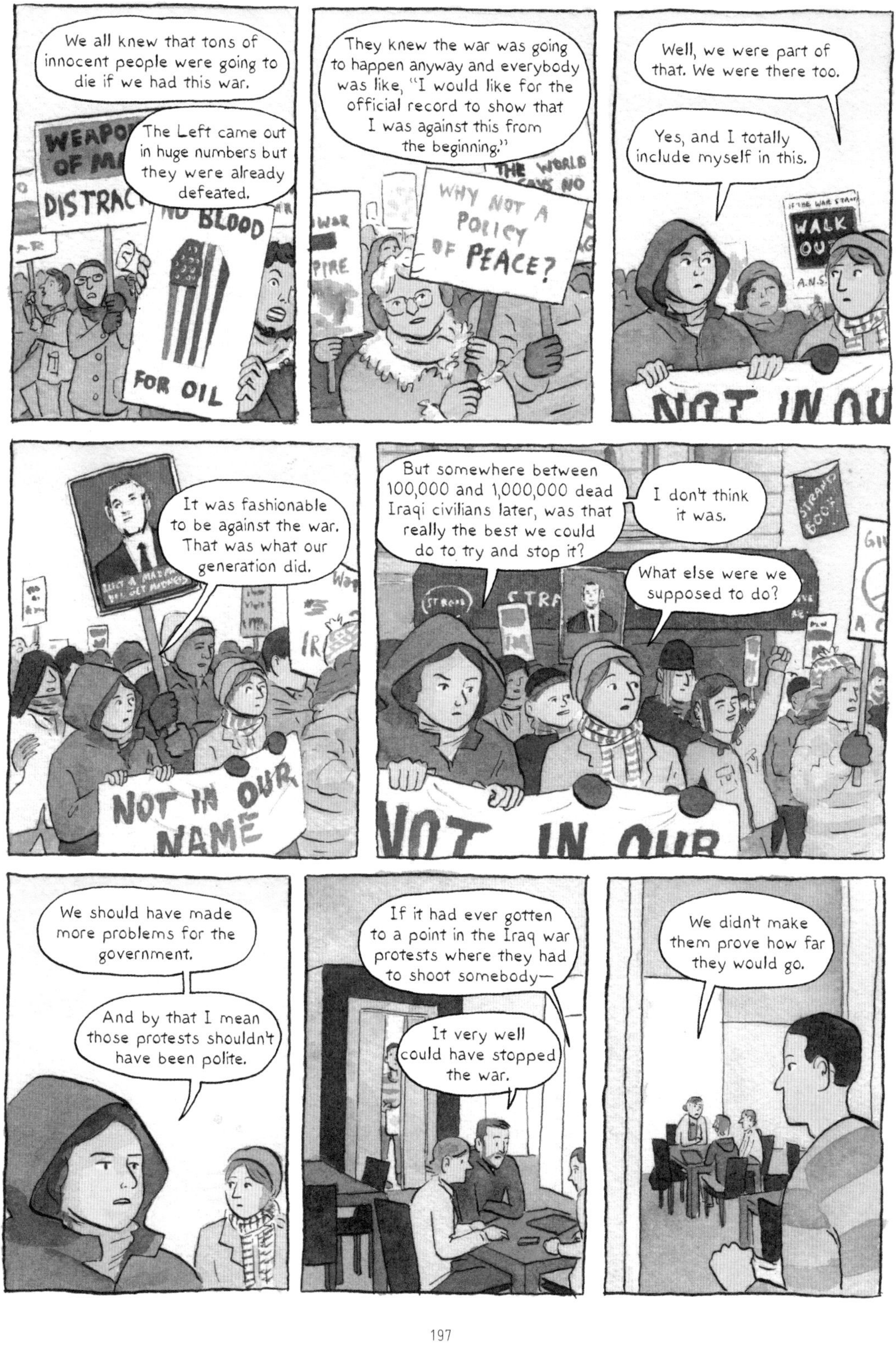
We all knew that tons of innocent people were going to die if we had this war.
The Left came out in huge numbers but they were already defeated.
NO BLOOD FOR OIL
They knew the war was going to happen anyway and everybody was like, "I would like for the official record to show that I was against this from the beginning."
WHY NOT A POLICY OF PEACE?
THE WORLD SAYS NO
Well, we were part of that. We were there too.
Yes, and I totally include myself in this.
WALK OUT
NOT IN OUR NAME
It was fashionable to be against the war. That was what our generation did.
But somewhere between 100,000 and 1,000,000 dead Iraqi civilians later, was that really the best we could do to try and stop it?
I don't think it was.
What else were we supposed to do?
We should have made more problems for the government.
And by that I mean those protests shouldn't have been polite.
If it had ever gotten to a point in the Iraq war protests where they had to shoot somebody—
It very well could have stopped the war.
We didn't make them prove how far they would go.

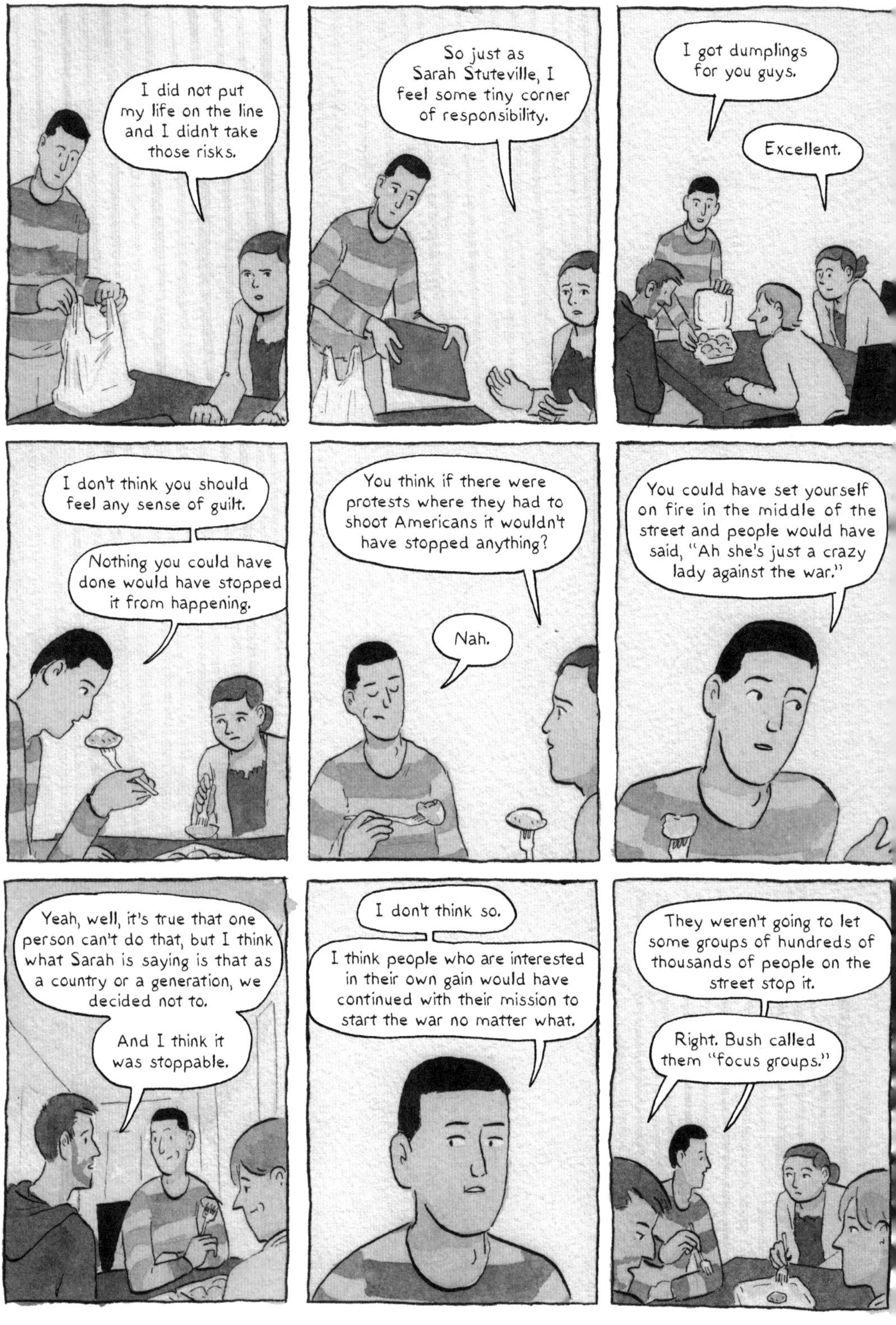
I did not put my life on the line and I didn't take those risks.
So just as Sarah Stuteville, I feel some tiny corner of responsibility.
I got dumplings for you guys.
Excellent.
I don't think you should feel any sense of guilt.
Nothing you could have done would have stopped it from happening.
You think if there were protests where they had to shoot Americans it wouldn't have stopped anything?
Nah.
You could have set yourself on fire in the middle of the street and people would have said, "Ah she's just a crazy lady against the war."
Yeah, well, it's true that one person can't do that, but I think what Sarah is saying is that as a country or a generation, we decided not to.
And I think it was stoppable.
I don't think so.
I think people who are interested in their own gain would have continued with their mission to start the war no matter what.
They weren't going to let some groups of hundreds of thousands of people on the street stop it.
Right. Bush called them "focus groups."

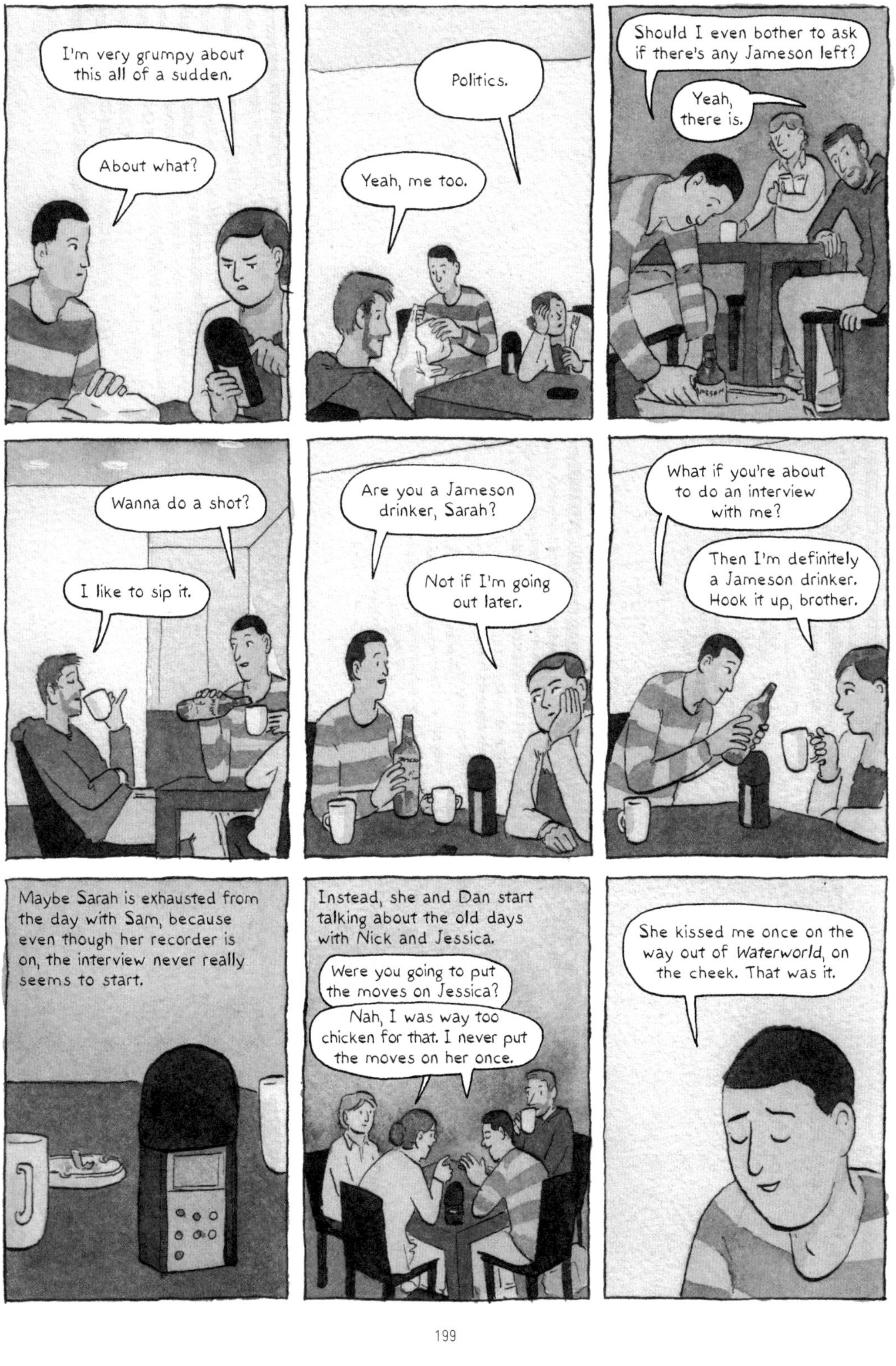

I'm very grumpy about this all of a sudden.
About what?
Politics.
Yeah, me too.
Should I even bother to ask if there's any Jameson left?
Yeah, there is.
Wanna do a shot?
I like to sip it.
Are you a Jameson drinker, Sarah?
Not if I'm going out later.
What if you're about to do an interview with me?
Then I'm definitely a Jameson drinker. Hook it up, brother.
Maybe Sarah is exhausted from the day with Sam, because even though her recorder is on, the interview never really seems to start.
Instead, she and Dan start talking about the old days with Nick and Jessica.
Were you going to put the moves on Jessica?
Nah, I was way too chicken for that. I never put the moves on her once.
She kissed me once on the way out of *Waterworld*, on the cheek. That was it.

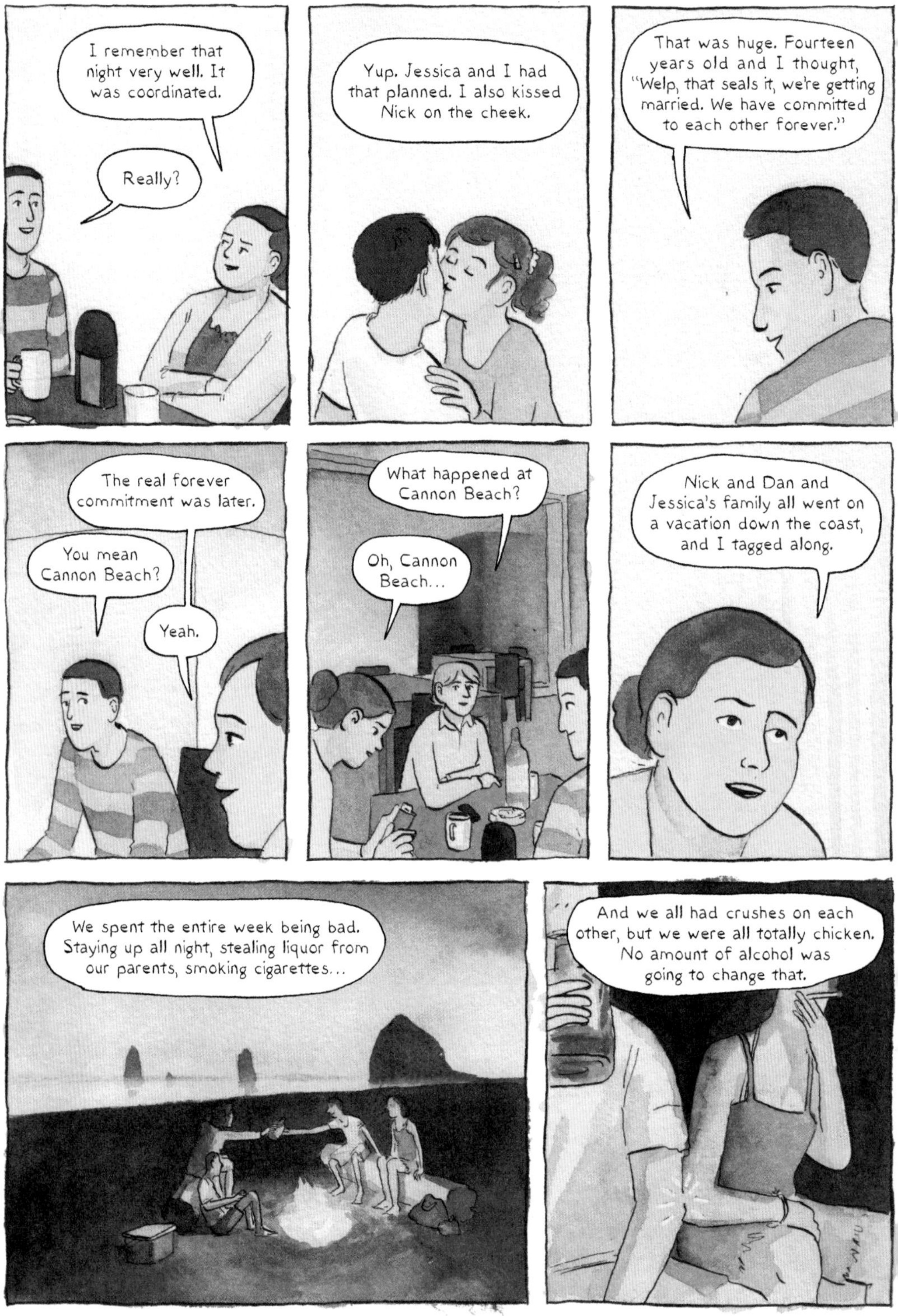
I remember that night very well. It was coordinated.
Really?
Yup. Jessica and I had that planned. I also kissed Nick on the cheek.
That was huge. Fourteen years old and I thought, "Welp, that seals it, we're getting married. We have committed to each other forever."
The real forever commitment was later.
You mean Cannon Beach?
Yeah.
What happened at Cannon Beach?
Oh, Cannon Beach...
Nick and Dan and Jessica's family all went on a vacation down the coast, and I tagged along.
We spent the entire week being bad. Staying up all night, stealing liquor from our parents, smoking cigarettes...
And we all had crushes on each other, but we were all totally chicken. No amount of alcohol was going to change that.

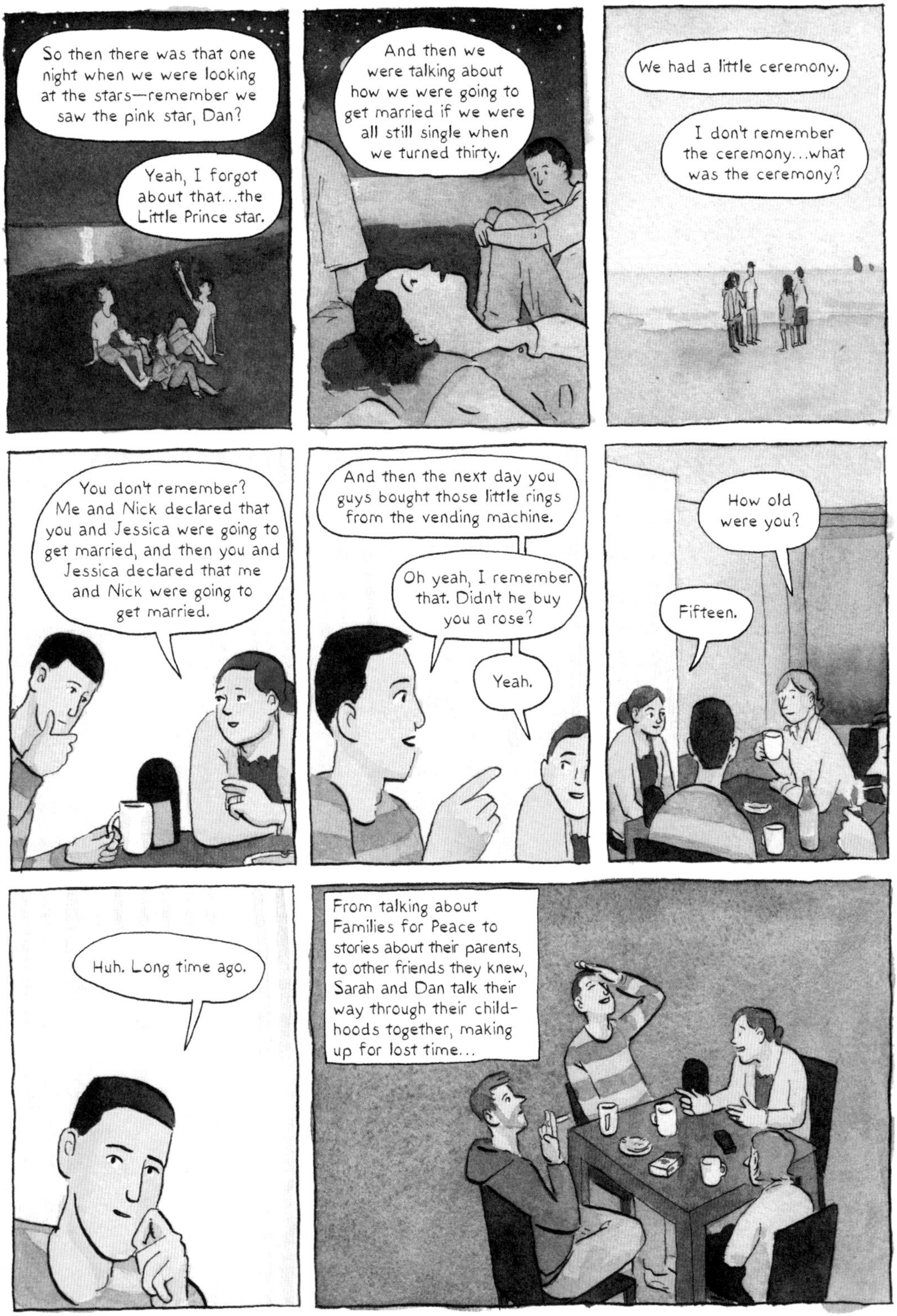

So then there was that one night when we were looking at the stars—remember we saw the pink star, Dan?
Yeah, I forgot about that...the Little Prince star.
And then we were talking about how we were going to get married if we were all still single when we turned thirty.
We had a little ceremony.
I don't remember the ceremony...what was the ceremony?
You don't remember? Me and Nick declared that you and Jessica were going to get married, and then you and Jessica declared that me and Nick were going to get married.
And then the next day you guys bought those little rings from the vending machine.
Oh yeah, I remember that. Didn't he buy you a rose?
Yeah.
How old were you?
Fifteen.
Huh. Long time ago.
From talking about Families for Peace to stories about their parents, to other friends they knew, Sarah and Dan talk their way through their childhoods together, making up for lost time...

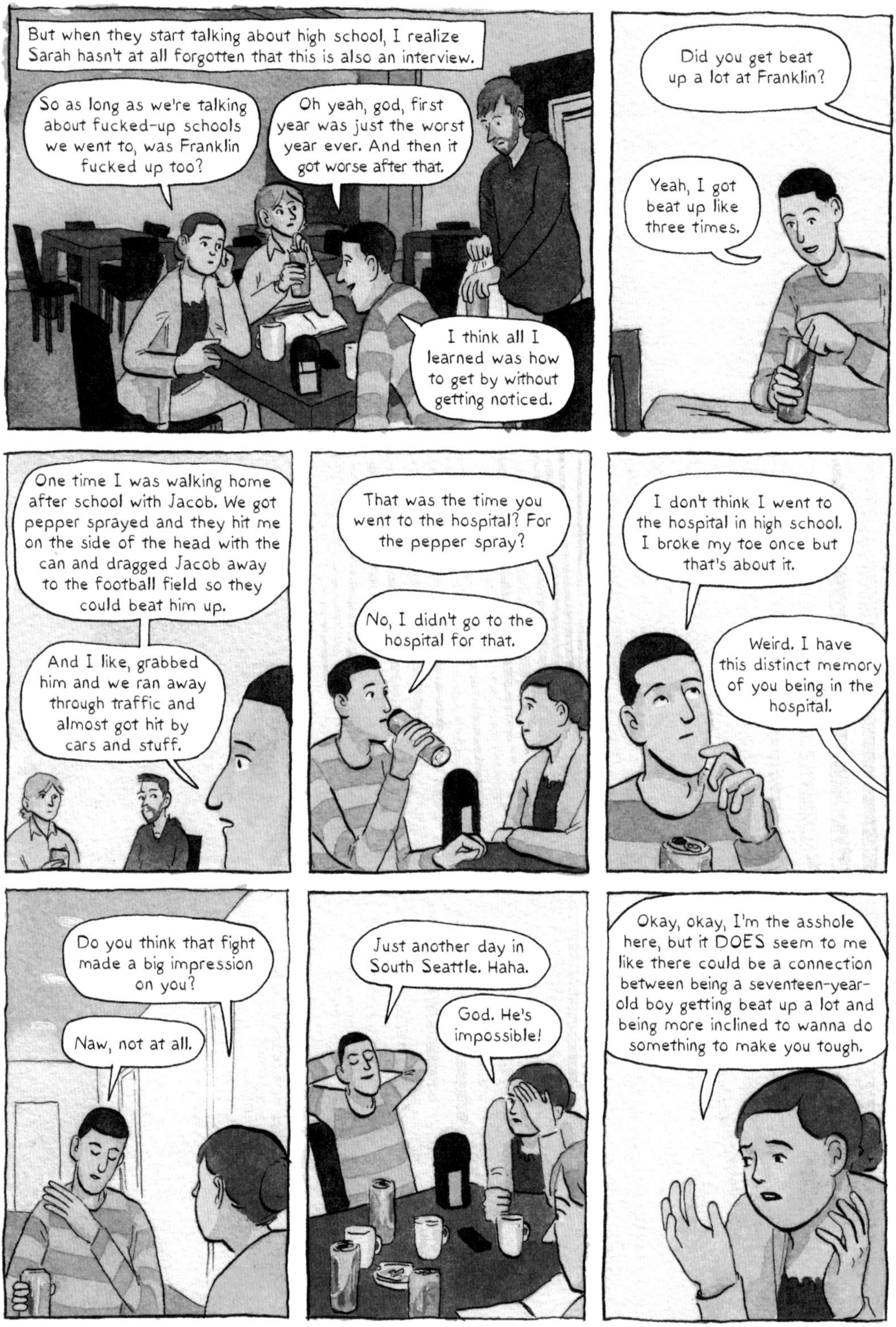
But when they start talking about high school, I realize Sarah hasn't at all forgotten that this is also an interview.
So as long as we're talking about fucked-up schools we went to, was Franklin fucked up too?
Oh yeah, god, first year was just the worst year ever. And then it got worse after that.
I think all I learned was how to get by without getting noticed.
Did you get beat up a lot at Franklin?
Yeah, I got beat up like three times.
One time I was walking home after school with Jacob. We got pepper sprayed and they hit me on the side of the head with the can and dragged Jacob away to the football field so they could beat him up.
And I like, grabbed him and we ran away through traffic and almost got hit by cars and stuff.
That was the time you went to the hospital? For the pepper spray?
No, I didn't go to the hospital for that.
I don't think I went to the hospital in high school. I broke my toe once but that's about it.
Weird. I have this distinct memory of you being in the hospital.
Do you think that fight made a big impression on you?
Naw, not at all.
Just another day in South Seattle. Haha.
God. He's impossible!
Okay, okay, I'm the asshole here, but it DOES seem to me like there could be a connection between being a seventeen-year-old boy getting beat up a lot and being more inclined to wanna do something to make you tough.

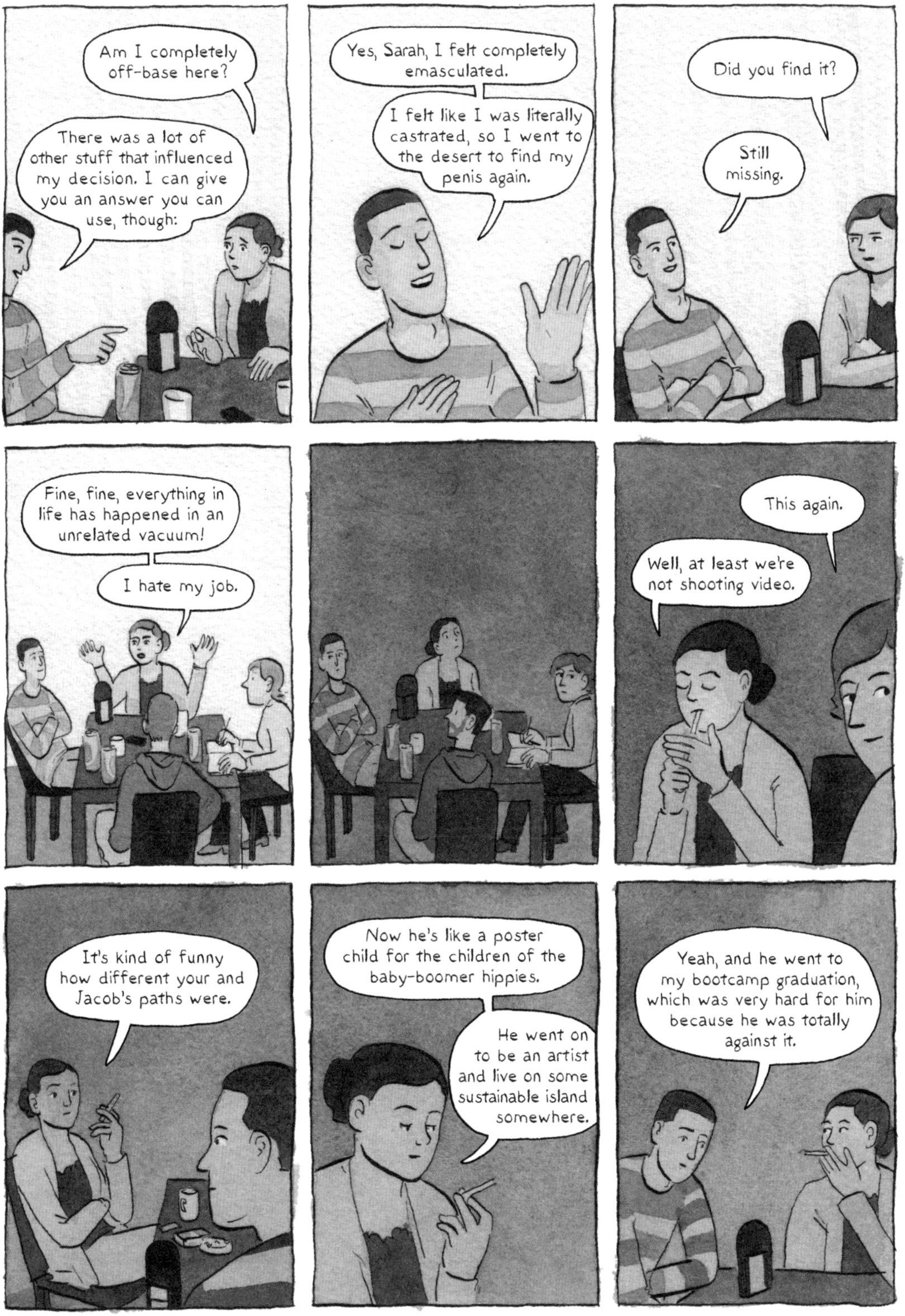
Am I completely off-base here?
There was a lot of other stuff that influenced my decision. I can give you an answer you can use, though:
Yes, Sarah, I felt completely emasculated.
I felt like I was literally castrated, so I went to the desert to find my penis again.
Did you find it?
Still missing.
Fine, fine, everything in life has happened in an unrelated vacuum!
I hate my job.
This again.
Well, at least we're not shooting video.
It's kind of funny how different your and Jacob's paths were.
Now he's like a poster child for the children of the baby-boomer hippies.
He went on to be an artist and live on some sustainable island somewhere.
Yeah, and he went to my bootcamp graduation, which was very hard for him because he was totally against it.

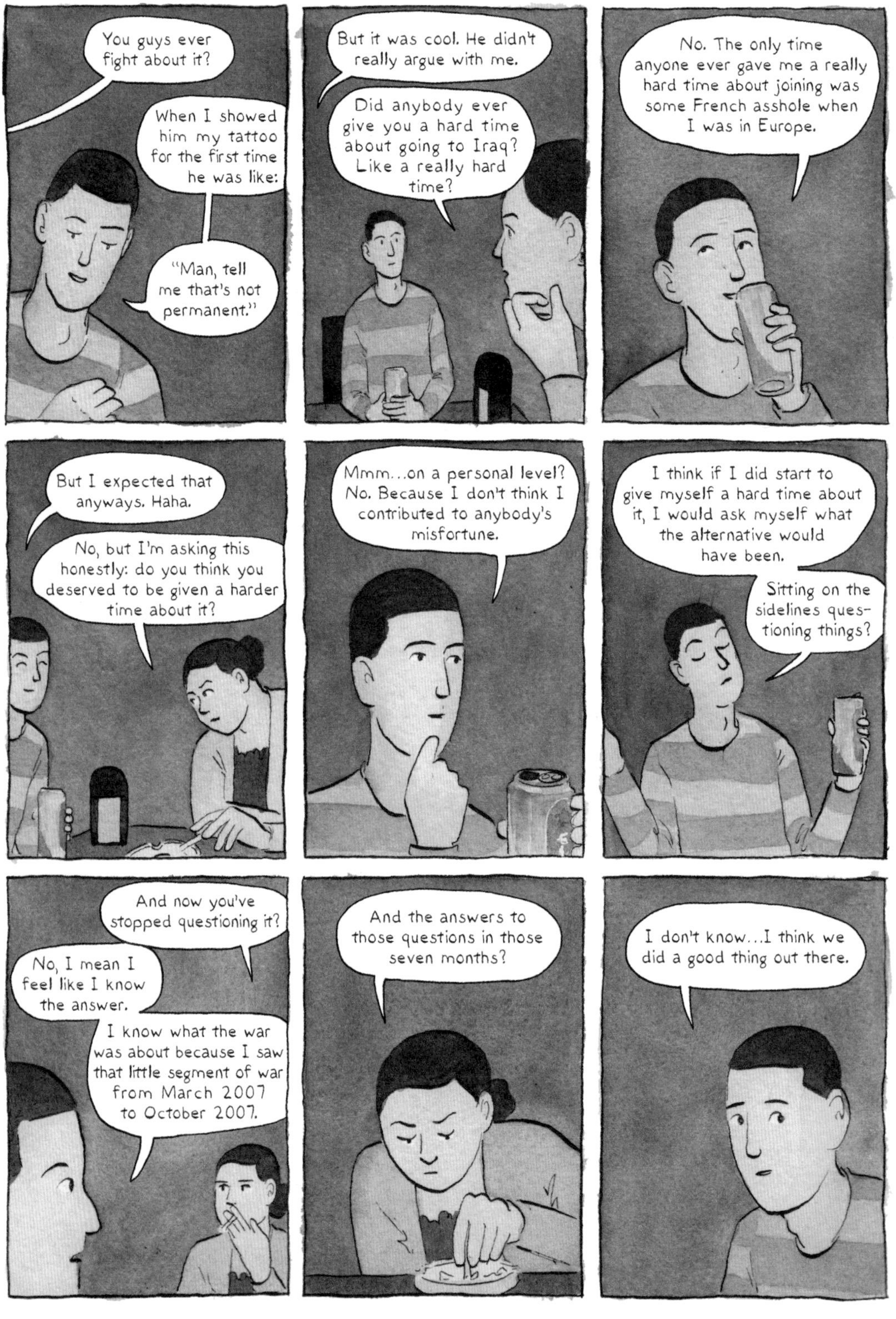
You guys ever fight about it?
When I showed him my tattoo for the first time he was like:
"Man, tell me that's not permanent."
But it was cool. He didn't really argue with me.
Did anybody ever give you a hard time about going to Iraq? Like a really hard time?
No. The only time anyone ever gave me a really hard time about joining was some French asshole when I was in Europe.
But I expected that anyways. Haha.
No, but I'm asking this honestly: do you think you deserved to be given a harder time about it?
Mmm...on a personal level? No. Because I don't think I contributed to anybody's misfortune.
I think if I did start to give myself a hard time about it, I would ask myself what the alternative would have been.
Sitting on the sidelines questioning things?
And now you've stopped questioning it?
No, I mean I feel like I know the answer.
I know what the war was about because I saw that little segment of war from March 2007 to October 2007.
And the answers to those questions in those seven months?
I don't know...I think we did a good thing out there.

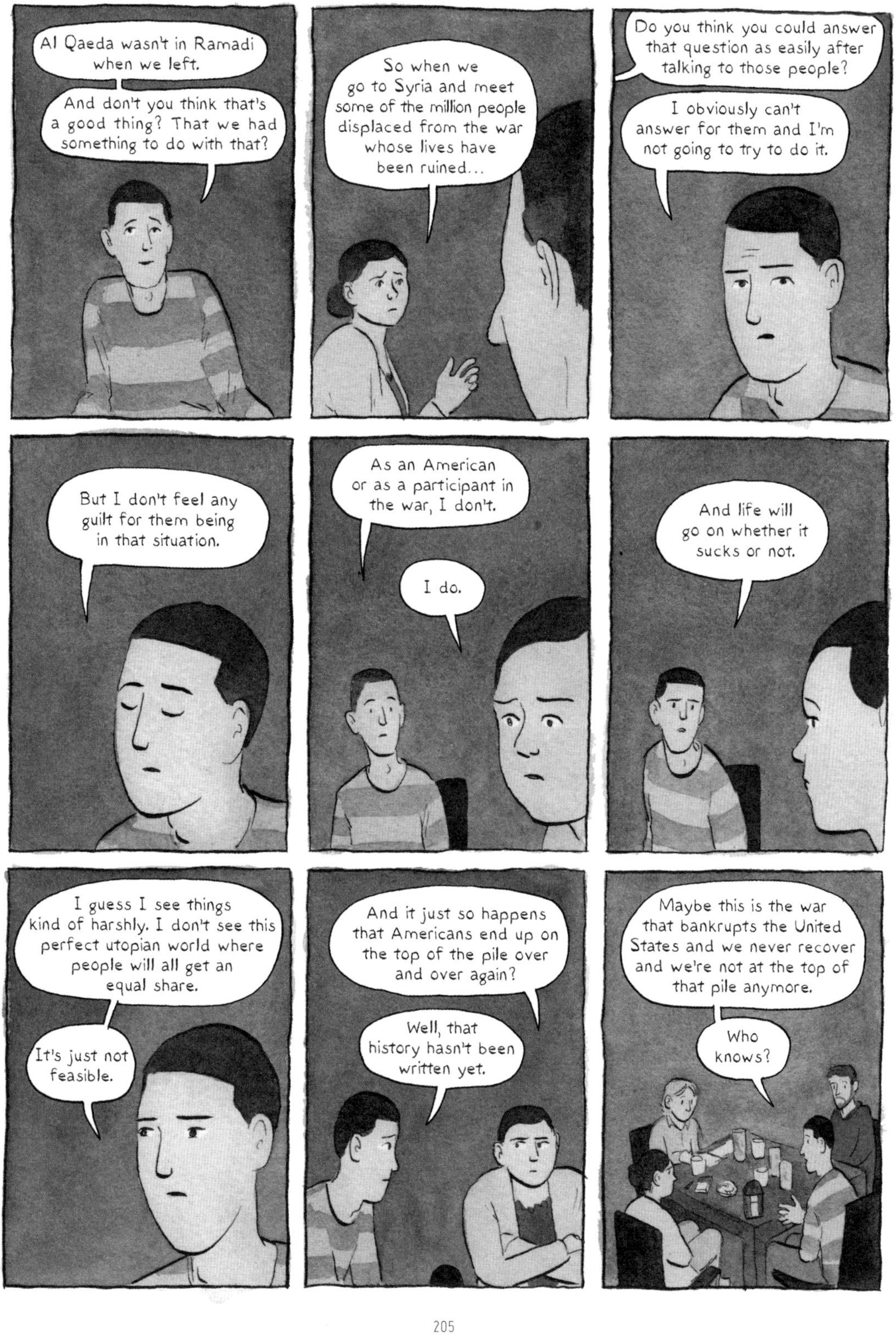

Al Qaeda wasn't in Ramadi when we left.
And don't you think that's a good thing? That we had something to do with that?
So when we go to Syria and meet some of the million people displaced from the war whose lives have been ruined...
Do you think you could answer that question as easily after talking to those people?
I obviously can't answer for them and I'm not going to try to do it.
But I don't feel any guilt for them being in that situation.
As an American or as a participant in the war, I don't.
I do.
And life will go on whether it sucks or not.
I guess I see things kind of harshly. I don't see this perfect utopian world where people will all get an equal share.
It's just not feasible.
And it just so happens that Americans end up on the top of the pile over and over again?
Well, that history hasn't been written yet.
Maybe this is the war that bankrupts the United States and we never recover and we're not at the top of that pile anymore.
Who knows?

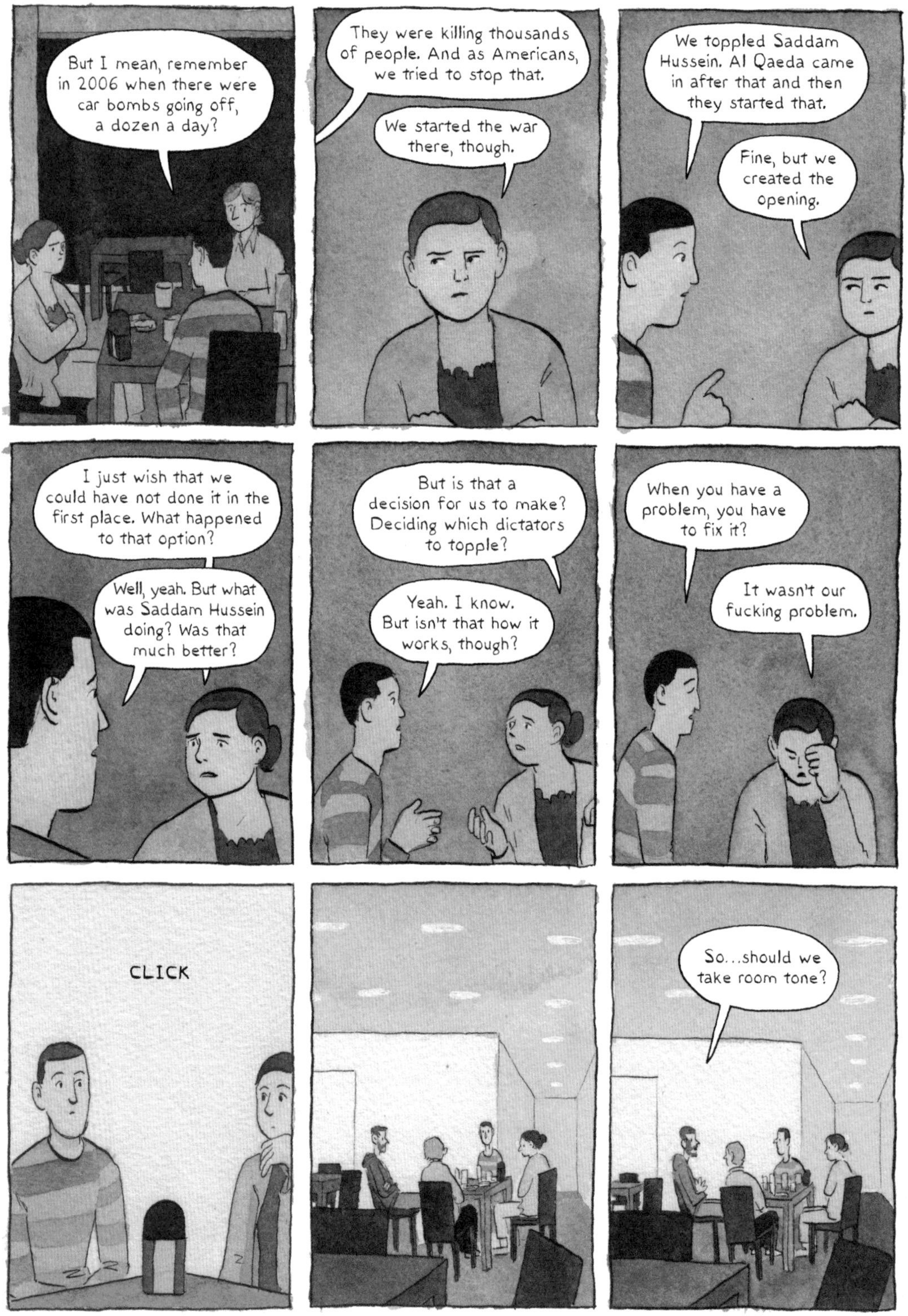
But I mean, remember in 2006 when there were car bombs going off, a dozen a day?
They were killing thousands of people. And as Americans, we tried to stop that.
We started the war there, though.
We toppled Saddam Hussein. Al Qaeda came in after that and then they started that.
Fine, but we created the opening.
I just wish that we could have not done it in the first place. What happened to that option?
Well, yeah. But what was Saddam Hussein doing? Was that much better?
But is that a decision for us to make? Deciding which dictators to topple?
Yeah. I know. But isn't that how it works, though?
When you have a problem, you have to fix it?
It wasn't our fucking problem.
CLICK
So...should we take room tone?

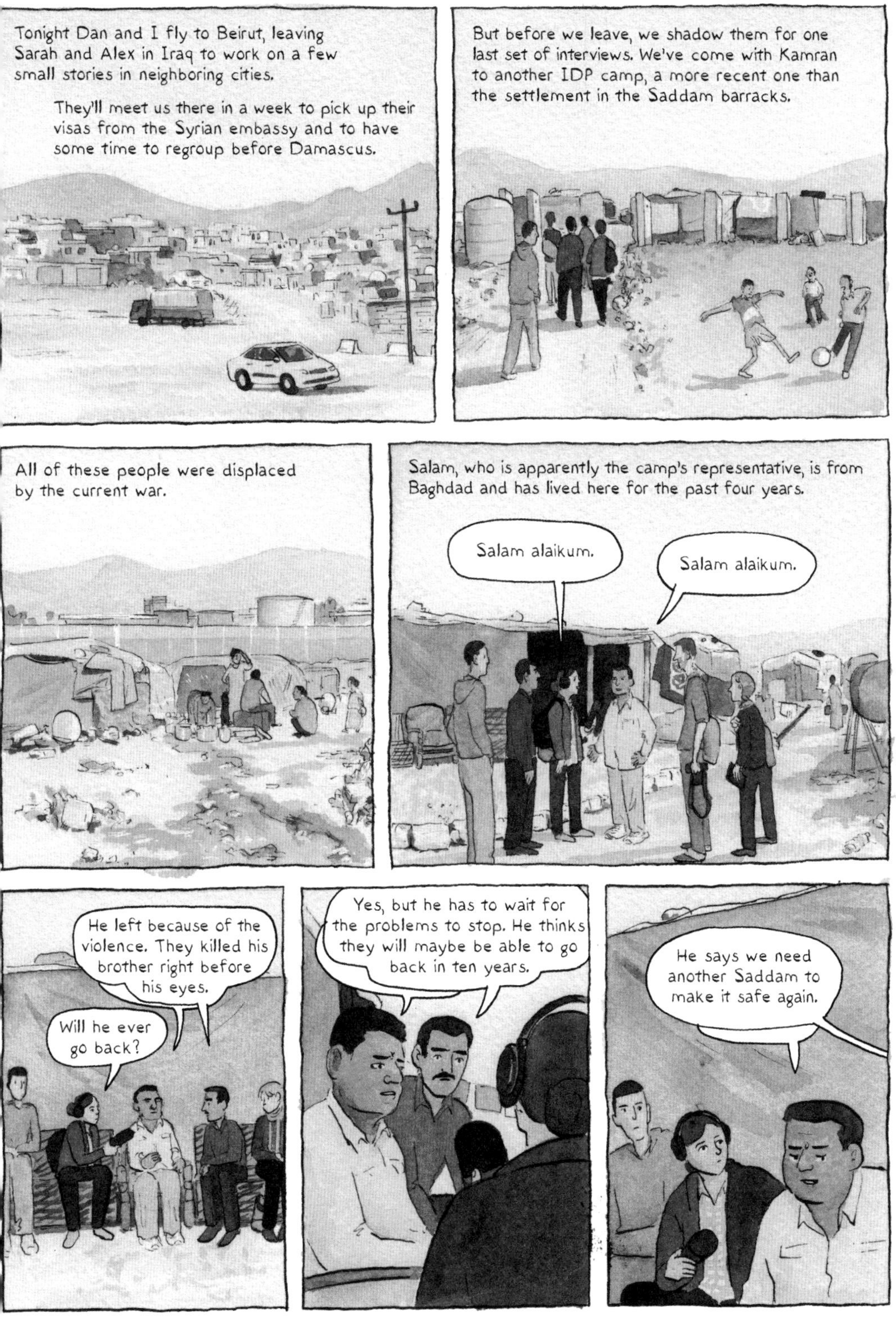

Tonight Dan and I fly to Beirut, leaving Sarah and Alex in Iraq to work on a few small stories in neighboring cities.
They'll meet us there in a week to pick up their visas from the Syrian embassy and to have some time to regroup before Damascus.
But before we leave, we shadow them for one last set of interviews. We've come with Kamran to another IDP camp, a more recent one than the settlement in the Saddam barracks.
All of these people were displaced by the current war.
Salam, who is apparently the camp's representative, is from Baghdad and has lived here for the past four years.
Salam alaikum.
Salam alaikum.
Will he ever go back?
He left because of the violence. They killed his brother right before his eyes.
Yes, but he has to wait for the problems to stop. He thinks they will maybe be able to go back in ten years.
He says we need another Saddam to make it safe again.

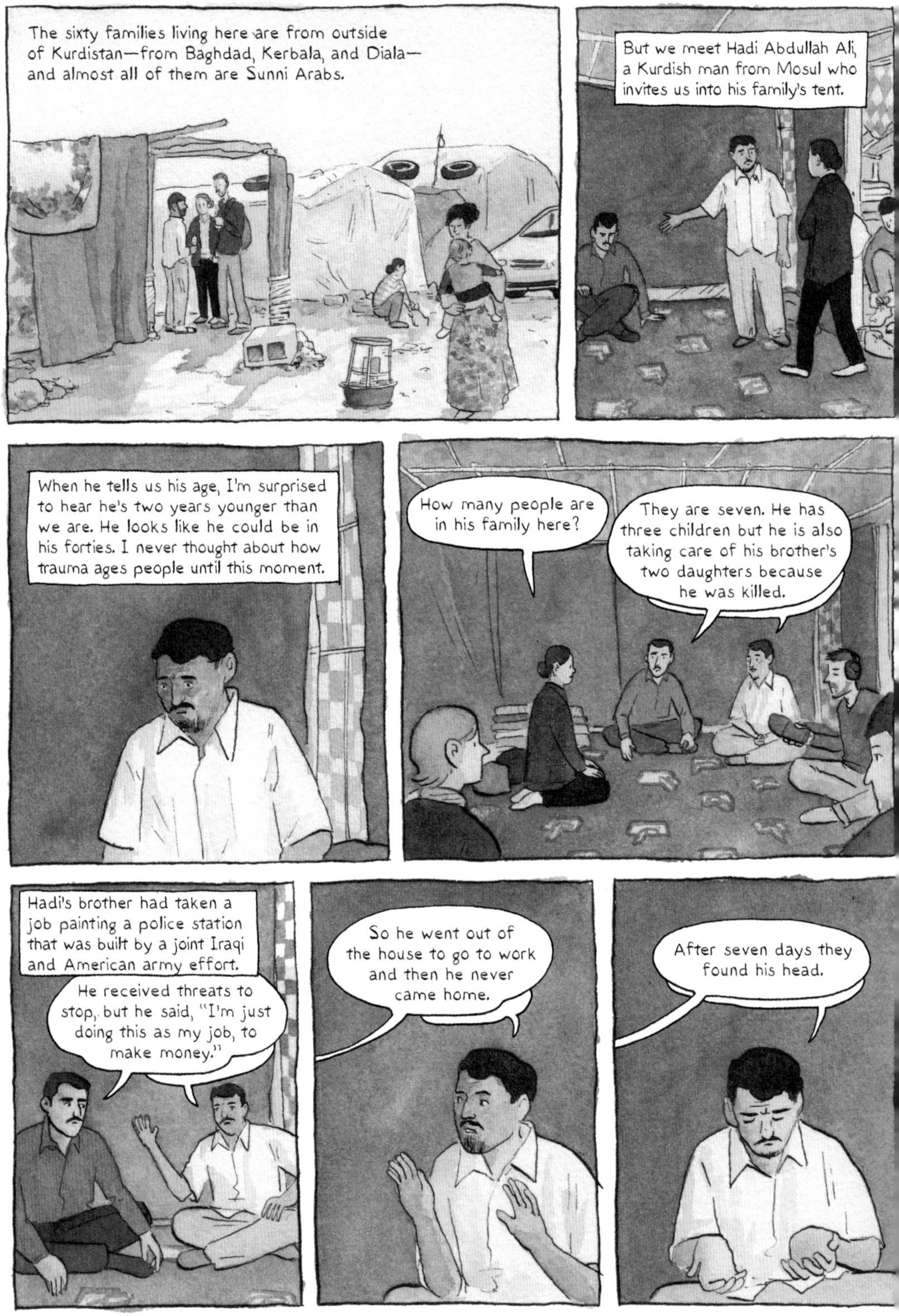
The sixty families living here are from outside of Kurdistan—from Baghdad, Kerbala, and Diala—and almost all of them are Sunni Arabs.
But we meet Hadi Abdullah Ali, a Kurdish man from Mosul who invites us into his family's tent.
When he tells us his age, I'm surprised to hear he's two years younger than we are. He looks like he could be in his forties. I never thought about how trauma ages people until this moment.
How many people are in his family here?
They are seven. He has three children but he is also taking care of his brother's two daughters because he was killed.
Hadi's brother had taken a job painting a police station that was built by a joint Iraqi and American army effort.
He received threats to stop, but he said, "I'm just doing this as my job, to make money."
So he went out of the house to go to work and then he never came home.
After seven days they found his head.

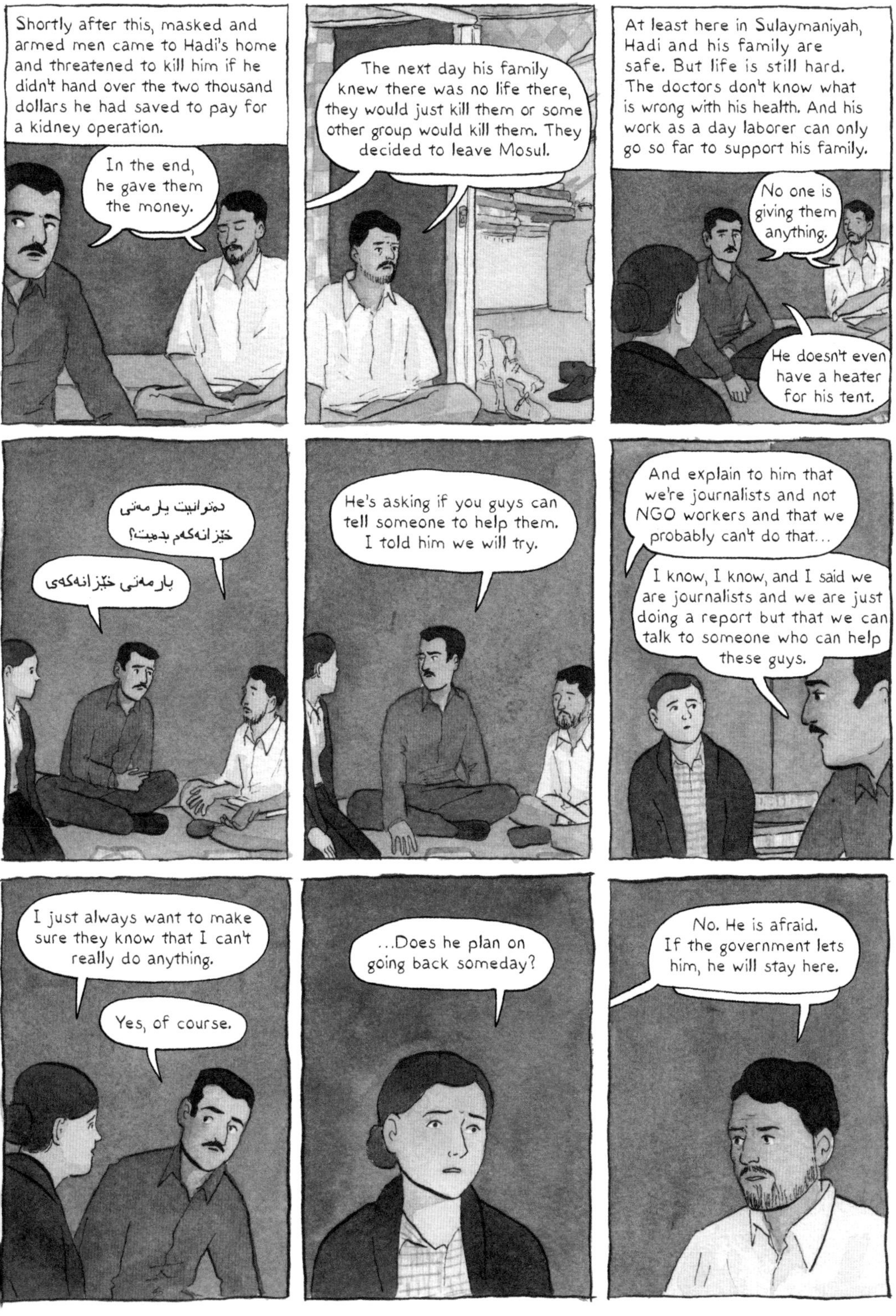
Shortly after this, masked and armed men came to Hadi's home and threatened to kill him if he didn't hand over the two thousand dollars he had saved to pay for a kidney operation.
In the end, he gave them the money.
The next day his family knew there was no life there, they would just kill them or some other group would kill them. They decided to leave Mosul.
At least here in Sulaymaniyah, Hadi and his family are safe. But life is still hard. The doctors don't know what is wrong with his health. And his work as a day laborer can only go so far to support his family.
No one is giving them anything.
He doesn't even have a heater for his tent.
دەتوانیت یارمەتی خێزانەکەم بدەیت؟
یارمەتی خێزانەکەی
He's asking if you guys can tell someone to help them. I told him we will try.
And explain to him that we're journalists and not NGO workers and that we probably can't do that...
I know, I know, and I said we are journalists and we are just doing a report but that we can talk to someone who can help these guys.
I just always want to make sure they know that I can't really do anything.
Yes, of course.
...Does he plan on going back someday?
No. He is afraid. If the government lets him, he will stay here.

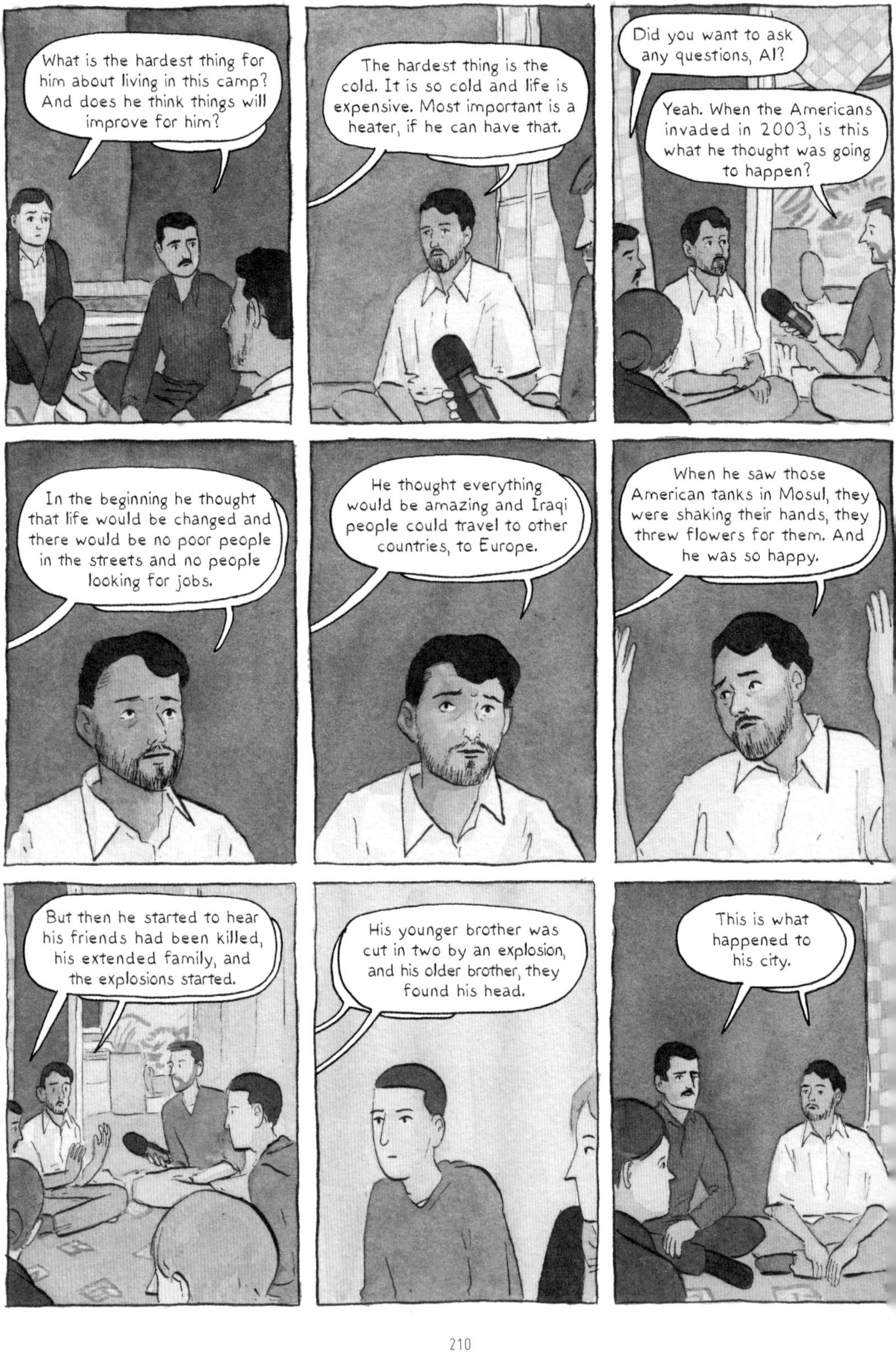
What is the hardest thing for him about living in this camp? And does he think things will improve for him?
The hardest thing is the cold. It is so cold and life is expensive. Most important is a heater, if he can have that.
Did you want to ask any questions, Al?
Yeah. When the Americans invaded in 2003, is this what he thought was going to happen?
In the beginning he thought that life would be changed and there would be no poor people in the streets and no people looking for jobs.
He thought everything would be amazing and Iraqi people could travel to other countries, to Europe.
When he saw those American tanks in Mosul, they were shaking their hands, they threw flowers for them. And he was so happy.
But then he started to hear his friends had been killed, his extended family, and the explosions started.
His younger brother was cut in two by an explosion, and his older brother, they found his head.
This is what happened to his city.

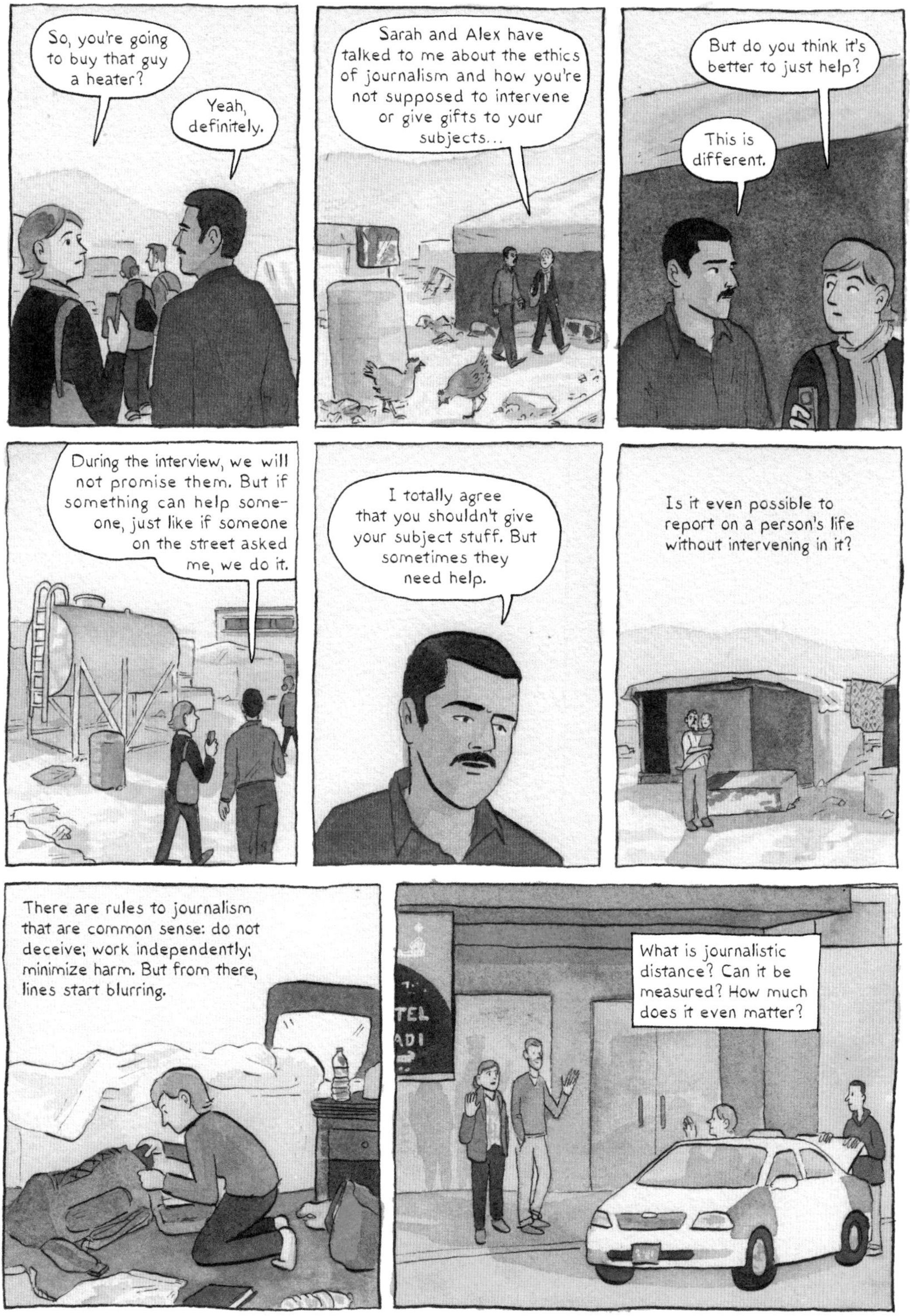
So, you're going to buy that guy a heater?
Yeah, definitely.
Sarah and Alex have talked to me about the ethics of journalism and how you're not supposed to intervene or give gifts to your subjects...
But do you think it's better to just help?
This is different.
During the interview, we will not promise them. But if something can help some-one, just like if someone on the street asked me, we do it.
I totally agree that you shouldn't give your subject stuff. But sometimes they need help.
Is it even possible to report on a person's life without intervening in it?
There are rules to journalism that are common sense: do not deceive; work independently; minimize harm. But from there, lines start blurring.
What is journalistic distance? Can it be measured? How much does it even matter?

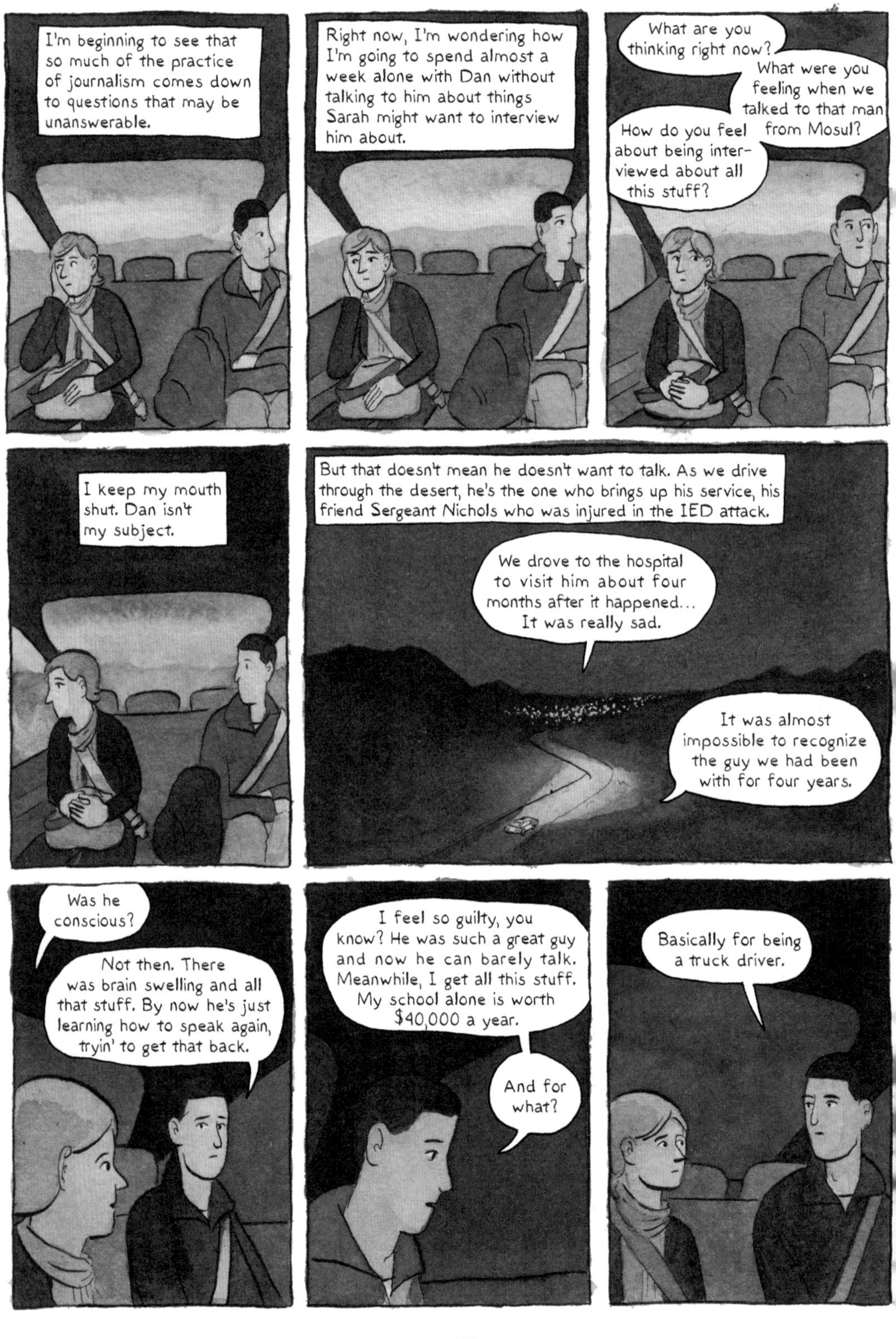

I'm beginning to see that so much of the practice of journalism comes down to questions that may be unanswerable.
Right now, I'm wondering how I'm going to spend almost a week alone with Dan without talking to him about things Sarah might want to interview him about.
What are you thinking right now?
What were you feeling when we talked to that man from Mosul?
How do you feel about being interviewed about all this stuff?
I keep my mouth shut. Dan isn't my subject.
But that doesn't mean he doesn't want to talk. As we drive through the desert, he's the one who brings up his service, his friend Sergeant Nichols who was injured in the IED attack.
We drove to the hospital to visit him about four months after it happened... It was really sad.
It was almost impossible to recognize the guy we had been with for four years.
Was he conscious?
Not then. There was brain swelling and all that stuff. By now he's just learning how to speak again, tryin' to get that back.
I feel so guilty, you know? He was such a great guy and now he can barely talk. Meanwhile, I get all this stuff. My school alone is worth $40,000 a year.
And for what?
Basically for being a truck driver.

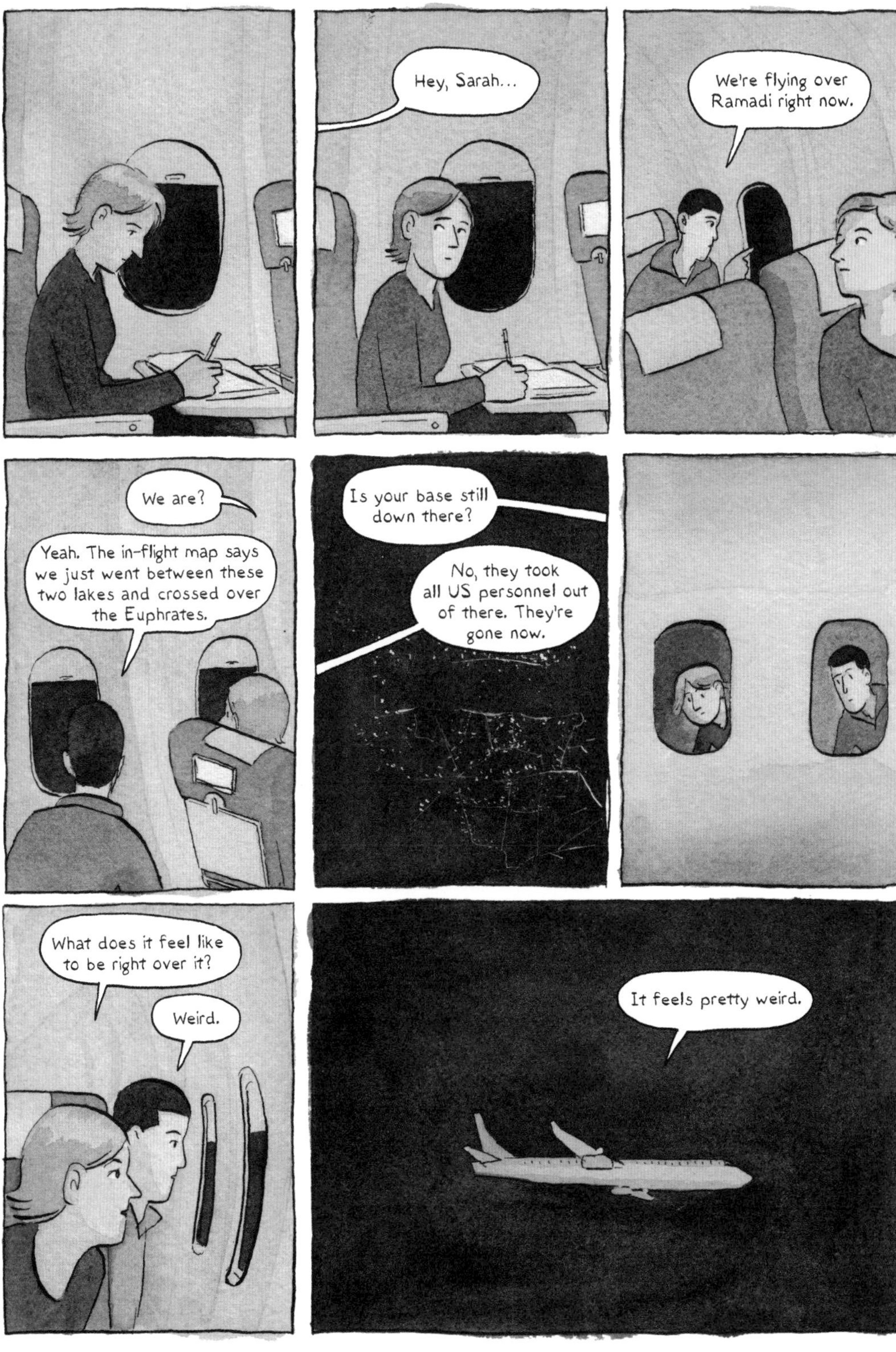

Hey, Sarah...
We're flying over Ramadi right now.
We are?
Yeah. The in-flight map says we just went between these two lakes and crossed over the Euphrates.
Is your base still down there?
No, they took all US personnel out of there. They're gone now.
What does it feel like to be right over it?
Weird.
It feels pretty weird.

DAMASCUS, SYRIA

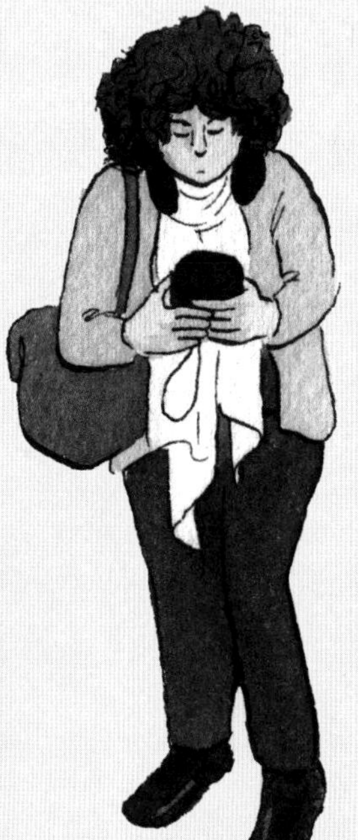

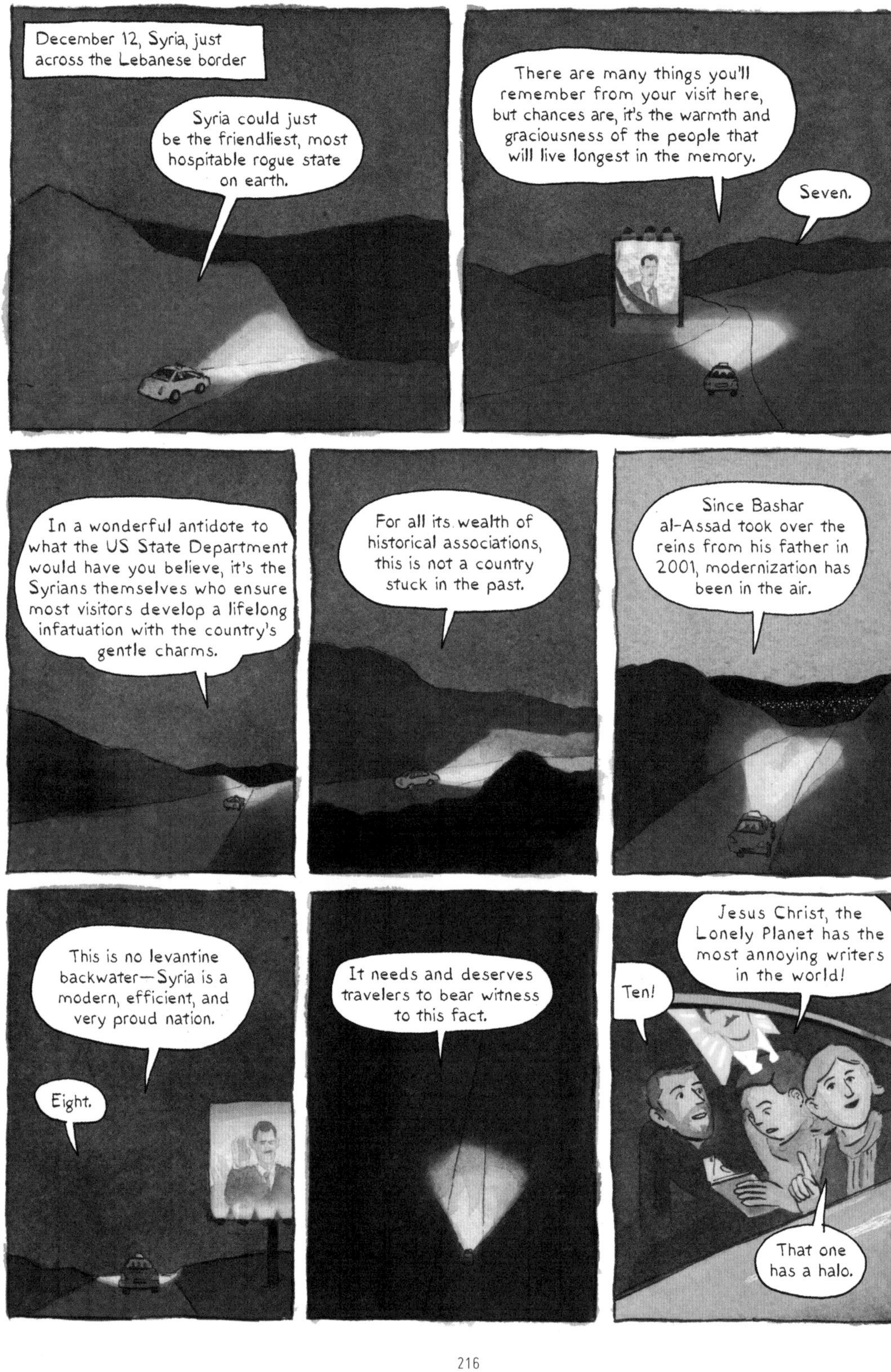
December 12, Syria, just across the Lebanese border
Syria could just be the friendliest, most hospitable rogue state on earth.
There are many things you'll remember from your visit here, but chances are, it's the warmth and graciousness of the people that will live longest in the memory.
Seven.
In a wonderful antidote to what the US State Department would have you believe, it's the Syrians themselves who ensure most visitors develop a lifelong infatuation with the country's gentle charms.
For all its wealth of historical associations, this is not a country stuck in the past.
Since Bashar al-Assad took over the reins from his father in 2001, modernization has been in the air.
This is no levantine backwater—Syria is a modern, efficient, and very proud nation.
Eight.
It needs and deserves travelers to bear witness to this fact.
Ten!
Jesus Christ, the Lonely Planet has the most annoying writers in the world!
That one has a halo.

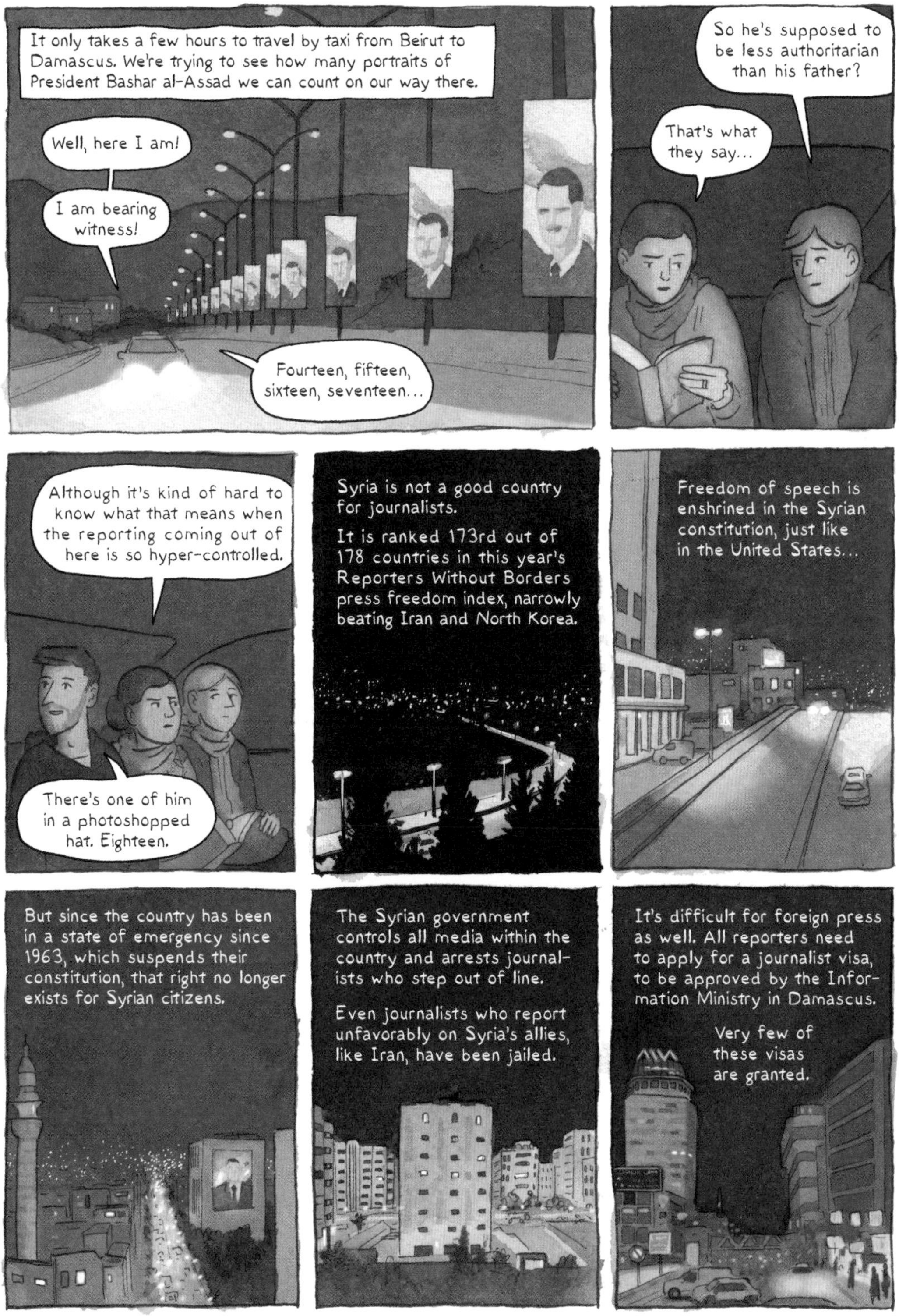

It only takes a few hours to travel by taxi from Beirut to Damascus. We're trying to see how many portraits of President Bashar al-Assad we can count on our way there.
Well, here I am!
I am bearing witness!
Fourteen, fifteen, sixteen, seventeen...
So he's supposed to be less authoritarian than his father?
That's what they say...
Although it's kind of hard to know what that means when the reporting coming out of here is so hyper-controlled.
There's one of him in a photoshopped hat. Eighteen.
Syria is not a good country for journalists.
It is ranked 173rd out of 178 countries in this year's Reporters Without Borders press freedom index, narrowly beating Iran and North Korea.
Freedom of speech is enshrined in the Syrian constitution, just like in the United States...
But since the country has been in a state of emergency since 1963, which suspends their constitution, that right no longer exists for Syrian citizens.
The Syrian government controls all media within the country and arrests journalists who step out of line.
Even journalists who report unfavorably on Syria's allies, like Iran, have been jailed.
It's difficult for foreign press as well. All reporters need to apply for a journalist visa, to be approved by the Information Ministry in Damascus.
Very few of these visas are granted.

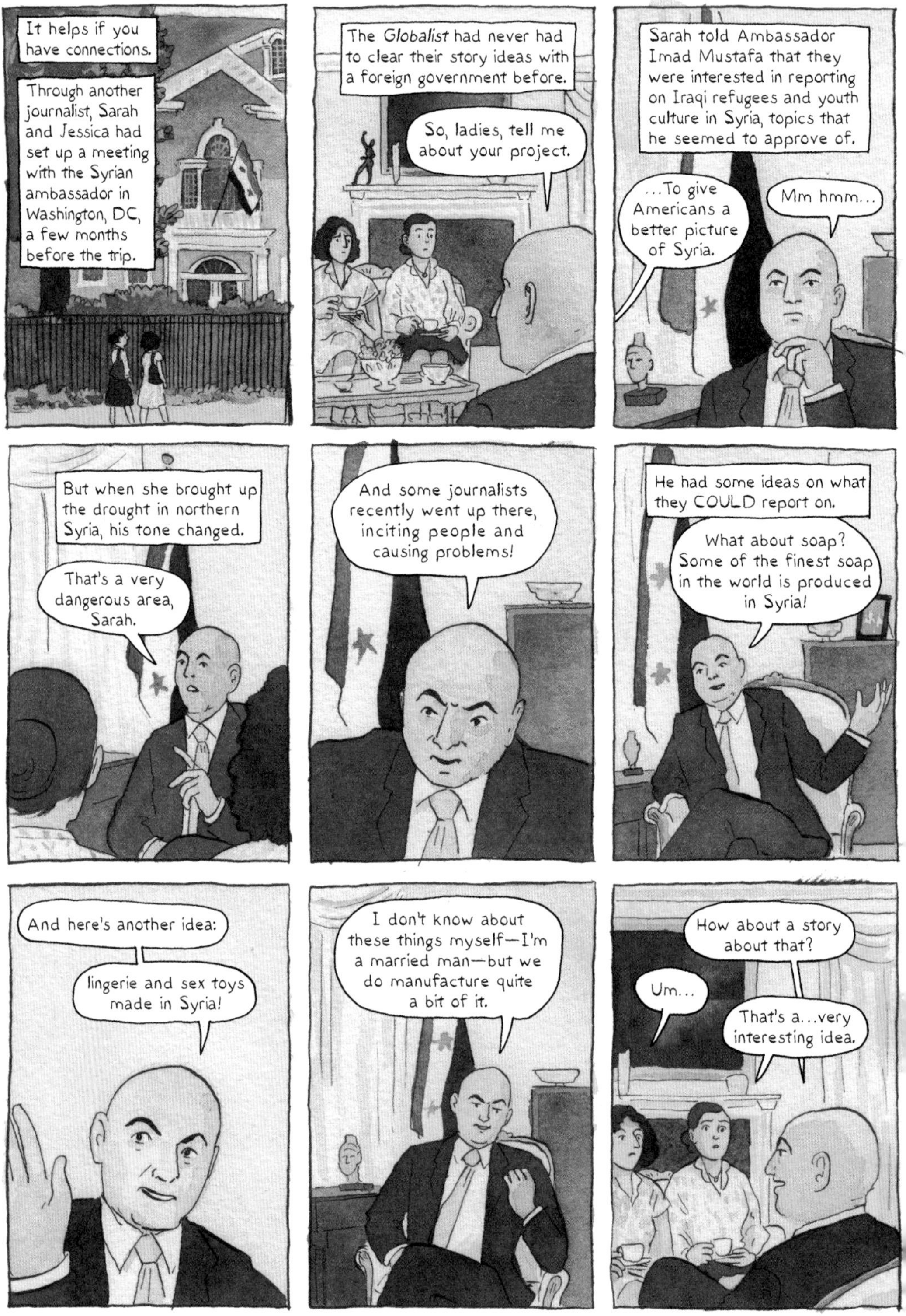
It helps if you have connections.
Through another journalist, Sarah and Jessica had set up a meeting with the Syrian ambassador in Washington, DC, a few months before the trip.
The *Globalist* had never had to clear their story ideas with a foreign government before.
So, ladies, tell me about your project.
Sarah told Ambassador Imad Mustafa that they were interested in reporting on Iraqi refugees and youth culture in Syria, topics that he seemed to approve of.
...To give Americans a better picture of Syria.
Mm hmm...
But when she brought up the drought in northern Syria, his tone changed.
That's a very dangerous area, Sarah.
And some journalists recently went up there, inciting people and causing problems!
He had some ideas on what they COULD report on.
What about soap? Some of the finest soap in the world is produced in Syria!
And here's another idea:
lingerie and sex toys made in Syria!
I don't know about these things myself—I'm a married man—but we do manufacture quite a bit of it.
How about a story about that?
Um...
That's a...very interesting idea.

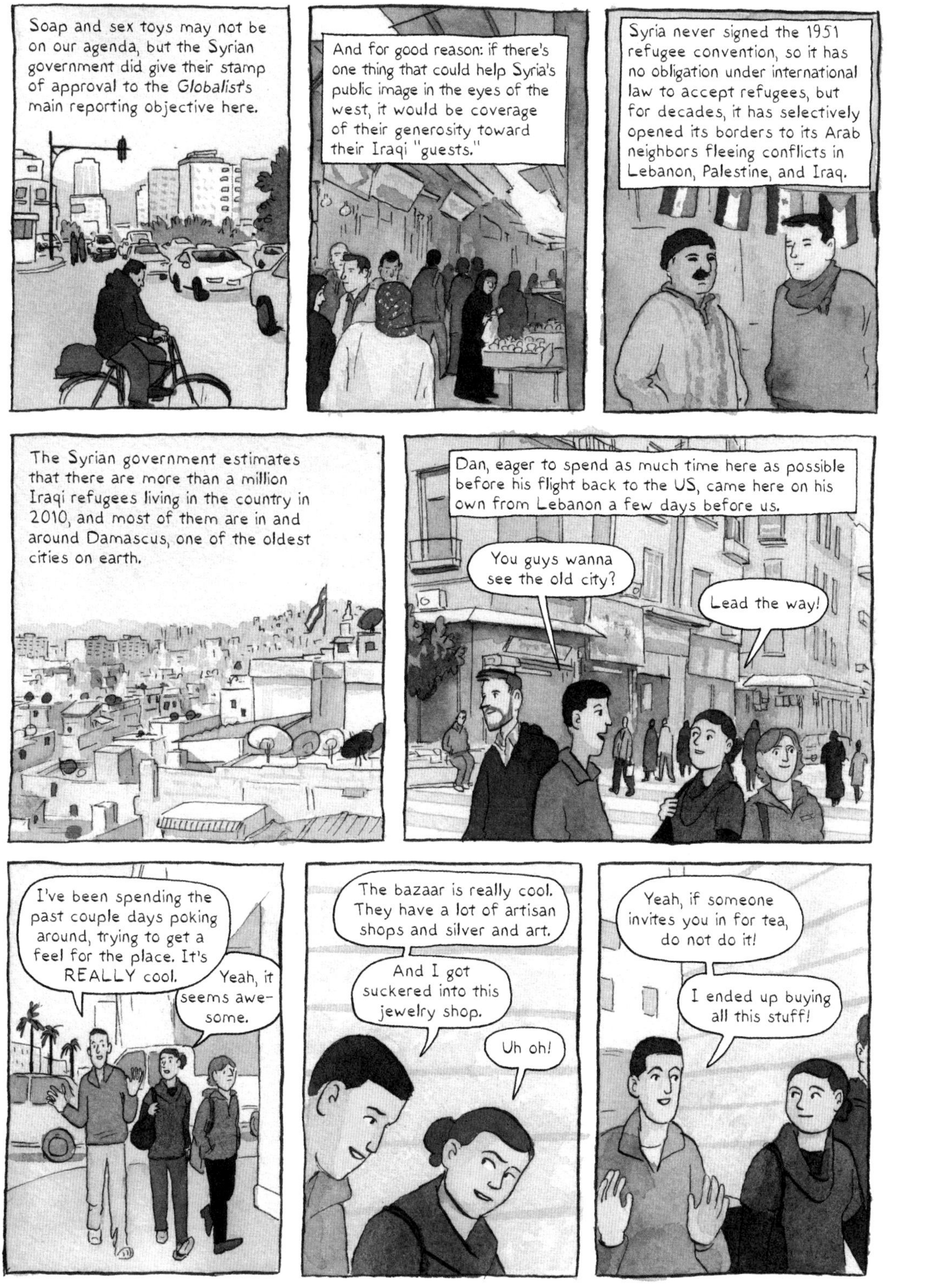
Soap and sex toys may not be on our agenda, but the Syrian government did give their stamp of approval to the *Globalist*'s main reporting objective here.
And for good reason: if there's one thing that could help Syria's public image in the eyes of the west, it would be coverage of their generosity toward their Iraqi "guests."
Syria never signed the 1951 refugee convention, so it has no obligation under international law to accept refugees, but for decades, it has selectively opened its borders to its Arab neighbors fleeing conflicts in Lebanon, Palestine, and Iraq.
The Syrian government estimates that there are more than a million Iraqi refugees living in the country in 2010, and most of them are in and around Damascus, one of the oldest cities on earth.
Dan, eager to spend as much time here as possible before his flight back to the US, came here on his own from Lebanon a few days before us.
You guys wanna see the old city?
Lead the way!
I've been spending the past couple days poking around, trying to get a feel for the place. It's REALLY cool.
Yeah, it seems awe-some.
The bazaar is really cool. They have a lot of artisan shops and silver and art.
And I got suckered into this jewelry shop.
Uh oh!
Yeah, if someone invites you in for tea, do not do it!
I ended up buying all this stuff!

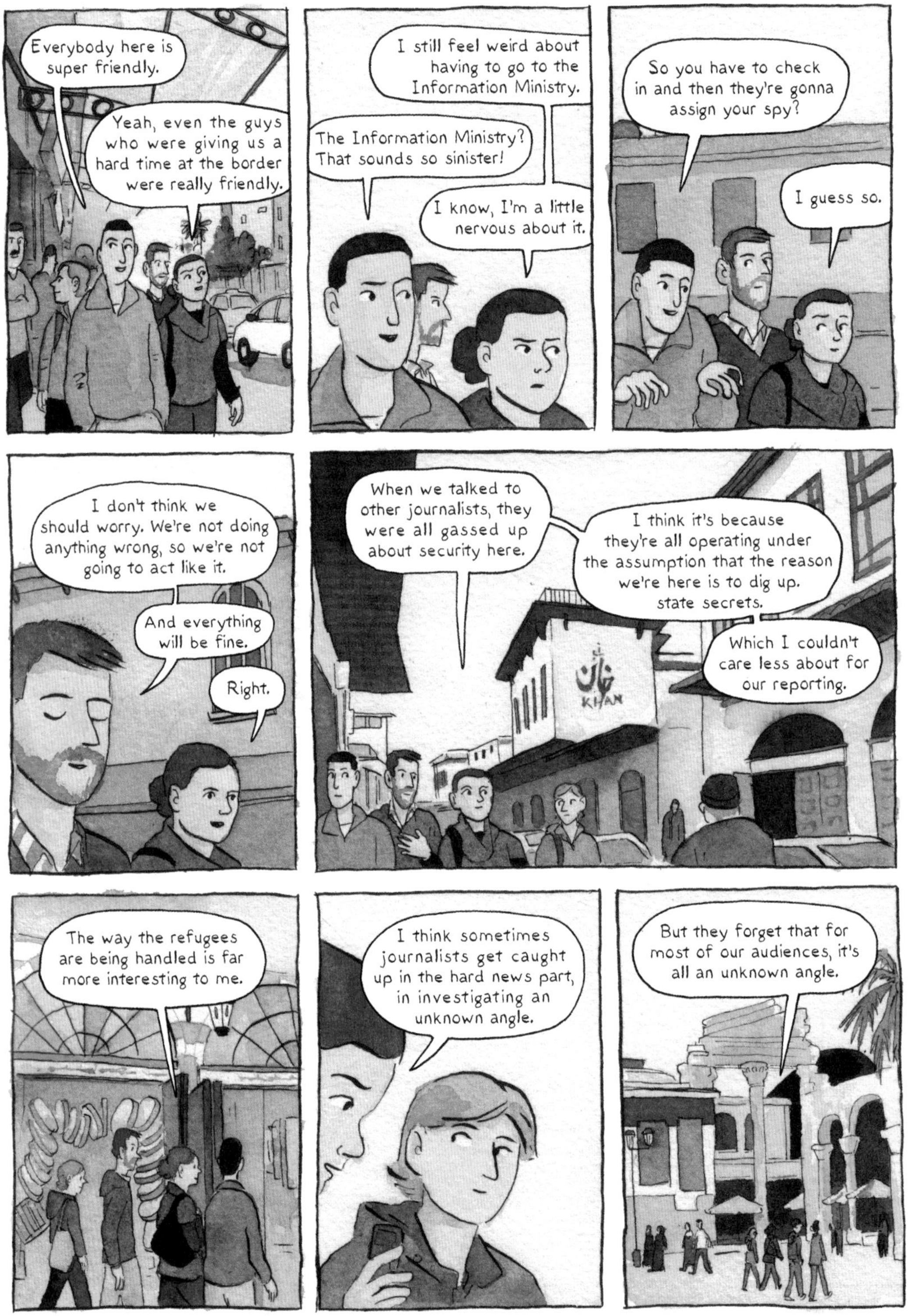
Everybody here is super friendly.
Yeah, even the guys who were giving us a hard time at the border were really friendly.
I still feel weird about having to go to the Information Ministry.
The Information Ministry? That sounds so sinister!
I know, I'm a little nervous about it.
So you have to check in and then they're gonna assign your spy?
I guess so.
I don't think we should worry. We're not doing anything wrong, so we're not going to act like it.
And everything will be fine.
Right.
When we talked to other journalists, they were all gassed up about security here.
I think it's because they're all operating under the assumption that the reason we're here is to dig up. state secrets.
Which I couldn't care less about for our reporting.
KHAN
The way the refugees are being handled is far more interesting to me.
I think sometimes journalists get caught up in the hard news part, in investigating an unknown angle.
But they forget that for most of our audiences, it's all an unknown angle.

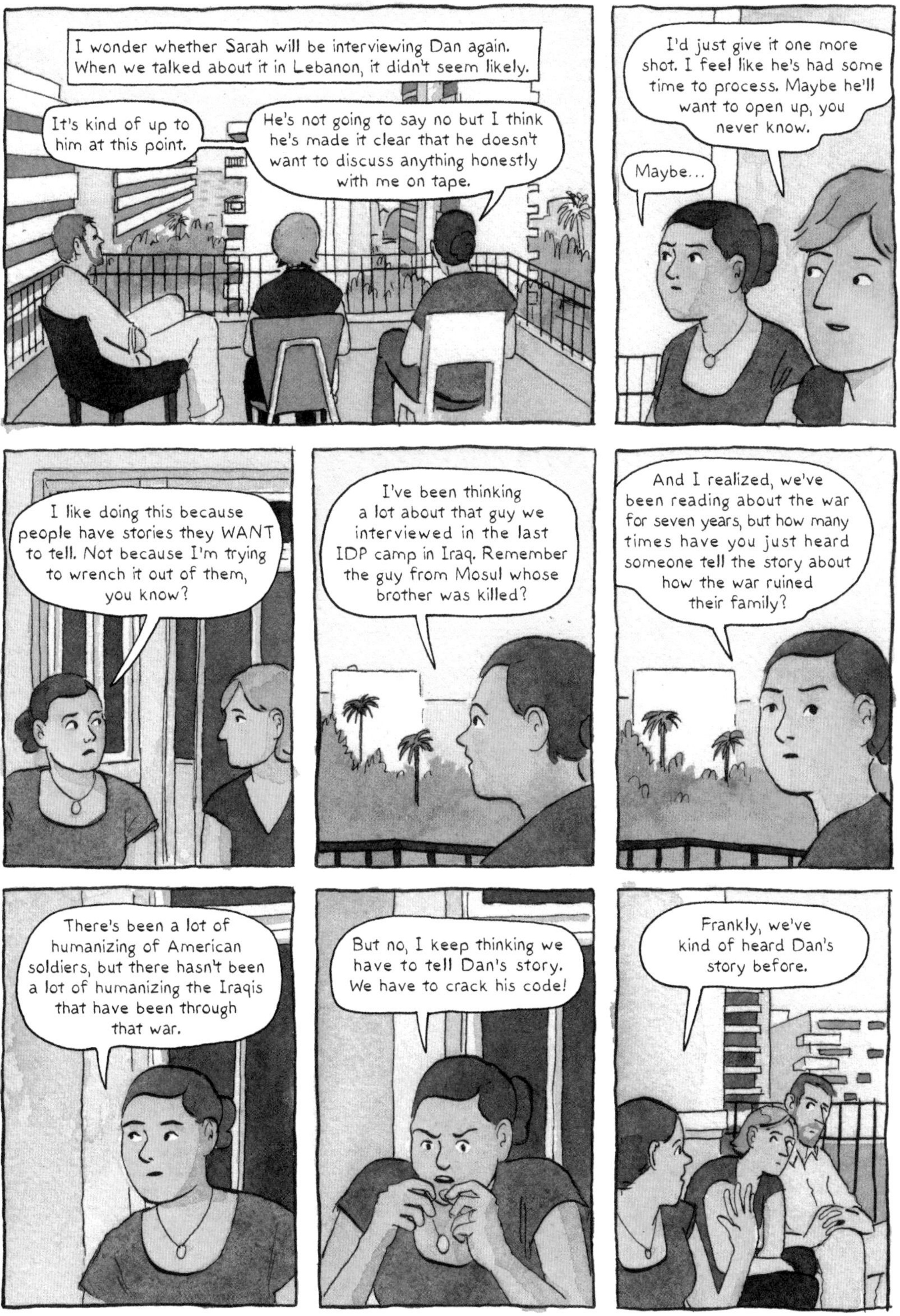
I wonder whether Sarah will be interviewing Dan again. When we talked about it in Lebanon, it didn't seem likely.
It's kind of up to him at this point.
He's not going to say no but I think he's made it clear that he doesn't want to discuss anything honestly with me on tape.
I'd just give it one more shot. I feel like he's had some time to process. Maybe he'll want to open up, you never know.
Maybe...
I like doing this because people have stories they WANT to tell. Not because I'm trying to wrench it out of them, you know?
I've been thinking a lot about that guy we interviewed in the last IDP camp in Iraq. Remember the guy from Mosul whose brother was killed?
And I realized, we've been reading about the war for seven years, but how many times have you just heard someone tell the story about how the war ruined their family?
There's been a lot of humanizing of American soldiers, but there hasn't been a lot of humanizing the Iraqis that have been through that war.
But no, I keep thinking we have to tell Dan's story. We have to crack his code!
Frankly, we've kind of heard Dan's story before.

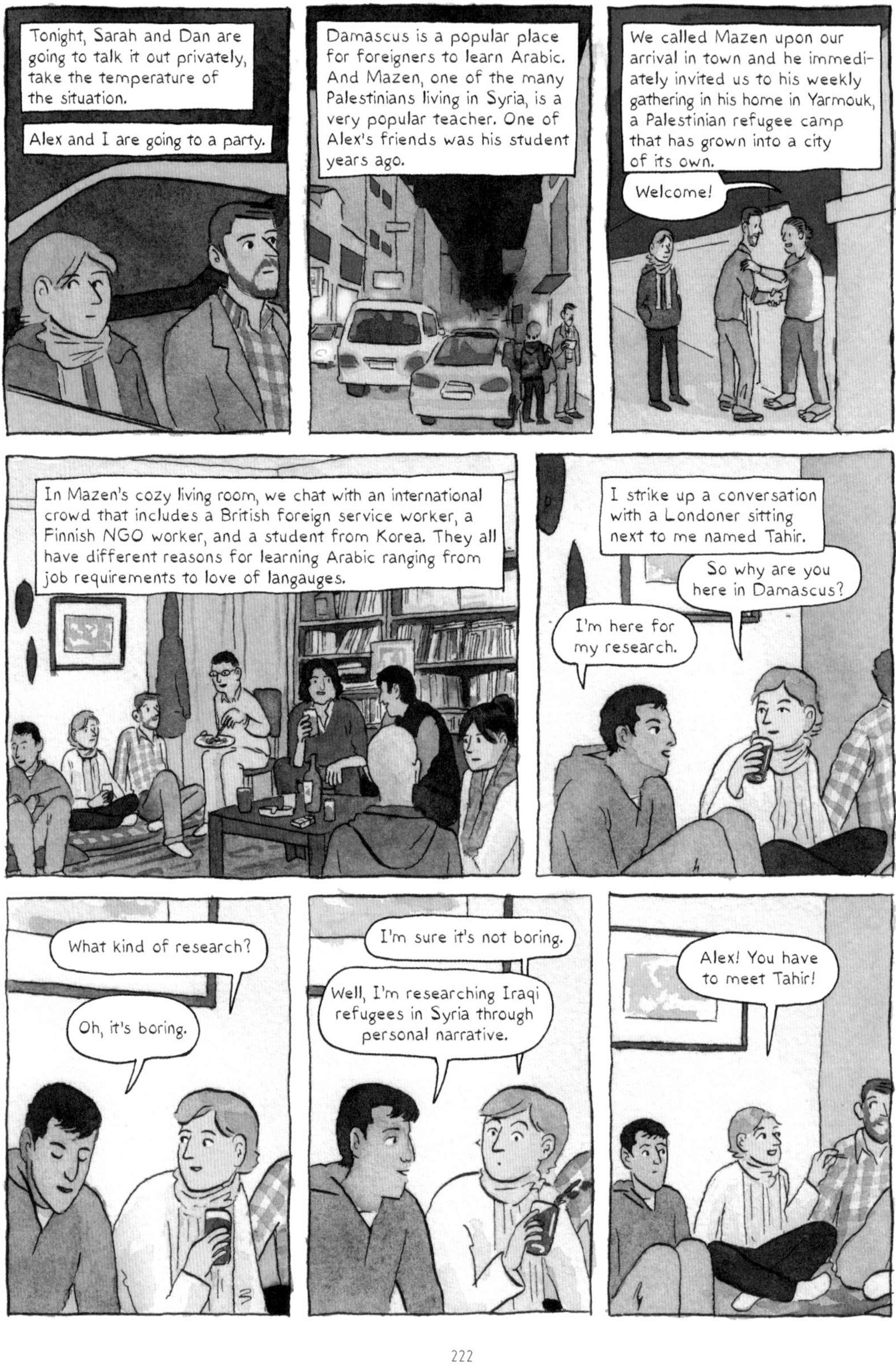
Tonight, Sarah and Dan are going to talk it out privately, take the temperature of the situation.
Alex and I are going to a party.
Damascus is a popular place for foreigners to learn Arabic. And Mazen, one of the many Palestinians living in Syria, is a very popular teacher. One of Alex's friends was his student years ago.
We called Mazen upon our arrival in town and he immediately invited us to his weekly gathering in his home in Yarmouk, a Palestinian refugee camp that has grown into a city of its own.
Welcome!
In Mazen's cozy living room, we chat with an international crowd that includes a British foreign service worker, a Finnish NGO worker, and a student from Korea. They all have different reasons for learning Arabic ranging from job requirements to love of langauges.
I strike up a conversation with a Londoner sitting next to me named Tahir.
So why are you here in Damascus?
I'm here for my research.
What kind of research?
Oh, it's boring.
I'm sure it's not boring.
Well, I'm researching Iraqi refugees in Syria through personal narrative.
Alex! You have to meet Tahir!

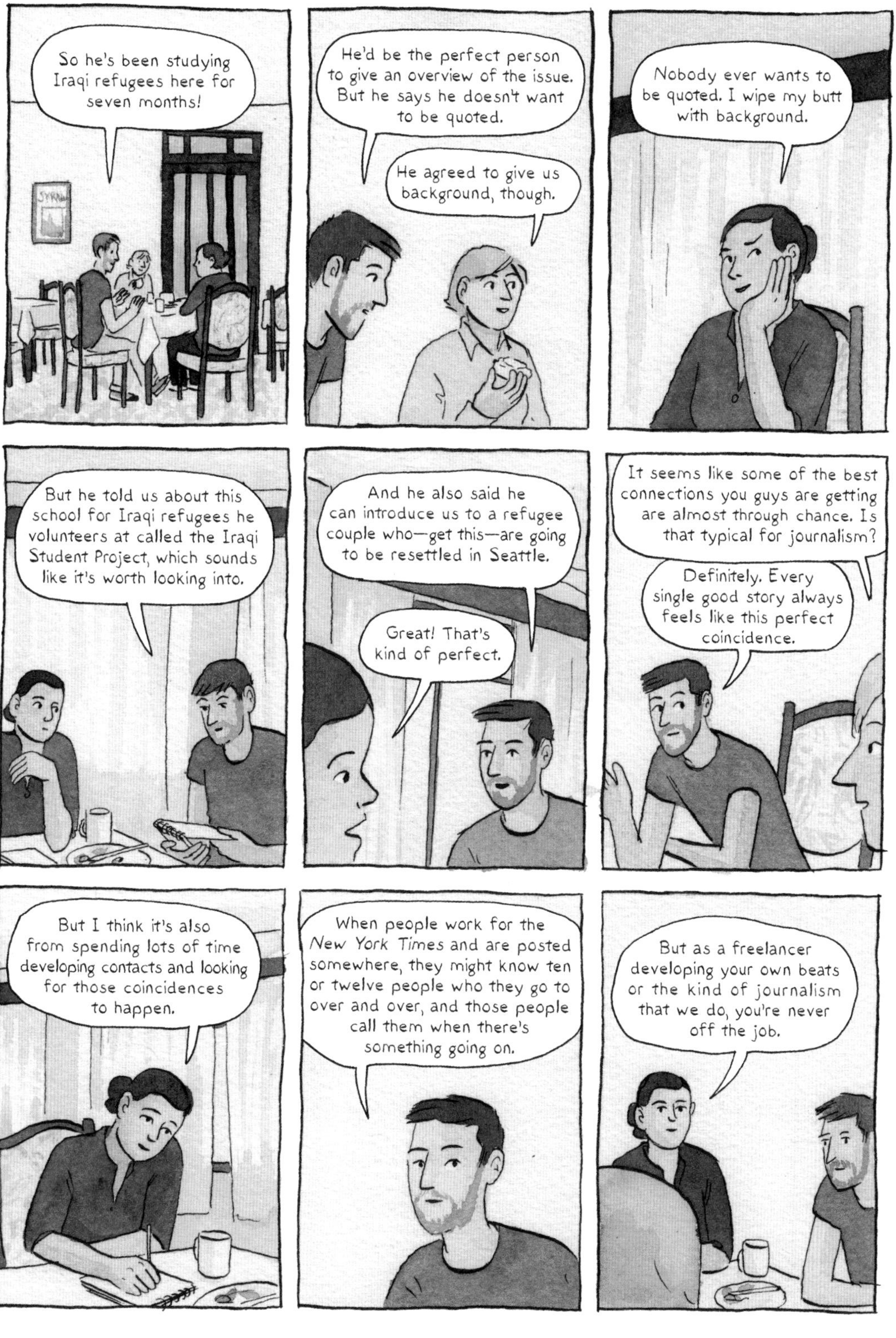
So he's been studying Iraqi refugees here for seven months!
SYRIA
He'd be the perfect person to give an overview of the issue. But he says he doesn't want to be quoted.
He agreed to give us background, though.
Nobody ever wants to be quoted. I wipe my butt with background.
But he told us about this school for Iraqi refugees he volunteers at called the Iraqi Student Project, which sounds like it's worth looking into.
And he also said he can introduce us to a refugee couple who—get this—are going to be resettled in Seattle.
Great! That's kind of perfect.
It seems like some of the best connections you guys are getting are almost through chance. Is that typical for journalism?
Definitely. Every single good story always feels like this perfect coincidence.
But I think it's also from spending lots of time developing contacts and looking for those coincidences to happen.
When people work for the *New York Times* and are posted somewhere, they might know ten or twelve people who they go to over and over, and those people call them when there's something going on.
But as a freelancer developing your own beats or the kind of journalism that we do, you're never off the job.

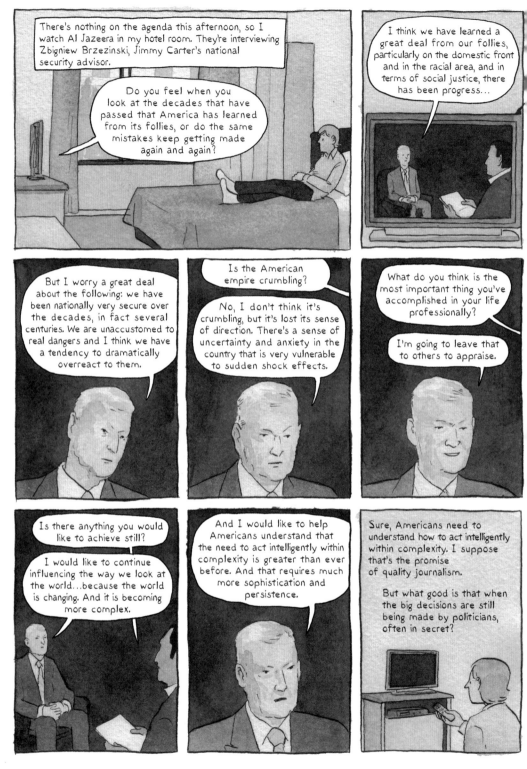

There's nothing on the agenda this afternoon, so I watch Al Jazeera in my hotel room. They're interviewing Zbigniew Brzezinski, Jimmy Carter's national security advisor.

Do you feel when you look at the decades that have passed that America has learned from its follies, or do the same mistakes keep getting made again and again?

I think we have learned a great deal from our follies, particularly on the domestic front and in the racial area, and in terms of social justice, there has been progress...

But I worry a great deal about the following: we have been nationally very secure over the decades, in fact several centuries. We are unaccustomed to real dangers and I think we have a tendency to dramatically overreact to them.

Is the American empire crumbling?

No, I don't think it's crumbling, but it's lost its sense of direction. There's a sense of uncertainty and anxiety in the country that is very vulnerable to sudden shock effects.

What do you think is the most important thing you've accomplished in your life professionally?

I'm going to leave that to others to appraise.

Is there anything you would like to achieve still?

I would like to continue influencing the way we look at the world...because the world is changing. And it is becoming more complex.

And I would like to help Americans understand that the need to act intelligently within complexity is greater than ever before. And that requires much more sophistication and persistence.

Sure, Americans need to understand how to act intelligently within complexity. I suppose that's the promise of quality journalism.

But what good is that when the big decisions are still being made by politicians, often in secret?

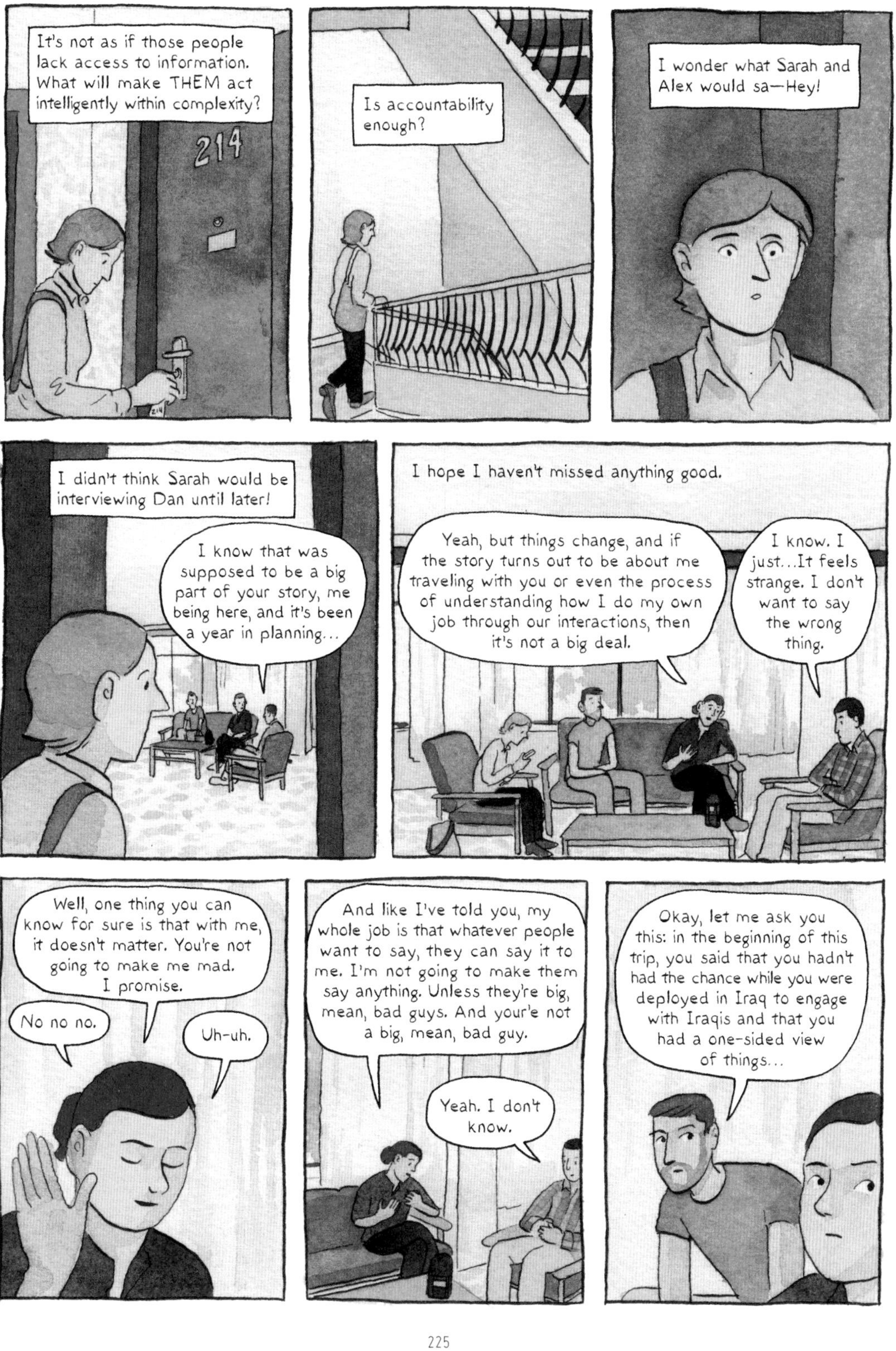
It's not as if those people lack access to information. What will make THEM act intelligently within complexity?
214
Is accountability enough?
I wonder what Sarah and Alex would sa—Hey!
I didn't think Sarah would be interviewing Dan until later!
I know that was supposed to be a big part of your story, me being here, and it's been a year in planning...
I hope I haven't missed anything good.
Yeah, but things change, and if the story turns out to be about me traveling with you or even the process of understanding how I do my own job through our interactions, then it's not a big deal.
I know. I just...It feels strange. I don't want to say the wrong thing.
Well, one thing you can know for sure is that with me, it doesn't matter. You're not going to make me mad. I promise.
No no no.
Uh-uh.
And like I've told you, my whole job is that whatever people want to say, they can say it to me. I'm not going to make them say anything. Unless they're big, mean, bad guys. And your'e not a big, mean, bad guy.
Yeah. I don't know.
Okay, let me ask you this: in the beginning of this trip, you said that you hadn't had the chance while you were deployed in Iraq to engage with Iraqis and that you had a one-sided view of things...

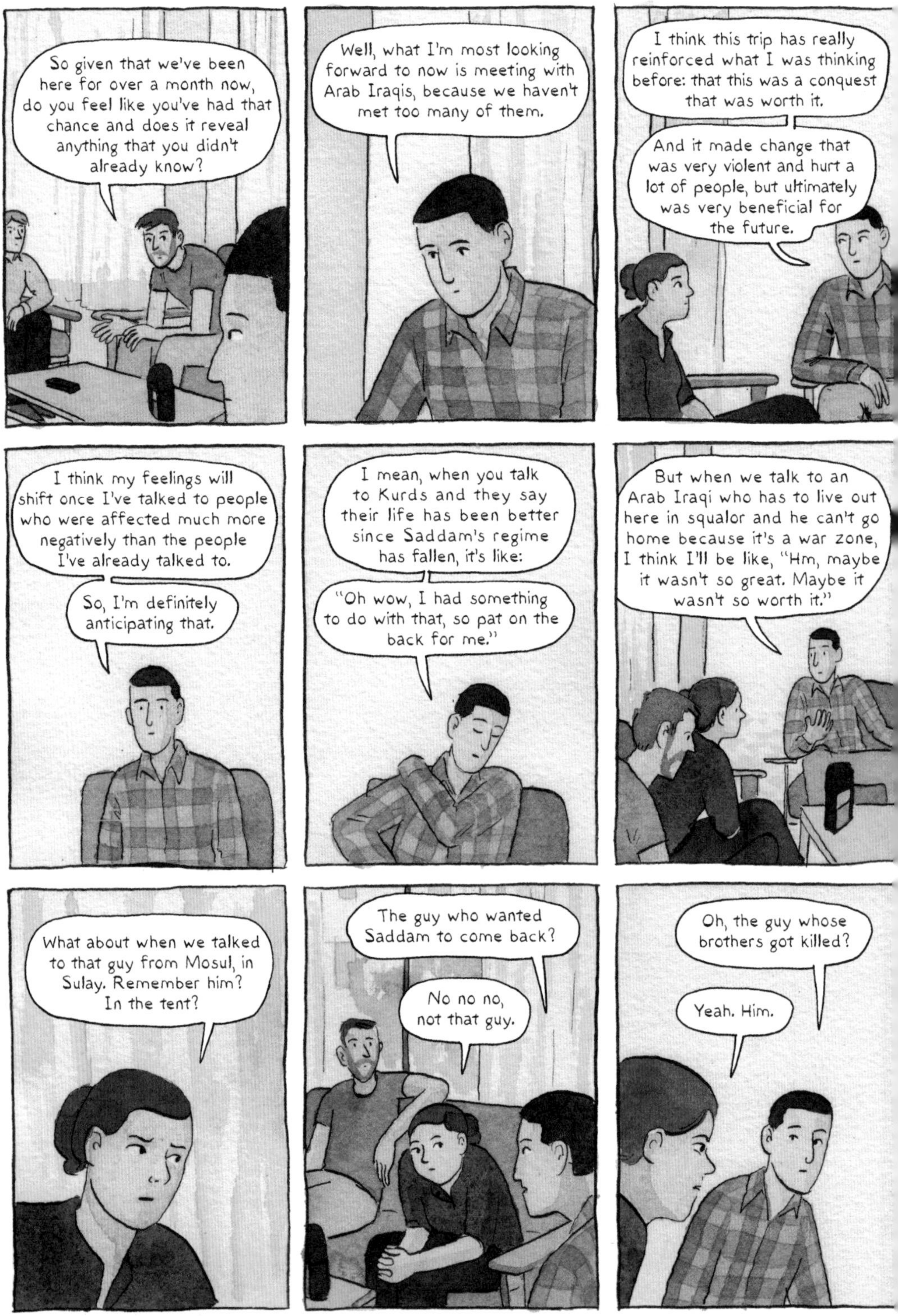
So given that we've been here for over a month now, do you feel like you've had that chance and does it reveal anything that you didn't already know?
Well, what I'm most looking forward to now is meeting with Arab Iraqis, because we haven't met too many of them.
I think this trip has really reinforced what I was thinking before: that this was a conquest that was worth it.
And it made change that was very violent and hurt a lot of people, but ultimately was very beneficial for the future.
I think my feelings will shift once I've talked to people who were affected much more negatively than the people I've already talked to.
So, I'm definitely anticipating that.
I mean, when you talk to Kurds and they say their life has been better since Saddam's regime has fallen, it's like:
"Oh wow, I had something to do with that, so pat on the back for me."
But when we talk to an Arab Iraqi who has to live out here in squalor and he can't go home because it's a war zone, I think I'll be like, "Hm, maybe it wasn't so great. Maybe it wasn't so worth it."
What about when we talked to that guy from Mosul, in Sulay. Remember him? In the tent?
The guy who wanted Saddam to come back?
No no no, not that guy.
Oh, the guy whose brothers got killed?
Yeah. Him.

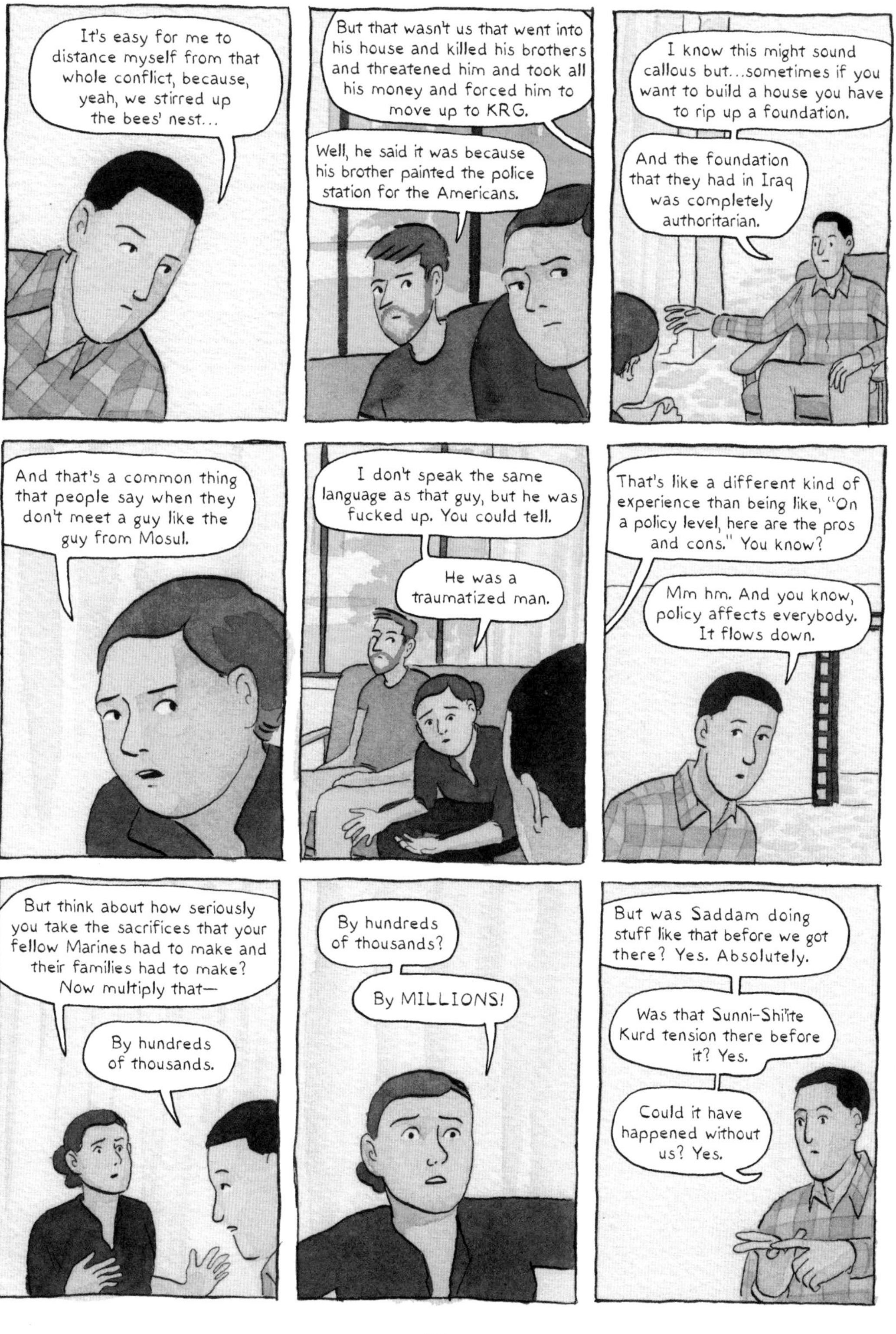
It's easy for me to distance myself from that whole conflict, because, yeah, we stirred up the bees' nest...
But that wasn't us that went into his house and killed his brothers and threatened him and took all his money and forced him to move up to KRG.
Well, he said it was because his brother painted the police station for the Americans.
I know this might sound callous but...sometimes if you want to build a house you have to rip up a foundation.
And the foundation that they had in Iraq was completely authoritarian.
And that's a common thing that people say when they don't meet a guy like the guy from Mosul.
I don't speak the same language as that guy, but he was fucked up. You could tell.
He was a traumatized man.
That's like a different kind of experience than being like, "On a policy level, here are the pros and cons." You know?
Mm hm. And you know, policy affects everybody. It flows down.
But think about how seriously you take the sacrifices that your fellow Marines had to make and their families had to make? Now multiply that—
By hundreds of thousands.
By hundreds of thousands?
By MILLIONS!
But was Saddam doing stuff like that before we got there? Yes. Absolutely.
Was that Sunni-Shi'ite Kurd tension there before it? Yes.
Could it have happened without us? Yes.

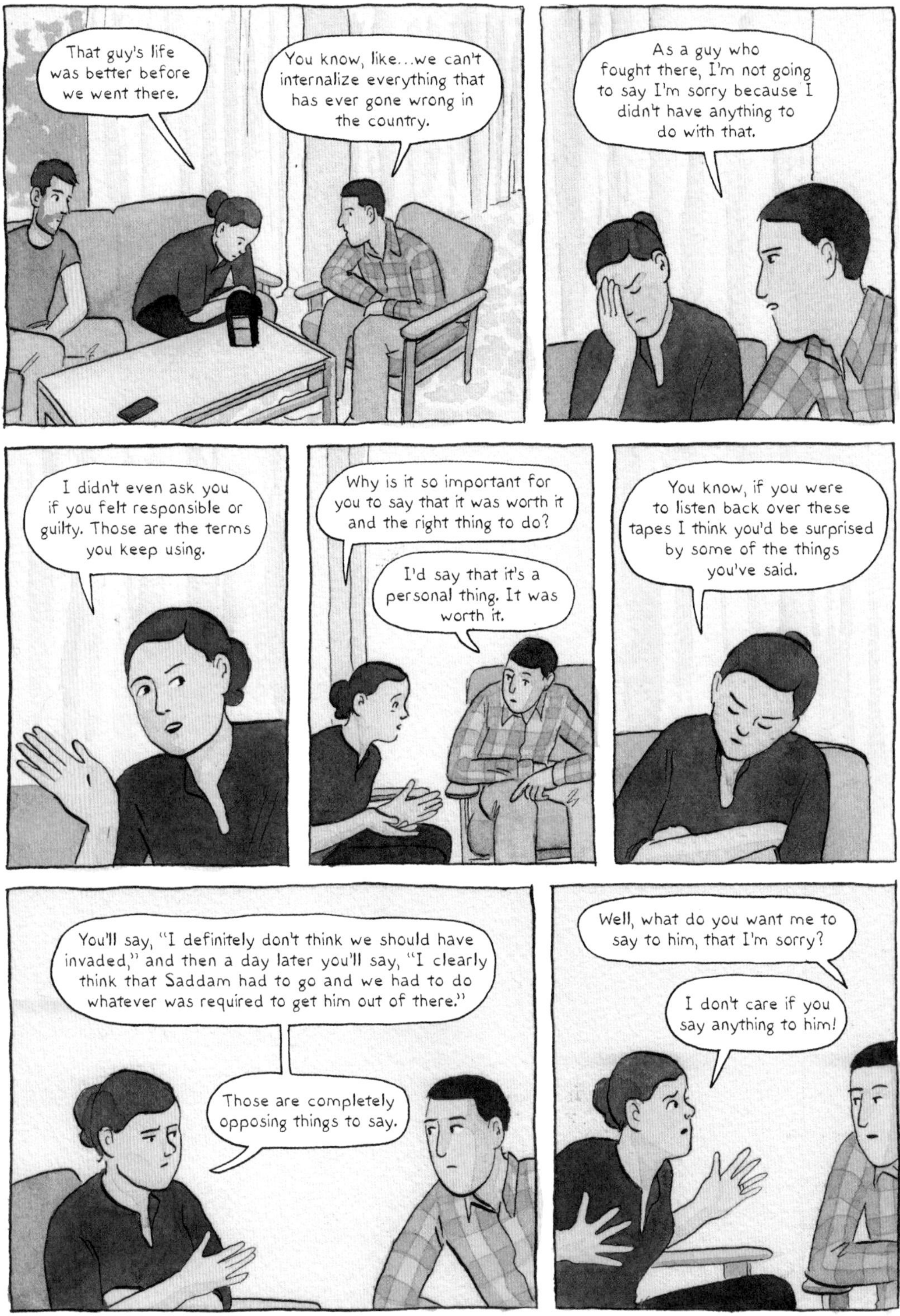
That guy's life was better before we went there.
You know, like...we can't internalize everything that has ever gone wrong in the country.
As a guy who fought there, I'm not going to say I'm sorry because I didn't have anything to do with that.
I didn't even ask you if you felt responsible or guilty. Those are the terms you keep using.
Why is it so important for you to say that it was worth it and the right thing to do?
I'd say that it's a personal thing. It was worth it.
You know, if you were to listen back over these tapes I think you'd be surprised by some of the things you've said.
You'll say, "I definitely don't think we should have invaded," and then a day later you'll say, "I clearly think that Saddam had to go and we had to do whatever was required to get him out of there."
Those are completely opposing things to say.
Well, what do you want me to say to him, that I'm sorry?
I don't care if you say anything to him!

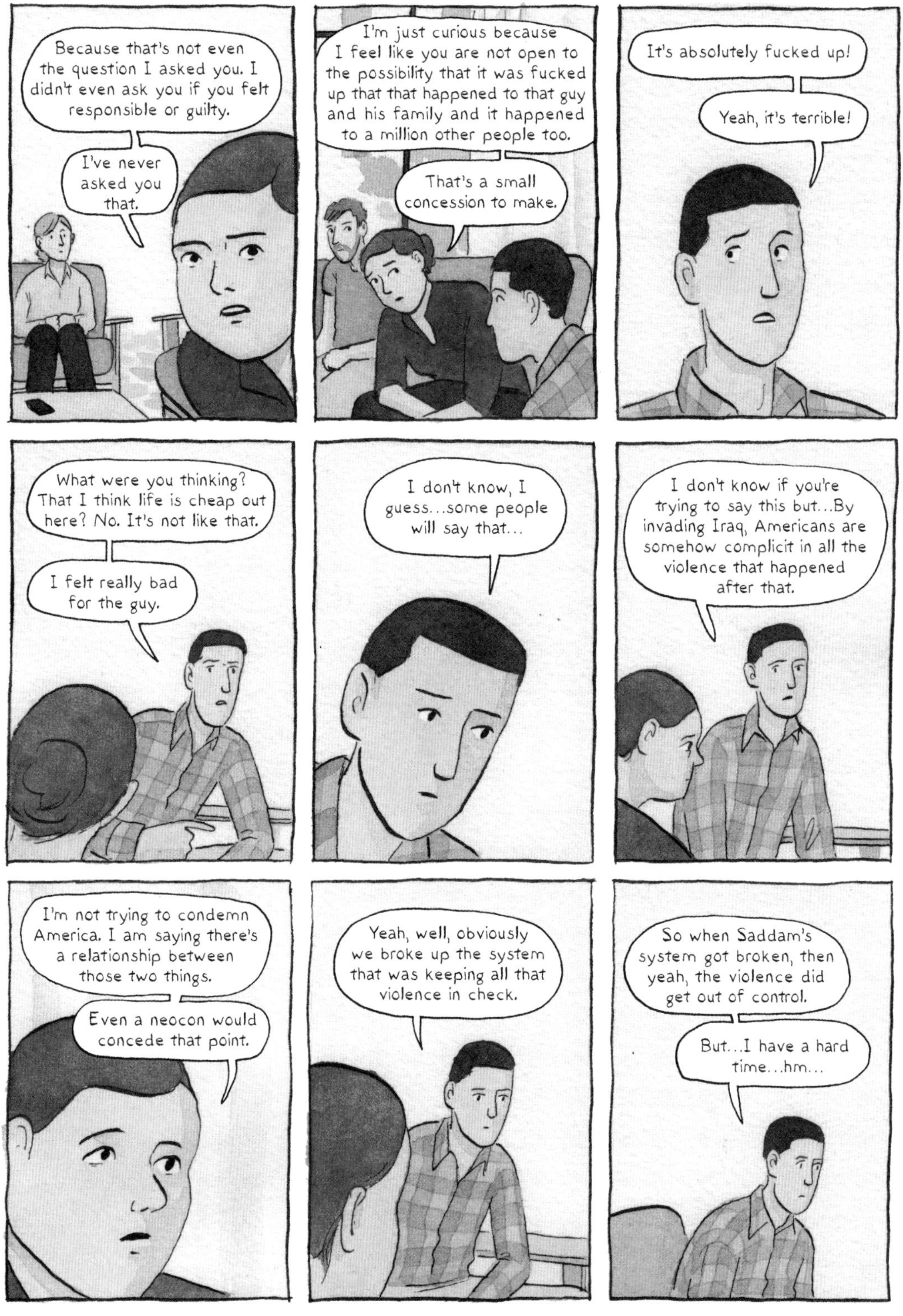
Because that's not even the question I asked you. I didn't even ask you if you felt responsible or guilty.
I've never asked you that.
I'm just curious because I feel like you are not open to the possibility that it was fucked up that that happened to that guy and his family and it happened to a million other people too.
That's a small concession to make.
It's absolutely fucked up!
Yeah, it's terrible!
What were you thinking? That I think life is cheap out here? No. It's not like that.
I felt really bad for the guy.
I don't know, I guess...some people will say that...
I don't know if you're trying to say this but...By invading Iraq, Americans are somehow complicit in all the violence that happened after that.
I'm not trying to condemn America. I am saying there's a relationship between those two things.
Even a neocon would concede that point.
Yeah, well, obviously we broke up the system that was keeping all that violence in check.
So when Saddam's system got broken, then yeah, the violence did get out of control.
But...I have a hard time...hm...

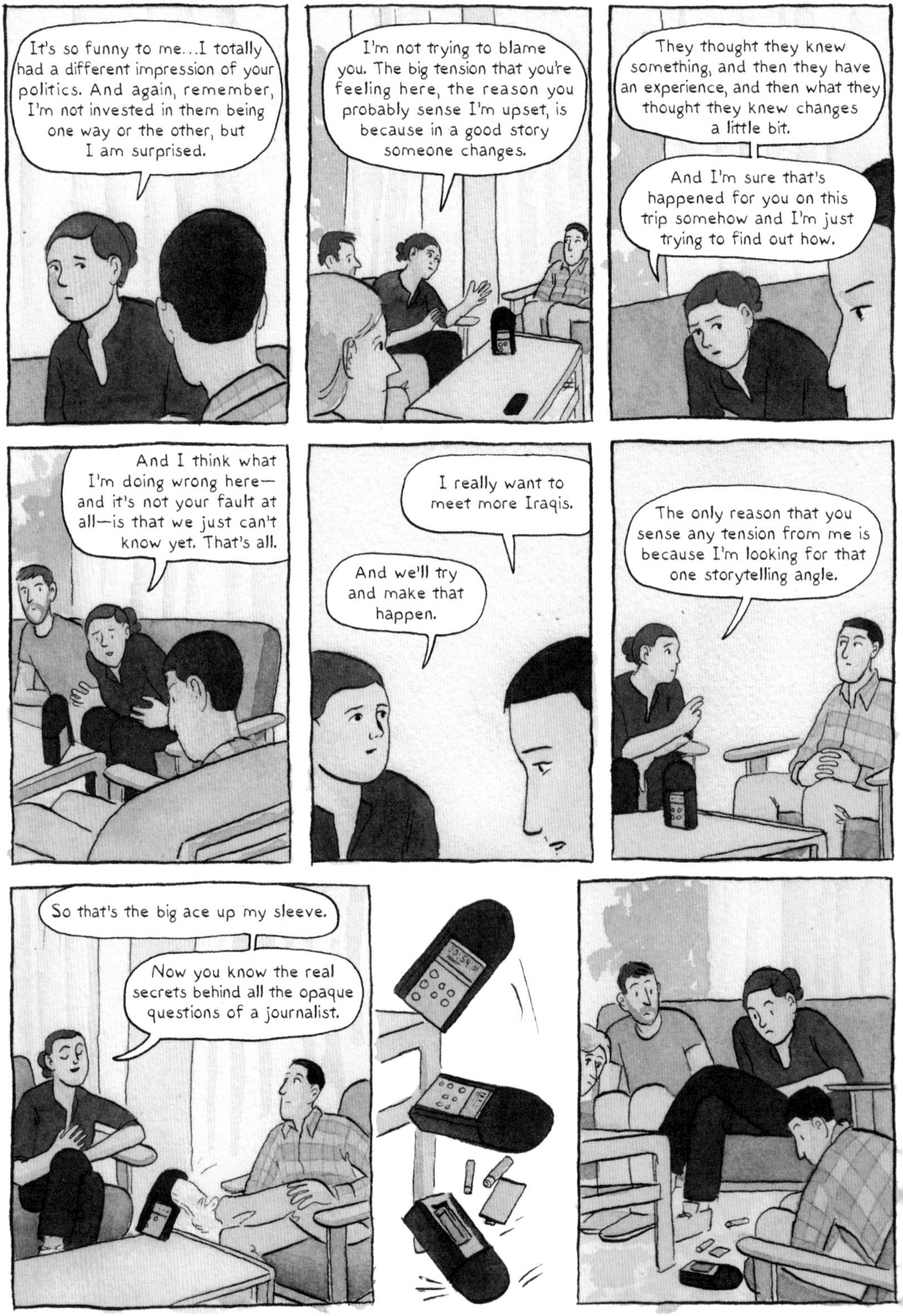
It's so funny to me...I totally had a different impression of your politics. And again, remember, I'm not invested in them being one way or the other, but I am surprised.
I'm not trying to blame you. The big tension that you're feeling here, the reason you probably sense I'm upset, is because in a good story someone changes.
They thought they knew something, and then they have an experience, and then what they thought they knew changes a little bit.
And I'm sure that's happened for you on this trip somehow and I'm just trying to find out how.
And I think what I'm doing wrong here—and it's not your fault at all—is that we just can't know yet. That's all.
I really want to meet more Iraqis.
And we'll try and make that happen.
The only reason that you sense any tension from me is because I'm looking for that one storytelling angle.
So that's the big ace up my sleeve.
Now you know the real secrets behind all the opaque questions of a journalist.

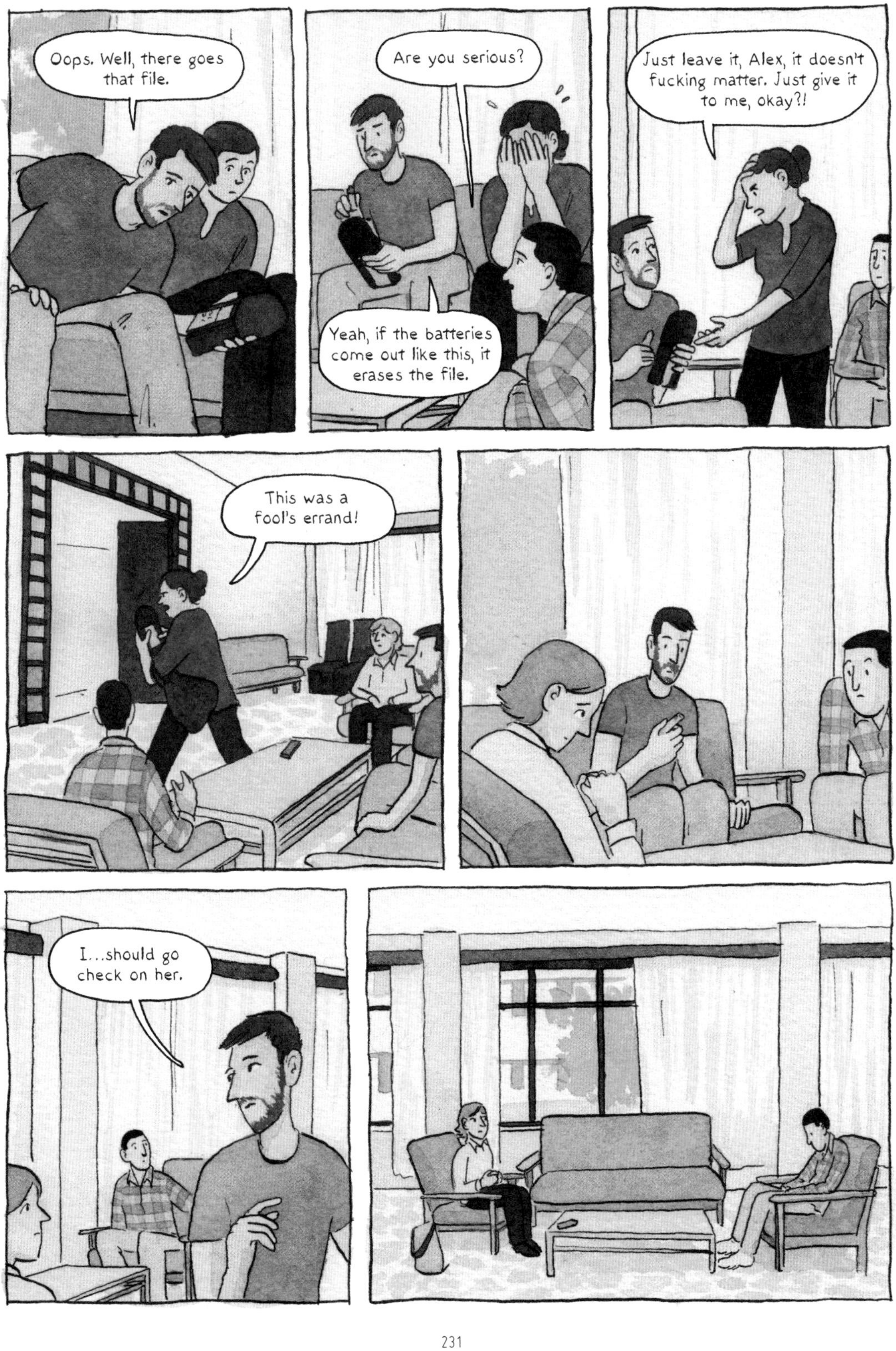
Oops. Well, there goes that file.
Are you serious?
Yeah, if the batteries come out like this, it erases the file.
Just leave it, Alex, it doesn't fucking matter. Just give it to me, okay?!
This was a fool's errand!
I...should go check on her.

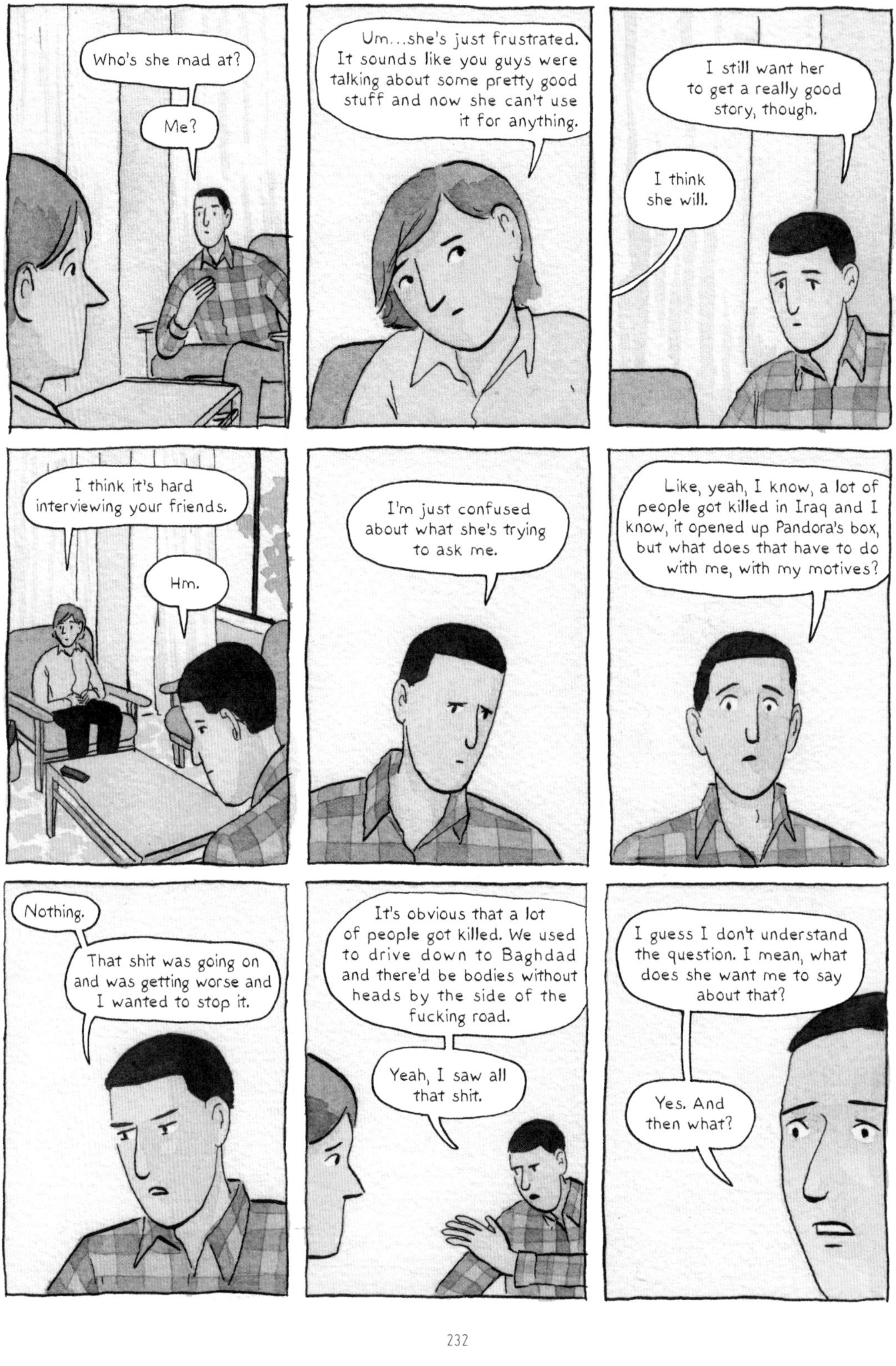

Who's she mad at?
Me?
Um...she's just frustrated. It sounds like you guys were talking about some pretty good stuff and now she can't use it for anything.
I still want her to get a really good story, though.
I think she will.
I think it's hard interviewing your friends.
Hm.
I'm just confused about what she's trying to ask me.
Like, yeah, I know, a lot of people got killed in Iraq and I know, it opened up Pandora's box, but what does that have to do with me, with my motives?
Nothing.
That shit was going on and was getting worse and I wanted to stop it.
It's obvious that a lot of people got killed. We used to drive down to Baghdad and there'd be bodies without heads by the side of the fucking road.
Yeah, I saw all that shit.
I guess I don't understand the question. I mean, what does she want me to say about that?
Yes. And then what?

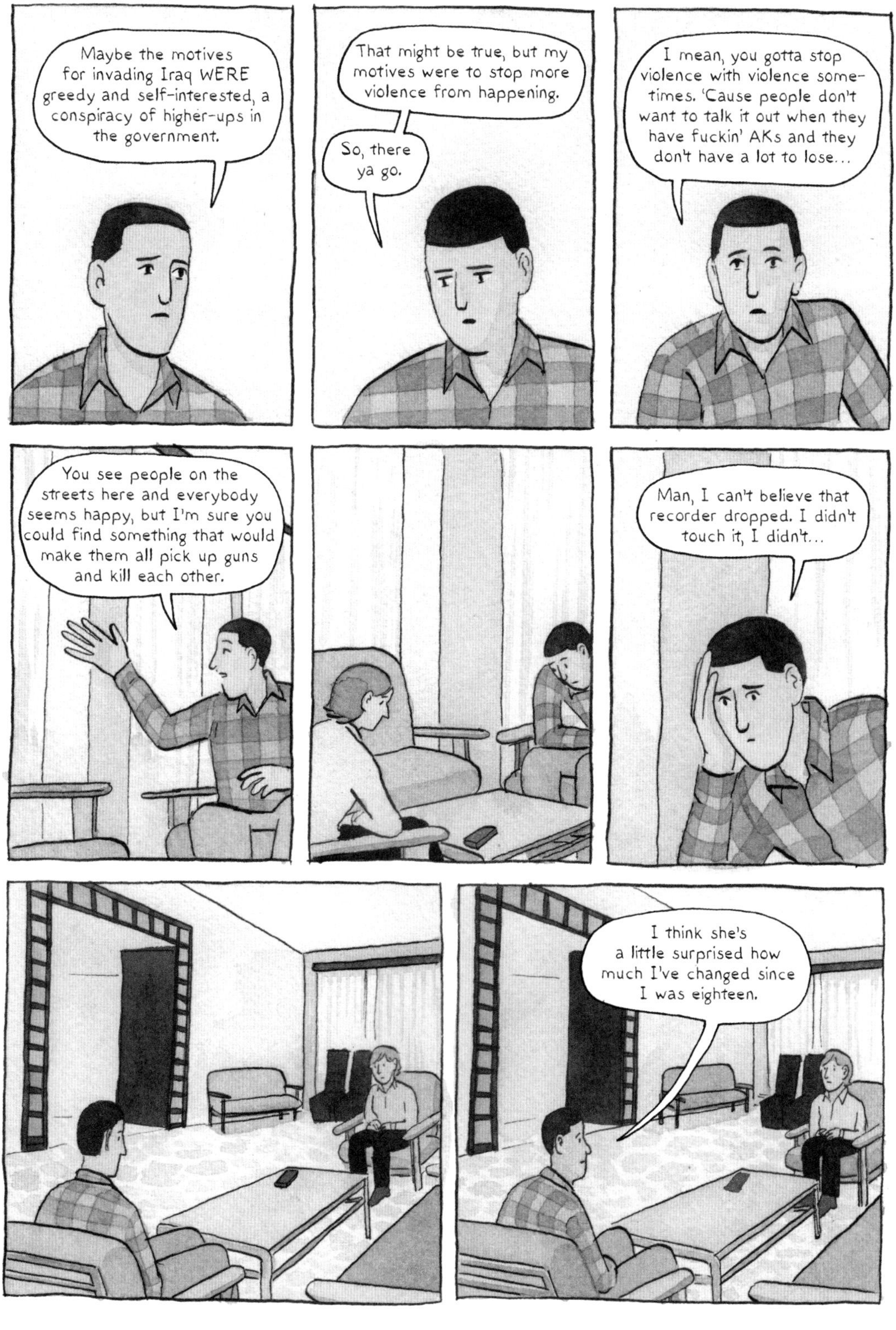
Maybe the motives for invading Iraq WERE greedy and self-interested, a conspiracy of higher-ups in the government.
That might be true, but my motives were to stop more violence from happening.
So, there ya go.
I mean, you gotta stop violence with violence sometimes. 'Cause people don't want to talk it out when they have fuckin' AKs and they don't have a lot to lose...
You see people on the streets here and everybody seems happy, but I'm sure you could find something that would make them all pick up guns and kill each other.
Man, I can't believe that recorder dropped. I didn't touch it, I didn't...
I think she's a little surprised how much I've changed since I was eighteen.

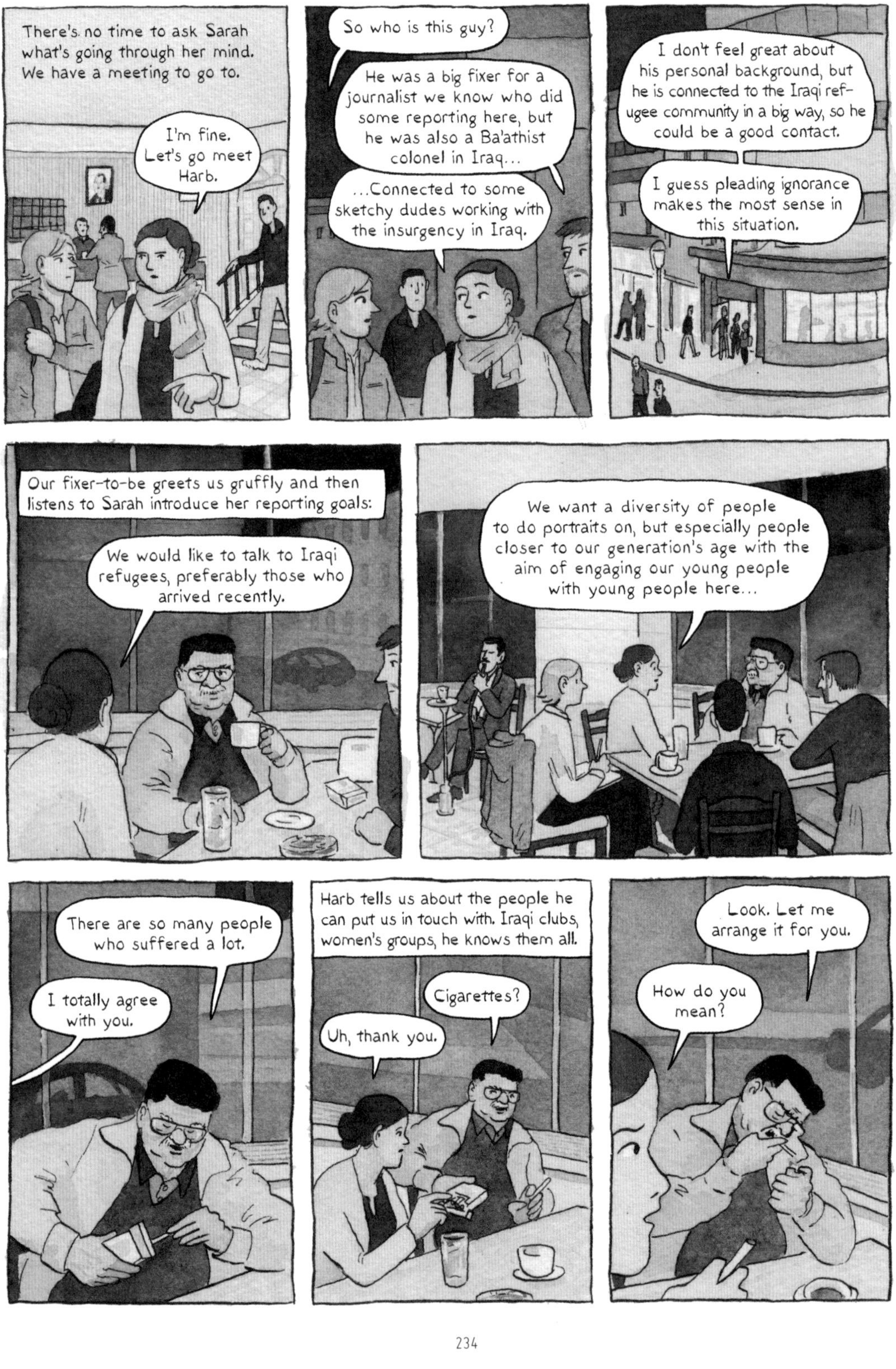

There's no time to ask Sarah what's going through her mind. We have a meeting to go to.
I'm fine. Let's go meet Harb.
So who is this guy?
He was a big fixer for a journalist we know who did some reporting here, but he was also a Ba'athist colonel in Iraq...
...Connected to some sketchy dudes working with the insurgency in Iraq.
I don't feel great about his personal background, but he is connected to the Iraqi refugee community in a big way, so he could be a good contact.
I guess pleading ignorance makes the most sense in this situation.
Our fixer-to-be greets us gruffly and then listens to Sarah introduce her reporting goals:
We would like to talk to Iraqi refugees, preferably those who arrived recently.
We want a diversity of people to do portraits on, but especially people closer to our generation's age with the aim of engaging our young people with young people here...
There are so many people who suffered a lot.
I totally agree with you.
Harb tells us about the people he can put us in touch with. Iraqi clubs, women's groups, he knows them all.
Cigarettes?
Uh, thank you.
Look. Let me arrange it for you.
How do you mean?

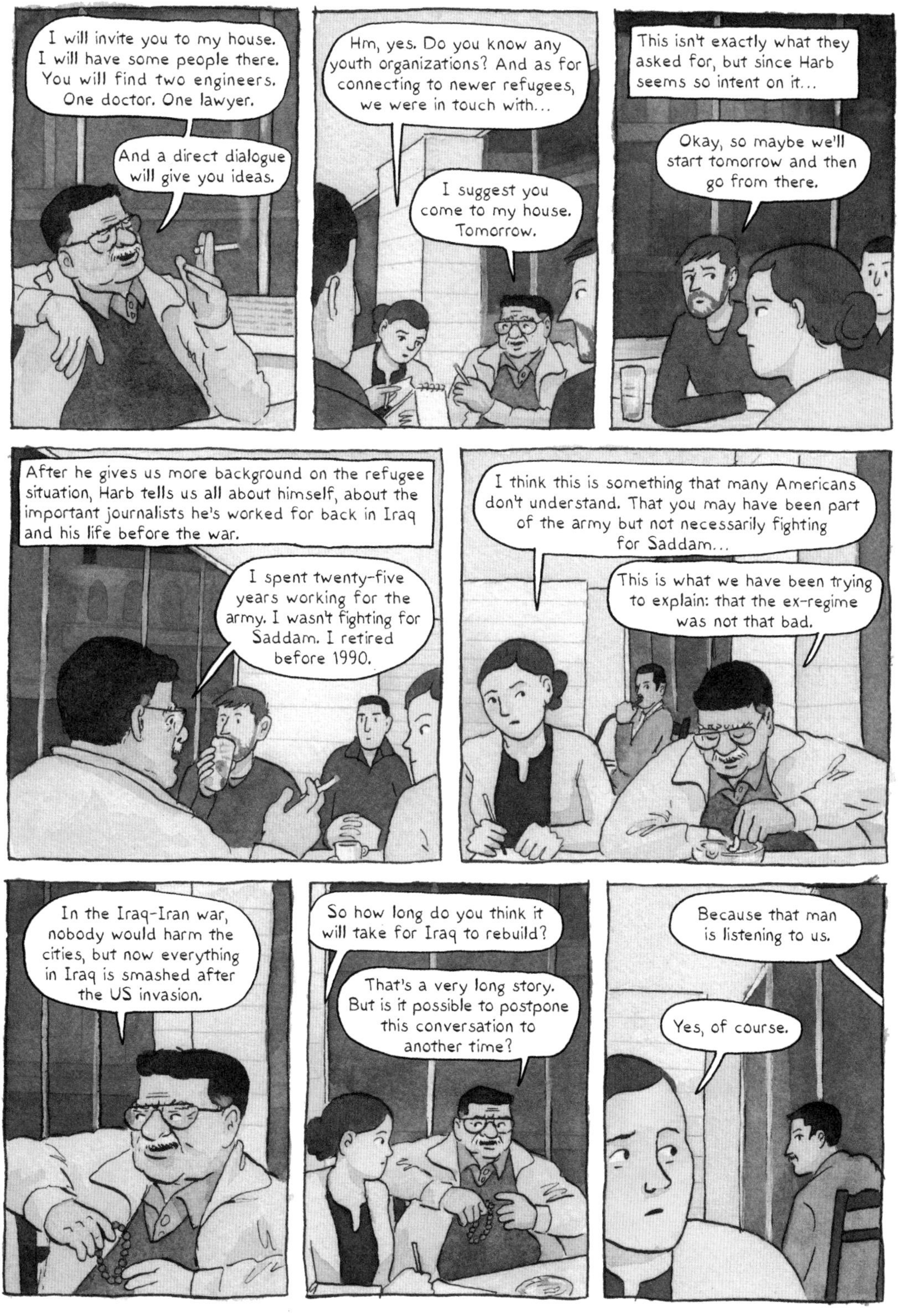
I will invite you to my house. I will have some people there. You will find two engineers. One doctor. One lawyer.
And a direct dialogue will give you ideas.
Hm, yes. Do you know any youth organizations? And as for connecting to newer refugees, we were in touch with...
I suggest you come to my house. Tomorrow.
This isn't exactly what they asked for, but since Harb seems so intent on it...
Okay, so maybe we'll start tomorrow and then go from there.
After he gives us more background on the refugee situation, Harb tells us all about himself, about the important journalists he's worked for back in Iraq and his life before the war.
I spent twenty-five years working for the army. I wasn't fighting for Saddam. I retired before 1990.
I think this is something that many Americans don't understand. That you may have been part of the army but not necessarily fighting for Saddam...
This is what we have been trying to explain: that the ex-regime was not that bad.
In the Iraq-Iran war, nobody would harm the cities, but now everything in Iraq is smashed after the US invasion.
So how long do you think it will take for Iraq to rebuild?
That's a very long story. But is it possible to postpone this conversation to another time?
Because that man is listening to us.
Yes, of course.

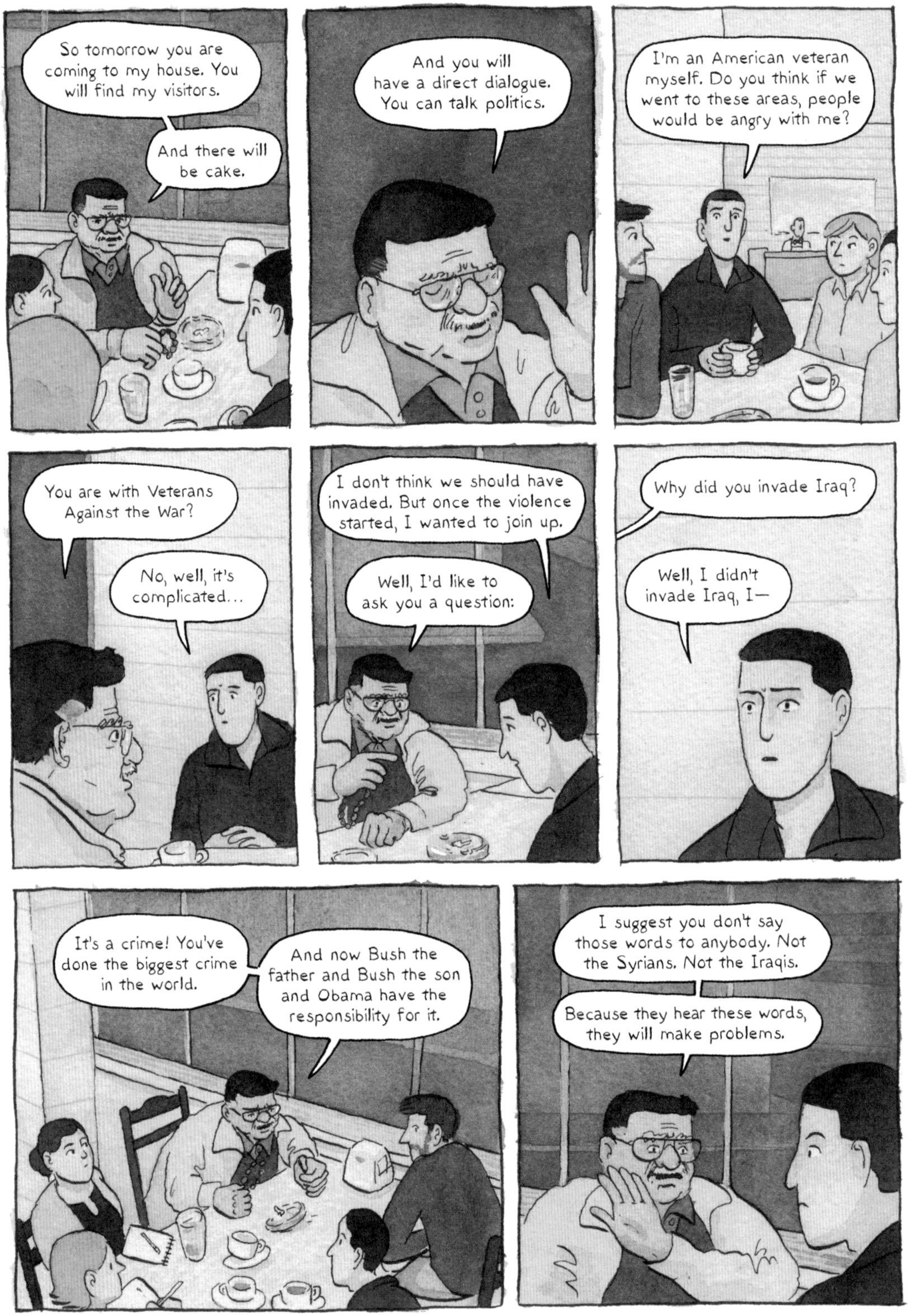
So tomorrow you are coming to my house. You will find my visitors.
And there will be cake.
And you will have a direct dialogue. You can talk politics.
I'm an American veteran myself. Do you think if we went to these areas, people would be angry with me?
You are with Veterans Against the War?
No, well, it's complicated...
I don't think we should have invaded. But once the violence started, I wanted to join up.
Well, I'd like to ask you a question:
Why did you invade Iraq?
Well, I didn't invade Iraq, I—
It's a crime! You've done the biggest crime in the world.
And now Bush the father and Bush the son and Obama have the responsibility for it.
I suggest you don't say those words to anybody. Not the Syrians. Not the Iraqis.
Because they hear these words, they will make problems.

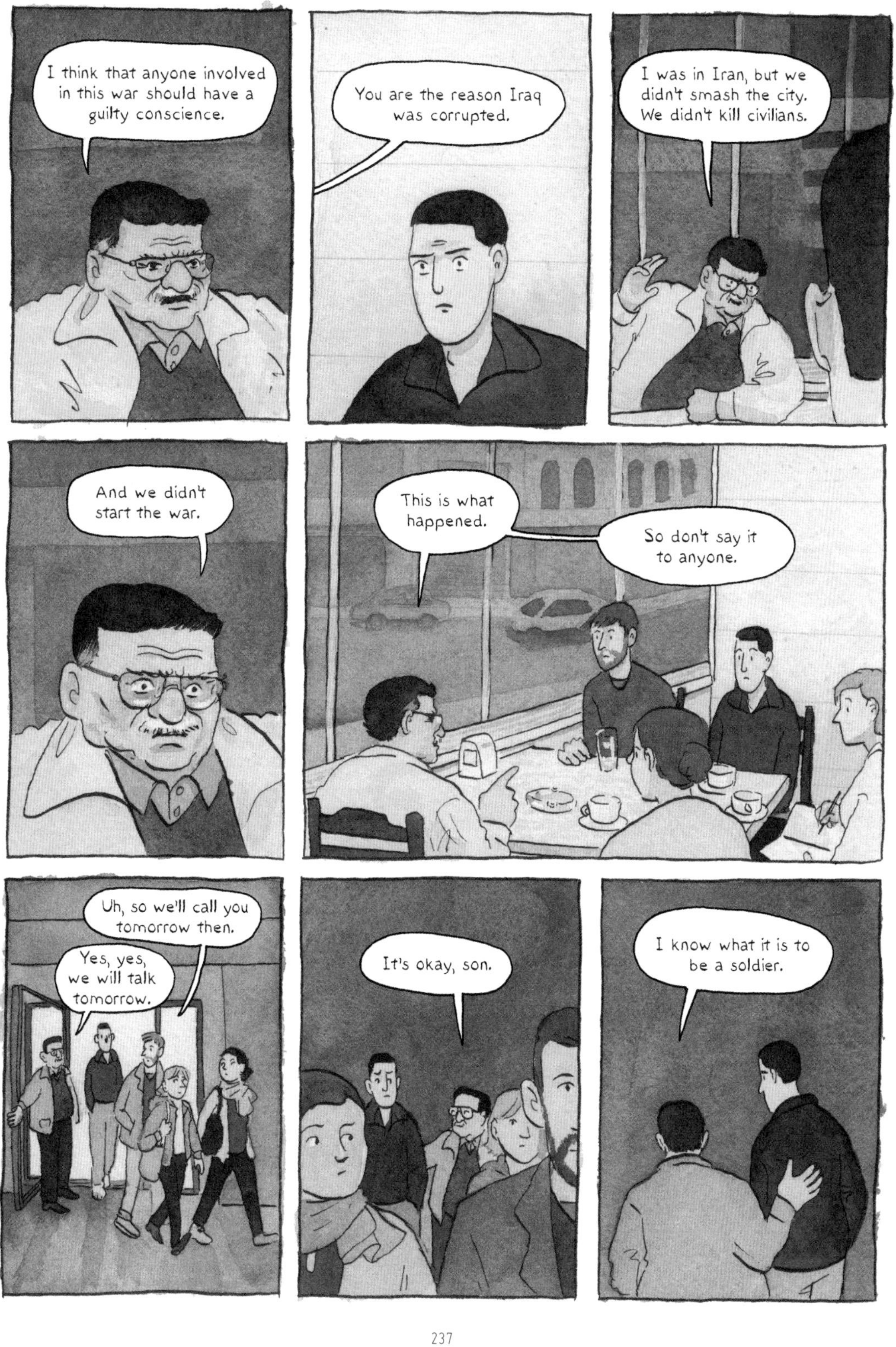
I think that anyone involved in this war should have a guilty conscience.
You are the reason Iraq was corrupted.
I was in Iran, but we didn't smash the city. We didn't kill civilians.
And we didn't start the war.
This is what happened.
So don't say it to anyone.
Uh, so we'll call you tomorrow then.
Yes, yes, we will talk tomorrow.
It's okay, son.
I know what it is to be a soldier.

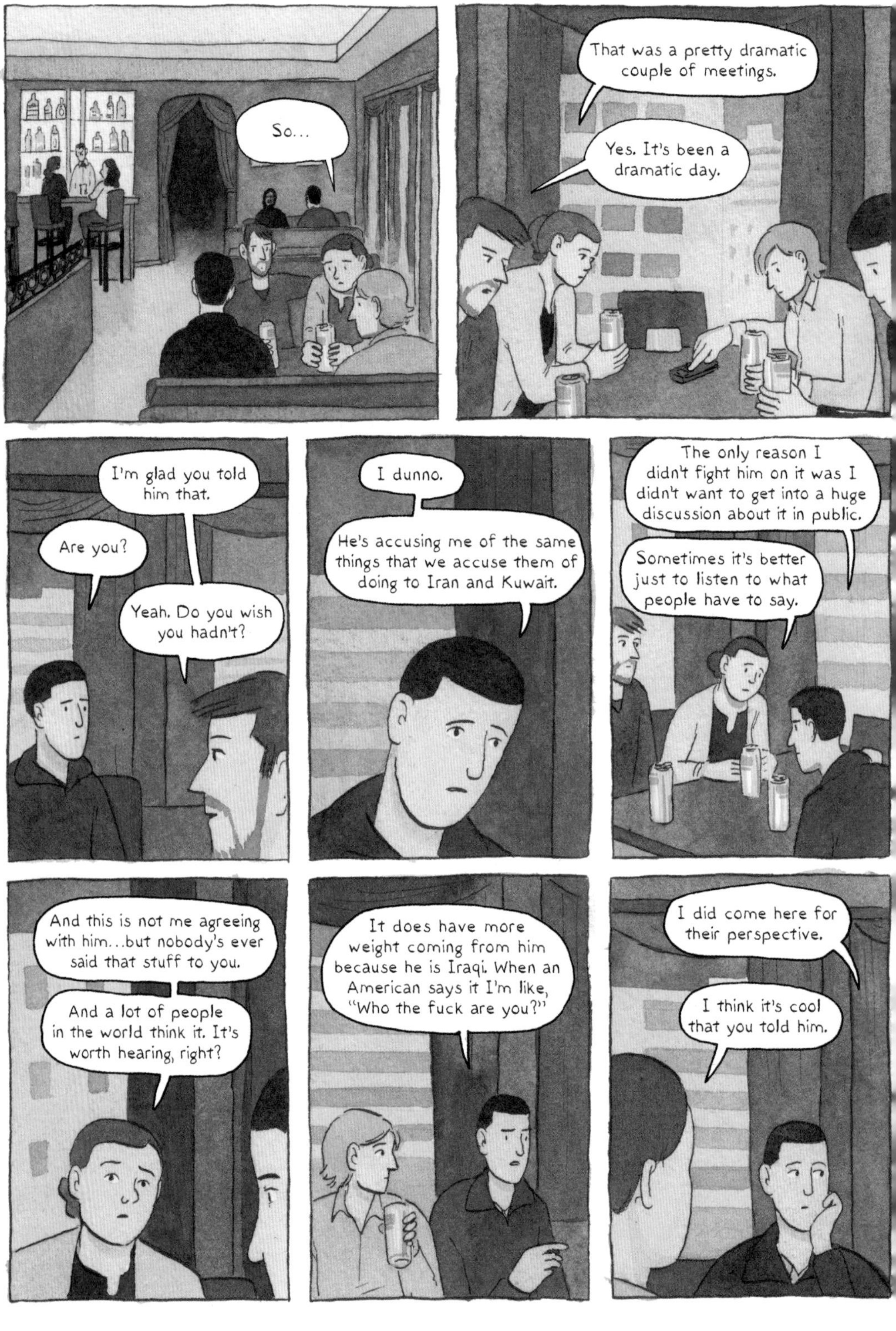
So...
That was a pretty dramatic couple of meetings.
Yes. It's been a dramatic day.
I'm glad you told him that.
Are you?
Yeah. Do you wish you hadn't?
I dunno.
He's accusing me of the same things that we accuse them of doing to Iran and Kuwait.
The only reason I didn't fight him on it was I didn't want to get into a huge discussion about it in public.
Sometimes it's better just to listen to what people have to say.
And this is not me agreeing with him...but nobody's ever said that stuff to you.
And a lot of people in the world think it. It's worth hearing, right?
It does have more weight coming from him because he is Iraqi. When an American says it I'm like, "Who the fuck are you?"
I did come here for their perspective.
I think it's cool that you told him.

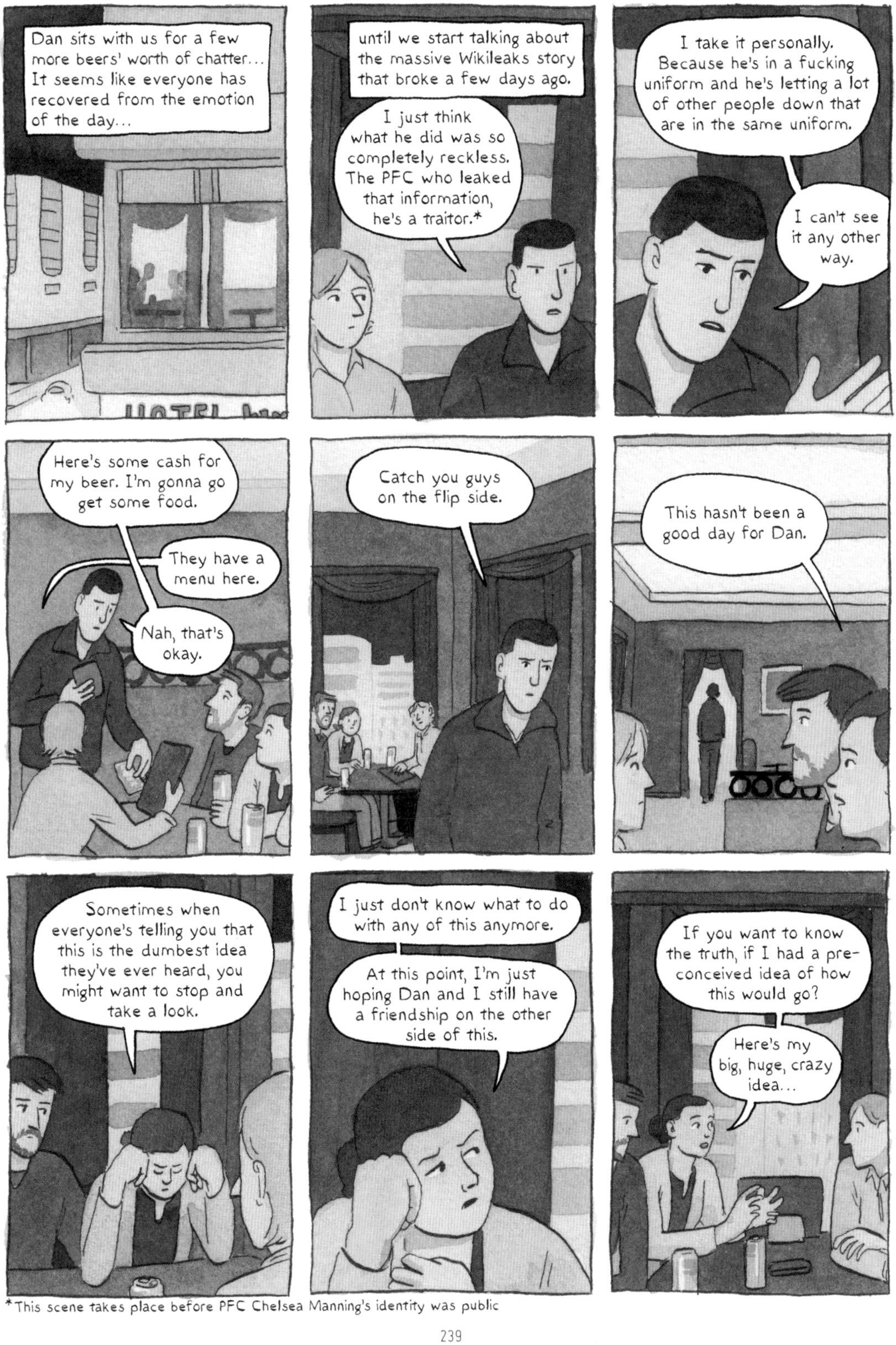
Dan sits with us for a few more beers' worth of chatter... It seems like everyone has recovered from the emotion of the day...
HOTEL
until we start talking about the massive Wikileaks story that broke a few days ago.
I just think what he did was so completely reckless. The PFC who leaked that information, he's a traitor.*
I take it personally. Because he's in a fucking uniform and he's letting a lot of other people down that are in the same uniform.
I can't see it any other way.
Here's some cash for my beer. I'm gonna go get some food.
They have a menu here.
Nah, that's okay.
Catch you guys on the flip side.
This hasn't been a good day for Dan.
Sometimes when everyone's telling you that this is the dumbest idea they've ever heard, you might want to stop and take a look.
I just don't know what to do with any of this anymore.
At this point, I'm just hoping Dan and I still have a friendship on the other side of this.
If you want to know the truth, if I had a preconceived idea of how this would go?
Here's my big, huge, crazy idea...

*This scene takes place before PFC Chelsea Manning's identity was public

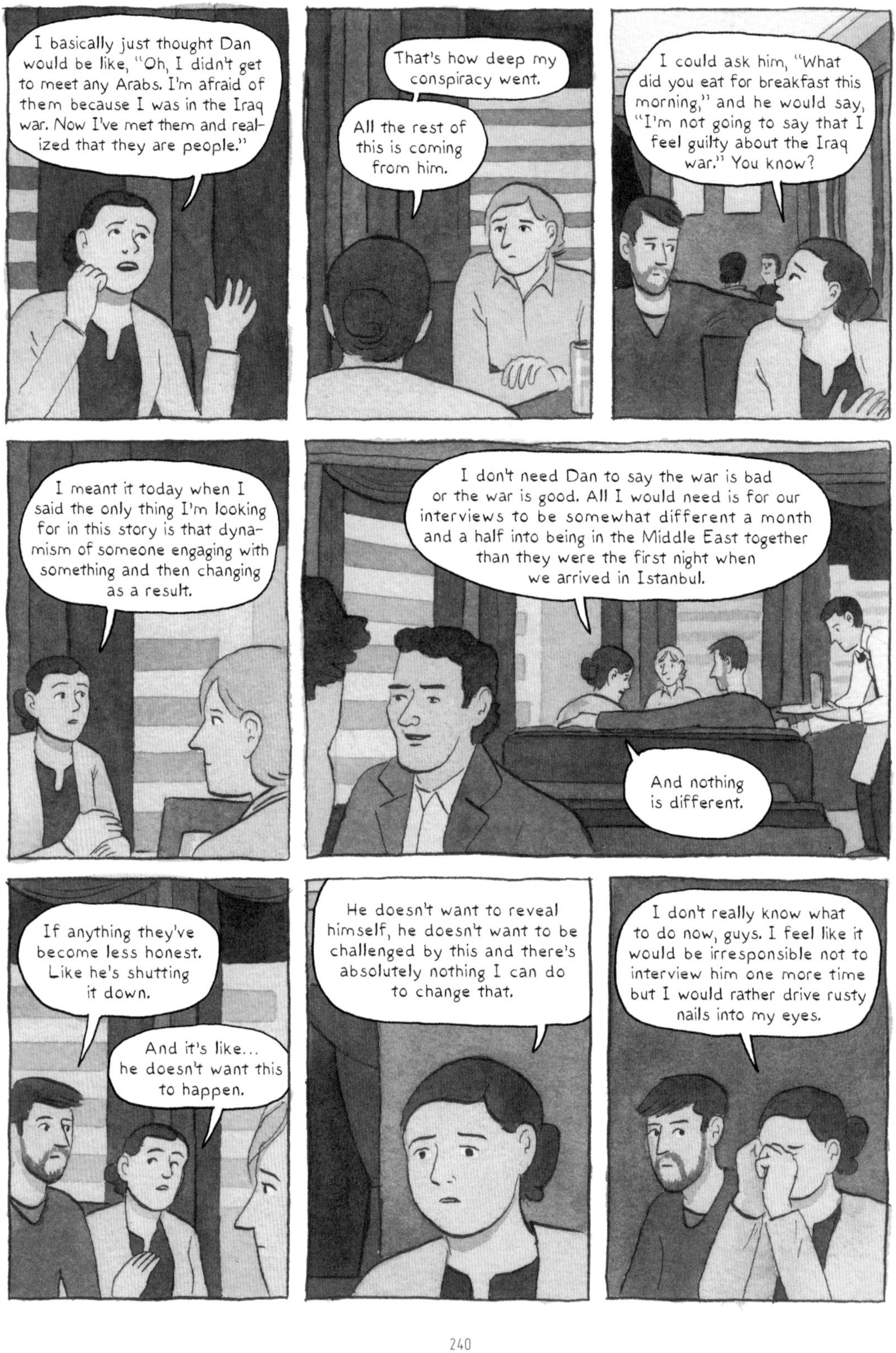

I basically just thought Dan would be like, "Oh, I didn't get to meet any Arabs. I'm afraid of them because I was in the Iraq war. Now I've met them and realized that they are people."
That's how deep my conspiracy went.
All the rest of this is coming from him.
I could ask him, "What did you eat for breakfast this morning," and he would say, "I'm not going to say that I feel guilty about the Iraq war." You know?
I meant it today when I said the only thing I'm looking for in this story is that dynamism of someone engaging with something and then changing as a result.
I don't need Dan to say the war is bad or the war is good. All I would need is for our interviews to be somewhat different a month and a half into being in the Middle East together than they were the first night when we arrived in Istanbul.
And nothing is different.
If anything they've become less honest. Like he's shutting it down.
And it's like... he doesn't want this to happen.
He doesn't want to reveal himself, he doesn't want to be challenged by this and there's absolutely nothing I can do to change that.
I don't really know what to do now, guys. I feel like it would be irresponsible not to interview him one more time but I would rather drive rusty nails into my eyes.

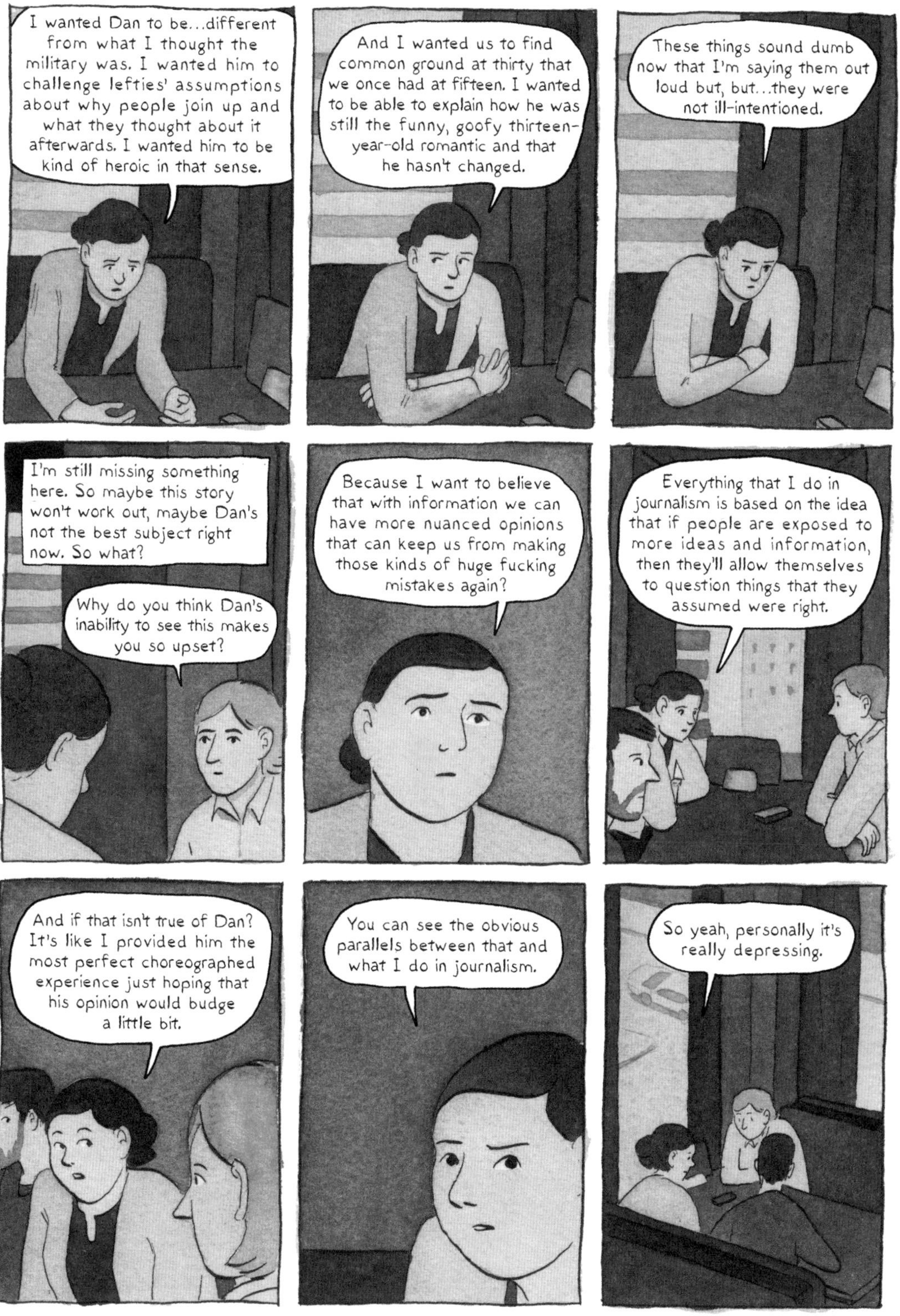
I wanted Dan to be...different from what I thought the military was. I wanted him to challenge lefties' assumptions about why people join up and what they thought about it afterwards. I wanted him to be kind of heroic in that sense.
And I wanted us to find common ground at thirty that we once had at fifteen. I wanted to be able to explain how he was still the funny, goofy thirteen-year-old romantic and that he hasn't changed.
These things sound dumb now that I'm saying them out loud but, but...they were not ill-intentioned.
I'm still missing something here. So maybe this story won't work out, maybe Dan's not the best subject right now. So what?
Why do you think Dan's inability to see this makes you so upset?
Because I want to believe that with information we can have more nuanced opinions that can keep us from making those kinds of huge fucking mistakes again?
Everything that I do in journalism is based on the idea that if people are exposed to more ideas and information, then they'll allow themselves to question things that they assumed were right.
And if that isn't true of Dan? It's like I provided him the most perfect choreographed experience just hoping that his opinion would budge a little bit.
You can see the obvious parallels between that and what I do in journalism.
So yeah, personally it's really depressing.

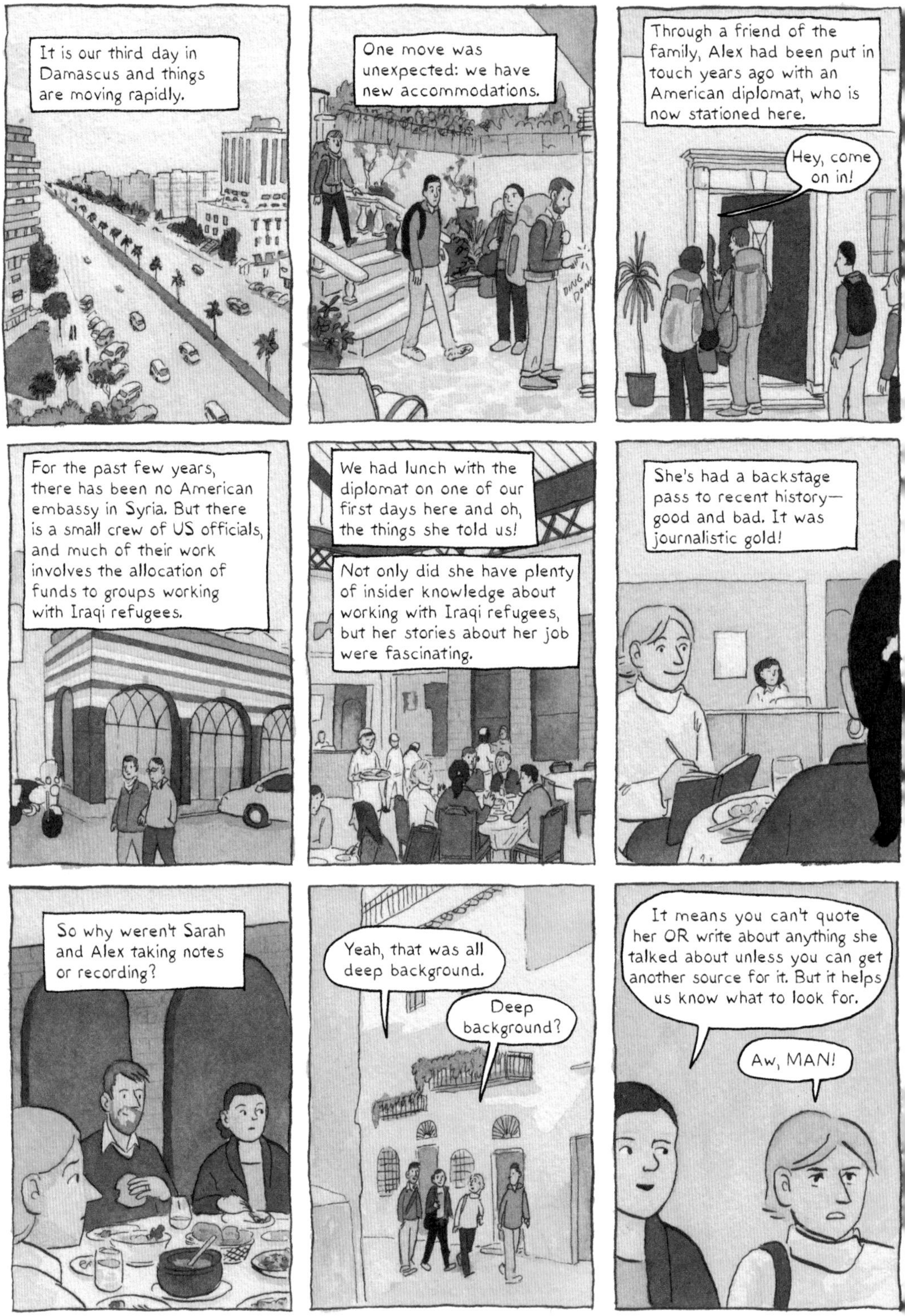
It is our third day in Damascus and things are moving rapidly.
One move was unexpected: we have new accommodations.
DING DONG
Through a friend of the family, Alex had been put in touch years ago with an American diplomat, who is now stationed here.
Hey, come on in!
For the past few years, there has been no American embassy in Syria. But there is a small crew of US officials, and much of their work involves the allocation of funds to groups working with Iraqi refugees.
We had lunch with the diplomat on one of our first days here and oh, the things she told us!
Not only did she have plenty of insider knowledge about working with Iraqi refugees, but her stories about her job were fascinating.
She's had a backstage pass to recent history—good and bad. It was journalistic gold!
So why weren't Sarah and Alex taking notes or recording?
Yeah, that was all deep background.
Deep background?
It means you can't quote her OR write about anything she talked about unless you can get another source for it. But it helps us know what to look for.
Aw, MAN!

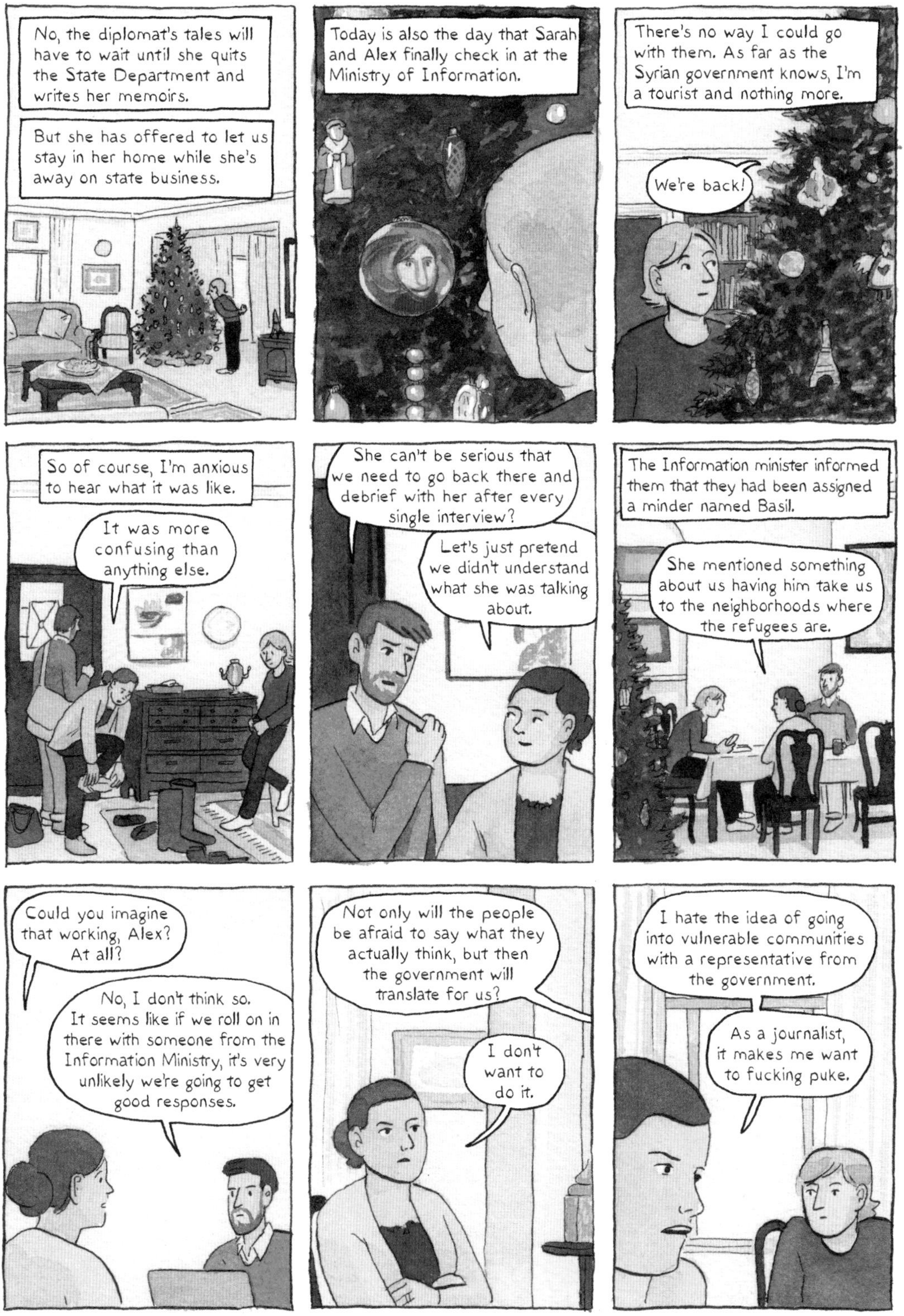
No, the diplomat's tales will have to wait until she quits the State Department and writes her memoirs.
But she has offered to let us stay in her home while she's away on state business.
Today is also the day that Sarah and Alex finally check in at the Ministry of Information.
There's no way I could go with them. As far as the Syrian government knows, I'm a tourist and nothing more.
We're back!
So of course, I'm anxious to hear what it was like.
It was more confusing than anything else.
She can't be serious that we need to go back there and debrief with her after every single interview?
Let's just pretend we didn't understand what she was talking about.
The Information minister informed them that they had been assigned a minder named Basil.
She mentioned something about us having him take us to the neighborhoods where the refugees are.
Could you imagine that working, Alex? At all?
No, I don't think so. It seems like if we roll on in there with someone from the Information Ministry, it's very unlikely we're going to get good responses.
Not only will the people be afraid to say what they actually think, but then the government will translate for us?
I don't want to do it.
I hate the idea of going into vulnerable communities with a representative from the government.
As a journalist, it makes me want to fucking puke.

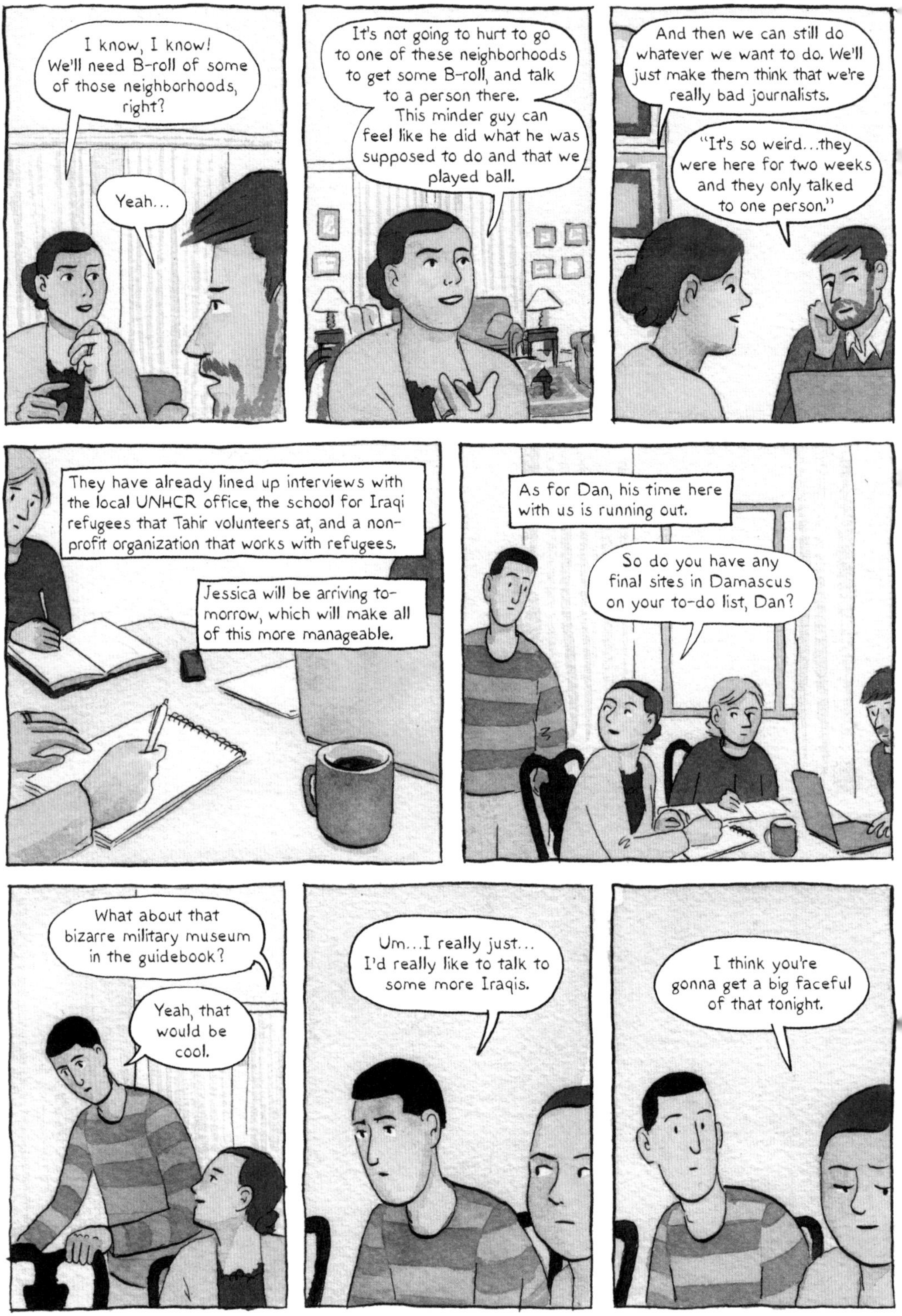
I know, I know! We'll need B-roll of some of those neighborhoods, right?
Yeah...
It's not going to hurt to go to one of these neighborhoods to get some B-roll, and talk to a person there.
This minder guy can feel like he did what he was supposed to do and that we played ball.
And then we can still do whatever we want to do. We'll just make them think that we're really bad journalists.
"It's so weird...they were here for two weeks and they only talked to one person."
They have already lined up interviews with the local UNHCR office, the school for Iraqi refugees that Tahir volunteers at, and a non-profit organization that works with refugees.
Jessica will be arriving tomorrow, which will make all of this more manageable.
As for Dan, his time here with us is running out.
So do you have any final sites in Damascus on your to-do list, Dan?
What about that bizarre military museum in the guidebook?
Yeah, that would be cool.
Um...I really just... I'd really like to talk to some more Iraqis.
I think you're gonna get a big faceful of that tonight.

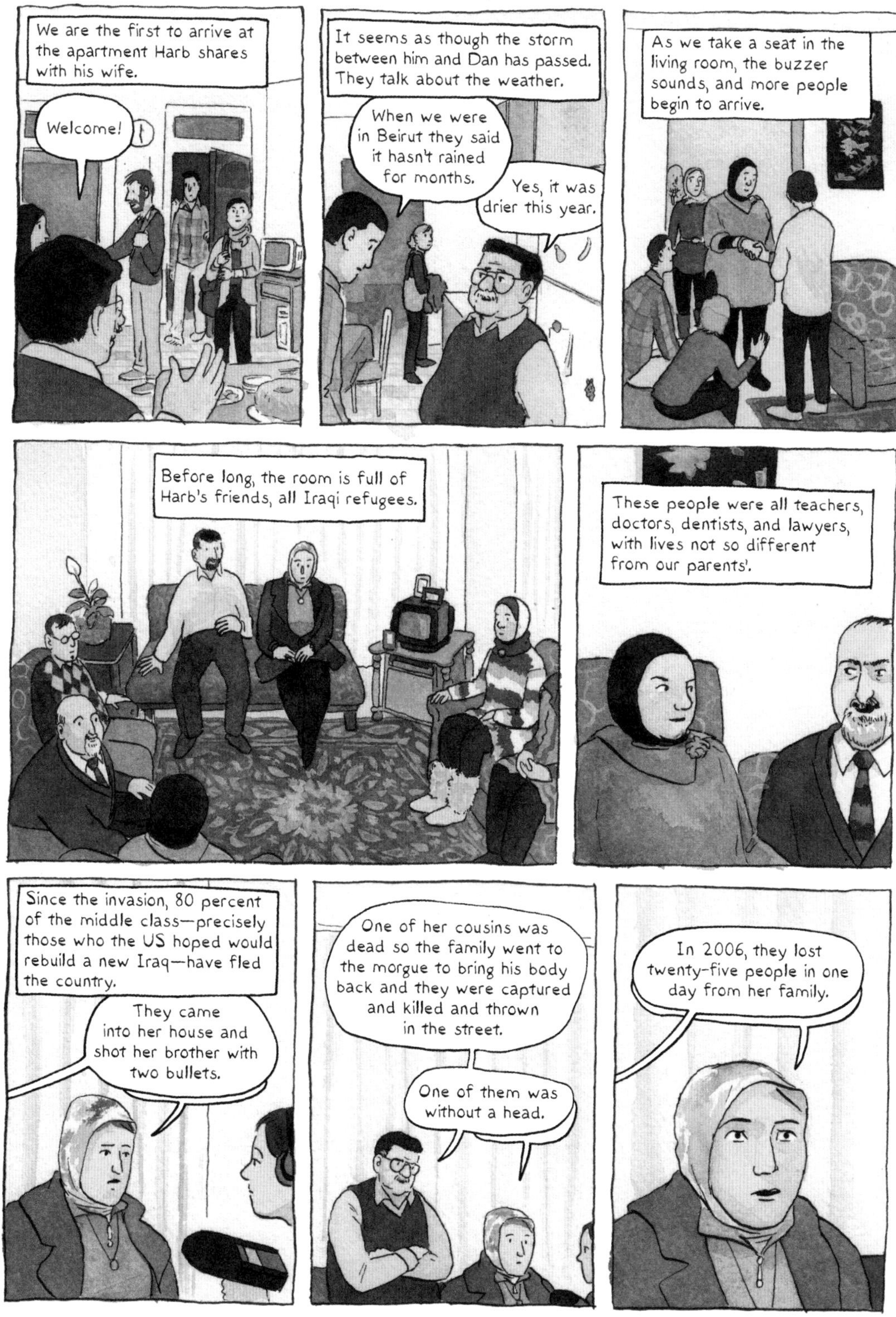

We are the first to arrive at the apartment Harb shares with his wife.
Welcome!
It seems as though the storm between him and Dan has passed. They talk about the weather.
When we were in Beirut they said it hasn't rained for months.
Yes, it was drier this year.
As we take a seat in the living room, the buzzer sounds, and more people begin to arrive.
Before long, the room is full of Harb's friends, all Iraqi refugees.
These people were all teachers, doctors, dentists, and lawyers, with lives not so different from our parents'.
Since the invasion, 80 percent of the middle class—precisely those who the US hoped would rebuild a new Iraq—have fled the country.
They came into her house and shot her brother with two bullets.
One of her cousins was dead so the family went to the morgue to bring his body back and they were captured and killed and thrown in the street.
One of them was without a head.
In 2006, they lost twenty-five people in one day from her family.

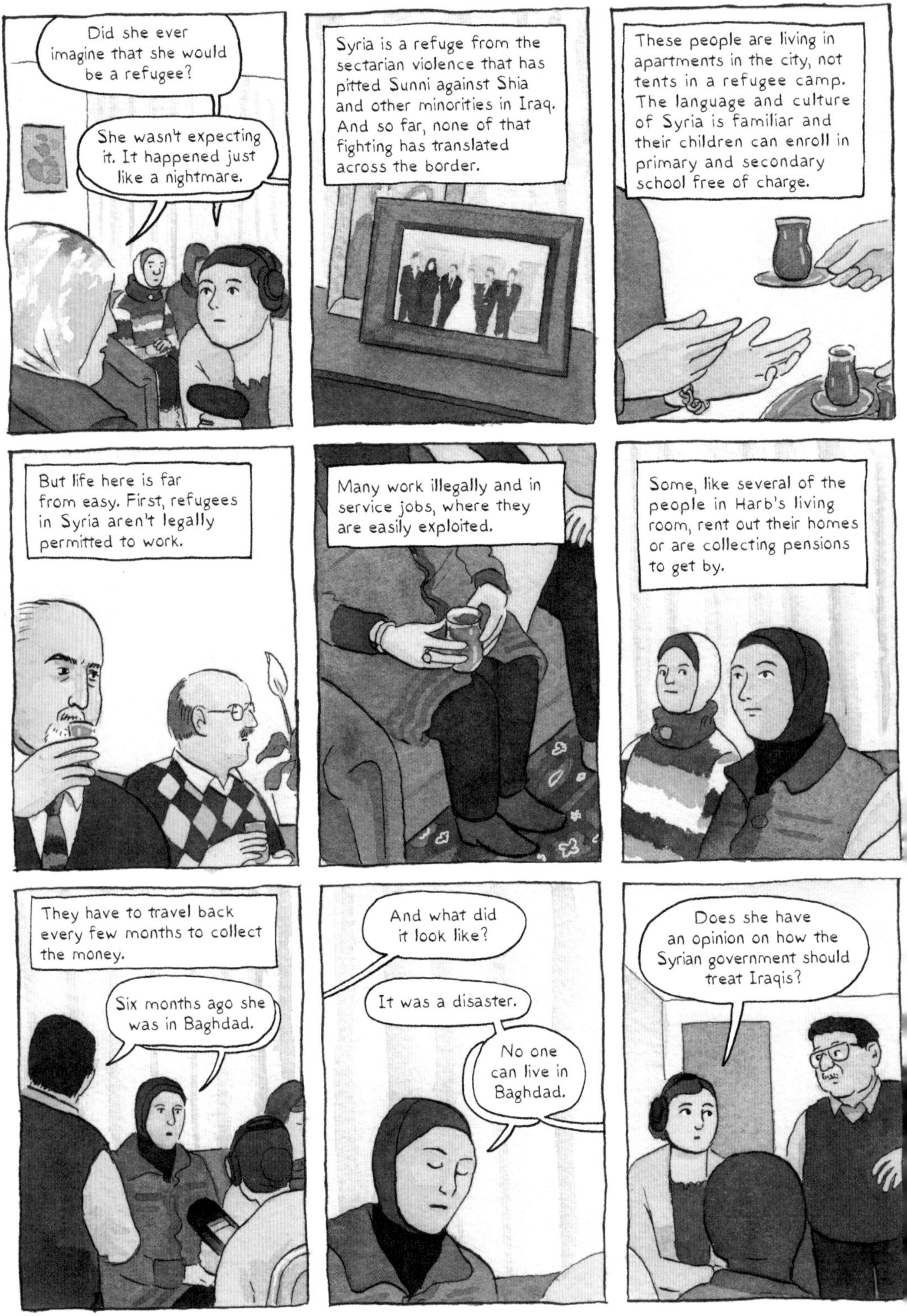

Did she ever imagine that she would be a refugee?
She wasn't expecting it. It happened just like a nightmare.
Syria is a refuge from the sectarian violence that has pitted Sunni against Shia and other minorities in Iraq. And so far, none of that fighting has translated across the border.
These people are living in apartments in the city, not tents in a refugee camp. The language and culture of Syria is familiar and their children can enroll in primary and secondary school free of charge.
But life here is far from easy. First, refugees in Syria aren't legally permitted to work.
Many work illegally and in service jobs, where they are easily exploited.
Some, like several of the people in Harb's living room, rent out their homes or are collecting pensions to get by.
They have to travel back every few months to collect the money.
Six months ago she was in Baghdad.
And what did it look like?
It was a disaster.
No one can live in Baghdad.
Does she have an opinion on how the Syrian government should treat Iraqis?

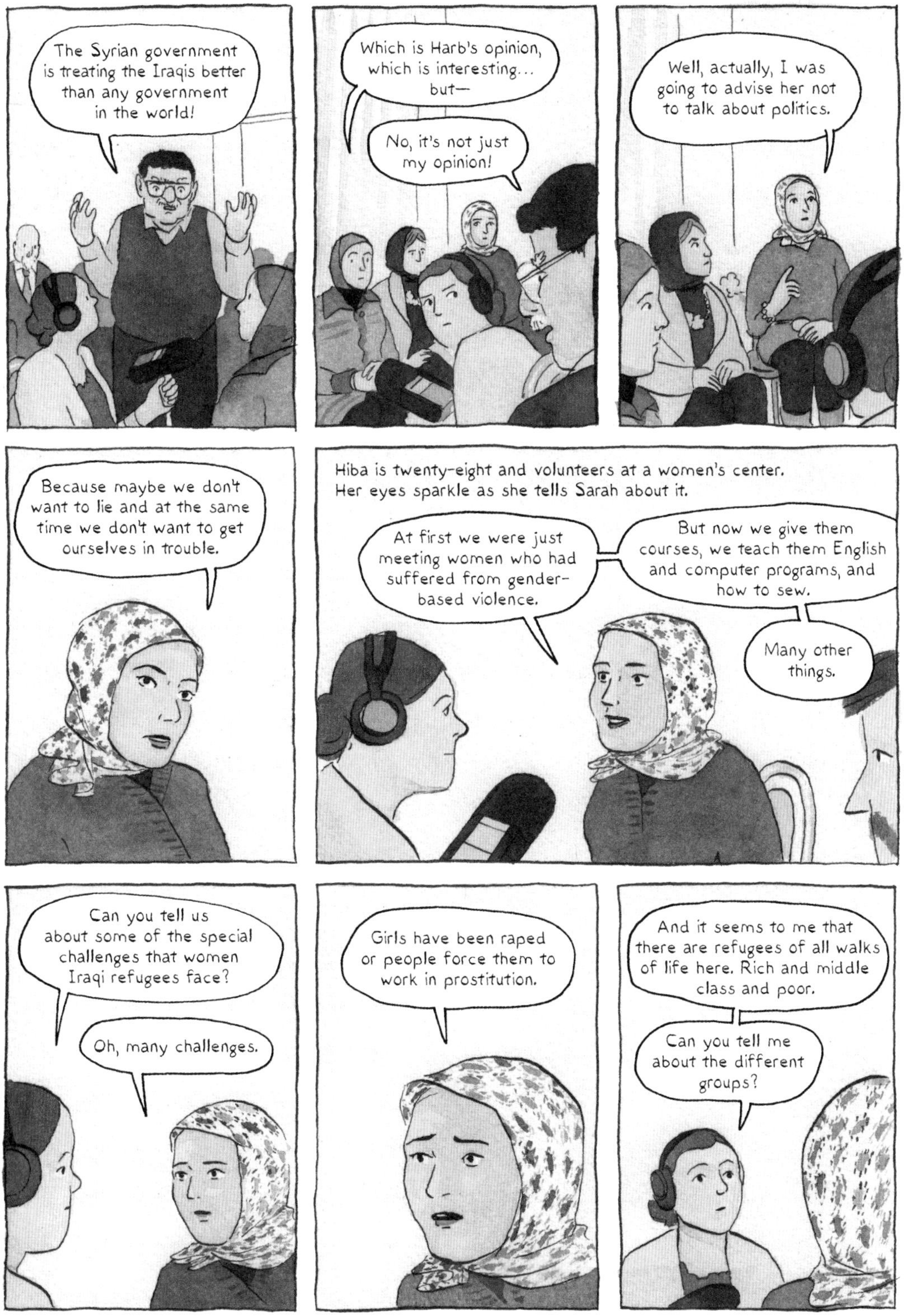
The Syrian government is treating the Iraqis better than any government in the world!
Which is Harb's opinion, which is interesting... but—
No, it's not just my opinion!
Well, actually, I was going to advise her not to talk about politics.
Because maybe we don't want to lie and at the same time we don't want to get ourselves in trouble.
Hiba is twenty-eight and volunteers at a women's center. Her eyes sparkle as she tells Sarah about it.
At first we were just meeting women who had suffered from gender-based violence.
But now we give them courses, we teach them English and computer programs, and how to sew.
Many other things.
Can you tell us about some of the special challenges that women Iraqi refugees face?
Oh, many challenges.
Girls have been raped or people force them to work in prostitution.
And it seems to me that there are refugees of all walks of life here. Rich and middle class and poor.
Can you tell me about the different groups?

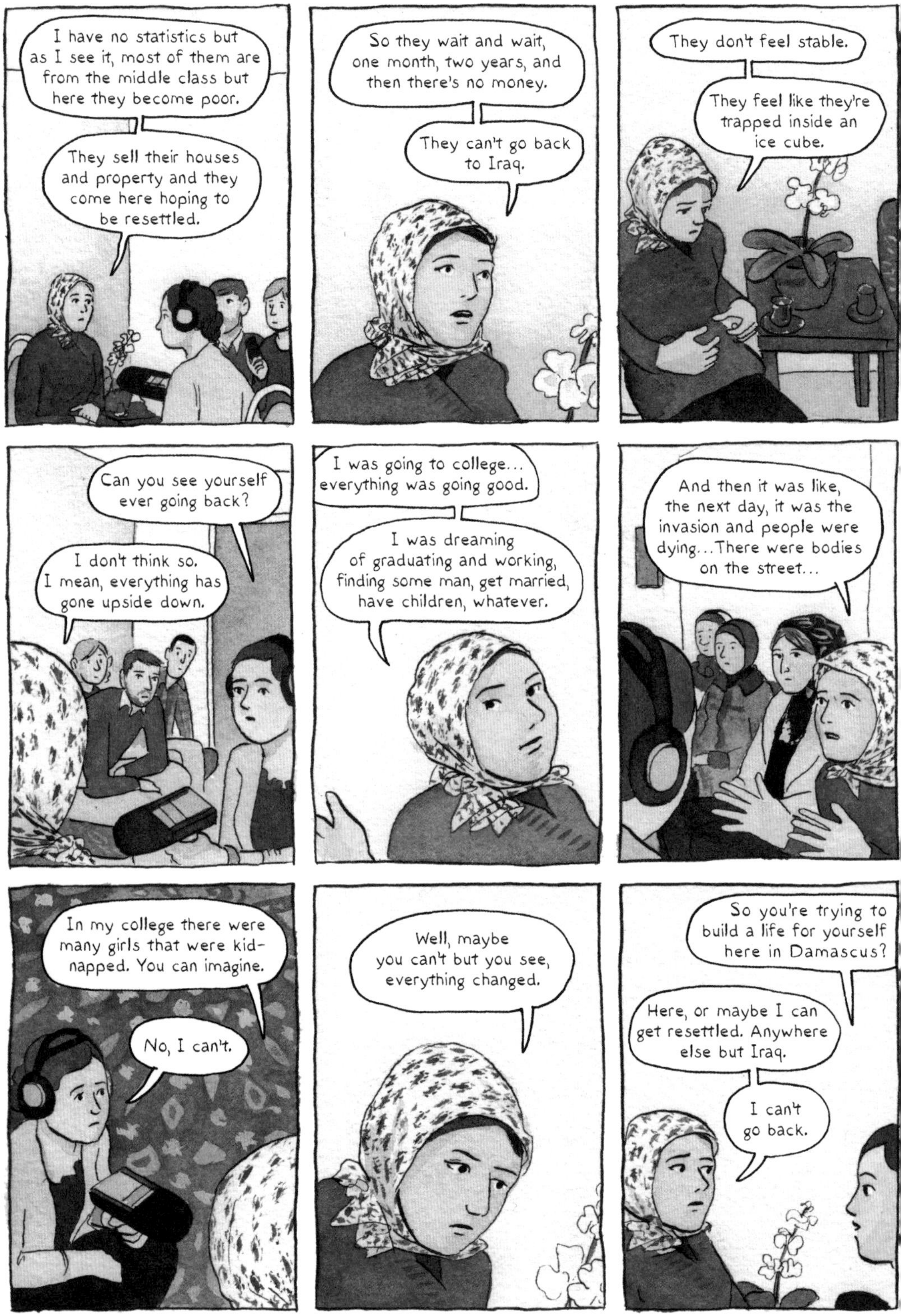
I have no statistics but as I see it, most of them are from the middle class but here they become poor.
They sell their houses and property and they come here hoping to be resettled.
So they wait and wait, one month, two years, and then there's no money.
They can't go back to Iraq.
They don't feel stable.
They feel like they're trapped inside an ice cube.
Can you see yourself ever going back?
I don't think so. I mean, everything has gone upside down.
I was going to college... everything was going good.
I was dreaming of graduating and working, finding some man, get married, have children, whatever.
And then it was like, the next day, it was the invasion and people were dying...There were bodies on the street...
In my college there were many girls that were kid-napped. You can imagine.
No, I can't.
Well, maybe you can't but you see, everything changed.
So you're trying to build a life for yourself here in Damascus?
Here, or maybe I can get resettled. Anywhere else but Iraq.
I can't go back.

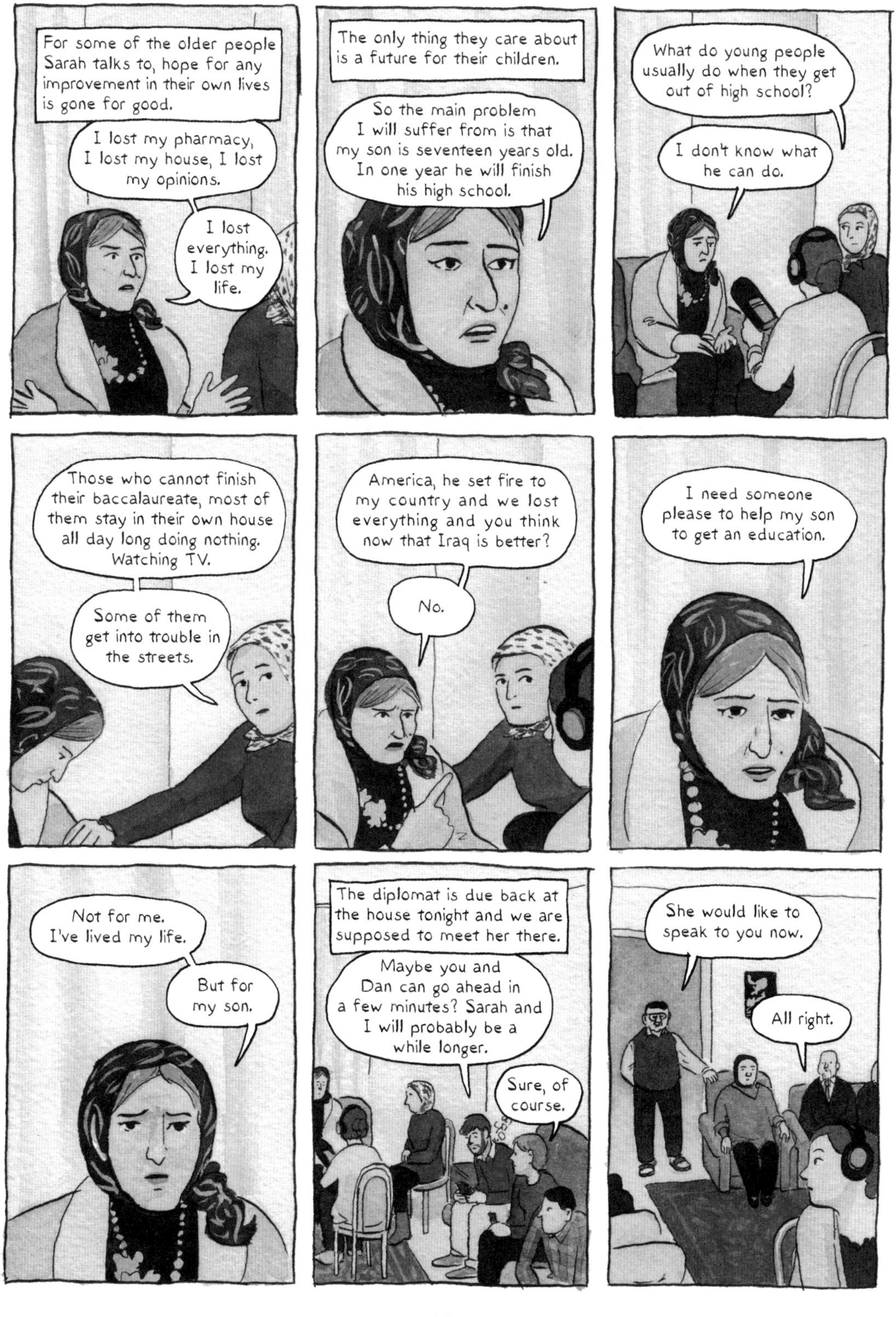
For some of the older people Sarah talks to, hope for any improvement in their own lives is gone for good.
I lost my pharmacy, I lost my house, I lost my opinions.
I lost everything. I lost my life.
The only thing they care about is a future for their children.
So the main problem I will suffer from is that my son is seventeen years old. In one year he will finish his high school.
What do young people usually do when they get out of high school?
I don't know what he can do.
Those who cannot finish their baccalaureate, most of them stay in their own house all day long doing nothing. Watching TV.
Some of them get into trouble in the streets.
America, he set fire to my country and we lost everything and you think now that Iraq is better?
No.
I need someone please to help my son to get an education.
Not for me. I've lived my life.
But for my son.
The diplomat is due back at the house tonight and we are supposed to meet her there.
Maybe you and Dan can go ahead in a few minutes? Sarah and I will probably be a while longer.
Sure, of course.
She would like to speak to you now.
All right.

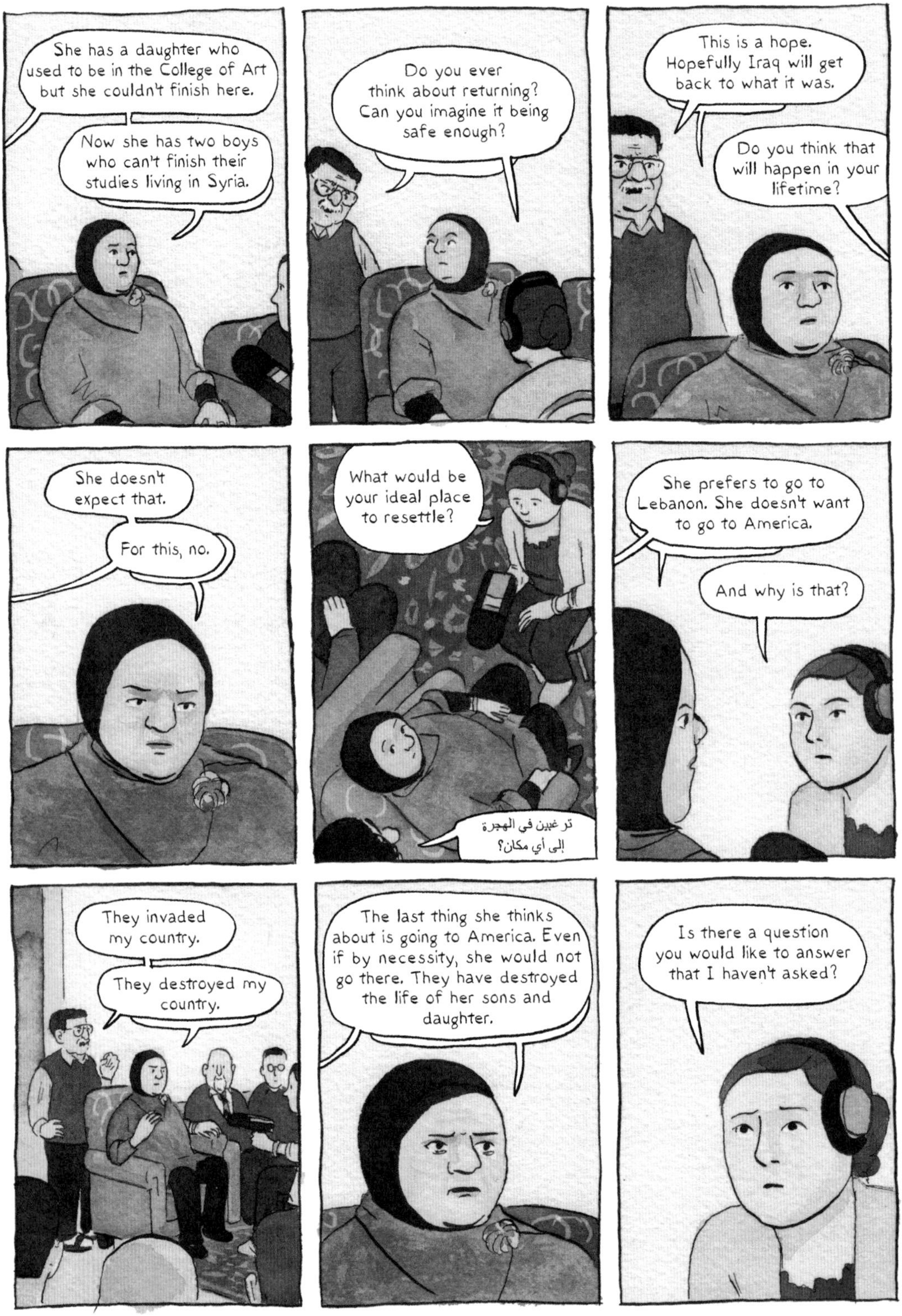
She has a daughter who used to be in the College of Art but she couldn't finish here.
Now she has two boys who can't finish their studies living in Syria.
Do you ever think about returning? Can you imagine it being safe enough?
This is a hope. Hopefully Iraq will get back to what it was.
Do you think that will happen in your lifetime?
She doesn't expect that.
For this, no.
What would be your ideal place to resettle?
ترغبين في الهجرة إلى أي مكان؟
She prefers to go to Lebanon. She doesn't want to go to America.
And why is that?
They invaded my country.
They destroyed my country.
The last thing she thinks about is going to America. Even if by necessity, she would not go there. They have destroyed the life of her sons and daughter.
Is there a question you would like to answer that I haven't asked?

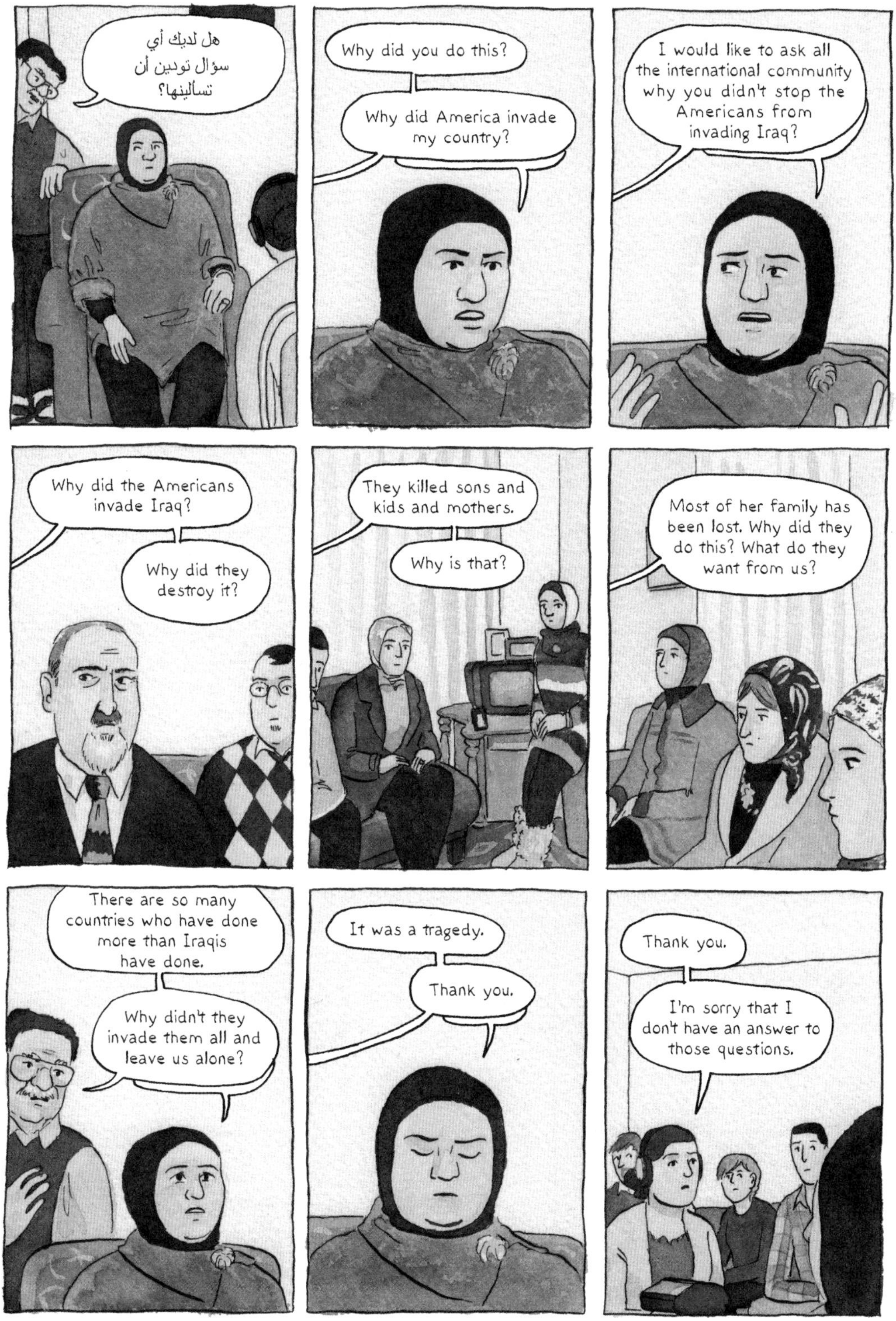
هل لديك أي سؤال تودين أن تسأليها؟
Why did you do this?
Why did America invade my country?
I would like to ask all the international community why you didn't stop the Americans from invading Iraq?
Why did the Americans invade Iraq?
Why did they destroy it?
They killed sons and kids and mothers.
Why is that?
Most of her family has been lost. Why did they do this? What do they want from us?
There are so many countries who have done more than Iraqis have done.
Why didn't they invade them all and leave us alone?
It was a tragedy.
Thank you.
Thank you.
I'm sorry that I don't have an answer to those questions.

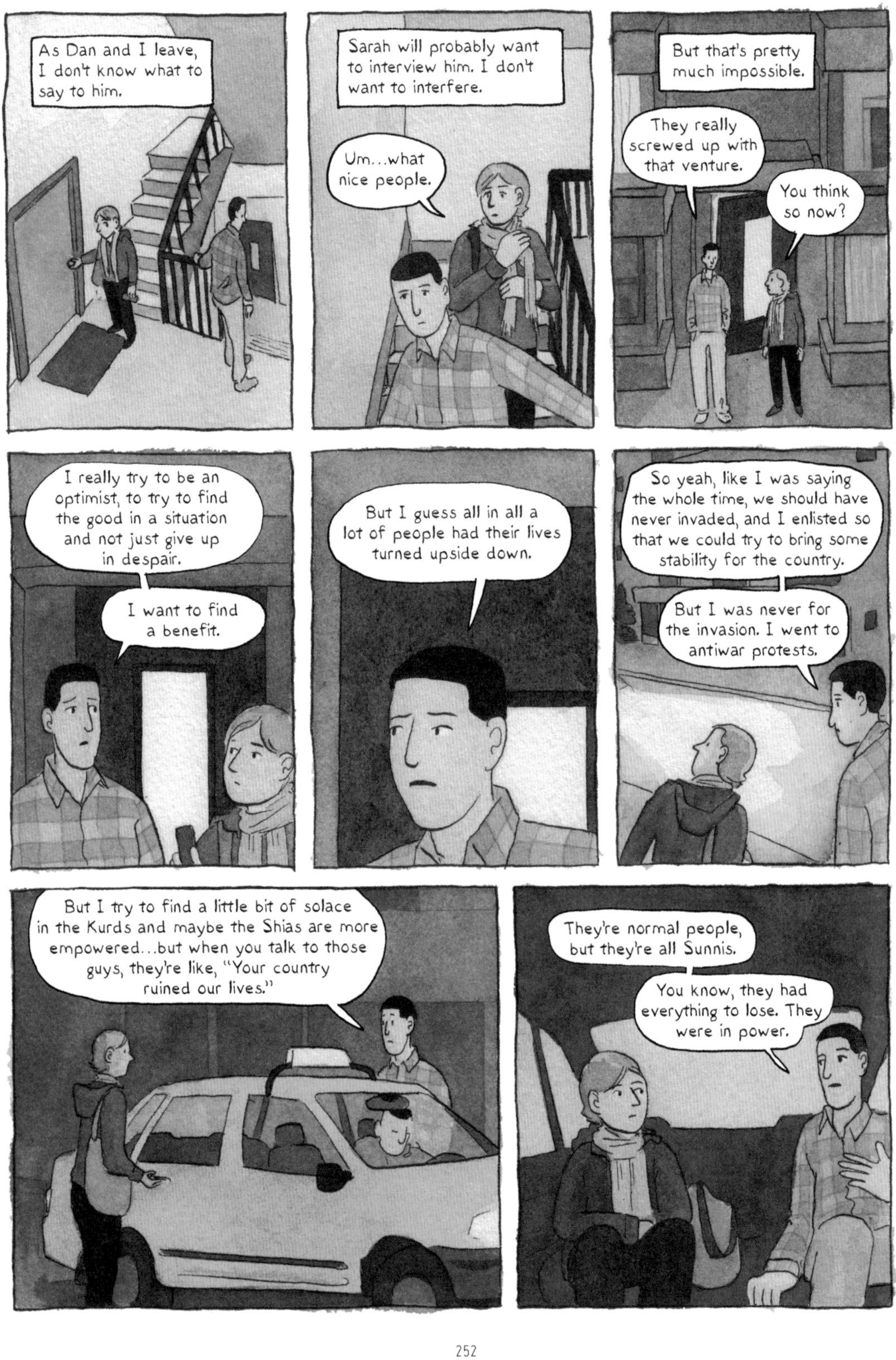
As Dan and I leave, I don't know what to say to him.
Sarah will probably want to interview him. I don't want to interfere.
Um...what nice people.
But that's pretty much impossible.
They really screwed up with that venture.
You think so now?
I really try to be an optimist, to try to find the good in a situation and not just give up in despair.
I want to find a benefit.
But I guess all in all a lot of people had their lives turned upside down.
So yeah, like I was saying the whole time, we should have never invaded, and I enlisted so that we could try to bring some stability for the country.
But I was never for the invasion. I went to antiwar protests.
But I try to find a little bit of solace in the Kurds and maybe the Shias are more empowered...but when you talk to those guys, they're like, "Your country ruined our lives."
They're normal people, but they're all Sunnis.
You know, they had everything to lose. They were in power.

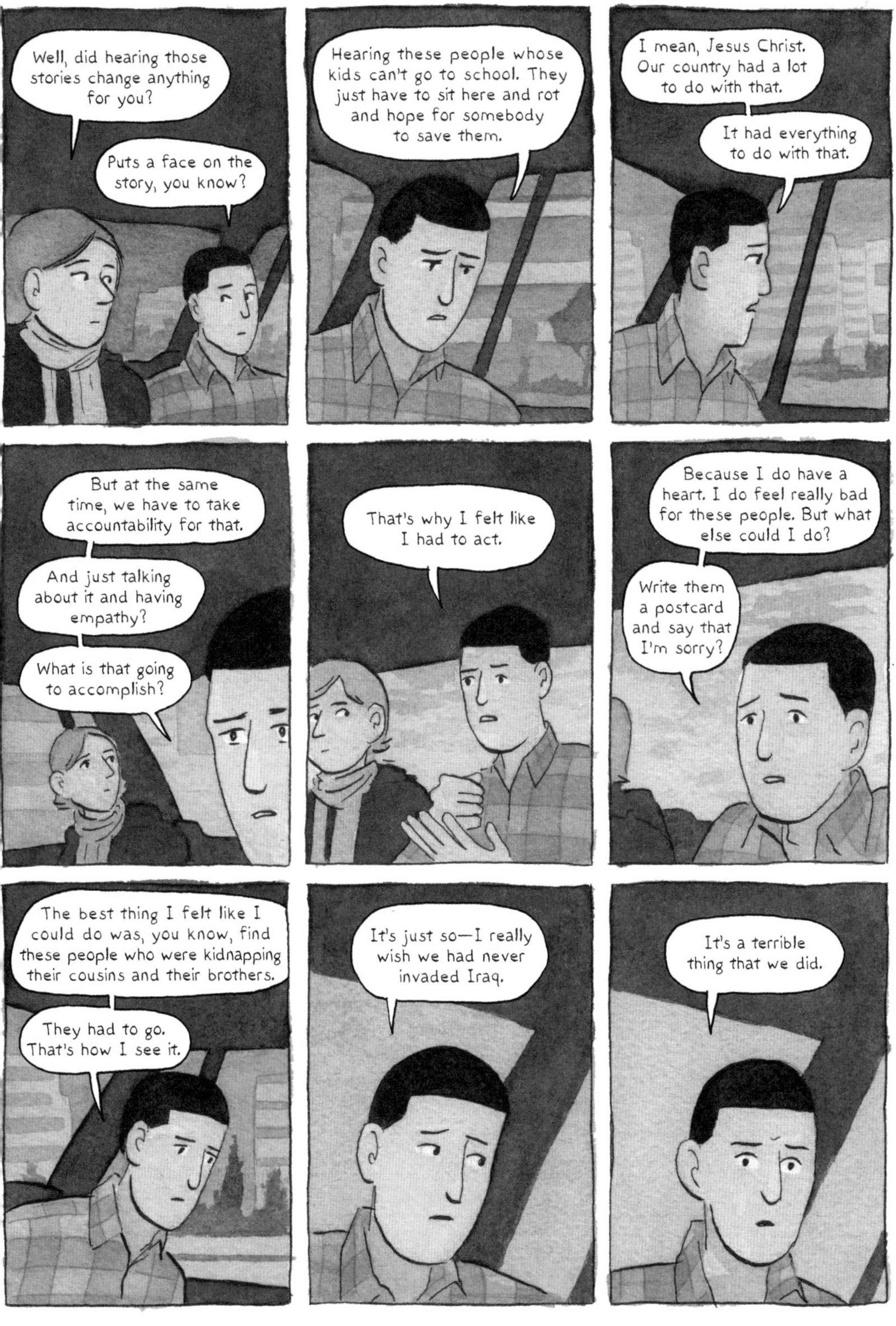
Well, did hearing those stories change anything for you?
Puts a face on the story, you know?
Hearing these people whose kids can't go to school. They just have to sit here and rot and hope for somebody to save them.
I mean, Jesus Christ. Our country had a lot to do with that.
It had everything to do with that.
But at the same time, we have to take accountability for that.
And just talking about it and having empathy?
What is that going to accomplish?
That's why I felt like I had to act.
Because I do have a heart. I do feel really bad for these people. But what else could I do?
Write them a postcard and say that I'm sorry?
The best thing I felt like I could do was, you know, find these people who were kidnapping their cousins and their brothers.
They had to go. That's how I see it.
It's just so—I really wish we had never invaded Iraq.
It's a terrible thing that we did.

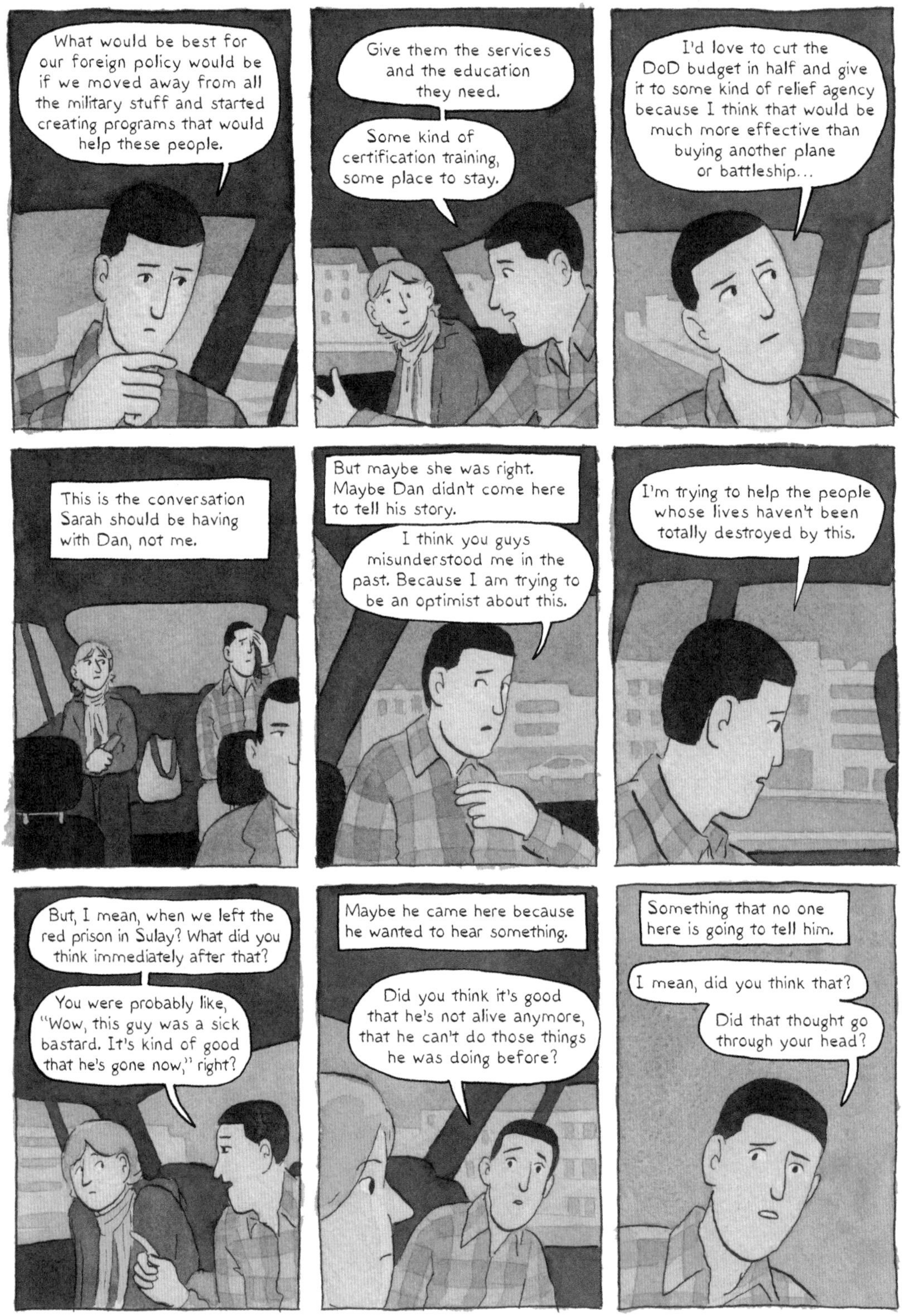
What would be best for our foreign policy would be if we moved away from all the military stuff and started creating programs that would help these people.
Give them the services and the education they need.
Some kind of certification training, some place to stay.
I'd love to cut the DoD budget in half and give it to some kind of relief agency because I think that would be much more effective than buying another plane or battleship...
This is the conversation Sarah should be having with Dan, not me.
But maybe she was right. Maybe Dan didn't come here to tell his story.
I think you guys misunderstood me in the past. Because I am trying to be an optimist about this.
I'm trying to help the people whose lives haven't been totally destroyed by this.
But, I mean, when we left the red prison in Sulay? What did you think immediately after that?
You were probably like, "Wow, this guy was a sick bastard. It's kind of good that he's gone now," right?
Maybe he came here because he wanted to hear something.
Did you think it's good that he's not alive anymore, that he can't do those things he was doing before?
Something that no one here is going to tell him.
I mean, did you think that?
Did that thought go through your head?

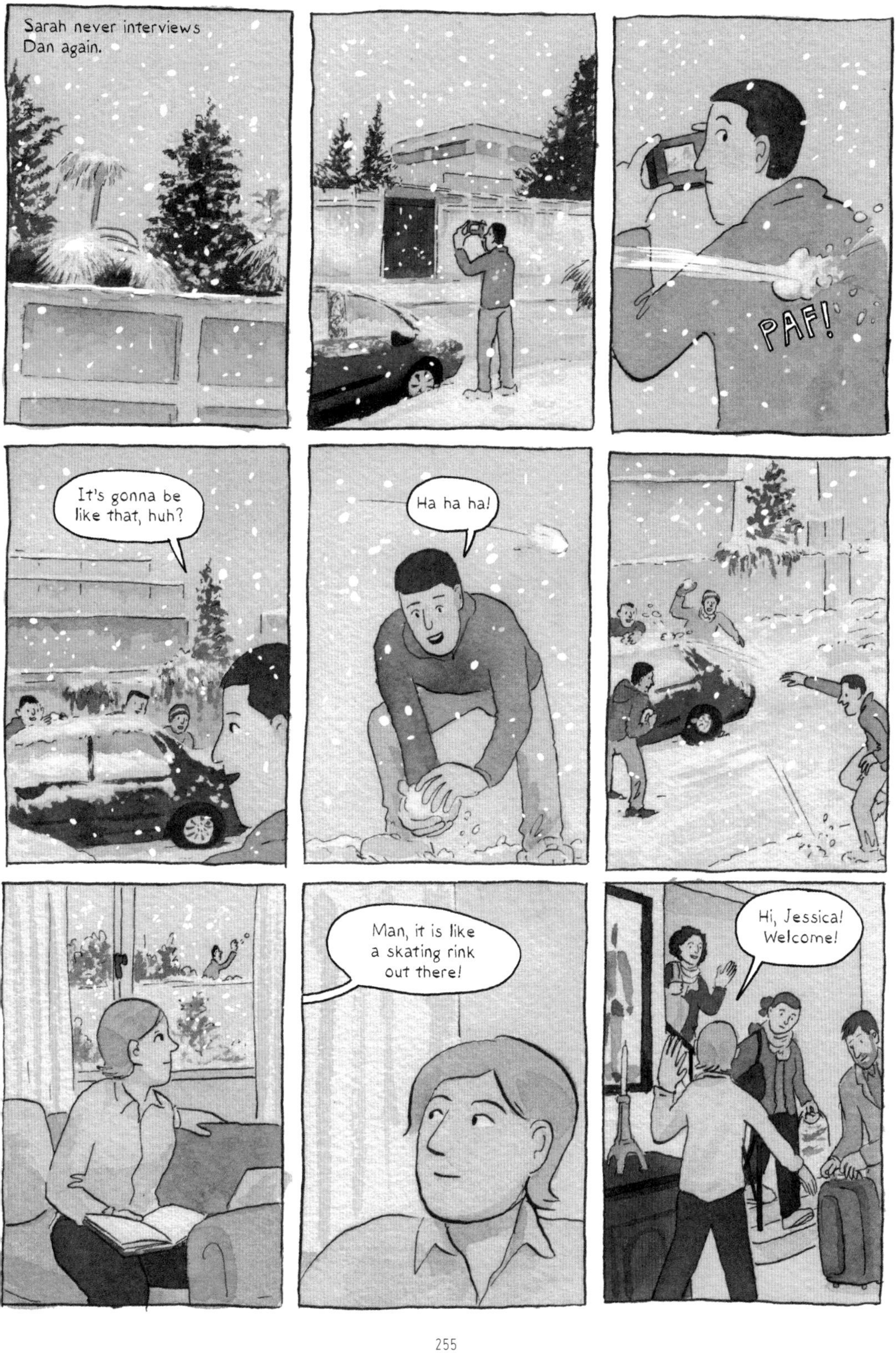
Sarah never interviews Dan again.
PAF!
It's gonna be like that, huh?
Ha ha ha!
Man, it is like a skating rink out there!
Hi, Jessica! Welcome!

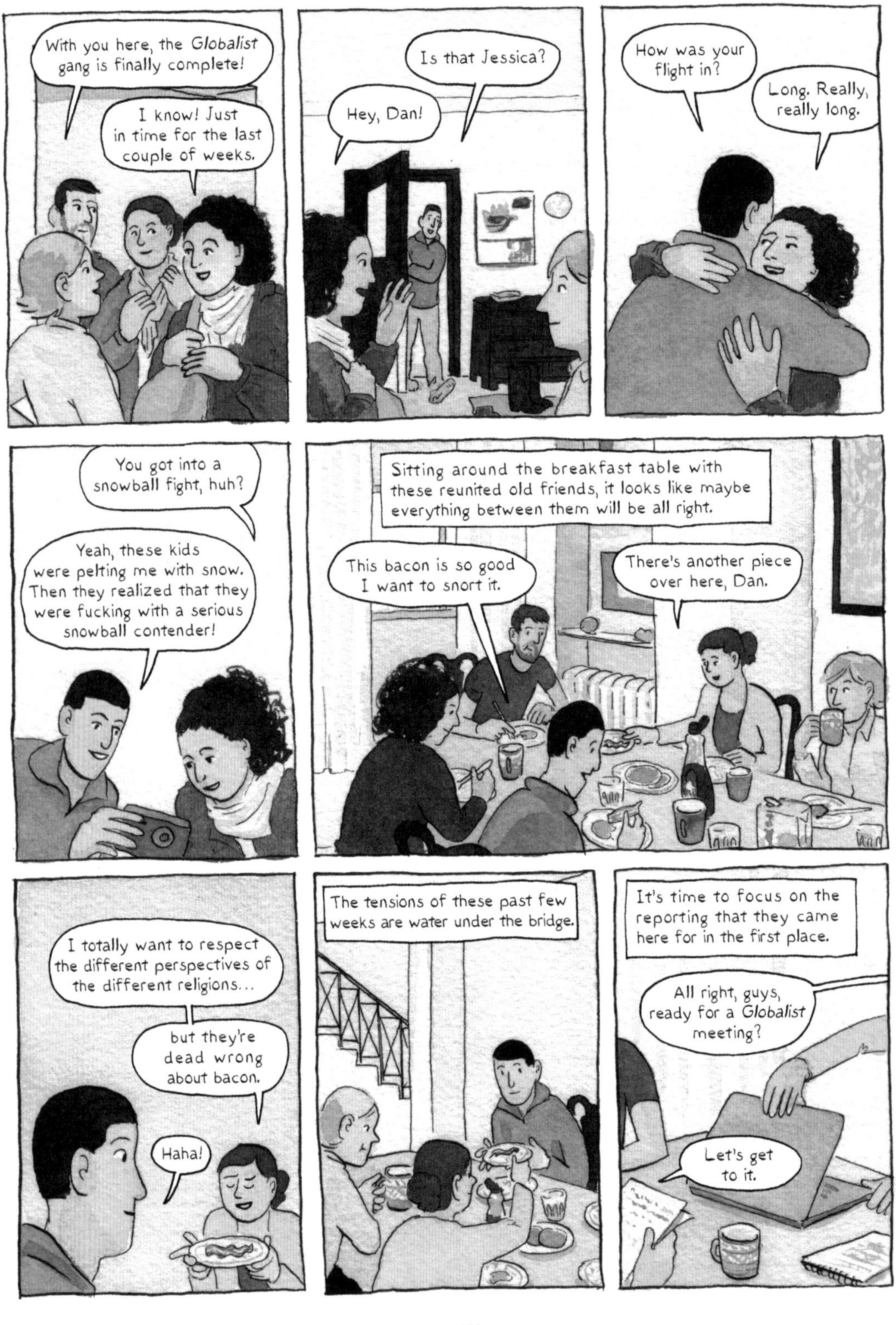

With you here, the *Globalist* gang is finally complete!
I know! Just in time for the last couple of weeks.
Is that Jessica?
Hey, Dan!
How was your flight in?
Long. Really, really long.
You got into a snowball fight, huh?
Yeah, these kids were pelting me with snow. Then they realized that they were fucking with a serious snowball contender!
Sitting around the breakfast table with these reunited old friends, it looks like maybe everything between them will be all right.
This bacon is so good I want to snort it.
There's another piece over here, Dan.
I totally want to respect the different perspectives of the different religions...
but they're dead wrong about bacon.
Haha!
The tensions of these past few weeks are water under the bridge.
It's time to focus on the reporting that they came here for in the first place.
All right, guys, ready for a *Globalist* meeting?
Let's get to it.

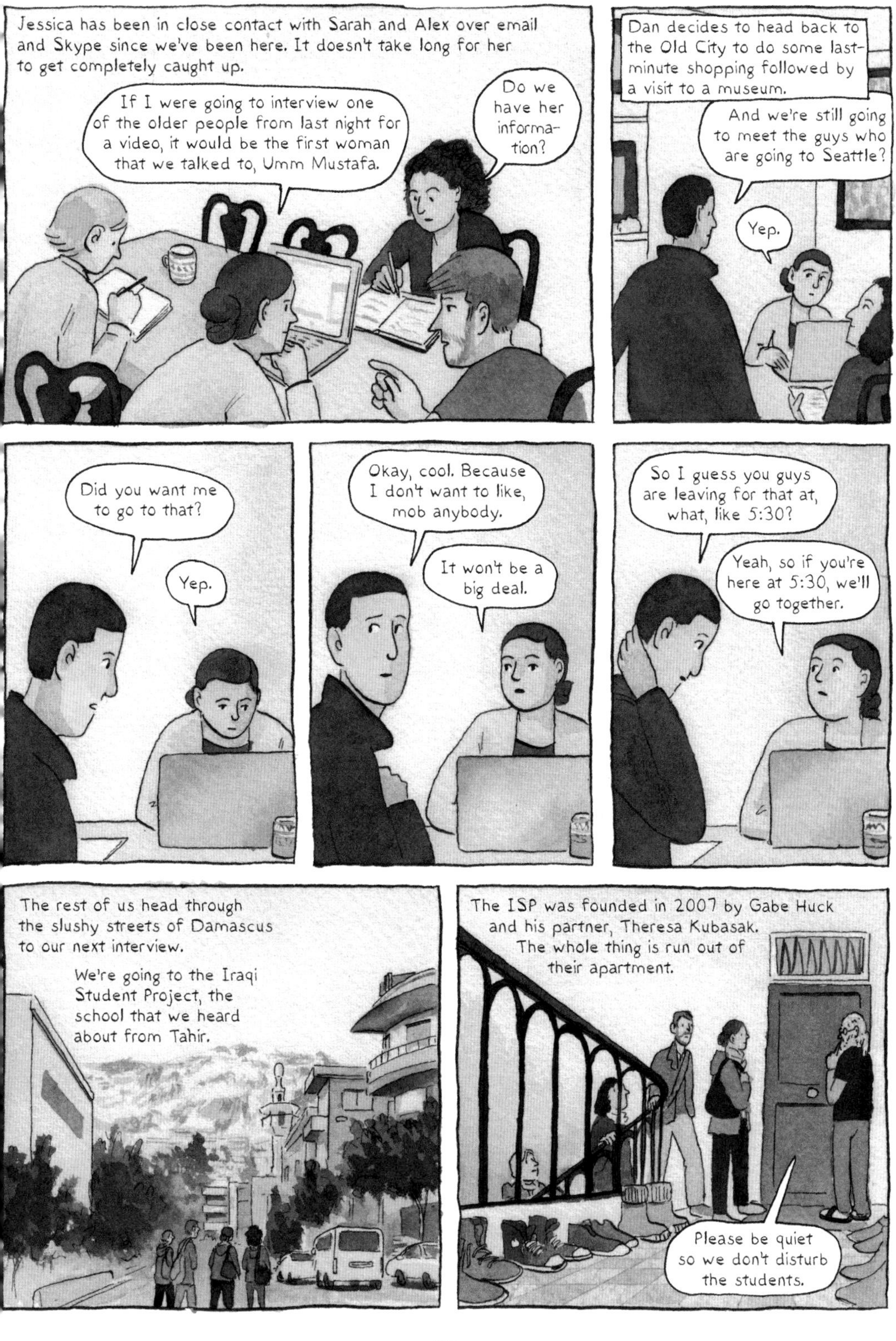
Jessica has been in close contact with Sarah and Alex over email and Skype since we've been here. It doesn't take long for her to get completely caught up.
If I were going to interview one of the older people from last night for a video, it would be the first woman that we talked to, Umm Mustafa.
Do we have her information?
Dan decides to head back to the Old City to do some last-minute shopping followed by a visit to a museum.
And we're still going to meet the guys who are going to Seattle?
Yep.
Did you want me to go to that?
Yep.
Okay, cool. Because I don't want to like, mob anybody.
It won't be a big deal.
So I guess you guys are leaving for that at, what, like 5:30?
Yeah, so if you're here at 5:30, we'll go together.
The rest of us head through the slushy streets of Damascus to our next interview.
We're going to the Iraqi Student Project, the school that we heard about from Tahir.
The ISP was founded in 2007 by Gabe Huck and his partner, Theresa Kubasak. The whole thing is run out of their apartment.
Please be quiet so we don't disturb the students.

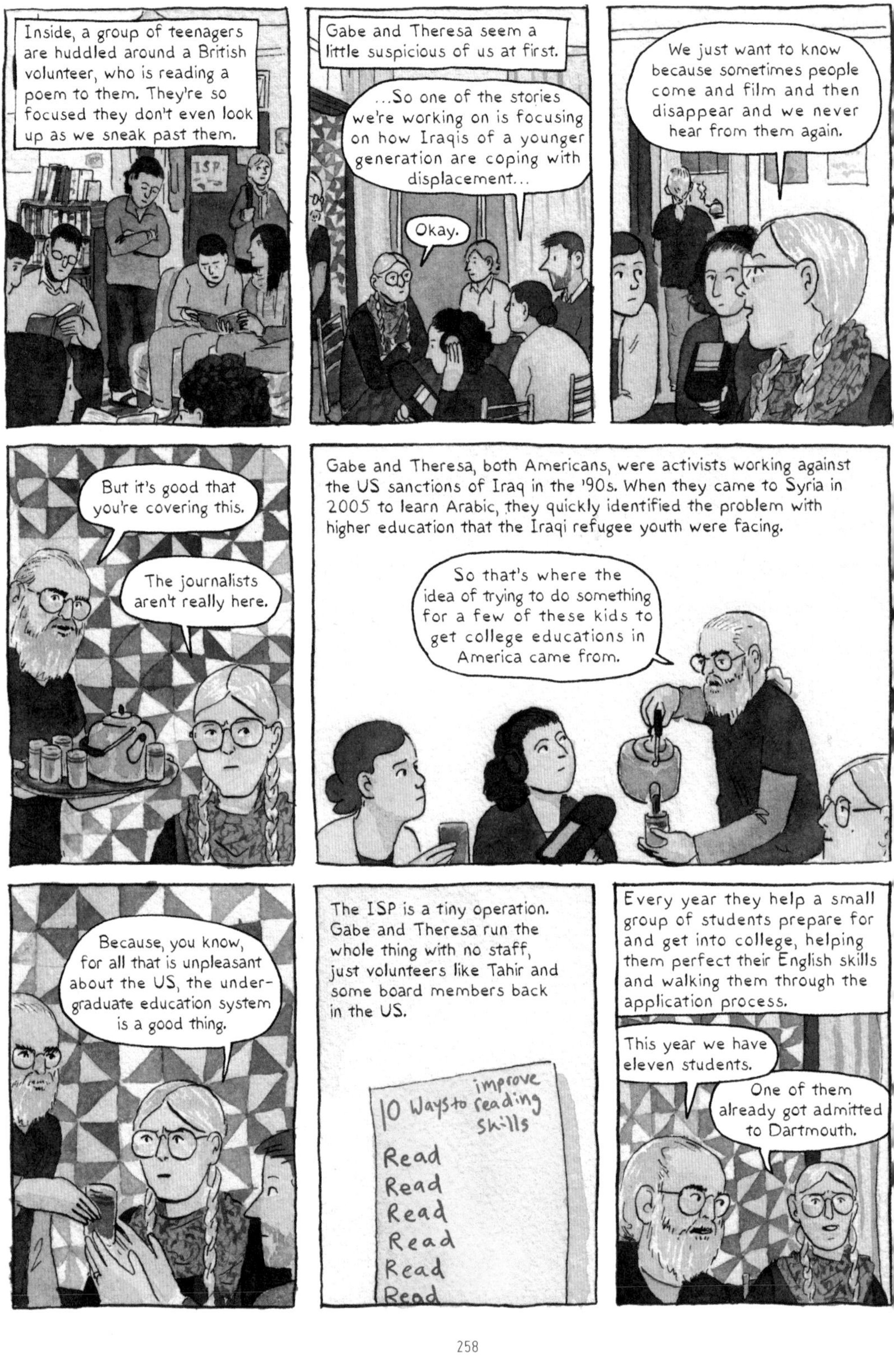
Inside, a group of teenagers are huddled around a British volunteer, who is reading a poem to them. They're so focused they don't even look up as we sneak past them.
ISP
Gabe and Theresa seem a little suspicious of us at first.
...So one of the stories we're working on is focusing on how Iraqis of a younger generation are coping with displacement...
Okay.
We just want to know because sometimes people come and film and then disappear and we never hear from them again.
But it's good that you're covering this.
The journalists aren't really here.
Gabe and Theresa, both Americans, were activists working against the US sanctions of Iraq in the '90s. When they came to Syria in 2005 to learn Arabic, they quickly identified the problem with higher education that the Iraqi refugee youth were facing.
So that's where the idea of trying to do something for a few of these kids to get college educations in America came from.
Because, you know, for all that is unpleasant about the US, the undergraduate education system is a good thing.
The ISP is a tiny operation. Gabe and Theresa run the whole thing with no staff, just volunteers like Tahir and some board members back in the US.
10 Ways to improve reading skills
Read
Read
Read
Read
Read
Every year they help a small group of students prepare for and get into college, helping them perfect their English skills and walking them through the application process.
This year we have eleven students.
One of them already got admitted to Dartmouth.

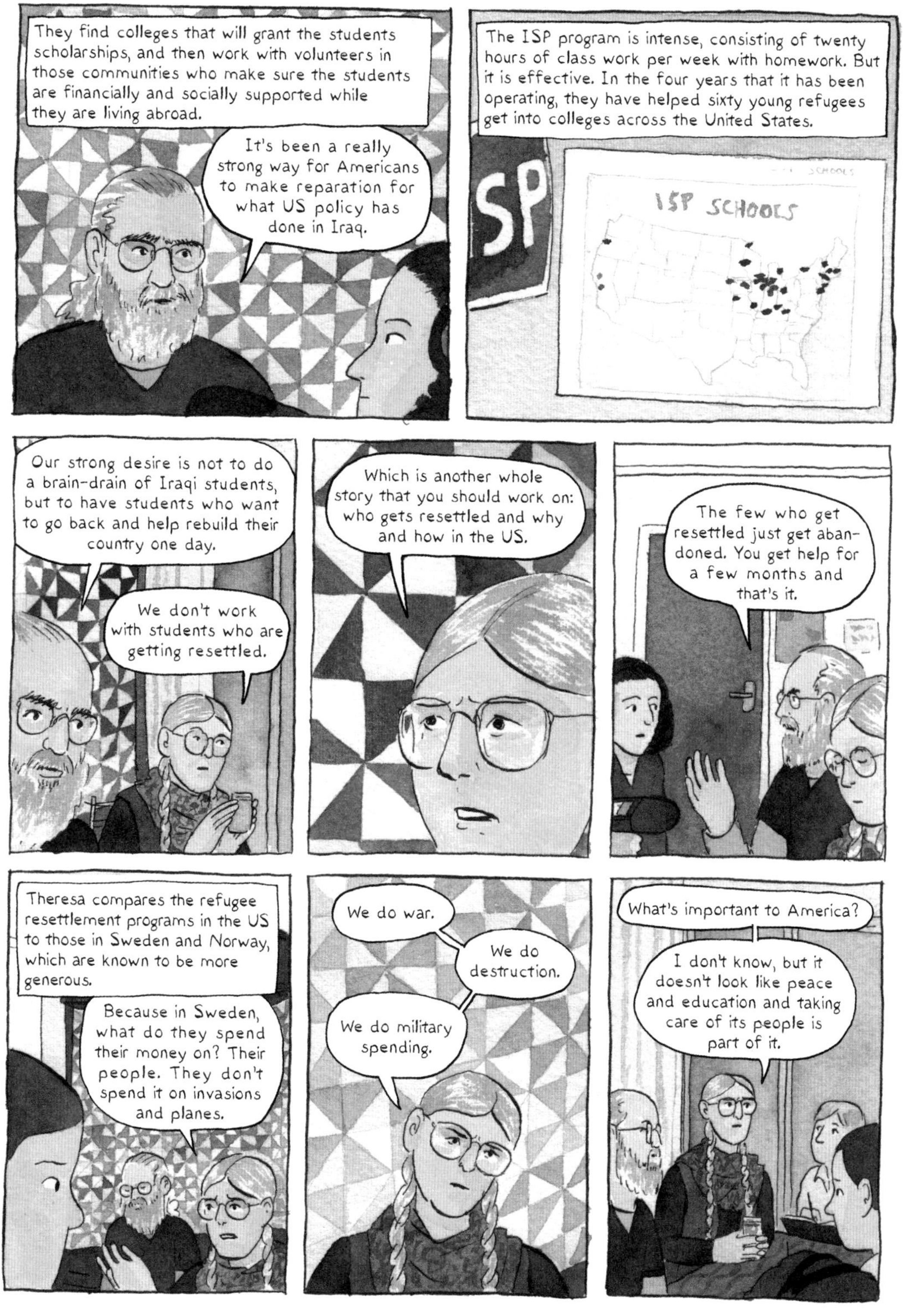
They find colleges that will grant the students scholarships, and then work with volunteers in those communities who make sure the students are financially and socially supported while they are living abroad.
It's been a really strong way for Americans to make reparation for what US policy has done in Iraq.
The ISP program is intense, consisting of twenty hours of class work per week with homework. But it is effective. In the four years that it has been operating, they have helped sixty young refugees get into colleges across the United States.
SP
ISP SCHOOLS
Our strong desire is not to do a brain-drain of Iraqi students, but to have students who want to go back and help rebuild their country one day.
We don't work with students who are getting resettled.
Which is another whole story that you should work on: who gets resettled and why and how in the US.
The few who get resettled just get abandoned. You get help for a few months and that's it.
Theresa compares the refugee resettlement programs in the US to those in Sweden and Norway, which are known to be more generous.
Because in Sweden, what do they spend their money on? Their people. They don't spend it on invasions and planes.
We do war.
We do destruction.
We do military spending.
What's important to America?
I don't know, but it doesn't look like peace and education and taking care of its people is part of it.

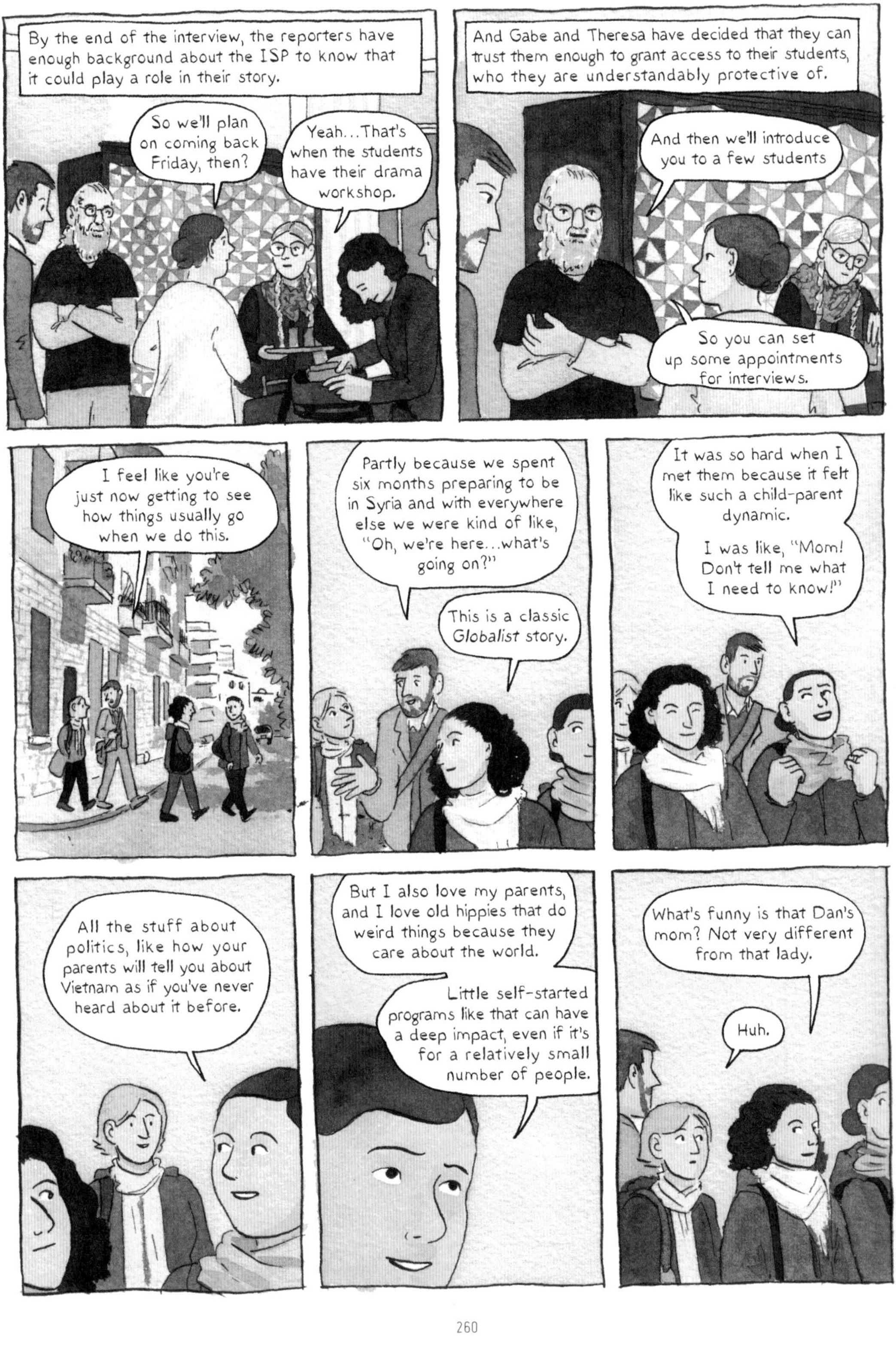
By the end of the interview, the reporters have enough background about the ISP to know that it could play a role in their story.
So we'll plan on coming back Friday, then?
Yeah...That's when the students have their drama workshop.
And Gabe and Theresa have decided that they can trust them enough to grant access to their students, who they are understandably protective of.
And then we'll introduce you to a few students
So you can set up some appointments for interviews.
I feel like you're just now getting to see how things usually go when we do this.
Partly because we spent six months preparing to be in Syria and with everywhere else we were kind of like, "Oh, we're here...what's going on?"
This is a classic *Globalist* story.
It was so hard when I met them because it felt like such a child-parent dynamic.
I was like, "Mom! Don't tell me what I need to know!"
All the stuff about politics, like how your parents will tell you about Vietnam as if you've never heard about it before.
But I also love my parents, and I love old hippies that do weird things because they care about the world.
Little self-started programs like that can have a deep impact, even if it's for a relatively small number of people.
What's funny is that Dan's mom? Not very different from that lady.
Huh.

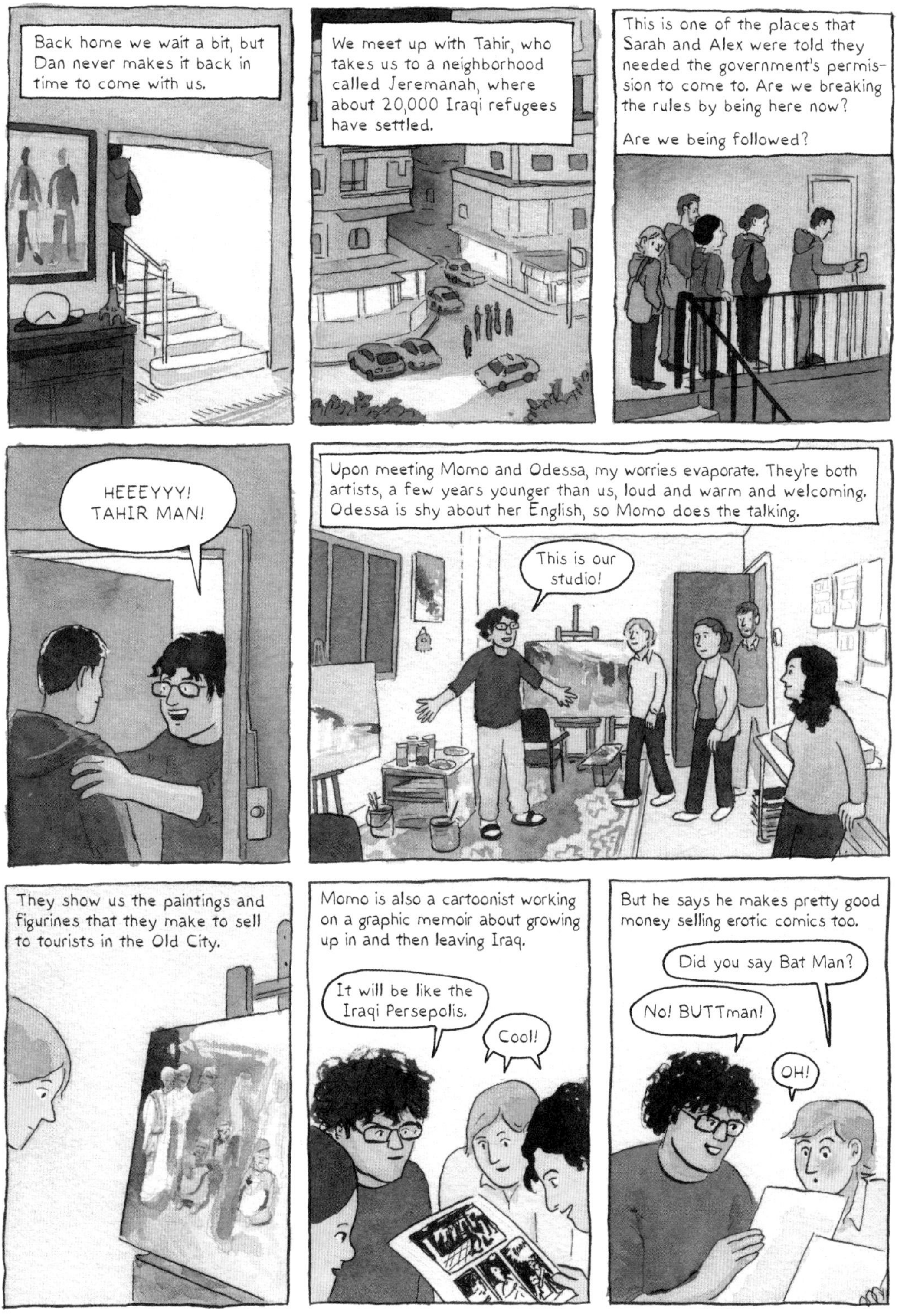

Back home we wait a bit, but Dan never makes it back in time to come with us.
We meet up with Tahir, who takes us to a neighborhood called Jeremanah, where about 20,000 Iraqi refugees have settled.
This is one of the places that Sarah and Alex were told they needed the government's permission to come to. Are we breaking the rules by being here now?
Are we being followed?
HEEEYYY! TAHIR MAN!
Upon meeting Momo and Odessa, my worries evaporate. They're both artists, a few years younger than us, loud and warm and welcoming. Odessa is shy about her English, so Momo does the talking.
This is our studio!
They show us the paintings and figurines that they make to sell to tourists in the Old City.
Momo is also a cartoonist working on a graphic memoir about growing up in and then leaving Iraq.
It will be like the Iraqi Persepolis.
Cool!
But he says he makes pretty good money selling erotic comics too.
Did you say Bat Man?
No! BUTTman!
OH!

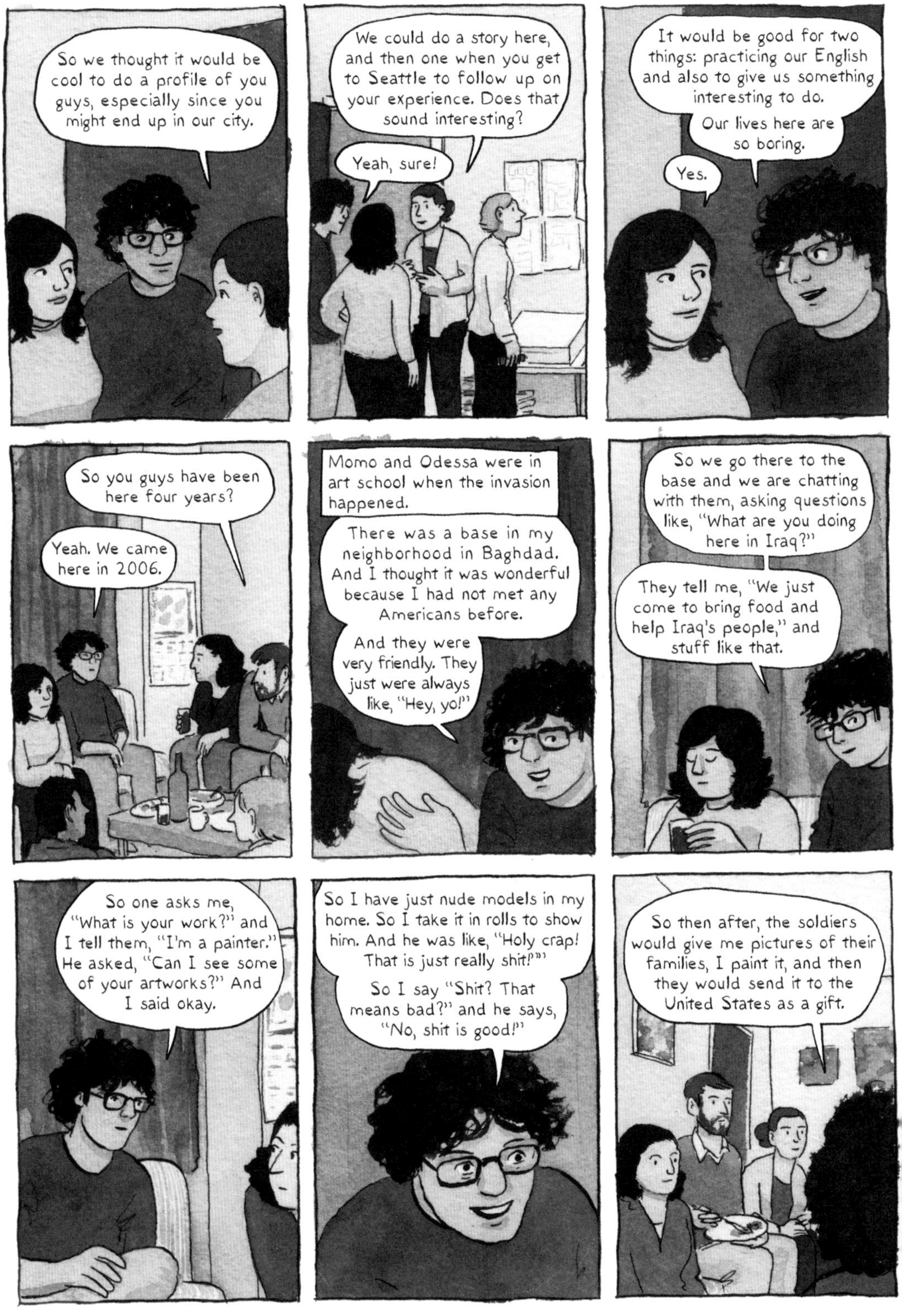
So we thought it would be cool to do a profile of you guys, especially since you might end up in our city.
We could do a story here, and then one when you get to Seattle to follow up on your experience. Does that sound interesting?
Yeah, sure!
It would be good for two things: practicing our English and also to give us something interesting to do.
Our lives here are so boring.
Yes.
So you guys have been here four years?
Yeah. We came here in 2006.
Momo and Odessa were in art school when the invasion happened.
There was a base in my neighborhood in Baghdad. And I thought it was wonderful because I had not met any Americans before.
And they were very friendly. They just were always like, "Hey, yo!"
So we go there to the base and we are chatting with them, asking questions like, "What are you doing here in Iraq?"
They tell me, "We just come to bring food and help Iraq's people," and stuff like that.
So one asks me, "What is your work?" and I tell them, "I'm a painter." He asked, "Can I see some of your artworks?" And I said okay.
So I have just nude models in my home. So I take it in rolls to show him. And he was like, "Holy crap! That is just really shit!"
So I say "Shit? That means bad?" and he says, "No, shit is good!"
So then after, the soldiers would give me pictures of their families, I paint it, and then they would send it to the United States as a gift.

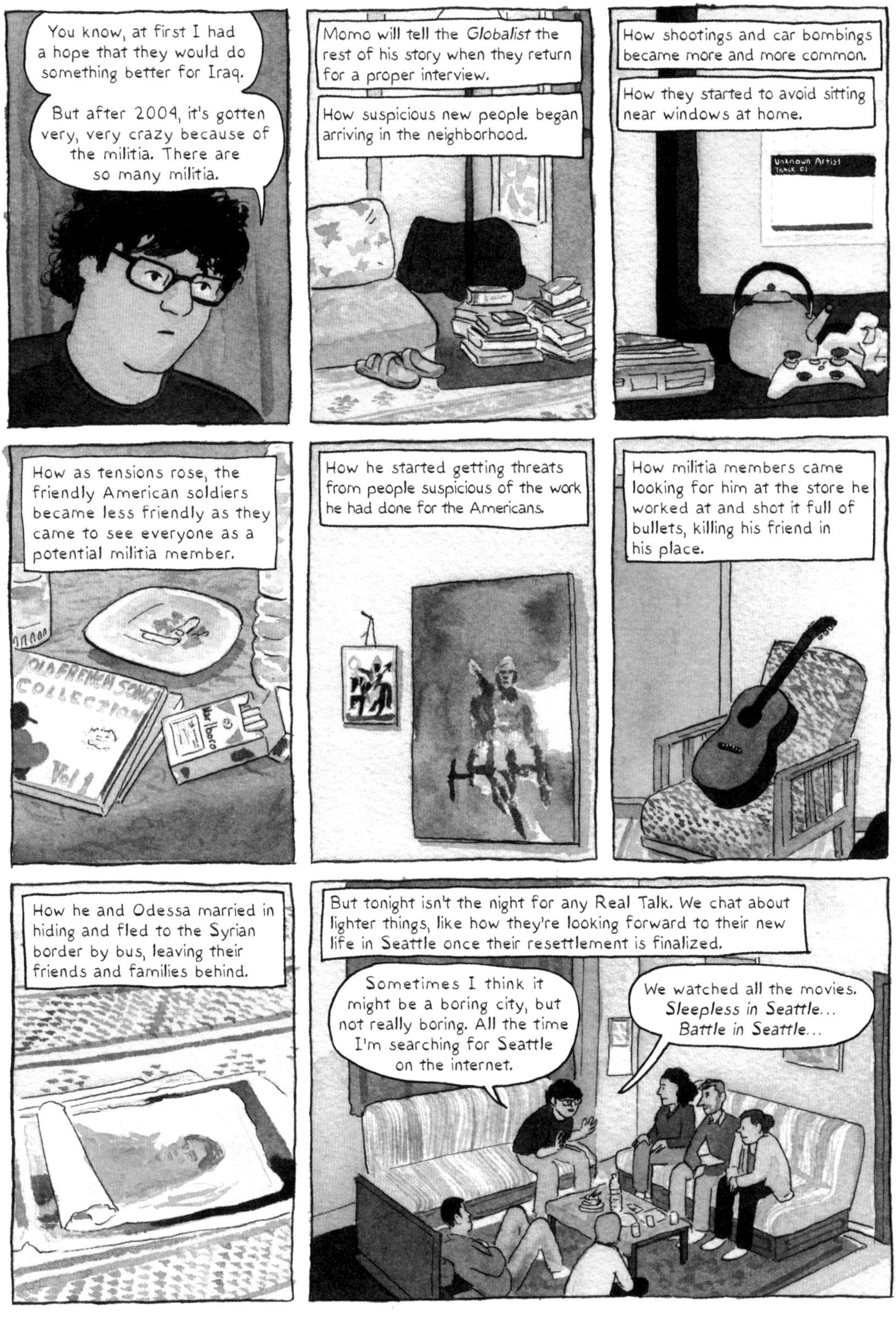

You know, at first I had a hope that they would do something better for Iraq.
But after 2004, it's gotten very, very crazy because of the militia. There are so many militia.
Momo will tell the *Globalist* the rest of his story when they return for a proper interview.
How suspicious new people began arriving in the neighborhood.
How shootings and car bombings became more and more common.
How they started to avoid sitting near windows at home.
Unknown Artist
TRACK 01
How as tensions rose, the friendly American soldiers became less friendly as they came to see everyone as a potential militia member.
OLD FRENCH SONGS COLLECTION
Vol 1
Marlboro
How he started getting threats from people suspicious of the work he had done for the Americans.
How militia members came looking for him at the store he worked at and shot it full of bullets, killing his friend in his place.
How he and Odessa married in hiding and fled to the Syrian border by bus, leaving their friends and families behind.
But tonight isn't the night for any Real Talk. We chat about lighter things, like how they're looking forward to their new life in Seattle once their resettlement is finalized.
Sometimes I think it might be a boring city, but not really boring. All the time I'm searching for Seattle on the internet.
We watched all the movies. *Sleepless in Seattle*... *Battle in Seattle*...

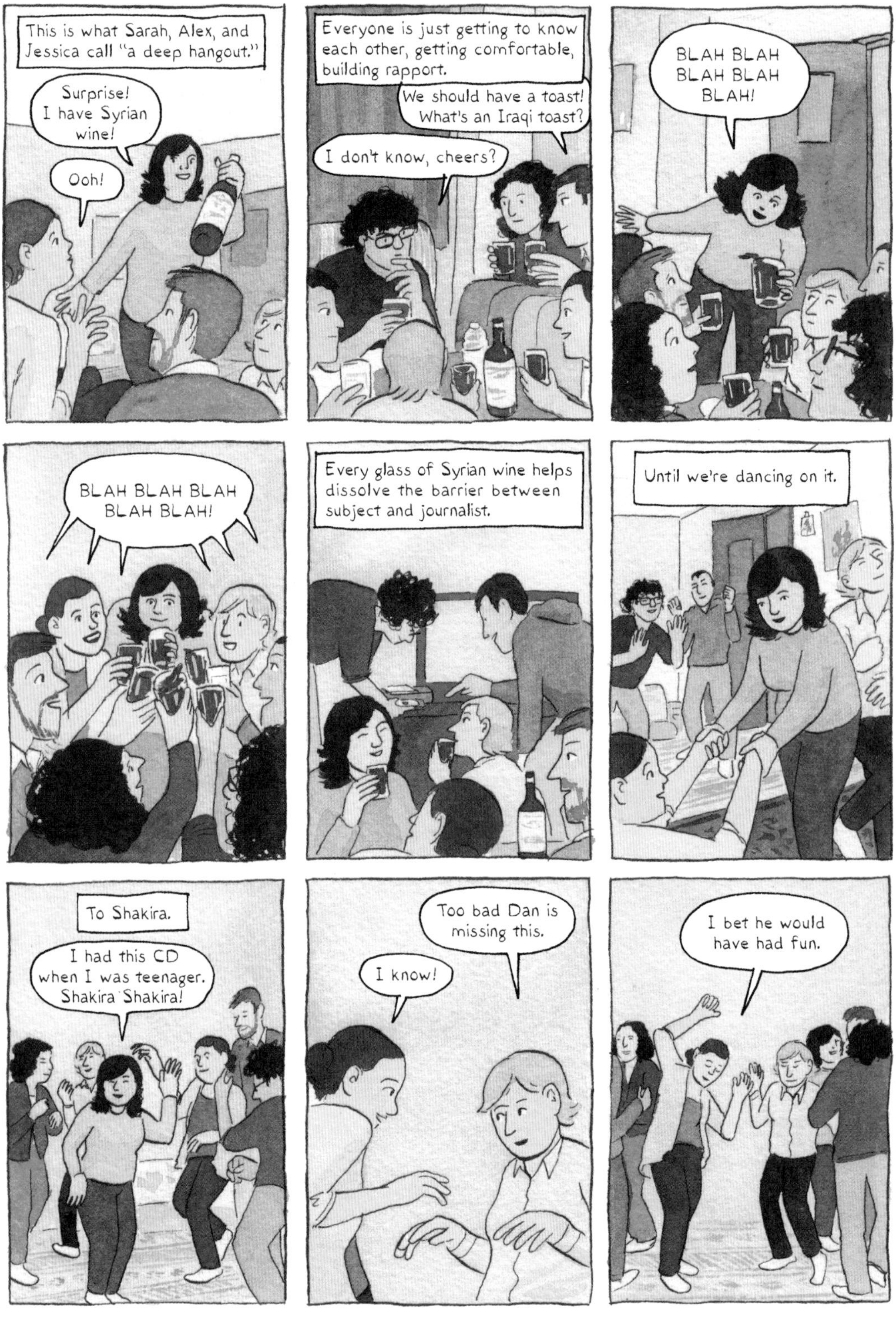
This is what Sarah, Alex, and Jessica call "a deep hangout."
Surprise! I have Syrian wine!
Ooh!
Everyone is just getting to know each other, getting comfortable, building rapport.
We should have a toast! What's an Iraqi toast?
I don't know, cheers?
BLAH BLAH BLAH BLAH BLAH!
BLAH BLAH BLAH BLAH BLAH!
Every glass of Syrian wine helps dissolve the barrier between subject and journalist.
Until we're dancing on it.
To Shakira.
I had this CD when I was teenager. Shakira Shakira!
Too bad Dan is missing this.
I know!
I bet he would have had fun.

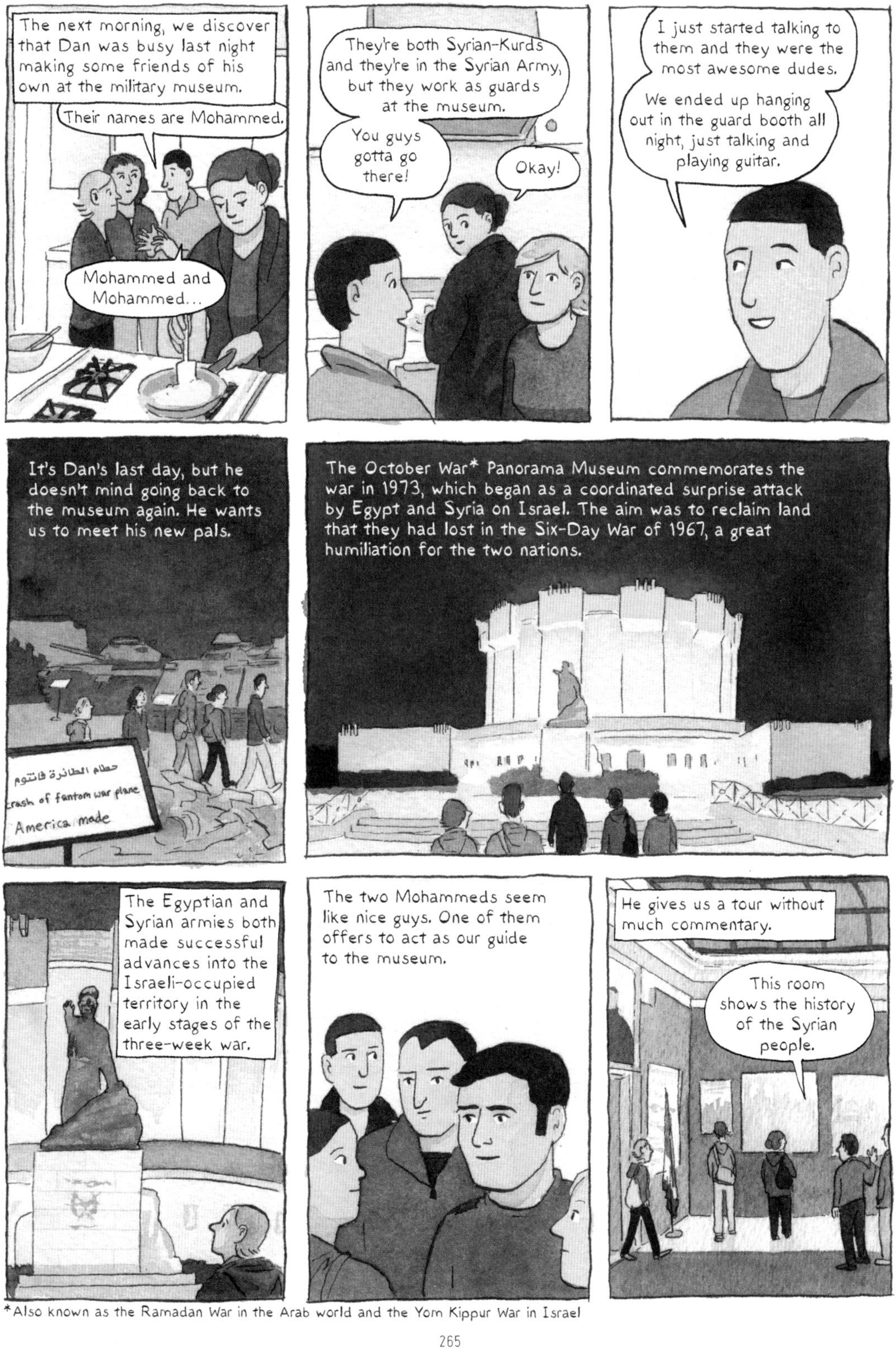
The next morning, we discover that Dan was busy last night making some friends of his own at the military museum.
Their names are Mohammed.
Mohammed and Mohammed...
They're both Syrian-Kurds and they're in the Syrian Army, but they work as guards at the museum.
You guys gotta go there!
Okay!
I just started talking to them and they were the most awesome dudes.
We ended up hanging out in the guard booth all night, just talking and playing guitar.
It's Dan's last day, but he doesn't mind going back to the museum again. He wants us to meet his new pals.
حطام الطائرة فانتوم
rash of fantom war plane
America made
The October War* Panorama Museum commemorates the war in 1973, which began as a coordinated surprise attack by Egypt and Syria on Israel. The aim was to reclaim land that they had lost in the Six-Day War of 1967, a great humiliation for the two nations.
The Egyptian and Syrian armies both made successful advances into the Israeli-occupied territory in the early stages of the three-week war.
The two Mohammeds seem like nice guys. One of them offers to act as our guide to the museum.
He gives us a tour without much commentary.
This room shows the history of the Syrian people.

*Also known as the Ramadan War in the Arab world and the Yom Kippur War in Israel

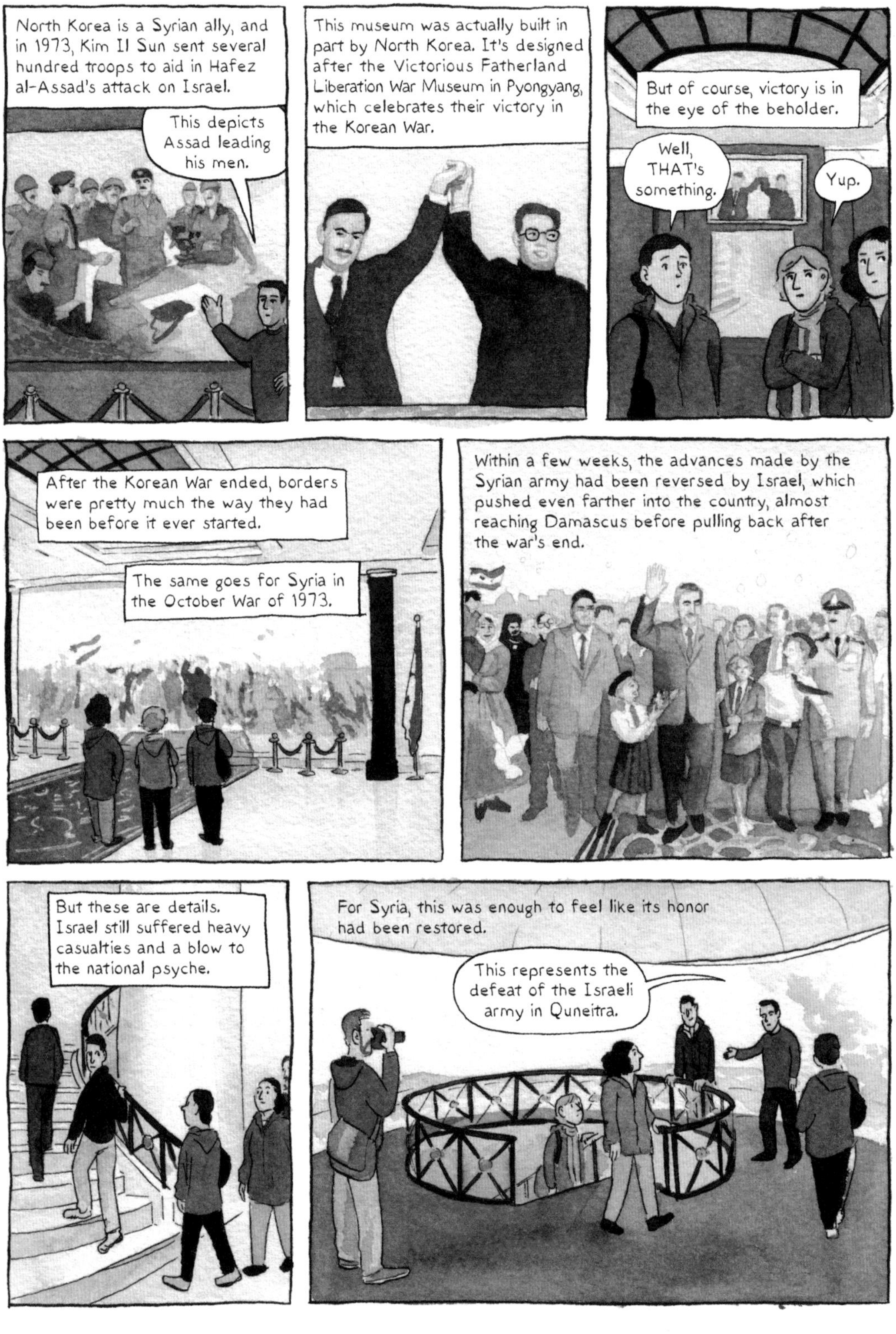
North Korea is a Syrian ally, and in 1973, Kim Il Sun sent several hundred troops to aid in Hafez al-Assad's attack on Israel.
This depicts Assad leading his men.
This museum was actually built in part by North Korea. It's designed after the Victorious Fatherland Liberation War Museum in Pyongyang, which celebrates their victory in the Korean War.
But of course, victory is in the eye of the beholder.
Well, THAT's something.
Yup.
After the Korean War ended, borders were pretty much the way they had been before it ever started.
The same goes for Syria in the October War of 1973.
Within a few weeks, the advances made by the Syrian army had been reversed by Israel, which pushed even farther into the country, almost reaching Damascus before pulling back after the war's end.
But these are details. Israel still suffered heavy casualties and a blow to the national psyche.
For Syria, this was enough to feel like its honor had been restored.
This represents the defeat of the Israeli army in Quneitra.

The centerpiece of the museum is a rotating panorama that shows the battle in which the Syrian army regained control of Quneitra, a city that was once the capitol of the Syrian Golan Heights until Israel captured it in 1967. Syria held it for four days before Israel launched their successful counteroffensive.

Military music accompanies a recording of Hafez al-Assad giving a rousing speech as the fighting wheels before us.

This is...

Fucked up and surreal? Yeah.

After the ceasefire, the Israeli military withdrew, but not before bulldozing the buildings and selling off anything of value. Assad ordered that the town be left in ruins as a memorial to its destruction.

But I won't find this out until I read about Quneitra later.

Neither Dan nor Mohammed seems very interested in the panorama, or in telling us about the politics it represents.

They chat and wait for us to finish looking around like counselors supervising a group of campers.

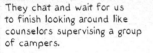

I can't help but wonder what they talked about last night.

Dan says he didn't tell them he was in the American military.

But he suspects they might have guessed.

He's been re-reading *Catch-22* on this trip, a book he said was influential to him while he was on his tour of Iraq. When we leave, he gives it to the Mohammeds as a parting gift.

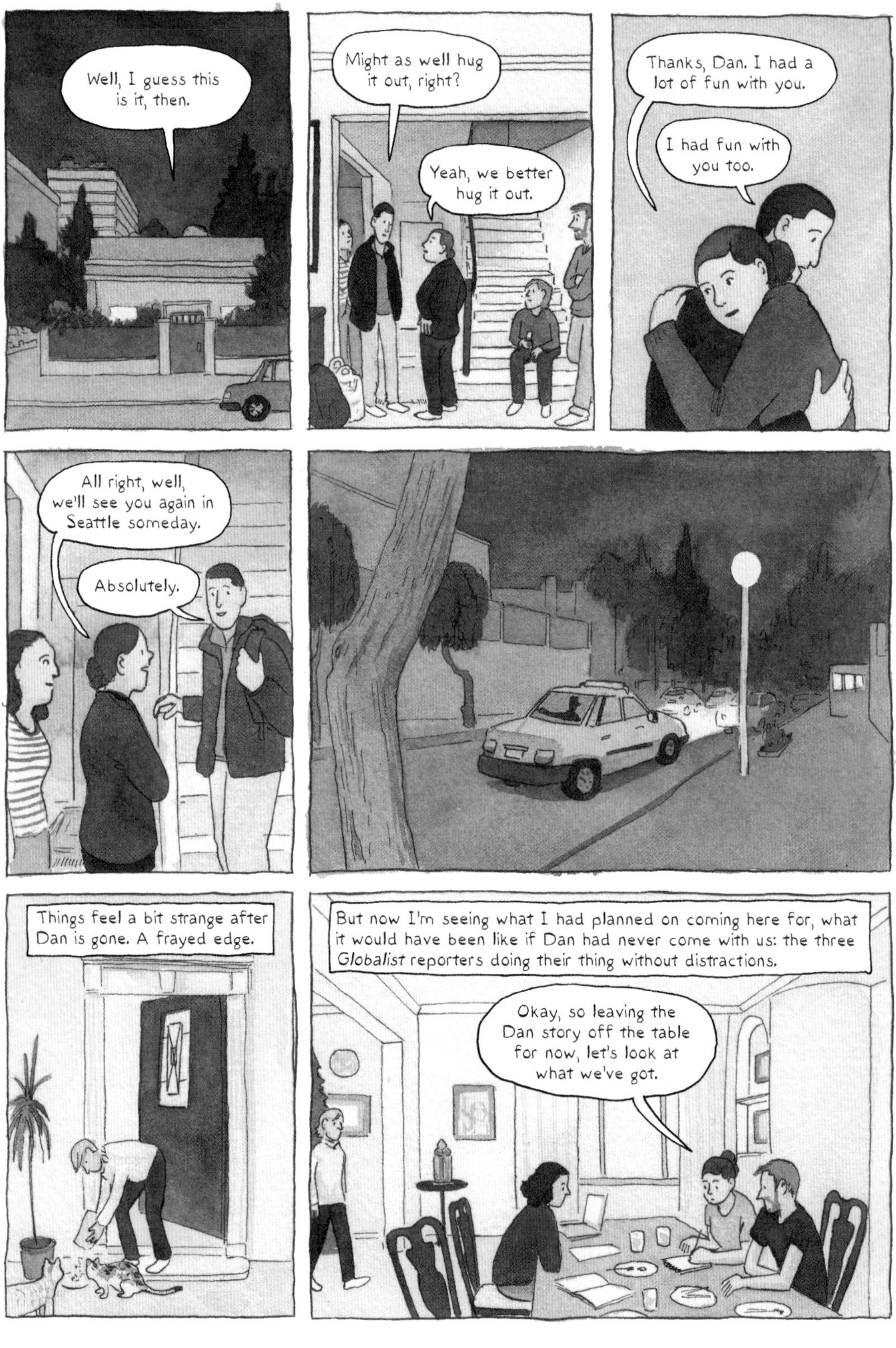
Well, I guess this is it, then.
Might as well hug it out, right?
Yeah, we better hug it out.
Thanks, Dan. I had a lot of fun with you.
I had fun with you too.
All right, well, we'll see you again in Seattle someday.
Absolutely.
Things feel a bit strange after Dan is gone. A frayed edge.
But now I'm seeing what I had planned on coming here for, what it would have been like if Dan had never come with us: the three *Globalist* reporters doing their thing without distractions.
Okay, so leaving the Dan story off the table for now, let's look at what we've got.

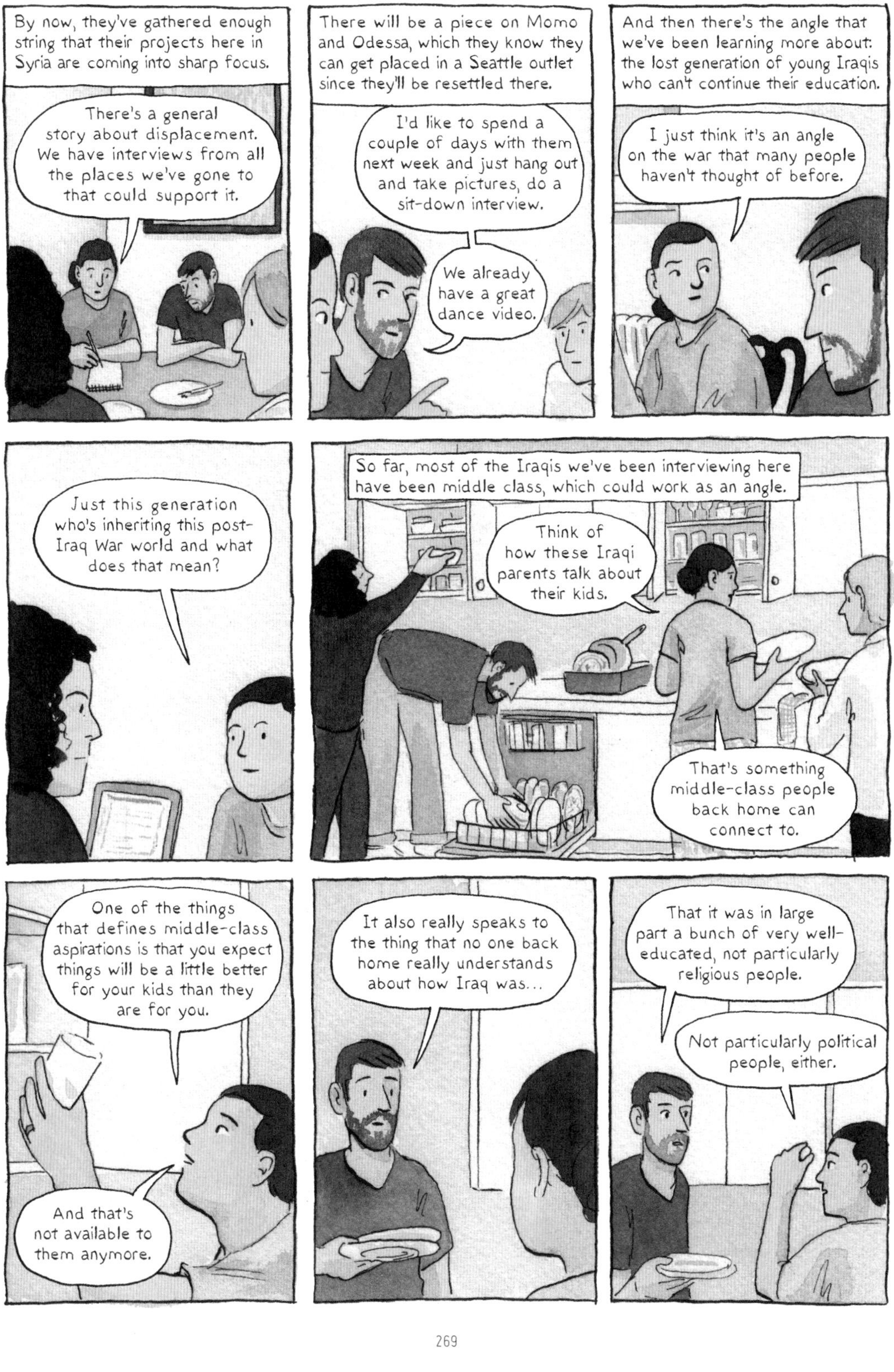

By now, they've gathered enough string that their projects here in Syria are coming into sharp focus.
There's a general story about displacement. We have interviews from all the places we've gone to that could support it.
There will be a piece on Momo and Odessa, which they know they can get placed in a Seattle outlet since they'll be resettled there.
I'd like to spend a couple of days with them next week and just hang out and take pictures, do a sit-down interview.
We already have a great dance video.
And then there's the angle that we've been learning more about: the lost generation of young Iraqis who can't continue their education.
I just think it's an angle on the war that many people haven't thought of before.
Just this generation who's inheriting this post-Iraq War world and what does that mean?
So far, most of the Iraqis we've been interviewing here have been middle class, which could work as an angle.
Think of how these Iraqi parents talk about their kids.
That's something middle-class people back home can connect to.
One of the things that defines middle-class aspirations is that you expect things will be a little better for your kids than they are for you.
And that's not available to them anymore.
It also really speaks to the thing that no one back home really understands about how Iraq was...
That it was in large part a bunch of very well-educated, not particularly religious people.
Not particularly political people, either.

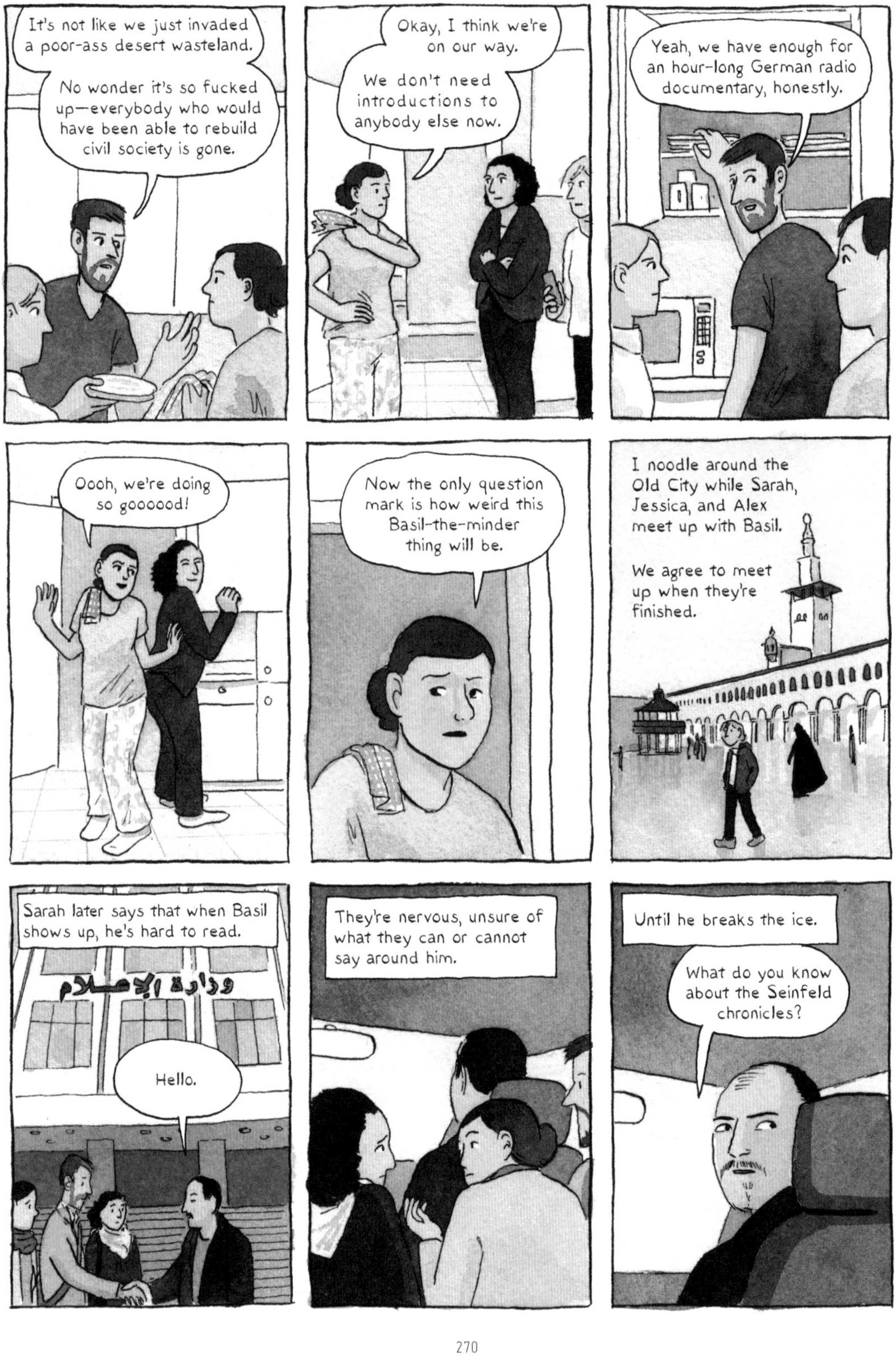
It's not like we just invaded a poor-ass desert wasteland.
No wonder it's so fucked up—everybody who would have been able to rebuild civil society is gone.
Okay, I think we're on our way.
We don't need introductions to anybody else now.
Yeah, we have enough for an hour-long German radio documentary, honestly.
Oooh, we're doing so goooood!
Now the only question mark is how weird this Basil-the-minder thing will be.
I noodle around the Old City while Sarah, Jessica, and Alex meet up with Basil.
We agree to meet up when they're finished.
Sarah later says that when Basil shows up, he's hard to read.
وزارة الإعلام
Hello.
They're nervous, unsure of what they can or cannot say around him.
Until he breaks the ice.
What do you know about the Seinfeld chronicles?

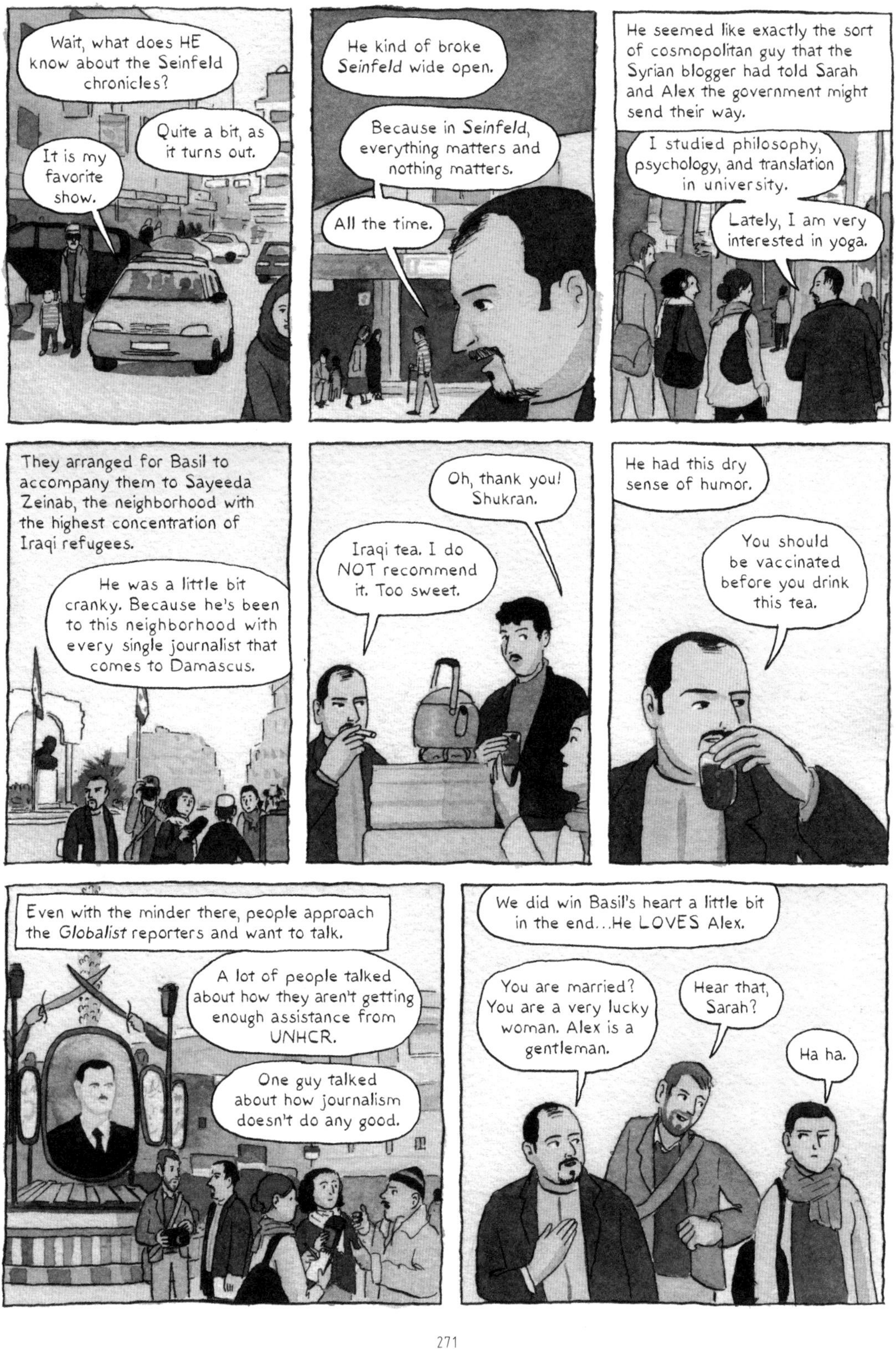

Wait, what does HE know about the Seinfeld chronicles?
Quite a bit, as it turns out.
It is my favorite show.
He kind of broke Seinfeld wide open.
Because in Seinfeld, everything matters and nothing matters.
All the time.
He seemed like exactly the sort of cosmopolitan guy that the Syrian blogger had told Sarah and Alex the government might send their way.
I studied philosophy, psychology, and translation in university.
Lately, I am very interested in yoga.
They arranged for Basil to accompany them to Sayeeda Zeinab, the neighborhood with the highest concentration of Iraqi refugees.
He was a little bit cranky. Because he's been to this neighborhood with every single journalist that comes to Damascus.
Oh, thank you! Shukran.
Iraqi tea. I do NOT recommend it. Too sweet.
He had this dry sense of humor.
You should be vaccinated before you drink this tea.
Even with the minder there, people approach the Globalist reporters and want to talk.
A lot of people talked about how they aren't getting enough assistance from UNHCR.
One guy talked about how journalism doesn't do any good.
We did win Basil's heart a little bit in the end...He LOVES Alex.
You are married? You are a very lucky woman. Alex is a gentleman.
Hear that, Sarah?
Ha ha.

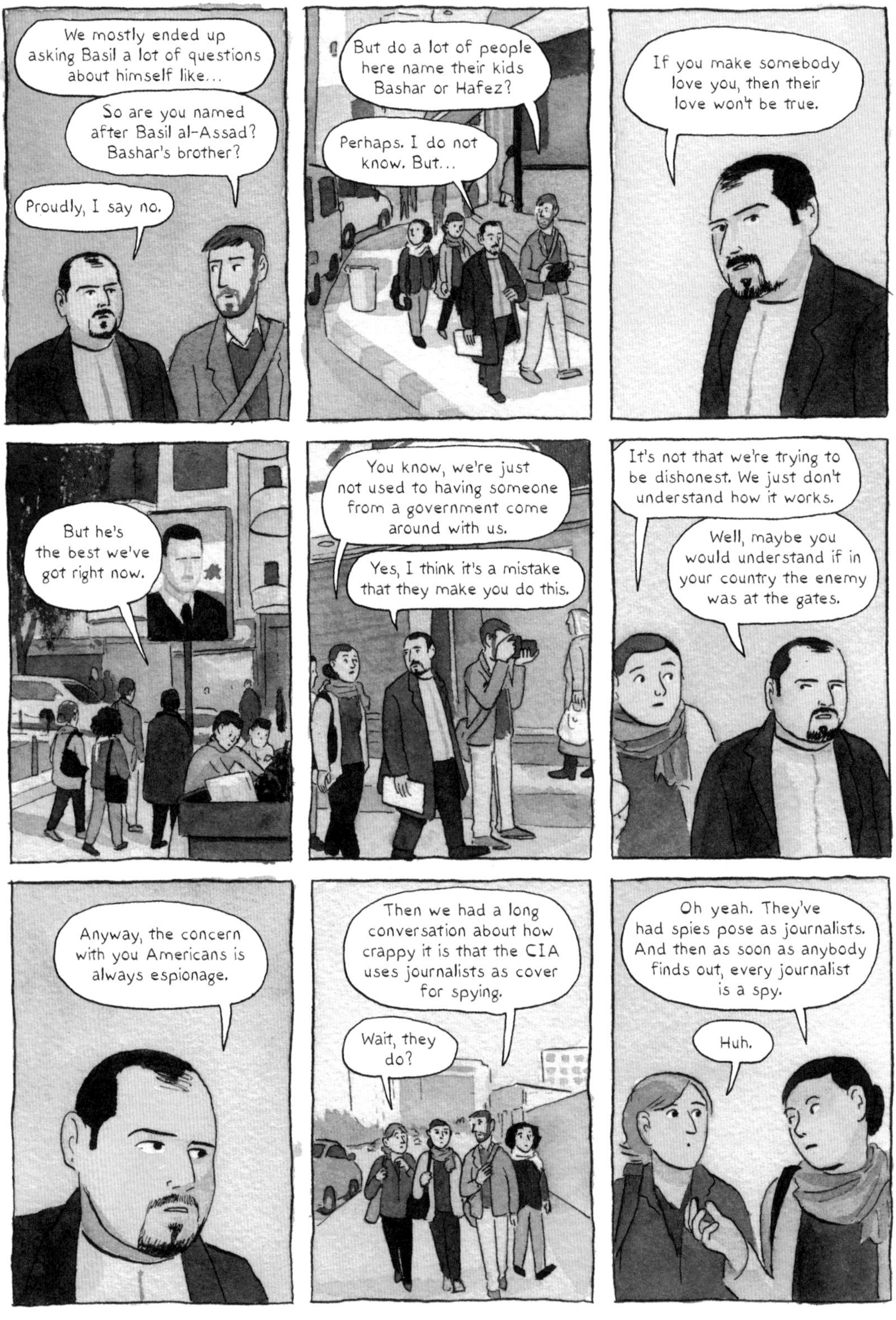
We mostly ended up asking Basil a lot of questions about himself like...
So are you named after Basil al-Assad? Bashar's brother?
Proudly, I say no.
But do a lot of people here name their kids Bashar or Hafez?
Perhaps. I do not know. But...
If you make somebody love you, then their love won't be true.
But he's the best we've got right now.
You know, we're just not used to having someone from a government come around with us.
Yes, I think it's a mistake that they make you do this.
It's not that we're trying to be dishonest. We just don't understand how it works.
Well, maybe you would understand if in your country the enemy was at the gates.
Anyway, the concern with you Americans is always espionage.
Then we had a long conversation about how crappy it is that the CIA uses journalists as cover for spying.
Wait, they do?
Oh yeah. They've had spies pose as journalists. And then as soon as anybody finds out, every journalist is a spy.
Huh.

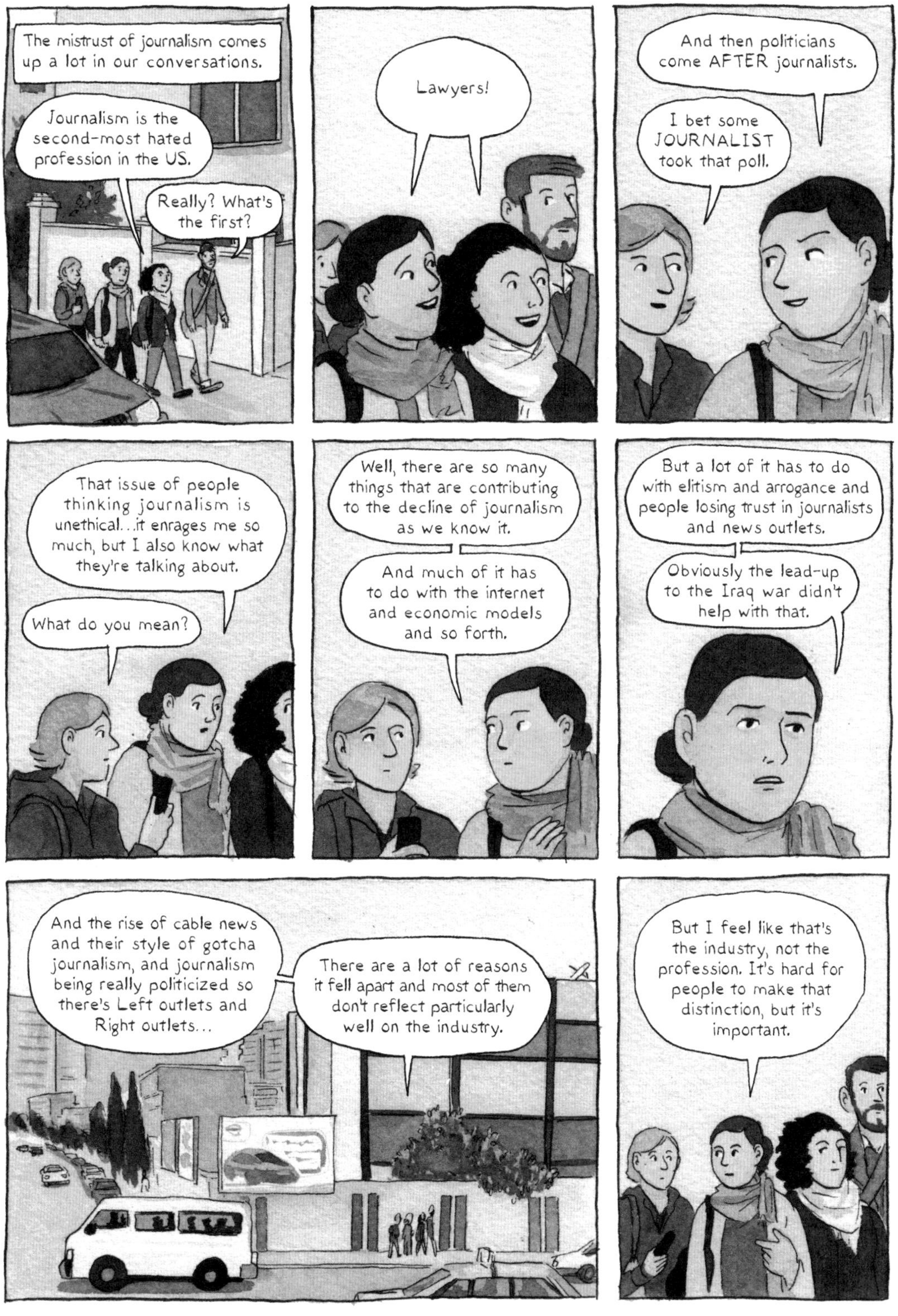
The mistrust of journalism comes up a lot in our conversations.
Journalism is the second-most hated profession in the US.
Really? What's the first?
Lawyers!
And then politicians come AFTER journalists.
I bet some JOURNALIST took that poll.
That issue of people thinking journalism is unethical...it enrages me so much, but I also know what they're talking about.
What do you mean?
Well, there are so many things that are contributing to the decline of journalism as we know it.
And much of it has to do with the internet and economic models and so forth.
But a lot of it has to do with elitism and arrogance and people losing trust in journalists and news outlets.
Obviously the lead-up to the Iraq war didn't help with that.
And the rise of cable news and their style of gotcha journalism, and journalism being really politicized so there's Left outlets and Right outlets...
There are a lot of reasons it fell apart and most of them don't reflect particularly well on the industry.
But I feel like that's the industry, not the profession. It's hard for people to make that distinction, but it's important.

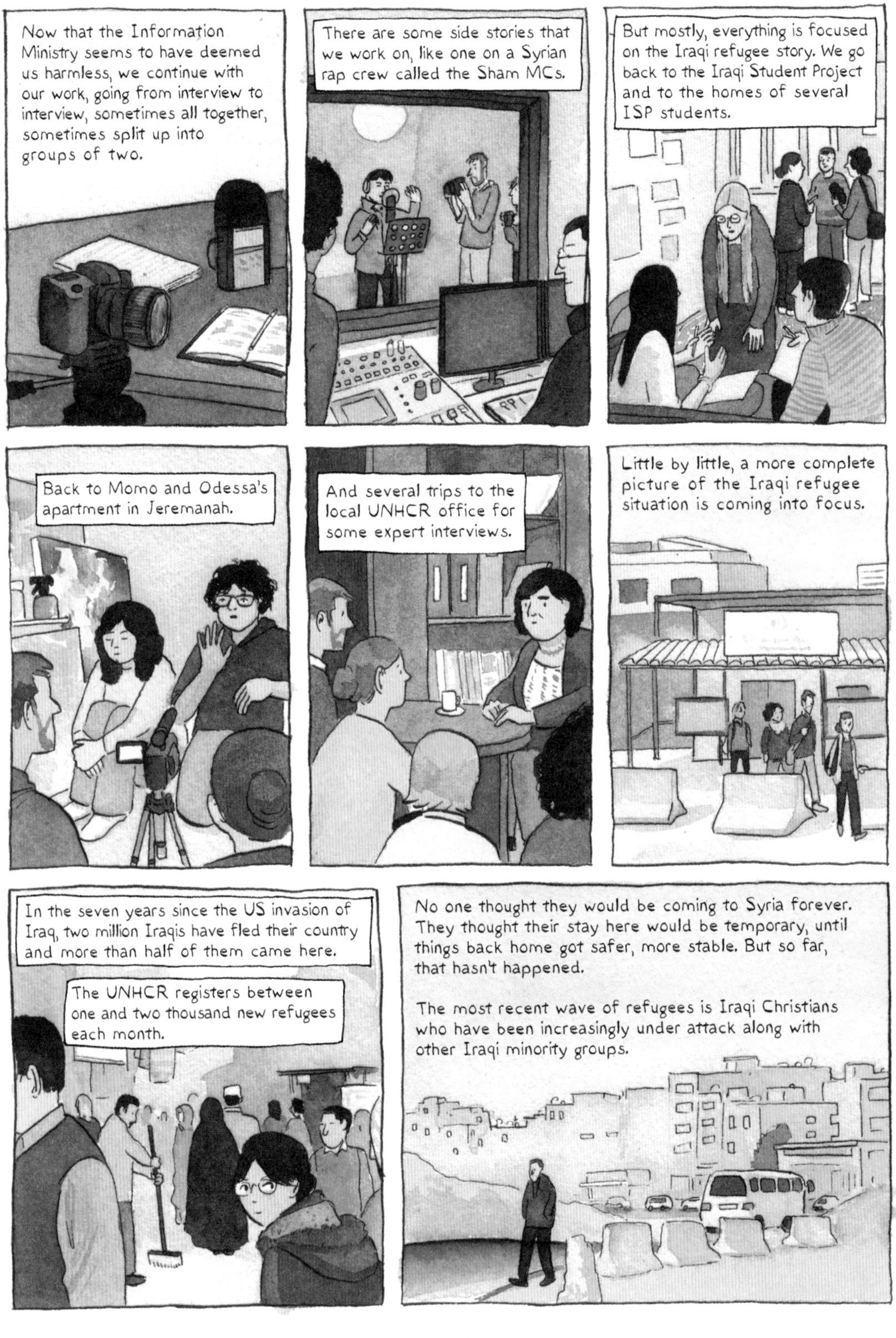
Now that the Information Ministry seems to have deemed us harmless, we continue with our work, going from interview to interview, sometimes all together, sometimes split up into groups of two.
There are some side stories that we work on, like one on a Syrian rap crew called the Sham MCs.
But mostly, everything is focused on the Iraqi refugee story. We go back to the Iraqi Student Project and to the homes of several ISP students.
Back to Momo and Odessa's apartment in Jeremanah.
And several trips to the local UNHCR office for some expert interviews.
Little by little, a more complete picture of the Iraqi refugee situation is coming into focus.
In the seven years since the US invasion of Iraq, two million Iraqis have fled their country and more than half of them came here.
The UNHCR registers between one and two thousand new refugees each month.
No one thought they would be coming to Syria forever. They thought their stay here would be temporary, until things back home got safer, more stable. But so far, that hasn't happened.
The most recent wave of refugees is Iraqi Christians who have been increasingly under attack along with other Iraqi minority groups.

In Syria, refugees at least feel safe. They have access to free medical care and education for their children.

But being safe from the violence of war does not mean a person gets their life back. We hear over and over again that one of the biggest dangers for refugees is a lack of hope for a future, and there is no future here.

There are 42,000 Iraqis between the ages of eighteen and thirty-five who can't go to university and can't get a job.

Even though children have access to primary and secondary school, many of them do not go because they end up becoming the bread-winners for their families.

We are told that men who used to support their families have lost their pride. Aid agencies tie this to an uptick in cases of domestic violence.

Almost every refugee has either witnessed or themselves suf-fered extreme acts of violence or rape, but there is almost no mental health support in Syria and people are afraid to seek counseling anyway because of its social stigma.

According to the UNHCR, about 16,000 Iraqi refugees residing in Syria have been approved for resettlement in 2011, with the majority of those going to the United States.

The US is also responsible for 80 percent of the UNHCR's funding for refugees. For now.

There's a major fear that the US will either cut funding or reduce the number of refugees they resettle. Or that the Syrian government will lose patience with their Iraqi guests.

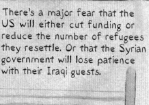

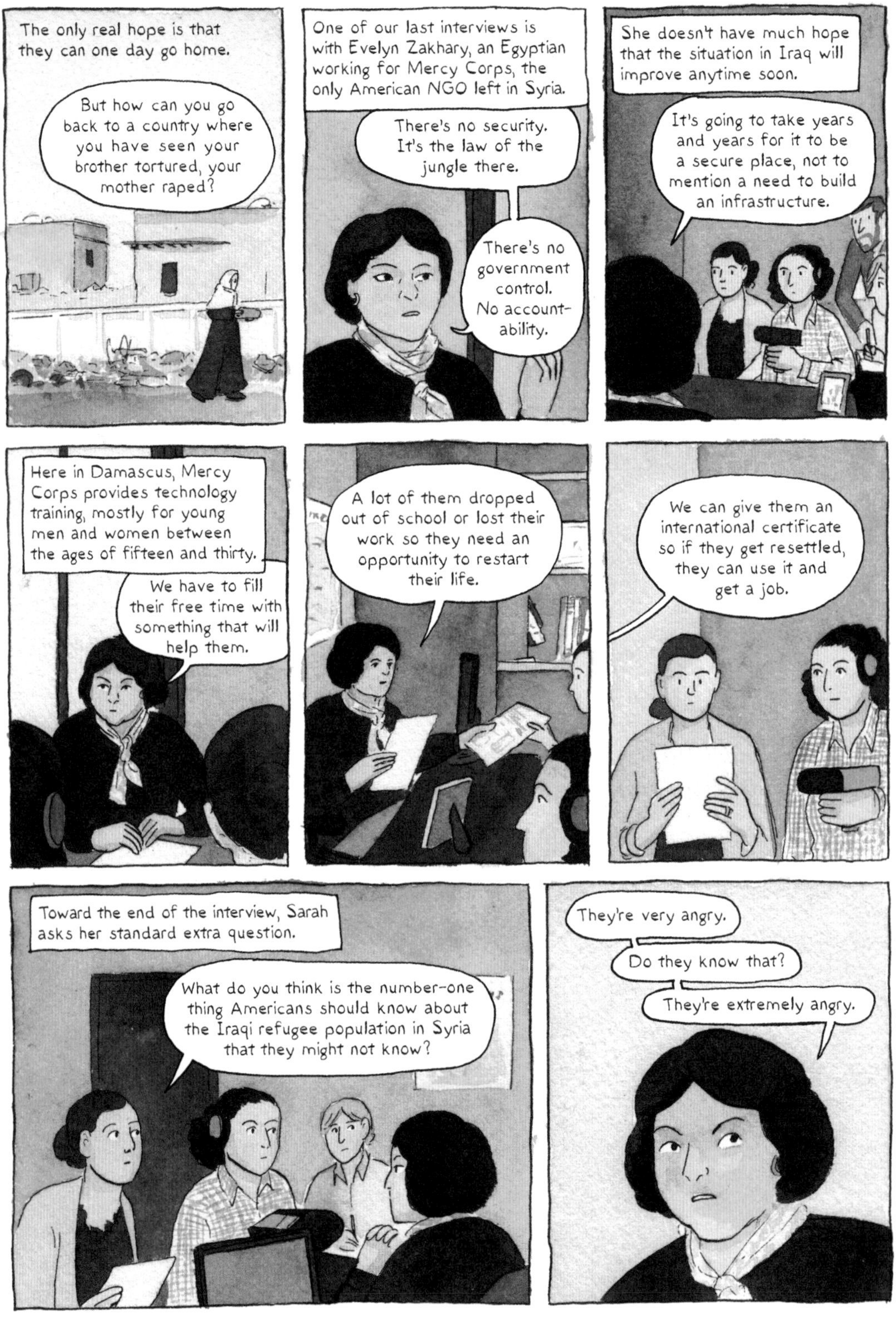
The only real hope is that they can one day go home.
But how can you go back to a country where you have seen your brother tortured, your mother raped?
One of our last interviews is with Evelyn Zakhary, an Egyptian working for Mercy Corps, the only American NGO left in Syria.
There's no security. It's the law of the jungle there.
There's no government control. No accountability.
She doesn't have much hope that the situation in Iraq will improve anytime soon.
It's going to take years and years for it to be a secure place, not to mention a need to build an infrastructure.
Here in Damascus, Mercy Corps provides technology training, mostly for young men and women between the ages of fifteen and thirty.
We have to fill their free time with something that will help them.
A lot of them dropped out of school or lost their work so they need an opportunity to restart their life.
We can give them an international certificate so if they get resettled, they can use it and get a job.
Toward the end of the interview, Sarah asks her standard extra question.
What do you think is the number-one thing Americans should know about the Iraqi refugee population in Syria that they might not know?
They're very angry.
Do they know that?
They're extremely angry.

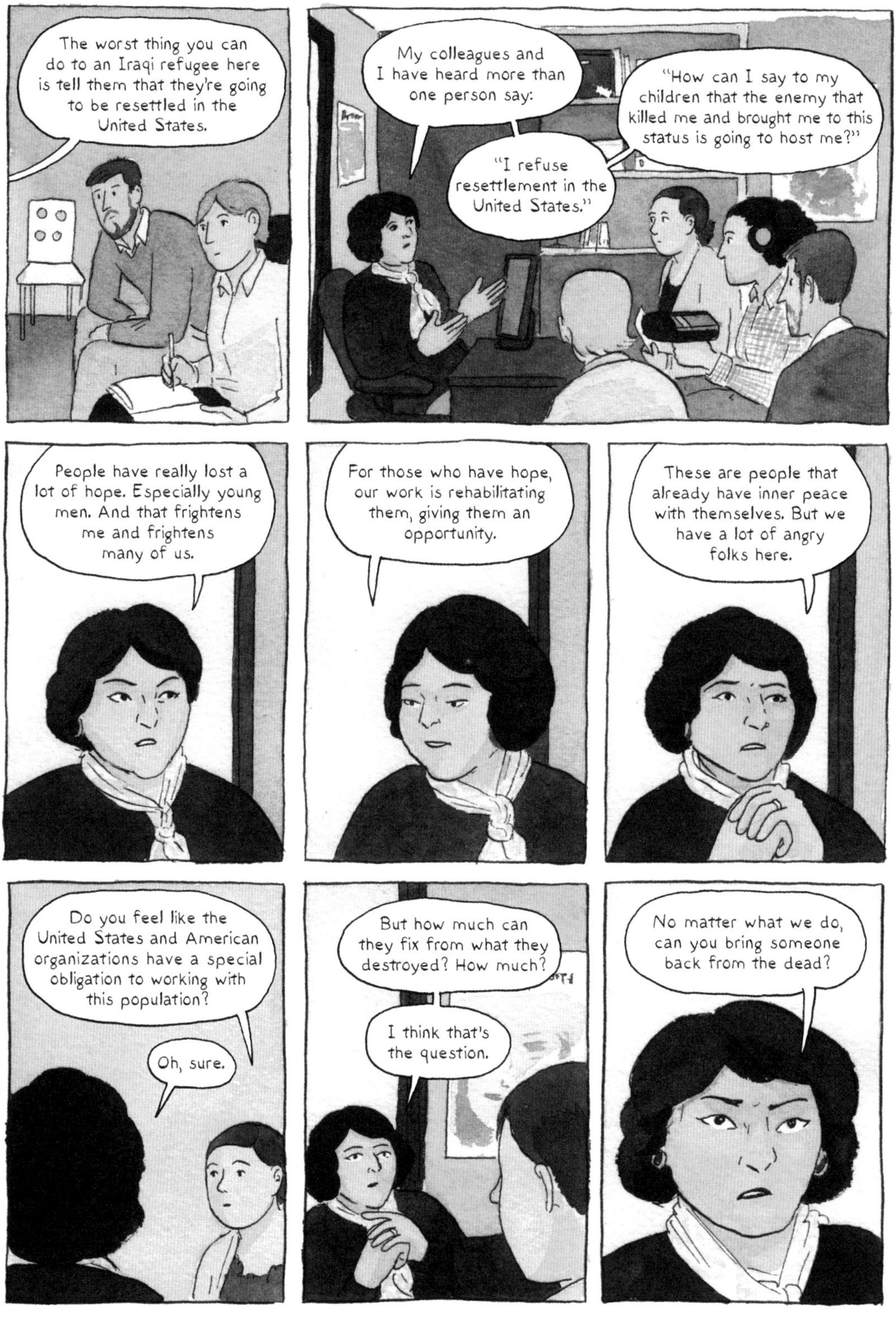
The worst thing you can do to an Iraqi refugee here is tell them that they're going to be resettled in the United States.
My colleagues and I have heard more than one person say:
"I refuse resettlement in the United States."
"How can I say to my children that the enemy that killed me and brought me to this status is going to host me?"
People have really lost a lot of hope. Especially young men. And that frightens me and frightens many of us.
For those who have hope, our work is rehabilitating them, giving them an opportunity.
These are people that already have inner peace with themselves. But we have a lot of angry folks here.
Do you feel like the United States and American organizations have a special obligation to working with this population?
Oh, sure.
But how much can they fix from what they destroyed? How much?
I think that's the question.
No matter what we do, can you bring someone back from the dead?

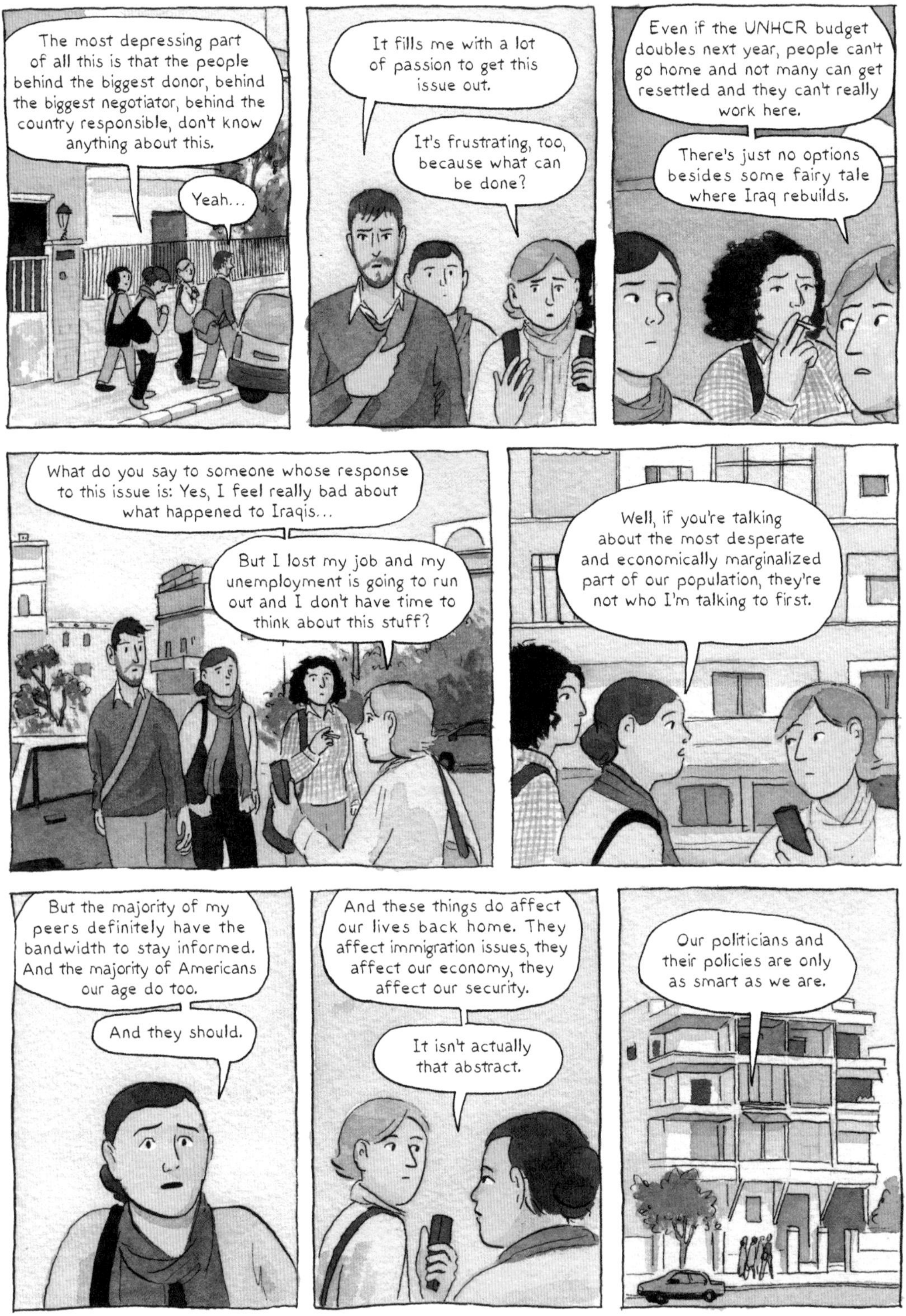
The most depressing part of all this is that the people behind the biggest donor, behind the biggest negotiator, behind the country responsible, don't know anything about this.
Yeah...
It fills me with a lot of passion to get this issue out.
It's frustrating, too, because what can be done?
Even if the UNHCR budget doubles next year, people can't go home and not many can get resettled and they can't really work here.
There's just no options besides some fairy tale where Iraq rebuilds.
What do you say to someone whose response to this issue is: Yes, I feel really bad about what happened to Iraqis...
But I lost my job and my unemployment is going to run out and I don't have time to think about this stuff?
Well, if you're talking about the most desperate and economically marginalized part of our population, they're not who I'm talking to first.
But the majority of my peers definitely have the bandwidth to stay informed. And the majority of Americans our age do too.
And they should.
And these things do affect our lives back home. They affect immigration issues, they affect our economy, they affect our security.
It isn't actually that abstract.
Our politicians and their policies are only as smart as we are.

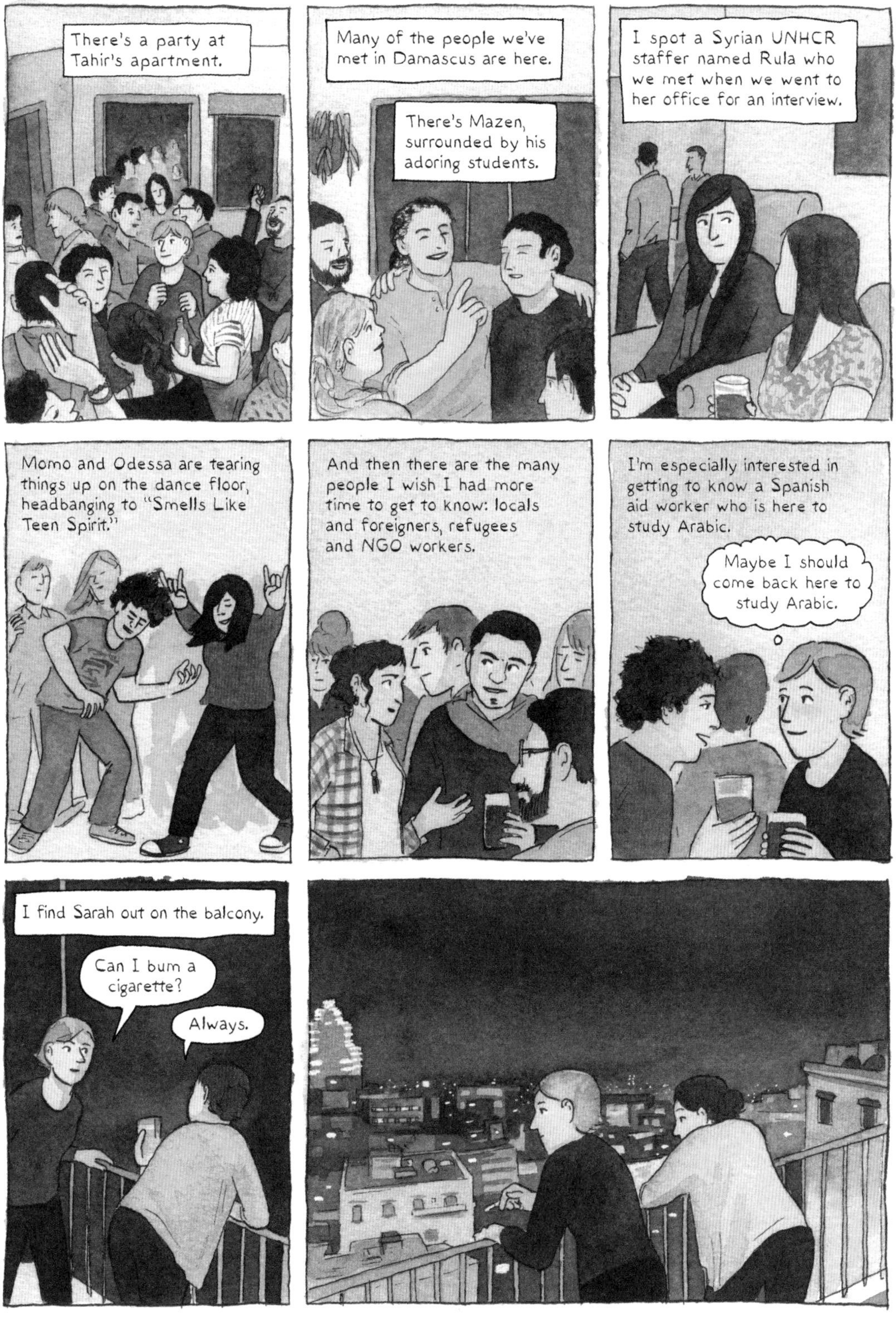
There's a party at Tahir's apartment.
Many of the people we've met in Damascus are here.
There's Mazen, surrounded by his adoring students.
I spot a Syrian UNHCR staffer named Rula who we met when we went to her office for an interview.
Momo and Odessa are tearing things up on the dance floor, headbanging to "Smells Like Teen Spirit."
And then there are the many people I wish I had more time to get to know: locals and foreigners, refugees and NGO workers.
I'm especially interested in getting to know a Spanish aid worker who is here to study Arabic.
Maybe I should come back here to study Arabic.
I find Sarah out on the balcony.
Can I bum a cigarette?
Always.

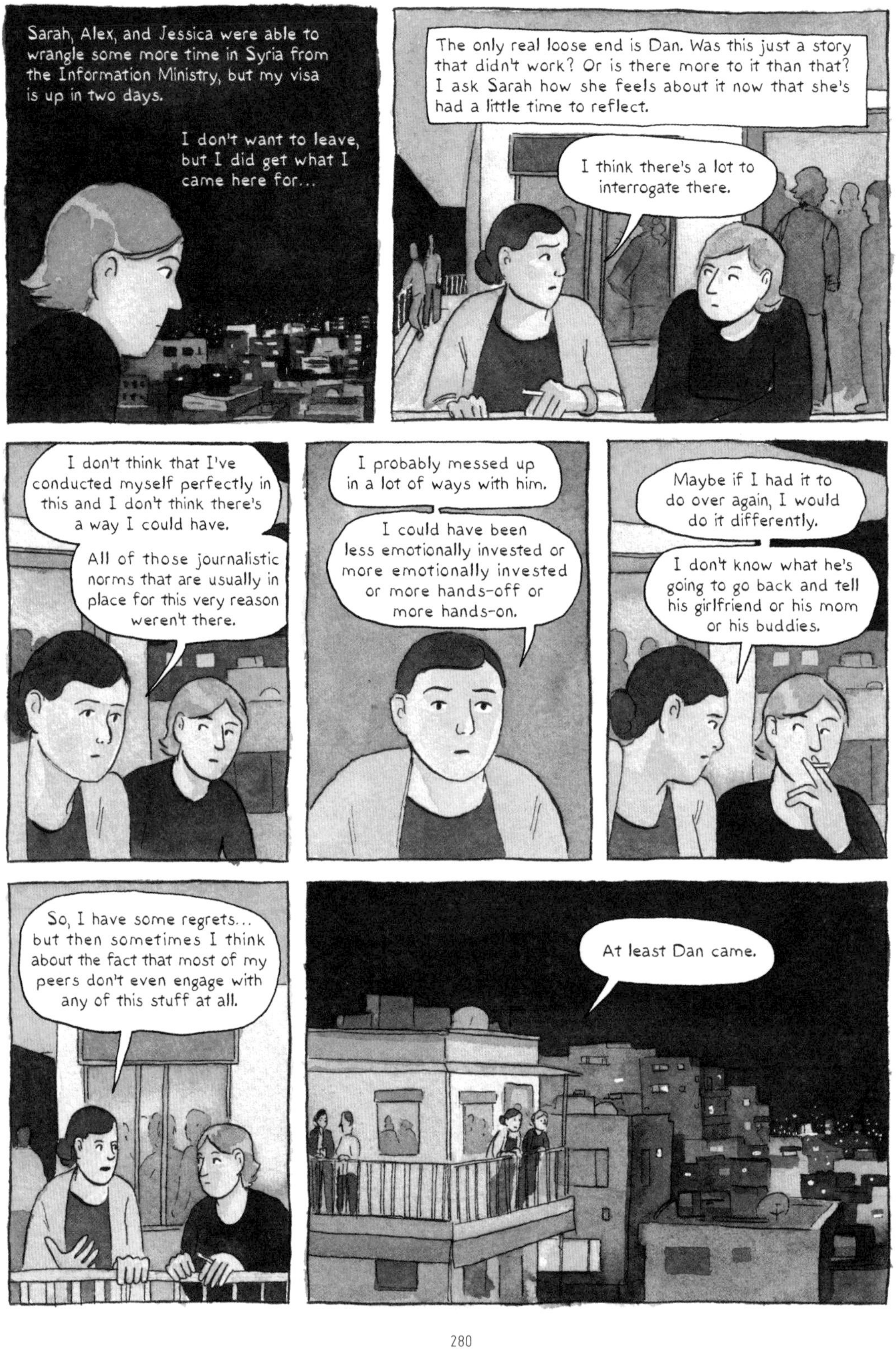
Sarah, Alex, and Jessica were able to wrangle some more time in Syria from the Information Ministry, but my visa is up in two days.
I don't want to leave, but I did get what I came here for...
The only real loose end is Dan. Was this just a story that didn't work? Or is there more to it than that? I ask Sarah how she feels about it now that she's had a little time to reflect.
I think there's a lot to interrogate there.
I don't think that I've conducted myself perfectly in this and I don't think there's a way I could have.
All of those journalistic norms that are usually in place for this very reason weren't there.
I probably messed up in a lot of ways with him.
I could have been less emotionally invested or more emotionally invested or more hands-off or more hands-on.
Maybe if I had it to do over again, I would do it differently.
I don't know what he's going to go back and tell his girlfriend or his mom or his buddies.
So, I have some regrets... but then sometimes I think about the fact that most of my peers don't even engage with any of this stuff at all.
At least Dan came.

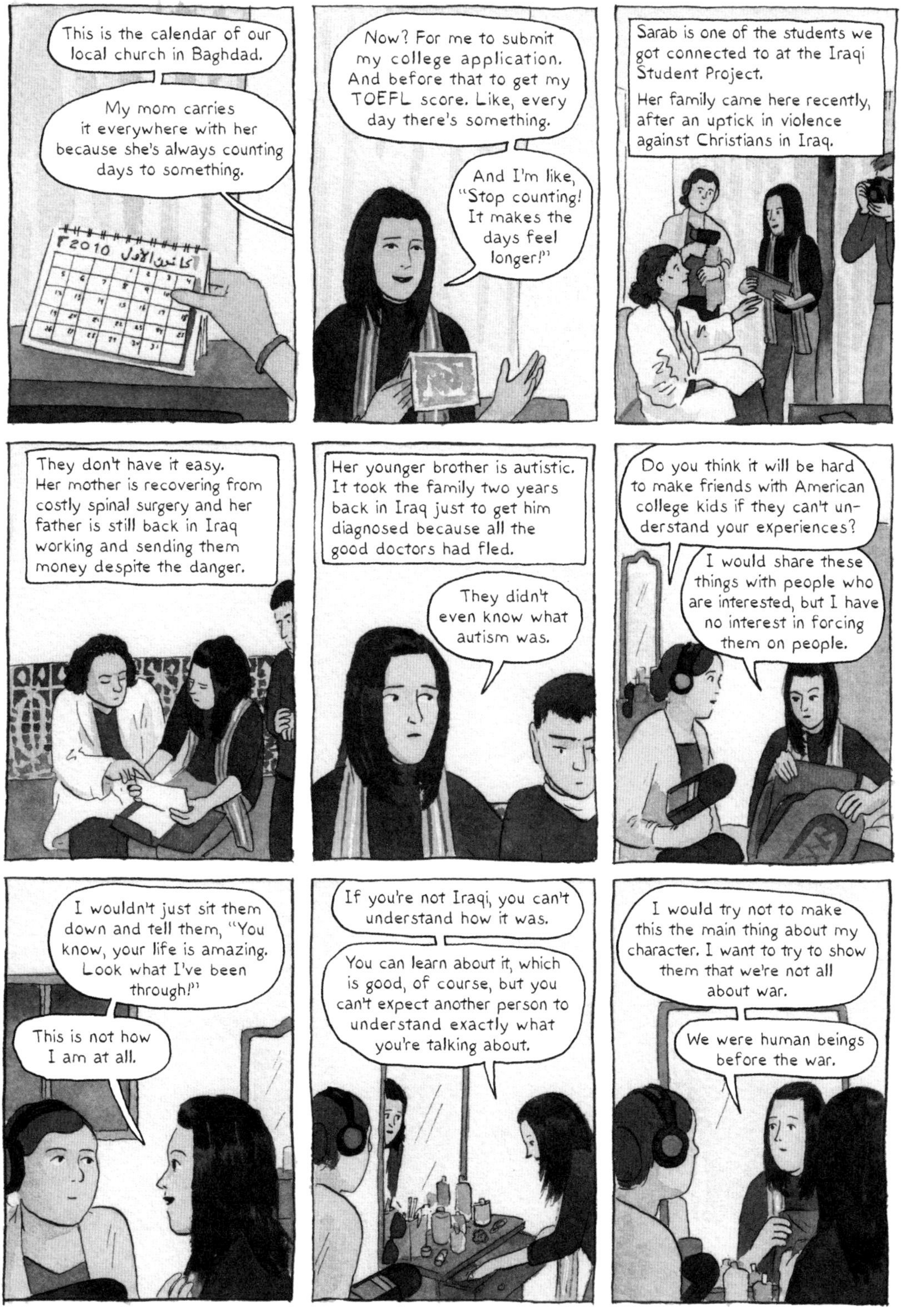
This is the calendar of our local church in Baghdad.
My mom carries it everywhere with her because she's always counting days to something.
2010 كانون الاول
Now? For me to submit my college application. And before that to get my TOEFL score. Like, every day there's something.
And I'm like, "Stop counting! It makes the days feel longer!"
Sarab is one of the students we got connected to at the Iraqi Student Project.
Her family came here recently, after an uptick in violence against Christians in Iraq.
They don't have it easy. Her mother is recovering from costly spinal surgery and her father is still back in Iraq working and sending them money despite the danger.
Her younger brother is autistic. It took the family two years back in Iraq just to get him diagnosed because all the good doctors had fled.
They didn't even know what autism was.
Do you think it will be hard to make friends with American college kids if they can't understand your experiences?
I would share these things with people who are interested, but I have no interest in forcing them on people.
I wouldn't just sit them down and tell them, "You know, your life is amazing. Look what I've been through!"
This is not how I am at all.
If you're not Iraqi, you can't understand how it was.
You can learn about it, which is good, of course, but you can't expect another person to understand exactly what you're talking about.
I would try not to make this the main thing about my character. I want to try to show them that we're not all about war.
We were human beings before the war.

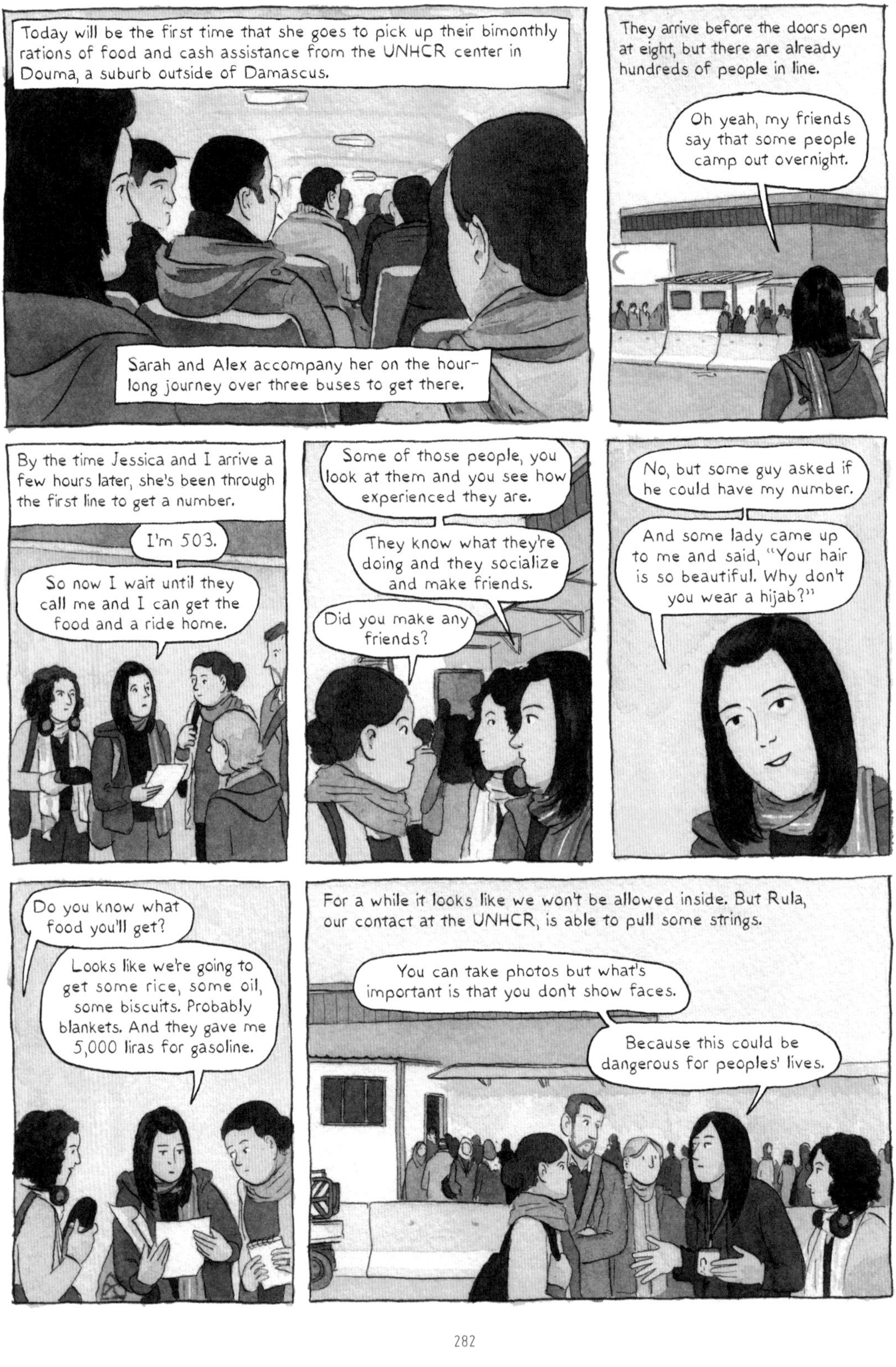
Today will be the first time that she goes to pick up their bimonthly rations of food and cash assistance from the UNHCR center in Douma, a suburb outside of Damascus.
Sarah and Alex accompany her on the hour-long journey over three buses to get there.
They arrive before the doors open at eight, but there are already hundreds of people in line.
Oh yeah, my friends say that some people camp out overnight.
By the time Jessica and I arrive a few hours later, she's been through the first line to get a number.
I'm 503.
So now I wait until they call me and I can get the food and a ride home.
Some of those people, you look at them and you see how experienced they are.
They know what they're doing and they socialize and make friends.
Did you make any friends?
No, but some guy asked if he could have my number.
And some lady came up to me and said, "Your hair is so beautiful. Why don't you wear a hijab?"
Do you know what food you'll get?
Looks like we're going to get some rice, some oil, some biscuits. Probably blankets. And they gave me 5,000 liras for gasoline.
For a while it looks like we won't be allowed inside. But Rula, our contact at the UNHCR, is able to pull some strings.
You can take photos but what's important is that you don't show faces.
Because this could be dangerous for peoples' lives.

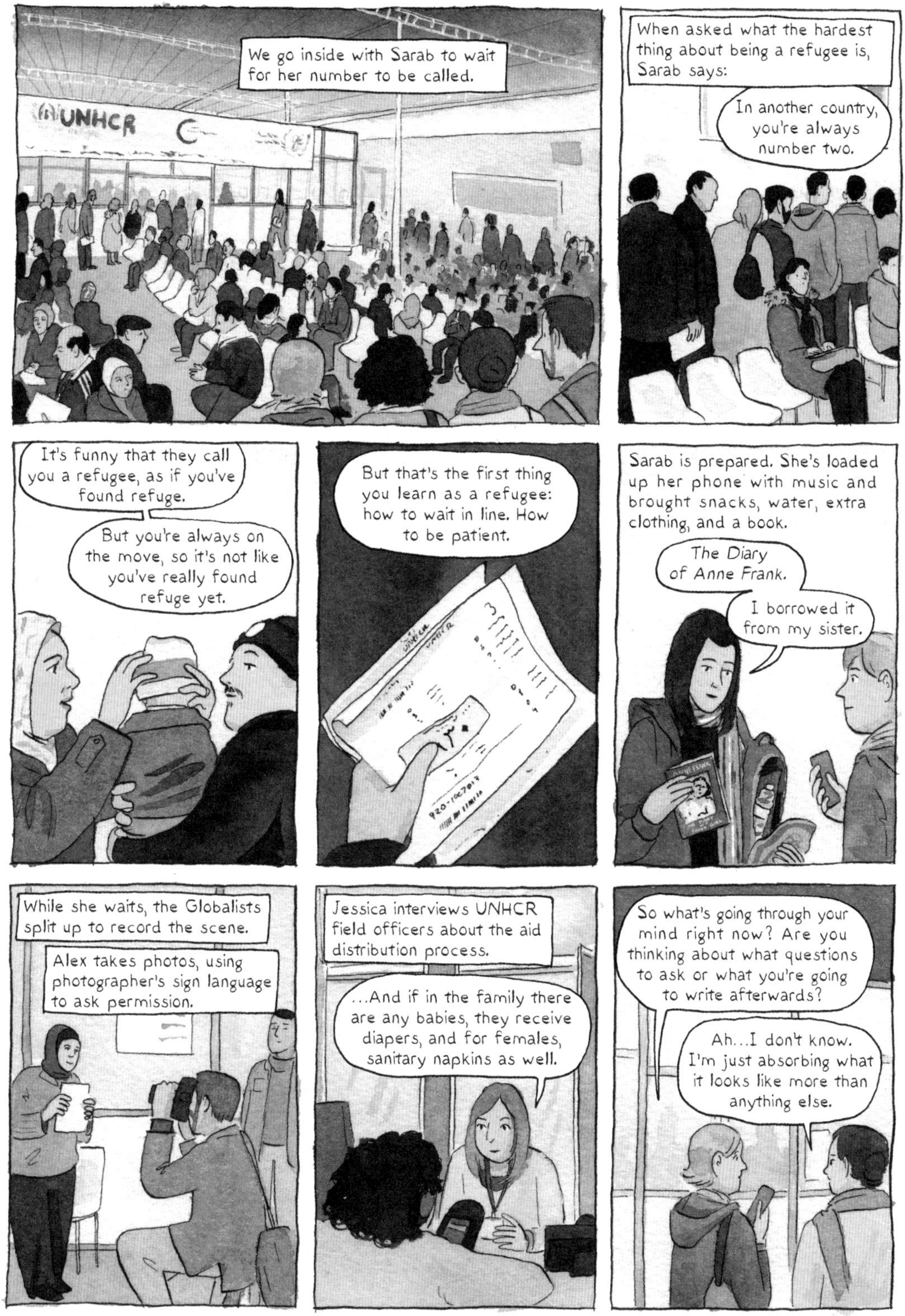
We go inside with Sarab to wait for her number to be called.
UNHCR
When asked what the hardest thing about being a refugee is, Sarab says:
In another country, you're always number two.
It's funny that they call you a refugee, as if you've found refuge.
But you're always on the move, so it's not like you've really found refuge yet.
But that's the first thing you learn as a refugee: how to wait in line. How to be patient.
Sarab is prepared. She's loaded up her phone with music and brought snacks, water, extra clothing, and a book.
The Diary of Anne Frank.
I borrowed it from my sister.
While she waits, the Globalists split up to record the scene.
Alex takes photos, using photographer's sign language to ask permission.
Jessica interviews UNHCR field officers about the aid distribution process.
...And if in the family there are any babies, they receive diapers, and for females, sanitary napkins as well.
So what's going through your mind right now? Are you thinking about what questions to ask or what you're going to write afterwards?
Ah...I don't know. I'm just absorbing what it looks like more than anything else.

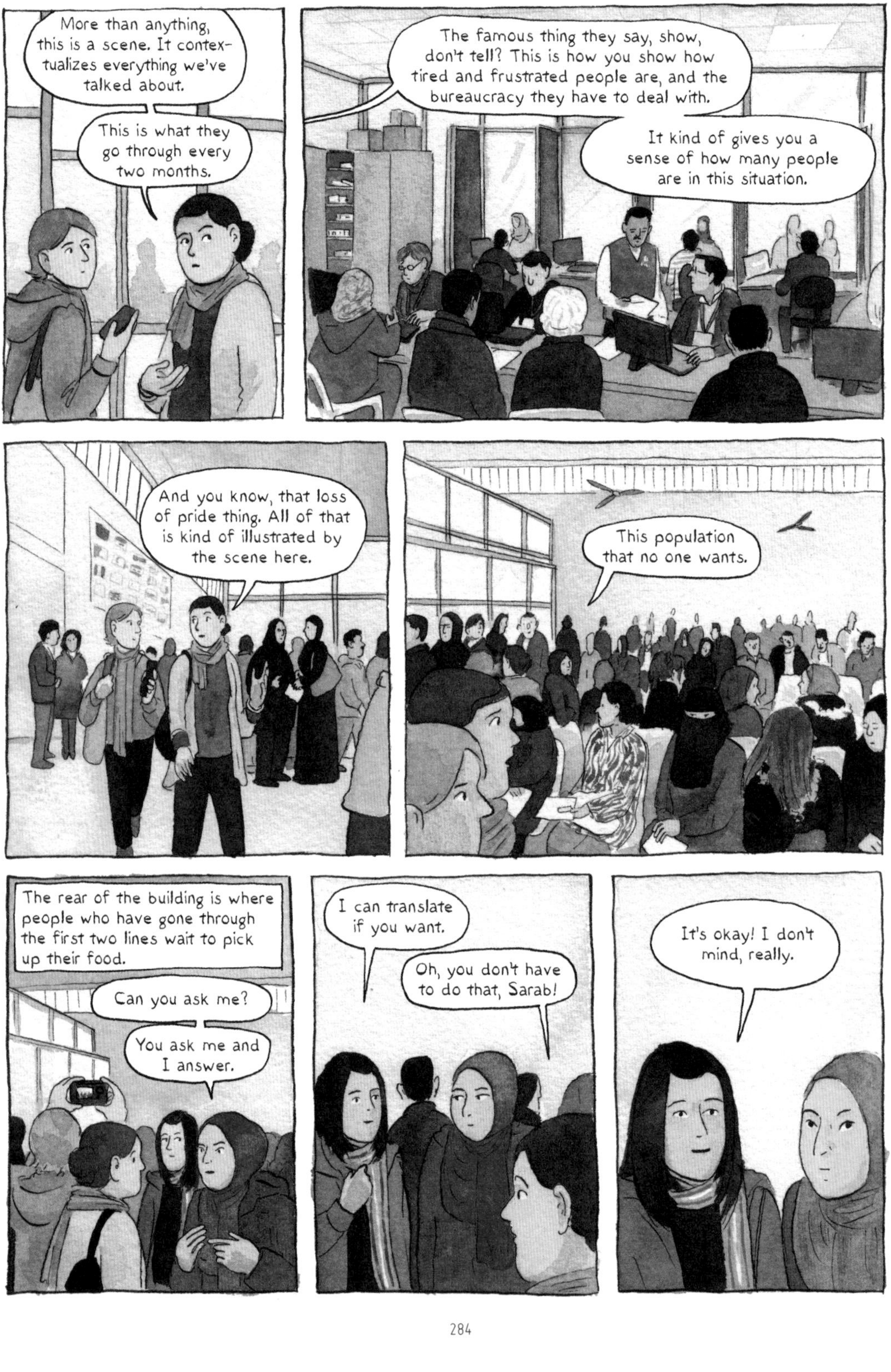
More than anything, this is a scene. It contextualizes everything we've talked about.
This is what they go through every two months.
The famous thing they say, show, don't tell? This is how you show how tired and frustrated people are, and the bureaucracy they have to deal with.
It kind of gives you a sense of how many people are in this situation.
And you know, that loss of pride thing. All of that is kind of illustrated by the scene here.
This population that no one wants.
The rear of the building is where people who have gone through the first two lines wait to pick up their food.
Can you ask me?
You ask me and I answer.
I can translate if you want.
Oh, you don't have to do that, Sarab!
It's okay! I don't mind, really.

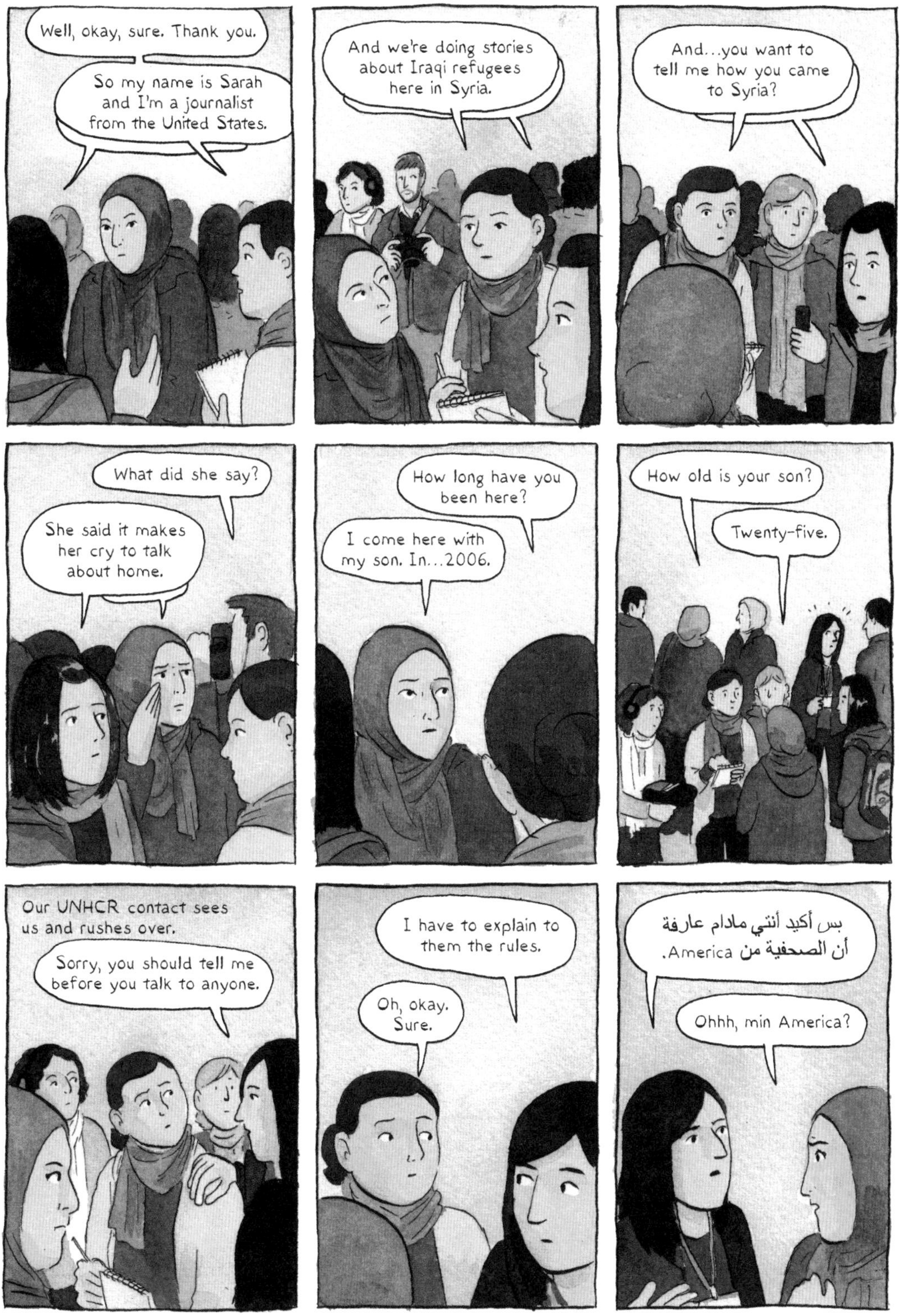

Well, okay, sure. Thank you.
So my name is Sarah and I'm a journalist from the United States.
And we're doing stories about Iraqi refugees here in Syria.
And...you want to tell me how you came to Syria?
What did she say?
She said it makes her cry to talk about home.
How long have you been here?
I come here with my son. In...2006.
How old is your son?
Twenty-five.
Our UNHCR contact sees us and rushes over.
Sorry, you should tell me before you talk to anyone.
I have to explain to them the rules.
Oh, okay. Sure.
بس أكيد أنتي مادام عارفة
أن الصحفية من America.
Ohhh, min America?

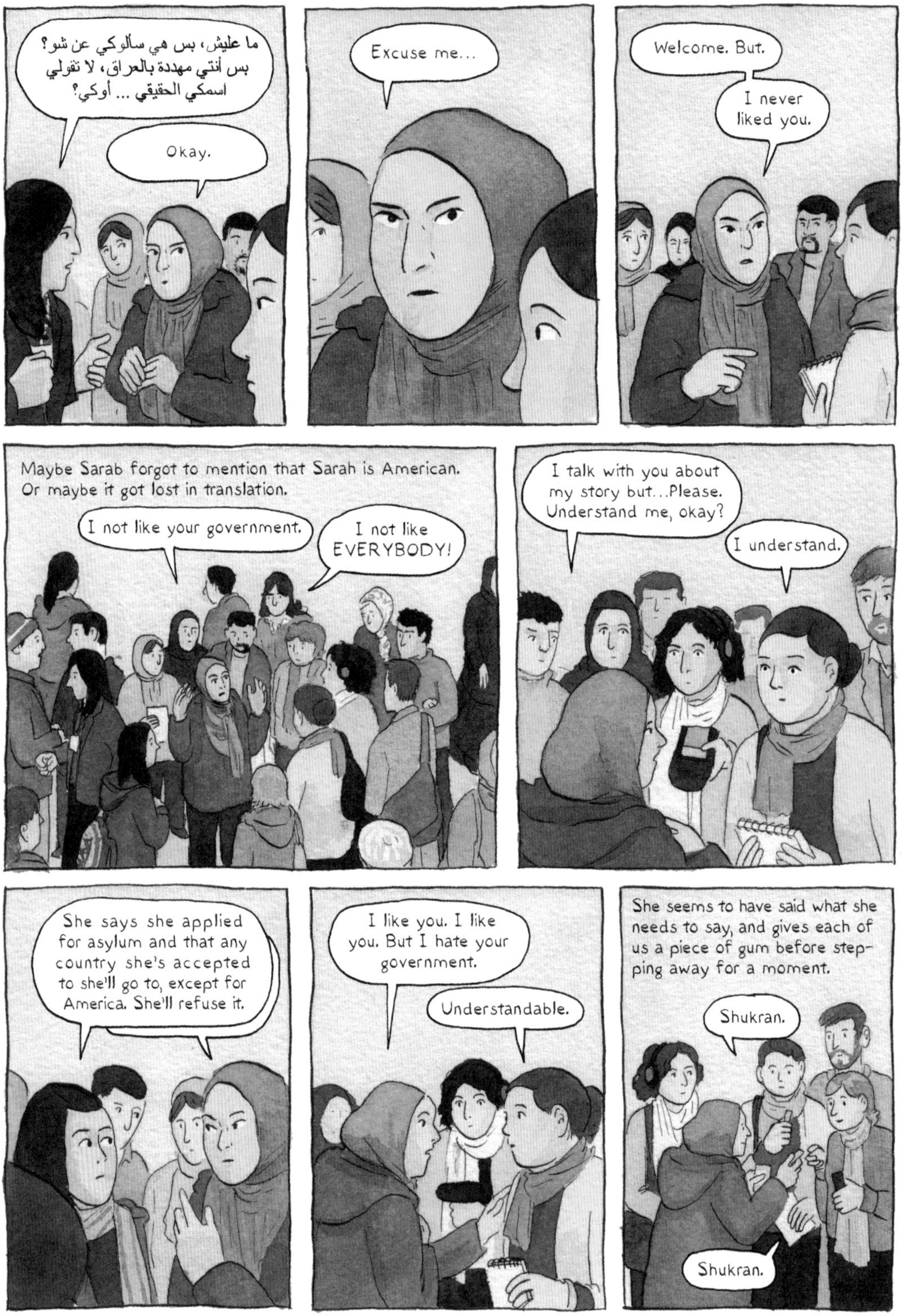
ما عليش، بس هي سالوكي عن شو؟ بس أنتي مهددة بالعراق، لا تقولي اسمكي الحقيقي ... أوكي؟
Okay.
Excuse me...
Welcome. But.
I never liked you.
Maybe Sarab forgot to mention that Sarah is American. Or maybe it got lost in translation.
I not like your government.
I not like EVERYBODY!
I talk with you about my story but...Please. Understand me, okay?
I understand.
She says she applied for asylum and that any country she's accepted to she'll go to, except for America. She'll refuse it.
I like you. I like you. But I hate your government.
Understandable.
She seems to have said what she needs to say, and gives each of us a piece of gum before stepping away for a moment.
Shukran.
Shukran.

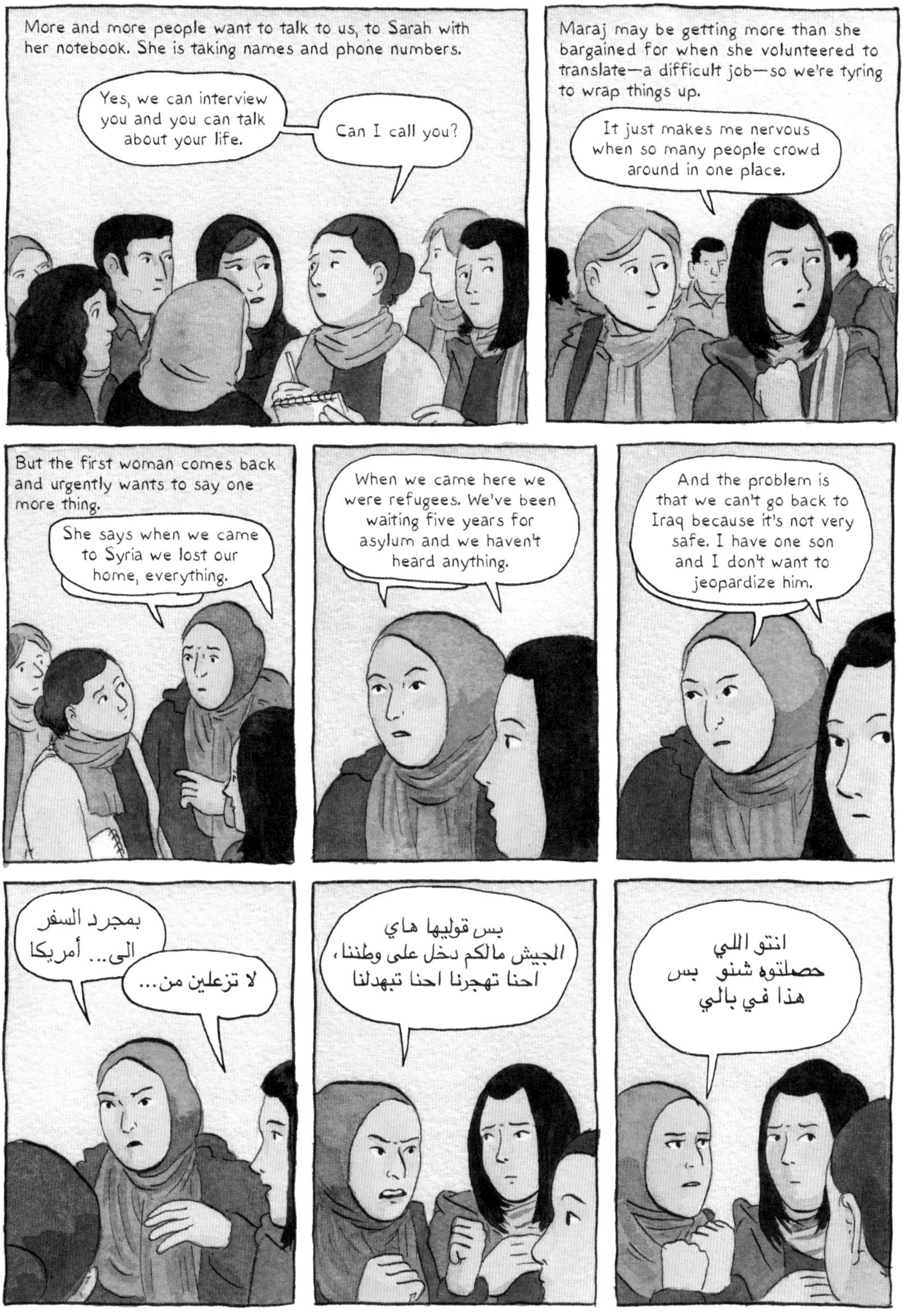
More and more people want to talk to us, to Sarah with her notebook. She is taking names and phone numbers.
Yes, we can interview you and you can talk about your life.
Can I call you?
Maraj may be getting more than she bargained for when she volunteered to translate—a difficult job—so we're tyring to wrap things up.
It just makes me nervous when so many people crowd around in one place.
But the first woman comes back and urgently wants to say one more thing.
She says when we came to Syria we lost our home, everything.
When we came here we were refugees. We've been waiting five years for asylum and we haven't heard anything.
And the problem is that we can't go back to Iraq because it's not very safe. I have one son and I don't want to jeopardize him.
بمجرد السفر الى... أمريكا
لا تزعلين من...
بس قوليها هاي الجيش مالكم دخل على وطننا، احنا تهجرنا احنا تبهدلنا
انتو اللي حصلتوه شنو بس هذا في بالي

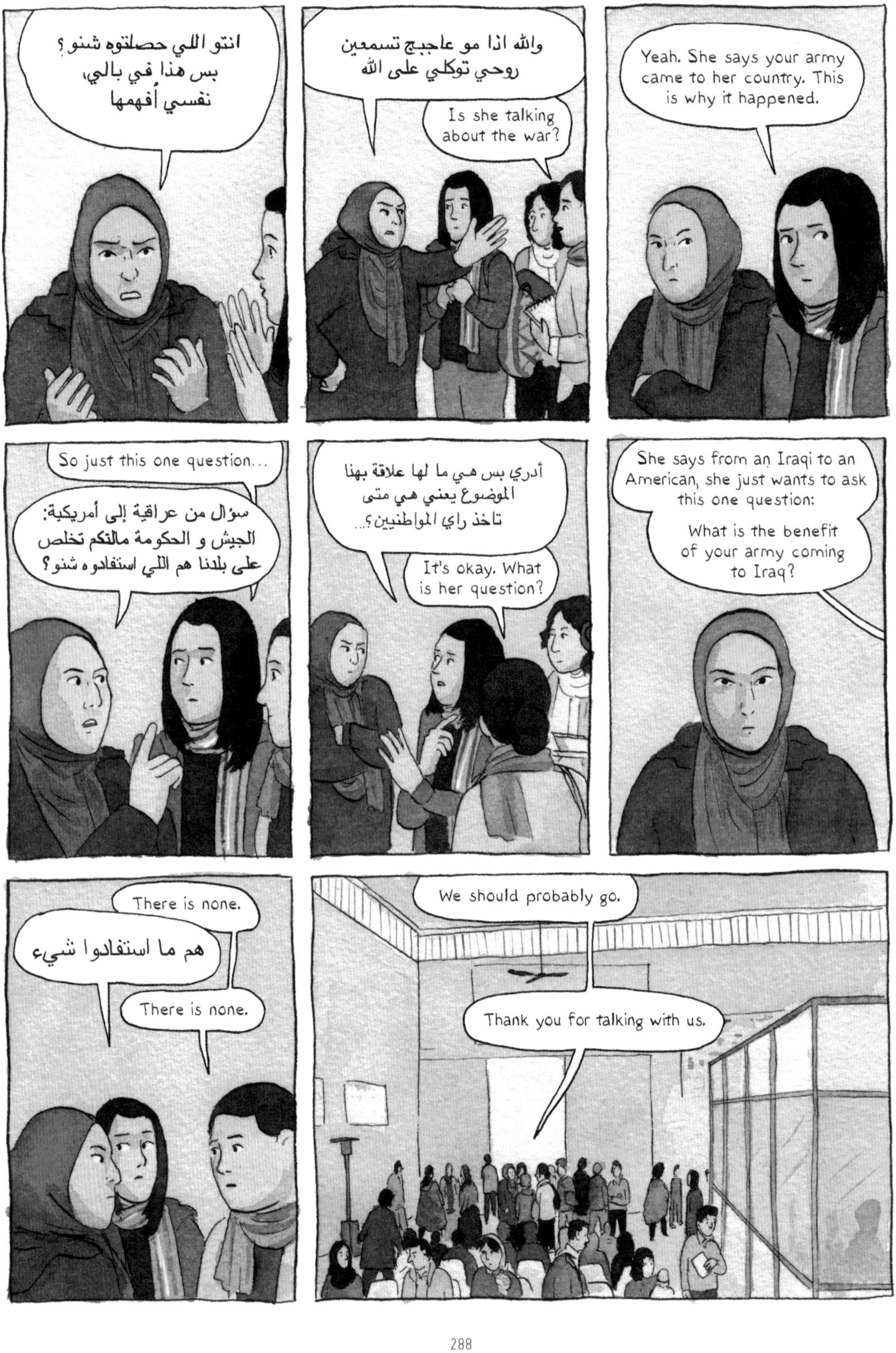
انتو اللي حصلتوه شنو؟
بس هذا في بالي،
نفسي أُفهمها
والله اذا مو عاجبج تسمعين
روحي توكلي على الله
Is she talking about the war?
Yeah. She says your army came to her country. This is why it happened.
So just this one question...
سؤال من عراقية إلى أمريكية:
الجيش و الحكومة مالتكم تخلص
على بلدنا هم اللي استفادوه شنو؟
أدري بس هي ما لها علاقة بهنا
الموضوع يعني هي متى
تاخذ راي المواطنين؟...
It's okay. What is her question?
She says from an Iraqi to an American, she just wants to ask this one question:
What is the benefit of your army coming to Iraq?
There is none.
هم ما استفادوا شيء
There is none.
We should probably go.
Thank you for talking with us.

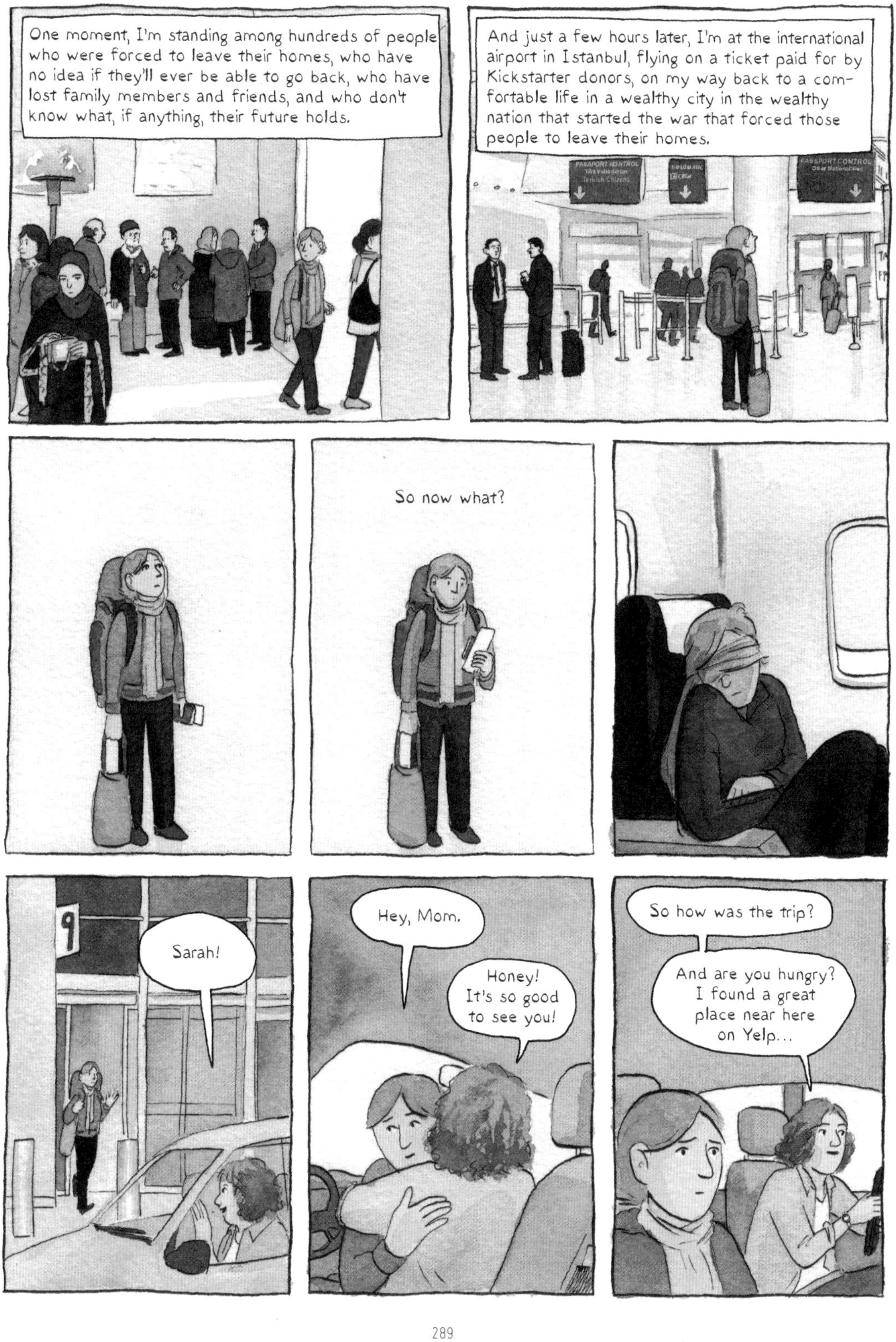
One moment, I'm standing among hundreds of people who were forced to leave their homes, who have no idea if they'll ever be able to go back, who have lost family members and friends, and who don't know what, if anything, their future holds.
And just a few hours later, I'm at the international airport in Istanbul, flying on a ticket paid for by Kickstarter donors, on my way back to a comfortable life in a wealthy city in the wealthy nation that started the war that forced those people to leave their homes.
PASSPORT CONTROL
So now what?
Sarah!
Hey, Mom.
Honey! It's so good to see you!
So how was the trip?
And are you hungry? I found a great place near here on Yelp...

HOME

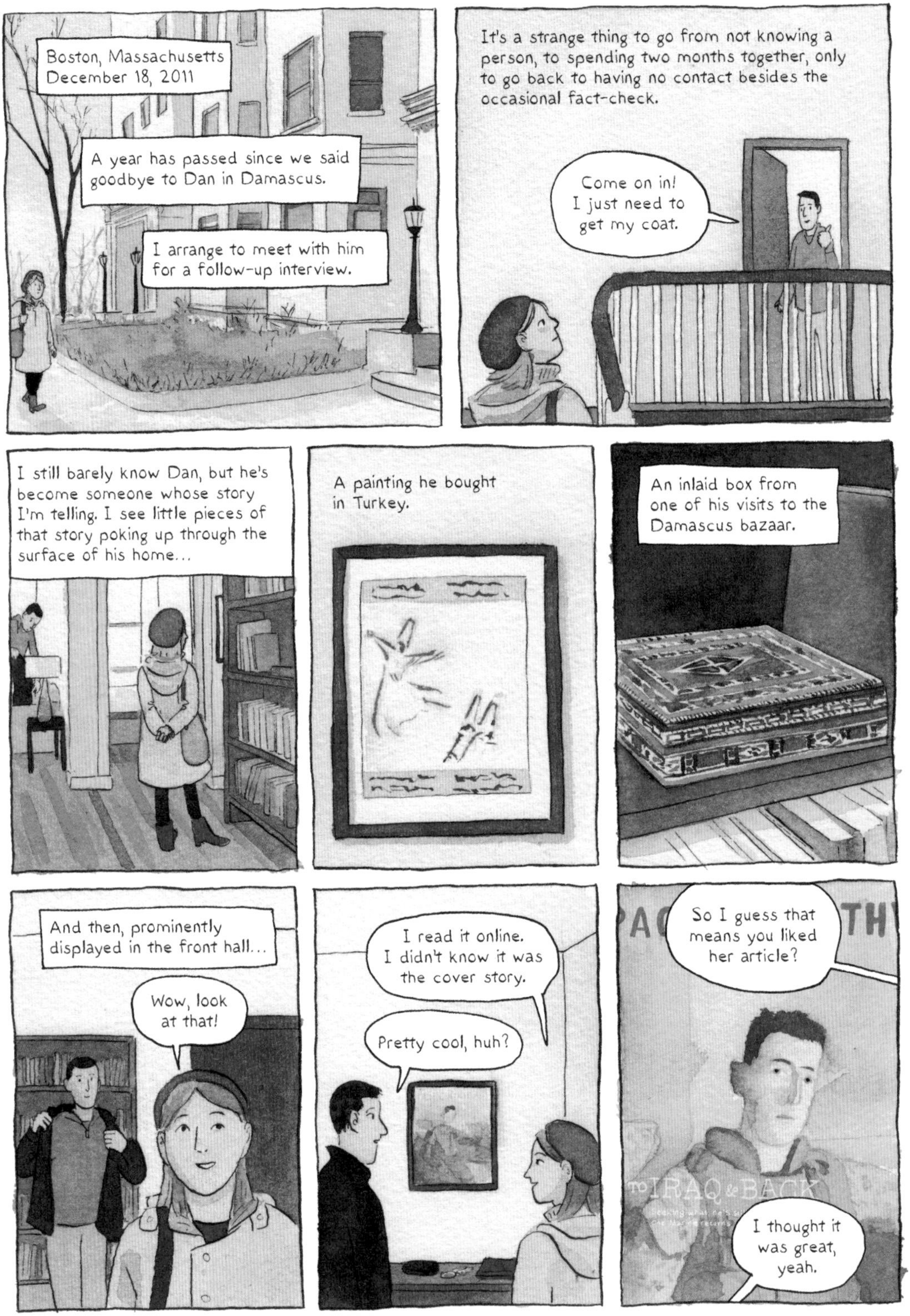
Boston, Massachusetts
December 18, 2011
A year has passed since we said goodbye to Dan in Damascus.
I arrange to meet with him for a follow-up interview.
It's a strange thing to go from not knowing a person, to spending two months together, only to go back to having no contact besides the occasional fact-check.
Come on in! I just need to get my coat.
I still barely know Dan, but he's become someone whose story I'm telling. I see little pieces of that story poking up through the surface of his home...
A painting he bought in Turkey.
An inlaid box from one of his visits to the Damascus bazaar.
And then, prominently displayed in the front hall...
Wow, look at that!
I read it online. I didn't know it was the cover story.
Pretty cool, huh?
So I guess that means you liked her article?
TO IRAQ & BACK
I thought it was great, yeah.

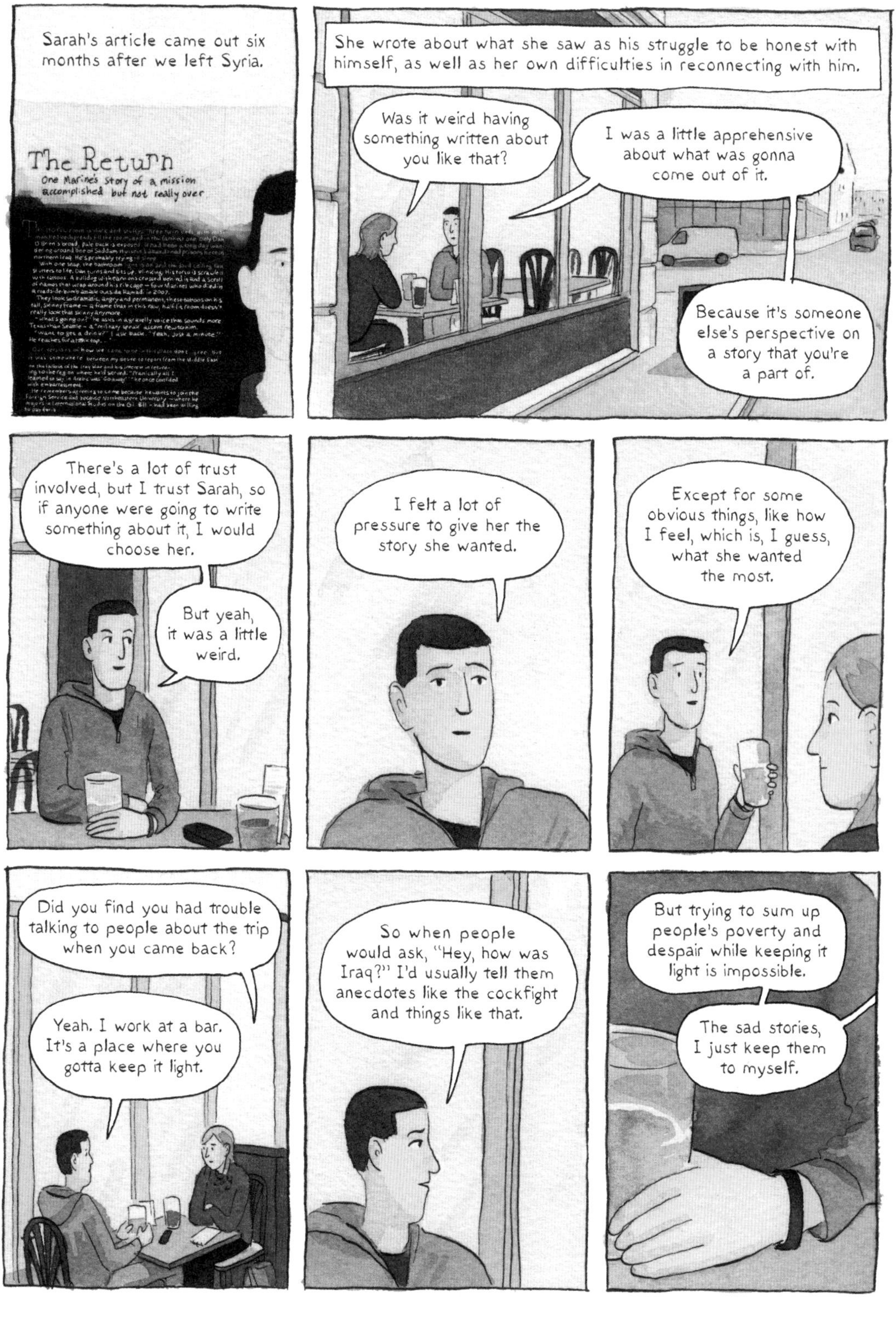
Sarah's article came out six months after we left Syria.
The Return
One Marine's story of a mission accomplished but not really over
She wrote about what she saw as his struggle to be honest with himself, as well as her own difficulties in reconnecting with him.
Was it weird having something written about you like that?
I was a little apprehensive about what was gonna come out of it.
Because it's someone else's perspective on a story that you're a part of.
There's a lot of trust involved, but I trust Sarah, so if anyone were going to write something about it, I would choose her.
But yeah, it was a little weird.
I felt a lot of pressure to give her the story she wanted.
Except for some obvious things, like how I feel, which is, I guess, what she wanted the most.
Did you find you had trouble talking to people about the trip when you came back?
Yeah. I work at a bar. It's a place where you gotta keep it light.
So when people would ask, "Hey, how was Iraq?" I'd usually tell them anecdotes like the cockfight and things like that.
But trying to sum up people's poverty and despair while keeping it light is impossible.
The sad stories, I just keep them to myself.

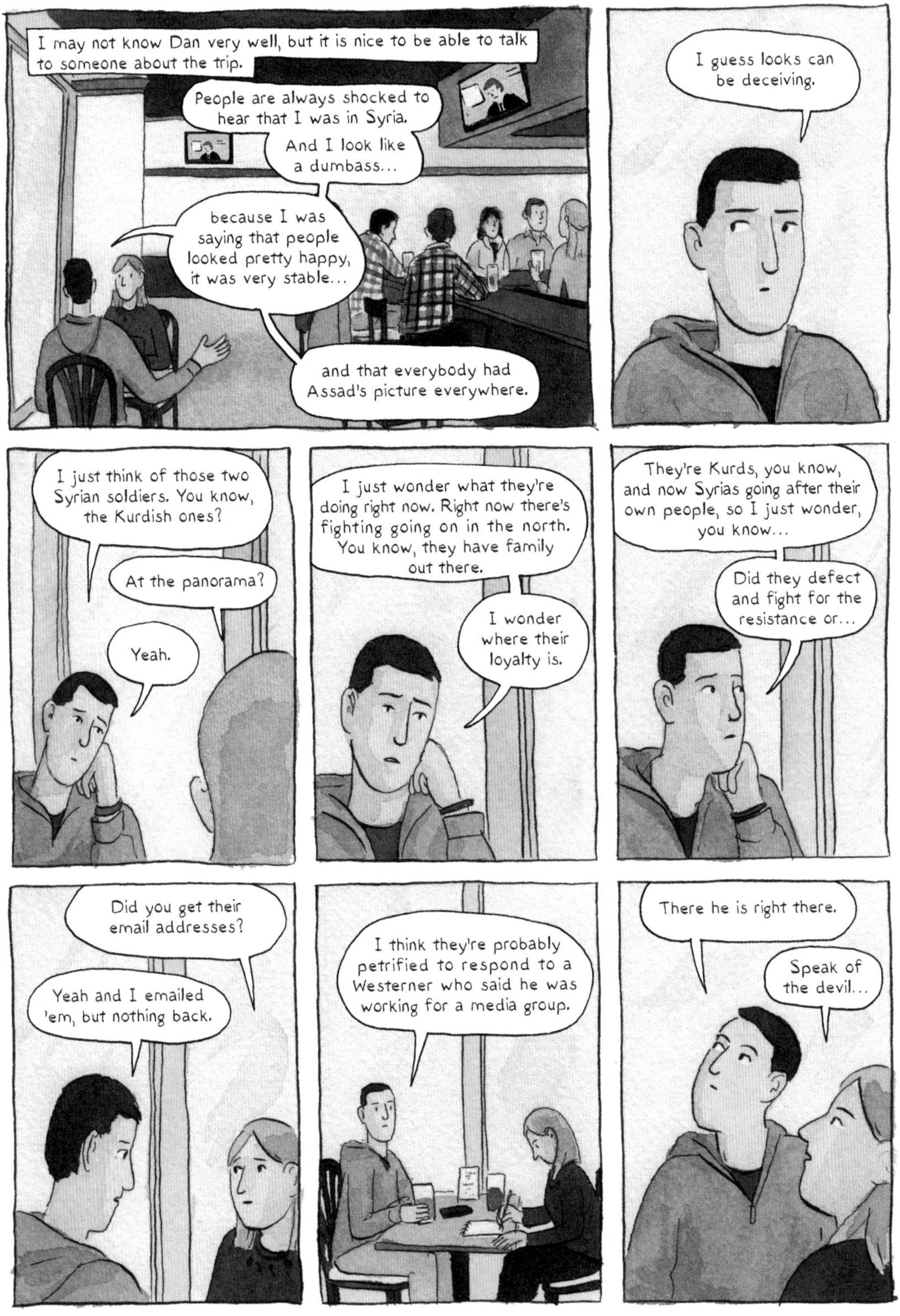

I may not know Dan very well, but it is nice to be able to talk to someone about the trip.
People are always shocked to hear that I was in Syria.
And I look like a dumbass...
because I was saying that people looked pretty happy, it was very stable...
and that everybody had Assad's picture everywhere.
I guess looks can be deceiving.
I just think of those two Syrian soldiers. You know, the Kurdish ones?
At the panorama?
Yeah.
I just wonder what they're doing right now. Right now there's fighting going on in the north. You know, they have family out there.
I wonder where their loyalty is.
They're Kurds, you know, and now Syrias going after their own people, so I just wonder, you know...
Did they defect and fight for the resistance or...
Did you get their email addresses?
Yeah and I emailed 'em, but nothing back.
I think they're probably petrified to respond to a Westerner who said he was working for a media group.
There he is right there.
Speak of the devil...

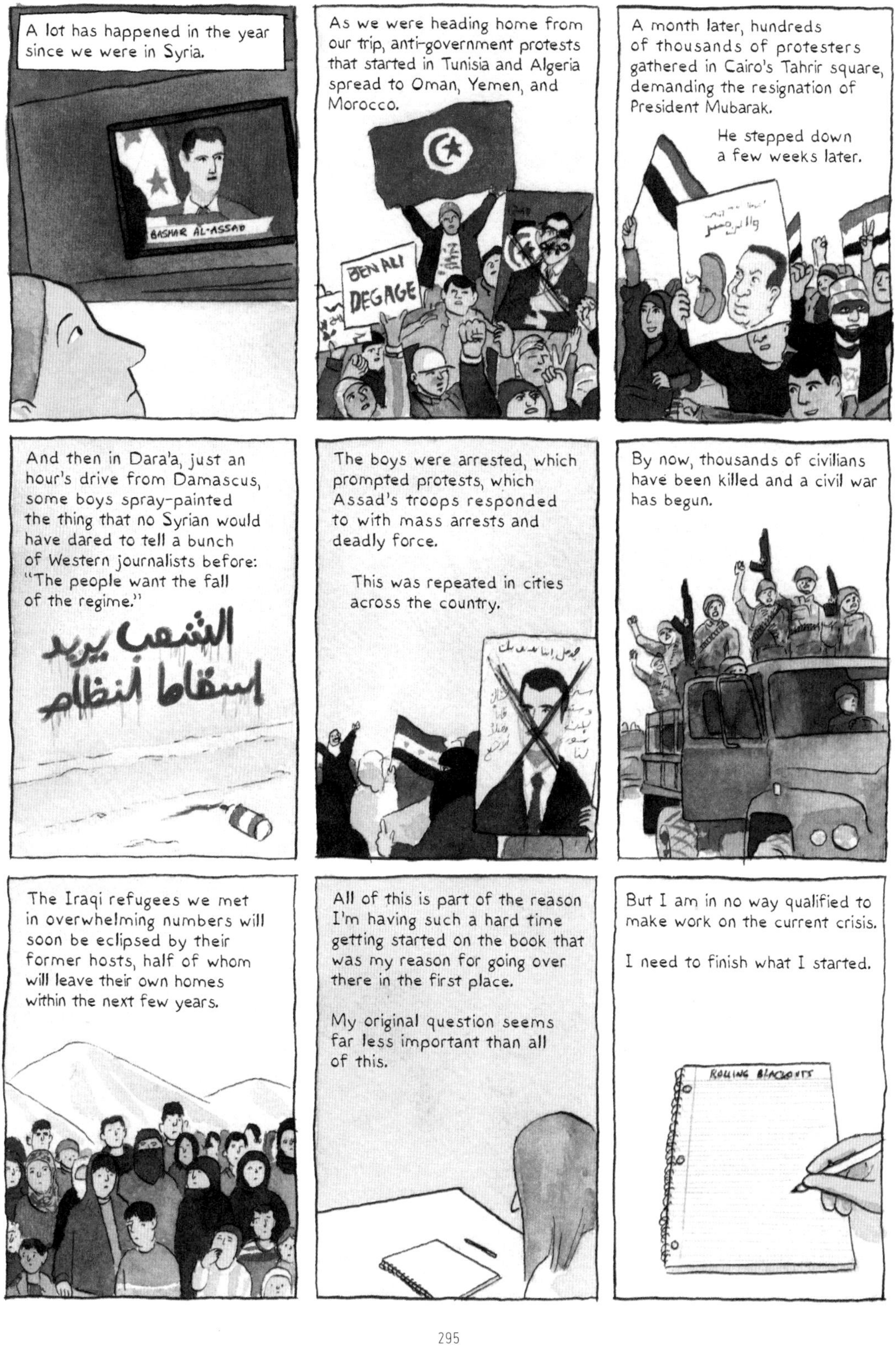
A lot has happened in the year since we were in Syria.
BASHAR AL-ASSAD
As we were heading home from our trip, anti-government protests that started in Tunisia and Algeria spread to Oman, Yemen, and Morocco.
BEN ALI DEGAGE
A month later, hundreds of thousands of protesters gathered in Cairo's Tahrir square, demanding the resignation of President Mubarak.
He stepped down a few weeks later.
And then in Dara'a, just an hour's drive from Damascus, some boys spray-painted the thing that no Syrian would have dared to tell a bunch of Western journalists before: "The people want the fall of the regime."
الشعب يريد
اسقاط النظام
The boys were arrested, which prompted protests, which Assad's troops responded to with mass arrests and deadly force.
This was repeated in cities across the country.
By now, thousands of civilians have been killed and a civil war has begun.
The Iraqi refugees we met in overwhelming numbers will soon be eclipsed by their former hosts, half of whom will leave their own homes within the next few years.
All of this is part of the reason I'm having such a hard time getting started on the book that was my reason for going over there in the first place.
My original question seems far less important than all of this.
But I am in no way qualified to make work on the current crisis.
I need to finish what I started.
ROLLING BLACKOUTS

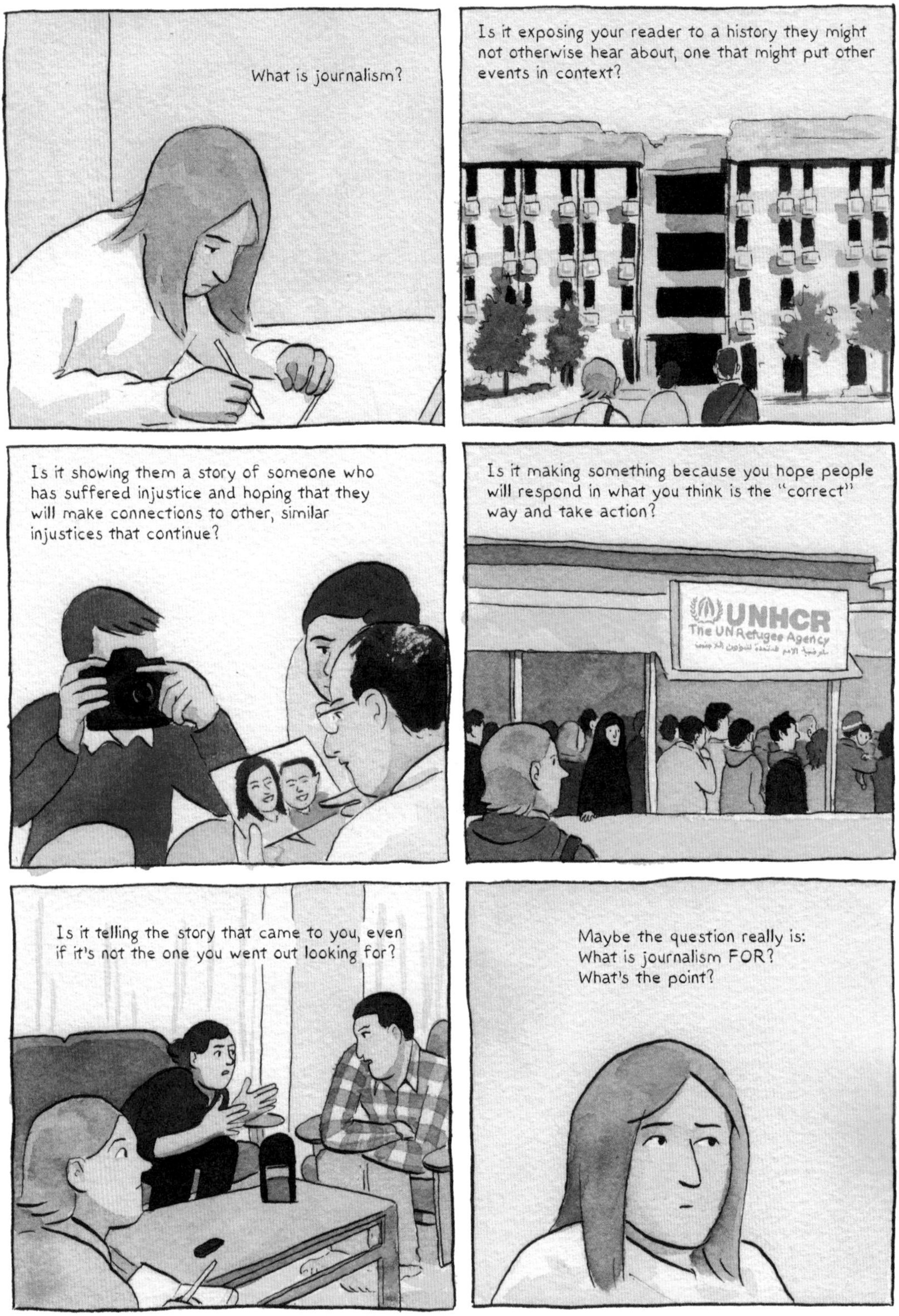
What is journalism?
Is it exposing your reader to a history they might not otherwise hear about, one that might put other events in context?
Is it showing them a story of someone who has suffered injustice and hoping that they will make connections to other, similar injustices that continue?
Is it making something because you hope people will respond in what you think is the "correct" way and take action?
UNHCR
The UN Refugee Agency
Is it telling the story that came to you, even if it's not the one you went out looking for?
Maybe the question really is:
What is journalism FOR?
What's the point?

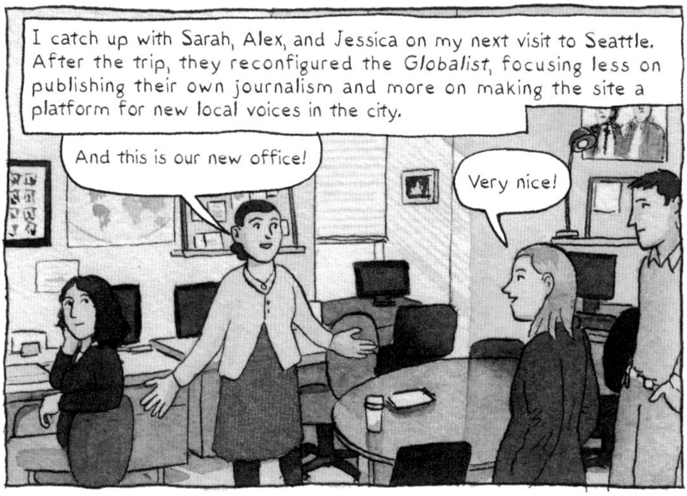
I catch up with Sarah, Alex, and Jessica on my next visit to Seattle. After the trip, they reconfigured the *Globalist*, focusing less on publishing their own journalism and more on making the site a platform for new local voices in the city.
And this is our new office!
Very nice!

They're finishing up work on a feature-length documentary about Sam's story called Barzan.

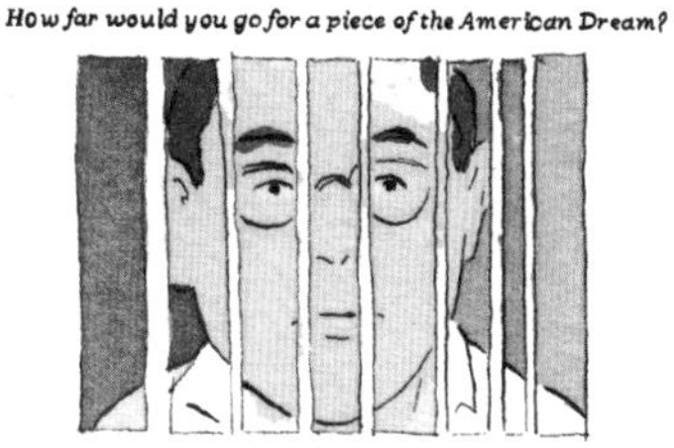
How far would you go for a piece of the American Dream?

Besides that, they produced thirteen other stories and blog posts from the reporting done during that trip.

We even collaborated on a story together, with me using their reporting to make a comic about Iraqi refugees in limbo in Damascus.

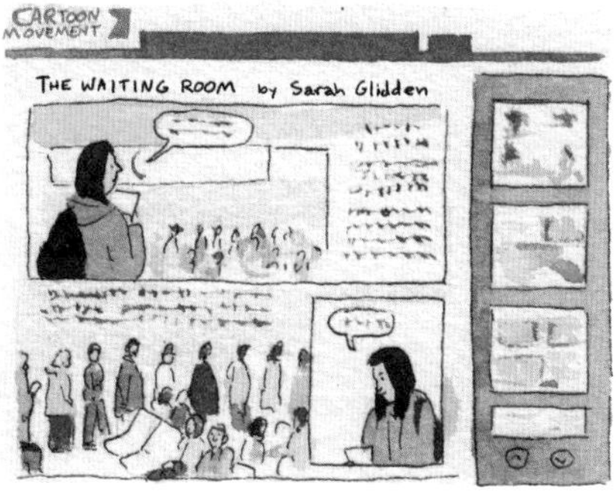
CARTOON MOVEMENT
THE WAITING ROOM by Sarah Glidden

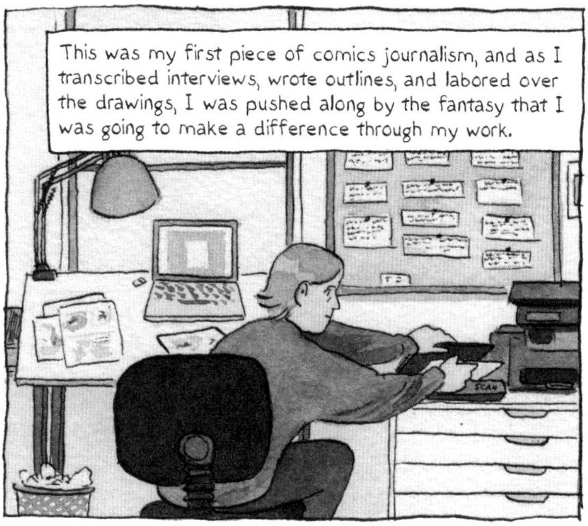
This was my first piece of comics journalism, and as I transcribed interviews, wrote outlines, and labored over the drawings, I was pushed along by the fantasy that I was going to make a difference through my work.
SCAN

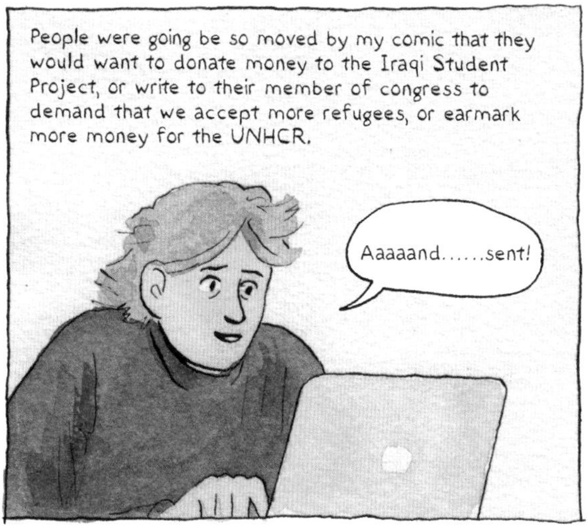
People were going be so moved by my comic that they would want to donate money to the Iraqi Student Project, or write to their member of congress to demand that we accept more refugees, or earmark more money for the UNHCR.
Aaaaand......sent!

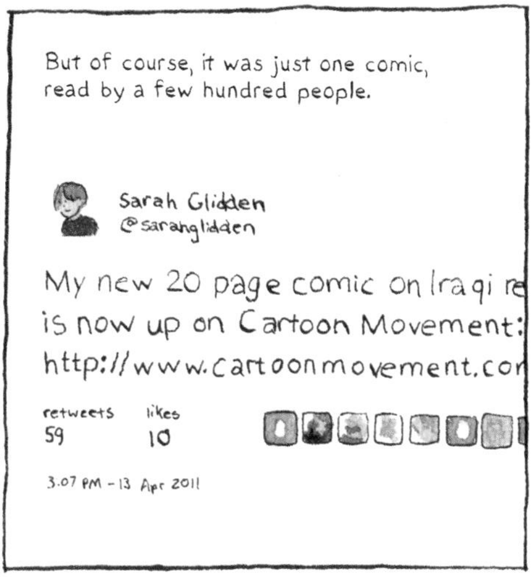
But of course, it was just one comic, read by a few hundred people.
Sarah Glidden
@sarahglidden
My new 20 page comic on Iraqi re
is now up on Cartoon Movement:
http://www.cartoonmovement.co
retweets
59
likes
10
3.07 PM - 13 Apr 2011

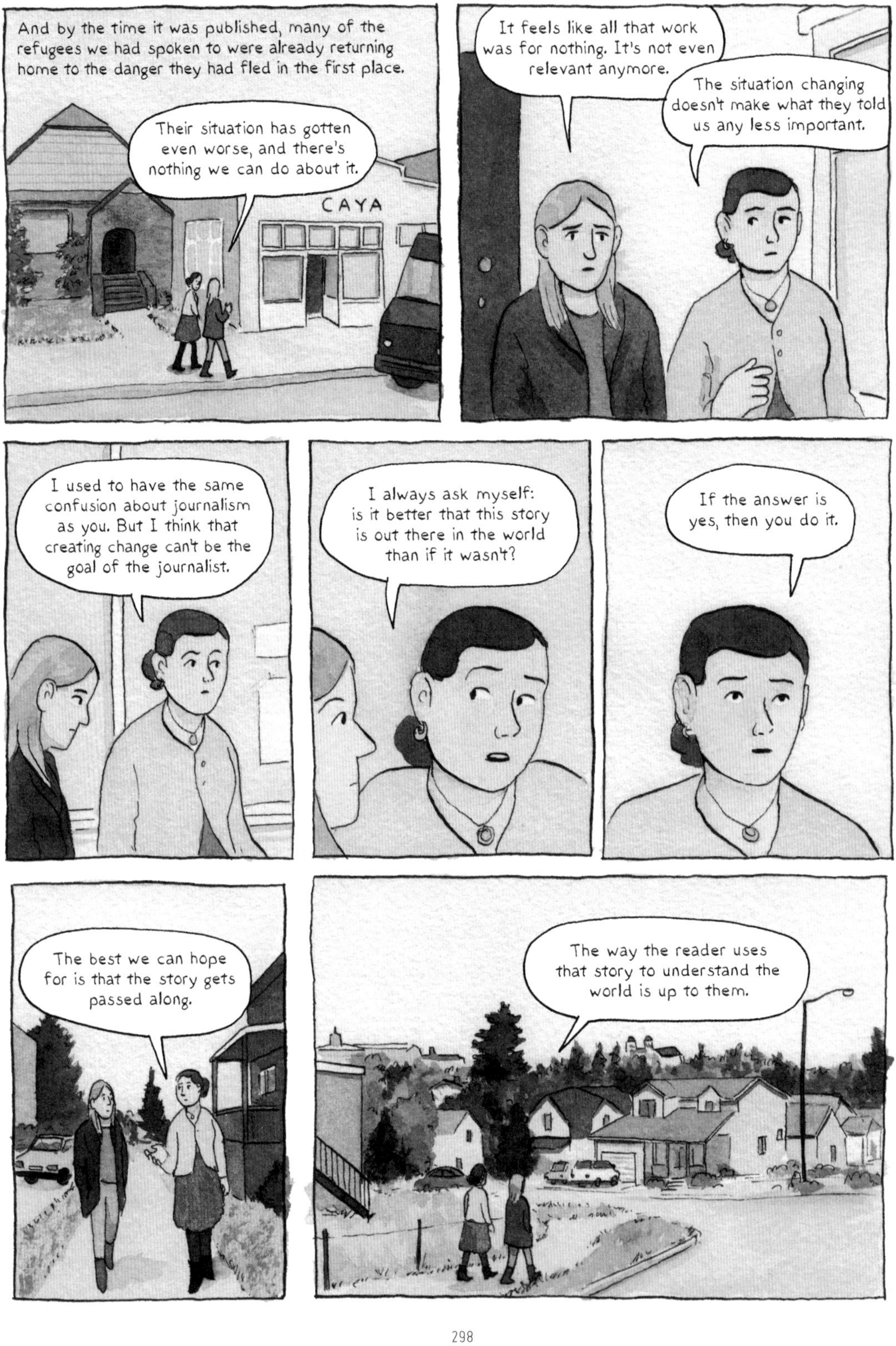
And by the time it was published, many of the refugees we had spoken to were already returning home to the danger they had fled in the first place.
Their situation has gotten even worse, and there's nothing we can do about it.
CAYA
It feels like all that work was for nothing. It's not even relevant anymore.
The situation changing doesn't make what they told us any less important.
I used to have the same confusion about journalism as you. But I think that creating change can't be the goal of the journalist.
I always ask myself: is it better that this story is out there in the world than if it wasn't?
If the answer is yes, then you do it.
The best we can hope for is that the story gets passed along.
The way the reader uses that story to understand the world is up to them.

NOTES

At the time of the 2010 trip, the *Globalist* was using their former name, the *Common Language Project*. As they changed the name shortly after our return, they have asked that I use the *Globalist* in its place for the book.

PAGE 14: This dialogue was not recorded at the time, but I remember Sarah telling me this story. When I was writing the book, I asked her to tell it to me again in her own words via email.

PAGES 15–16: I made a recording of this conversation but the file got lost. These pages have been rewritten to the best of my memory and partially taken from dialogue recorded later.

PAGES 33–34: All dialogue here is taken directly from quotations in Sarah's article for the *Independent*.

PAGE 46: This dialogue was written from a secondhand account by Sarah shortly after this took place.

PAGE 59: Amin and Mina asked that their names be changed. A friend of theirs, also an Iranian refugee, was sitting in on this interview but asked not to be part of the *Globalist*'s story or the comic.

PAGE 123: Panel four is referenced from a photograph by photojournalist Bruno Barbey.

PAGE 186: The scenes of the detention center in panels one to three are referenced from photos taken by Alex Stonehill for a story on the Northwest Detention Center.

PAGE 192: Dan's video blog at this point was actually still a script, which we read over in the Yadi, but for storytelling's sake I've added shots from the video he completed several days later.

PAGE 218: This dialogue was recreated through Sarah and Jessica's account of their meeting with Ambassador Mustafa and should not be taken as direct quotes.

PAGE 261: Momo and Odessa have requested that we use fake names. A friend of Tahir's, Ali, was also present but I omitted him for clarity's sake.

PAGES 270–272: The day the *Globalist* spent with Basil was not recorded, so dialogue is based on recollections from Sarah, Alex, and Jessica, which I recorded shortly after their meeting.

PAGE 275: All the panels on this page are referenced from photos taken by Alex Stonehill while reporting on Iraqi refugees in Damascus.

PAGE 275: Although the US accepts the most refugees worldwide in absolute number, other countries like Australia, Canada, and Norway receive a higher proportion of refugees per capita according to UNHCR data.

PAGE 281: I was not present for this home interview with Sarab, but this dialogue is taken from Sarah's recording.

PAGE 298: While we did have a conversation similar to this on this particular visit to Seattle, I did not record it. This dialogue is written from notes taken later while talking to Sarah about the same topic.

Links to all of the *Seattle Globalist* articles, photoessays, documentaries, and radio pieces referenced in this book can be found on my website at sarahglidden.com.

THANK YOU

To my family and friends who gave me their support while I worked on this book.

To my husband, Fran López, who deserves a medal for tolerating my stormier moments of self-doubt, indecision, and writer's block, for reading over every page multiple times and offering editorial advice, and for knowing when I just needed someone to listen as I worked out a problem on my own.

To Chris Oliveros, Peggy Burns, Tom Devlin, Tracy Hurren, Julia Pohl-Miranda, Marcela Huerta, and everyone else at Drawn & Quarterly who helped turn this book into a thing that exists in the world.

To the cartoonists and writers who inspired me with their work, cheered me along, and helped me make artistic decisions, especially Julia Wertz, Lisa Hanawalt, Domitille Collardey-Adebimpe, Julie Maroh, Tom Hart, Tim Kreider, Eroyn Franklin, Nathan Schreiber, Matt Bors, Sophie Yanow, Josh Neufeld, and Joe Sacco.

To everyone who supported me on my Kickstarter campaign to help fund my trip, especially those whose backer rewards were more than a little late.

To Ahmed Yahya Hussein and Shoayb Zohrabi, who helped me with translations. To Karen O'Reilly, Anna Mudd, Paul Beran, and Ranen Omer-Sherman for looking over specific segments of the book with expert eyes. And a big thanks to the many people who through social media were so generous with their help on small translations, links to resources, and many other gestures that may have seemed small taken individually, but were actually huge and essential to this work.

To all the people we met in Turkey, Iraq, Lebanon, and Syria who helped us with our work: Pouya Alagheband, Sebastian Meyer, Kamran Najm Ibrahim, and Sanayeh House.

To Dan O'Brien, Sarah Stuteville, Alex Stonehill, and Jessica Partnow for giving me access to two months of their lives.

To all the people we met who gave us their time and shared their stories.

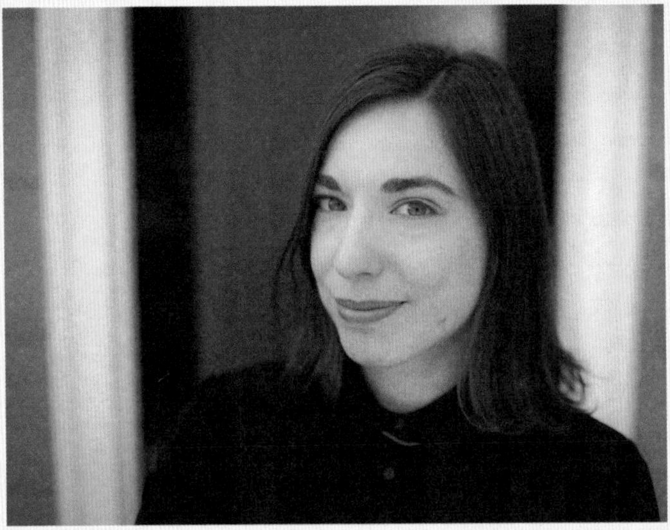

PHOTO CREDIT: ALEX STONEHILL

Sarah Glidden was born in 1980 in Massachusetts and studied painting at Boston University. She started making comics in 2006 when she was living at the Flux Factory artists collective in Queens, New York, and soon began working on her first book, *How to Understand Israel in 60 Days or Less*. She spent a year as an artist in residence at the Maison des Auteurs in Angoulême, France. She currently lives in Seattle.